AMERICAN THOUGHT AND WRITING

VOLUME TWO

The Revolution and the Early Republic

✌§ ?✌

RIVERSIDE EDITIONS

RIVERSIDE EDITIONS

UNDER THE GENERAL EDITORSHIP OF

Gordon N. Ray

American Thought and Writing

VOLUME TWO

The Revolution and the Early Republic

EDITED BY

RUSSEL B. NYE, *Michigan State University*

AND

NORMAN S. GRABO, *University of California, Berkeley*

HOUGHTON MIFFLIN COMPANY · BOSTON

The Riverside Press Cambridge

Acknowledgment is made to the following for permission to reprint material from their publications:

American Book Company — Selections from Hugh Henry Brackenridge, *Modern Chivalry*, ed. Claude M. Newlin (New York: American Book Company, 1937).

Appleton-Century — *André* by William Dunlap, from Arthur H. Quinn, *Representative American Plays* (3d ed.), copyright, 1925, The Century Company; reprinted by permission of Appleton-Century.

Harry Hayden Clark and Hafner Publishing Company — Selections from *Poems of Freneau*, ed. Harry Hayden Clark (New York: Harcourt, Brace, 1929; reprint edition, Hafner Publishing Company, 1960).

Columbia University Press — Letters of Turgot and Richard Price, from Louis M. Hacker, *The Shaping of the American Tradition* (New York: Columbia University Press, 1947); selection from Courtney R. Hall, *A Scientist in the Early Republic: Samuel Latham Mitchill* (New York: Columbia University Press, 1934).

Duke University Press — Selection from David Lee Clark, *Charles Brockden Brown, Pioneer Voice of America* (Durham: Duke University Press, 1952).

Vernon L. Parrington, Jr., and Archon Books–The Shoe String Press, Inc. — Selections from *The Connecticut Wits*, ed. Vernon Louis Parrington (New York: Harcourt, Brace, 1926; reprint edition, Archon Books–The Shoe String Press, Inc., 1963).

Philosophical Library, Inc. — Selection from *The Selected Writings of Benjamin Rush*, ed. Dagobert D. Runes (New York: Philosophical Library, 1947).

The Scarecrow Press, Inc. — Selection from *The Prose of Philip Freneau*, ed. Philip Marsh (New Brunswick, N.J.: The Scarecrow Press, Inc., 1955).

CONTENTS

v

A More Perfect Union

Contents vii

Nature and Deity

The Beginnings of a National Literature

The Nationalistic Impulse

The Beginnings of the American Novel

Early American Poetry

INTRODUCTION

The Contexts of American Thought

The framework of ideas within which the United States achieved its independence was constructed of materials furnished by two great European intellectual movements, Neoclassicism and Romanticism. American thought, as it took shape in the crucial years of its creation between 1776 and 1820, shared in both. The period is, therefore, one of transition and combination, an era poised between the close of the Enlightenment and the full opening of the Romantic movement. The motivations and patterns of the Age of Reason persisted, at the same time that they were being challenged, tested, and to some extent displaced by other ways of looking at man, society, and experience.

The colonial American of the early eighteenth century was very much a child of the Age of Reason. John Locke wrote a charter for the Carolinas; Rousseau, Franklin, Montesquieu, Cotton Mather, and Sir Isaac Newton were contemporaries; Voltaire lived to see the signing of the American Declaration of Independence. Puritanism, though still a powerful force, was fast losing its thrust. The Enlightenment, as it arrived in America, was the first nationalized ideological movement in the American experience. Whereas Puritanism was parochial, and largely restricted to New England, the ideas of the Age of Reason permeated the colonies, attracting leaders of thought from John Adams of Massachusetts, to Benjamin Franklin of Pennsylvania, to Thomas Jefferson of Virginia.

The Enlightenment rested on five general beliefs: the inevitability of progress; the perfectibility of man and his institutions; the efficacy of reason; the beneficence of God; and the plenitude and perfection of nature. It stressed the primacy of science over theology, skepticism over authority, reason over faith. The philosophers of the Enlightenment were convinced that it was within man's capacity, by applying reason to his problems, to discover those great laws by which all human and natural activity could be explained. Possessing such knowledge, men could then direct their efforts toward building a society in which progress was certain and continuous. The temper of the Enlightenment was orderly, progressive, hopeful. As the Reverend Charles Backus, reflecting on his era's sense of achievement, wrote in 1788: "The present age is an enlightened one. Theories capable of being corrected and improved by experiment, have been greatly elucidated. Principles venerable for their antiquity have been freely examined, and their absurdities exposed." Those Americans who, after their successful revolution, set out to build a new state and a new culture, responded to the challenge with confidence and optimism.

American thought, however, much as it drew from Europe, was not simply a transatlantic reflection. The American version of the Enlightenment was late, eclectic, and native. First of all, the natural lag in the transfer of ideas across the ocean meant that patterns of thought conceived in Britain and France were employed to their greatest effect in America a half-century later (or more) under different circumstances, in response to different needs. Americans worked with ideas already old by European standards, in another part of the world, for new purposes, and more often than not with changed meanings attached to them. It is worthwhile to note, in describing the patterns of later eighteenth- and early nineteenth-century American thought, that Goethe, Schiller, Wordsworth, Coleridge, and Kant were at work at almost the same time that Americans were quoting Newton, Locke, Voltaire, and Pufendorf.

Second, the English Enlightenment was a relatively conservative compromise of new and old ideas with current conditions. The British produced a few genuine radicals — William Godwin, Horne Tooke, Thomas Paine, Joseph Priestley (these last two exported to America) — but its Age of Reason was better represented by such reasonable men as Charles James Fox and Edmund Burke. The *philosophes* across the channel — among them Diderot, Holbach, Helvetius, and Voltaire — translated the French version of the Age of Reason into quite un-British extremes. Americans, who needed positive rules to justify a revolution and a new kind of society, found French interpretations of the Enlightenment much more to their satisfaction. American intellectuals read the French and British radicals, praised them, and hoped to turn their thinking to American uses. They took what they needed from British and European thought — using, for example, Locke's explanation of an old English revolution to justify their own against a different England, or adopting French "radicalism," aimed at the long tyranny of royal France, to overthrow a much less tyrannical King and Parliament on another continent. They shaped the Enlightenment to their advantage, and put an American stamp on it.

The rise of Romanticism in England and Europe introduced another factor into later eighteenth-century American thought. The basic concepts of the Romantic movement were not new, but a revival of interest, beginning about 1750, brought about a re-examination and extension of them, which in turn led men on both sides of the Atlantic to question and to alter some of the ideas of the Enlightenment. The Romantics, while never wholly consistent among themselves, tended to agree on three essential principles. First, on the organic nature of life — men, ideas, and institutions were conceived of as wholes or units, each with its own rules of development and governance. Second, on the dynamic quality of life — which was conceived of as fluid, changing, constantly in adaptation and permutation. Third, on the diversity of life — with emphasis on differences in cultures, tastes, societies, principles, and individuals, in contrast to the uniformitarian standards of the Enlightenment. Where the Age of Reason recognized that man was a mixture of passion and reason, and stressed the need for control of the former by the latter power, the Romantics emphasized the validity of human emotions, intuitions, and fancies, or (as they often called it) of the Imagination. Because of this, they believed deeply in the importance of the individual, his private judgment, and his capacity for growth and improvement.

There were a number of reasons, of course, for the popularity of these ideas in the latter decades of the eighteenth century. Among them was the fact that Romanticism reflected something of the rising strength of the European and American middle class, who found in it new proof of the worth of the average man and his ability to make his own world. Recent advances in science showed the power of human reason, and how knowledge might accrue to men by their own efforts without the need of religious revelation. Just as Newton and the scientists pushed out the limits of the physical universe, so the new psychology of Locke, Hartley, and others seemed to demonstrate man's ability to control and improve himself and his environment.

Much of Romanticism fitted the facts of American life; some of it did not. On the soil of a revolutionary, frontier, agrarian society — an open society developed out of Calvinist-evangelical theology and set in an immense new land — the seeds of British and European Romanticism quickly bore American fruit. American Romantics had less reason to demolish, more to build. Unlike any other modern Western nation, the United States began its history without having to overthrow a nobility, a state church, an entrenched landed class, or any other of the apparatus of feudalism. Romanticism in America, therefore, turned out to be a much more constructive, individualistic, and democratically based movement than in either Britain or Europe. It produced not Byron but Emerson, not Marx but Thoreau, not Napoleon but Jackson.

American thinking and writing of the period, of course, displayed certain inconsistencies and individualities. Drawing from his education in Enlightened rationalism, the American saw a number of analogies between his civilization and that of the classic world; he hoped in his national culture to combine something of the intellectual symmetry and beauty of Greek thought with the Roman sense of law, control, and arrangement. The Newtonian vision of a perfectly machined universe, to his mind, paralleled the classic concept of universal order and beauty. As the classics — and the Puritans — taught him, the eighteenth-century American valued ideas and institutions in terms of their usefulness. Franklin's "Nothing is good or beautiful but in the measure that it is useful" is as much the expression of the American neoclassic mode as it is of the functional pragmatism of a frontier society. Like their British and French instructors, American artists placed great emphasis on structure, channeling their creative energies within the limits of form established by the masters of the past. And of course, in good Augustan fashion, they believed in the virtues of discipline, reasonableness, clarity, and uniformity, accepting the need for standards of taste, propriety, and decorum in settling life's matters. Much of the politics and art of the American eighteenth century reflects these concepts, derived and adapted from the Age of Reason.

Though the classical tradition remained the cultural anchor of American intellectual life for another generation, American thought after 1780 began to show clear effects of the new Romanticism — its enlargement of man's inward boundaries to include a wider range of imaginative and sensual knowledge; its renewed interest in direct and concrete observation; its awareness of nature and the face of the American land; its emphasis on the validity of ordinary, average, common-held experience; its recognition of nonconformity; its fascination with the exotic, strange, faraway, and "Gothic." Romanticism broadened every man's scope, and opened windows out into the world. Thus Philip Freneau found in the powers of fancy

> Endless images of things,
> Fluttering each on golden wings,
> Ideal objects, such a store,
> The universe could hold no more:

while young William Cullen Bryant spoke for many of his generation when he refused to be "condemned to tinkle the same eternal tune . . . , the imagination confined to one trodden circle."

The American people, over the years 1765 to 1814, confronted three of the most difficult and intricate problems in politics ever faced by any people in the history of the Western world. The first, which occupied their energies to 1776, was how to make and to justify a revolution against the world's greatest military and economic power. The second, paramount during the years 1776 to 1783, was how to execute a revolution and control it. The third, dominating the postwar years until the close of the War of 1812, was how to consolidate a revolution — how to bring out of it a just and stable government that would stand in proper relationships to its own citizens and to the rest of a hostile world which (for the most part) did not believe in it. Each phase raised new questions and posed new difficulties on whose solution survival depended; there was little room for error, and everything was being done for the first time. In addition, those involved in this great experiment believed sincerely that everything that was done carried consequences of tremendous importance for the future of the nation, the world, and perhaps for mankind.

The Backgrounds of Independence

At the close of the Seven Years' War in 1763 (known in its American phase as the French and Indian War) Great Britain, having defeated France in India and driven her from North America, was indisputably the master of the Western world. American colonists were proud to have played a crucial role in the victory and equally proud to be British. As Franklin wrote after the victories at Quebec and Montreal, "No one can more sincerely rejoice than I do, on the reduction of Canada, and this is not merely as I am a colonist, but as I am a Briton." Yet in less than twenty years Franklin and thousands of other proud and loyal Britons rejected their King, repudiated their Parliament, and declared war on their fellow Englishmen. Small wonder that John Adams wrote on July 3, 1776, as he paused to reflect on "the whole period from that time to this, and recollect the series of political events, the chain of causes and effect," that "I am surprised at the suddenness as well as the greatness of this revolution." What moved these men from patriotic loyalty to defiance and open rebellion?

There were two complementary sets of reasons, the one political and economic, the other ideological. In the first instance, the argument between Britain and the colonies after 1763 centered on matters of imperial organization and the rights of the colonist within the empire. In the second, the conflict involved different concepts of the rights of man and the contractual nature of governments, both of which were parts of the great intellectual heritage of the Age of Reason.

After the signing of the peace with France in 1763, the American colonies — prosperous, expanding, confident — were in an excellent position within the empire. Under the British policy of "salutary neglect" they had long enjoyed a liberal measure of political and economic autonomy which they expected to retain and hoped to expand. Over the war years they had gained a good deal of political experience, had developed strong leaders, and had begun to evolve a feeling of unity and purpose. But with the succession of George III, and especially after the close of the French wars, the British inaugurated a different colonial policy, or, more accurately, decided to enforce more rigidly the policy they had allowed to lapse for a half-century. This was accomplished in a series of measures — the Proclamation Line (1763), the Currency Act (1764), the Stamp Act (1765), the Quartering Act (1765), the Townshend Acts (1767), the "Intolerable" Acts (1774) and others — which introduced new and direct taxes; placed curbs on colonial manufacturing, trade, and currency; closed off the West; and restricted the authority of colonial legislatures. In addition, the British enforced these acts by strict legal and military means.

The American colonists, with some bitterness, saw their present and future gains jeopardized by Britain's new colonial attitude. Each act of colonial resistance brought coercive countermeasures from London, which in turn aroused greater resistance. Each conflict between colony and mother country inflamed tempers a little more, eroded respect for imperial authority, and introduced new issues. What were the rights of Englishmen who happened to live in the colonies, not in England? What was the proper relationship between colonial legislatures and Parliament? Who possessed what taxing powers, and who should make what kinds of laws for colonial government? There seemed to be no satisfactory answers, and as King and Parliament tightened the imperial reins, the colonists claimed greater freedom from them. The argument moved from the right of colonists to tax themselves, to their right to govern themselves internally through their own elected bodies, to their right to exist as an independent union of states, for which they were willing to declare revolution and war.

The period between the French and Indian War and the Declaration witnessed the development of a sharp struggle over the distribution of authority within the imperial framework. A conflict was also shaping between a set of colonies that were rapidly beginning to feel like a nation, and a central government that was determined to hold its empire together after the strain of a long, wearisome war. After 1763 the colonies unconsciously began to close ranks against England, as they had against the French danger, and to think of themselves as "Americans." It is impossible, of course, to point to a particular year and say, "Here Americanism began," but it is certain that by the middle of the eighteenth century the colonists conceived of themselves as a special kind of Briton, and that they possessed a common outlook and sense of relationship that could only be described as *American*. The term seemed to have, by Franklin's time, a meaning distinct from "British" or "English" that the term "West Indian," for example, clearly did not have. It was quite normal for Franklin's Poor Richard, who was by no means a revolutionary, to refer to his countrymen as "American patriots," or for Dr. William Smith of Philadelphia, long before the Revolution, to speak of the colonies as "our nation," with no sense of disloyalty to England. The growing national spirit provided a wider dimension to the arguments with Britain, and undoubtedly contributed greatly to the colonial will to resist. This is what John Adams meant when he remarked later that "The revolution was effected before the war commenced. The revolution was in the hearts and minds of the people."

The issues at stake, however, were not limited to the rights of Englishmen or colonists. There was also a broader conflict over general political principles, arising from different interpretations of the twin theories of natural rights and government by social contract, both of which stemmed from Enlightenment philosophy. It was assumed that in the beginning man was endowed by his Creator with certain natural rights, which antedated the existence of governments and were superior to them. They were, as Thomas Paine called them, "those rights which always appertain to man in right of his existence." These rights were never exactly enumerated and defined, but they included the protection of life, the acquisition and security of property, freedom of movement, equal justice before law, and the freedom to speak and think within certain limits.

The social contract theory grew from the natural rights concept, for since these rights were not self-enforcing, some form of government seemed necessary to maintain them. To accomplish this, it was also assumed that men consented to a contract with the state for the furtherance and defense of their natural rights. A government was, then, in the definition of the English jurist Blackstone, "a voluntary compact between a ruler and the ruled . . . , liable to such limitations as are necessary for the security of the absolute rights of the latter." The aim of this contract, as James Otis of Pennsylvania explained it, was "above all things to provide for the security, the quiet and happy enjoyment of life, liberty, and property." Implicit in the terms of this contract were three things: that the primary power of government remain with the people; that the authority of government rest on the consent of the governed; and that violations of the contract by the state render that government null and void. The Declaration of Independence defined these theories best, and for all time.

The nationalism of the pre-Revolutionary years was a natural product of the French and Indian War, and of the arguments with England over colonial rights and imperial policies. The Revolution itself, obviously, raised patriotic fervor to a high pitch, but after the war, as memories of military action receded, other factors emerged to keep alive the incandescent nationalism of 1776. The Revolution forced the colonists to consider much more carefully what "America" and "Americanism" meant, and why they deserved independent existence. They entered the war as a nation, with strong convictions that they knew what they were fighting for; having won, they now had to define that nation. As Dr. David Ramsay of South Carolina wrote, in celebrating the second anniversary of the Declaration, "We have laid the foundations of a new empire, which promises to enlarge itself into vast dimensions, and to give happiness to a great continent. It is our time to figure on the face of the earth, and in the annals of the world."

For though the Revolution settled the right of the United States to exist legally as a nation, there still remained a number of unanswered questions. Consistent (and sometimes savage) attacks by British and European critics forced Americans to defend and define themselves, their ideas and ideals, their way of life. Again and again they tried to answer the question of the Frenchman Crèvecoeur, "What is an American?" and in the process they slowly evolved a set of answers to what an American was, and hoped to be.

Americans themselves, at the end of the Revolution, looked ahead with a feeling of fresh beginnings. They held great hope for the present, for they had no record of failure in their past; they were impatient of traditions and institutions, for they had just finished over-throwing some old ones and establishing new ones of their own. They were especially conscious of the importance of their actuality as a nation — of existing not simply as England or Europe projected to another continent, but as a different civilization with its own being and futurity. British and European travelers and commentators constantly criticized the United States for being new, different, and un-European (charges which no American could deny) — until Americans gradually began to realize that being so was not necessarily shameful. Indeed, it occurred to them that the United States, because of its newness, its difference, and its American-ness, was far superior to Britain or Europe.

Nor was this all. The evidence of history, closely examined, seemed to show that God had willed the United States to be different, so that it might play a special role in the future. It seemed plain to many Americans, as it did to a Connecticut magazine contributor in 1786, that God "had reserved this country to be the last and greatest theater in the improvement of mankind," while Dr. Richard Price, Franklin's friend, somewhat extravagantly ranked the American Revolution as second in importance only to the introduction of Christianity on earth. Europe, where "human reason and the rights of human nature had been the sport of chance and the prey of ambition," as Joel Barlow wrote, offered men little hope. The United States was intended by God to be the model of a New World, whose mission, Barlow continued, was "to excite emulation among the kingdoms of the earth, and meliorate the condition of the human race." In order to fulfill this assignment, it was imperative that America emphasize its nationality, reject the prejudices and patterns of the corrupt Old World, and construct its own civilization to fit the nation's divine purpose. In other words, the United States must be American, if it were to succeed in what Jefferson called man's greatest experiment, to determine whether "men may be trusted to govern themselves without a master."

American Society and the Revolution

The American colonist in 1760 lived in an environment that was not substantially different from his grandfather's. He owned the same kind of house, traveled in the same fashion, communicated with his fellows in much the same way, drew power for his production from similar sources, and for that matter produced and consumed much the same kinds of goods. The span between the close of the French and Indian War and the Treaty of Ghent measured only fifty-one years — but they were years of incredibly swift change. Between lay two major revolutions, the rise and fall of Napoleon, the attainment of American independence, the ratification of the Constitution, an explosion of scientific knowledge, the culmination of the Industrial Revolution, the formation of modern urban society, and a complete change in methods of transportation and communication. The American of 1820 lived in what was almost literally a new society, so recently built that one man's lifetime might have spanned it all.

At the center of this period of change was the American Revolution, a relatively conservative revolution fought to protect certain rights and practices the colonists believed they already possessed. Its aim was not to destroy an established order, but rather to be allowed to create a new order without interference. American radicals, by European standards, were no more than cautious liberals; yet their Revolution was a true revolution which wrought irrevocable alterations in American society, in some cases simply by allowing movements already under way to continue without hindrance, in others by initiating wholly new trends.

The Revolution did not create an egalitarian, level, homogeneous American society. The war disturbed but did not substantially rearrange the colonial class structure which, by the mid-eighteenth century, was already different from that of England and Europe. Wealth, talent, education, language, manners, lineage, and such things still counted in the America of 1800 as they had in 1750 (the Jacksonian "common man" had not yet arrived) but never so much as they did abroad, and not quite so much as they had a half-century earlier. Enlightened Americans, like Jefferson, believed in leadership by "a natural aristocracy of worth" and in the social and political guidance of "gentlemen" — which was not the same as the British "gentry." Most would probably have agreed with John Adams, who, though a committed revolutionary, felt that there had to be stability and order in the new society, "decency and respect and veneration introduced for persons in authority, at every rank."

On the other hand, this postwar society was by far the most open and flexible in the world. It included, of course, both rich and poor, educated and ignorant, gentleman and boor, but, as Lafayette noted,

the gap between them was much narrower than in Europe. In a
general way, almost everyone within it had a chance to better himself
and his children; there were too many roads to success for any group
or class to monopolize them. The war and its subsequent contest for
wealth and power opened the way upward for men of relatively humble origins — Patrick Henry, George Clinton, Alexander Hamilton,
John Marshall, to name a few; or the two richest men of the era, John
Jacob Astor, a penniless German boy, and Stephen Girard, a French-
born emigré tradesman. Land, resources, and opportunities were too
plentiful to be appropriated for the benefit of a few.

Other social changes could be traced, in one way or another, to the
revolutionary impetus. The discrediting and departure of the royalist-
loyalist element removed the most conservative group from the American scene. It was estimated that about 60,000 loyalists took refuge
elsewhere during the war, few of whom returned afterwards. The
confiscation and sale of their estates, among them some of the largest
in the colonies, speeded a trend toward the distribution of land ownership perceptible in prewar years. The postwar abolition of quitrents,
primogeniture, and entail (the last vestiges of feudalism) removed the
means of building such estates again, while cheap land to the west
made everybody a prospective landholder. The war also hastened the
separation of church and state, visible in the theological arguments of
mid-century and practically complete by the 1790's. Only in New
England, where the clergy had supported the Revolution and Calvinism's hold was still strong, was the actual legal division of civil and
religious authority delayed for another twenty years.

At the time of the Revolution, the American colonies had been settled for more than a century and a half. Since the beginning of the
eighteenth century they had shown signs of social and cultural division
and a tendency to group themselves along regional lines. Postwar
geographers usually identified a central "middle" group of states, a
"northern" or "New England" group, a Southern bloc, and occasionally
a "coastal" and "back" region. Delegates to the Continental Congress
referred to themselves as representing Northern, Middle, or Southern
states; likewise, the Continental Army command divided the nation
into three military districts, Eastern (New England), Middle, and
Southern. After 1800 standard geographies usually identified a fourth
or "western" region. Jedidiah Morse, whose *American Geography* in
1793 listed "the grand division of the United States" as Northern,
Middle, and Southern, in his 1819 edition added "the Western States
and Territories."

Within these regions there were a number of generally accepted
social and cultural divisions — the Boston area as separate from the
New England mountain states or the Connecticut Valley; upstate New
York as distinct from New York City or the Hudson Valley; the division

of Pennsylvania into western (Pittsburgh) and eastern (Philadelphia); the Chesapeake Bay area; the deep South; the Kentucky-Tennessee frontier; and so on. Each of these had its temperamental traits, its personality, its presumably "typical" character such as the canny Yankee, the Dutch New Yorker, the contentious Philadelphian, the cavalier Southerner, the hearty Westerner — who probably did not exist at all except in the popular imagination, but who illustrated the variety of ways by which Americans saw themselves. Even in its youth American society showed great diversity and cultural differentiation. The motto *E Pluribus Unum* had its basis in fact.

One of the most far-reaching consequences of the Revolution was its effect on American economic and industrial life. The United States matured suddenly, within two generations, into a business civilization. Nowhere was a nation quite so ready as the United States to accept the Industrial Revolution. Lacking any deeply entrenched economic group, it had vast natural resources, a rapidly growing population of producers and consumers, relative political stability and unity, and the protection of a government friendly to business.

Colonial trade and manufacturing were severely limited by British law. It was possible to build a fortune in the colonies, as "King" Derby of Salem and John Hancock of Boston did, but colonial bankers, merchants, and planters were for the most part tightly shut within the walls of the British mercantile system. It was perfectly evident that the function of the American economy was to furnish cheap materials for British industry in return for more expensive manufactured goods; colonial economic life must always supplement, never compete with the mother country's. Pre-Revolutionary business organizations were therefore uncomplicated, usually no more than simple partnerships operating under primitive credit and investment techniques. Before the Revolution the American colonies possessed all the elements necessary for large-scale economic development — surplus capital, an expanding labor force, huge natural resources, generous sources of power, a growing population, a flourishing marine trade — but all were confined by British restrictions.

The act of independence released these pent-up forces, placing the United States in a completely different economic relationship to Britain and Europe. No longer a colony within an imperial system, the United States at once became an independent unit in the world competition for markets. There was a great demand for manufactured goods to replace British trade, as well as for new banking and investment systems, and immediately after the war a need for more complex business organizations, such as the joint-stock company and the corporation. The rapid expansion of American business is graphically illustrated by the increase in corporation charters issued by the new states. From 1781 to 1790, there were thirty-three; from 1791 to

1795, one hundred and two; from 1795 to 1820, five hundred and fifty-seven. The war trained hundreds of young men in organizing and financing a revolution, and supplied the businessmen of the next generation, who replaced the landed gentlemen and merchant princes as the leaders of American economic life. The risks of the entrepreneur in postwar business were great, but so were the rewards. "We have one material that constitutes aristocracy," John Adams noted in 1808, "and that material is wealth."

"All the world," commented Jefferson as he looked about him in 1783, "is becoming commercial." The spread of factories, the introduction of improved machinery and production methods, the establishment of tariffs and other government aids, the growth of banking and credit systems, the opening of the West, and the revolution in transportation combined to make the United States into a burgeoning business society. The conversion from a mercantile to a manufacturing economy was under way, the pattern of nineteenth-century industrial America virtually complete.

The Growth of the Republic

The extensive changes wrought in American life during the early decades of independence were accompanied by an astonishing enlargement in the sheer size of the nation. Three states (Vermont, Kentucky, and Tennessee) entered the union between 1789 and 1801; Ohio, Louisiana, Indiana, Illinois, Mississippi, Alabama, Maine, and Missouri joined over the next twenty years. Jefferson's purchase of Louisiana in 1803 more than doubled the size of the country overnight; by a single stroke the United States became proprietor of nearly one-half of North America, master of the continental navigational system, and owner of the western world's greatest storehouse of untapped natural wealth. At the same time the population of the nation more than doubled between 1790 and 1820, rising from 3,900,000 to 9,600,000 in thirty years. The West grew even faster, from a few thousand to more than three million over the same period, so that one-third of the people of the United States, by 1820, lived beyond the mountains.

Postwar America was overwhelmingly rural. In 1790 less than five percent of the population lived in towns of more than 8,000, and even by 1800 there were only five cities of more than 10,000 population. Philadelphia, the largest (and also the second largest in the English-speaking world) had 70,000, New York 60,000, Boston 25,000, Charleston 18,000 and Baltimore 13,000. Within a decade American cities, large and small alike, began a period of phenomenal expansion. New York passed Philadelphia by adding 36,000 people, and Baltimore moved up to third place, while the western cities mushroomed. It took Boston two hundred years to reach 30,000; it took Cincinnati only fifty years to count five times that many. Though the United States still remained a predominantly agrarian nation of farms and small settlements, the cities provided focal points for trade, immigration, and political organization that had lasting effects on the configuration of American society. It was in the cities that the patterns of emergent American culture were largely shaped and directed.

The early nineteenth century saw sweeping changes in transportation and communication, essential for the movement of people, goods, and information in a land of immense distances and scattered population. To unify the country economically and politically, and to join its separate sections into a common society under one government, the new United States needed to construct at least three east-west lines of travel, each six hundred to a thousand miles long, across a mountain range into wild country inhabited by savages; and a similar north-south line about a thousand miles long. Unlike Europe, where a network of roads and canals had been in the making for seven hundred years, the United States was expected to accomplish this at once. Actually, it took less than fifty years. It was possible for a child who had ridden a packhorse into Kentucky to ride within his lifetime from New York to St. Louis on a train.

At the time of the Revolution, the best American roads were bad in good weather and impassable in bad; in the 1750's, for example, the Boston-Philadelphia mail run often took three weeks. The need for good roads led several states to charter private turnpike corporations, which built toll roads over the routes most in demand. The Philadelphia and Lancaster Turnpike Company, chartered in 1792, opened a sixty-two-mile stretch that was so useful and profitable that similar corporations sprang up everywhere. By 1814 there were nearly a thousand miles of turnpike, and over a hundred companies in Massachusetts alone. In another five years a network of reasonably good toll roads connected all the major cities and reached out into the West, while bridge companies spanned the streams and rivers with toll bridges. The state and federal governments entered the road-building business, too; in 1811 Congress let contracts for a turnpike from Cumberland, Maryland, to Wheeling, Virginia, connecting the coast with the Ohio Valley. The National (or Cumberland) Pike, completed in 1818, soon extended into Ohio and finally into Illinois.

Though turnpikes speeded and cheapened transportation, water travel still remained the best way to move heavy freight. In 1786 the Virginia legislature chartered a company to improve navigation on the Potomac, opening an era of waterway and canal construction. The Erie Canal, the greatest engineering project in early American history, built between 1817 and 1825, linked the Hudson Valley with the Great Lakes. Meanwhile, the steamboat changed the nature of water transport. Fulton's *Clermont* made its historic run in 1807; four years later the first steamer made its way from Pittsburgh to New Orleans; eleven years later the *Walk-in-the-Water* appeared on the Great Lakes.

The effects of this new transportation system on American economic life were incalculable. The Erie Canal cut shipping costs from New York to Ohio in half and the time by one-third. Turnpikes chopped days and dollars from freight shipments — it cost ten dollars to send one hundred pounds from Baltimore to Pittsburgh in 1790; on the Cumberland Pike, two dollars. In 1783 a letter from Boston to New York took seven to ten days; in 1800, less than three days. When Thomas Tucker came from South Carolina to Philadelphia to attend the Constitutional Convention, his journey covered sixteen days, whereas thirteen years later the "Flying Coach" made a regularly scheduled New York-Philadelphia run in two days.

Not only goods, but ideas, opinions, and people moved over these roads and waterways. One of the most important factors in the diffusion of information throughout the new republic was the spread of newspapers. Colonial newspapers usually maintained editorial neutrality — and for good reason, since a controversial paper was likely to be suppressed. With the Stamp Act of 1765 (which taxed newspapers too) neutrality disappeared and the press became a potent force in forming revolutionary opinion. Furthermore, Americans developed quickly into a newspaper-reading people. In 1775 there were fewer than 40 papers in the colonies. Between 1783 and 1800 about 450 new ones were started, many of them ephemeral, but the best estimates show 90 to 100 in regular publication in 1790. In 1800 there were 187; Thomas' *History of Printing*, in 1811, listed 366. By 1833 there were twelve hundred newspapers in the United States publishing six million issues each year, giving the country the largest number of newspapers and the widest per capita circulation of any nation in the world. Magazines proliferated in the same fashion. Between 1783 and the turn of the century about seventy-five of them were published over varying lengths of time. Several hundred were founded after 1800, among them such influential journals as *The Portfolio, The North American Review, The American Magazine,* and *The Southern Literary Messenger*. The same expansion took place in book publishing — Americans seemed to demand books, a Philadelphia printer observed in 1798, "as a thirsty man demands drink." That year Boston listed 41 publishers, New York 56, and Philadelphia 88. In 1820 there were nearly 700 presses in the country (345 of them in Boston), including flourishing presses in Pittsburgh, Cincinnati, and St. Louis.

People moved by the thousands — chiefly westward — over the land and water routes. When John Jay remarked in 1785 on "the rage for emigrating to the westward country," the first wave of migration was already sweeping into the back counties of the settled states and across the mountains into western Pennsylvania, Kentucky, and Tennessee. Virginia counted 400,000 people in 1775 and 750,000 in 1790, with most of the increase concentrated in its western counties. Kentucky, which had a few hundred people in 1770, listed 73,000 in the 1790 census. This first wave, however, was a mere ripple in comparison to the flood that streamed into the Northwest, the Southwest, and the Mississippi Valley in the years directly ahead. It seemed to the English traveler Morris Birkbeck in 1817 that the entire country was "breaking up and moving westward." A farmer in upstate New York, for example, during nine days in 1813, counted 260 wagons filing past his farm, filled with families moving west. Some impression of the size of this great population shift may be gained from the national census reports. Two-fifths of South Carolina's entire population left the state for the West, one-third of Virginia's, and one-third of North Carolina's. Ohio doubled and Indiana tripled its population in the ten years 1810–1820. By 1821 the nine new Western states contained slightly more than one-quarter of the entire national population. Meanwhile, exploring parties probed beyond the Mississippi into the plains; Lewis and Clark's expedition crossed the continent in 1804–6, and John Jacob Astor set up fur posts on the Pacific coast in 1811 and 1812. For the next century the drive westward and the gradual movement with it of the frontier were facts of primary (perhaps dominant) importance in the development of American society.

Defining the Terms of Nationality

Since the Declaration of Independence abolished the entire governmental system under which the colonies existed, the Continental Congress moved swiftly to provide another. The British governed their colonies under a dual system, that is, by means of a strong central government in London, which made major decisions in colonial affairs, and a subordinate government in the colony itself. The central issue of the Revolution, reduced to its simplest terms, was the degree and quality of subordination that should characterize this relationship. In setting up the government of the newly independent nation, the Founding Fathers retained the dual nature of British policy, replaced the colonial law-making bodies with state legislatures, Parliament with Congress, and wrote new documents spelling out the powers and functions of each.

The Revolutionary leaders agreed that they wanted a government which guaranteed natural rights, states' rights, and all those other individual and political privileges which they believed the British colonial system had denied them. They assumed that, since they had been unable to govern themselves as they wished under a strong centralized British government in London, they could possibly do so under a weaker American government in Philadelphia; furthermore, their whole colonial experience had taught them, long before, to distrust any political authority very far beyond their reach. As inheritors of the Enlightenment, as well as of generations of British political theory, they also believed that government was most effective and trustworthy when kept close to the people, the original source of sovereignty. "Where can the power be lodged so Safe as in the Hands of the people?" a Massachusetts meeting asked in 1778. "The oftener power Returns to the hands of the people, the Better." Thus when the state constitutions were drawn up between 1776 and 1780, they placed the essentials of political control — taxes, currency, militia, voting rights, appointments, guarantees of civil and natural rights — in the state legislatures. These new constitutions translated the principles of the Revolution and the Declaration from general to practical political terms. Not only were these the primary contracts under which the nation governed itself during its first decisive decade; they also established precedents and processes of great usefulness for its later political life. The device of the convention, employed by most of the states in evolving their constitutions, still remains the best political method for the actual making of a social compact. The manner of forming constitutions, as developed in the United States, became the model for establishing or revising constitutional governments all over the Western world. In addition, these documents introduced into politics the American conviction, truly novel to the eighteenth century, that government should be based on a written document, which spelled out the principles on which it was founded, and which must have the approval of those who were to live under it. The careful, specific construction of written instruments of government on such a grand scale was an important contribution to the science of politics.

At the same time that the Continental Congress adopted the Declaration of Independence, it also resolved that "a plan of confederation be prepared and transmitted to the respective colonies for their consideration and approbation." A committee headed by John Dickinson of Pennsylvania prepared a set of Articles of Confederation, which the Congress approved in 1777. After ratification by the necessary number of states, these Articles supplied the machinery by which the United States governed itself as a nation until 1789. With the states exerting control over local matters, and the Congress over national and foreign affairs, the United States, wrote the editor of the *Pennsylvania Packet* in 1781, formed "a well-constructed arch, whose parts, harmonizing and mutually supporting each other, are all the more closely united the greater the pressure is upon them."

The trouble was that the system did not work that way. The Articles of Confederation denied Congress certain indispensable powers over finance, diplomatic affairs, and commerce, distributing them instead among the states. Congress, as a result, became little more than an advisory body, with insufficient authority to act on key national issues or to force cooperation from the reluctant states on domestic ones. Still, it is no doubt true that the Articles provided precisely what the American people then wanted — that is, an assembly of equal states, with a weak central government to serve as a coordinating agency to enable the nation, when the need arose, to confront common problems with some sort of unity. In the language of the Articles, the United States was "a firm league of friendship," nothing more, in which "each state retains its sovereignty, freedom, and independence." In John Adams' pungent phrase, it was the problem of "making thirteen clocks strike together."

Congress found itself in severe difficulties long before the war ended. After the war, quantities of worthless paper money caused constant financial crisis; interstate rivalries hampered internal commerce; foreign trade suffered from British competition and confusing trade laws; the states argued bitterly over the ownership of western lands and the payment of war debts; Spanish and Indians harassed the frontier in the face of an ineffective army. Congress lacked authority to deal decisively with any of these matters, and the worsening situation convinced a number of leaders that a stronger central government was necessary. Neither Congress, nor the executive, nor the judiciary possessed sufficient jurisdiction where it was needed most. Some argued that the Articles could be amended into an effective document; others (among them Alexander Hamilton, James Madison, John Jay, and Henry Knox) thought that the only solution lay in greater federal control. In 1787 Congress, responding to urgent appeals for action, authorized a convention "for the sole and express purpose of revising the Articles of Confederation and reporting to Congress and the several legislatures therein." From that moment the Articles, for all useful purposes, were obsolescent and the Congress a lame duck. Yet though the Articles were apparently insufficient to meet the needs of the postwar years, they were not a complete failure. Under their authority Congress carried the nation through the war, negotiated a favorable peace, contracted valuable foreign alliances, established a procedure for settling the West, created a nationalized citizenship, and survived three years of desperate postwar readjustment.

The convention which met in Philadelphia on May 25, 1787, did much more than the charge from Congress suggested. The fifty-five delegates who attended (some arrived late) represented a cross-section of the groups that had provided political leadership since the early eighteenth century — landowners, planters, lawyers, businessmen, shippers, bankers. Forty-one of them had served in Congress, seven were former state governors. Washington, who commanded unanimous respect, was chosen presiding officer. Jefferson, Jay, and John Adams were absent on diplomatic service, but the powerful state

leaders were present — Hamilton of New York; James Wilson, Robert
Morris, and the elderly Benjamin Franklin from Pennsylvania; Gerry
and King of Massachusetts; Roger Sherman of Connecticut; Luther
Martin of Maryland; and the brilliant Virginia delegation of Edmund
Randolph, George Mason, George Wythe, and James Madison. In
attempting one of the most delicate tasks of political history, the
formation of a stable union of independent states under a written body
of fundamental law, the delegates had few precedents from which to
work; they could draw upon the histories of the Greek confederacies,
the colonial charters and state constitutions, the British and classical
traditions of law and philosophy, their own colonial past, and little else.
The materials which went into the Constitution were not new; the
delegates gathered them from the total of Western political experience.
But the convention, in an act of creative statesmanship, blended them
into new and meaningful combinations, bringing them to bear directly
on the specific problems of their place and time.

The delegates did not all agree exactly on what kind of document
the convention should produce, but there seemed to be a general
consensus on three things. First, the national government would be
republican in form and aim, consistent with the substance of the
American revolutionary philosophy. No one had the slightest intention
of repealing the Declaration of Independence. Second, the national
government would derive its powers from the consent of the governed
and rest on the rights of man. Third, the national authority would be
sufficiently increased (and that of the states correspondingly lessened)
to meet the requirements of an expanding nation, yet without infringement of the rights of states and individuals. The result was not absolute perfection, but perhaps as close to it as a group of mortal men
could achieve under the circumstances. John Adams, assessing what
had been done at Philadelphia, found it well done; the American
system, he wrote, "will last forever, govern the globe, and introduce
the perfection of man."

When it came to the states for ratification, the new Constitution
found strong favor and almost equally strong opposition. Many of its
proponents, called "Federalists," were drawn from the same mercantile,
financial, and social classes that controlled the convention; a number
of the Anti-Federalists, who opposed it, came from the ranks of farmers, laborers, debtors, and small tradesmen, who feared the domination
of government by the wealthy groups. Five states (Delaware, New
Jersey, Georgia, Connecticut, and Pennsylvania) ratified the Constitution almost at once. Massachusetts (where the vote was close),
Maryland, and South Carolina followed in quick succession. New
Hampshire, the ninth state to ratify, did so in June 1788, providing
the majority needed to place the Constitution in operation. But since
New York and Virginia, the two most powerful states remaining, had

not yet given approval, it was clear that, however legal the new government might be, it could not function until they ratified. In both states the contest was hard and close. The Virginia Federalists won by a small margin in late June, while Hamilton and his New York contingent narrowly pulled it through in July. Though North Carolina and Rhode Island held out until 1789 and 1790, the Constitution for all practical purposes was now the basis for the government of the United States. After the balloting for President and Congress, the presidential electors met in 1789 to choose Washington as first President, and John Adams as Vice President. The United States was now fully launched on the second phase of its existence.

Under the Federalist administrations of Washington and his successor John Adams, and then under Republicans Jefferson and Madison, the federal and state governments settled their differences and slowly hammered out the nation's problems. The most pressing issues facing the country, once its internal stability was established, were those of foreign policy. What should be the American posture toward Europe, and what the American role in world affairs? Federalists and Jeffersonians alike agreed that the United States should avoid entanglements and follow a neutral policy in foreign disputes — something which, under prevailing diplomatic conditions, was more easily said than done. Britain, France, and Spain still controlled large areas on three sides of the American boundary, while Britain and France between them controlled the oceans of the world, so vital to American trade. In the long war that broke out in 1793 between the French Republic and England, Spain, and Holland, the United States maintained a shaky neutrality, which Jefferson managed to keep intact through the early years of the Napoleonic wars.

An accumulation of grievances eventually forced President Madison to declare war against Britain in 1812, a war which no one really wanted, which was poorly fought, and which decided none of the major problems which caused it. Nevertheless the conflict, which ended in 1814, brought certain major changes in America's point of view toward itself and Europe. It was not a "second war of independence," as some called it, but in a broader sense it put an end to the lingering colonial complex and the sense of inferiority that had colored American relations with Britain and Europe since independence. "In 1815," the historian Henry Adams wrote, "for the first time Americans ceased to doubt the path they were to follow." Never again did any power treat the United States with the contempt displayed by the British and French prior to 1812, and never again were American domestic policies quite so dominated and disrupted by events abroad.

By settling the question, for some years at least, of America's position in the world, the war allowed the United States to turn its attention to the conquest and absorption of the great West, a task which occupied it for another seventy-five years. Most of all, the conflict knit together and matured the American people. "It has renewed and reinstated the national feeling and character which the Revolution had given, and which were daily lessening," concluded Albert Gallatin, Jefferson's former Secretary of the Treasury. "The people now have more general objects of attachment with which their pride and political opinions are connected. They are more American, and feel and act more as a nation."

The Frontiers of American Science

The most direct expression of the rationalistic spirit of the Enlightenment came in the advancement of eighteenth-century science. The Age of Reason might perhaps be called the Age of Science, for it coincided with a tremendous burst of scientific knowledge that erupted in the late seventeenth century. The American colonies were children of this age, settled in the era of Bacon, Kepler, and Galileo, matured in the era of Newton and Leibnitz. Americans were never far from the stream of scientific knowledge that flowed through the eighteenth century, and men of scientific attainments, such as John Winthrop of Harvard, Cotton Mather, and Benjamin Franklin were representative products of the American Enlightenment.

The eighteenth-century attitude toward science was founded on four generally accepted principles: the belief that all natural and human problems responded to the application of scientific investigation; a belief in the unity of science, that all knowledge was fundamentally scientific; a belief in a mechanistic universe, governed by consistent natural law which was discoverable by human reason; a belief in the efficacy of the inductive method, and a corresponding distrust of dogmatism and authority. This scientific point of view seemed to provide the best and most understandable pattern by which the affairs of God, man, and nature might be explained; therefore the eighteenth-century philosopher worked outward from this set of beliefs, probing into the social world and the universe in search of laws and principles. In the process of settling America, there were always new observations to be made, new conditions to be met, new adjustments to the ever-changing frontiers of discovery; hence the American experience proved especially receptive to the implications of scientific method, to the testing and proving of theories by conformity to facts. American conditions, too, favored science that was useful, emphasizing such branches as cartography, surveying, navigational mathematics, astronomy, agriculture, metallurgy, medicine, chemistry, and physics.

The Revolution suspended scientific work (Rittenhouse, the great mathematician, helped manufacture gunpowder, and Benjamin Rush, the foremost colonial physician, served as an army surgeon) but afterwards science prospered. At the news of the peace, Dr. Amos Eaton said, "A thirst for natural science seemed to pervade the United States like the progress of an epidemic." Americans believed that science was vitally important to the development of their new continent and new society, for it not only gave man the means to control nature but assisted him in gaining mastery over his own troublesome problems. "To this source of improvement," Elihu Palmer wrote in 1800, "no limits can be assigned — it is indefinite and incalculable." Many also believed that science was the instrument by which America could achieve world leadership: the poet Joel Barlow hailed the day when

> Science bright
> Through shadowy nature leads with surer light . . . ;
> Gives each effect its own indubious cause,
> Divides her moral from her physic laws,
> Shows where the virtues find their nurturing food,
> And men their motives to be just and good.

It seemed particularly urgent, therefore, that American science be encouraged; in fact, there seemed reason to believe that science was particularly destined to flourish in America, since its institutions were peculiarly adapted to scientific study. Only in the United States, said Samuel Cooper, where "liberty unfetters and expands the human mind, can science flourish."

The United States was fortunate in receiving a number of brilliant emigrés during and shortly after the war. Thomas Cooper, a chemist, geologist, and economist of repute, came from England to become eventually president of the College of South Carolina. Joseph Priestley, one of the world's great chemists and the discoverer of oxygen, settled near Philadelphia after being harried from England for his religious unorthodoxy. Chemist Pierre du Pont de Nemours, Jefferson's friend, came from France; botanist Constantine Rafinesque from Italy; geologist William Maclure and ornithologist Alexander Wilson from Scotland. American science benefited immeasurably from the work of these men and others like them. At the same time, the United States was developing its own group of highly competent scientists — medical men Benjamin Rush and Benjamin Waterhouse; William Bartram, the Quaker naturalist; geographer Jedidiah Morse; botanists and ornithologists Thomas Say and Benjamin Smith Barton; Samuel Latham Mitchill, Benjamin Silliman, and James Woodhouse, chemists; Rittenhouse, astronomer and mathematician; Nathaniel Bowditch, the mathematician whose *Practical Navigator* (1792) became the seaman's bible. President Thomas Jefferson, for that matter, was a scientist of more than amateur attainments; nor should it be forgotten that the Lewis and Clark expedition, which Jefferson sent westward in 1804, was one of the most significant scientific projects in American history.

The most important development in American science during these postwar years was the change in attitude of the public and the scientists alike toward scientific study and its application. Long neglected by the colleges and universities, scientific subjects began to appear in the curriculum in the late eighteenth century. Men such as Waterhouse at Brown, Mitchill at Columbia, Silliman at Yale, and Rush at Philadelphia gave instruction in the sciences shortly after the Revolution, but few colleges could boast men of such caliber on their faculties. Nevertheless the trend continued, so that within another thirty years at least some scientific study was virtually mandatory at most of the qualified educational institutions.

Meanwhile, science itself was becoming a profession, no longer a hobby for talented amateurs but a field demanding a man's full time and energy. There was no longer a place for the "natural philosopher" who took all knowledge as his province. Moreover, the wealth of data pressing in upon the scientist forced him to concentrate his area of investigation. The tendency was toward narrower, more specialized branches such as genetics, inorganic and organic chemistry, entomology, paleontology, and so on. The day of the old-time jack-of-all-trades (like Samuel Latham Mitchill, who wrote papers in medicine, chemistry, mathematics, botany, zoology, and anthropology, as well as Popean verse and light essays) was over.

It was true that American scientists, as they themselves admitted, had made fewer theoretical contributions to science than practical ones, and that their main achievements lay in the identification of the flora and fauna of the new continent and the classification of its natural resources. Nevertheless, this was in itself an achievement, for everywhere one looked in the land there were distant horizons of knowledge, so much unknown. In the United States, as in Britain and Europe, these were years of scientific consolidation, rather than discovery. In certain areas, such as chemistry, biology, botany, and zoology, old theories were being demolished and new ones tested; in the better-established disciplines, such as astronomy, physics, and mathematics, scientists were extending lines of research already marked out a century earlier. The Reverend Samuel Miller, writing his *Retrospect of the Eighteenth Century* in 1802, concluded that while American science had matured in the half-century just past, it still derived its impetus from abroad, and that it was not yet "properly self-reliant and independent." This would come in time.

The Search for a National Culture

The early years of American independence produced a great deal of writing, of which only a small part could be called artistically distinguished. It was an age of persuasion and argument, rather than of belles-lettres, and much of what was produced seems amateurish and labored. But whatever its literary value, the writing that Americans did in these years is of utmost importance to an understanding of what they thought and felt as their society took shape — as American ideas were germinating, as a national style was forming, as key issues were being hammered out on the anvil of day-to-day experience. The attainments of the age were not small. Within the span of half a century these men knit thirteen disparate colonies into a unit, erected a government, and launched a nation. What they wrote reflects and expresses much of this achievement.

Having won their political independence, Americans searched for ways to create a culture of their own to express the sense and spirit of their new civilization. They were inheritors of the great Western, classical, Christian tradition they shared with Britain and Europe. Yet they were no longer British and European, but American. How, then, might this inheritance be absorbed and used, rather than simply borrowed or imitated? Editors, critics, authors, orators, and politicians alike agreed with those like Nathan Appleton of New England, who after the Revolution reminded his fellow citizens that they must "sing a New song, a Song that neither We nor our Fathers were ever able to sing before," and the historian David Ramsay, who called for "poets, orators, critics and historians equal to the most celebrated of the ancient commonwealths of Greece and Italy."

Exhortations, unfortunately, did not immediately produce great literary accomplishments. Potential American Homers and Shakespeares faced a number of hurdles and handicaps. A great deal of the creative energy of the times was channeled into political and business life; with a government to construct and a continent to subdue, there was little opportunity to pause for poems. Philip Freneau's advice to young poets to find a job lest they starve had the ring of bitter truth. There were some who felt also that the United States did not have the necessary resources for a distinctive culture and must always lean on Europe. It had no usable past, no tradition of literary patronage, no social diversity; as Washington Irving wrote, it lacked "the charms of storied and poetical associations . . . , the accumulated treasures of age." Neither did the United States have an adequate copyright law. As late as 1830 two of every three books sold came from British or continental presses, and the American market was glutted with cheap, pirated editions of foreign books.

Nevertheless, the outlook for authors was not wholly dark. The American public was literate and well-educated, and, in contrast to Europe, the reading habit was not restricted to the upper classes. Americans, an observer remarked in 1772, had "a taste for books that made almost every man a reader," and foreign travelers rarely failed to note the avidity of newspaper consumption. The cities had numbers of bookstores (Boston alone had fifty in the 1770's) and after 1800 the spread of circulating libraries made books available to almost any American who really wanted to read them. The famous "Coonskin" Library on the Ohio frontier rented books for pelts, and the traveling book-agent poked his way into the remotest log-town hamlet.

To produce its own culture, the United States had first to declare its intellectual independence of Britain. Since no educated American could conceivably wish to reject the great tradition of English letters, his problem became one of what to reject and what to retain that might be made American. As Noah Webster said, no amount of national pride could make him lay aside his beloved Addison. At the outset, the critics decided that Americans should accept Milton, Shakespeare, Addison, Pope, and the rest, but that they must avoid what Webster called "servile imitation" of foreign writing. They must shun anything untrue, immoral, or useless, and things which, in Joel Barlow's phrase, "might prove false and destructive" to American minds.

Simply to avoid European models was not enough. What positive steps might be taken to encourage an *American* artistic tradition? First, though Americans did not have Rob Roy, the Thames, or Cromwell to write about, they decided that they did have a number of things that neither Britain nor Europe could equal. The Indian, the frontier, the Revolution and its heroes, especially the American land itself — these were subjects to challenge and excite the finest artists. The robin, the whippoorwill, and the whispering brook were as inspiring materials for poets, Joseph Dennie thought, "as nightingales, or skylarks, dingles or dells." The Yankee, the Dutchman, the frontiersman, the Southern yeoman, and other national types were as promising literary timber as any of Scott's knights in armor or Germany's young Werthers. The American writer must, then, find the right way to use these unique resources, so that he might create from them a true, correct, and American art. To do so he need only to discover, John Neal wrote, "the abundant and hidden sources of fertility in our own brave earth." Thus the novelist Charles Brockden Brown advised the American writer to observe his own land directly, to "examine objects with his own eyes, employ European models merely for the improvement of his own taste," and to build his art about "all that is genuine and peculiar in the scene before him." In this way, predicted *The Columbian Orator* (1807), "Columbia's soil" might

> Rear Men as great as Britain's isle;
> Exceed what Greece and Rome have done,
> Or any land beneath the sun.

The post-Revolutionary period was one of intense literary activity, marking the beginnings of a strong (if not always first-rate) belletristic tradition, the emergence of a profession of letters, and the slow recognition by artist and public that literature was art as well as utility. The writing of the period is not easily classifiable. It has been called "pre-Romantic," "late Neoclassic," "transitional," "Federalistic," and other terms, all proper but only partially descriptive. It was heavily derivative, filled with echoes of Addison, Pope, Goldsmith, Richardson, and others, as the writing of a generation later would echo Scott, Wordsworth, Burns, and Byron. It was distinguished by two general trends: first, the dominance of political writing; and second, the decreasing importance of certain older forms and the increased popularity of others.

Politics naturally bulked large, since the overriding issues of the times were centered on political rights, independence, and survival. Government and law (as theology earlier) attracted the best minds of the Revolutionary generation, and the level of their writing was high. John Adams' *Novanglus*, or Dickinson's *Letters*, or Paine's pamphlets, or the *Federalist* papers, belong in the first rank of political literature in any century. Jefferson's Declaration of Independence, with its adjustment of reason to emotion, its balance of theory with application, and its magnificent rhetoric, cannot be matched.

Among the forms which lost considerable ground after the Revolution were the diary and the journal, both favorite means of self-expression in an earlier, more introspective era. The published sermon rapidly declined in popularity (soon to be replaced by the secular oration), and though travel narratives were still fairly common, they were no longer so widely read as earlier. The promotional tract, its purpose gone, quickly disappeared. The "captivity" tale, favorite American reading since Captain John Smith's adventures, was absorbed into the novel. Such changes were natural reflections of the shifting nature of American society and taste. Those forms of writing of a more direct artistic purpose, in which the ideas of the writer were shaped within the pattern of novel, poem, essay, or play, increased in popularity and their practitioners in skill and sophistication. Also, as one might expect, the postwar drive for nationalism and patriotism caused great activity in both biography and history, culminating in such works as Ramsay's *History of South Carolina* (1786), Belknap's *American Biography* (1794–98), "Parson" Weems's famous *Washington* (1800), Mrs. Mercy Warren's *Rise, Progress, and Termination of the American Revolution* (1805), and John Marshall's monumental *Life of Washington* (1804–7).

The development of the American essay depended largely on the growth of magazines and newspapers. American writers copied Addison, Steele, Goldsmith, Butler, and the other great English satirists in profusion; few newspapers were without a "Tatler" or a "Scriblerus" imitating their masters. The essay attracted the best authors of the time, as well as the least talented; among those who wrote essays of superior literary quality were Franklin, Freneau, Noah Webster, Joseph Dennie, and James Paulding. The essay was not only an accepted form within which one could imitate or experiment without much risk; it was also a useful vehicle for moral instruction, political comment, satire, burlesque, criticism, or casual pleasure. Washington Irving, after serving an apprenticeship with his *Jonathan Oldstyle* (1802) and *Salmagundi* (1807–8) series, became with *The Sketch-Book* (1819–20) the first identifiably American essayist, in spirit, style, and subject, and unquestionably the best. His popularity, abroad and at home, gave a swift answer to the English critic Sidney Smith's sneer of 1820, "Who reads an American book?"

Although the novel encountered less public and ecclesiastical opposition after the war than earlier in the century, few men of substance believed it worthy of serious consideration as an art form. Ministers cautioned against fiction that might "inflame the passions and corrupt the heart," and even so sophisticated a poet as John Trumbull expressed distrust of

> . . . books that poison all the mind,
> Novels and plays (where shines display'd
> A world that nature never made.)

For that matter, some believed that there was really very little in America for the novelist to write about. "A novel describing these savage barbarians (*Indians*), their squaws and papooses," wrote one critic (a few years before James Fenimore Cooper), "would not be very interesting." The American who wanted to write a novel also had to compete against the whole established array of British novelists in pirated editions, as well as against the lingering snobbishness and Anglophilia of segments of the reading public. It was easier and safer to imitate Richardson or Scott than to write an American book. Cooper himself found it advisable to foster the rumor that his first novel was by "a prominent Englishman."

Nevertheless, the demand for novels increased so swiftly that bookstores could hardly stock them fast enough, and magazines printed them serially by scores. Following British models, American novels tended to fall into four classes: the novel of morality and sentiment, derived from Richardson and Sterne; the "Gothic" novel of suspense and emotion, modeled on Ann Radcliffe, Walpole, and Godwin; the picaresque-satiric novel, drawn from Smollett, Swift, and Fielding; and the historical romance, inspired by Sir Walter Scott. William Hill Brown's *Power of Sympathy* (1789), the first successful American sentimental novel, was followed by Susannah Rowson's *Charlotte Temple* (1790), which ran subsequently to nearly two hundred editions. After Charlotte opened the floodgates, the magazines were filled with despairing but virtuous heroines, rascally villains, and hapless orphans. Royall Tyler's *Algerine Captive* (1797) and H. H. Brackenridge's *Modern Chivalry* (1792–97) were satiric novels, but the type never attained popularity. The Gothic tradition attracted Charles Brockden Brown, the most gifted novelist of the pre-Cooper years, whose *Wieland* (1798) and *Ormond* (1799) were excellent if uneven books.

Sir Walter Scott's novels took the United States by storm; adapted, memorized, summarized, dramatized, and imitated, they sold more than a half-million copies in America by 1823. The notice of a forth-coming Scott novel, one bookseller reported, excited "a greater sensation in the United States than some of Napoleon's battles." Since Scott's powerful nationalism and his superb use of history represented exactly what Americans hoped to do with their own national experience, dozens of novelists tried to apply the Scott formula to native materials. Aside from thirty-five towns named Waverley, several side-wheel steamers named *Marmion,* and hundreds of little girls named Rowena, the success of the Scott imitators was negligible. James Fenimore Cooper, beginning with *The Spy* in 1821 and *The Pioneers* in 1823, did more than imitate Scott; he naturalized him, so that the historical romance became American. When Leatherstocking walked into fiction with his long rifle, the American novel came of age.

The shift of opinion concerning the theater after 1750 reflected parallel changes in American society. The lessening of religious prejudices against plays, the growth of urban playgoing audiences, the emergence of professional management and the star system, among other things, had much to do with the growing interest in the stage. English companies played fairly regular tours of the colonies, and a few American plays had been produced before the Revolution, notably Thomas Godfrey's pseudo-Jacobean tragedy, *The Prince of Parthia* (1767). However, since the theaters were closed as a wartime measure and the British occupied the major cities, the drama practically vanished until 1783. At the close of the war acting groups quickly reappeared, and within fifteen years several new playhouses were built. Boston's Federal Street Theater and Philadelphia's Chestnut Street Theater opened in 1794, New York's Park Theater in 1798, and both New York and Philadelphia had permanent acting companies by 1800. But the American stage still leaned heavily on imported plays and players, with a few notable exceptions such as Thomas Wignell, who made a career of playing the down-east Yankee, and Lewis Hallam junior, who played everything.

Of the numerous American playwrights who attempted to compete with imported British plays, only Royall Tyler and William Dunlap found much success. Tyler, a Boston lawyer who later sat on the Vermont Supreme Court, wrote a witty comedy of manners, *The Contrast,* first performed in 1787, that merits being called the first American dramatic hit. Dunlap, who wrote at least sixty-five plays, adapted dozens more, and managed two stage companies, wrote and produced *André*, the best tragic play of the period. Despite the popularity of a few dramatists and players, however, the theater found hard going. It had not yet outgrown its dependence on Britain; playgoing audiences, complained the dramatist James Nelson Barker, were still "mental colonists" in the theater. The American stage needed good plays, regular seasons, and solid financing, for all of which it had to wait another generation.

Poets had the most difficult task. "Of all the fools that haunt our coast," wrote Philip Freneau, "the scribbling tribe I pity most." There were no doubt many young men of poetic gifts in the new nation, but the muse attracted few disciples in a climate of revolution and political strife. Some wrote a limited amount of verse, but gave up and turned to law, politics, theology, or education, for, as Freneau commented, "An age employed in edging steel, can no poetic raptures feel." The poetic tradition was trapped in imitation — of Pope, Dryden, Churchill, the "graveyard" school, and later of Scott, Byron, Moore, Leigh Hunt — for it was more convenient and much safer for an American to copy approved models than to strike out for himself, notwithstanding the clamor of critics for "bards of native style."

Since satire was especially suited to the uses of war and politics, lampoons, burlesques, mock epics, hudibrastics, and other combative poetic types flooded out nearly everything else. The contemporary obsession with nationalism led a number of poets, such as Joel Barlow and Timothy Dwight, to expend their limited gifts on awkward patriotic odes and national epics. Yet there were a few authentic American voices. John Trumbull's impish satires showed more than passing talent; Timothy Dwight's inflated pomposities displayed some effective moments of power and dignity; Joel Barlow's "American epic" never came off, but his attempt was not a total failure. Philip Freneau, sea captain, journalist, and poet, produced the best lyric poetry of his generation, combining an unusual freshness and originality with consummate technique. The skill and delicacy of his better verse was unmatched by any American poet of his era and few British, and despite his restlessness and uneven discipline he deserves to be called the first major American poet.

American literature, taken as a whole from 1776 to 1820, was only partially American, still to a large extent derivative, imitative, dependent on British models and standards. It was, however, self-consciously searching for a mode and style of its own, testing ways of using its own materials and expressing its own attitudes. The real liberation of American literature was yet to come.

A NOTE ON THE TEXTS

The problems of establishing authoritative texts for much of the material in this anthology, and particularly in the first volume, are manifold and complex. Twentieth-century editions from manuscript, as those of William Bradford, Edward Taylor, and John Woolman, are generally trustworthy; but they are few. Modern editions of work originally printed in the seventeenth and eighteenth centuries, as for example the fine Yale edition of Benjamin Franklin's *Papers*, sometimes differ substantially from earlier "standard" editions, but do not record the differences, and force the reader back to original publications to determine correct readings. Widely used and respected editions, rightly termed standard, such as the Original Narratives of Early American History series, generally prove to be excellent reprints of nineteenth-century reprints. And while the student of early American thought and writing cannot review the materials preserved in the *Collections* and the *Proceedings* of the Massachusetts Historical Society without gratitude and admiration, he is still obliged to confirm the accuracy of these printings by recourse to original publications where they exist.

Fortunately, the American Antiquarian Society's project of microfilming all the verifiable titles in Charles Evans' *American Bibliography* has made copies of American publications to 1820 widely available, and must stand as the most authoritative source for many of the selections in this anthology. But given the irregularities of early American printing, the variations among existing copies of these books, the lack of thoroughgoing collations, and the fact that some important works by Americans were printed in England but not in America, the Evans microfilms can only be a first step in securing definitive texts. The problem is complicated further by the fact that books of the same title often appeared in considerably different form when published in England (as in the case of Thomas Hooker's *The Application of Redemption*), that piracies and posthumous editions of questionable authority were common, that works like Robert Beverley's *The History and Present State of Virginia* were sometimes mutilated by the author himself in revised editions, and that when writers like Jonathan Edwards gained sufficient stature to be collected into *Works*, their language was frequently "improved" by their editors. The present efforts of the National Historical Commission and the Center for Editions of American Authors of the Modern Language Association are doing much to solve these problems, but it will be years before any but the major figures of American history and literature will be represented by definitive readings.

The present editors have therefore attempted, on a variety of grounds, to use the best or most representative texts in the selections that follow, giving priority to first editions and modern critical editions, and comparing texts when variant lifetime or other putatively authoritative editions exist. The authorities for the verbal sequence of the selections are cited in the headnotes. Colonial printing practice regarding capitals, abbreviations, italics, and spelling was often whimsical and inconsistent. For this reason, the editors have generally modernized the texts in these respects, retaining unusual spellings, however, when they may be presumed to distinguish colonial pronunciation from modern American English (e.g., *shew* for *show*, *then* for *than*, *learnt* for *learned*), and allowing the consequent irregularities to stand; special care has been taken not to impair the pronunciation of the poetry. To maintain the rhythms of early American writing, we have in general retained the punctuation of the source texts, emending only occasionally to remove impediments to understanding.

R. B. N.
N. S. G.

Making a Revolution

⊛ John Wise (1652–1725)

JOHN WISE of Massachusetts belonged to the first native-born generation of New Englanders. A Harvard graduate of 1673, he studied theology and accepted a pulpit at Ipswich, Massachusetts. When Governor Andros, the royal governor, attempted to levy a tax on the colony in order to raise money for the treasury, Wise was one of the leaders of resistance.

Wise was arrested in 1687 by order of the Governor, tried, found guilty, fined fifty pounds, put under bond of a thousand pounds, and forbidden to preach. Later he was allowed to return to his pulpit, and after Andros was recalled, Wise was a delegate from Ipswich in the reorganized colonial legislature.

From 1705 to 1717 he engaged in an acrid pamphlet battle with the Mathers over what he considered their reactionary policies of church organization. A writer of clear, persuasive, powerful prose, Wise was also a pulpit orator of great effectiveness. His sermons on political and religious liberty, directed against Andros and the Mathers, were reprinted in 1772 and widely distributed as part of the colonial argument with England.

TEXT: John Wise, *A Vindication of the Government of New England Churches* (Boston, 1717).

Original Liberty

[From *A Vindication of the Government of New England Churches*, 1717]

The second great immunity of man is an original liberty instampt upon his rational nature. He that intrudes upon this liberty, violates the law of nature. In this discourse I shall waive the consideration of man's moral turpitude, but shall view him physically as a creature which God has made and furnished essentially with many ennobling immunities, which render him the most august animal in the world, and still, whatever has happened since his creation, he remains at the upper end of nature, and as such is a creature of a very noble character. For as to his dominion, the whole frame of the lower part of the universe is devoted to his use, and at his command; and his liberty under the conduct of right reason, is equal with his trust. Which liberty may be briefly considered, internally as to his mind, and externally as to his person.

3

1. The internal native liberty of man's nature in general implies, a faculty of doing or omitting things according to the direction of his judgment. But in a more special meaning, this liberty does not consist in a loose and ungovernable freedom, or in an unbounded license of acting. Such license is disagreeing with the condition and dignity of man, and would make man of a lower and meaner constitution than brute creatures; who in all their liberties are kept under a better and more rational government, by their instincts. Therefore as Plutarch says, Those persons only who live in obedience to reason, are worthy to be accounted free: They alone live as they will, who have learnt what they ought to will. So that the true natural liberty of man, such as really and truly agrees to him, must be understood, as he is guided and restrained by the ties of reason, and laws of nature; all the rest is brutal, if not worse.

2. Man's external personal, natural liberty, antecedent to all humane parts, or alliances must also be considered. And so every man must be conceived to be perfectly in his own power and disposal, and not to be controlled by the authority of any other. And thus every man must be acknowledged equal to every man, since all subjection and all command are equally banished on both sides; and considering all men thus at liberty, every man has a prerogative to judge for himself, viz., what shall be most for his behalf, happiness and well-being.

The third capital immunity belonging to man's nature, is an equality amongst men; which is not to be denied by the law of nature, till man has resigned himself with all his rights for the sake of a civil state; and then his personal liberty and equality is to be cherished, and preserved to the highest degree, as will consist with all just distinctions amongst men of honor, and shall be agreeable with the public good. For man has a high valuation of himself, and the passion seems to lay its first foundation really in the high and admirable frame and constitution of humane nature. The word man, says my author, is thought to carry somewhat of dignity in its sound; and we commonly make use of this as the most proper and prevailing argument against a rude insulter, viz., I am not a beast or a dog, but am a man as well as yourself. Since then humane nature agrees equally with all persons; and since no one can live a sociable life with another that does not own or respect him as a man; it follows as a command of the law of nature, that every man esteem and treat another as one who is naturally his equal, or who is a man as well as he. There be many popular or plausible reasons that greatly illustrate this equality, viz., that we all derive our being from one stock, the same common father of the humane race. On this consideration *Boethius* checks the pride of the insulting nobility.

> *Quid genus et proavos strepitis?*
> *Si primordia vestra,*

Auteremque deum spectas,
Nullus degener extat
Nisi vitiis perjura fovens,
Proprium deserat ortum.

Fondly our first descent we boast;
If whence at first our breath we drew
The common springs of life we view,
The airy notion soon is lost.

The Almighty made us equal all;
But he that slavishly complies
To do the drudgery of vice,
Denies his high original.

And also that our bodies are composed of matter, frail, brittle, and liable to be destroyed by a thousand accidents; we all owe our existence to the same method of propagation. The noblest mortal in his entrance on to the stage of life, is not distinguished by any pomp or of passage from the lowest of mankind; and our life hastens to the same general mark: Death observes no ceremony, but knocks as loud at the barriers of the court, as at the door of the cottage. This equality being admitted, bears a very great force in maintaining peace and friendship amongst men.

✑ Jonathan Mayhew (1720–1766)

JONATHAN MAYHEW, born on Martha's Vineyard and a Harvard theology graduate, was pastor of Boston's West Church. A vigorous preacher, Mayhew was an avowed liberal in his theology; in fact, his reputation as an agitator was such that when he was ordained in 1747, only two other ministers appeared for the ceremonies. His strong belief in the responsibility of the individual and the right of private judgment placed him in the center of a number of theological arguments. An admirer of John Milton and John Locke, Mayhew preached powerful sermons against what he believed were Parliamentary encroachments on colonial rights. He was especially angry at the Stamp Act, and, with Samuel Adams, was one of the most prominent leaders of the Bostonian opposition.

Mayhew's sermon *A Discourse Concerning Unlimited Submission and Non-resistance to the Higher Powers* was given, significantly, on January 30, 1750, the anniversary of the execution of Charles I by the Cromwellian Puritans.

TEXT: Jonathan Mayhew, A *Discourse Concerning Unlimited Submission and Non-resistance to the Higher Powers* (Boston, 1750).

On the Righteousness of Rebellion

[From A *Discourse Concerning Unlimited Submission,* 1750]

If we calmly consider the nature of the thing itself, nothing can well be imagined more directly contrary to common sense than to suppose that millions of people should be subjected to the arbitrary, precarious pleasure of *one single man,* — who has naturally no superiority over them in point of authority, — so that their estates, and everything that is valuable in life, and even their lives also, shall be absolutely at his disposal, if he happens to be wanton and capricious enough to demand them. What unprejudiced man can think that God made ALL to be thus subservient to the lawless pleasure and frenzy of ONE, so that it shall always be a sin to resist him? Nothing but the most plain and express revelation from heaven could make a sober, impartial man believe such a monstrous, unaccountable doctrine; and, indeed, the thing itself appears so shocking, so out of all *proportion,* that it may be questioned whether all the miracles that ever were wrought could make it credible that this doctrine really came from God. At present there is not the least syllable in Scripture which gives any countenance to it. The hereditary, indefeasible, divine right of kings, and the doctrine of non-resistance, which is built upon the supposition of such a right, are altogether as fabulous and chimerical as transubstantiation, or any of the most absurd reveries of ancient or modern visionaries. These notions are fetched neither from divine revelation nor human reason; and, if they are derived from neither of those sources, it is not much matter from *whence they come or whither they go.* . . .

We may very safely assert these two things in general, without undermining government: One is, that no civil rulers are to be obeyed when they enjoin things that are inconsistent with the commands of God. All such disobedience is lawful and glorious; particularly if persons refuse to comply with any *legal establishment of religion,* because it is a gross perversion and corruption — as to doctrine, worship, and discipline — of a pure and divine religion, brought from heaven to earth by the *Son of God,* — the only King and Head of the Christian Church, — and propagated through the word by his inspired apostles. All commands running counter to the declared will of the Supreme Legislator of heaven and earth are null and void, and therefore disobedience to them is a duty, not a crime. Another thing that may be asserted with equal truth and safety is, that no government is to be submitted to at the expense of that which is the sole end of all government — the common good and safety of society. Because to submit in this case, if it should ever happen, would evidently be to set up the means as more valuable and above the end, than which there cannot be a greater solecism and contradiction. The only reason of the institution of civil government, and the only rational ground of submission to it, is the common safety and utility. If, therefore, in any case, the common safety and utility would not be promoted by submission to government, but the contrary, there is no ground or motive for obedience and submission, but for the contrary.

Whoever considers the nature of civil government, must indeed be sensible that a great degree of *implicit confidence* must unavoidably be placed in those that bear rule: this is implied in the very notion of authority's being originally a *trust*, committed by the people, to those who are vested with it, — as all just and righteous authority is. All besides is mere lawless force and usurpation; neither God nor nature having given any man a right of dominion over any society independently of that society's approbation and consent to be governed by him. — Now, as all men are fallible, it cannot be supposed that the public affairs of any state should be always administered in the best manner possible, even by persons of the greatest wisdom and integrity. Nor is it sufficient to legitimate disobedience to the *higher powers* that they are not so administered, or that they are in some instances very ill-managed; for, upon this principle, it is scarcely supposable that any government at all could be supported, or subsist. Such a principle manifestly tends to the dissolution of government, and to throw all things into confusion and anarchy. But it is equally evident, upon the other hand, that those in authority may abuse their trust and power to *such a degree*, that neither the law of reason nor of religion requires that any obedience or submission should be paid to them; but, on the contrary, that they should be totally *discarded*, and the authority which they were before vested with transferred to others, who may exercise it more to those good purposes for which it is given. Nor is this principle, that resistance to the higher powers is in some extraordinary cases justifiable, so liable to abuse as many persons seem to apprehend it. For, although there will be always some petulant, querulous men in every state, — men of factious, turbulent, and carping dispositions, glad to lay hold of any trifle to justify and legitimate their caballing against their rulers, and other seditious practices, — yet there are, comparatively speaking, but few men of this *contemptible* character. It does not appear but that mankind in general have a disposition to be as submissive and passive and tame under government as they ought to be. Witness a great, if not the greatest, part of the known world, who are now groaning, but not murmuring, under the heavy yoke of tyranny! While those who govern do it with any tolerable degree of moderation and justice, and in any good measure act up to their office and character by being public benefactors, the people will generally be easy and peaceable, and be rather inclined to flatter and adore than to insult and resist them. Nor was there ever any *general* complaint against any administration, which *lasted long,* but what there was good reason for. Till people find themselves greatly abused and oppressed by their governors, they are not apt to complain; and whenever they do, in fact, find themselves thus abused and oppressed, they must be stupid not to complain. To say that subjects in general are not proper judges when their governors oppress them and play the tyrant, and when they defend their rights, administer justice impartially, and promote the public welfare, is as great *treason* as ever man uttered. 'Tis treason, not against one *single* man, but the state — against the whole body politic; 'tis treason against mankind, 'tis treason against common sense, 'tis treason against God. And this impious principle lays the foundation for justifying all the tyranny and oppression that ever any prince was guilty of. The people know for what end they set up and maintain their governors, and they are the proper judges when they execute their *trust* as they ought to do it; — when their prince exercises an equitable and paternal authority over them; when from a prince and common father he exalts himself into a tyrant; when from subjects and children he degrades them into the classes of slaves, plunders them, makes them his prey, and unnaturally sports himself with their lives and fortunes.

⟡ Samuel Adams (1722–1803)

BOSTON-BORN, and a cousin of John Adams, Samuel Adams graduated from Harvard, studied law, and entered business. He had small success in either law or business, but soon discovered that he possessed political skill of a high order. By the 1760's he was a power in Boston politics, and as the contest with Britain took shape, Sam Adams emerged as undisputed leader of the "radical" or "independence" party in Massachusetts.

Adams helped to organize the Boston "Sons of Liberty," drew up the Boston "Bill of Rights," had a hand in the Boston Tea Party, and led the opposition to the Sugar Act, the Stamp Act, and the Boston Port Bill. "I doubt whether there is a greater incendiary in the King's dominion," Governor Hutchinson wrote of him.

At the beginning of his terms in the Massachusetts House of Representatives (1765–74), Adams introduced a set of resolutions intended to write out "the laws of God and nature" and man's consequent rights in clear and unmistakable terms. As the break with Britain approached, he instituted the system of Committees of Correspondence which had much to do with organizing and consolidating anti-British opposition in New England. He served in the Continental Congress as one of the representatives of Massachusetts, signed the Declaration of Independence, and remained in Congress until 1781. After the war he was elected lieutenant governor and later governor of Massachusetts.

Adams' skill in identifying and phrasing basic principles in clear, incisive, inspiring language and his gift for political leadership were of great importance in framing and executing a revolution. He was less effective as a peacetime leader, and his influence in Massachusetts waned after the war.

TEXTS: Harry Alonzo Cushing, ed., *The Writings of Samuel Adams* (New York, 1905–8), I, 444–446; II, 351–355.

The American Position

[Resolutions of the House of Representatives of Massachusetts,
October 29, 1765]

Whereas the just rights of his Majesty's subjects of this Province, derived to them from the British Constitution, as well as the royal charter, have been lately drawn into question: in order to ascertain the same, this House do unanimously come into the following resolves: —

1. *Resolved,* That there are certain essential rights of the British Constitution of government, which are founded in the law of God and nature, and are the common rights of mankind; — therefore,

2. *Resolved,* That the inhabitants of this Province are unalienably entitled to those essential rights in common with all men: and that no law of society can, consistent with the law of God and nature, divest them of those rights.

3. *Resolved,* That no man can justly take the property of another without his consent; and that upon this original principle, the right of representation in the same body which exercises the power of making laws for levying taxes, which is one of the main pillars of the British Constitution, is evidently founded.

4. *Resolved,* That this inherent right, together with all other essential rights, liberties, privileges, and immunities of the people of Great Britain, have been fully confirmed to them by Magna Charta, and by former and by later acts of Parliament.

5. *Resolved,* That his Majesty's subjects in America are, in reason and common sense, entitled to the same extent of liberty with his Majesty's subjects in Britain.

6. *Resolved,* That by the declaration of the royal charter of this Province, the inhabitants are entitled to all the rights, liberties, and immunities of free and natural subjects of Great Britain to all intents, purposes, and constructions whatever.

7. *Resolved,* That the inhabitants of this Province appear to be entitled to all the rights aforementioned by an act of Parliament, 13th of Geo. II.

8. *Resolved,* That those rights do belong to the inhabitants of this Province upon the principle of common justice; their ancestors having settled this country at their sole expense, and their posterity having approved themselves most loyal and faithful subjects of Great Britain.

9. *Resolved,* That every individual in the Colonies is as advantageous to Great Britain as if he were in Great Britain and held to pay his full proportion of taxes there; and as the inhabitants of this Province pay their full proportion of taxes for the support of his Majesty's government here, it is unreasonable for them to be called upon to pay any part of the charges of the government there.

10. *Resolved,* That the inhabitants of this Province are not, and never have been, represented in the Parliament of Great Britain; and that such a representation there as the subjects in Britain do actually and rightfully enjoy *is impracticable* for the subjects in America; — and further, that in the opinion of this House, the several subordinate powers of legislation in America were constituted upon the apprehensions of this *impracticability.*

11. *Resolved,* That the only method whereby the constitutional rights of the subjects of this Province can be secure, consistent with a subordination to the supreme power of Great Britain, is by the continued exercise of such powers of government as are granted in the royal charter, and a firm adherence to the privileges of the same.

12. *Resolved,* — as a just conclusion from some of the foregoing resolves, — That all acts made by any power whatever, other than the General Assembly of this Province, imposing taxes on the inhabitants, are infringements of our inherent and unalienable rights as men and British subjects, and render void the most valuable declarations of our charter.

13. *Resolved,* That the extension of the powers of the Court of Admiralty within this Province is a most violent infraction of the right of trials by juries, — a right which this House, upon the principles of their British ancestors, hold most dear and sacred; it being the only security of the lives, liberties, and properties of his Majesty's subjects here.

14. *Resolved,* That this House owe the strictest allegiance to his most sacred Majesty King George the Third; that they have the greatest veneration for the Parliament; and that they will, after the example of all their predecessors from the settlement of this country, exert themselves to their utmost in supporting his Majesty's authority in the Province, in promoting the true happiness of his subjects, and in enlarging the extent of his dominion.

Ordered, That all the foregoing resolves be kept in the records of this House, that a just sense of liberty and the firm sentiments of loyalty be transmitted to posterity.

The Natural Rights of Colonists

[From *Statement of the Rights of Colonists* . . . , 1772]

Among the Natural Rights of the Colonists are these: first, a right to *Life;* secondly to *Liberty;* thirdly to *Property;* together with the right to support and defend them in the best manner they can — Those are evident branches of, rather than deductions from the Duty of Self Preservation, commonly called the first Law of Nature. ——

All men have a right to remain in a state of nature as long as they please: and in case of intolerable oppression, civil or religious, to leave the society they belong to, and enter into another. ——

When men enter into society, it is by voluntary consent; and they have a right to demand and insist upon the performance of such conditions and previous limitations as form an equitable *original compact.* ——

Every natural right not expressly given up or from the nature of a social compact necessarily ceded remains. ——

All positive and civil laws should conform as far as possible to the law of natural reason and equity. ——

As neither reason requires, nor religion permits the contrary, every man living in or out of a state of civil society has a right peaceably and quietly to worship God according to the dictates of his conscience. ——

"Just and true liberty, equal and impartial liberty" in matters spiritual and temporal, is a thing that all men are clearly entitled to, by the eternal and immutable laws of God and nature, as well as by the law of Nations, and all well-grounded municipal laws, which must have their foundation in the former. ——

In regard to religion, mutual toleration in the different professions thereof is what all good and candid minds in all ages have ever practiced; and both by precept and example inculcated on mankind. And

it is now generally agreed among Christians that this spirit of toleration in the fullest extent consistent with the being of civil society "is
the chief characteristical mark of the true church," and in so much that
Mr. Locke has asserted, and proved beyond the possibility of contradiction on any solid ground, that such toleration ought to be extended to all whose doctrines are not subversive of society. The only
sects which he thinks ought to be, and which by all wise laws are
excluded from such toleration, are those who teach doctrines subversive of the civil government under which they live. The Roman
Catholics or Papists are excluded by reason of such doctrines as these,
"that princes excommunicated may be deposed, and those they call
heretics may be destroyed without mercy; besides their recognizing
the Pope in so absolute a manner, in subversion of government, by
introducing as far as possible into the states, under whose protection
they enjoy life, liberty, and property, that solecism in politics, *Im-
perium in imperio,* leading directly to the worst anarchy and confusion,
civil discord, war and bloodshed." ——

The natural liberty of men by entering into society is abridged or
restrained so far only as is necessary for the great end of society the
best good of the whole. ——

In the state of nature, every man is, under God, judge and sole
judge of his own rights and the injuries done him. By entering into
society, he agrees to an arbiter or indifferent judge between him and
his neighbors; but he no more renounces his original right, than by
taking a cause out of the ordinary course of law, and leaving the decision to referees or indifferent arbitrations. In the last case he must
pay the referees for time and trouble; he should be also willing to pay
his just quota for the support of government, the law and constitution;
the end of which is to furnish indifferent and impartial judges in all
cases that may happen, whether civil, ecclesiastical, marine, or military. ——

"The natural liberty of man is to be free from any superior power
on earth, and not to be under the will or legislative authority of man;
but only to have the law of nature for his rule." ——

In the state of nature men may as the Patriarchs did, employ hired
servants for the defense of their lives, liberty, and property; and they
should pay them reasonable wages. Government was instituted for the
purposes of common defense; and those who hold the reins of government have an equitable natural right to an honorable support from the
same principle "that the laborer is worthy of his hire"; but then the
same community which they serve ought to be assessors of their pay.
Governors have no right to seek what they please; by this, instead of
being content with the station assigned them, that of honorable
servants of the society, they would soon become absolute masters,

despots, and tyrants. Hence as a private man has a right to say what wages he will give in his private affairs, so has a community to determine what they will give and grant of their substance, for the administration of public affairs. And in both cases more are ready generally to offer their service at the proposed and stipulated price than are able and willing to perform their duty. ——

In short, it is the greatest absurdity to suppose it in the power of one or any number of men at the entering into society, to renounce their essential natural rights, or the means of preserving those rights when the great end of civil government from the very nature of its institution is for the support, protection, and defense of those very rights: the principal of which, as is before observed, are life, liberty, and property. If men through fear, fraud, or mistake, should *in terms* renounce and give up any essential natural right, the eternal law of reason and the great end of society would absolutely vacate such renunciation; the right to freedom being *the gift* of God Almighty, it is not in the power of man to alienate this gift, and voluntarily become a slave. ——

◌ James Wilson (1742–1798)

SCOTTISH-BORN James Wilson studied at Glasgow and Edinburgh before coming to Philadelphia in 1767. He read law in John Dickinson's law office, and by reason of his talent as writer and speaker soon became known as a young political leader of promise. He threw himself into the revolutionary cause with fervor, and in 1774 wrote a pamphlet, *Considerations on the Nature and Extent of Legislative Authority of the British Parliament,* which was perhaps the best statement of the colonial contention that Parliament had no authority over the colonies, since they were separate states governed only by a common King. Wilson served in the Continental Congress, signed the Declaration of Independence, and enlisted in the army. After the war he practiced law successfully and played an important part in the Constitutional Convention of 1787. Washington appointed him an Associate Justice of the Supreme Court, a post he filled with great distinction until his death.

TEXT: E. C. Stedman and E. M. Hutchinson, *A Library of American Literature* (New York, 1889–90), III, 260–261.

Loyalty to Law

[From a Speech in Vindication of the Colonies, delivered in
the Convention for the Province of Pennsylvania, January 1775]

Are we deficient in loyalty to his majesty? Let our conduct convict,
for it will fully convict, the insinuation that we are, of falsehood. Our
loyalty has always appeared in the true form of loyalty; in obeying our
sovereign according to law: let those who would require it in any other
form, know that we call the persons who execute his commands, when
contrary to law, disloyal and traitors. Are we enemies to the power of
the Crown? No, sir, we are its best friends: this friendship prompts us
to wish that the power of the Crown may be firmly established on the
most solid basis; but we know that the constitution alone will perpetuate the former, and securely uphold the latter. Are our principles
irreverent to majesty? They are quite the reverse: we ascribe to it
perfection almost divine. We say that the king can do no wrong: we
say that to do wrong is the property, not of power, but of weakness.
We feel oppression, and will oppose it; but we know, for our constitution tells us, that oppression can never spring from the throne. We
must, therefore, search elsewhere for its source: our infallible guide
will direct us to it. Our constitution tells us that all oppression springs
from the ministers of the throne. The attributes of perfection ascribed
to the king, are, neither by the constitution nor in fact, communicable
to his ministers. They may do wrong; they have often done wrong;
they have been often punished for doing wrong.

Here we may discern the true cause of all the impudent clamor
and unsupported accusations of the ministers and of their minions, that
have been raised and made against the conduct of the Americans.
Those ministers and minions are sensible that the opposition is directed,
not against his majesty, but against them; because they have abused
his majesty's confidence, brought discredit upon his government, and
derogated from his justice. They see the public vengeance collected
in dark clouds around them: their consciences tell them that it should
be hurled, like a thunder-bolt, at their guilty heads. Appalled with
guilt and fear, they skulk behind the throne. Is it disrespectful to drag
them into public view, and make a distinction between them and his
majesty, under whose venerable name they daringly attempt to shelter
their crimes? Nothing can more effectually contribute to establish his
majesty on the throne, and to secure to him the affections of his people,
than this distinction. By it we are taught to consider all the blessings
of government as flowing from the throne; and to consider every instance of oppression as proceeding, which in truth is oftenest the case,
from the ministers.

If, now, it is true that all force employed for the purposes so often mentioned, is force unwarranted by any act of Parliament; unsupported by any principle of the common law; unauthorized by any commission from the Crown; that, instead of being employed for the support of the constitution and his majesty's government, it must be employed for the support of oppression and ministerial tyranny; if all this is true (and I flatter myself it appears to be true), can any one hesitate to say that to resist such force is lawful; and that both the letter and the spirit of the British constitution justify such resistance?

Resistance, both by the letter and the spirit of the British constitution, may be carried further, when necessity requires it, than I have carried it. Many examples in the English history might be adduced, and many authorities of the greatest weight might be brought to show that when the king, forgetting his character and his dignity, has stepped forth and openly avowed and taken a part in such iniquitous conduct as has been described; in such cases, indeed, the distinction above mentioned, wisely made by the constitution for the security of the Crown, could not be applied; because the Crown had unconstitutionally rendered the application of it impossible. What has been the consequence? The distinction between him and his ministers has been lost; but they have not been raised to his situation; he has sunk to theirs.

◄ℜ Benjamin Franklin (1706–1790)

FRANKLIN, when he retired from business, hoped to lead a quiet, contemplative life in his library and laboratory. However, he was almost immediately appointed deputy postmaster for the colonies, a post he held from 1753 to 1774. He was very early concerned with the colonial cause in the rapidly developing argument between colonies and mother country, and in 1754 was instrumental in arranging the Albany Congress, which found no solution to the problem. After 1757 he served in London as agent for Pennsylvania, representing that colony's interests before Parliament and King, and from 1770 to 1775 he represented not only Pennsylvania, but also Georgia, New Jersey, and Massachusetts. In 1775, having given up any hopes for compromising or averting the great colonial-imperial clash to come, he returned to America.

As if he had not already lived enough lives for one man, Franklin at sixty-nine joined the revolutionary cause, served on the Pennsylvania Committee of Correspondence, as delegate to the Second Continental Congress, and as one of the committee appointed to draw up the Declaration of Independence. The next year he went to France as the first representative of the United States, serving with great effectiveness. In 1778 he secured the French alliance, which was the greatest single factor in the ultimate military and naval victory of the Revolution, and in 1783 he was, with John Adams and John Jay, a member of the committee which wrote the peace treaty at Paris.

Franklin returned to the new country to serve two terms as president of Pennsylvania, and finally, at eighty-one, he sat in the Philadelphia convention, with men half his age, to write the American Constitution. Franklin's career in the service of his country remains unmatched.

TEXTS: Albert H. Smyth, ed., *The Writings of Benjamin Franklin* (New York, 1905–7), VI, 127–137, 407; VII, 27–30.

Rules by Which a Great Empire May Be Reduced to a Small One

PRESENTED TO A LATE MINISTER, WHEN HE ENTERED UPON HIS ADMINISTRATION

[1773]

An ancient Sage boasted, that, tho' he could not fiddle, he knew how to make a *great city* of a *little one*. The science that I, a modern simpleton, am about to communicate, is the very reverse.

I address myself to all ministers who have the management of extensive dominions, which from their very greatness are become troublesome to govern, because the multiplicity of their affairs leaves no time for *fiddling*.

I. In the first place, gentlemen, you are to consider, that a great empire, like a great cake, is most easily diminished at the edges. Turn your attention, therefore, first to your *remotest* provinces; that, as you get rid of them, the next may follow in order.

II. That the possibility of this separation may always exist, take special care the provinces are never incorporated with the mother country; that they do not enjoy the same common rights, the same privileges in commerce; and that they are governed by *severer* laws, all of *your enacting*, without allowing them any share in the choice of the legislators. By carefully making and preserving such distinctions, you will (to keep to my simile of the cake) act like a wise gingerbread-baker, who, to facilitate a division, cuts his dough half through in those places where, when baked, he would have it *broken to pieces*.

III. Those remote provinces have perhaps been acquired, purchased, or conquered, at the *sole expence* of the settlers, or their ancestors, without the aid of the mother country. If this should happen to increase her *strength*, by their growing numbers, ready to join in her wars; her *commerce*, by their growing demand for her manufactures; or her *naval power*, by greater employment for her ships and seamen, they may probably suppose some merit in this, and that it entitles them to some favour; you are therefore to *forget it all, or resent it*, as if they had done you injury. If they happen to be zealous whigs, friends of liberty, nurtured in revolution principles, *remember all that* to their prejudice, and resolve to punish it; for such principles, after a revolution is thoroughly established, are of *no more use;* they are even *odious* and *abominable*.

IV. However peaceably your colonies have submitted to your government, shewn their affection to your interests, and patiently borne their grievances; you are to *suppose* them always inclined to revolt, and treat them accordingly. Quarter troops among them, who by their insolence may *provoke* the rising of mobs, and by their bullets and bayonets *suppress* them. By this means, like the husband who uses his wife ill *from suspicion,* you may in time convert your *suspicions* into *realities*.

V. Remote provinces must have *Governors* and *Judges*, to represent the Royal Person, and execute everywhere the delegated parts of his office and authority. You ministers know, that much of the strength of government depends on the *opinion* of the people; and much of that opinion on the *choice of rulers placed* immediately over them. If you send them wise and good men for governors, who study the interest of the colonists, and advance their prosperity, they will think their King wise and good, and that he wishes the welfare of his subjects. If you send them learned and upright men for Judges, they will think him a lover of justice. This may attach your provinces more to his government. You are therefore to be careful whom you recommend for those offices. If you can find prodigals, who have ruined their fortunes, broken gamesters or stockjobbers, these may do well as *governors;* for they will probably be rapacious, and provoke the people by their extortions. Wrangling proctors and pettifogging lawyers, too, are not amiss; for they will be for ever disputing and quarrelling with their little parliaments. If withal they should be ignorant, wrong-headed, and insolent, so much the better. Attornies' clerks and Newgate solicitors will do for *Chief Justices*, especially if they hold their places *during your pleasure;* and all will contribute to impress those ideas of your government, that are proper for a people *you would wish to renounce it*.

VI. To confirm these impressions, and strike them deeper, whenever the injured come to the capital with complaints of mal-administration, oppression, or injustice, punish such suitors with long delay, enormous expence, and a final judgment in favour of the oppressor. This will have an admirable effect every way. The trouble of future complaints will be prevented, and Governors and Judges will be encouraged to farther acts of oppression and injustice; and thence the people may become more disaffected, and at length desperate.

VII. When such Governors have crammed their coffers, and made themselves so odious to the people that they can no longer remain among them, with safety to their persons, *recall and reward* them with pensions. You may make them *baronets* too, if that respectable order should not think fit to resent it. All will contribute to encourage new governors in the same practice, and make the supreme government, *detestable*.

VIII. If, when you are engaged in war, your colonies should vie in liberal aids of men and money against the common enemy, upon your simple requisition, and give far beyond their abilities, reflect that a penny taken from them by your power is more honourable to you, than a pound presented by their benevolence; despise therefore their voluntary grants, and resolve to harass them with novel taxes. They will probably complain to your parliaments, that they are taxed by a body in which they have no representative, and that this is contrary to common right. They will petition for redress. Let the Parliaments flout their claims, reject their petitions, refuse even to suffer the reading of them, and treat the petitioners with the utmost contempt. Nothing can have a better effect in producing the alienation proposed; for though many can forgive injuries, *none ever forgave contempt.*

IX. In laying these taxes, never regard the heavy burthens those remote people already undergo, in defending their own frontiers, supporting their own provincial governments, making new roads, building bridges, churches, and other public edifices, which in old countries have been done to your hands by your ancestors, but which occasion constant calls and demands on the purses of a new people. Forget the *restraints* you lay on their trade for *your own* benefit, and the advantage a *monopoly* of this trade gives your exacting merchants. Think nothing of the wealth those merchants and your manufacturers acquire by the colony commerce; their encreased ability thereby to pay taxes at home; their accumulating, in the price of their commodities, most of those taxes, and so levying them from their consuming customers; all this, and the employment and support of thousands of your poor by the colonists, you are *intirely to forget*. But remember to make your arbitrary tax more grievous to your provinces, by public declarations importing that your power of taxing them has *no limits;* so that when you take from them without their consent one shilling in the pound, you have a clear right to the other nineteen. This will probably weaken every idea of *security in their property*, and convince them, that under such a government they *have nothing they can call their own;* which can scarce fail of producing the *happiest consequence!*

X. Possibly, indeed, some of them might still comfort themselves, and say, "Though we have no property, we have yet *something* left that is valuable; we have constitutional *liberty*, both of person and of conscience. This King, these Lords, and these Commons, who it seems are too remote from us to know us, and feel for us, cannot take from us our *Habeas Corpus* right, or our right of trial *by a jury of our neighbours;* they cannot deprive us of the exercise of our religion, alter our ecclesiastical constitution, and compel us to be Papists, if they please, or Mahometans." To annihilate this comfort, begin by laws to perplex their commerce with infinite regulations, impossible to be remembered and observed; ordain seizures of their property for every failure; take away the trial of such property by Jury, and give it to arbitrary Judges of your own appointing, and of the lowest characters in the country, whose salaries and emoluments are to arise out of the duties or condemnations, and whose appointments are *during pleasure*. Then let there be a formal declaration of both Houses, that opposition to your edicts is *treason*, and that any person suspected of treason in the provinces may, according to some obsolete law, be seized and sent to the metropolis of the empire for trial; and pass an act, that those there charged with certain other offences, shall be sent away in chains from their friends and country to be tried in the same manner for felony. Then erect a new Court of Inquisition among them, accompanied by an armed force, with instructions to transport all such suspected persons; to be ruined by the expence, if they bring over evidences to prove their innocence, or be found guilty and hanged, if they cannot afford it. And, lest the people should think you cannot possibly go any farther, pass another solemn declaratory act, "that King, Lords, Commons had, hath, and of right ought to have, full power and authority to make statutes of sufficient force and validity to bind the unrepresented provinces IN ALL CASES WHATSOVER." This will include *spiritual* with temporal, and, taken together, must operate wonderfully to your purpose; by convincing them, that they are at present under a power something like that spoken of in the scriptures, which can not only *kill their bodies*, but *damn their souls* to all eternity, by compelling them, if it pleases, *to worship the Devil*.

XI. To make your taxes more odious, and more likely to procure resistance, send from the capital a board of officers to superintend the collection, composed of the most *indiscreet, ill-bred,* and *insolent* you can find. Let these have large salaries out of the extorted revenue, and live in open, grating luxury upon the sweat and blood of the industrious; whom they are to worry continually with groundless and expensive prosecutions before the abovementioned arbitrary revenue Judges; *all at the cost of the party prosecuted,* tho' acquitted, because *the King is to pay no costs.* Let these men, *by your order,* be exempted from all the common taxes and burthens of the province, though they and their property are protected by its laws. If any revenue officers are *suspected* of the least tenderness for the people, discard them. If others are justly complained of, protect and reward them. If any of the under officers behave so as to provoke the people to drub them, promote those to better offices: this will encourage others to procure for themselves such profitable drubbings, by multiplying and enlarging such provocations, and *all will work towards the end you aim at.*

XII. Another way to make your tax odious, is to misapply the produce of it. If it was originally appropriated for the *defence* of the provinces, the better support of government, and the administration of justice, where it may be *necessary,* then apply none of it to that *defence,* but bestow it where it is *not necessary,* in augmented salaries or pensions to every governor, who has distinguished himself by his enmity to the people, and by calumniating them to their sovereign. This will make them pay it more unwillingly, and be more apt to quarrel with those that collect it and those that imposed it, who will quarrel again with them, and all shall contribute to your *main purpose,* of making them *weary of your government.*

XIII. If the people of any province have been accustomed to support their own Governors and Judges to satisfaction, you are to apprehend that such Governors and Judges may be thereby influenced to treat the people kindly, and to do them justice. This is another reason for applying part of that revenue in larger salaries to such Governors and Judges, given, as their commissions are, *during your pleasure* only; forbidding them to take any salaries from their provinces; that thus the people may no longer hope any kindness from their Governors, or (in Crown cases) any justice from their Judges. And, as the money thus misapplied in one province is extorted from all, probably *all will resent the misapplication.*

XIV. If the parliaments of your provinces should dare to claim rights, or complain of your administration, order them to be harrassed with *repeated dissolutions.* If the same men are continually returned by new elections, adjourn their meetings to some country village, where they cannot be accommodated, and there keep them *during pleasure;* for this, you know, is your PREROGATIVE; and an excellent one it is, as you may manage it to promote discontents among the people, diminish their respect, and *increase their disaffection.*

XV. Convert the brave, honest officers of your *navy* into pimping tide-waiters and colony officers of the *customs.* Let those, who in time

of war fought gallantly in defence of the commerce of their countrymen, in peace be taught to prey upon it. Let them learn to be corrupted by great and real smugglers; but (to shew their diligence)
scour with armed boats every bay, harbour, river, creek, cove, or
nook throughout the coast of your colonies; stop and detain every
coaster, every wood-boat, every fisherman, tumble their cargoes and
even their ballast inside out and upside down; and, if a penn'orth of
pins is found un-entered, let the whole be seized and confiscated.
Thus shall the trade of your colonists suffer more from their friends in
time of peace, than it did from their enemies in war. Then let these
boats crews land upon every farm in their way, rob the orchards,
steal the pigs and the poultry, and insult the inhabitants. If the
injured and exasperated farmers, unable to procure other justice,
should attack the aggressors, drub them, and burn their boats; you
are to call this *high treason and rebellion*, order fleets and armies into
their country, and threaten to carry all the offenders three thousand
miles to be hanged, drawn, and quartered. *O! this will work admirably!*

XVI. If you are told of discontents in your colonies, never believe
that they are general, or that you have given occasion for them; therefore do not think of applying any remedy, or of changing any offensive
measure. Redress no grievance, lest they should be encouraged to
demand the redress of some other grievance. Grant no request that is
just and reasonable, lest they should make another that is unreasonable. Take all your informations of the state of the colonies from your
Governors and officers in enmity with them. Encourage and reward
these *leasing-makers;* secrete their lying accusations, lest they should be
confuted; but act upon them as the clearest evidence; and believe
nothing you hear from the friends of the people: suppose all *their*
complaints to be invented and promoted by a few factious demagogues, whom if you could catch and hang, all would be quiet. Catch
and hang a few of them accordingly; and the *blood of the Martyrs*
shall *work miracles* in favour of your purpose.

XVII. If you see *rival nations* rejoicing at the prospect of your dis-
union with your provinces, and endeavouring to promote it; if they
translate, publish, and applaud all the complaints of your discontented
colonists, at the same time privately stimulating you to severer measures, let not that *alarm* or offend you. Why should it, since you all
mean *the same thing?*

XVIII. If any colony should at their own charge erect a fortress to
secure their port against the fleets of a foreign enemy, get your Governor to betray that fortress into your hands. Never think of paying
what it cost the country, for that would look, at least, like some regard
for justice; but turn it into a citadel to awe the inhabitants and curb

their commerce. If they should have lodged in such fortress the very arms they bought and used to aid you in your conquests, seize them all; it will provoke like *ingratitude* added to *robbery*. One admirable effect of these operations will be, to discourage every other colony from erecting such defences, and so your enemies may more easily invade them; to the great disgrace of your government, and of course *the furtherance of your project*.

XIX. Send armies into their country under pretence of protecting the inhabitants; but, instead of garrisoning the forts on their frontiers with those troops, to prevent incursions, demolish those forts, and order the troops into the heart of the country, that the savages may be encouraged to attack the frontiers, and that the troops may be protected by the inhabitants. This will seem to proceed from your ill will or your ignorance, and contribute farther to produce and strengthen an opinion among them, *that you are no longer fit to govern them*.

XX. Lastly, invest the General of your army in the provinces, with great and unconstitutional powers, and free him from the controul of even your own Civil Governors. Let him have troops enow under his command, with all the fortresses in his possession; and who knows but (like some provincial Generals in the Roman empire, and encouraged by the universal discontent you have produced) he may take it into his head to set up for himself? If he should, and you have carefully practised these few *excellent rules* of mine, take my word for it, all the provinces will immediately join him; and you will that day (if you have not done it sooner) get rid of the trouble of governing them, and all the *plagues* attending their *commerce* and connection from henceforth and for ever.   Q. E. D.

The Sale of the Hessians

FROM THE COUNT DE SCHAUMBERGH TO THE BARON HOHENDORF,
COMMANDING THE HESSIAN TROOPS IN AMERICA

ROME, February 18, 1777.

MONSIEUR LE BARON: — On my return from Naples, I received at Rome your letter of the 27th December of last year. I have learned with unspeakable pleasure the courage our troops exhibited at Trenton, and you cannot imagine my joy on being told that of the 1,950 Hessians engaged in the fight, but 345 escaped. There were just 1,605 men killed, and I cannot sufficiently commend your prudence in sending an exact list of the dead to my minister in London. This precaution was the more necessary, as the report sent to the English ministry does not give but 1,455 dead. This would make 483,450 florins instead of 643,500 which I am entitled to demand under our convention. You will comprehend the prejudice which such an error would work in my finances, and I do not doubt you will take the necessary pains to prove that Lord North's list is false and yours correct.

The court of London objects that there were a hundred wounded who ought not to be included in the list, nor paid for as dead; but I trust you will not overlook my instructions to you on quitting Cassel, and that you will not have tried by human succor to recall the life of the unfortunates whose days could not be lengthened but by the loss of a leg or an arm. That would be making them a pernicious present, and I am sure they would rather die than live in a condition no longer fit for my service. I do not mean by this that you should assassinate them; we should be humane, my dear Baron, but you may insinuate to the surgeons with entire propriety that a crippled man is a reproach to their profession, and that there is no wiser course than to let every one of them die when he ceases to be fit to fight.

I am about to send to you some new recruits. Don't economize them. Remember glory before all things. Glory is true wealth. There is nothing degrades the soldier like the love of money. He must care only for honour and reputation, but this reputation must be acquired in the midst of dangers. A battle gained without costing the conqueror any blood is an inglorious success, while the conquered cover themselves with glory by perishing with their arms in their hands. Do you remember that of the 300 Lacedæmonians who defended the defile of Thermopylæ, not one returned? How happy should I be could I say the same of my brave Hessians!

It is true that their king, Leonidas, perished with them: but things have changed, and it is no longer the custom for princes of the empire to go and fight in America for a cause with which they have no concern. And besides, to whom should they pay the thirty guineas per man if I did not stay in Europe to receive them? Then, it is necessary also that I be ready to send recruits to replace the men you lose. For this purpose I must return to Hesse. It is true, grown men are becoming scarce there, but I will send you boys. Besides, the scarcer the commodity the higher the price. I am assured that the women and little girls have begun to till our lands, and they get on not badly. You did right to send back to Europe that Dr. Crumerus who was so successful in curing dysentery. Don't bother with a man who is subject to looseness of the bowels. That disease makes bad soldiers. One coward will do more mischief in an engagement than ten brave men will do good. Better that they burst in their barracks than fly in a battle, and tarnish the glory of our arms. Besides, you know that they pay me as killed for all who die from disease, and I don't get a farthing for runaways. My trip to Italy, which has cost me enormously, makes it desirable that there should be a great mortality among them. You will therefore promise promotion to all who expose themselves; you will exhort them to seek glory in the midst of dangers; you will say to Major Maundorff that I am not at all content with his saving the 345 men who escaped the massacre of Trenton. Through the whole campaign he has not had ten men killed in consequence of his orders. Finally, let it be your principal object to prolong the war and avoid a decisive engagement on either side, for I have made arrangements for a grand Italian opera, and I do not wish to be obliged to give it up. Meantime I pray God, my dear Baron de Hohendorf, to have you in his holy and gracious keeping.

Letter to an Englishman

PHILADELPHIA, July 5, 1775.

MR. STRAHAN,

You are a Member of Parliament, and one of that Majority which has doomed my Country to Destruction. — You have begun to burn our Towns and murder our People. — Look upon your Hands! They are stained with the Blood of your Relations! — You and I were long Friends: — You are now my Enemy, — and I am

Yours,

B. FRANKLIN.

[To William Strahan]

⪻ John Dickinson (1732–1808)

JOHN DICKINSON, a well-to-do Philadelphia lawyer, was an essentially conservative man. Well aware of the growing rift between the colonies and the British government, and at the same time a loyal Englishman, Dickinson did his best to heal it. He wrote a series of articles, *Letters from a Farmer in Pennsylvania to the Inhabitants of the British Colonies,* which he published in the *Pennsylvania Gazette* in 1767 and 1768. The *Letters* pointed out the grievances of the colonies and the advantage of imperial membership, and appealed to both sides of the controversy for understanding, reliance on law, and reasonableness. He continued to counsel moderation while the argument grew in heat, and hoped until the last for a reconciliation between colonists and Crown.

Dickinson served in both Continental Congresses; since he did not favor war, he voted against the Declaration of Independence, but he later served as a private in the Continental Army. After the Revolution he was elected president of the Supreme Executive Councils of both Delaware and Pennsylvania, and delegate to the Constitutional Convention, where he led the moderate group from his state. Dickinson was largely responsible for breaking the deadlock between large and small states by suggesting the compromise principle on which representation in the House and Senate is based.

TEXTS: *The Political Writings of John Dickinson, Esq.* (Wilmington, 1814). *Letters from a Farmer in Pennsylvania . . . ,* 3d ed. (London, 1779).

A Warning to the Colonists in 1766

[From *The Political Writings of John Dickinson,* 1814]

Though I always reflect with a high pleasure on the integrity and understanding of my countrymen, which, joined with a pure and humble devotion to the great and gracious Author of every blessing they enjoy, will, I hope, insure to them and their posterity all temporal and eternal happiness; yet when I consider that in every age and country there have been bad men, my heart at this threatening period is so full of apprehension as not to permit me to believe, but that there may be some on this continent against whom you ought to be upon your guard. Men, who either hold, or expect to hold certain advantages by setting examples of servility to their countrymen. Men, who trained to the employment, or self-taught by a natural versatility of genius serve as decoys for drawing the innocent and unwary into snares. It is not to be doubted but that such men will diligently bestir themselves on this and every like occasion to spread the infection of their meanness as far as they can. On the plans they have adopted, this is their course. This is the method to recommend themselves to their patrons. They act consistently in a bad cause. They run well in a mean race.

From them we shall learn how pleasant and profitable a thing it is for our submissive behavior to be well spoken of at St. James's or St. Stephen's; at Guildhall or the Royal Exchange. Specious fallacies will be dressed up with all the arts of delusion to persuade one colony to distinguish herself from another by unbecoming condescensions, which will serve the ambitious purposes of great men at home, and therefore will be thought by them to entitle their assistants in obtaining them to considerable rewards.

Our fears will be excited. Our hopes will be awakened. It will be insinuated to us, with a plausible affectation of wisdom and concern, how prudent it is to please the powerful — how dangerous to provoke them — and then comes in the perpetual incantation that freezes up every generous purpose of the soul in cold, inactive expectation — "that if there is any request to be made, compliance will obtain a favorable attention."

Our vigilance and our union are success and safety. Our negligence and our division are distress and death. They are worse — they are shame and slavery. Let us equally shun the benumbing stillness of overweening sloth, and the feverish activity of that ill-informed zeal which busies itself in maintaining little, mean and narrow opinions. Let us, with a truly wise generosity and charity, banish and discourage all illiberal distinctions which may arise from differences in situation, forms of government, or modes of religion. Let us consider ourselves as men — freemen — Christian freemen — separated from the rest of the world and firmly bound together by the same rights, interests and dangers. Let these keep our attention inflexibly fixed on the great objects which we must continually regard in order to preserve those rights, to promote those interests, and to avert those dangers.

Let these truths be indelibly impressed on our minds — that we cannot be happy without being free — that we cannot be free without being secure in our property — that we cannot be secure in our property, if, without our consent others may, as by right, take it away — that taxes imposed on us by parliament do thus take it away — that duties laid for the sole purpose of raising money are taxes — that attempts to lay such duties should be instantly and firmly opposed — that this opposition can never be effectual unless it is the united effort of these provinces — that therefore benevolence of temper towards each other and unanimity of counsels are essential to the welfare of the whole — and lastly, that for this reason every man amongst us who in any manner would encourage either dissension, diffidence, or indifference between these colonies, is an enemy to himself, and to his country.

From
Letters from a Farmer in Pennsylvania
[Letter III, 1767]

MY DEAR COUNTRYMEN,

I rejoice to find that my two former letters to you have been generally received with so much favor, by such of you whose sentiments
I have had an opportunity of knowing. Could you look into my heart,
you would instantly perceive an ardent affection for your persons, a
zealous attachment to your interests, a lively resentment of every insult
and injury offered to your honor or happiness; and an inflexible resolution to assert your rights, to the utmost of my weak power, to be
the only motives that have engaged me to address you.

I am no farther concerned in any thing affecting America, than any
one of you, and when liberty leaves it, I can quit it much more conveniently than most of you. But while Divine Providence that gave
me existence in a land of freedom, permits my head to think, my lips
to speak, and my hand to move, I shall so highly and gratefully value
the blessing received, as to take care, that my silence and inactivity
shall not give my implied assent to any act, degrading my brethren
and myself from the birthright, wherewith Heaven itself "hath made
us free."

Sorry I am to learn, that there are some few persons, who shake
their heads with solemn motion, and pretend to wonder, what can be
the meaning of these letters. "Great Britain," they say, "is too powerful to contend with; she is determined to oppress us; it is in vain to
speak of right on one side, when there is power on the other; when
we are strong enough to resist, we shall attempt it; but now we are
not strong enough, and therefore we had better be quiet; it signifies
nothing to convince us that our rights are invaded, when we cannot
defend them; and if we should get into riots and tumults about the
late act, it will only draw down heavier displeasure upon us."

What can such men design? What do their grave observations
amount to, but this — "That these colonies totally regardless of their
liberties, should commit them with humble resignation to *chance,
time,* and the tender mercies of *ministers.*"

Are these men ignorant that usurpations which might have been
successfully opposed at first, acquire strength by continuance, and
thus become irresistible? Do they condemn the conduct of the colonies concerning the Stamp Act? Or have they forgot its successful
issue? Ought the colonies at that time, instead of acting as they did,
to have trusted for relief to the fortuitous events of futurity? If it is

needless "to speak of *rights*" now, it was as needless then. If the behavior of the colonies was prudent and glorious then, and successful
too; it will be equally prudent and glorious to act in the same manner
now, if our rights are equally invaded, and may be as successful. —
Therefore it becomes necessary to enquire, whether "our rights *are*
invaded." To talk of "defending" them, as if they could be no otherwise "defended" than by arms, is as much out of the way, as if a man
having a choice of several roads, to reach his journey, and should
prefer the worst, for no other reason but because it *is* the worst.

As to "riots and tumults," the gentlemen who are so apprehensive
of them, are much mistaken if they think, that grievances cannot be
redressed without such assistance.

I will now tell the gentlemen what is "the meaning of these letters."
The meaning of them is, to convince the people of these colonies that
they are, at this moment, exposed to the most imminent dangers; and
to persuade them immediately, vigorously, unanimously to exert themselves, in the most firm, and most peaceable manner, for obtaining
relief.

The cause of liberty is a "cause of too much dignity, to be sullied
by turbulence and tumults." It ought to be maintained in a manner
suitable to her nature. Those who engage in it, should breathe a
sedate yet fervent spirit, animating them to actions of prudence, justice, modesty, bravery, humanity and magnanimity.

To such a wonderful degree were the ancient Spartans, as brave
and free a people as ever existed, inspired by this happy temperature
of soul, that rejecting even in their battles the use of trumpets, and
other instruments, for exciting heat and rage, they marched up to
scenes of havoc and horror, with the sound of flutes, to the tunes of
which their steps kept pace — "exhibiting," as Plutarch says, "at once
a terrible and delightful sight, and proceeding, with a deliberate valor,
full of hope and good assurance, as if some divinity had sensibly assisted them."

I hope, my dear countrymen, that you will in every colony be upon
your guard against those who may at any time endeavor to stir you
up, under pretenses of patriotism, to any measures disrespectful to
our sovereign and our mother-country. Hot, rash, disorderly proceedings injure the reputation of a people as to wisdom, valor, and virtue,
without procuring them the least benefit. I pray GOD that he may be
pleased to inspire you and your posterity to the latest ages with that
spirit, of which I have an idea, but find a difficulty to express: To
express in the best manner I can, I mean a spirit that shall so guide
you, that it will be impossible to determine whether an American's
character is most distinguishable for his loyalty to his sovereign, his

duty to his mother-country, his love of freedom, or his affection for his native soil.

Every government, at some time or other, falls into wrong measures; these may proceed from mistake or passion. But every such measure does not dissolve the obligation between the governors and the governed; the mistake may be corrected; the passion may pass over. It is the duty of the governed, to endeavor to rectify the mistake, and to appease the passion. They have not at first any other right, than to represent their grievances, and to pray for redress, unless an emergency is so pressing as not to allow time for receiving an answer to their applications, which rarely happens. If their applications are disregarded, *then* that kind of opposition becomes justifiable, which can be made without breaking the laws, or disturbing the public peace. This consists in the prevention of the oppressors reaping advantage from their oppressions, and not in their punishment. For experience may teach them what reason did not; and harsh methods cannot be proper till milder ones have failed.

If at length it becomes UNDOUBTED, that an inveterate resolution is formed to annihilate the liberties of the governed, the English history affords frequent examples of resistance by force. What particular circumstances will in any future case justify such resistance, can never be ascertained till they happen. Perhaps it may be allowable to say, generally, that it never can be justifiable, until the people are FULLY CONVINCED, that any further submission will be destructive to their happiness.

When the appeal is made to the sword, highly probable is it, that the punishment will exceed the offense; and the calamities attending on war outweigh those preceding it. These considerations of justice and prudence will always have great influence with good and wise men.

To these reflections on this subject, it remains to be added, and ought forever to be remembered; that resistance in the case of colonies against their mother-country, is extremely different from the resistance of a people against their prince. A nation may change their kings, or race of kings, and retaining their ancient form of government, be gainers by changing. Thus Great Britain, under the illustrious house of Brunswick, a house that seems to flourish for the happiness of mankind, has found a felicity, unknown in the reigns of the Stuarts. But if once *we* are separated from our mother-country, what new form of government shall we accept, or where shall we find another Britain to supply our loss? Torn from the body to which we are united by religion, liberty, laws, affections, relations, language and commerce, we must bleed at every vein.

In truth, the prosperity of these provinces is founded in their dependence on Great Britain; and when she returns to "her old good humor, and old good nature," as Lord Clarendon expresses it, I hope they will always esteem it their duty and interest, as it most certainly will be, to promote her welfare by all the means in their power.

We cannot act with too much caution in our disputes. Anger produces anger; and differences that might be accommodated by kind and respectful behavior, may by imprudence be enlarged to an incurable rage.

In quarrels between countries, as well as in those between individuals, when they have risen to a certain height, the first cause of dissension is no longer remembered, the minds of the parties being wholly engaged in recollecting and resenting the mutual expressions of their dislike. When feuds have reached that fatal point, all considerations of reason and equity vanish; and a blind fury governs, or rather confounds all things. A people no longer regards their interest, but the gratification of their wrath. The sway of the Cleons, and Clodius's, the designing and detestable flatterers of the prevailing passion, becomes confirmed. Wise and good men in vain oppose the storm, and may think themselves fortunate, if endeavoring to preserve their ungrateful fellow-citizens, they do not ruin themselves. Their *prudence* will be called *baseness;* their *moderation, guilt;* and if their virtue does not lead them to destruction, as that of many other great and excellent persons has done, they may survive to receive from their expiring country, the mournful glory of her acknowledgment, that their councils, if regarded, would have saved her.

The *constitutional* modes of obtaining relief, are those which I would wish to see pursued on the present occasion; that is, by petitions of our Assemblies, or, where they are not permitted to meet, of the people, to the powers that can afford us relief.

We have an excellent prince, in whose good dispositions toward us we may confide. We have a generous, sensible and humane nation, to whom we may apply. They *may* be deceived: They may, by artful men, be provoked to anger against us; but I cannot yet believe they will be cruel or unjust, or that their anger will be implacable. Let us behave like dutiful children, who have received unmerited blows from a beloved parent. Let us complain to our parents; but let our complaints speak, at the same time, the language of affliction and veneration.

If, however, it shall happen by an unfortunate course of affairs, that our applications to his Majesty and the Parliament for redress prove ineffectual, let us *then* take another step, by withholding from Great Britain, all the advantages she has been used to receive from us. *Then* let us try, if our ingenuity, industry and frugality, will not give weight to our remonstrances. Let us all be united with one spirit in one cause. Let us invent; let us work; let us save; let us, at the same time, keep up our claims, and unceasingly repeat our complaints; but above all, let us implore the protection of that infinitely good and gracious Being, "by whom kings reign and princes decree justice."

"Nil desperandum."

A FARMER.

The Declaration of the Representatives of the United Colonies

[1775]

Our forefathers, inhabitants of the island of Great Britain, left their native land, to seek on these shores a residence for civil and religious freedom. At the expense of their blood, at the hazard of their fortunes, without the least charge to the country from which they removed, by unceasing labor and an unconquerable spirit they effected settlements in the distant and inhospitable wilds of America, then filled with numerous and warlike nations of barbarians. Societies or governments vested with perfect legislatures were formed under charters from the crown, and an harmonious intercourse was established between the colonies and the kingdom from which they derived their origin. The mutual benefits of this union became in a short time so extraordinary, as to excite astonishment. It is universally confessed, that the amazing increase of the wealth, strength, and navigation of the realm, arose from this source; and the minister who so wisely and successfully directed the measures of Great Britain in the late war, publicly declared that these colonies enabled her to triumph over her enemies. Towards the conclusion of that war, it pleased our sovereign to make a change in his counsels. From that fatal moment the affairs of the British Empire began to fall into confusion, and gradually sliding from the summit of glorious prosperity to which they had been advanced by the virtues and abilities of one man, are at length distracted by the convulsions that now shake it to its deepest foundations. The new ministry, finding the brave foes of Britain though frequently defeated yet still contending, took up the unfortunate idea of granting them a hasty peace, and of then subduing her faithful friends.

These devoted colonies were judged to be in such a state, as to present victories without bloodshed, and all the easy emoluments of statutable plunder. The uninterrupted tenor of their peaceable and respectful behavior from the beginning of colonization, their dutiful, zealous, and useful services during the war, though so recently and amply acknowledged in the most honorable manner by his majesty, by the late king, and by parliament, could not save them from the meditated innovations. Parliament was influenced to adopt the pernicious project, and assuming a new power over them, have in the course of eleven years given such decisive specimens of the spirit and consequences attending this power, as to leave no doubt concerning the effects of acquiescence under it. They have undertaken to give and grant our money without our consent, though we have ever exercised an exclusive right to dispose of our own property; statutes have been passed for extending the jurisdiction of courts of admiralty and vice admiralty beyond their ancient limits; for depriving us of the accustomed and inestimable privilege of trial by jury in cases affecting both life and property; for suspending the legislature of one of the colonies; for interdicting all commerce to the capital of another; and for altering fundamentally the form of government established by charter, and secured by acts of its own legislature solemnly confirmed by the crown; for exempting the murderers of colonists from legal trial, and in effect, from punishment; for erecting in a neighboring province, acquired by the joint arms of Great Britain and America, a despotism dangerous to our very existence; and for quartering soldiers upon the colonists in time of profound peace. It has also been resolved in parliament, that colonists charged with committing certain offences, shall be transported to England to be tried.

But why should we enumerate our injuries in detail? By one statute it is declared, that parliament can "of right make laws to bind us in all cases whatsoever." What is to defend us against so enormous, so unlimited a power? Not a single man of those who assume it is chosen by us; or is subject to our control or influence; but on the contrary, they are all of them exempt from the operation of such laws, and an American revenue, if not diverted from the ostensible purposes for which it is raised, would actually lighten their own burdens in proportion as they increase ours. We saw the misery to which such despotism would reduce us. We for ten years incessantly and ineffectually besieged the throne as supplicants; we reasoned, we remonstrated with parliament in the most mild and decent language.

Administration, sensible that we should regard these oppressive measures as freemen ought to do, sent over fleets and armies to enforce them. The indignation of the Americans was roused, it is true; but it was the indignation of a virtuous, loyal, and affectionate people. A Congress of delegates from the United Colonies was assembled at Philadelphia, on the fifth day of last September. We resolved again to offer an humble and dutiful petition to the king, and also addressed our fellow-subjects of Great Britain. We have pursued every temperate, every respectful measure; we have even proceeded to break off our commercial intercourse with our fellow-subjects as the last peaceable admonition that our attachment to no nation upon earth should supplant our attachment to liberty. This, we flattered ourselves, was the ultimate step of the controversy: but subsequent events have shown how vain was this hope of finding moderation in our enemies. . . .

In brief, a part of these colonies now feel, and all of them are sure of feeling, as far as the vengeance of administration can inflict them, the complicated calamities of fire, sword and famine. We are reduced to the alternative of choosing an unconditional submission to the tyranny of irritated ministers, or resistance by force. — The latter is our choice. *We have counted the cost of this contest, and find nothing so dreadful as voluntary slavery.* Honor, justice and humanity forbid us tamely to surrender that freedom which we received from our gallant ancestors, and which our innocent posterity have a right to receive from us. We cannot endure the infamy and guilt of resigning succeeding generations to that wretchedness which inevitably awaits them, if we basely entail hereditary bondage upon them.

Our cause is just. Our union is perfect. Our internal resources are great, and, if necessary, foreign assistance is undoubtedly attainable. We gratefully acknowledge, as signal instances of the Divine favor toward us, that his providence would not permit us to be called into this severe controversy until we were grown up to our present strength, had been previously exercised in warlike operations, and possessed the means of defending ourselves. With hearts fortified by these animating reflections, we most solemnly, before God and the world, declare that, exerting the utmost energy of those powers which our beneficent Creator hath graciously bestowed upon us, the arms we have been compelled by our enemies to assume, we will in defiance of every hazard, with unabating firmness and perseverance, employ for the preservation of our liberties; being with one mind resolved to die freemen rather than to live slaves.

⤷ Joseph Galloway (1731–1803)

JOSEPH GALLOWAY's political career provides an excellent example of the problems which faced a colonial American who was also a loyal British subject. Galloway was a wealthy Marylander, well-educated, a man of good taste, interested in science and the classics, a member of the American Philosophical Society. He entered business in Philadelphia with great success, and soon became an important figure in Pennsylvania politics. From 1766 to 1775 he served as speaker of the Pennsylvania Assembly, where he saw the breach between colony and Crown widen year by year.

Caught between his deep allegiance to the Crown and his passionate colonial patriotism, Galloway searched vainly for some ground of compromise. As Pennsylvania delegate to the First Continental Congress in 1774, he submitted to it a plan for a British imperial system, with a written constitution, under which the American colonies might live in peace and harmony. However, Galloway's suggestion was rejected, and he refused to serve in the Second Continental Congress.

Outspoken in his opposition to independence, for he was certain that the American cause would lose, Galloway joined General Howe's army when it occupied Philadelphia, in the hope that he could assist in reorganizing the colonial governments when the British won. In 1778, when the Continental Army took Philadelphia, he sailed for England. His estates were confiscated, his request to return to the United States in 1793 was refused, and he died a broken man after twenty-five years of exile.

TEXTS: Joseph Galloway, *Historical and Political Reflections on the Rise and Progress of the American Rebellion* (London, 1780). Worthington C. Ford, ed., *Journals of the Continental Congress, 1774–1789* (Washington, 1904), Vol. I.

A Plea for Compromise

[1774]

Upon the meeting of Congress, two parties were immediately formed, with different views, and determined to act upon different principles. One intended candidly and clearly to define American rights, and explicitly and dutifully to petition for the remedy which would redress the grievances justly complained of — to form a more solid and constitutional union between the two countries, and to avoid every measure which tended to sedition, or acts of violent opposition. The other consisted of persons whose design, from the beginning of their opposition to the Stamp Act, was to throw off all subordination and connection with Great Britain; who meant by every fiction, falsehood and fraud, to delude the people from their due allegiance, to throw the subsisting Governments into anarchy, to incite the ignorant and vulgar to arms, and with those arms to establish American Independence. The one were men of loyal principles, and possessed the greatest fortunes in America; the other were congregational and presbyterian republicans, or men of bankrupt fortunes, overwhelmed in debt to the British merchants. The first suspected the designs of the last, and were therefore cautious; but as they meant to do nothing but what was reasonable and just, they were open and ingenuous. The second, fearing the opposition of the first, were secret and hypocritical, and left no art, no falsehood, no fraud unessayed to conceal their intentions. The loyalists rested, for the most part, on the defensive, and opposed, with success, every measure which tended to violent opposition. Motions were made, debated and rejected, and nothing was carried by either.

While the two parties in Congress remained thus during three weeks on an equal balance, the republicans were calling to their assistance the aid of their factions without. Continual expresses were employed between Philadelphia and Boston. These were under the management of Samuel Adams — a man, who though by no means remarkable for brilliant abilities, yet is equal to most men in popular intrigue, and the management of a faction. He eats little, drinks little, sleeps little, thinks much, and is most decisive and indefatigable in the pursuit of his objects. It was this man, who by his superior application managed at once the faction in Congress at Philadelphia, and the factions in New England. Whatever these patriots in Congress wished to have done by their colleagues without, to induce General Gage, then at the head of his Majesty's army at Boston, to give them a pretext for violent opposition, or to promote their measures in Congress, Mr. Adams advised and directed to be done; and when done, it was dispatched by express to Congress. By one of these expresses came the inflammatory resolves of the county of Suffolk, which contained a complete declaration of war against Great Britain. . . .

Upon these resolves being read, a motion was made that the Congress should give them their sanction. Long and warm debates ensued between the parties. At this time the republican faction in Congress had provided a mob, ready to execute their secret orders. The cruel practice of tarring and feathering had been long since introduced. This lessened the firmness of some of the loyalists; the vote was put and carried. Two of the dissenting members presumed to offer their protest against it in writing, which was negatived. They next insisted that the tender of their protest and its negative should be entered on the minutes; this was also rejected.

By this treasonable vote the foundation of military resistance throughout America was effectually laid. The example was now set by the people of Suffolk, and the measure was approved of by those who called themselves the representatives of all America. The loyal party, although they knew a great majority of the colonists were adverse to the measure, perceived the improbability of stemming the torrent.

They had no authority, no means in their own power to resist it; they saw those who held the powers of Government inactive spectators, and either shrinking from their duty, or uniting in the measures of sedition; they saw the flame of rebellion spreading with more rapidity in a province under the eye of his Majesty's army than in any other; and that no effectual measures were taken by Government in Britain to suppress it; and yet, as a petition to his Majesty had been ordered to be brought in, they resolved to continue their exertions. They hoped to prevail in stating the rights of America on just and constitutional principles; in proposing a plan for uniting the two countries on those principles, and in a clear, definitive and decent prayer, to ask for what a majority of the colonies wished to obtain; and as they had no reason to doubt the success of this measure in a British Parliament, they further hoped, that it would stop the effusion of blood and the ruin of their country.

With this view, as well as to probe the ultimate design of the republicans, and to know with certainty whether any proposal, short of the absolute independence of the Colonies, would satisfy them, a plan of union was drawn by a member[1] of the loyal party, and approved by the rest. It was so formed as to leave no room for any reasonable objection on the part of the republicans, if they meant to be united to Great Britain on any grounds whatever. It included a restoration of all their rights, and a redress of all their grievances, on constitutional principles; and it accorded with all the instructions given to them as members of Congress.

SPEECH DELIVERED IN THE CONTINENTAL CONGRESS, SEPTEMBER 28, 1774

. . . Desirous as I am to promote the freedom of the Colonies, and to prevent the mischiefs which will attend a military contest with Great Britain, I must intreat you to desert the measures which have been so injudiciously and ineffectually pursued by antecedent Assemblies. Let us thoroughly investigate the subject matter in dispute, and endeavor to find from that investigation the means of perfect and permanent redress. In whatever we do, let us be particular and explicit, and not wander in general allegations. These will lead us to no point, nor can produce any relief; they are besides dishonorable and insidious. I would therefore acknowledge the necessity of the supreme authority of Parliament over the Colonies, because it is a proposition which we cannot deny without manifest contradiction, while we confess that we are subjects of the British Government; and if we do not approve of a representation in Parliament, let us ask for a participation in the

[1] Galloway.

freedom and power of the English constitution in some other mode of incorporation: for I am convinced, by long attention to the subject, that let us deliberate, and try what other expedients we may, we shall find none that can give to the Colonies substantial freedom, but some such incorporation. I therefore beseech you, by the respect you are bound to pay to the instructions of your constituents, by the regard you have for the honor and safety of your country, and as you wish to avoid a war with Great Britain, which must terminate, at all events in the ruin of America, not to rely on a denial of the authority of Parliament, a refusal to be represented, and on a non-importation agreement; because whatever protestations, in that case, may be made to the contrary, it will prove to the world that we intend to throw off our allegiance to the State, and to involve the two countries in all the horrors of a civil war.

With a view to promote the measure I have so earnestly recommended, I have prepared the draught of a plan for uniting America more intimately, in constitutional policy, with Great Britain. . . .

A Plan of a Proposed Union between Great Britain and the Colonies, September 28, 1774.

That a British and American legislature, for regulating the administration of the general affairs of America, be proposed and established in America, including all the said colonies; within, and under which government, each colony shall retain its present constitution, and powers of regulating and governing its own internal police, in all cases whatever.

That the said government be administered by a President-General, to be appointed by the King, and a Grand Council, to be chosen by the Representatives of the people of the several colonies, in their respective assemblies, once in every three years. . . .

That the Grand Council shall meet once in every year, if they shall think it necessary, and oftener, if occasions shall require, at such time and place as they shall adjourn to, at the last preceding meeting, or as they shall be called to meet at, by the President-General, on any emergency.

That the Grand Council shall have power to choose their Speaker, and shall hold and exercise all the like rights, liberties and privileges, as are held and exercised by and in the House of Commons of Great Britain.

That the President-General shall hold his office during the pleasure of the King, and his assent shall be requisite to all acts of the Grand Council, and it shall be his office and duty to cause them to be carried into execution.

That the President-General, by and with the advice and consent of the Grand Council hold and exercise all the legislative rights, powers, and authorities, necessary for regulating and administering all the general police and affairs of the colonies, in which Great Britain and the colonies, or any of them, the colonies in general, or more than one colony, are in any manner concerned, as well civil and criminal as commercial.

That the said President-General and the Grand Council, be an inferior and distinct branch of the British legislature, united and incorporated with it, for the aforesaid general purposes; and that any of the said general regulations may originate and be formed and digested, either in the Parliament of Great Britain, or in the said Grand Council, and being prepared, transmitted to the other for their approbation or dissent; and that the assent of both shall be requisite to the validity of all such general acts or statutes.

That in time of war, all bills for granting aid to the crown, prepared by the Grand Council, and approved by the President-General, shall be valid and passed into a law, without the assent of the British Parliament.

◆ Jonathan Boucher (1737–1804)

JONATHAN BOUCHER, an Anglican clergyman, was born in England and came to Virginia in 1759. He served as tutor to the sons of various wealthy Virginia families, among them Jackie Custis, George Washington's stepson. In 1770 Boucher was appointed rector of a well-to-do parish in Annapolis, Maryland, where he soon became chaplain to the Maryland Assembly and a leader in the colony's Anglican circles.

Boucher believed in the sanctity of established authority, and from the outset of the colonial controversy with the British he counseled obedience and nonresistance. His outspoken Toryism elicited a good deal of ill-feeling, and after a number of threats against his life he preached on Sundays with a brace of loaded pistols in the pulpit. By 1775 his position was so precarious that he left for England, never to return. In 1797 he published thirteen sermons he had preached in 1775, at the height of the cry for independence, under the title A View of the Cause and Consequences of the American Revolution, still one of the best statements of the Loyalist position.

TEXT: Jonathan Boucher, A View of the Cause and Consequences of the American Revolution, in Thirteen Discourses . . . (London, 1797).

On Civil Liberty, Passive Obedience, and Nonresistance
[From a sermon of 1775]

"Civil liberty," says an excellent writer, "is a severe and a restrained thing; implies, in the notion of it, authority, settled subordinations, subjection, and obedience; and is altogether as much hurt by too little of this kind, as by too much of it. And the love of liberty, when it is indeed the love of liberty, which carries us to withstand tyranny, will as much carry us to reverence authority, and to support it; for this most obvious reason, that one is as necessary to the being of liberty, as the other is destructive of it. And, therefore, the love of liberty which does not produce this effect, the love of liberty which is not a real principle of dutiful behavior towards authority, is as hypocritical as the religion which is not productive of a good life. Licentiousness is, in truth, such an excess of liberty as is of the same nature with tyranny. For what is the difference betwixt them, but that one is lawless power exercised under pretense of authority, or by persons vested with it; the other, lawless power exercised under pretense of liberty, or without any pretense at all? A people, then, must always be less free in proportion as they are more licentious; licentiousness being not only different from liberty, but directly contrary to it — a direct breach upon it."

True liberty, then, is a liberty to do every thing that is right, and the being restrained from doing any thing that is wrong. So far from our having a right to do every thing that we please, under a notion of liberty, liberty itself is limited and confined — but limited and confined only by laws which are at the same time both its foundation and its support. It can, however, hardly be necessary to inform you, that ideas and notions respecting liberty, very different from these, are daily suggested in the speeches and the writings of the times; and also that some opinions on the subject of government at large, which appear to me to be particularly loose and dangerous, are advanced in the sermon now under consideration; and that, therefore, you will acknowledge the propriety of my bestowing some farther notice on them both.

It is laid down in this sermon, as a settled maxim, that the end of government is "the common good of mankind." I am not sure that the position itself is indisputable; but, if it were, it would by no means follow that, "this common good being matter of common feeling, government must therefore have been instituted by common consent." There is an appearance of logical accuracy and precision in this statement; but it is only an appearance. The position is vague and loose; and the assertion is made without an attempt to prove it. If by men's "common feelings" we are to understand that principle in the human mind called common sense, the assertion is either unmeaning and insignificant, or it is false. In no instance have mankind ever yet agreed as to what is, or is not, "the common good." A form or mode of government cannot be named, which these "common feelings" and "common consent," the sole arbiters, as it seems, of "common good," have not, at one time or another, set up and established, and again pulled down and reprobated. What one people in one age have concurred in establishing as the "common good," another in another age have voted to be mischievous and big with ruin. The premises, therefore, that "the common good is a matter of common feeling," being false, the consequence drawn from it, viz. that government was instituted by "common consent," is of course equally false.

This popular notion, that government was originally formed by the consent or by a compact of the people, rests on, and is supported by, another similar notion, not less popular, nor better founded. This other notion is, that the whole human race is born equal; and that no man is naturally inferior, or, in any respect, subjected to another; and that he can be made subject to another only by his own consent. The position is equally ill-founded and false both in its premises and conclusions. In hardly any sense that can be imagined is the position strictly true; but, as applied to the case under consideration, it is demonstrably not true. Man differs from man in every thing that can be supposed to lead to supremacy and subjection, *as one star differs from another star in glory*. It was the purpose of the Creator, that man should be social; but, without government, there can be no society; nor, without some relative inferiority and superiority, can there be any government. A musical instrument composed of chords, keys, or pipes, all perfectly equal in size and power, might as well be expected to produce harmony, as a society composed of members all perfectly equal to be productive of order and peace. If (according to the idea of the advocates of this chimerical scheme of equality) no man could rightfully *be compelled to come in* and be a member even of a government to be formed by a regular compact, but by his own individual consent; it clearly follows, from the same principles, that neither could he rightfully be made or compelled to submit to the ordinances of any government already formed, to which he has not individually or actually consented. On the principle of equality, neither his parents, nor even the vote of a majority of the society, (however virtuously and honorably that vote might be obtained,) can have any such authority over any man. Neither can it be maintained that acquiescence implies consent; because acquiescence may have been extorted from impotence or incapacity. Even an explicit consent can bind a man no longer than he chooses to be bound. The same principle of equality that exempts him from being governed without his own consent, clearly entitles him to recall and resume that consent whenever he sees fit; and he alone has a right to judge when and for what reasons it may be resumed.

Any attempt, therefore, to introduce this fantastic system into practice, would reduce the whole business of social life to the wearisome, confused, and useless talk of mankind's first expressing, and then withdrawing, their consent to an endless succession of schemes of government. Governments, though always forming, would never be completely formed: for, the majority today, might be the minority tomorrow; and, of course, that which is now fixed might and would be soon unfixed. Mr. Locke indeed says, that, "by consenting with others to make one body-politic under government, a man puts himself under an obligation to every one of that society to submit to the determination of the majority, and to be concluded by it." For the sake of the peace of society, it is undoubtedly reasonable and necessary that this should be the case: but, on the principles of the system now under consideration, before Mr. Locke or any of his followers can have authority to say that it actually is the case, it must be stated and proved that every individual man, on entering into the social compact, did first consent, and declare his consent, to be concluded and bound in all cases by the vote of the majority. In making such a declaration, he would certainly consult both his interest and his duty; but at the same time he would also completely relinquish the principle of equality, and eventually subject himself to the possibility of being governed by ignorant and corrupt tyrants. Mr. Locke himself afterwards disproves his own position respecting this supposed obligation to submit to the "determination of the majority," when he argues that a right of resistance still exists in the governed: for, what is resistance but a recalling and resuming the consent heretofore supposed to have been given, and in fact refusing to submit to the "determination of the majority"? It does not clearly appear what Mr. Locke exactly meant by what he calls "the determination of the majority": but the only rational and practical public manner of declaring "the determination of the majority," is by law: the laws, therefore, in all countries, even in those that are despotically governed, are to be regarded as the declared "determination of a majority" of the members of that community; because, in such cases, even acquiescence only must be looked upon as equivalent to a declaration. A right of resistance, therefore, for which Mr. Locke contends, is incompatible with the duty of submitting to the determination of "the majority," for which he also contends.

It is indeed impossible to carry into effect any government which, even by compact, might be framed with this reserved right of resistance. Accordingly there is no record that any such government ever was so formed. If there had, it must have carried the seeds of its decay in its very constitution. For, as those men who make a government (certain that they have the power) can have no hesitation to vote that they also have the right to unmake it; and as the people, in all circumstances, but more especially when trained to make and unmake governments, are at least as well disposed to do the latter as the former, it is morally impossible that there should be any thing like permanency or stability in a government so formed. Such a system, therefore, can produce only perpetual dissensions and contests, and bring back mankind to a supposed state of nature; arming every man's hand, like Ishmael's, against every man, and rendering the world an *aceldama,* or field of blood. — Such theories of government seem to give something like plausibility to the notions of those other modern theorists, who regard all governments as invasions of the natural rights of men, usurpations, and tyranny. On this principle it would follow, and could not be denied, that government was indeed fundamentally, as our people are sedulously taught it still is, an evil. Yet it is to government that mankind owe their having, after their fall and corruption, been again reclaimed, from a state of barbarity and war, to the conveniency and the safety of the social state: and it is by means of government that society is still preserved, the weak protected from the strong, and the artless and innocent from the wrongs of proud oppressors. It was not without reason, then, that Mr. Locke asserted, that a greater wrong cannot be done to prince and people, than is done by "propagating wrong notions concerning government."

Ashamed of this shallow device, that government originated in superior strength and violence, another party, hardly less numerous, and certainly not less confident than the former, fondly deduce it from some imaginary compact. They suppose that, in the decline perhaps of some fabulous age of gold, a multitude of human beings, who, like their brother beasts, had hitherto ranged the forests, *without guide, overseer, or ruler* — at length convinced, by experience, of the impossibility of living either alone with any degree of comfort or security, or together in society, with peace, without government, had (in some lucid interval of reason and reflection) met together in a spacious plain, for the express purpose of framing a government. Their first step must have been the transferring to some individual, or individuals, some of those rights which are supposed to have been inherent in each of them: of these it is essential to government that they should be divested; yet can they not, rightfully, be deprived of them, otherwise than by their own consent. Now, admitting this whole supposed assembly to be perfectly equal as to rights, yet all agreed as to the propriety of ceding some of them, on what principles of equality is it possible to determine, either who shall relinquish such a portion of his rights, or who shall be invested with such new accessory rights? By asking another to exercise jurisdiction over me, I clearly confess that I do not think myself his equal; and by his consenting to exercise such authority, he also virtually declares that he thinks himself superior. And, to establish this hypothesis of a compact, it is farther necessary that the whole assembly should concur in this opinion — a concurrence so extremely improbable, that it seems to be barely possible. The supposition that a large concourse of people, in a rude and imperfect state of society, or even a majority of them, should thus rationally and unanimously concur to subject themselves to various restrictions, many of them irksome and unpleasant, and all of them contrary to all their former habits, is to suppose them possessed of more wisdom and virtue than multitudes in any instance in real life have ever shewn. Another difficulty respecting this notion may yet be mentioned. Without a power of life and death, it will, I presume, be readily admitted that there could be no government. Now, admitting it to be possible that men, from motives of public and private utility, may be induced to submit to many heavy penalties, and even to corporal punishment, inflicted by the sentence of the law, there is an insuperable objection to any man's giving to another a power over his life: this objection is, that no man has such a power over his own life; and cannot therefore transfer to another, or to others, be they few or many, on any conditions, a right which he does not himself possess. He only who gave life, can give the authority to take it away: and as such authority is essential to government, this argument seems very decidedly to prove, not only that government did not originate in any compact, but also that it was originally from God.

This visionary idea of a government by compact was, as Filmer says, "first hatched in the schools; and hath, ever since, been fostered by Papists, for good divinity." For some time, the world seemed to regard it merely as another Utopian fiction; and it was long confined to the disciples of Rome and Geneva, who, agreeing in nothing else, yet agreed in this. In an evil hour it gained admittance into the Church of England; being first patronized by her during the civil wars, by "a few miscreants, who were as far from being true Protestants, as true Subjects." Mankind have listened, and continue to listen to it with a predilection and partiality, just as they do to various other exceptionable notions, which are unfavorable to true religion and sound morals; merely from imagining, that if such doctrines be true, they shall no longer be subjected to sundry restraints, which, however wholesome and proper, are too often unpalatable to our corrupt natures. What we wish to be true, we easily persuade ourselves is true. On this principle it is not difficult to account for our thus eagerly following these *ignes fatui* of our own fancies or "feelings," rather than the sober steady light of the word of God; which (in this instance as well as in others) lies under this single disadvantage, that it proposes no doctrines which may conciliate our regards by flattering our pride.

If, however, we can ever resolve no longer to be bewildered by these vain imaginations, still the interesting question presses on us, "Where," in the words of Plato, "where shall we look for the origin of government?" Let Plato himself instruct us. Taught then by this oracle of heathen wisdom, "we will take our stations there, where the prospect of it is most easy and most beautiful." Of all the theories respecting the origin of government with which the world has ever been either puzzled, amused, or instructed, that of the Scriptures alone is accompanied by no insuperable difficulties.

It was not to be expected from an all-wise and all-merciful Creator, that, having formed creatures capable of order and rule, he should turn them loose into the world under the guidance only of their own unruly wills; that, like so many wild beasts, they might tear and worry one another in their mad contests for pre-eminence. His purpose from the first, no doubt, was, that men should *live godly and sober lives*. But, such is the sad estate of our corrupted nature, that, ever since the Fall, we have been averse from good, and prone to evil. We are, indeed, so disorderly and unmanageable, that, were it not for the restraints and the terrors of human laws, it would not be possible for us to dwell together. But as men were clearly formed for society, and to dwell together, which yet they cannot do without the restraints of law, or, in other words, without government, it is fair to infer that government was also the original intention of God, who never decrees the end, without also decreeing the means. Accordingly, when man was made, his Maker did not turn him adrift into a shoreless ocean, without star or compass to steer by. As soon as there were some to be governed, there were also some to govern: and the first man, by virtue of that paternal claim, on which all subsequent governments have been founded, was first invested with the power of government. For, we are not to judge of the Scriptures of God, as we do of some other writings; and so, where no express precept appears, hastily to conclude that none was given. On the contrary, in commenting on the Scriptures, we are frequently called upon to find out the precept from the practice. Taking this rule, then, for our direction in the present instance, we find, that, copying after the fair model of heaven itself, wherein there was government even among the angels, the families of the earth were subjected to rulers, at first set over them by God: *for, there is no power, but of God; the powers that be are ordained of God.* The first father was the first king: and if (according to the rule just laid down) the law may be inferred from the practice, it was thus that all government originated; and monarchy is its most ancient form.

Little risk is run in affirming that this idea of the patriarchal origin of government has not only the most and best authority of history, as far as history goes, to support it; but that it is also by far the most natural, most consistent, and most rational idea. Had it pleased God not to have interfered at all in the case, neither directly nor indirectly, and to have left mankind to be guided only by their own uninfluenced judgments, they would naturally have been led to the government of a community, or a nation, from the natural and obvious precedent of the government of a family. In confirmation of this opinion, it may be observed, that the patriarchal scheme is that which always has prevailed, and still does prevail, among the most enlightened people: and (what is no slight attestation of its truth) it has also prevailed, and still does prevail, among the most unenlightened. According to Vitruvius, the rudiments of architecture are to be found in the cottage: and, according to Aristotle, the first principles of government are to be traced to private families. Kingdoms and empires are but so many larger families: and hence it is that our Church, in perfect conformity with the doctrine here inculcated, in her explication of the fifth commandment, from the obedience due to parents, wisely derives the congenial duty of *honoring the king and all that are put in authority under him.*

◄↛ Alexander Hamilton (1757–1804)

ALEXANDER HAMILTON was born in the West Indies, and at the age of fifteen was sent by friends of the family to King's College (later Columbia) in New York City. Here he joined a group of youths deep in the colonial argument with Britain. In answer to the letters of a Loyalist who signed himself "A Westchester Farmer," Hamilton, barely seventeen, wrote *A Full Vindication of the Measures of Congress* in 1774, and followed it with *The Farmer Refuted,* an effective reply and a clear statement of the American case. During the Revolutionary War he served on Washington's staff and led a charge that captured a redoubt at Yorktown. In *A Full Vindication* Hamilton shows the beginnings of the tightly-reasoned, incisively-cadenced style that later became the trademark of his public papers.

TEXT: Henry Cabot Lodge, ed., *The Works of Alexander Hamilton* (New York, 1904), I, 5–7.

The Issue Stated

[From *A Full Vindication*, 1774]

. . . The only distinction between freedom and slavery consists in this: In the former state a man is governed by the laws to which he has given his consent, either in person or by his representative; in the latter, he is governed by the will of another. In the one case, his life and property are his own; in the other, they depend upon the pleasure of his master. It is easy to discern which of these two states is preferable. No man in his senses can hesitate in choosing to be free, rather than a slave.

That Americans are entitled to freedom is incontestable on every rational principle. All men have one common original: they participate in one common nature, and consequently have one common right. No reason can be assigned why one man should exercise any power or pre-eminence over his fellow-creatures more than another; unless they have voluntarily vested him with it. Since, then, Americans have not, by any act of theirs, empowered the British Parliament to make laws for them, it follows they can have no just authority to do it.

Besides the clear voice of natural justice in this respect, the fundamental principles of the English constitution are in our favor. It has been repeatedly demonstrated that the idea of legislation or taxation, when the subject is not represented, is inconsistent with *that*. Nor is this all; our charters, the express conditions on which our progenitors relinquished their native countries, and came to settle in this, preclude every claim of ruling and taxing us without our assent.

Every subterfuge that sophistry has been able to invent, to evade or obscure this truth, has been refuted by the most conclusive reasonings; so that we may pronounce it a matter of undeniable certainty, that the pretensions of Parliament are contradictory to the law of nature, subversive of the British constitution, and destructive of the faith of the most solemn compacts.

What, then, is the subject of our controversy with the mother country? It is this: Whether we shall preserve that security to our lives and properties, which the law of nature, the genius of the British constitution, and our charters, afford us; or whether we shall resign them into the hands of the British House of Commons, which is no more privileged to dispose of them than the Great Mogul. What can actuate those men who labor to delude any of us into an opinion that the object of contention between the parent state and the colonies is only three pence duty upon tea; or that the commotions in America originate in a plan, formed by some turbulent men, to erect it into a republican government? The Parliament claims a right to tax us in all cases whatsoever; its late acts are in virtue of that claim. How ridiculous, then, is it to affirm that we are quarrelling for the trifling sum of three pence a pound on tea, when it is evidently the principle against which we contend.

◁ Patrick Henry (1736–1799)

PATRICK HENRY, descended from Virginia frontiersmen, came to the Virginia House of Burgesses in 1765 as an unknown, shy, awkward young man from the backcountry. His famous speech against the Stamp Act, delivered that year, electrified Virginia by its outspoken attack on the Crown, concluding with the famous climax, "Caesar had his Brutus, Charles the First had his Cromwell, and George the Third — may he profit by their example!" Immediately projected into prominence in the colonial cause against Britain, Henry was an acknowledged leader of the revolutionary faction in Virginia, and in 1775, in the Virginia convention, delivered his famous "Liberty or Death" speech.

Unfortunately, few of Henry's speeches were preserved in authentic form, and although he was undoubtedly one of the most eloquent and convincing orators of his time, his speeches exist chiefly in shorthand notes and reporters' second-hand versions. The 1775 speech as reconstructed by William Wirt in his *Life of Patrick Henry* (1817), whatever the final authenticity of its language, apparently retained much of Henry's style and ideas.

Henry served as one of Virginia's delegates to the Continental Congress, but he declined membership in the Constitutional Convention after the war and also in the Senate. Washington also offered him two positions in the government, which he refused.

TEXT: William Wirt, *The Life of Patrick Henry*, rev. ed. (New York, 1860), pp. 138–142.

Liberty or Death

[From William Wirt, *The Life of Patrick Henry*]

[Mr. Henry] was a spirit fitted to raise the whirlwind, as well as to ride in and direct it. His was that comprehensive view, that unerring prescience, that perfect command over the actions of men, which qualified him not merely to guide, but almost to create the destinies of nations.

He rose at this time with a majesty unusual to him in an exordium, and with all that self-possession by which he was so invariably distinguished. "No man," he said, "thought more highly than he did of the patriotism, as well as abilities, of the very worthy gentlemen who had just addressed the house. But different men often saw the same subject in different lights; and, therefore, he hoped it would not be thought disrespectful to those gentlemen, if, entertaining as he did, opinions of a character very opposite to theirs, he should speak forth *his* sentiments freely, and without reserve. This," he said, "was no time for ceremony. The question before this house was one of awful moment to the country. For his own part, he considered it as nothing less than a question of freedom or slavery. And in proportion to the magnitude of the subject, ought to be the freedom of the debate. It was only in this way that they could hope to arrive at truth, and fulfil the great responsibility which they held to God and their country. Should he keep back his opinions at such a time, through fear of giving offence, he should consider himself as guilty of treason toward his country, and of an act of disloyalty toward the majesty of heaven, which he revered above all earthly kings."

"Mr. President," said he, "it is natural to man to indulge in the illusions of hope. We are apt to shut our eyes against a painful truth — and listen to the song of that siren, till she transforms us into beasts. Is this," he asked, "the part of wise men, engaged in a great and arduous struggle for liberty? Were we disposed to be of the number of those, who having eyes, see not, and having ears, hear not, the things which so nearly concern their temporal salvation? For his part, whatever anguish of spirit it might cost, *he* was willing to know the whole truth; to know the worst, and to provide for it."

"He had," he said, "but one lamp by which his feet were guided; and that was the lamp of experience. He knew of no way of judging of the future but by the past. And judging by the past, he wished to know what there had been in the conduct of the British ministry for the last ten years, to justify those hopes with which gentlemen had been pleased to solace themselves and the house? Is it that insidious smile with which our petition has been lately received? Trust it not, sir; it will prove a snare to your feet. Suffer not yourselves to be betrayed with a kiss. Ask yourselves how this gracious reception of our petition comports with those warlike preparations which cover our waters and darken our land. Are fleets and armies necessary to a work of love and reconciliation? Have we shown ourselves so unwilling to be reconciled, that force must be called in to win back our love? Let us not deceive ourselves, sir. These are the implements of war and subjugation — the last arguments to which kings resort. I ask gentlemen, sir, what means this martial array, if its purpose be not to force us to submission? Can gentlemen assign any other possible motive for it? Has Great Britain any enemy in this quarter of the world, to call for all this accumulation of navies and armies? No, sir, she has none. They are meant for us: they can be meant for no other. They are sent over to bind and rivet upon us those chains which the British ministry have been so long forging. And what have we to oppose them? Shall we try argument? Sir, we have been trying that for the last ten years. Have we any thing new to offer upon the subject? Nothing. We have held the subject up in every light of which it is capable; but it has been all in vain. Shall we resort to entreaty and humble supplication? What terms shall we find, which have not been already exhausted? Let us not, I beseech you, sir, deceive ourselves longer. Sir, we have done every thing that could be done, to avert the storm which is now coming on. We have petitioned — we have remonstrated — we have supplicated — we have prostrated ourselves before the throne, and have implored its interposition to arrest the tyrannical hands of the ministry and parliament. Our petitions have been slighted; our remonstrances have produced additional violence and insult; our supplications have been disregarded; and we have been spurned, with contempt, from the foot of the throne. In vain, after these things, may we indulge the fond hope of peace and reconciliation. *There is no longer any room for hope.* If we wish to be free — if we mean to preserve inviolate those inestimable privileges for which we have been so long contending — if we mean not basely to abandon the noble struggle in which we have been so long engaged, and which we have pledged ourselves never to abandon, until the glorious object of our contest shall be obtained — we must fight! — I repeat it, sir, we must fight! ! An appeal to arms and to the God of hosts, is all that is left us!"[1]

"They tell us, sir," continued Mr. Henry, "that we are weak — unable to cope with so formidable an adversary. But when shall we be stronger. Will it be the next week or the next year? Will it be when we are totally disarmed, and when a British guard shall be stationed in every house? Shall we gather strength by irresolution and inaction? Shall we acquire the means of effectual resistance by lying supinely on our backs, and hugging the delusive phantom of hope, until our

[1] "Imagine to yourself," says my correspondent, (Judge Tucker,) "this sentence delivered with all the calm dignity of Cato, of Utica — imagine to yourself the Roman senate, assembled in the capitol, when it was entered by the profane Gauls, who, at first, were awed by their presence, as if they had entered an assembly of the gods! — imagine that you heard that Cato addressing such a senate — imagine that you saw the handwriting on the wall of Belshazzar's palace — imagine you heard a voice as from heaven uttering the words: 'We *must* fight,' as the doom of fate, and you may have some idea of the speaker, the assembly to whom he addressed himself, and the auditory, of which I was one." [Wirt's note]

enemies shall have bound us hand and foot? Sir, we are not weak, if we make a proper use of those means which the God of nature hath placed in our power. Three millions of people armed in the holy cause of liberty and in such a country as that which we possess, are invincible by any force which our enemy can send against us. Besides, sir, we shall not fight our battles alone. There is a just God who presides over the destinies of nations, and who will raise up friends to fight our battles for us. The battle, sir, is not to the strong alone; it is to the vigilant, the active, the brave. Besides, sir, we have no election. If we were base enough to desire it, it is now too late to retire from the contest. There is no retreat but in submission and slavery! Our chains are forged. Their clanking may be heard on the plains of Boston! The war is inevitable — and let it come!! I repeat it, sir, let it come!!!

"It is vain, sir, to extenuate the matter. Gentlemen may cry, peace, peace — but there is no peace. The war is actually begun! The next gale that sweeps from the north will bring to our ears the clash of resounding arms! Our brethren are already in the field! Why stand we here idle? What is it that gentlemen wish? What would they have? Is life so dear, or peace so sweet, as to be purchased at the price of chains and slavery? Forbid it, Almighty God — I know not what course others may take; but as for me," cried he, with both his arms extended aloft, his brows knit, every feature marked with the resolute purpose of his soul, and his voice swelled to its boldest note of exclamation — "give me liberty, or give me death!"

He took his seat. No murmur of applause was heard. The effect was too deep. After the trance of a moment, several members started from their seats. The cry, "to arms!" seemed to quiver on every lip, and gleam from every eye. Richard H. Lee arose and supported Mr. Henry, with his usual spirit and elegance. But his melody was lost amid the agitations of that ocean, which the master-spirit of the storm had lifted up on high. That supernatural voice still sounded in their ears, and shivered along their arteries. They heard, in every pause, the cry of liberty or death. They became impatient of speech — their souls were on fire for action.

✑ Thomas Jefferson (1743–1826)

THOMAS JEFFERSON, thirty-seven years Franklin's junior, was like him a perfect product of the American Enlightenment. Trained as a lawyer, Jefferson ranged easily over science, history, philosophy, architecture, art, music, and almost every aspect of knowledge of his age. Yet it is for his political philosophy, and for his services to his country as revolutionary patriot, Secretary of State, and President, that he is best remembered. His statement to Benjamin Rush, in 1800, is the keynote of his life: "I have sworn," he wrote, "upon the altar of God, eternal hostility against every form of tyranny over the mind of man."

Jefferson spent forty years of his life in service to his colony, his state, and his country. He first entered public life as a member of the Virginia House of Burgesses in 1769. He represented Virginia in the Second Continental Congress in 1775, and in 1776 was chosen, with John Adams, Franklin, Sherman, and Livingston, to draft the Declaration of Independence. He served once more in the Virginia legislature, was wartime governor of Virginia, and was Virginia delegate to Congress under the Confederation. After the peace he succeeded Franklin as American minister in Paris, returning to the United States in 1790 to become the first Secretary of State. He also served as Vice President under John Adams, and two terms as President from 1801 to 1809. Perhaps no one man, with the possible exception of Washington, had more influence on the early history of the United States.

The final draft of the Declaration of Independence represented the thinking of all the members of the committee appointed to draw it up. But the precision, power, and grace of the prose are Jefferson's and his alone.

TEXT: A. A. Lipscomb and A. E. Bergh, eds., *The Writings of Thomas Jefferson* (Washington, 1903–5), I, 25–38.

The Framing of the Declaration

[From *Autobiography*]

It appearing in the course of these debates, that the colonies of New York, New Jersey, Pennsylvania, Delaware, Maryland, and South Carolina were not yet matured for falling from the parent stem, but that they were fast advancing to that state, it was thought most prudent to wait a while for them, and to postpone the final decision to July 1st; but, that this might occasion as little delay as possible, a committee was appointed to prepare a Declaration of Independence. The committee were John Adams, Dr. Franklin, Roger Sherman, Robert R. Livingston, and myself. Committees were also appointed, at the same time, to prepare a plan of confederation for the colonies, and to state the terms proper to be proposed for foreign alliance. The committee for drawing the Declaration of Independence, desired me to do it. It was accordingly done, and being approved by them, I

reported it to the House on Friday, the 28th of June, when it was
read, and ordered to lie on the table. On Monday, the 1st of July, the
House resolved itself into a committee of the whole, and resumed the
consideration of the original motion made by the delegates of Virginia,
which, being again debated through the day, was carried in the
affirmative by the votes of New Hampshire, Connecticut, Massachusetts, Rhode Island, New Jersey, Maryland, Virginia, North Carolina
and Georgia. South Carolina and Pennsylvania voted against it.
Delaware had but two members present, and they were divided. The
delegates from New York declared they were for it themselves, and
were assured their constituents were for it; but that their instructions
having been drawn near a twelve-month before, when reconciliation
was still the general object, they were enjoined by them to do nothing
which should impede that object. They, therefore, thought themselves
not justifiable in voting on either side, and asked leave to withdraw
from the question; which was given them. The committee rose and
reported their resolution to the House. Mr. Edward Rutledge, of South
Carolina, then requested the determination might be put off to the
next day, as he believed his colleagues, though they disapproved of
the resolution, would then join in it for the sake of unanimity. The
ultimate question, whether the House would agree to the resolution
of the committee, was accordingly postponed to the next day, when it
was again moved, and South Carolina concurred in voting for it. In
the meantime, a third member had come post from the Delaware
counties, and turned the vote of that colony in favor of the resolution.
Members of a different sentiment attending that morning from
Pennsylvania also, her vote was changed, so that the whole twelve
colonies who were authorized to vote at all, gave their voices for it;
and, within a few days,[1] the convention of New York approved of it,
and thus supplied the void occasioned by the withdrawing of her
delegates from the vote.

Congress proceeded the same day to consider the Declaration of
Independence, which had been reported and lain on the table the
Friday preceding, and on Monday referred to a committee of the
whole. The pusillanimous idea that we had friends in England worth
keeping terms with, still haunted the minds of many. For this reason,
those passages which conveyed censures on the people of England
were struck out, lest they should give them offence. The clause too,
reprobating the enslaving the inhabitants of Africa, was struck out in
complaisance to South Carolina and Georgia, who had never attempted
to restrain the importation of slaves, and who, on the contrary, still
wished to continue it. Our northern brethren also, I believe, felt a little
tender under those censures; for though their people had very few

[1] July 9.

slaves themselves, yet they had been pretty considerable carriers of them to others. The debates, having taken up the greater parts of the 2d, 3d, and 4th days of July, were, on the evening of the last, closed; the Declaration was reported by the committee, agreed to by the House, and signed by every member present, except Mr. Dickinson. As the sentiments of men are known not only by what they receive, but what they reject also, I will state the form of the Declaration as originally reported. The parts struck out by Congress shall be distinguished by a black line drawn under them;[2] and those inserted by them shall be placed in the margin, or in a concurrent column.

A Declaration by the Representatives of the United States of America, in *General* Congress assembled.

When, in the course of human events, it becomes necessary for one people to dissolve the political bands which have connected them with another, and to assume among the powers of the earth the separate and equal station to which the laws of nature and of nature's God entitle them, a decent respect to the opinions of mankind requires that they should declare the causes which impel them to the separation.

We hold these truths to be self evident: that all men are created equal; that they are endowed by their Creator with [*inherent and*] inalienable rights;   certain that among these are life, liberty, and the pursuit of happiness; that to secure these rights, governments are instituted among men, deriving their just powers from the consent of the governed; that whenever any form of government becomes destructive of these ends, it is the right of the people to alter or to abolish it, and to institute new government, laying its foundation on such principles, and organizing its powers in such form, as to them shall seem most likely to effect their safety and happiness. Prudence, indeed, will dictate that governments long established should not be changed for light and transient causes; and accordingly all experience hath shown that mankind are more disposed to suffer while evils are sufferable, than to right themselves by abolishing the forms to which they are accustomed. But when a long train of abuses and usurpations, [*begun at a distinguished*

[2 In this publication, the parts struck out are printed in *Italics* and inclosed in brackets.]

period and] pursuing invariably the same object, evinces a design to reduce them under absolute despotism, it is their right, it is their duty to throw off such government, and to provide new guards for their future security. Such has been the patient sufferance of these colonies; and such is now the

alter

necessity which constrains them to [*expunge*] their former systems of government. The history of the present king of Great Britain is a history of [*unre-*

repeated

mitting] injuries and usurpations, [*among which*

all having

appears no solitary fact to contradict the uniform tenor of the rest, but all have] in direct object the establishment of an absolute tyranny over these states. To prove this, let facts be submitted to a candid world [*for the truth of which we pledge a faith yet unsullied by falsehood.*]

He has refused his assent to laws the most wholesome and necessary for the public good.

He has forbidden his governors to pass laws of immediate and pressing importance, unless suspended in their operation till his assent should be obtained; and, when so suspended, he has utterly neglected to attend to them.

He has refused to pass other laws for the accommodation of large districts of people, unless those people would relinquish the right of representation in the legislature, a right inestimable to them, and formidable to tyrants only.

He has called together legislative bodies at places unusual, uncomfortable, and distant from the depository of their public records, for the sole purpose of fatiguing them into compliance with his measures.

He has dissolved representative houses repeatedly [*and continually*] for opposing with manly firmness his invasions on the rights of the people.

He has refused for a long time after such dissolutions to cause others to be elected, whereby the legislative powers, incapable of annihilation, have returned to the people at large for their exercise, the state remaining, in the meantime, exposed to all the dangers of invasion from without and convulsions within.

He has endeavored to prevent the population of these states; for that purpose obstructing the laws for naturalization of foreigners, refusing to pass others to encourage their migrations hither, and raising the conditions of new appropriations of lands.

He has [*suffered*] the administration of justice [*totally to cease in some of these states*] refusing his assent to laws for establishing judiciary powers.
obstructed by

He has made [*our*] judges dependent on his will alone for the tenure of their offices, and the amount and payment of their salaries.

He has erected a multitude of new offices, [*by a self-assumed power*] and sent hither swarms of new officers to harass our people and eat out their substance.

He has kept among us in times of peace standing armies [*and ships of war*] without the consent of our legislatures.

He has affected to render the military independent of, and superior to, the civil power.

He has combined with others to subject us to a jurisdiction foreign to our constitutions and unacknowledged by our laws, giving his assent to their acts of pretended legislation for quartering large bodies of armed troops among us; for protecting them by a mock trial from punishment for any murders which they should commit on the inhabitants of these states; for cutting off our trade with all parts of the world; for imposing taxes on us without our consent; for depriving us [ ] of the benefits of trial by jury; for transporting us beyond seas to be tried for pretended offences; for abolishing the free system of English laws in a neighboring province, establishing therein an arbitrary government, and enlarging its boundaries, so as to render it at once an example and fit instrument for introducing the same absolute rule into these [*states*]; for taking away our charters, abolishing our most valuable laws, and altering fundamentally the forms of our governments; for suspending our own legislatures, and declaring themselves invested with power to legislate for us in all cases whatsoever.
in many cases

colonies

He has abdicated government here [*withdrawing his governors, and declaring us out of his allegiance and protection.*]
by declaring us out of his protection, and waging war against us.

He has plundered our seas, ravaged our coasts,

burnt our towns, and destroyed the lives of our people.

He is at this time transporting large armies of foreign mercenaries to complete the works of death, desolation and tyranny already begun with circumstances of cruelty and perfidy [ ] unworthy the head of a civilized nation.

He has constrained our fellow citizens taken captive on the high seas, to bear arms against their country, to become the executioners of their friends and brethren, or to fall themselves by their hands.

He has [ ] endeavored to bring on the inhabitants of our frontiers, the merciless Indian savages, whose known rule of warfare is an undistinguished destruction of all ages, sexes and conditions [*of existence*].

[*He has incited treasonable insurrections of our fellow citizens, with the allurements of forfeiture and confiscation of our property.*

He has waged cruel war against human nature itself, violating its most sacred rights of life and liberty in the persons of a distant people who never offended him, captivating and carrying them into slavery in another hemisphere, or to incur miserable death in their transportation thither. This piratical warfare, the opprobrium of INFIDEL *powers, is the warfare of the* CHRISTIAN *king of Great Britain. Determined to keep open a market where* MEN *should be bought and sold, he has prostituted his negative for suppressing every legislative attempt to prohibit or to restrain this execrable commerce. And that this assemblage of horrors might want no fact of distinguished die, he is now exciting those very people to rise in arms among us, and to purchase that liberty of which he has deprived them, by murdering the people on whom he also obtruded them: thus paying off former crimes committed against the* LIBERTIES *of one people, with crimes which he urges them to commit against the* LIVES *of another.*]

In every stage of these oppressions we have petitioned for redress in the most humble terms: our repeated petitions have been answered only by repeated injuries.

A prince whose character is thus marked by every

act which may define a tyrant is unfit to be the ruler
of a [ ] people [*who mean to be free.* *Future ages*   free
will scarcely believe that the hardiness of one man
adventured, within the short compass of twelve years
only, to lay a foundation so broad and so undisguised
for tyranny over a people fostered and fixed in
principles of freedom].

Nor have we been wanting in attentions to our
British brethren. We have warned them from time
to time of attempts by their legislature to extend   an unwarrantable
[*a*] jurisdiction over [*these our states*]. We have   us
reminded them of the circumstances of our emigration and settlement here, [*no one of which could*
warrant so strange a pretension: that these were
effected at the expense of our own blood and treasure,
unassisted by the wealth or the strength of Great
Britain: that in constituting indeed our several forms
of government, we had adopted one common king,
thereby laying a foundation for perpetual league and
amity with them: but that submission to their parlia-
ment was no part of our constitution, nor ever in
idea, if history may be credited: and,] we [ ] ap-   have
pealed to their native justice and magnanimity [*as*   and we have
                                                            conjured them
well as to] the ties of our common kindred to dis-   by
avow these usurpations which [*were likely to*] inter-   would inevit-
                                                            ably
rupt our connection and correspondence. They too
have been deaf to the voice of justice and of
consanguinity, [*and when occasions have been given*
them, by the regular course of their laws, of removing
from their councils the disturbers of our harmony,
they have, by their free election, re-established them
in power. At this very time too, they are permitting
their chief magistrate to send over not only soldiers of
our common blood, but Scotch and foreign mer-
cenaries to invade and destroy us. These facts have
given the last stab to agonizing affection, and manly
spirit bids us to renounce forever these unfeeling
brethren. We must endeavor to forget our former
love for them, and hold them as we hold the rest of
mankind, enemies in war, in peace friends. We might
have been a free and a great people together; but a
communication of grandeur and of freedom, it seems,
is below their dignity. Be it so, since they will have
it. The road to happiness and to glory is open to us,

too. We will tread it apart from them, and] acquiesce in the necessity which denounces our [*eter-
nal]* separation [ ]!

We must
therefore
and hold them
as we hold the
rest of mankind,
enemies in war,
in peace friends.

We therefore the representatives of the United States of
America in General Congress assembled, do in the name, and by
the authority of the good people
of these [*states reject and renounce all allegiance and subjection to the kings of Great Britain
and all others who may hereafter
claim by, through or under them;
we utterly dissolve all political
connection which may heretofore
have subsisted between us and
the people or parliament of Great
Britain: and finally we do assert
and declare these colonies to be
free and independent states,]* and
that as free and independent
states, they have full power to
levy war, conclude peace, contract
alliances, establish commerce, and
to do all other acts and things
which independent states may of
right do.

And for the support of this
declaration, we mutually pledge
to each other our lives, our fortunes, and our sacred honor.

We, therefore, the representatives of the United States of
America in General Congress assembled, appealing to the supreme judge of the world for the
rectitude of our intentions, do in
the name, and by the authority of
the good people of these colonies,
solemnly publish and declare, that
these united colonies are, and of
right ought to be free and independent states; that they are ab-
solved from all allegiance to the
British crown, and that all political connection between them and
the state of Great Britain is, and
ought to be, totally dissolved; and
that as free and independent
states, they have full power to
levy war, conclude peace, contract alliances, establish commerce, and to do all other acts
and things which independent
states may of right do.

And for the support of this
declaration, with a firm reliance
on the protection of divine providence, we mutually pledge to
each other our lives, our fortunes,
and our sacred honor.

The Declaration thus signed on the 4th, on paper, was engrossed
on parchment, and signed again on the 2d of August.

⚔ Thomas Paine (1737–1809)

THOMAS PAINE was born in England; after failing as a corset-
maker, a sailor, and an excise officer, he came to America in
1774, bearing circumspect letters of introduction from Franklin.
He had already developed a passion for liberty, a clear and persuasive pamphlet style, and an acute knowledge of propagandist
techniques. The controversy between colonies and Crown over
rights and liberties was exactly fitted to Paine's interests and
talents. He plunged into the argument, and in January 1776
published *Common Sense,* which had much to do with crystal-
lizing support for independence. It sold nearly 100,000 copies in
three months, and Paine was on the way toward becoming the
most effective pamphleteer of the times.

Paine served in the Continental Army on General Greene's
staff. At intervals from 1776 to 1783 he brought out sixteen
pamphlets called "The American Crisis," in which he commented
on the course of events and exhorted the public to greater war
efforts. The first of the "Crisis" papers (written in camp with
a drumhead for a desk) appeared in December 1776, after
Washington's retreat across New Jersey, at the darkest hour of
the Revolution. After the war, acclaimed by the Congress and
the people for his services to the nation, Paine went to Europe,
where he plunged into the French Revolutionary cause with the
same fervor.

Paine was made an honorary citizen of France and served in the
Revolutionary convention, but because he opposed the execution
of the king he was imprisoned and almost guillotined himself.
His deist book, *The Age of Reason,* brought violent attacks
from the theologically orthodox, and on his return to the United
States in 1802 he was greeted with obloquy and abuse. He died,
poor and unpopular, in 1809.

TEXTS: Moncure D. Conway, ed., *The Writings of Thomas Paine*
(New York, 1894), I, 84–89, 170–175.

The Issue Joined

[From *Common Sense,* Part II, 1776]

In the following pages I offer nothing more than simple facts, plain
arguments, and common sense: and have no other preliminaries to
settle with the reader, than that he will divest himself of prejudice
and prepossession, and suffer his reason and his feelings to determine

for themselves: that he will put on, or rather that he will not put off, the true character of a man, and generously enlarge his views beyond the present day.

Volumes have been written on the subject of the struggle between England and America. Men of all ranks have embarked in the controversy, from different motives, and with various designs; but all have been ineffectual, and the period of debate is closed. Arms as the last resource decide the contest; the appeal was the choice of the King, and the Continent has accepted the challenge.

It hath been reported of the late Mr. Pelham (who tho' an able minister was not without his faults) that on his being attacked in the House of Commons on the score that his measures were only of a temporary kind, replied, *"they will last my time."* Should a thought so fatal and unmanly possess the Colonies in the present contest, the name of ancestors will be remembered by future generations with detestation.

The Sun never shined on a cause of greater worth. 'Tis not the affair of a City, a County, a Province, or a Kingdom; but of a Continent — of at least one eighth part of the habitable Globe. 'Tis not the concern of a day, a year, or an age; posterity are virtually involved in the contest, and will be more or less affected even to the end of time, by the proceedings now. Now is the seed-time of Continental union, faith and honour. The least fracture now will be like a name engraved with the point of a pin on the tender rind of a young oak; the wound would enlarge with the tree, and posterity read it in full grown characters.

By referring the matter from argument to arms, a new æra for politics is struck — a new method of thinking hath arisen. All plans, proposals, &c. prior to the nineteenth of April, *i. e.* to the commencement of hostilities, are like the almanacks of the last year; which tho' proper then, are superseded and useless now. Whatever was advanced by the advocates on either side of the question then, terminated in one and the same point, viz. a union with Great Britain; the only difference between the parties was the method of effecting it; the one proposing force, the other friendship; but it hath so far happened that the first hath failed, and the second hath withdrawn her influence.

As much hath been said of the advantages of reconciliation, which, like an agreeable dream, hath passed away and left us as we were, it is but right that we should examine the contrary side of the argument, and enquire into some of the many material injuries which these Colonies sustain, and always will sustain, by being connected with and dependant on Great Britain. To examine that connection and dependance, on the principles of nature and common sense, to see

what we have to trust to, if separated, and what we are to expect, if
dependant.

I have heard it asserted by some, that as America has flourished
under her former connection with Great Britain, the same connection
is necessary towards her future happiness, and will always have the
same effect. Nothing can be more fallacious than this kind of argument. We may as well assert that because a child has thrived upon
milk, that it is never to have meat, or that the first twenty years of
our lives is to become a precedent for the next twenty. But even this
is admitting more than is true; for I answer roundly, that America
would have flourished as much, and probably much more, had no
European power taken any notice of her. The commerce by which
she hath enriched herself are the necessaries of life, and will always
have a market while eating is the custom of Europe.

But she has protected us, say some. That she hath engrossed us is
true, and defended the Continent at our expense as well as her own,
is admitted; and she would have defended Turkey from the same
motive, *viz.* for the sake of trade and dominion.

Alas! we have been long led away by ancient prejudices and made
large sacrifices to superstition. We have boasted the protection of
Great Britain, without considering, that her motive was *interest* not
attachment; and that she did not protect us from *our enemies* on *our
account;* but from *her enemies* on *her own account,* from those who
had no quarrel with us on any *other account,* and who will always be
our enemies on the *same account.* Let Britain waive her pretensions
to the Continent, or the Continent throw off the dependance, and we
should be at peace with France and Spain, were they at war with
Britain. The miseries of Hanover's last war ought to warn us against
connections.

It hath lately been asserted in parliament, that the Colonies have
no relation to each other but through the Parent Country, *i. e.* that
Pennsylvania and the Jerseys, and so on for the rest, are sister Colonies
by the way of England; this is certainly a very roundabout way of
proving relationship, but it is the nearest and only true way of proving
enmity (or enemyship, if I may so call it.) France and Spain never
were, nor perhaps ever will be, our enemies as *Americans,* but as our
being the *subjects of Great Britain.*

But Britain is the parent country, say some. Then the more shame
upon her conduct. Even brutes do not devour their young, nor savages
make war upon their families; Wherefore, the assertion, if true, turns
to her reproach; but it happens not to be true, or only partly so, and
the phrase *parent* or *mother country* hath been jesuitically adopted by
the King and his parasites, with a low papistical design of gaining
an unfair bias on the credulous weakness of our minds. Europe, and

not England, is the parent country of America. This new World hath been the asylum for the persecuted lovers of civil and religious liberty from *every part* of Europe. Hither have they fled, not from the tender embraces of the mother, but from the cruelty of the monster; and it is so far true of England, that the same tyranny which drove the first emigrants from home, pursues their descendants still.

In this extensive quarter of the globe, we forget the narrow limits of three hundred and sixty miles (the extent of England) and carry our friendship on a larger scale; we claim brotherhood with every European Christian, and triumph in the generosity of the sentiment.

It is pleasant to observe by what regular gradations we surmount the force of local prejudices, as we enlarge our acquaintance with the World. A man born in any town in England divided into parishes, will naturally associate most with his fellow parishioners (because their interests in many cases will be common) and distinguish him by the name of *neighbour;* if he meet him but a few miles from home, he drops the narrow idea of a street, and salutes him by the name of *townsman;* if he travel out of the county and meet him in any other, he forgets the minor divisions of street and town, and calls him *countryman, i. e. countyman:* but if in their foreign excursions they should associate in France, or any other part of *Europe,* their local remembrance would be enlarged into that of *Englishmen.* And by a just parity of reasoning, all Europeans meeting in America, or any other quarter of the globe, are *countrymen;* for England, Holland, Germany, or Sweden, when compared with the whole, stand in the same places on the larger scale, which the divisions of street, town, and county do on the smaller ones; Distinctions too limited for Continental minds. Not one third of the inhabitants, even of this province, [Pennsylvania], are of English descent. Wherefore, I reprobate the phrase of Parent or Mother Country applied to England only, as being false, selfish, narrow and ungenerous.

But, admitting that we were all of English descent, what does it amount to? Nothing. Britain, being now an open enemy, extinguishes every other name and title: and to say that reconciliation is our duty, is truly farcical. The first king of England, of the present line (William the Conqueror) was a Frenchman, and half the peers of England are descendants from the same country; wherefore, by the same method of reasoning, England ought to be governed by France.

Much hath been said of the united strength of Britain and the Colonies, that in conjunction they might bid defiance to the world: But this is mere presumption; the fate of war is uncertain, neither do the expressions mean any thing; for this continent would never suffer itself to be drained of inhabitants, to support the British arms in either Asia, Africa, or Europe.

Besides, what have we to do with setting the world at defiance? Our plan is commerce, and that, well attended to, will secure us the peace and friendship of all Europe; because it is the interest of all Europe to have America a free port. Her trade will always be a protection, and her barrenness of gold and silver secure her from invaders.

I challenge the warmest advocate for reconciliation to show a single advantage that this continent can reap by being connected with Great Britain. I repeat the challenge; not a single advantage is derived. Our corn will fetch its price in any market in Europe, and our imported goods must be paid for buy them where we will.

But the injuries and disadvantages which we sustain by that connection, are without number; and our duty to mankind at large, as well as to ourselves, instruct us to renounce the alliance: because, any submission to, or dependance on, Great Britain, tends directly to involve this Continent in European wars and quarrels, and set us at variance with nations who would otherwise seek our friendship, and against whom we have neither anger nor complaint. As Europe is our market for trade, we ought to form no partial connection with any part of it. It is the true interest of America to steer clear of European contentions, which she never can do, while, by her dependance on Britain, she is made the makeweight in the scale of British politics.

Europe is too thickly planted with Kingdoms to be long at peace, and whenever a war breaks out between England and any foreign power, the trade of America goes to ruin, *because of her connection with Britain.* The next war may not turn out like the last, and should it not, the advocates for reconciliation now will be wishing for separation then, because neutrality in that case would be a safer convoy than a man of war. Every thing that is right or reasonable pleads for separation. The blood of the slain, the weeping voice of nature cries, 'TIS TIME TO PART. Even the distance at which the Almighty hath placed England and America is a strong and natural proof that the authority of the one over the other, was never the design of Heaven. The time likewise at which the Continent was discovered, adds weight to the argument, and the manner in which it was peopled, encreases the force of it. The Reformation was preceded by the discovery of America: As if the Almighty graciously meant to open a sanctuary to the persecuted in future years, when home should afford neither friendship nor safety. . . .

The Times That Try Men's Souls

[From *The American Crisis*, I, 1776]

These are the times that try men's souls. The summer soldier and the sunshine patriot will, in this crisis, shrink from the service of their country; but he that stands it *now*, deserves the love and thanks of man and woman. Tyranny, like hell, is not easily conquered; yet we have this consolation with us, that the harder the conflict, the more glorious the triumph. What we obtain too cheap, we esteem too lightly: it is dearness only that gives every thing its value. Heaven knows how to put a proper price upon its goods; and it would be strange indeed if so celestial an article as FREEDOM should not be highly rated. Britain, with an army to enforce her tyranny, has declared that she has a right (*not only to* TAX) but "to BIND *us in* ALL CASES WHATSOEVER," and if being *bound in that manner,* is not slavery, then is there not such a thing as slavery upon earth. Even the expression is impious; for so unlimited a power can belong only to God.

Whether the independence of the continent was declared too soon, or delayed too long, I will not now enter into as an argument; my own simple opinion is, that had it been eight months earlier, it would have been much better. We did not make a proper use of last winter, neither could we, while we were in a dependant state. However, the fault, if it were one, was all our own;[1] we have none to blame but ourselves. But no great deal is lost yet. All that Howe has been doing for this month past, is rather a ravage than a conquest, which the spirit of the Jerseys, a year ago, would have quickly repulsed, and which time and a little resolution will soon recover.

I have as little superstition in me as any man living, but my secret opinion has ever been, and still is, that God Almighty will not give up a people to military destruction, or leave them unsupportedly to perish, who have so earnestly and so repeatedly sought to avoid the calamities of war, by every decent method which wisdom could invent. Neither have I so much of the infidel in me, as to suppose that He has relinquished the government of the world, and given us up to the care of devils; and as I do not, I cannot see on what grounds the king of Britain can look up to heaven for help against us: a common murderer, a highwayman, or a house-breaker, has as good a pretence as he.

'Tis surprising to see how rapidly a panic will sometimes run

---

1 The present winter is worth an age, if rightly employed; but, if lost or neglected, the whole continent will partake of the evil; and there is no punishment that man does not deserve, be he who, or what, or where he will, that may be the means of sacrificing a season so precious and useful. [Paine's note — a citation from his *Common Sense*.]

through a country. All nations and ages have been subject to them: Britain has trembled like an ague at the report of a French fleet of flat bottomed boats; and in the fourteenth [fifteenth] century the whole English army, after ravaging the kingdom of France, was driven back like men petrified with fear; and this brave exploit was performed by a few broken forces collected and headed by a woman, Joan of Arc. Would that heaven might inspire some Jersey maid to spirit up her countrymen, and save her fair fellow sufferers from ravage and ravishment! Yet panics, in some cases, have their uses; they produce as much good as hurt. Their duration is always short; the mind soon grows through them, and acquires a firmer habit than before. But their peculiar advantage is, that they are the touchstones of sincerity and hypocrisy, and bring things and men to light, which might otherwise have lain forever undiscovered. In fact, they have the same effect on secret traitors, which an imaginary apparition would have upon a private murderer. They sift out the hidden thoughts of man, and hold them up in public to the world. Many a disguised tory has lately shown his head, that shall penitentially solemnize with curses the day on which Howe arrived upon the Delaware.

As I was with the troops at Fort Lee, and marched with them to the edge of Pennsylvania, I am well acquainted with many circumstances, which those who live at a distance know but little or nothing of. Our situation there was exceedingly cramped, the place being a narrow neck of land between the North River and the Hackensack. Our force was inconsiderable, being not one fourth so great as Howe could bring against us. We had no army at hand to have relieved the garrison, had we shut ourselves up and stood on our defence. Our ammunition, light artillery, and the best part of our stores, had been removed, on the apprehension that Howe would endeavor to penetrate the Jerseys, in which case Fort Lee could be of no use to us; for it must occur to every thinking man, whether in the army or not, that these kind of field forts are only for temporary purposes, and last in use no longer than the enemy directs his force against the particular object, which such forts are raised to defend. Such was our situation and condition at Fort Lee on the morning of the 20th of November, when an officer arrived with information that the enemy with 200 boats had landed about seven miles above: Major General [Nathanael] Green[e], who commanded the garrison, immediately ordered them under arms, and sent express to George Washington at the town of Hackensack, distant by the way of the ferry = six miles. Our first object was to secure the bridge over the Hackensack, which laid up the river between the enemy and us, about six miles from us, and three from them. General Washington arrived in about three quarters of an hour, and marched at the head of the troops towards the bridge, which place I expected we should have a brush for; however, they did not choose to dispute it with us, and the greatest part of our troops went over the bridge, the rest over the ferry, except some which passed at a mill on a small creek, between the bridge and the ferry, and made their way through some marshy grounds up to the town of Hackensack, and there passed the river. We brought off as much baggage as the wagons could contain, the rest was lost. The simple object was to bring off the garrison, and march them on till they could be strengthened by the Jersey or Pennsylvania militia, so as to be enabled to make a stand. We staid four days at Newark, collected our out-posts with some of the Jersey militia, and marched out twice to meet the enemy, on being informed that they were advancing, though our numbers were greatly inferior to theirs. Howe, in my little opinion, committed a great error in generalship in not throwing a body of forces off from Staten Island through Amboy, by which means he might have seized all our stores at Brunswick, and intercepted our march into Pennsylvania; but if we believe the power of hell to be limited, we must likewise believe that their agents are under some providential controul.

I shall not now attempt to give all the particulars of our retreat to the Delaware; suffice it for the present to say, that both officers and men, though greatly harassed and fatigued, frequently without rest, covering, or provision, the inevitable consequences of a long retreat, bore it with a manly and martial spirit. All their wishes centred in one, which was, that the country would turn out and help them to drive the enemy back. Voltaire has remarked that King William never appeared to full advantage but in difficulties and in action; the same remark may be made on General Washington, for the character fits him. There is a natural firmness in some minds which cannot be unlocked by trifles, but which, when unlocked, discovers a cabinet of fortitude; and I reckon it among those kind of public blessings, which we do not immediately see, that God hath blessed him with uninterrupted health, and given him a mind that can even flourish upon care.

I shall conclude this paper with some miscellaneous remarks on the state of our affairs; and shall begin with asking the following question, Why is it that the enemy have left the New-England provinces, and made these middle ones the seat of war? The answer is easy: New-England is not infested with tories, and we are. I have been tender in raising the cry against these men, and used numberless arguments to show them their danger, but it will not do to sacrifice a world either to their folly or their baseness. The period is now arrived, in which either they or we must change our sentiments, or one or both must fall. And what is a tory? Good God! what is he? I should not be afraid to go with a hundred whigs against a thousand tories, were they to attempt to get into arms. Every tory is a coward; for servile, slavish, self-interested fear is the foundation of toryism; and a man under such influence, though he may be cruel, never can be brave.

But, before the line of irrecoverable separation be drawn between us, let us reason the matter together: Your conduct is an invitation to the enemy, yet not one in a thousand of you has heart enough to join him. Howe is as much deceived by you as the American cause is injured by you. He expects you will all take up arms, and flock to his standard, with muskets on your shoulders. Your opinions are of no use to him, unless you support him personally, for 'tis soldiers, and not tories, that he wants.

I once felt all that kind of anger, which a man ought to feel, against the mean principles that are held by the tories: a noted one, who kept a tavern at Amboy,[2] was standing at his door, with as pretty a child in his hand, about eight or nine years old, as I ever saw, and after speaking his mind as freely as he thought was prudent, finished with this unfatherly expression, *"Well! give me peace in my day."* Not a man lives on the continent but fully believes that a separation must some time or other finally take place, and a generous parent should have said, *"If there must be trouble, let it be in my day, that my child may have peace;"* and this single reflection, well applied, is sufficient to awaken every man to duty. Not a place upon earth might be so happy as America. Her situation is remote from all the wrangling world, and she has nothing to do but to trade with them. A man can distinguish himself between temper and principle, and I am as confident, as I am that God governs the world, that America will never be happy till she gets clear of foreign dominion. Wars, without ceasing, will break out till that period arrives, and the continent must in the end be conqueror; for though the flame of liberty may sometimes cease to shine, the coal can never expire.

⌘ Thomas Pownall (1722–1805)

THOMAS POWNALL, Lincolnshire-born and Cambridge-educated, accompanied his brother-in-law, who was Royal Governor of New York, to his new post as his secretary in 1753. He remained in America as an official of the Board of Trade, and became friends with a number of colonists, among them Benjamin Franklin. For his services in the French and Indian wars and his knowledge of American affairs, he was appointed by William Pitt to be governor

2 Early in August, 1776, Paine enlisted in a Pennsylvania division of the Flying Camp, under Gen. Roberdeau, and was first stationed at Amboy, New Jersey.

of Massachusetts in 1757. He knew America well, and enjoyed the confidence of colonial leaders, so much so that John Adams later described him as "the most constitutional and national Governor" who ever represented the Crown in Massachusetts. Removed in 1759, he was offered the governorship of South Carolina and also of Jamaica, but he declined and remained in England.

Pownall wrote *The Administration of the Colonies,* which first appeared in 1764, an exceptionally able analysis of the colonial mind and the issues at dispute in the controversy between the Americans and England. Though sympathetic to the colonial cause, Pownall could not countenance rebellion; convinced in 1777, however, that the Americans would win, he counseled negotiation and a quick end to the war. His pamphlet, *A Memorial, Most Humbly Addressed to the Sovereigns of Europe* (1780), predicted not only victory but world power for the new country across the Atlantic.

TEXT: Thomas Pownall, *A Memorial, Most Humbly Addressed to the Sovereigns of Europe, on the Present State of Affairs, between the Old and New World,* 2d ed. (London, 1780).

The United States as a World Power

[From *A Memorial,* 1780]

North America is become a new *primary planet* in the system of the world, which while it takes its own course, in its own orbit, must have effect on the orbit of every other planet, and shift the common center of gravity of the whole system of the European world.

North America is *de facto* AN INDEPENDENT POWER *which has taken its equal station with other powers,* and must be so *de jure.* The politicians of the Governments of Europe may reason or negotiate upon this idea, as a matter *sub lite.* The powers of those Governments may fight about it as a new Power coming into establishment; such negotiations, and such wars, are of no consequence either to the right or the fact. It would be just as wise, and just as effectual, if they were to go to war to decide, or set on foot negotiations to settle, to whom for the future the sovereignty of the moon should belong. The moon hath been long common to them all, and they may all in their turns profit of her reflected light. The independence of America is fixed as fate; she is mistress of her own fortune; — knows that she is so, and will actuate that power which she feels she hath, so as to establish her own system, and to change the system of Europe. . . .

If the Powers of Europe will view the state of things *as they do really exist,* and will treat them *as being what they are,* the lives of thousands may be spared; the happiness of millions may be secured; and, the peace of the whole world preserved. If they will not, they will be plunged into a sea of troubles, a sea of blood, fathomless and boundless. The war that has begun to rage betwixt Britain, France, and Spain, which is almost gorged betwixt Britain and America, will extend itself to all the maritime, and most likely, afterwards, to all the inland powers of Europe: and like the *thirty years war* of the sixteenth and seventeenth centuries, will not end, but as that did, by a new and general resettlement of powers and interests, according to the new spirit of the new system which hath taken place. . . .

There is nowhere in the European part of the old world such a greatness of interwoven and combined interest, communicating through such largeness of territory, as that in North America, possessed and actuated by the English nation. The northern and southern parts of Europe, are possessed by different nations, actuated by different spirits, and conducted under very different systems. . . .

On the contrary, when the site and circumstances of the large extended territories of North America are examined; one finds every thing united in it which forms greatness of dominions, *amplitude and growth of state.*

The nature of the coast and of the winds upon that coast, is such as renders marine navigation, from one end of its extent to the other, a perpetually moving intercourse of communion: and the nature of the rivers which open (where marine navigation ends) an inland navigation which, with short interruptions, carries on a circulation throughout the whole, renders such inland navigation but a further process of that communion; all which becomes, as it were, a one vital principle of life, extended through a one organized being. . . .

In this new world we see all the inhabitants not only free, but allowing an universal naturalization to all who wish to be so; and an uncontrolled liberty of using any mode of life they choose, or any means of getting a livelihood that their talents lead them to. Free of all restraints, which take the property of themselves out of their own hands, their souls are their own, and their reason; they are their own masters, and they act; their labor is employed on their own property, and what they produce is their own. In a country like this, where every man has the full and free exertion of his powers, where every man may acquire any share of the good things thereof, or of interest and power which his spirit can work him up to; there, an unabated application of the powers of individuals, and a perpetual struggle of their spirits, sharpens their wits, and gives constant training to the mind. The acquirement of information in things and business, which becomes necessary to this mode of life, gives the mind, thus sharpened, and thus exercised, a turn of inquiry and investigation which forms a *character peculiar to these people,* which is not to be met with, nor ever did exist in any other to the same degree, unless in some of the ancient republics, where the people were under the same predicament. This turn of character, which, in the ordinary occurrences of life, is called *inquisitiveness,* and which, when exerted about trifles, goes even to a degree of ridicule in many instances; is yet, in matters of business and commerce, a most useful and efficient talent. . . .

. . . In America, the wisdom and not the man is attended to; and *America is peculiarly a poor man's country.* . . . They find themselves at liberty to follow what mode they like; they feel that they can venture to try experiments, and that the advantages of their discoveries are their own. They, therefore, try what the soil claims, what the climate permits, and what both will produce and sustain to the greatest advantage. . . .

Although the civilizing activity of America does not, by artificial and false helps, contrary to the natural course of things, inconsistent with, and checking the first applications of, its natural labor, and before the community is ripe for such endeavor, attempt to force the establishment of manufactures: yet following, as Use and Experience lead, the natural progress of improvement, it is every year producing a surplus profit; which surplus, as it enters again into the circulation of productive employment, creates an accumulating accelerated progressive series of surpluses. *With these accumulated surpluses* of the produce of the earth and seas, *and not with manufactures,* the Americans carry on their *commercial* exertions. Their fish, wheat, flour, rice, tobacco, indigo, live stock, barrel pork and beef (some of these articles being peculiar to the country and staple commodities) form the exports of their commerce. This has given them a direct trade to Europe; and, with some additional articles, a circuitous trade to Africa and the West Indies.

The same ingenuity of mechanic handicraft, which arises concomitant with agriculture, doth here also rise concomitant with commerce, and is exerted in SHIP-BUILDING: it is carried on, not only to serve all the purposes of their own carriage, and that of the West Indies in part, but to an extent of sale, so as to supply great part of the shipping of Britain; and further, if it continues to advance with the same progress, it will supply great part of the trade of Europe also with shipping, at cheaper rates than they can any where, or by any means, supply themselves.

Thus their commerce, although subsisting (while they were subordinate provinces) under various restrictions, by its advancing progress in *ship-building,* hath been striking deep root, and is now shot forth an *active commerce,* growing into *amplitude of state* and great power. . . .

I will here, therefore, from this comparison of the spirit of civilizing activity in the old and in the new world, as one sees it in its application to agriculture, handicrafts, and mechanics, and finally in an active commerce, spatiating on an amplitude of base, the natural communion of a great country, and rising in a natural progression, venture to assert, that in this point, NORTH AMERICA HAS ADVANCED, AND IS EVERY DAY ADVANCING, TO GROWTH OF STATE, WITH A STEADY AND CONTINUALLY ACCELERATING MOTION, OF WHICH THERE HAS NEVER YET BEEN ANY EXAMPLE IN EUROPE.

But farther; when one looks to the progressive POPULATION which this fostering happiness doth, of course, produce, one cannot but see, in North America, that God's first blessing, *"Be fruitful and multiply; replenish the earth and subdue it,"* hath operated in full manifestation of his will. . . .

This might have been, indeed, the spirit of the British Empire, America being a part of it: *This is the spirit* of the government of the new Empire of America, Great Britain being no part of it. It is a vitality, liable, indeed, to many disorders, many dangerous diseases; but it is young and strong, and will struggle, by the vigor of internal healing principles of life, against those evils, and surmount them; like the infant Hercules, it will strangle these serpents in its cradle. Its strength will grow with its years, and it will establish its constitution, and perfect adultness in growth of state.

To this greatness of empire it will certainly arise. That it is removed three thousand miles distant from its enemy; that it lies on another side of the globe where it has no enemy; that it is earth-born, and like a giant ready to run its course, are not alone the grounds and reasons on which a speculatist may pronounce this. The fostering care with which the rival Powers of Europe will nurse it, ensures its establishment beyond all doubt or danger.

৶ Anne Robert Jacques Turgot (1727–1781)

Richard Price (1723–1791)

THERE were a number of Englishmen and Europeans who regarded the American war for independence as one of the great moral turning points of history, the first of a series of revolutions which would conclude only when men were free all over the world. Turgot, in France, although he had been educated for the church, joined with a group of liberal young political economists, philosophers, and writers who demanded widespread reforms in social and political life. Dr. Richard Price of London, a friend of both Turgot and Franklin, was also a liberal reformer, strongly opposed to British policy toward the American colonies. Price's two books, *Observations on Civil Liberty and Justice and Policy of War with America* (1776) and *Observations on the Importance of the American Revolution* (1785), were among the most enlightened and sympathetic of European reactions to the American revolutionary experience.

TEXTS: Louis M. Hacker, *The Shaping of the American Tradition* (New York, 1947), pp. 226–229.

Anne Robert Jacques Turgot
The American Revolution
[Letter to Dr. Price, March 22, 1778]

TO DR. PRICE, *London*

... I have been led to judge thus by the infatuation of your people in the absurd project of subduing America, till the affair of Burgoyne began to open their eyes; and by the system of monopoly and exclusion which has been recommended by all your writers on Commerce, (except Mr. Adam Smith and Dean Tucker); a system which has been the true source of your separation from your Colonies. I have also been led to this opinion by all your controversial writings upon the questions which have occupied your attention these twenty years, and in which, till your observations appeared, I scarce recollect to have read one that took up these questions on their proper ground. I cannot conceive how a nation which has cultivated every branch of natural knowledge with such success, should have made so little progress in the most interesting of all sciences, that of the public good: A science, in which the liberty of the Press, which she alone enjoys, ought to have given her a prodigious advantage over every other nation in Europe. Was it national pride which prevented you from profiting by this advantage? Or was it, because you were not altogether in so bad a condition as other nations, that you have imposed upon yourselves in your speculations so far as to be persuaded that your arrangements were compleat? Is it party spirit and a desire of being supported by popular opinion which has retarded your progress, by inducing your political writers to treat as vain Metaphysics all those speculations which aim at establishing the rights and true interests of nations and individuals upon fixed principles? How comes it that you are almost the first of the writers of your country, who has given a just idea of

liberty, and shewn the falsity of the notion so frequently repeated by
almost all Republican Writers, "that liberty consists in being subject
only to the laws," as if a man could be free while oppressed by an
unjust law. This would not be true, even if we could suppose that
all the laws were the work of an assembly of the whole nation; for
certainly every individual has his rights, of which the nation cannot
deprive him, except by violence and an unlawful use of the general
power. Though you have attended to this truth and have explained
yourself upon this head, perhaps it would have merited a more minute
explanation, considering how little attention is paid to it even by the
most zealous friends of liberty.

It is likewise extraordinary that it was not thought a trivial matter
in England to assert "that one nation never can have a right to govern
another nation" — "that a government where such a principle is
admitted can have no foundation but that of force, which is equally
the foundation of robbery and tyranny" — "and that the tyranny of
a people is the most cruel and intolerable, because it leaves the fewest
resources to the oppressed." — A despot is restrained by a sense of his
own interest. He is checked by remorse or by the public opinion. But
the multitude never calculate. The multitude are never checked by
remorse, and will even ascribe to themselves the highest honour when
they deserve only disgrace.

What a dreadful commentary on your book are the events which
have lately befallen the English nation? — For some months they have
been running headlong to ruin. — The fate of America is already
decided — Behold her independent beyond recovery. — But will She
be free and happy? — Can this new people, so advantageously placed
for giving an example to the world of a constitution under which man
may enjoy his rights, freely exercise all his faculties, and be governed
only by nature, reason and justice — Can they form such a Constitution? — Can they establish it upon a neverfailing foundation, and
guard against every source of division and corruption which may
gradually undermine and destroy it? . . .

It is impossible not to wish ardently that this people may attain to
all the prosperity of which they are capable. They are the *hope* of the
world. They may become a *model* to it. They *may* prove by fact that
men can be free and yet tranquil; and that it is in their power to rescue
themselves from the chains in which tyrants and knaves of all descriptions have presumed to bind them under the pretence of the public
good. They may exhibit an example of *political* liberty, of *religious*
liberty, of *commercial* liberty, and of industry. The *Asylum* they open
to the oppressed of all nations should console the earth. The ease with
which the injured may escape from oppressive governments, will com-

pel Princes to become just and cautious; and the rest of the world will gradually open their eyes upon the empty illusions with which they have been hitherto cheated by politicians. But for this purpose *America* must preserve *herself* from these illusions; and take care to avoid being what your ministerial writers are frequently saying She *will* be — an image of our *Europe* — a mass of divided powers contending for territory and commerce, and continually cementing the slavery of the people with their own blood.

All enlightened men — All the friends of humanity ought at this time to unite their lights to those of the *American* sages, and to assist them in the great work of legislation. This, sir, would be a work worthy of you. I wish it was in my power to animate your zeal in this instance. If I have in this letter indulged too free an effusion of my sentiments, this has been my only motive; and it will, I hope, induce you to pardon me for tiring you. I wish indeed that the blood which has been spilt, and which will continue for some time to be spilt in this contest, may not be without its use to the human race.

Our two nations are about doing much harm to each other, and probably without the prospect to either of any real advantage. An increase of debts and public burthens, (perhaps a national bankruptcy), and the ruin of a great number of individuals, will prove the result. England seems to me to be more likely to suffer by these evils, and much nearer to them, than France. — If instead of going to war, you had at the commencement of your disputes endeavoured to retreat with a good grace; if your Statesmen had then consented to make those concessions, which they will infallibly be obliged to make at last; if the national opinion would have permitted your government to anticipate events which might have been foreseen; if, in short, you had immediately yielded to the independence of America without entering into any hostilities; I am firmly persuaded your nation would have lost nothing. — But you will *now* lose what you have already expended, and what you are still to expend; you will experience a great diminution of your commerce for some time, and great interior commotions, if driven to a bankruptcy; and, at any rate, a great diminution of weight in foreign politics. But this last circumstance I think of little consequence to the real happiness of a people; for I cannot agree with the *Abbe Raynal* in your motto. I do not believe all this will make you a contemptible nation or throw you into slavery. — On the contrary; your misfortunes may have the effect of a necessary amputation. They are perhaps the only means of saving you from the gangrene of luxury and corruption. And if they should terminate in the amendment of your constitution, by restoring annual elections, and distributing the right of suffrages for representation so as to render it more equal and better proportioned to the interests of the represented, you will perhaps gain as much as America by this revolution; for you will preserve your liberty, and with your liberty, and by means of it, all your other losses will be speedily repaired.

By the freedom with which I have opened myself to you, sir, upon these delicate points, you will judge of the esteem with which you have inspired me; and the satisfaction I feel in thinking there is some resemblance between our sentiments and views. I depend on your confining this confidence to yourself. I even beg that you will not be particular in answering me by the Post, for your letter will certainly be opened at our Post-Offices, and I shall be found much too great a friend to liberty for a minister, even though a discarded minister.

I have the honour to be with all possible respect,

Sir,

Your most humble,

and most obedient Servant,

Turgot

Richard Price

The Meaning of the Revolution

[From *Observations on the Importance of the American Revolution,* 1785]

Having, from pure conviction, taken a warm part in favour of the *British* colonies (now the United States of America) during the late war; and been exposed, in consequence of this, to *much* abuse and *some* danger; it must be supposed that I have been waiting for the issue with anxiety — I am thankful that my anxiety is removed; and that I have been spared to be a witness to that very issue of the war which has been all along the object of my wishes. With heart-felt satisfaction, I see the revolution in favour of universal liberty which has taken place in *America;* — a revolution which opens a new prospect in human affairs, and begins a new æra in the history of mankind; — a revolution by which *Britons* themselves will be the greatest gainers, if wise enough to improve properly the check that has been given to the despotism of their ministers, and to catch the flame of virtuous liberty which has saved their American brethren.

The late war, in its *commencement and progress,* did great good by disseminating just sentiments of the rights of mankind, and the nature of legitimate government; by exciting a spirit of resistance to tyranny which has emancipated one *European* country, and is likely to emancipate others; and by occasioning the establishment in *America* of forms of government more equitable and more liberal than any that the world has yet known. But, in its *termination,* the war has done still greater good by preserving the new governments from that destruction in which they must have been involved, had Britain conquered; by providing, in a sequestered continent possessed of many singular advantages, a place of refuge for opprest men in every region of the world; and by laying the foundation there of an empire which may be the seat of liberty, science and virtue, and from whence there is reason to hope these sacred blessings will spread, till they become universal, and the time arrives when kings and priests shall have no more power to oppress, and that ignominious slavery which has hitherto debased the world is exterminated. I therefore, think I see the hand of Providence in the late war working for the general good. . . .

But among the events in modern times tending to the elevation of mankind, there are none probably of so much consequence as the recent one which occasions these observations. Perhaps, I do not go too far when I say that, next to the introduction of Christianity among mankind, the American revolution may prove the most important step in the progressive course of human improvement. It is an event which may produce a general diffusion of the principles of humanity, and become the means of setting free mankind from the shackles of superstition and tyranny, by leading them to see and know "that nothing is *fundamental* but impartial enquiry, an honest mind, and virtuous practice — that state policy ought not to be applied to the support of speculative opinions and formularies of faith." — "That the members of a civil community are *confederates*, not *subjects;* and their rulers, *servants*, not *masters*. — And that all legitimate government consists in the dominion of equal laws made with common consent; that is, in the dominion of men over *themselves;* and not in the dominion of communities over communities, or of any men over other men."

Happy will the world be when these truths shall be every where acknowledged and practised upon. Religious bigotry, that cruel demon, will be then laid asleep. Slavish governments and slavish Hierarchies will then sink; and the old prophecies be verified, "that the last universal empire upon earth shall be the empire of reason and virtue, under which the gospel of peace (better understood) *shall have free course and be glorified, many will run to and fro and knowledge be increased, the wolf dwell with the lamb and the leopard with the kid, and nation no more lift up a sword against nation."

It is a conviction I cannot resist, that the independence of the *English* colonies in America is one of the steps ordained by Providence to introduce these times; and I can scarcely be deceived in this conviction, if the United States should escape some dangers which threaten them, and will take proper care to throw themselves open to future improvements, and to make the most of the advantages of their present. . . .

◁R George Washington (1732–1799)

THE British surrender at Yorktown, as the Revolutionary leaders knew, did not mark the end of the Revolution. The problem of completing the peace and of consolidating wartime gains into an acceptable treaty, and the even greater problem of creating a stable government out of thirteen wartorn and disunited colonies still remained.

In the spring of 1783, with the final negotiations of the peace treaty nearly reached, George Washington looked forward to civilian life after eight years of military service. He had seen, in these years, bickering, self-interest, and even treason as well as bravery, idealism, and dedication to the cause of independence. He had himself refused offers of a limited monarchy and had destroyed schemes for a military dictatorship. Aware that no other American enjoyed such great influence and prestige as himself, he used these in this appeal to the nation (in the form of a letter to the governors of the new states) to put aside all selfishness and differences in the great task of uniting the United States.

TEXT: John C. Fitzpatrick, ed., *The Writings of George Washington* (Washington, 1931–44), XXVI, 483–487, 494–496.

Advice for the Future

[From a circular letter to the Governors of all the States, on disbanding the Army, June 8, 1783]

The great object for which I had the honor to hold an appointment in the Service of my Country, being accomplished, I am now preparing to resign it into the hands of Congress, and to return to that domestic retirement, which, it is well known, I left with the greatest reluctance, a Retirement for which I have never ceased to sigh through a long and painful absence, and in which (remote from the noise and trouble of the World) I meditate to pass the remainder of life in a state of undisturbed repose. But before I carry this resolution into effect, I think it a duty incumbent on me, to make this my last official communication, to congratulate you on the glorious events which Heaven has been pleased to produce in our favor, to offer my sentiments respecting some important subjects, which appear to me, to be intimately connected with the tranquillity of the United States, to take my leave of your Excellency as a public Character, and to give my final blessing to that Country, in whose service I have spent the prime of my life, for whose sake I have consumed so many anxious days and watchfull nights, and whose happiness being extremely dear to me, will always constitute no inconsiderable part of my own.

Impressed with the liveliest sensibility on this pleasing occasion, I will claim the indulgence of dilating the more copiously on the subjects of our mutual felicitation. When we consider the magnitude of the prize we contended for, the doubtful nature of the contest, and the favorable manner in which it has terminated, we shall find the greatest possible reason for gratitude and rejoicing; this is a theme that will afford infinite delight to every benevolent and liberal mind, whether the event in contemplation, be considered as the source of present enjoyment or the parent of future happiness; and we shall have equal occasion to felicitate ourselves on the lot which Providence has assigned us, whether we view it in a natural, a political or moral point of light.

The Citizens of America, placed in the most enviable condition, as the sole Lords and Proprietors of a vast Tract of Continent, comprehending all the various soils and climates of the World, and abounding with all the necessaries and conveniencies of life, are now by the late satisfactory pacification, acknowledged to be possessed of absolute freedom and Independency. They are, from this period, to be considered as the Actors on a most conspicuous Theatre, which seems to be peculiarly designated by Providence for the display of human greatness and felicity. Here, they are not only surrounded with every thing which can contribute to the completion of private and domestic enjoyment, but Heaven has crowned all its other blessings, by giving a fairer opportunity for political happiness, than any other Nation has ever been favored with. Nothing can illustrate these observations more forcibly, than a recollection of the happy conjuncture of times and circumstances, under which our Republic assumed its rank among the Nations. The foundation of our Empire was not laid in the gloomy age of Ignorance and Superstition, but at an Epoch when the rights of mankind were better understood and more clearly defined, than at any former period; the researches of the human mind, after social happiness, have been carried to a great extent, the Treasures of knowledge, acquired by the labours of Philosophers, Sages and Legislatures, through a long succession of years, are laid open for our use, and their collected wisdom may be happily applied in the Establishment of our forms of Government; the free cultivation of Letters, the unbounded extension of Commerce, the progressive refinement of Manners, the growing liberality of sentiment, and above all, the pure and benign light of Revelation, have had a meliorating influence on mankind and increased the blessings of Society. At this auspicious period, the United States came into existence as a Nation, and if their Citizens should not be completely free and happy, the fault will be intirely their own.

Such is our situation, and such are our prospects: but notwithstanding the cup of blessing is thus reached out to us, notwithstanding happiness is ours, if we have a disposition to seize the occasion and make it our own; yet, it appears to me there is an option still left to the United States of America, that it is in their choice, and depends upon their conduct, whether they will be respectable and prosperous, or contemptible and miserable as a Nation. This is the time of their political probation, this is the moment when the eyes of the whole World are turned upon them, this is the moment to establish or ruin their national Character forever, this is the favorable moment to give such a tone to our Federal Government, as will enable it to answer the ends of its institution, or this may be the ill-fated moment for relaxing the powers of the Union, annihilating the cement of the Confederation, and exposing us to become the sport of European politics, which may play one State against another to prevent their growing importance, and to serve their own interested purposes. For, according to the system of Policy the States shall adopt at this moment, they will stand or fall, and by their confirmation or lapse, it is yet to be decided, whether the Revolution must ultimately be considered as a blessing or a curse: a blessing or a curse, not to the present age alone, for with our fate will the destiny of unborn Millions be involved. . . .

There are four things, which I humbly conceive, are essential to the well being, I may even venture to say, to the existence of the United States as an Independent Power:

1st. An indissoluble Union of the States under one Federal Head.

2dly. A Sacred regard to Public Justice.

3dly. The adoption of a proper Peace Establishment, and

4thly. The prevalence of that pacific and friendly Disposition, among the People of the United States, which will induce them to forget their local prejudices and policies, to make those mutual concessions which are requisite to the general prosperity, and in some instances, to sacrifice their individual advantages to the interest of the Community.

These are the Pillars on which the glorious Fabrick of our Independency and National Character must be supported. Liberty is the Basis, and whoever would dare to sap the foundation, or overturn the Structure, under whatever specious pretexts he may attempt it, will merit the bitterest execration, and the severest punishment which can be inflicted by his injured Country. . . .

. . . Here I might speak with the more confidence from my actual observations, and, if it would not swell this Letter (already too prolix) beyond the bounds I had prescribed myself: I could demonstrate to every mind open to conviction, that in less time and with much less expence than has been incurred, the War might have been brought to the same happy conclusion, if the resources of the Continent could have been properly drawn forth, that the distresses and disappointments which have very often occurred, have in too many instances, resulted more from a want of energy, in the Continental Government, than a deficiency of means in the particular States. That the inefficiency of measures, arising from the want of an adequate authority in the Supreme Power, from a partial compliance with the Requisitions of Congress in some of the States, and from a failure of punctuality in others, while it tended to damp the zeal of those which were more willing to exert themselves, served also to accumulate the expences of the War, and to frustrate the best concerted Plans; and that the discouragement occasioned by the complicated difficulties and embarrassments, in which our affairs were by this means involved, would have long ago produced the dissolution of any Army, less patient, less virtuous and less persevering, than that which I have had the honor to command. . . .

I now make it my earnest prayer, that God would have you, and the State over which you preside, in his holy protection, that he would incline the hearts of the Citizens to cultivate a spirit of subordination and obedience to Government, to entertain a brotherly affection and love for one another, for their fellow Citizens of the United States at large, and particularly for their brethren who have served in the Field, and finally, that he would most graciously be pleased to dispose us all, to do Justice, to love mercy, and to demean ourselves with that Charity, humility and pacific temper of mind, which were the Characteristicks of the Divine Author of our blessed Religion, and without an humble imitation of whose example in these things, we can never hope to be a happy Nation.

ᴄᴿ Ezra Stiles (1727–1795)

EZRA STILES, son of a Congregational clergyman, was born at North Haven, Connecticut. He graduated from Yale in 1746, and in 1755 accepted a post as pastor of the Second Congregational Church at Newport, Rhode Island. A man of tremendous intellectual vitality and broad interests, who read widely in six languages, Stiles helped to found Rhode Island College (later Brown University). A strong supporter of the cause of independence, he was forced to flee Newport ahead of a threatened

British landing in 1776. Elected president of Yale in 1777, he kept the college together during the difficult war years. Stiles wrote much, but published little. His sermon "The United States Elevated to Glory and Honor" was given at Election Day exercises on May 8, 1783, and later appeared in pamphlet form.

TEXT: E. C. Stedman and E. M. Hutchinson, *A Library of American Literature* (New York, 1889–90), III, 116–118.

The Results of the War

[From *The United States Elevated to Glory and Honor,* 1783]

This war has decided, not by the *jus maritimum* of Rhodes, Oleron, or Britain, but on the principles of commercial utility and public right, that the navigation of the Atlantic Ocean shall be free: and so probably will be that of all the oceans of the terraqueous globe. All the European powers will henceforth, from national and commercial interests, naturally become an united and combined guaranty for the free navigation of the Atlantic and free commerce with America. Interest will establish a free access for all nations to our shores, and for us to all nations. The armed neutrality will disarm even war itself of hostilities against trade; will form a new chapter in the laws of nations, and preserve a free commerce among powers at war. Fighting armies will decide the fate of empires by the sword without interrupting the civil, social, and commercial intercourse of subjects. The want of anything to take will prove a natural abolition of privateering when the property shall be covered with neutral protection. Even the navies will, within a century, become useless. A generous and truly liberal system of national connection, in the spirit of the plan conceived and nearly executed by the great Henry IV, of France, will almost annihilate war itself.

We shall have a communication with all nations in commerce, manners, and science, beyond anything heretofore known in the world. Manufacturers and artisans, and men of every description may, perhaps, come and settle among us. They will be few indeed in comparison with the annual thousands of our natural increase, and will be incorporated with the prevailing hereditary complexion of the first settlers. We shall not be assimilated to them, but they to us; especially in the second and third generations. This fermentation and communion of nations will doubtless produce something very new, singular, and glorious. Upon the conquest of Alexander the Great, statuary, painting, architecture, philosophy, and the other fine arts were transplanted in perfection from Athens to Tarsus, from Greece to Syria, where they immediately flourished in even greater perfection than in the parent state. Not in Greece herself are there to be found specimens of a sublimer or more magnificent architecture, even in the Grecian style, than in the ruins of Baalbec and Palmyra. So all the arts may be transplanted from Europe and Asia, and flourish in America with an augmented lustre; not to mention the augment of the sciences from American inventions and discoveries, of which there have been as capital ones here, the last half century, as in all Europe.

The rough, sonorous diction of the English language may here take its Athenian polish, and receive its Attic urbanity; as it will probably become the vernacular tongue of more numerous millions than ever yet spake one language on earth. It may continue for ages to be the prevailing and general language of North America. The intercommunion of the United States with all the world in travels, trade, and politics, and the infusion of letters into our infancy, will probably preserve us from the provincial dialects risen into inexterminable habit before the invention of printing. The Greek never became the language of the Alexandrine, nor the Turkish of the Ottoman conquests, nor yet the Latin that of the Roman empire. The Saracenic conquests have already lost the pure and elegant Arabic of the Koreish tribe, or the family of Ishmael, in the corrupted dialects of Egypt, Syria, Persia, and Hindostan. Different from these, the English language will grow up with the present American population into great purity and elegance, unmutilated by the foreign dialects of foreign conquests.

A More Perfect Union

◆ John Adams (1735–1826)

How far one might trust human nature, and to what extent man might be entrusted with his own government, were questions of great importance to the men who, after the close of the War for Independence, were faced with the problems of establishing a just, stable, and free government consistent with the principles for which the war was fought.

John Adams, though as ardent a believer in human freedom and dignity as any man, was never fully convinced of the unselfishness and wisdom of man in the mass. "All men," he once wrote, "are men and not angels," adding bluntly that "whoever would found a state . . . must presume that all men are bad by nature." There was and always would be, in his opinion, an "aristocracy" in any society which, by one means or another, would rule; to protect the principles of republican government it would be best to recognize, legalize, and control this ruling minority. Adams' *Defence of the Constitutions of the United States* (1787–88) and his *Discourses on Davila* (1790–91) both supported a conservative-centered political system, in which an experienced, wealthy, and wise minority governed under a system of checks and balances designed to prevent autocratic or democratic excesses.

Though Adams and Jefferson were political opponents for twenty years, the two men in later life began a correspondence in which they discussed the recent past and speculated on the future of the new nation they had both done so much to construct. The problem of aristocracy versus democracy formed the subject of one of their most famous exchanges.

TEXTS: Charles Francis Adams, ed., *The Works of John Adams* (Boston, 1850–56), VI, 279–281; X, 282–284. A. A. Lipscomb and A. E. Bergh, eds., *The Writings of Thomas Jefferson* (Washington, 1903–5), XIV, 1–2, 5–8.

A Balanced Government

[From *Discourses on Davila,* 1791]

. . . Amidst all their exultations, Americans and Frenchmen should remember that the perfectibility of man is only human and terrestrial perfectibility. Cold will still freeze, and fire will never cease to burn; disease and vice will continue to disorder, and death to terrify mankind. Emulation next to self-preservation will forever be the great spring of human actions, and the balance of a well-ordered government will alone be able to prevent that emulation from degenerating into dangerous ambition, irregular rivalries, destructive factions, wasting seditions, and bloody, civil wars.

The great question will forever remain, *who shall work?* Our species cannot all be idle. Leisure for study must ever be the portion of a few. The number employed in government must forever be very small. Food, raiment, and habitations, the indispensable wants of all, are not to be obtained without the continual toil of ninety-nine in a hundred of mankind. As rest is rapture to the weary man, those who labor little will always be envied by those who labor much, though the latter in reality be probably the most enviable. With all the encouragements, public and private, which can ever be given to general education, and it is scarcely possible they should be too many or too great, the laboring part of the people can never be learned. The controversy between the rich and the poor, the laborious and the idle, the learned and the ignorant, distinctions as old as the creation, and as extensive as the globe, distinctions which no art or policy, no degree of virtue or philosophy can ever wholly destroy, will continue, and rivalries will spring out of them. These parties will be represented in the legislature, and must be balanced, or one will oppress the other. There will never probably be found any other mode of establishing such an equilibrium, than by constituting the representation of each an independent branch of the legislature, and an independent executive authority, such as that in our government, to be a third branch and a mediator or an arbitrator between them. Property must be secured, or liberty cannot exist. But if unlimited or unbalanced power of disposing property, be put into the hands of those who have no property, France will find, as we have found, the lamb committed to the custody of the wolf. In such a case, all the pathetic exhortations and addresses of the national assembly to the people, to respect property, will be regarded no more than the warbles of the songsters of the forest. The great art of lawgiving consists in balancing the poor against the rich in the legislature, and in constituting the legislative a perfect balance against the executive power, at the same time that no individual or party can become its rival. The essence of a free government consists in an effectual control of rivalries. The executive and the legislative powers are natural rivals; and if each has not an effectual control over the other, the weaker will ever be the lamb in the paws of the wolf. The nation which will not adopt an equilibrium of power must adopt a despotism. There is no other alternative. Rivalries must be controlled, or they will throw all things into confusion; and there is nothing but despotism or a balance of power which can control them. Even in the simple monarchies, the nobility and the judicatures constitute a balance, though a very imperfect one, against the royalties.

Let us conclude with one reflection more which shall barely be hinted at, as delicacy, if not prudence, may require, in this place, some degree of reserve. Is there a possibility that the government of nations may fall into the hands of men who teach the most disconsolate of all creeds, that men are but fireflies, and that this *all* is without a father? Is this the way to make man, as man, an object of respect? Or is it to make murder itself as indifferent as shooting a plover, and the extermination of the Rohilla nation as innocent as the swallowing of mites on a morsel of cheese? If such a case should happen, would not one of these, the most credulous of all believers, have reason to pray to his eternal nature or his almighty chance (the more absurdity there is in this address the more in character) *give us again the gods of the Greeks; give us again the more intelligible as well as more comfortable systems of Athanasius and Calvin; nay, give us again our popes and hierarchies, Benedictines and Jesuits, with all their superstition and fanaticism, impostures and tyranny.* A certain duchess, of venerable years and masculine understanding, said of some of the philosophers of the eighteenth century, admirably well, — *"On ne croit pas dans le Christianisme, mais on croit toutes les sottises possibles."*

A Natural Aristocracy

[From a letter to Thomas Jefferson, November 15, 1813][1]

We are now explicitly agreed upon one important point, viz., that there is a natural aristocracy among men, the grounds of which are virtue and talents. You very justly indulge a little merriment upon this solemn subject of aristocracy. I often laugh at it too, for there is nothing in this laughable world more ridiculous than the management of it by all the nations of the earth; but while we smile, mankind have reason to say to us, as the frogs said to the boys, what is sport to you, are wounds and death to us. When I consider the weakness, the folly, the pride, the vanity, the selfishness, the artifice, the low craft and mean cunning, the want of principle, the avarice, the unbounded ambition, the unfeeling cruelty of a majority of those (in all nations) who are allowed an aristocratical influence, and, on the other hand, the stupidity with which the more numerous multitude not only become their dupes, but even love to be taken in by their tricks, I feel a stronger disposition to weep at their destiny, than to laugh at their folly. But though we have agreed in one point, in words, it is

[1] See page 130 for Jefferson's letter to Adams, October 28, 1813.

not yet certain that we are perfectly agreed in sense. Fashion has introduced an indeterminate use of the word talents. Education, wealth, strength, beauty, stature, birth, marriage, graceful attitudes and motions, gait, air, complexion, physiognomy, are talents, as well as genius, science, and learning. Any one of these talents that in fact commands or influences two votes in society, gives to the man who possesses it the character of an aristocrat, in my sense of the word. Pick up the first hundred men you meet, and make a republic. Every man will have an equal vote; but when deliberations and discussions are opened, it will be found that twenty-five, by their talents, virtues being equal, will be able to carry fifty votes. Every one of these twenty-five is an aristocrat in my sense of the word; whether he obtains his one vote in addition to his own, by his birth, fortune, figure, eloquence, science, learning, craft, cunning, or even his character for good fellowship, and a *bon vivant*. . . .

. . . Your distinction between natural and artificial aristocracy, does not appear to me well founded. Birth and wealth are conferred upon some men as imperiously by nature as genius, strength, or beauty. The heir to honors, and riches, and power, has often no more merit in procuring these advantages, than he has in obtaining a handsome face, or an elegant figure. When aristocracies are established by human laws, and honor, wealth and power are made hereditary by municipal laws and political institutions, then I acknowledge artificial aristocracy to commence; but this never commences till corruption in elections become dominant and uncontrollable. But this artificial aristocracy can never last. The everlasting envies, jealousies, rivalries, and quarrels among them; their cruel rapacity upon the poor ignorant people, their followers, compel them to set up Caesar, a demagogue, to be a monarch, a master; *pour mettre chacun à sa place*. Here you have the origin of all artificial aristocracy, which is the origin of all monarchies. And both artificial aristocracy and monarchy, and civil, military, political, and hierarchical despotism, have all grown out of the natural aristocracy of virtues and talents. . . .

You suppose a difference of opinion between you and me on the subject of aristocracy. I can find none. I dislike and detest hereditary honors, offices, emoluments, established by law. So do you. I am for excluding legal, hereditary distinctions from the United States as long as possible. So are you. I only say that mankind have not yet discovered any remedy against irresistible corruption in elections to offices of great power and profit, but making them hereditary.

The Meaning of the Revolution

[From a letter to Hezekiah Niles, February 13, 1818]

The American Revolution was not a common event. Its effects and consequences have already been awful over a great part of the globe. And when and where are they to cease?

But what do we mean by the American Revolution? Do we mean the American war? The Revolution was effected before the war commenced. The Revolution was in the minds and hearts of the people; a change in their religious sentiments of their duties and obligations. While the king, and all in authority under him, were believed to govern in justice and mercy, according to the laws and constitution derived to them from the God of nature and transmitted to them by their ancestors, they thought themselves bound to pray for the king and queen and all the royal family, and all in authority under them, as ministers ordained of God for their good; but when they saw these powers renouncing all the principles of authority, and bent upon the destruction of all the securities of their lives, liberties, and properties, they thought it their duty to pray for the continental congress and all the thirteen State congresses, &c.

There might be, and there were others who thought less about religion and conscience, but had certain habitual sentiments of allegiance and loyalty derived from their education; but believing allegiance and protection to be reciprocal, when protection was withdrawn, they thought allegiance was dissolved.

Another alteration was common to all. The people of America had been educated in an habitual affection for England, as their mother country; and while they thought her a kind and tender parent, (erroneously enough, however, for she never was such a mother,) no affection could be more sincere. But when they found her a cruel beldam, willing like Lady Macbeth, to "dash their brains out," it is no wonder if their filial affections ceased, and were changed into indignation and horror.

This radical change in the principles, opinions, sentiments, and affections of the people, was the real American Revolution.

By what means this great and important alteration in the religious, moral, political, and social character of the people of the thirteen colonies, all distinct, unconnected, and independent of each other, was begun, pursued, and accomplished, it is surely interesting to humanity to investigate, and perpetuate to posterity.

To this end, it is greatly to be desired, that young men of letters in all the States, especially in the thirteen original States, would undertake the laborious, but certainly interesting and amusing task, of searching and collecting all the records, pamphlets, newspapers, and even hand-bills, which in any way contributed to change the temper and views of the people, and compose them into an independent nation.

The colonies had grown up under constitutions of government so different, there was so great a variety of religions, they were composed of so many different nations, their customs, manners, and habits had so little resemblance, and their intercourse had been so rare, and their knowledge of each other so imperfect, that to unite them in the same principles in theory and the same system of action, was certainly a very difficult enterprise. The complete accomplishment of it, in so short a time and by such simple means, was perhaps a singular example in the history of mankind. Thirteen clocks were made to strike together — a perfection of mechanism, which no artist had ever before effected.

In this research, the gloriole of individual gentlemen, and of separate States, is of little consequence. The *means and the measures* are the proper objects of investigation. These may be of use to posterity, not only in this nation, but in South America and all other countries. They may teach mankind that revolutions are no trifles; that they ought never to be undertaken rashly; not without deliberate consideration and sober reflection; nor without a solid, immutable, eternal foundation of justice and humanity; nor without a people possessed of intelligence, fortitude, and integrity sufficient to carry them with steadiness, patience, and perseverance, through all the vicissitudes of fortune, the fiery trials and melancholy disasters they may have to encounter. . . .

⚓ Samuel Adams (1722–1803)

SAMUEL ADAMS did not agree with his cousin John in his attitude toward government by the many rather than the few. The people might, Adams admitted, occasionally err, but he trusted their ultimate good sense and their ability to perceive and rectify their mistakes. Like Jefferson, Samuel Adams perceived the importance of education in the creation of an enlightened majority, and like the Virginian he stressed the necessity of recognizing and nurturing talent and wisdom wherever it occurred, irrespective of class.

Adams' great skill lay less in political theory than in political organization, and in phrasing in swift and decisive terms the prevailing attitudes of the people. He drafted a number of important revolutionary documents, and fanned the sparks of colonial rebellion with effective and timely pamphleteering. After the close of the war, his influence decreased, since he was more the agitator than the statesman; nevertheless, his contributions to the American political tradition were both real and important.

TEXT: William V. Wells, *The Life and Public Services of Samuel Adams* (Boston, 1865), III, 308–313.

Popular Government

[From a letter to John Adams, November 20, 1790]

. . . I lately received your letter of the 18th of October. The sentiments and observations contained in it demand my attention.

A republic, you tell me, is a government in which "the people have an essential *share* in the sovereignty." Is not the *whole* sovereignty, my friend, essentially in the people? Is not government designed for the welfare and happiness of all the people? and is it not the uncontrollable, essential right of the people to amend and alter or annul their Constitution, and frame a new one, whenever they shall think it will better promote their own welfare and happiness to do it? That the sovereignty resides in the people, is a political doctrine which I have never heard an American politician seriously deny. The Constitutions of the American States reserve to the people the exercise of the rights of sovereignty by the annual or biennial election of their governors, senators, and representatives; and by empowering their own representatives to impeach the greatest officers of the State before the senators, who are also chosen by themselves. *We the people,* is the style of the Federal Constitution: they adopted it; and, conformably to it, they delegate the exercise of the powers of government to particular persons, who, after short intervals, resign their powers to the people; and they will re-elect them, or appoint others, as they think fit.

The American Legislatures are nicely balanced. They consist of two branches, each having a check upon the determinations of the other. They sit in different chambers, and probably often reason differently in their respective chambers on the same question: if they disagree in their decisions, by a conference their reasons and arguments are mutually communicated to each other; candid explanations tend to bring them to agreement; and then, according to the Massachusetts Constitution, the matter is laid before the First Magistrate for his revision. He states objections, if he has any, with his reasons, and returns them to the legislators, who, by larger majorities, ultimately decide. Here is a mixture of three powers, founded in the nature of man, calculated to call forth the rational faculties, in the great points of legislation, into exertion, to cultivate mutual friendship and good

humor, and, finally, to enable them to decide, not by the impulse of
passion or party prejudice, but by the calm voice of reason, which is
the voice of God. In this mixture you may see your "natural and
actual aristocracy among mankind," operating among the several
powers in legislation, and producing the most happy effects. But the
son of an excellent man may never inherit the great qualities of his
father; this is a common observation, and there are many instances of
its truth. Should we not, therefore, conclude that hereditary nobility
is a solecism in government? . . . Much safer is it, and much more
does it tend to promote the welfare and happiness of society, to fill
up the offices of government, after the mode prescribed in the American Constitutions, by frequent elections of the people. They may,
indeed, be deceived in their choice; they sometimes are. But the evil
is not incurable, the remedy is always near; they will feel their mistakes
and correct them.

I am very willing to agree with you in thinking that improvements
in knowledge and benevolence receive much assistance from the principles and systems of good government. But is it not as true that, without knowledge and benevolence, men would neither have been capable
nor disposed to search for the principles or form the system? Should
we not, my friend, bear a grateful remembrance of our pious and
benevolent ancestors, who early laid plans of education, by which
means wisdom, knowledge, and virtue have been generally diffused
among the body of the people, and they have been enabled to form
and establish a civil Constitution calculated for the preservation of
their rights and liberties? This Constitution was evidently founded in
the expectation of the further progress and *extraordinary* degrees of
virtue. It enjoins the encouragement of all seminaries of literature,
which are the nurseries of virtue, depending upon these for the support
of government, rather than titles, splendor, or force. Mr. Hume may
call this a "chimerical project;" I am far from thinking the people can
be deceived by urging upon them a dependence on the more general
prevalence of knowledge and virtue. . . .

"It is a fixed principle that all good government is, and must be,
republican." You have my hearty concurrence; and I believe we are
well enough acquainted with each other's ideas to understand what we
respectively mean when we "use the word with approbation." The
body of the people in this country are not so ignorant as those in
England were in the time of the Interregnum Parliament. They are
better educated. . . . So well assured are they that their liberties are
best secured by their own frequent and free election of fit persons to
be the essential sharers in the administration of their government, and
that this form of government is truly *republican*, that the body of the
people will not be persuaded nor compelled to "renounce, detest, and
execrate" the very word *republican*, "as the English do." Their educa-

tion has "confirmed them in the opinion of the necessity of preserving and strengthening the dikes against the ocean, its tides and storms;" and I think they have made more safe and more durable dikes than the English have done. . . .

"The people who have no property feel the power of governing by a majority, and ever attack those who have property." "The injured men of property recur to *finesse*, trick, and stratagem to outwit them." True: these may proceed from a lust of domination in *some* of both parties. Be this as it may, it has been known that such deceitful tricks have been practised by some of the rich upon their unsuspecting fellow-citizens, to turn the determination of questions so as to answer their own selfish purposes. To plunder or filch the rights of men are crimes equally immoral and nefarious, though committed in different manners. Neither of them is confined to the rich or the poor; they are too common among both. The Lords as well as the Commons of Great Britain, by continued large majorities endeavored by *finesse*, tricks, and stratagems, as well as threats, to prevail on the American Colonies to surrender their liberty and property to their disposal. These failing, they attempted to *plunder* our rights by force of arms. We feared their arts more than their arms. Did the members of that hereditary House of Lords, who constituted those repeated majorities, then possess the spirit of nobility? Not so, I think. That spirit resided in the illustrious minorities in both Houses.

But "by nobles," who have prevented "one hideous despotism as horrid as that of Turkey from falling to the lot of every nation of Europe," you mean, "not peculiarly an hereditary nobility, or any particular modification, but the natural and actual aristocracy among mankind," the existence of which I am not disposed to deny. Where is this aristocracy found? Among men of all ranks and conditions. The cottager may beget a wise son; the noble, a fool. The one is capable of great improvement; the other is not. Education is within the power of men and societies of men; wise and judicious modes of education, patronized and supported by communities, will draw together the sons of the rich and the poor, among whom it makes no distinction; it will cultivate the natural genius, elevate the soul, excite laudable emulation to excel in knowledge, piety, and benevolence; and finally it will reward its patrons and benefactors by shedding its benign influence on the public mind. Education inures men to thinking and reflection, to reasoning and demonstration. It discovers to them the moral and religious duties they owe to God, their country, and to all mankind. Even savages might, by the means of education, be instructed to frame the best civil and political institutions with as much skill and ingenuity as they now shape their arrows. Education leads youth to "the study of human nature, society, and universal history," from whence they may "draw all the principles" of political architecture which ought to be regarded. All men are "interested in the truth;" education, by showing them "the end of all its consequences," would induce at least the greatest numbers to enlist on its side. The man of good understanding, who has been well educated, and improves these advantages as far as his circumstances will allow, in promoting the happiness of mankind, in my opinion, and I am inclined to think in yours, is indeed "well born."

Robert Goodloe Harper (1765–1825)

BORN in Virginia, Robert Goodloe Harper grew to young manhood in North Carolina. His early schooling was casual, interrupted by service during the Revolution in the cavalry as part of General Greene's army. After the war he taught school for a time, and then, imbued with a desire for more education, he entered Princeton and graduated in 1785.

Harper settled in Charleston, South Carolina, studied law, and in 1789 entered politics as an Antifederalist. In 1795 he ran successfully for Congress as a Republican, but during his stay in Philadelphia he began to shift his political allegiance toward the Federalists. He soon became generally known as one of the more influential Southern Federalists. An ardent advocate of the Alien and Sedition Acts, he was violently anti-French and a strong supporter of Adams. Aware of the fact that the Federalist party in South Carolina had little hope of re-electing him, he did not run in 1800, but moved to Maryland to take up a successful career in law. In 1816 he returned to politics as a member of the Senate from Maryland and as Federalist candidate for Vice President. His reasoned explanation of what his party stood for is one of the better expositions of the conservative political point of view.

TEXT: E. C. Stedman and E. M. Hutchinson, *A Library of American Literature* (New York, 1889–90), III, 204–207.

Federalist Maxims

[From *Select Works*, 1814]

In the management of our domestic affairs their system has been, in the first place to support vigorously the independence and authority of the federal government; which alone is capable of insuring our safety from abroad, by opposing to foreign nations the barrier of our united strength, and of maintaining our peace at home, by checking the ambition and repressing the passions of the several states, and balancing their forces, so as to prevent the greater from overpowering and subduing the lesser. They well knew this government, being under the necessity of laying and collecting considerable taxes, of raising and supporting armies and fleets, of maintaining numerous officers, and of carrying on all those expensive operations which its superintendence of our general affairs require, and from which the state governments are wholly exempt, is far more likely than those governments to incur unpopularity, to become subject to the imputation of extravagance, oppression, and ambitious views, and to be deprived of the public confidence. They well knew that this government, being removed to a greater distance than the state governments from the people, was more apt to be viewed with jealousy and considered as a foreign government; and that there never would be wanting ambitious and restless men, who failing to obtain that share of influence in the federal government, or those honors and employments under it, to which they might think themselves entitled, would take refuge in the state governments, and avail themselves of all these circumstances to render the federal government odious, to excite against it the public resentment, and even to overrule and control it by means of the state governments. Well knowing this, the federalists considered it as a principle of the utmost importance for the preservation of the federal government, to render it as independent as possible of state influence; to give it a movement of its own, and complete power to enforce its own laws; to resist state encroachments; and to restrain the state governments within their just and proper bounds. In every struggle between the federal and the state governments, they considered the latter as possessing infinitely the greatest natural strength; and therefore thought it their duty to take part with the former, in order to preserve the balance.

As to the federal government itself, their second great maxim was to support the executive power against the encroachments, the ambition and the superior strength of the popular branch. The power of a popular assembly, being little suspected by the people, is always little watched; and as no one member is to bear the blame of any excesses which the whole body may commit its power is but little restrained by personal responsibility and a regard to character, and of course is very likely to be abused. Hence has resulted, in every age and nation where the form of government admitted popular assemblies, a constant effort on the part of those assemblies to get all power into their own hands, and to exercise it according to their own passions and caprice. This has everywhere produced the necessity of checking the power of those assemblies, by confining it wholly to legislation, by dividing it between two houses, and by giving the judicial and executive powers to persons independent of the legislature. This has been done by our constitution, which gives the executive power to the President, a single magistrate, places the judicial power in the courts, and divides the legislative power between the Senate and House of Representatives. This House of Representatives, being the most numerous and the most popular body, is subject to the same passions and dispositions which popular bodies ever feel; and consequently has a perpetual tendency to encroach on the executive powers, and to direct and control the President in the exercise of his authority. As the President, being a single magistrate, is much more apt to be suspected and viewed with a jealous eye than this popular assembly, which the people consider as nearer to themselves and more under their control, he would have the people against him in these contests, and must finally submit absolutely to the control of the House, were there not always some members of it, whose just way of thinking and regard to the constitution induce them to oppose the improper enterprizes of their own body, and to defend the executive power against its perpetual attacks. This was the conduct of the federalists. Knowing the executive power to be absolutely essential for preserving the due balance of the constitution and for conducting the affairs of the nation with prudence, steadiness and success, and knowing it also to be in itself much weaker than its antagonist, they made themselves its defenders, and by their perseverance and talents have thus far succeeded in preserving to it the weight and authority designed for it by the constitution.

It was a third maxim in the system of the federalists, to give liberal not large compensations to men in office: well knowing that in a country where there are but few fortunes, and where almost every man of talents and character depends on his industry for supporting and providing for his family, the contrary system has a constant and powerful tendency to throw the most important offices into the hands of unworthy or unqualified persons, who either neglect or mismanage the public business, or resort to dishonest means for supplying the deficiencies in their regular compensation. Nothing is more true than that men of talents and character will not long leave their homes and devote their time to the public service, unless they are at least supported decently; and that if we wish for able and faithful services we must pay their price. This the federal government has never done. The first officers under it do not receive enough to support them and their families in a proper manner. Hence in part the difficulty which has been constantly experienced, in prevailing on men of high character and qualifications to fill those offices. The Secretary of State for instance, or the Secretary of the Treasury, receives but little more from his office, than half as much as a lawyer of talents can derive from his practice, with half the labor and confinement. The federalists have constantly endeavored to remedy this abuse. They have done something, but never were able to do enough. The expense is constantly made an objection; but it is a most futile objection. To compensate liberally, and even handsomely, all the principal officers of the government, would require an additional expense of perhaps thirty thousand dollars annually; which is less than a man without talents, in one of those offices, may waste or lose through mismanagement in a month.

◆❧ Timothy Dwight (1752–1817)

TIMOTHY DWIGHT, pastor of the Congregational Church at Greenfield Hill, Connecticut, believed with Hamilton in the virtues of strong, responsible, federalized government. As discussions opened in Philadelphia on the new instrument of government, Dwight published an exhortation, in somewhat stilted verse, to the assembled Convention. Later president of Yale and a staunch Federalist, Dwight was a powerful conservative force in New England theology and politics.

TEXT: *The Columbian Muse* (New York, 1794).

Advice to the Constitutional Convention

[From "Address of the Genius of Columbia, to the Members
of the Constitutional Convention," 1787]

Be then your counsels, as your subject, great,
A world their sphere, and time's long reign their date.
　　Each party-view, each private good, disclaim,
Each petty maxim, each colonial aim;
Let all Columbia's weal your views expand,
A mighty system rule a mighty land;
Yourselves her genuine sons let Europe own,
Not the small agents of a paltry town.
　　Learn, cautious, what to alter, where to mend;
See to what close projected measures tend.
From pressing wants the mind averting still,
Thinks good remotest from the present ill:
From feuds anarchial to oppression's throne,
Misguided nations hence for safety run;
And through the miseries of a thousand years,
Their fatal folly mourn in bloody tears.
　　Ten thousand follies thro' Columbia spread;

Ten thousand wars her darling realms invade.
The private interest of each jealous state;
Of rule the impatience, and of law the hate.
But ah! from narrow springs these evils flow,
A few base wretches mingle general woe;
Still the same mind her manly race pervades;
Still the same virtues haunt the hallow'd shades.
But when the peals of war her centre shook,
All private aims the anxious mind forsook.
In danger's iron-bond her race was one,
Each separate good, each little view unknown.
Now rule, unsystem'd, drives the mind astray;
Now private interest points the downward way:
Hence civil discord pours her muddy stream,
And fools and villains float upon the brim;
O'er all, the sad spectator casts his eye,
And wonders where the gems and minerals lie.
      But ne'er of freedom, glory, bliss, despond:
Uplift your eyes those little clouds beyond;
See there returning suns, with gladdening ray,
Roll on fair spring to chase this wint'ry day.
      'Tis yours to bid those days of Eden shine:
First, then, and last, the federal bands entwine:
To this your every aim and effort bend:
Let all your efforts here commence and end.
      O'er state concerns, let every state preside;
Its private tax controul; its justice guide;
Religion aid; the morals to secure;
And bid each private right thro' time endure.
Columbia's interests public sway demand,
Her commerce, impost, unlocated land;
Her war, her peace, her military power;
Treaties to seal with every distant shore;
      To bid contending states their discord cease;
To send thro' all the calumet of peace;
Science to wing thro' every noble flight;
And lift desponding genius into light.
      Thro' every state to spread each public law,
Interest must animate, and force must awe.
Persuasive dictates realms will ne'er obey;
Sway, uncoercive, is the shade of sway.
      Be then your task to alter, aid, amend;
The weak to strengthen, and the rigid bend;
The prurient lop; what's wanted to supply;
And graft new scions from each friendly sky.
      Slow, by degrees, politic systems rise;
Age still refines them, and experience tries.
This, this alone consolidates, improves;

Their sinews strengthens; their defects removes;
Gives that consistence time alone can give;
Habituates men by law and right to live;
To gray-hair'd rules increasing reverence draws;
And wins the slave to love e'en tyrant laws.
But should Columbia, with distracted eyes,
See o'er her ruins one proud monarch rise;
Should vain partitions her fair realms divide,
And rival empires float on faction's tide;
Lo fix'd opinions 'gainst the fabric rage!
What wars, fierce passions with fierce passions wage!
From Cancer's glowing wilds, to Brunswick's shore,
Hark, how the alarms of civil discord roar!
"To arms," the trump of kindled warfare cries,
And kindred blood smokes upward to the skies.
As Persia, Greece, so Europe bids her flame,
And smiles, with eye malignant, o'er her shame.
Seize then, oh! seize Columbia's golden hour;
Perfect her federal system, public power;
For this stupendous realm, this chosen race,
With all the improvements of all lands its base,
The glorious structure build; its breadth extend;
Its columns lift, its mighty arches bend!
[On] freedom, science, arts, its stories shine,
Unshaken pillars of a frame divine;
Far o'er the Atlantic wild its beams aspire,
The world approves it, and the heavens admire;
O'er clouds, and suns, and stars, its splendours rise,
Till the bright top-stone vanish in the skies.

✒ Alexander Hamilton (1757–1804)

ALEXANDER HAMILTON, like Jefferson, had long political experience, despite his comparative youth. A handsome, arrogant,
and not always tactful man, Hamilton aroused strong feelings of
admiration or enmity in his relations with his fellows, but both
his friends and enemies conceded his political ability. He possessed a hard, incisive, brilliant (if somewhat narrow) mind, and
was a thorough realist in his political theories and attitudes.
Unlike Jefferson, who was always a Virginian, Hamilton had no
strong sectional attachments and rarely thought in terms of state
or locality. The state governments, in fact, he believed were so
dangerously partisan and localized in interest as to constitute a
real danger to national unity.

Hamilton's attachments were to the traditions of English political thought, to the practical, cautious spirit of British liberalism, and to Locke's emphasis on property rights and stability. He did not trust man in the mass, and believed "the amazing violence and turbulence of the democratic spirit" to be the greatest hazard of the new nation. "The people are turbulent and changing," he is supposed to have said at Philadelphia; "they seldom judge or determine right." Therefore he advocated a strong central government of checks and balances, so that men's self-interests might be used, as Hobbes thought, to check each other.

This did not mean that Hamilton was an enemy of the people; it meant, rather, that he did not trust them with the delicate, important business of government. Power belonged to the class equipped to use it properly, that is, to the propertied, upper class of "the wise, the rich, and the well-born." Temperamentally an aristocrat, he thought that the British government was perhaps "the best in the world," for it conserved best the values of property and liberty against popular instability and encroachment.

Yet Hamilton was by no means a royalist or dictator, as his enemies accused him of being, nor "un-American" — he admired order, hierarchy, and control in politics as he did elsewhere in human affairs. He stated his idea of government clearly and succinctly: "First, the necessity of union to the respectability and happiness of this country, and second, the necessity of an efficient government to maintain the union." Hamilton's world was constructed about the concept of discipline, of things and people in their right places.

TEXT: Henry Cabot Lodge, ed., *The Works of Alexander Hamilton* (New York, 1904), I, 305–314.

The Demand for a New Constitution

[Resolutions for a General Convention, 1783]

Whereas, in the opinion of this Congress, the Confederation of the United States is defective in the following essential points, to wit:

Firstly, and generally: In confining the power of the Federal Government within too narrow limits; withholding from it that efficacious authority and influence, in all matters of general concern, which are indispensable to the harmony and welfare of the whole; embarrassing general provisions by unnecessary details and inconvenient exceptions incompatible with their nature, tending only to create jealousies and disputes respecting the proper bounds of the authority of the United States, and of that of the particular States, and a mutual interference of the one with the other.

Secondly: In confounding legislative and executive powers in a single body: as, that of determining on the number and quantity of force, land and naval, to be employed for the common defence, and of directing their operations when raised and equipped, with that of ascertaining and making requisitions for the necessary sums or quantities of money to be paid by the respective States into the common treasury; contrary to the most approved and well-founded maxims of free government, which require that the legislative, executive, and judicial authorities should be deposited in distinct and separate hands.

Thirdly: In want of a Federal Judicature, having cognizance of all matters of general concern in the last resort, especially those in which foreign nations and their subjects are interested; from which defect, by the interference of the local regulations of particular States militating directly or indirectly against the powers vested in the Union, the national treaties will be liable to be infringed, the national faith to be violated, and the public tranquillity to be disturbed.

Fourthly: In vesting the United States in Congress assembled with the *power of general taxation,* comprehended in that of "ascertaining the necessary sums of money to be raised for the common defence, and of appropriating and applying the same, for defraying the public expenses"; and yet rendering that power, so essential to the existence of the Union, nugatory, by withholding from them all control over either the imposition or the collection of the taxes for raising the sums required: whence it happens that the inclinations, not the abilities, of the respective States are, in fact, the criterion of their contributions to the common expense; and the public burthen has fallen, and will continue to fall, with very unequal weight.

Fifthly: In fixing a rule for determining the proportion of each State towards the common expense, which, if practicable at all, must, in the execution, be attended with great expense, inequality, uncertainty, and difficulty.

Sixthly: In authorizing Congress "to borrow money, or emit bills on the credit of the United States," without the power of establishing funds to secure the repayment of the money borrowed, or the redemption of the bills emitted; from which must result one of these evils: Either a want of sufficient credit, in the first instance, to borrow, or to circulate the bills emitted, whereby, in great national exigencies, the public safety may be endangered; or, in the second instance, frequent infractions of the public engagements, disappointments to lenders, repetitions of the calamities of depreciating paper, a continuance of the injustice and mischiefs of an unfunded debt, and, first or last, the annihilation of public credit.

Indeed, in authorizing Congress at all to emit an *unfunded* paper as the sign of value, a resource which, though useful in the infancy of this country, and indispensable in the commencement of the revolution, ought not to continue a formal part of the Constitution, nor ever, hereafter, to be employed, being, in its nature, pregnant with abuses, and liable to be made the engine of imposition and fraud, holding out temptations equally pernicious to the integrity of government and to the morals of the people.

Seventhly: In not making proper or competent provisions for interior or exterior defence. For interior defence, by leaving it to the individual States to appoint all regimental officers of the land-forces; to raise the men in their own way; to clothe, arm, and equip them at the expense of the United States: from which circumstances have resulted, and will hereafter result, great confusion in the military department; continual disputes of rank; languid and disproportionate levies of men; an enormous increase of expense, for want of system and uniformity in the manner of conducting them, and from the competitions of State bounties; by an ambiguity in the fourth clause of the sixth article, susceptible of a construction which would devolve upon the particular States in time of peace the care of their own defence, both by sea and land, and would preclude the United States from raising a single regiment, or building a single ship, before a declaration of war or an actual commencement of hostilities, — a principle dangerous to the Confederacy in different respects, by leaving the United States at all times unprepared for the defence of their common rights, obliging them to begin to raise an army and to build and equip a navy at the moment they would have occasion to employ them, and by putting into the hands of a few States, who, from their local situations, are more immediately exposed, all the standing forces of the country; thereby, not only leaving the care of the safety of the whole to a part which will naturally be both unwilling and unable to make effectual provision at its particular expense, but also furnishing grounds of jealousy and distrust between the States; unjust, in its operation, to those States in whose hands they are, by throwing the exclusive burthen of maintaining those forces upon them, while their neighbors, immediately, and all the States, ultimately, would share the benefits of their services.

For exterior defence, in authorizing Congress to "build and equip a navy" without providing any means of manning it, either by requisitions of the States, by the power of registering and draughting the seamen in rotation, or by embargoes in cases of emergency to induce them to accept employment on board the ships of war; the omission of all of which, leaves no other resource than voluntary enlistment, — a resource which has been found ineffectual in every country, and, for reasons of peculiar force, in this.

Eighthly: In not vesting in the United States, a general superintendence of trade, equally necessary in the view of revenue and regulation. Of revenue, because duties on commerce, when moderate, are one of the most agreeable and productive species of it; which cannot, without great disadvantages, be imposed by particular States while others refrain from doing it, but must be imposed in concert, and by laws operating upon the same principles, at the same moment, in all the States, otherwise those States which should not impose them would engross the commerce of such of their neighbors as did. Of regulation, because by general prohibitions of particular articles, by a judicious arrangement of duties, sometimes by bounties on the manufacture or exportation of certain commodities, injurious branches of commerce might be discouraged, favorable branches encouraged, useful products and manufactures promoted, none of which advantages can be as effectually attained by separate regulations, without a general superintending power; because, also, it is essential to the due observance of the commercial stipulations of the United States with foreign powers, an interference with which will be unavoidable if the different States have the exclusive regulation of their own trade, and, of course, the construction of the treaties entered into.

Ninthly: In defeating essential powers by provisions and limitations inconsistent with their nature, as the power of making treaties with foreign nations, *"provided* that no treaty of commerce shall be made whereby the legislative power of the respective States shall be restrained from imposing such imposts and duties on foreigners as their own people are subjected to, or from prohibiting the importation or exportation of any species of goods or commodities whatsoever"; a proviso, susceptible of an interpretation which includes a constitutional possibility of defeating the treaties of commerce entered into by the United States. As also the power "of regulating the trade and managing all affairs with the Indians, not members of any of the States, *provided* that the legislative right of any State, within its own limits, be not infringed or violated"; and others of a similar nature.

Tenthly: In granting the United States the sole power "of regulating the alloy and value of coin struck by their own authority or by that of the respective States," without the power of regulating the foreign coin in circulation; though the one is essential to the due exercise of the other, as there ought to be such proportions maintained, between the national and foreign coin as will give the former preference in all internal negotiations; and without the latter power the operations of government, in a matter of primary importance to the commerce and finances of the United States, will be exposed to numberless obstructions.

Eleventhly: In requiring the assent of *nine* States to matters of principal importance, and of seven to all others, except adjournments from day to day; a rule destructive of vigor, consistency, or expedition in the administration of affairs; tending to subject the sense of the majority to that of the minority, by putting it in the power of a small combination to retard, and even to frustrate, the most necessary measures; and to oblige the greater number, in cases which require speedy determinations, as happens in the most interesting concerns of the community, to come into the views of the smaller; the evils of which have been felt in critical conjunctures, and must always make the spirit of government a spirit of compromise and expedient rather than of system and energy.

Twelfthly: In vesting in the Federal Government the sole direction of the interests of the United States, in their intercourse with foreign nations, without empowering it to pass all general laws in aid and support of the laws of nations; for the want of which authority the faith of the United States may be broken, their reputation sullied, and their peace interrupted by the negligence or misconception of any particular State.

And whereas, experience hath clearly manifested that the powers reserved to the Union in the Confederation are unequal to the purpose of effectually drawing forth the resources of the respective members, for the common welfare and defence: whereby the United States have, upon several occasions, been exposed to the most critical and alarming situations; have wanted an army adequate to their defence, and pro-portioned to the abilities of the country; have, on account of that deficiency, seen essential posts reduced, others eminently endangered, whole States, and large parts of others overrun and ravaged by small bodies of the enemy's forces; have been destitute of sufficient means of feeding, clothing, paying, and appointing that army; by which the troops, rendered less efficient for military operations, have been ex-posed to sufferings which nothing but unparalleled patience, persever-ance, and patriotism could have endured; whereby, also, the United States have been too often compelled to make the administration of their affairs a succession of temporary expedients, inconsistent with order, economy, energy, or a scrupulous adherence to the public engagements; and now find themselves, at the close of a glorious struggle for independence, without any certain means of doing justice to those who have been its principal supporters, — to an army which has bravely fought and patiently suffered, to citizens who have cheer-fully lent their money, and to others who have in different ways con-tributed their property and their personal service to the common cause; obliged to rely, for the only effectual mode of doing that justice, by funding the debt on solid securities, on the precarious concurrence of thirteen distinct deliberatives, the dissent of either of which may defeat the plan, and leave these States, at this early period of their existence, involved in all the disgrace and mischiefs of violated faith and national bankruptcy.

And whereas, notwithstanding we have, by the blessing of Providence, so far happily escaped the complicated dangers of such a situation, and now see the object of our wishes secured by an honorable peace, it would be unwise to hazard a repetition of the same dangers and embarrassments in any future war in which these States may be engaged, or to continue this extensive empire under a government unequal to its protection and prosperity.

And whereas, it is essential to the happiness and security of these States, that their union should be established on the most solid foundations; and it is manifest that this desirable object cannot be effected but by a government capable, both in peace and war, of making every member of the Union contribute, in just proportion, to the common necessities, and of combining and directing the forces and wills of the several parts to a general end; to which purposes, in the opinion of Congress, the present Confederation is altogether inadequate.

And whereas, on the spirit which may direct the councils and measures of these States at the present juncture may depend their future safety and welfare, Congress conceives it to be their duty freely to state to their constituents the defects which, by experience, have been discovered in the present plan of the Federal Union, and solemnly to call their attention to a revisal and amendment of the same.

Therefore, *Resolved,* That it be earnestly recommended to the several States to appoint a Convention to meet at   , on the   day of   , with full powers to revise the Confederation, and to adopt and propose such alterations as to them shall appear necessary; to be finally approved or rejected by the States respectively; and that a Committee of   be appointed to prepare an address upon the subject.

⚜ *The Federalist Papers* (1787–1788)

THE proposed new Constitution, intended to replace the Articles of Confederation, emerged from the Philadelphia Convention on September 27, 1787. As soon as nine of the thirteen states ratified the document, it would become effective. Ratification proceeded fairly swiftly in the smaller states: by January 1788, five states (Delaware, New Jersey, Georgia, Connecticut, and Pennsylvania) had ratified. In Massachusetts, the sixth state, the struggle was long and hard, with ratification succeeding only after a close vote. Maryland and South Carolina followed, and the

ninth state, New Hampshire, finally adopted the document on
June 21, 1788. Legally, the Constitution was now in force,
although it was obvious that without the approval of the two
powerful states of New York and Virginia it could never successfully operate.

In New York State the opposition was led by Governor Clinton,
who attacked the Constitution in a New York newspaper. To
counteract the skillful and effective arguments put up against
ratification by Clinton and his supporters, Alexander Hamilton
asked John Jay of New York, Secretary of Foreign Affairs under
the Confederation, and James Madison of Virginia to assist him
in writing a series of essays explaining and defending the new instrument of government.

The *Federalist* series, numbering eighty-five papers in all, appeared between October 1787 and April 1788. Of the total,
Hamilton wrote fifty-one, Madison twenty-six, and Jay five; the
authorship of three is uncertain, perhaps a collaboration. The
central argument of the series is that the Articles did not provide
the national government with sufficient authority to maintain
liberty, security, and property; and that the Constitution, which
remedies those deficiencies, ought therefore to be adopted in its
place. While the *Federalist* papers were undoubtedly influential
in consolidating support for the Constitutional forces, not a little
of the success of the outcome was due to Hamilton's skill in
political maneuvering. At that, the margin of victory in New
York, in July 1788, was breathtakingly small, 30–27, and the
convention in approving the document demanded, as had several
other states, that a bill of rights be included with it.

Federalist No. IV, by Jay, examines the military advantages of
stronger national authority in defending the nation against foreign
aggression. No. X, by Madison, is one of the most important of
all. In it Madison points out the advantages of a strong Union for
"its tendency to break and control the violence of faction," and
addresses himself to the problem of majority and minority rights
in a majority government. In No. XXIII Hamilton argues that
the objectives of the United States require a stronger general
government, "at least equally energetic with the one proposed,"
and one that allows both national and state governments "the
most ample authority for fulfilling the objects of its charge."

Text: *The Federalist, or The New Constitution, written in
the Year 1788* . . . (Washington, 1818, 1837).

No. IV

BY JOHN JAY

My last paper assigned several reasons, why the safety of the people would be best secured by union against the danger it may be exposed to by *just* causes of war given to other nations; and those reasons show, that such causes would not only be more rarely given, but would also be more easily accommodated by a national government, than either by the state governments, or the proposed confederacies.

But the safety of the people of America against dangers from *foreign* force, depends not only on their forbearing to give *just* causes of war to other nations, but also on their placing and continuing themselves in such a situation as not to *invite* hostility or insult; for it need not be observed, that there are *pretended* as well as just causes of war.

It is too true, however disgraceful it may be to human nature, that nations in general will make war whenever they have a prospect of getting any thing by it; nay, that absolute monarchs will often make war when their nations are to get nothing by it, but for purposes and objects merely personal, such as a thirst for military glory, revenge for personal affronts, ambition, or private compacts to aggrandize or support their particular families, or partisans. These, and a variety of motives, which affect only the mind of the sovereign, often lead him to engage in wars not sanctioned by justice, or the voice and interests of his people. But independent of these inducements to war, which are most prevalent in absolute monarchies, but which well deserve our attention, there are others which affect nations as often as kings; and some of them will on examination be found to grow out of our relative situation and circumstances.

With France and with Britain, we are rivals in the fisheries, and can supply their markets cheaper than they can themselves, notwithstanding any efforts to prevent it by bounties on their own, or duties on foreign fish.

With them and with most other European nations, we are rivals in navigation and the carrying trade; and we shall deceive ourselves, if we suppose that any of them will rejoice to see these flourish in our hands: for as our carrying trade cannot increase, without in some degree diminishing theirs, it is more their interest, and will be more their policy, to restrain, than to promote it.

In the trade to China and India, we interfere with more than one nation, inasmuch as it enables us to partake in advantages which they had in a manner monopolized, and as we thereby supply ourselves with commodities which we used to purchase from them.

The extension of our own commerce, in our own vessels, cannot give pleasure to any nations who possess territories on or near this continent, because the cheapness and excellence of our productions, added to the circumstance of vicinity, and the enterprise and address of our merchants and navigators, will give us a greater share in the advantages which those territories afford, than consists with the wishes or policy of their respective sovereigns.

Spain thinks it convenient to shut the Mississippi against us on the one side, and Britain excludes us from the Saint Lawrence on the other; nor will either of them permit the other waters, which are between them and us, to become the means of mutual intercourse and traffic.

From these and like considerations, which might, if consistent with prudence, be more amplified and detailed, it is easy to see that jealousies and uneasinesses may gradually slide into the minds and cabinets of other nations; and that we are not to expect they should regard our advancement in union, in power and consequence by land and by sea, with an eye of indifference and composure.

The people of America are aware, that inducements to war may arise out of these circumstances, as well as from others not so obvious at present; and that whenever such inducements may find fit time and opportunity for operation, pretences to colour and justify them will not be wanting. Wisely therefore do they consider union and a good national government as necessary to put and keep them in *such a situation,* as, instead of *inviting* war will tend to repress and discourage it. That situation consists in the best possible state of defence, and necessarily depends on the government, the arms, and the resources of the country.

As the safety of the whole is the interest of the whole, and cannot be provided for without government, either one or more or many, let us imagine whether one good government is not, relative to the object in question, more competent than any other given number whatever.

One government can collect and avail itself of the talents and experience of the ablest men, in whatever part of the union they may be found. It can move on uniform principles of policy. It can harmonize, assimilate, and protect the several parts and members, and extend the benefit of its foresight and precautions to each. In the formation of treaties it will regard the interest of the whole, and the particular interests of the parts as connected with that of the whole. It can apply the resources and power of the whole to the defence of any particular part, and that more easily and expeditiously than state governments, or separate confederacies can possibly do, for want of concert and unity of system. It can place the militia under one plan of discipline, and by putting their officers in a proper line of subordination to the chief magistrate, will in a manner consolidate them into one corps, and thereby render them more efficient than if divided into thirteen or into three or four distinct independent bodies.

What would the militia of Britain be, if the English militia obeyed the government of England, if the Scotch militia obeyed the government of Scotland, and if the Welch militia obeyed the government of Wales? Suppose an invasion: would those three governments (if they agreed at all) be able with all their respective forces, to operate against the enemy so effectually as the single government of Great Britain would?

We have heard much of the fleets of Britain; and if we are wise, the time may come, when the fleets of America may engage attention. But if one national government had not so regulated the navigation of Britain as to make it a nursery for seamen . . . if one national government had not called forth all the national means and materials for forming fleets, their prowess and their thunder would never have been celebrated. Let England have its navigation and fleet . . . let Scotland have its navigation and fleet . . . let Wales have its navigation and fleet . . . let Ireland have its navigation and fleet . . . let those four of the constituent parts of the British empire be under four independent governments, and it is easy to perceive, how soon they would each dwindle into comparative insignificance.

Apply these facts to our own case. Leave America divided into thirteen, or if you please into three or four independent governments, what armies could they raise and pay, what fleets could they ever hope to have? If one was attacked, would the others fly to its succor, and spend their blood and money in its defence? Would there be no danger of their being flattered into neutrality by specious promises, or seduced by a too great fondness for peace to decline hazarding their tranquillity and present safety for the sake of neighbours, of whom perhaps they have been jealous, and whose importance they are content to see diminished? Although such conduct would not be wise, it would nevertheless be natural. The history of the states of Greece, and of other countries, abound with such instances; and it is not improbable, that what has so often happened would, under similar circumstances, happen again.

But admit that they might be willing to help the invaded state or confederacy. How, and when, and in what proportion shall aids of men and money be afforded? Who shall command the allied armies, and from which of the associates shall he receive his orders? Who shall settle the terms of peace, and in case of disputes what umpire shall decide between them, and compel acquiescence? Various difficulties and inconveniences would be inseparable from such a situation;

whereas one government, watching over the general and common interests, and combining and directing the powers and resources of the whole, would be free from all these embarrassments, and conduce far more to the safety of the people.

But whatever may be our situation, whether firmly united under one national government, or split into a number of confederacies, certain it is, that foreign nations will know and view it exactly as it is, and they will act towards us accordingly. If they see that our national government is efficient and well administered . . . our trade prudently regulated . . . our militia properly organized and disciplined . . . our resources and finances discreetly managed . . . our credit re-established . . . our people free, contented, and united, they will be much more disposed to cultivate our friendship, than to provoke our resentment. If, on the other hand, they find us either destitute of an effectual government, (each state doing right or wrong as to its rulers may seem convenient,) or split into three or four independent and probably discordant republics or confederacies, one inclining to Britain, another to France, and a third to Spain, and perhaps played off against each other by the three, what a poor pitiful figure will America make in their eyes! How liable would she become not only to their contempt, but to their outrage; and how soon would dear-bought experience proclaim that when a people or family so divide, it never fails to be against themselves!   PUBLIUS.

No. X

BY JAMES MADISON

Among the numerous advantages promised by a well constructed union, none deserves to be more accurately developed than its tendency to break and control the violence of faction. The friend of popular governments, never finds himself so much alarmed for their character and fate, as when he contemplates their propensity to this dangerous vice. He will not fail, therefore, to set a due value on any plan which, without violating the principles to which he is attached, provides a proper cure for it. The instability, injustice, and confusion, introduced into the public councils, have, in truth, been the mortal diseases under which popular governments have everywhere perished; as they continue to be the favorite and fruitful topics from which the adversaries to liberty derive their most specious declamations. The valuable improvements made by the American constitutions on the popular models, both ancient and modern, cannot certainly be too much admired; but it would be an unwarrantable partiality, to contend that they have as effectually obviated the danger on this side, as was wished and expected. Complaints are everywhere heard from our most considerate and virtuous citizens, equally the friends of public and private faith, and of public and personal liberty, that our governments are too unstable; that the public good is disregarded in the conflicts of rival parties; and that measures are too often decided, not according to the rules of justice, and the rights of the minor party, but by the superior force of an interested and overbearing majority. However anxiously we may wish that these complaints had no foundation, the evidence of known facts will not permit us to deny that they are in some degree true. It will be found, indeed, on a candid review of our situation, that some of the distresses under which we labor, have been erroneously charged on the operation of our governments; but it will be found, at the same time, that other causes will not alone account for many of our heaviest misfortunes; and, particularly, for that prevailing and increasing distrust of public engagements, and alarm for private rights, which are echoed from one end of the continent to the other. These must be chiefly, if not wholly, effects of the unsteadiness and injustice, with which a factious spirit has tainted our public administrations.

By a faction, I understand a number of citizens, whether amounting to majority or minority of the whole, who are united and actuated by some common impulse of passion, or of interest, adverse to the rights of other citizens, or to the permanent and aggregate interests of the community.

There are two methods of curing the mischiefs of faction: The one, by removing its causes; the other, by controlling its effects.

There are again two methods of removing the causes of faction: The one, by destroying the liberty which is essential to its existence; the other, by giving to every citizen the same opinions, the same passions, and the same interests.

It could never be more truly said, than of the first remedy, that it was worse than the disease. Liberty is to faction what air is to fire, an aliment without which it instantly expires. But it could not be a less folly to abolish liberty, which is essential to political life, because it nourishes faction, than it would be to wish the annihilation of air, which is essential to animal life, because it imparts to fire its destructive agency.

The second expedient is as impracticable, as the first would be unwise. As long as the reason of man continues fallible, and he is at liberty to exercise it, different opinions will be formed. As long as the connection subsists between his reason and his self-love, his opinions and his passions will have a reciprocal influence on each other; and the former will be objects to which the latter will attach themselves. The diversity in the faculties of men, from which the rights of property originate, is not less an insuperable obstacle to an uniformity of interests. The protection of these faculties is the first object of government. From the protection of different and unequal faculties of acquiring property, the possession of different degrees and kinds of property immediately results; and from the influence of these on the sentiments and views of the respective proprietors, ensues a division of the society into different interests and parties.

The latent causes of faction are thus sown in the nature of man; and we see them everywhere brought into different degrees of activity, according to the different circumstances of civil society. A zeal for different opinions concerning religion, concerning government, and many other points, as well of speculation as of practice; an attachment to different leaders, ambitiously contending for pre-eminence and power; or to persons of other descriptions, whose fortunes have been interesting to the human passions, have, in turn, divided mankind into parties, inflamed them with mutual animosity, and rendered them much more disposed to vex and oppress each other, than to cooperate for their common good. So strong is this propensity of mankind, to fall into mutual animosities, that where no substantial occasion presents itself, the most frivolous and fanciful distinctions have been sufficient to kindle their unfriendly passions, and excite their most violent conflicts. But the most common and durable source of factions, has been the various and unequal distribution of property. Those who hold, and those who are without property, have ever formed distinct interests in society. Those who are creditors, and those who are debtors, fall under a like discrimination. A landed interest, a manufacturing interest, a mercantile interest, a moneyed interest, with many lesser interests, grow up of necessity in civilized nations, and divide them into different classes, actuated by different sentiments and views. The regulation of these various and interfering interests forms the principal task of modern legislation, and involves the spirit of party and faction in the necessary and ordinary operations of the government.

No man is allowed to be a judge in his own cause; because his interest will certainly bias his judgment, and, not improbably, corrupt his integrity. With equal, nay, with greater reason, a body of men are unfit to be both judges and parties at the same time; yet what are many of the most important acts of legislation, but so many judicial determinations, not indeed concerning the rights of single persons, but concerning the rights of large bodies of citizens? and what are the different classes of legislators, but advocates and parties to the causes which they determine? Is a law proposed concerning private debts? It is a question to which the creditors are parties on one side, and the debtors on the other. Justice ought to hold the balance between them. Yet the parties are, and must be, themselves the judges; and the most numerous party, or, in other words, the most powerful faction, must be expected to prevail. Shall domestic manufactures be encouraged, and in what degree, by restrictions on foreign manufactures? are questions which would be differently decided by the landed and the manufacturing classes; and probably by neither with a sole regard to justice and the public good. The apportionment of taxes, on the various descriptions of property, is an act which seems to require the most exact impartiality; yet there is, perhaps, no legislative act, in which greater opportunity and temptation are given to a predominant party, to trample on the rules of justice. Every shilling, with which they overburden the inferior number, is a shilling saved to their own pockets.

It is in vain to say, that enlightened statesmen will be able to adjust these clashing interests, and render them all subservient to the public good. Enlightened statesmen will not always be at the helm: nor, in many cases, can such an adjustment be made at all, without taking into view indirect and remote considerations, which will rarely prevail over the immediate interest which one party may find in disregarding the rights of another, or the good of the whole.

The inference to which we are brought is, that the *causes* of faction cannot be removed; and that relief is only to be sought in the means of controlling its *effects*.

If a faction consists of less than a majority, relief is supplied by the republican principle, which enables the majority to defeat its sinister views, by regular vote. It may clog the administration, it may convulse the society; but it will be unable to execute and mask its violence under the forms of the constitution. When a majority is included in a faction, the form of popular government, on the other hand, enables it to sacrifice to its ruling passion or interest, both the public good and the rights of other citizens. To secure the public good, and private rights, against the danger of such a faction, and at the same time to preserve the spirit and the form of popular government, is then the great object to which our inquiries are directed. Let me add, that it is the great desideratum, by which alone this form of government can be rescued from the opprobrium under which it has so long laboured, and be recommended to the esteem and adoption of mankind.

By what means is this object attainable? Evidently by one of two only. Either the existence of the same passion or interest in a majority, at the same time, must be prevented; or the majority, having such coexistent passions or interest, must be rendered, by their number and local situation, unable to concert and carry into effect schemes of oppression. If the impulse and the opportunity be suffered to coincide, we well know, that neither moral nor religious motives can be relied on as an adequate control. They are not found to be such on the injustice and violence of individuals, and lose their efficacy in proportion to the number combined together; that is, in proportion as their efficacy becomes needful.

From this view of the subject, it may be concluded, that a pure democracy, by which I mean a society consisting of a small number of citizens, who assemble and administer the government in person, can admit of no cure from the mischiefs of faction. A common passion or interest will, in almost every case, be felt by a majority of the whole; a communication and concert, results from the form of government itself; and there is nothing to check the inducements to sacrifice the weaker party, or an obnoxious individual. Hence it is, that such democracies have ever been spectacles of turbulence and contention; have ever been found incompatible with personal security, or the rights of property; and have, in general, been as short in their lives, as they have been violent in their deaths. Theoretic politicians, who have patronized this species of government, have erroneously supposed, that by reducing mankind to a perfect equality in their political rights, they would, at the same time be perfectly equalized and assimilated in their possessions, their opinions, and their passions.

A republic, by which I mean a government in which the scheme of representation takes place, opens a different prospect, and promises the cure for which we are seeking. Let us examine the points in which it varies from pure democracy, and we shall comprehend both the nature of the cure and the efficacy which it must derive from the union.

The two great points of difference, between a democracy and a republic, are, first, the delegation of the government, in the latter, to a small number of citizens elected by the rest; secondly, the greater number of citizens, and greater sphere of country, over which the latter may be extended.

The effect of the first difference is, on the one hand, to refine and enlarge the public views, by passing them through the medium of a chosen body of citizens, whose wisdom may best discern the true interest of their country, and whose patriotism and love of justice, will be least likely to sacrifice it to temporary or partial considerations. Under such a regulation, it may well happen, that the public voice, pronounced by the representatives of the people, will be more consonant to the public good, than if pronounced by the people themselves, convened for the purpose. On the other hand the effect may be inverted. Men of factious tempers, of local prejudices, or of sinister designs, may by intrigue, by corruption, or by other means, first obtain the suffrages, and then betray the interests of the people. The question resulting is, whether small or extensive republics are most favourable to the election of proper guardians of the public weal; and it is clearly decided in favour of the latter by two obvious considerations.

In the first place, it is to be remarked, that however small the republic may be, the representatives must be raised to a certain number, in order to guard against the cabals of a few; and that however large it may be, they must be limited to a certain number, in order to guard against the confusion of a multitude. Hence, the number of representatives in the two cases not being in proportion to that of the constituents, and being proportionally greatest in the small republic, it follows, that if the proportion of fit characters be not less in the large than in the small republic, the former will present a greater option, and consequently a greater probability of a fit choice.

In the next place, as each representative will be chosen by a greater number of citizens in the large than in the small republic, it will be more difficult for unworthy candidates to practise with success the vicious arts, by which elections are too often carried; and the suffrages of the people being more free, will be more likely to centre in men who possess the most attractive merit, and the most diffusive and established characters.

It must be confessed, that in this, as in most other cases, there is a mean, on both sides of which inconveniences will be found to lie. By enlarging too much the number of electors, you render the representative too little acquainted with all their local circumstances and lesser interests; as by reducing it too much, you render him unduly attached to these, and too little fit to comprehend and pursue great and national objects. The federal constitution forms a happy combination in this respect; the great and aggregate interests being referred to the national, the local and particular to the state legislatures.

The other point of difference is, the greater number of citizens, and extent of territory, which may be brought within the compass of republican, than of democratic government; and it is this circumstance principally which renders factious combinations less to be dreaded in the former, than in the latter. The smaller the society, the fewer probably will be the distinct parties and interests composing it; the fewer the distinct parties and interests, the more frequently will a majority be found of the same party; and the smaller the number of individuals composing a majority, and the smaller the compass within which they are placed, the more easily they concert and execute their plans of oppression. Extend the sphere, and you take in a greater variety of parties and interests; you make it less probable that a majority of the whole will have a common motive to invade the rights of other citizens, or if such a common motive exists, it will be more difficult for all who feel it to discover their own strength, and to act in unison with each other. Besides other impediments, it may be remarked, that where there is a consciousness of unjust or dishonourable purposes, communication is always checked by distrust, in proportion to the number whose concurrence is necessary.

Hence, it clearly appears, that the same advantage, which a republic has over a democracy, in controlling the effects of faction, is enjoyed by a large over a small republic — is enjoyed by the union over the states composing it. Does this advantage consist in the substitution of representatives, whose enlightened views and virtuous sentiments render them superior to local prejudices, and to schemes of injustice? It will not be denied, that the representation of the union will be most likely to possess these requisite endowments. Does it consist in the greater security afforded by a greater variety of parties, against the event of any one party being able to outnumber and oppress the rest? In an equal degree does the increased variety of parties, comprised within the union, increase this security. Does it, in fine, consist in the greater obstacles opposed to the concert and accomplishment of the secret wishes of an unjust and interested majority? Here, again, the extent of the union gives it the most palpable advantage.

The influence of factious leaders may kindle a flame within their particular states, but will be unable to spread a general conflagration through the other states: a religious sect may degenerate into a political faction in a part of the confederacy; but the variety of sects dispersed over the entire face of it, must secure the national councils against any danger from that source: a rage for paper money, for an abolition of debts, for an equal division of property, or for any other improper or wicked project, will be less apt to pervade the whole body of the union than a particular member of it; in the same proportion as such a malady is more likely to taint a particular county or district, than an entire state.

In the extent and proper structure of the union, therefore, we behold a republican remedy for the diseases most incident to republican government. And according to the degree of pleasure and pride we feel in being republicans, ought to be our zeal in cherishing the spirit, and supporting the character of federalists.   PUBLIUS.

No. XXIII

BY ALEXANDER HAMILTON

The necessity of a constitution, at least equally energetic with the one proposed, to the preservation of the union, is the point, at the examination of which we are now arrived.

This inquiry will naturally divide itself into three branches. The objects to be provided for by the federal government; the quantity of power necessary to the accomplishment of those objects; the persons upon whom that power ought to operate. Its distribution and organization will more properly claim our attention under the succeeding head.

The principal purposes to be answered by union, are these: the common defence of the members; the preservation of the public peace, as well against internal convulsions as external attacks; the regulation of commerce with other nations, and between the states; the superintendence of our intercourse, political and commercial, with foreign countries.

The authorities essential to the care of the common defence, are these: to raise armies; to build and equip fleets; to prescribe rules for the government of both; to direct their operations; to provide for their support. These powers ought to exist without limitation; because it is impossible to foresee or to define the extent and variety of national exigencies, and the correspondent extent and variety of the means which may be necessary to satisfy them. The circumstances that endanger the safety of nations are infinite; and for this reason, no constitutional shackles can wisely be imposed on the power to which the care of it is committed. This power ought to be coextensive with all the possible combinations of such circumstances; and ought to be under the direction of the same councils which are appointed to preside over the common defence.

This is one of those truths which, to a correct and unprejudiced mind, carries its own evidence along with it; and may be obscured, but cannot be made plainer by argument or reasoning. It rests upon axioms, as simple as they are universal — the *means* ought to be proportioned to the *end;* the persons from whose agency the attainment of any *end* is expected, ought to possess the *means* by which it is to be attained.

Whether there ought to be a federal government entrusted with the care of the common defence, is a question, in the first instance, open to discussion; but the moment it is decided in the affirmative, it will follow, that that government ought to be clothed with all the powers requisite to the complete execution of its trust. And unless it can be shown, that the circumstances which may affect the public safety, are reducible within certain determinate limits; unless the contrary of this position can be fairly and rationally disputed, it must be admitted as a necessary consequence, that there can be no limitation of that authority, which is to provide for the defence and protection of the community, in any matter essential to its efficacy; that is, in any matter essential to the *formation, direction,* or *support* of the NATIONAL FORCES.

Defective as the present confederation has been proved to be, this principle appears to have been fully recognised by the framers of it; though they have not made proper or adequate provision for its exercise. Congress have an unlimited discretion to make requisitions of men and money; to govern the army and navy; to direct their operations. As their requisitions are made constitutionally binding upon the states, who are in fact under the most solemn obligations to furnish the supplies required of them, the intention evidently was, that the United States should command whatever resources were by them judged requisite to the "common defence and general welfare." It was presumed, that a sense of their true interests, and a regard to the dictates of good faith, would be found sufficient pledges for the punctual performance of the duty of the members to the federal head.

The experiment has, however, demonstrated, that this expectation was ill founded and illusory; and the observations made under the last head will, I imagine, have sufficed to convince the impartial and discerning, that there is an absolute necessity for an entire change in the first principles of the system. That if we are in earnest about giving the union energy and duration, we must abandon the vain project of legislating upon the states in their collective capacities; we must extend the laws of the federal government to the individual citizens of America; we must discard the fallacious scheme of quotas and requisitions, as equally impracticable and unjust. The result from all this is, that the union ought to be invested with full power to levy troops; to build and equip fleets; and to raise the revenues which will be required for the formation and support of an army and navy, in the customary and ordinary modes practised in other governments.

If the circumstances of our country are such as to demand a compound, instead of a simple — a confederate, instead of a sole government, the essential point which will remain to be adjusted, will be to discriminate the OBJECTS, as far as it can be done, which shall appertain to the different provinces or departments of power: allowing to each the most ample authority for fulfilling THOSE which may be committed to its charge. Shall the union be constituted the guardian of the common safety? Are fleets, and armies, and revenues, necessary to this purpose? The government of the union must be empowered to pass all laws, and to make all regulations which have relation to them. The same must be the case in respect to commerce, and to every other matter to which its jurisdiction is permitted to extend. Is the administration of justice between the citizens of the same state, the proper department of the local governments? These must possess all the authorities which are connected with this object, and with every other that may be allotted to their particular cognizance and direction. Not to confer in each case a degree of power commensurate to the end, would be to violate the most obvious rules of prudence and propriety, and improvidently to trust the great interests of the nation to hands which are disabled from managing them with vigour and success.

Who so likely to make suitable provisions for the public defence, as that body to which the guardianship of the public safety is confided; which, as the centre of information, will best understand the extent and urgency of the dangers that threaten; as the representative of the WHOLE, will feel itself most deeply interested in the preservation of every part; which from the responsibility implied in the duty assigned to it, will be most sensibly impressed with the necessity of proper exertions; and which, by the extension of its authority throughout the states, can alone establish uniformity and concert in the plans and measures, by which the common safety is to be secured? Is there not a manifest inconsistency in devolving upon the federal government the care of the general defence, and leaving in the state governments the *effective* powers, by which it is to be provided for? Is not a want of cooperation the infallible consequence of such a system? And will not weakness, disorder, an undue distribution of the burthens and calamities of war, an unnecessary and intolerable increase of expense, be its natural and inevitable concomitants? Have we not had unequivocal experience of its effects in the course of the revolution which we have just achieved?

Every view we may take of the subject, as candid inquirers after truth, will serve to convince us, that it is both unwise and dangerous to deny the federal government an unconfined authority in respect to all those objects which are entrusted to its management. It will indeed deserve the most vigilant and careful attention of the people, to see that it be modelled in such a manner as to admit of its being safely vested with the requisite powers. If any plan which has been, or may be, offered to our consideration, should not, upon a dispassionate inspection, be found to answer this description, it ought to be rejected. A government, the constitution of which renders it unfit to be entrusted with all the powers which a free people *ought to delegate to any government,* would be an unsafe and improper depository of the NATIONAL INTERESTS. Wherever THESE can with propriety be confided, the coincident powers may safely accompany them. This is the true result of all just reasoning upon the subject. And the adversaries of the plan promulgated by the convention, would have given a better impression of their candour if they had confined themselves to showing, that the internal structure of the proposed government was such as to render it unworthy of the confidence of the people. They ought not to have wandered into inflammatory declamations and unmeaning cavils, about the extent of the powers. The POWERS are not too extensive for the OBJECTS of federal administration, or, in other words, for the management of our NATIONAL INTERESTS; nor can any satisfactory argument be framed to show that they are chargeable with such an excess. If it be true, as has been insinuated by some of the writers on the other side, that the difficulty arises from the nature of the thing, and that the extent of the country will not permit us to form a government in which such ample powers can safely be reposed, it would prove that we ought to contract our views, and resort to the expedient of separate confederacies, which will move within more practicable spheres. For the absurdity must continually stare us in the face, of confiding to a government the direction of the most essential national concerns, without daring to trust it with the authorities which are indispensable to their proper and efficient management. Let us not attempt to reconcile contradictions, but firmly embrace a rational alternative.

I trust, however, that the impracticability of one general system cannot be shown. I am greatly mistaken, if any thing of weight has yet been advanced of this tendency; and I flatter myself, that the observations which have been made in the course of these papers, have served to place the reverse of that position in as clear a light as any matter, still in the womb of time and experience, is susceptible of. This, at all events, must be evident, that the very difficulty itself, drawn from the extent of the country, is the strongest argument in favour of an energetic government; for any other can certainly never preserve the union of so large an empire. If we embrace, as the standard of our political creed, the tenets of those who oppose the adoption of the proposed constitution, we cannot fail to verify the gloomy doctrines, which predict the impracticability of a national system, pervading the entire limits of the present confederacy.

PUBLIUS.

Patrick Henry (1736–1799)

OPPOSITION to the proposed Constitution came chiefly from small farmers, debtors, the landless and the workers in the West and South (as well as in the cities and on the farms of the Middle States) who feared Eastern domination, "moneyed aristocracy," and overbearing centralized political authority. A number of state officials, naturally loath to surrender any of their own powers, also campaigned against ratification. The Antifederalists, as they came to be called, were by no means so well organized as their opponents, but they could count among their leaders such men as Luther Martin of Maryland, Sam Adams and John Hancock of Massachusetts, and James Monroe, George Mason, and Patrick Henry of Virginia. Claiming that the nation could achieve prosperity and progress under the revised Articles, they charged that the Convention at Philadelphia had grossly exceeded its authority, and that the Constitution created a form of government that might deteriorate into autocracy. The Constitution lacked a bill of rights, reduced the rights of the states, and endangered those of the common people.

The Virginia ratifying convention met in June 1788, with Governor Edmund Randolph, James Madison, George Wythe, and John Marshall leading the pro-ratification group, opposed by the redoubtable Patrick Henry and George Mason. Henry's attack on the document expressed most of the fears felt by the Antifederalist opposition: that it removed the national government from the reach of the people, dangerously consolidated power, and placed liberty and property under the control of a government which could, under some conditions, take either or both away. On June 26, however, the assembly ratified the Constitution, though by a margin of only ten votes.

TEXT: Jonathan Elliot, ed., *The Debates in the Several State Conventions on the Adoption of the Federal Constitution* (Washington, 1840), III, 21–66 *passim*.

The Defects of the New Constitution

[From a speech to the Virginia Ratifying Convention, 1788]

MR. HENRY. Mr. Chairman, the public mind as well as my own, is extremely uneasy at the proposed change of government. Give me leave to form one of the number of those who wish to be thoroughly acquainted with the reasons of this perilous and uneasy situation, and why we are brought hither to decide on this great national question. I consider myself as the servant of the people of this commonwealth, as a sentinel over their rights, liberty, and happiness. I represent their feelings when I say that they are exceedingly uneasy at being brought from that state of full security, which they enjoyed, to the present delusive appearance of things. A year ago, the minds of our citizens were at perfect repose. Before the meeting of the late federal Convention at Philadelphia, a general peace and a universal tranquillity prevailed in this country; but, since that period, they are exceedingly uneasy and disquieted. When I wished for an appointment to this Convention, my mind was extremely agitated for the situation of public affairs. I conceived the republic to be in extreme danger. If our situation be thus uneasy, whence has arisen this fearful jeopardy? It arises from this fatal system; it arises from a proposal

to change our government — a proposal that goes to the utter annihilation of the most solemn engagements of the states. . . .

. . . Make the best of this new government — say it is composed
by any thing but inspiration — you ought to be extremely cautious,
watchful, jealous of your liberty; for, instead of securing your rights,
you may lose them forever. If a wrong step be now made, the republic
may be lost forever. If this new government will not come up to the
expectation of the people, and they shall be disappointed, their liberty
will be lost, and tyranny must and will arise. I repeat it again, and
I beg gentlemen to consider, that a wrong step, made now, will plunge
us into misery, and our republic will be lost. It will be necessary for
this Convention to have a faithful historical detail of the facts that
preceded the session of the federal Convention, and the reasons that
actuated its members in proposing an entire alteration of government,
and to demonstrate the dangers that awaited us. If they were of such
awful magnitude as to warrant a proposal so extremely perilous as
this, I must assert, that this Convention has an absolute right to a
thorough discovery of every circumstance relative to this great event.
And here I would make this inquiry of those worthy characters who
composed a part of the late federal Convention. I am sure they were
fully impressed with the necessity of forming a great consolidated
government, instead of a confederation. That this is a consolidated
government is demonstrably clear; and the danger of such a government is, to my mind, very striking. I have the highest veneration for
those gentlemen; but, sir, give me leave to demand, What right had
they to say, *We, the people?* My political curiosity, exclusive of my
anxious solicitude for the public welfare, leads me to ask: Who authorized them to speak the language of, *We, the people,* instead of, *We,
the states?* States are the characteristics and the soul of a confederation. If the states be not the agents of this compact, it must be one
great, consolidated, national government, of the people of all the
states. . . .

. . . Here is a resolution as radical as that which separated us from
Great Britain. It is radical in this transition; our rights and privileges
are endangered, and the sovereignty of the states will be relinquished:
and cannot we plainly see that this is actually the case? The rights
of conscience, trial by jury, liberty of the press, all your immunities
and franchises, all pretensions to human rights and privileges, are
rendered insecure, if not lost, by this change, so loudly talked of by
some, and inconsiderately by others. Is this tame relinquishment of
rights worthy of freemen? Is it worthy of that manly fortitude that
ought to characterize republicans? It is said eight states have adopted
this plan. I declare that if twelve states and a half had adopted it, I
would, with manly firmness, and in spite of an erring world, reject it.

You are not to inquire how your trade may be increased, nor how you are to become a great and powerful people, but how your liberties can be secured; for liberty ought to be the direct end of your government. . . .

. . . We are come hither to preserve the poor commonwealth of Virginia, if it can be possibly done: something must be done to preserve your liberty and mine. The Confederation, this same despised government, merits, in my opinion, the highest encomium: it carried us through a long and dangerous war; it rendered us victorious in that bloody conflict with a powerful nation; it has secured us a territory greater than any European monarch possesses: and shall a government which has been thus strong and vigorous, be accused of imbecility, and abandoned for want of energy? Consider what you are about to do before you part with the government. Take longer time in reckoning things; revolutions like this have happened in almost every country in Europe; similar examples are to be found in ancient Greece and ancient Rome — instances of the people losing their liberty by their own carelessness and the ambition of a few. We are cautioned by the honorable gentleman, who presides, against faction and turbulence. I acknowledge that licentiousness is dangerous, and that it ought to be provided against: I acknowledge, also, the new form of government may effectually prevent it: yet there is another thing it will as effectually do — it will oppress and ruin the people. . . .

. . . An opinion has gone forth, we find, that we are contemptible people: the time has been when we were thought otherwise. Under the same despised government, we commanded the respect of all Europe: wherefore are we now reckoned otherwise? The American spirit has fled from hence: it has gone to regions where it has never been expected; it has gone to the people of France, in search of a splendid government — a strong, energetic government. Shall we imitate the example of those nations who have gone from a simple to a splendid government? Are those nations more worthy of our imitation? What can make an adequate satisfaction to them for the loss they have suffered in attaining such a government — for the loss of their liberty? If we admit this consolidated government, it will be because we like a great, splendid one. Some way or other we must be a great and mighty empire; we must have an army, and a navy, and a number of things. When the American spirit was in its youth, the language of America was different: liberty, sir, was then the primary object. We are descended from a people whose government was founded on liberty: our glorious forefathers of Great Britain made liberty the foundation of every thing. That country is become a great, mighty, and splendid nation; not because their government is strong and energetic, but, sir, because liberty is its direct end and foundation. We drew the spirit of liberty from our British ancestors: by that spirit we have triumphed over every difficulty. But now, sir, the American spirit, assisted by the ropes and chains of consolidation, is about to convert this country into a powerful and mighty empire. If you make the citizens of this country agree to become the subjects of one great consolidated empire of America, your government will not have sufficient energy to keep them together. Such a government is incompatible with the genius of republicanism. There will be no checks, no real balances, in this government. What can avail your specious, imaginary balances, your rope-dancing, chain-rattling, ridiculous ideal checks and contrivances? But, sir, we are not feared by foreigners; we do not make nations tremble. Would this constitute happiness, or secure liberty? I trust, sir, our political hemisphere will ever direct their operations to the security of those objects.

Consider our situation, sir: go to the poor man, and ask him what he does. He will inform you that he enjoys the fruits of his labor, under his own fig-tree, with his wife and children around him, in peace and security. Go to every other member of society — you will find the same tranquil ease and content; you will find no alarms or disturbances. Why, then, tell us of danger, to terrify us into an adoption of this new form of government? And yet who knows the dangers that this new system may produce? They are out of the sight of the common people: they cannot foresee latent consequences. I dread the operation of it on the middling and lower classes of people: it is for them I fear the adoption of this system. I fear I tire the patience of the committee; but I beg to be indulged with a few more observations. When I thus profess myself an advocate for the liberty of the people, I shall be told I am a designing man, that I am to be a great man, that I am to be a demagogue; and many similar illiberal insinuations will be thrown out: but, sir, conscious rectitude outweighs those things with me. I see great jeopardy in this new government. I see none from our present one. . . .

This Constitution is said to have beautiful features; but when I come to examine these features, sir, they appear to me horribly frightful. Among other deformities, it has an awful squinting; it squints towards monarchy; and does not this raise indignation in the breast of every true American?

Your President may easily become king. Your Senate is so imperfectly constructed that your dearest rights may be sacrificed by what may be a small minority; and a very small minority may continue forever unchangeably this government, although horridly defective. Where are your checks in this government? Your strongholds will be in the hands of your enemies. It is on a supposition that your American governors shall be honest, that all the good qualities of this government are founded, but its defective and imperfect construction puts it in their power to perpetrate the worst of mischiefs, should they be bad men; and, sir, would not all the world, from the eastern to the western hemisphere, blame our distracted folly in resting our rights upon the contingency of our rulers being good or bad? Show me that age and country where the rights and liberties of the people were placed on the sole chance of their rulers being good men, without a consequent loss of liberty! I say that the loss of that dearest privilege has ever followed, with absolute certainty, every such mad attempt.

If your American chief be a man of ambition and abilities, how easy is it for him to render himself absolute! The army is in his hands, and if he be a man of address, it will be attached to him, and it will be the subject of long meditation with him to seize the first auspicious moment to accomplish his design; and, sir, will the American spirit solely relieve you when this happens? I would rather infinitely — and I am sure most of this Convention are of the same opinion — have a king, lords, and commons, than a government so replete with such insupportable evils. If we make a king, we may prescribe the rules by which he shall rule his people, and interpose such checks as shall prevent him from infringing them; but the President, in the field, at the head of his army, can prescribe the terms on which he shall reign master, so far that it will puzzle any American ever to get his neck from under the galling yoke. I cannot with patience think of this idea. If ever he violates the laws, one of two things will happen: he will come at the head of his army, to carry every thing before him; or he will give bail, or do what Mr. Chief Justice will order him. If he be guilty, will not the recollection of his crimes teach him to make one bold push for the American throne? Will not the immense difference between being master of every thing, and being ignominiously tried and punished, powerfully excite him to make this bold push? But, sir, where is the existing force to punish him? Can he not, at the head of his army, beat down every opposition? Away with your President! we shall have a king: the army will salute him monarch: your militia will leave you, and assist in making him king, and fight against you: and what have you to oppose this force? What will then become of you and your rights? Will not absolute despotism ensue? . . .

I beg pardon of this house for having taken up more time than came to my share, and I thank them for the patience and polite attention with which I have been heard. If I shall be in the minority, I shall have those painful sensations which arise from a conviction of *being overpowered in a good cause.* Yet I will be a peaceable citizen. My head, my hand, and my heart, shall be at liberty to retrieve the loss of liberty, and remove the defects of that system in a constitutional way. I wish not to go to violence, but will wait with hopes that the spirit which predominated in the revolution is not yet gone, nor the cause of those who are attached to the revolution yet lost. I shall therefore patiently wait in expectation of seeing that government changed, so as to be compatible with the safety, liberty, and happiness, of the people.

ᴥᴿ Thomas Jefferson (1743–1826)

THOMAS JEFFERSON was, among many other things, a brilliant political philosopher. At the same time, with his long experience in practical politics and administration, he recognized that theory and practice could not be successfully separated in government. In his letters and public statements he formulated, over the years, what he believed to be "an expression of the American mind" in political affairs, still the most eloquent and thoughtful exposition of the American political faith.

Jefferson accepted the prevailing concepts of traditional British and European political thinking: that is, he believed in human equality, natural rights, the compact theory of government, popular sovereignty, the right of revolution, and a government of limited authority. The best republican government, he wrote, was a republican government, "a government by the citizens in the mass, acting directly, according to the rules established by the majority." Majority rule was to him vitally important to the wisdom and justice of government, for "absolute acquiescence in the rule of the majority," he thought, was "the vital principle of republics from which there is no appeal but to force."

Jefferson's faith in the majority rested on his basic belief (though he sometimes had doubts) that "morality, compassion, and generosity are innate elements of the human constitution," that man had "capacity for improvement, for learning and understanding himself and the world." He could not accept an unqualified belief in man's goodness, for he had too much experience with the world for that; but he was confident that, under proper conditions, men could be relied upon to think and do the right thing — if they were free, educated, and "habituated to think for themselves and to follow reason as their guides."

For this reason Jefferson favored a government which diffused political power through an educated, enlightened populace; the majority of men, "the people (by which is meant the mass of individuals composing the society)" are "competent to judge of the facts occurring in ordinary life. . . ." The way to "good and safe government," he wrote, "is not to trust all to one, but to divide it among the many." Jefferson feared the great corrupt cities of Europe, with their poor and propertyless proletariat and their merchant princes, visualizing instead in America an agrarian, egalitarian society of freeholders. His philosophy of government, if it could be reduced to a single key idea, was built about the concept of *liberation,* of *freedom.*

TEXTS: Paul L. Ford, ed., *The Writings of Thomas Jefferson* (New York, 1892–99), IV, 475–480. A. A. Lipscomb and A. E. Bergh, eds., *The Writings of Thomas Jefferson* (Washington, 1903–5), XIII, 396–402; XV, 36–38, 40–43.

Remarks on the Constitution

[From a letter to James Madison, December 20, 1787]

DEAR SIR, — . . . The season admitting only of operations in the Cabinet, and these being in a great measure secret, I have little to fill a letter. I will therefore make up the deficiency by adding a few words on the Constitution proposed by our Convention. I like much the general idea of framing a government which should go on of itself peaceably, without needing continual recurrence to the state legislatures. I like the organization of the government into Legislative, Judiciary and Executive. I like the power given the Legislature to levy taxes, and for that reason solely approve of the greater house being chosen by the people directly. For tho' I think a house chosen by them will be very illy qualified to legislate for the Union, for foreign nations &c., yet this evil does not weigh against the good of preserving inviolate the fundamental principle that the people are not to be taxed but by representatives chosen immediately by themselves. I am captivated by the compromise of the opposite claims of the great and little states, of the latter to equal, and the former to proportionate influence. I am much pleased too with the substitution of the method of voting by persons, instead of that of voting by states: and I like the negative given to the Executive with a third of either house, though I should have liked it better had the Judiciary been associated for that purpose, or invested with a similar and separate power. There are other good things of less moment. I will now add what I do not like. First the omission of a bill of rights providing clearly and without the aid of sophisms for freedom of religion, freedom of the press, protection against standing armies, restriction against monopolies, the eternal and unremitting force of the habeas corpus laws, and trials by jury in all matters of fact triable by the laws of the land and not by the law of nations. To say, as Mr. Wilson does, that a bill of rights was not necessary because all is reserved in the case of the general government which is not given, while in the particular ones all is given which is not reserved, might do for the audience to whom it was addressed, but is surely a *gratis dictum*, opposed by strong inferences from the body of the instrument, as well as from the omission of the clause of our present confederation which had declared that in express terms. It was a hard conclusion to say because there has been no uniformity among the states as to the cases triable by jury, because some have been so incautious as to abandon this mode of trial, therefore the more prudent states shall be reduced to the same level of calamity. It would have been much more just and wise to have concluded the other way that as most of the states had judiciously preserved this palladium, those who had wandered should be brought back to it, and to have established general right instead of general wrong. Let me add that a bill of rights is what the people are entitled to against every government on earth, general or particular, and what no just government should refuse, or rest on inferences. The second feature I dislike, and greatly dislike, is the abandonment in every instance of the necessity of rotation in office, and most particularly in the case of the President. Experience concurs with reason in concluding that the first magistrate will always be re-elected if the Constitution permits it. He is then an officer for life. This once observed, it becomes of so much consequence to certain nations to have a friend or a foe at the head of our affairs that they will interfere with money and with arms. A Galloman or an Angloman will be supported by the nation he befriends. If once elected, and at a second or third election out voted by one or two votes, he will pretend false votes, foul play, hold possession of the reins of government, be supported by the States voting for him, especially if they are the central ones lying in a compact body themselves and separating their opponents: and they will be aided by one nation of Europe, while the majority are aided by another. The election of a President of America some years hence will be much more interesting to certain nations of Europe than ever the election of a king of Poland was. Reflect on all the instances in history ancient and modern, of elective monarchies, and say if they do not give foundation for my fears. The Roman emperors, the popes, while they were of any importance, the German emperors till they became hereditary in practice, the kings of Poland, the Deys of the Ottoman dependances. It may be said that if elections are to be attended with these disorders, the seldomer they are renewed the better. But experience shews that the only way to prevent disorder is to render them uninteresting by frequent changes. An incapacity to be elected a second time would have been the only effectual preventative. The power of removing him every fourth year by the vote of the people is a power which will not be exercised. The king of Poland is removeable every day by the Diet, yet he is never removed. — Smaller objections are the Appeal in fact as well as law, and the binding all persons Legislative Executive and Judiciary by oath to maintain that constitution. I do not pretend to decide what would be the best method of procuring the establishment of the manifold good things in this constitution, and of getting rid of the bad. Whether by adopting it in hopes of future amendment, or, after it has been duly weighed and canvassed by the people, after seeing the parts they generally dislike, and those they generally approve, to say to them 'We see now what you wish. Send together your deputies again, let them frame a constitution for you omitting what you have condemned, and establishing the powers you approve. Even these will be a great addition to the energy of your government.' — At all events I hope you will not be discouraged from other trials, if the present one should fail of its full effect. — I have thus told you freely what I like and dislike: merely as a matter of curiosity, for I know your own judgment has been formed on all these points after having heard everything which could be urged on them. I own I am not a friend to a very energetic government. It is always oppressive. The late rebellion in Massachusetts has given more alarm than I think it should have done. Calculate that one rebellion in 13 states in the course of 11 years, is but one for each state in a century and a half. No country should be so long without one. Nor will any degree of power in the hands of government prevent insurrections. France, with all its despotism, and two or three hundred thousand men always in arms has had three insurrections in the three years I have been here[1] in every one of which greater numbers were engaged than in Massachusetts and a great deal more blood was spilt. In Turkey, which Montesquieu supposes more despotic, insurrections are the events of every day. In England, where the hand of power is lighter than here, but heavier than with us they happen every half dozen years. Compare again the ferocious depredations of their insurgents with the order, the moderation and the almost self-extinguishment of ours. — After all, it is my principle that the will of the majority should always prevail. If they approve the proposed Convention in all its parts, I shall concur in it cheerfully, in hopes that they will amend it whenever they shall find it work wrong. I think our governments will remain virtuous for many centuries; as long as they are chiefly agricultural; and this will be as long as there shall be vacant lands in any part of America. When they get piled upon one another in large cities, as in Europe, they will become corrupt as in Europe. Above all things I hope the edu-

[1] Jefferson was at this time the U.S. minister to France.

cation of the common people will be attended to; convinced that on
their good sense we may rely with the most security for the preservation of a due degree of liberty. I have tired you by this time with
my disquisitions and will therefore only add assurances of the sincerity
of those sentiments of esteem and attachment with which I am Dear
Sir your affectionate friend and servant.

P.S. The instability of our laws is really an immense evil. I think
it would be well to provide in our constitutions that there shall always
be a twelve-month between the ingrossing a bill and passing it: that
it should then be offered to its passage without changing a word:
and that if circumstances should be thought to require a speedier
passage, it should take two thirds of both houses instead of a bare
majority.

On a Natural Aristocracy

[From a letter to John Adams, October 28, 1813]

. . . For I agree with you that there is a natural aristocracy among
men. The grounds of this are virtue and talents. Formerly, bodily
powers gave place among the aristoi. But since the invention of
gunpowder has armed the weak as well as the strong with missile
death, bodily strength, like beauty, good humor, politeness and other
accomplishments, has become but an auxiliary ground of distinction.
There is also an artificial aristocracy, founded on wealth and birth,
without either virtue or talents; for with these it would belong to
the first class. The natural aristocracy I consider as the most precious
gift of nature, for the instruction, the trusts, and government of society.
And indeed, it would have been inconsistent in creation to have
formed man for the social state, and not to have provided virtue and
wisdom enough to manage the concerns of the society. May we not
even say, that that form of government is the best, which provides
the most effectually for a pure selection of these natural aristoi into
the offices of government? The artificial aristocracy is a mischievous
ingredient in government, and provision should be made to prevent its
ascendency. On the question, what is the best provision, you and I
differ; but we differ as rational friends, using the free exercise of our
own reason, and mutually indulging its errors. You think it best to
put the pseudo-aristoi into a separate chamber of legislation, where
they may be hindered from doing mischief by their co-ordinate
branches, and where, also, they may be a protection to wealth against
the agrarian and plundering enterprises of the majority of the people.
I think that to give them power in order to prevent them from doing

mischief, is arming them for it, and increasing instead of remedying the evil. For if the co-ordinate branches can arrest their action, so may they that of the co-ordinates. Mischief may be done negatively as well as positively. Of this, a cabal in the Senate of the United States has furnished many proofs. Nor do I believe them necessary to protect the wealthy; because enough of these will find their way into every branch of the legislation, to protect themselves. From fifteen to twenty legislatures of our own, in action for thirty years past, have proved that no fears of an equalization of property are to be apprehended from them. I think the best remedy is exactly that provided by all our constitutions, to leave to the citizens the free election and separation of the aristoi from the pseudo-aristoi, of the wheat from the chaff. In general they will elect the really good and wise. In some instances, wealth may corrupt, and birth blind them; but not in sufficient degree to endanger the society.

It is probable that our difference of opinion may, in some measure, be produced by a difference of character in those among whom we live. From what I have seen of Massachusetts and Connecticut myself, and still more from what I have heard, and the character given of the former by yourself, who know them so much better there seems to be in those two States a traditionary reverence for certain families, which has rendered the offices of the government nearly hereditary in those families. I presume that from an early period of your history, members of those families happening to possess virtue and talents, have honestly exercised them for the good of the people, and by their services have endeared their names to them. In coupling Connecticut with you, I meant it politically only, not morally. For having made the Bible the common law of their land, they seem to have modeled their morality on the story of Jacob and Laban. But although this hereditary succession to office with you, may, in some degree, be founded in real family merit, yet in a much higher degree, it has proceeded from your strict alliance of Church and State. These families are canonized in the eyes of the people on common principles, "you tickle me, and I will tickle you." In Virginia we have nothing of this. Our clergy, before the revolution, having been secured against rivalship by fixed salaries, did not give themselves the trouble of acquiring influence over the people. Of wealth, there were great accumulations in particular families, handed down from generation to generation, under the English law of entails. But the only object of ambition for the wealthy was a seat in the King's Council. All their court then was paid to the crown and its creatures; and they Philipized in all collisions between the King and the people. Hence they were unpopular; and that unpopularity continues attached to their names. A Randolph, a Carter, or a Bur-

well must have great personal superiority over a common competitor
to be elected by the people even at this day. At the first session of
our legislature after the Declaration of Independence, we passed a law
abolishing entails. And this was followed by one abolishing the privilege of primogeniture, and dividing the lands of intestates equally
among all their children, or other representatives. These laws, drawn
by myself, laid the axe to the foot of pseudo-aristocracy. And had
another which I prepared been adopted by the legislature, our work
would have been complete. It was a bill for the more general diffusion of learning. This proposed to divide every county into wards of
five or six miles square, like your townships; to establish in each
ward a free school for reading, writing and common arithmetic; to
provide for the annual selection of the best subjects from these schools,
who might receive, at the public expense, a higher degree of education
at a district school; and from these district schools to select a certain
number of the most promising subjects, to be completed at an university, where all the useful sciences should be taught. Worth and
genius would thus have been sought out from every condition of life,
and completely prepared by education for defeating the competition
of wealth and birth for public trusts. My proposition had, for a
further object, to impart to these wards those portions of self-government for which they are best qualified, by confiding to them the care
of their poor, their roads, police, elections, the nomination of jurors,
administration of justice in small cases, elementary exercises of militia;
in short, to have made them little republics, with a warden at the
head of each, for all those concerns which, being under their eye,
they would better manage than the larger republics of the county
or State. A general call of ward meetings by their wardens on the
same day through the State, would at any time produce the genuine
sense of the people on any required point, and would enable the State
to act in mass, as your people have so often done, and with so much
effect by their town meetings. The law for religious freedom, which
made a part of this system, having put down the aristocracy of the
clergy, and restored to the citizen the freedom of the mind, and those
of entails and descents nurturing an equality of condition among
them, this on education would have raised the mass of the people to
the high ground of moral respectability necessary to their own safety,
and to orderly government; and would have completed the great
object of qualifying them to select the veritable aristoi, for the trusts
of government, to the exclusion of the pseudalists; and the same
Theognis who has furnished the epigraphs of your two letters, assures
us that "Ουδεμιαν πω, Κυρν', αγαθοι πολιν ωλεσαν ανδρες." Although
this law has not yet been acted on but in a small and inefficient degree,
it is still considered as before the legislature, with other bills of the

revised code, not yet taken up, and I have great hope that some patriotic spirit will, at a favorable moment, call it up, and make it the keystone of the arch of our government.

With respect to aristocracy, we should further consider, that before the establishment of the American States, nothing was known to history but the man of the old world, crowded within limits either small or overcharged, and steeped in the vices which that situation generates. A government adapted to such men would be one thing; but a very different one, that for the man of these States. Here every one may have land to labor for himself, if he chooses; or, preferring the exercise of any other industry, may exact for it such compensation as not only to afford a comfortable subsistence, but wherewith to provide for a cessation from labor in old age. Every one, by his property, or by his satisfactory situation, is interested in the support of law and order. And such men may safely and advantageously reserve to themselves a wholesome control over their public affairs, and a degree of freedom, which, in the hands of the *canaille* of the cities of Europe, would be instantly perverted to the demolition and destruction of everything public and private. The history of the last twenty-five years of France, and of the last forty years in America, nay of its last two hundred years, proves the truth of both parts of this observation.

But even in Europe a change has sensibly taken place in the mind of man. Science had liberated the ideas of those who read and reflect, and the American example had kindled feelings of right in the people. An insurrection has consequently begun, of science, talents, and courage, against rank and birth, which have fallen into contempt. It has failed in its first effort, because the mobs of the cities, the instrument used for its accomplishment, debased by ignorance, poverty, and vice, could not be restrained to rational action. But the world will recover from the panic of this first catastrophe. Science is progressive, and talents and enterprise on the alert. Resort may be had to the people of the country, a more governable power from their principles and subordination; and rank, and birth, and tinsel-aristocracy will finally shrink into insignificance, even there. This, however, we have no right to meddle with. It suffices for us, if the moral and physical condition of our own citizens qualifies them to select the able and good for the direction of their government, with a recurrence of elections at such short periods as will enable them to displace an unfaithful servant, before the mischief he meditates may be irremediable.

The Foundations of Government

[From a letter to Samuel Kercheval, July 12, 1816]

... The true foundation of republican government is the equal right
of every citizen, in his person and property, and in their management.
Try by this, as a tally, every provision of our Constitution, and see if it
hangs directly on the will of the people. Reduce your legislature to a
convenient number for full, but orderly discussion. Let every man
who fights or pays, exercise his just and equal right in their election.
Submit them to approbation or rejection at short intervals. Let the
executive be chosen in the same way, and for the same term, by those
whose agent he is to be; and leave no screen of a council behind which
to skulk from responsibility. It has been thought that the people are
not competent electors of judges *learned in the law.* But I do not
know that this is true, and, if doubtful, we should follow principle.
In this, as in many other elections, they would be guided by reputation,
which would not err oftener, perhaps, than the present mode of
appointment. In one State of the Union, at least, it has long been
tried, and with the most satisfactory success. The judges of Connecticut have been chosen by the people every six months, for nearly two
centuries, and I believe there has hardly ever been an instance of
change; so powerful is the curb of incessant responsibility. If prejudice,
however, derived from a monarchical institution, is still to prevail
against the vital elective principle of our own, and if the existing
example among ourselves of periodical election of judges by the
people be still mistrusted, let us at least not adopt the evil, and reject
the good, of the English precedent; let us retain amovability on the
concurrence of the executive and legislative branches, and nomination
by the executive alone. Nomination to office is an executive function.
To give it to the legislature, as we do, is a violation of the principle of
the separation of powers. It swerves the members from correctness,
by temptations to intrigue for office themselves, and to a corrupt barter
of votes; and destroys responsibility by dividing it among a multitude.
By leaving nomination in its proper place, among executive functions,
the principle of the distribution of power is preserved, and responsibility weighs with its heaviest force on a single head.

The organization of our county administrations may be thought
more difficult. But follow principle, and the knot unties itself. Divide
the counties into wards of such size as that every citizen can attend,
when called on, and act in person. Ascribe to them the government of
their wards in all things relating to themselves exclusively. A justice,
chosen by themselves, in each, a constable, a military company, a
patrol, a school, the care of their own poor, their own portion of the

public roads, the choice of one or more jurors to serve in some court, and the delivery, within their own wards, of their own votes for all elective officers of higher sphere, will relieve the county administration of nearly all its business, will have it better done, and by making every citizen an acting member of the government, and in the offices nearest and most interesting to him, will attach him by his strongest feelings to the independence of his country, and its republican Constitution. The justices thus chosen by every ward, would constitute the county court, would do its judiciary business, direct roads and bridges, levy county and poor rates, and administer all the matters of common interest to the whole country. These wards, called townships in New England, are the vital principle of their governments, and have proved themselves the wisest invention ever devised by the wit of man for the perfect exercise of self-government, and for its preservation. We should thus marshal our government into, 1, the general federal republic, for all concerns foreign and federal; 2, that of the State, for what relates to our own citizens exclusively; 3, the county republics, for the duties and concerns of the county; and 4, the ward republics, for the small, and yet numerous and interesting concerns of the neighborhood; and in government, as well as in every other business of life, it is by division and subdivision of duties alone, that all matters, great and small, can be managed to perfection. And the whole is cemented by giving to every citizen, personally, a part in the administration of the public affairs. . . .

Some men look at constitutions with sanctimonious reverence, and deem them like the ark of the covenant, too sacred to be touched. They ascribe to the men of the preceding age a wisdom more than human, and suppose what they did to be beyond amendment. I knew that age well; I belonged to it, and labored with it. It deserved well of its country. It was very like the present, but without the experience of the present; and forty years of experience in government is worth a century of book-reading; and this they would say themselves, were they to rise from the dead. I am certainly not an advocate for frequent and untried changes in laws and constitutions. I think moderate imperfections had better be borne with; because, when once known, we accommodate ourselves to them, and find practical means of correcting their ill effects. But I know also, that laws and institutions must go hand in hand with the progress of the human mind. As that becomes more developed, more enlightened, as new discoveries are made, new truths disclosed, and manners and opinions change with the change of circumstances, institutions must advance also, and keep pace with the times. We might as well require a man to wear still the coat which fitted him when a boy, as civilized society to remain ever under the regimen of their barbarous ancestors. It is this preposterous idea which has lately deluged Europe in blood. Their monarchs, instead of wisely yielding to the gradual change of circumstances, of favoring progressive accommodation to progressive improvement, have clung to old abuses, entrenched themselves behind steady habits, and obliged their subjects to seek through blood and violence rash and ruinous innovations, which, had they been referred to the peaceful deliberations and collected wisdom of the nation, would have been put into acceptable and salutary forms. Let us follow no such examples, nor weakly believe that one generation is not as capable as another of taking care of itself, and of ordering its own affairs. Let us, as our sister States have done, avail ourselves of our reason and experience, to correct the crude essays of our first and unexperienced, although wise, virtuous, and well-meaning councils. And lastly, let us provide in our Constitution for its revision at stated periods. What these periods should be, nature herself indicates. By the European tables of mortality, of the adults living at any one moment of time, a majority will be dead in about nineteen years. At the end of that period then, a new majority is come into place; or, in other words, a new generation. Each generation is as independent of the one preceding, as that was of all which had gone before. It has then, like them, a right to choose for itself the form of government it believes most promotive of its own happiness; consequently, to accommodate to the circumstances in which it finds itself, that received from its predecessors; and it is for the peace and good of mankind, that a solemn opportunity of doing this every nineteen or twenty years, should be provided by the Constitution; so that it may be handed on, with periodical repairs, from generation to generation, to the end of time, if anything human can so long endure. It is now forty years since the constitution of Virginia was formed. The same tables inform us, that, within that period, two-thirds of the adults then living are now dead. Have then the remaining third, even if they had the wish, the right to hold in obedience to their will, and to laws heretofore made by them, the other two-thirds, who, with themselves, compose the present mass of adults? If they have not, who has? The dead? But the dead have no rights. They are nothing; and nothing cannot own something. Where there is no substance, there can be no accident. This corporeal globe, and everything upon it, belong to its present corporeal inhabitants, during their generation. They alone have a right to direct what is the concern of themselves alone, and to declare the law of that direction; and this declaration can only be made by their majority. That majority, then, has a right to depute representatives to a convention, and to make the Constitution what they think will be the best for themselves. But how collect their voice? This is the real difficulty. If invited by private authority, or county or district meetings, these divisions are so large that few will attend; and their voice will be imperfectly, or falsely, pronounced. Here, then, would be one of the advantages of the ward divisions I have proposed. The mayor of every ward, on a question like the present, would call his ward together, take the simple yea or nay of its members, convey these to the county court, who would hand on those of all its wards to the proper general authority; and the voice of the whole people would be thus fairly, fully, and peaceably expressed, discussed, and decided by the common reason of the society. If this avenue be shut to the call of sufferance, it will make itself heard through that of force, and we shall go on, as other nations are doing, in the endless circle of oppression, rebellion, reformation; and oppression, rebellion, reformation, again; and so on forever.

ᕦ Fisher Ames (1758–1808)

FISHER AMES, son of the famed New England almanac-maker Dr. Nathaniel Ames, was born near Boston and graduated from Harvard in the class of 1774. After the war he studied law and entered politics, serving in the state legislature and in Congress. Ames did not believe in democracy and was never hesitant to express his contempt for it as a political system. He soon emerged as the leader of New England Federalism, and in essay and debate was its most effective spokesman.

Ames's speeches, letters, and essays, couched in a clear, bristling prose, are the best expression of the arch-conservative point of view of his times. Man, he believed, as "the most ferocious of animals," needed a powerful government and a set of strong, realistic leaders to protect his rights from his own inbred tendency to violate them. At his best in attack, Ames was a difficult opponent for the Jeffersonians and a constant thorn in the Republican party's side.

TEXT: Seth Ames, ed., *The Works of Fisher Ames* (Boston, 1854), II, 345–347, 392–395.

The Dangers of American Liberty

[From *Works*, 1809 (written 1805)]

. . . The political sphere, like the globe we tread upon, never stands still, but with a silent swiftness accomplishes the revolutions which, we are too ready to believe, are effected by our wisdom, or might have been controlled by our efforts. There is a kind of fatality in the affairs of republics, that eludes the foresight of the wise as much as it frustrates the toils and sacrifices of the patriot and the hero. Events proceed, not as they were expected or intended, but as they are impelled by the irresistible laws of our political existence. Things inevitable happen, and we are astonished, as if they were miracles, and the course of nature had been overpowered or suspended to produce them. Hence it is, that, till lately, more than half our countrymen believed our public tranquillity was firmly established, and that our liberty did not merely rest upon dry land, but was wedged, or rather rooted high above the flood in the rocks of granite, as immovably as the pillars that prop the universe. They, or at least the discerning of them, are at length no less disappointed than terrified to perceive that we have all the time floated, with a fearless and unregarded course, down the stream of events, till we are now visibly drawn within the revolutionary suction of Niagara, and every thing that is liberty will be dashed to pieces in the descent.

We have been accustomed to consider the pretension of Englishmen to be free as a proof how completely they were broken to subjection, or hardened in imposture. We have insisted, that they had no constitution, because they never made one; and that their boasted government, which is just what time and accident have made it, was palsied with age, and blue with the plague-sores of corruption. We have believed that it derived its stability, not from reason, but from prejudice; that it is supported, not because it is favorable to liberty, but as it is dear to national pride; that it is reverenced, not for its excellence, but because ignorance is naturally the idolater of antiquity; that it is not sound and healthful, but derives a morbid energy from disease, and an unaccountable aliment from the canker that corrodes its vitals.

But we maintained that the federal Constitution, with all the bloom of youth and splendor of innocence, was gifted with immortality. For if time should impair its force, or faction tarnish its charms, the people, ever vigilant to discern its wants, ever powerful to provide for them, would miraculously restore it to the field, like some wounded hero of the epic, to take a signal vengeance on its enemies, or like Antæus, invigorated by touching his mother earth, to rise the stronger for a fall.

There is of course a large portion of our citizens who will not believe, even on the evidence of facts, that any public evils exist, or are impending. They deride the apprehensions of those who foresee that licentiousness will prove, as it ever has proved, fatal to liberty. They consider her as a nymph, who need not be coy to keep herself pure, but that on the contrary, her chastity will grow robust by frequent scuffles with her seducers. They say, while a faction is a minority it will remain harmless by being outvoted; and if it should become a majority, all its acts, however profligate or violent, are then legitimate. For with the democrats the people is a sovereign who can do no wrong, even when he respects and spares no existing right, and whose voice, however obtained or however counterfeited, bears all the sanctity and all the force of a living divinity. . . .

They are certainly blind who do not see that we are descending from a supposed orderly and stable republican government into a licentious democracy, with a progress that baffles all means to resist, and scarcely leaves leisure to deplore its celerity. The institutions and the hopes that Washington raised are nearly prostrate; and his name and memory would perish, if the rage of his enemies had any power over history. But they have not — history will give scope to her vengeance, and posterity will not be defrauded.

But if our experience had not clearly given warning of our approaching catastrophe, the very nature of democracy would inevitably produce it.

A government by the passions of the multitude, or, no less correctly, according to the vices and ambition of their leaders, is a democracy. We have heard so long of the indefeasible sovereignty of the people, and have admitted so many specious theories of the rights of man, which are contradicted by his nature and experience, that few will dread at all, and fewer still will dread as they ought, the evils of an American democracy. They will not believe them near, or they will think them tolerable or temporary. Fatal delusion!

When it is said, there may be a tyranny of the *many* as well as of the *few*, every democrat will yield at least a cold and speculative assent; but he will at all times act, as if it were a thing incomprehensible, that there should be any evil to be apprehended in the uncontrolled power of the people. He will say arbitrary power may make a tyrant, but how can it make its possessor a slave?

In the first place, let it be remarked, the power of individuals is a very different thing from their liberty. When I vote for the man I prefer, he may happen not to be chosen; or he may disappoint my expectations if he is; or he may be outvoted by others in the public body to which he is elected. I may then hold and exercise all the power that a citizen can have or enjoy, and yet such laws may be made and such abuses allowed as shall deprive me of all liberty. I may be tried by a jury, and that jury may be culled and picked out from my political enemies by a federal marshal. Of course, my life and liberty may depend on the good pleasure of the man who appoints that marshal. I may be assessed arbitrarily for my faculty, or upon conjectural estimation of my property, so that all I have shall be at the control of the government, whenever its displeasure shall exact the sacrifice. I may be told that I am a federalist, and as such bound to submit, in all cases whatsoever, to the will of the majority, as the ruling faction ever pretend to be. My submission may be tested by my resisting or obeying commands that will involve me in disgrace, or drive me to despair. I may become a fugitive, because the ruling party have made me afraid to stay at home; or, perhaps, while I remain at home, they may, nevertheless, think fit to inscribe my name on the list of emigrants and proscribed persons.

All this was done in France, and many of the admirers of French examples are impatient to imitate them. . . .

The people, as a body, cannot deliberate. Nevertheless, they will feel an irresistible impulse to act, and their resolutions will be dictated to them by their demagogues. The consciousness, or the opinion, that they possess the supreme power, will inspire inordinate passions; and the violent men, who are the most forward to gratify those passions, will be their favorites. What is called the government of the people is in fact too often the arbitrary power of such men. Here, then, we have the faithful portrait of democracy. What avails the boasted power of individual citizens? or of what value is the will of the majority, if that will is dictated by a committee of demagogues, and law and right are in fact at the mercy of a victorious faction? To make a nation free, the crafty must be kept in awe, and the violent in restraint. The weak and the simple find their liberty arise not from their own individual sovereignty, but from the power of law and justice over all. It is only by the due restraint of others, that I am free.

Popular sovereignty is scarcely less beneficent than awful, when it resides in their courts of justice; there its office, like a sort of human providence, is to warn, enlighten, and protect; when the people are inflamed to seize and exercise it in their assemblies, it is competent only to kill and destroy. Temperate liberty is like the dew, as it falls unseen from its own heaven; constant without excess, it finds vegetation thirsting for its refreshment, and imparts to it the vigor to take more. All nature, moistened with blessings, sparkles in the morning ray. But democracy is a water-spout that bursts from the clouds, and lays the ravaged earth bare to its rocky foundations. The labors of man lie whelmed with his hopes beneath masses of ruin, that bury not only the dead but their monuments.

It is the almost universal mistake of our countrymen, that democracy would be mild and safe in America. They charge the horrid excesses of France not so much to human nature, which will never act better, when the restraints of government, morals, and religion are thrown off, but to the characteristic cruelty and wickedness of Frenchmen.

The truth is, and let it humble our pride, the most ferocious of all animals, when his passions are roused to fury and are uncontrolled, is man; and of all governments, the worst is that which never fails to excite, but was never found to restrain those passions, that is, democracy. It is an illuminated hell, that in the midst of remorse, horror, and torture, rings with festivity; for experience shows, that one joy remains to this most malignant description of the damned, the power to make others wretched. When a man looks round and sees his neighbors mild and merciful, he cannot feel afraid of the abuse of their power over him; and surely if they oppress me, he will say, they will spare their own liberty, for that is dear to all mankind. It is so. The human heart is so constituted, that a man loves liberty as naturally as himself. Yet liberty is a rare thing in the world, though the love of it is so universal.

◢ Thomas Paine (1737–1809)

NEW YORK State, after the Revolution, gave Thomas Paine a confiscated Loyalist farm, and Pennsylvania awarded him £500 for his services to the country. Paine lived quietly in New York for a time, attempting to interest builders in an iron bridge he had invented. Failing to promote his bridge, and no doubt restless at inactivity, he went to England in 1787 and thence, when the French Revolution broke out, directly to the heart of it in Paris. For the next three years he alternated between London and Paris, serving as apologist and propagandist for the revolutionary cause and doing his best to interest English radicals in something similar.

Edmund Burke's *Reflections on the French Revolution* (1790), a brilliant and incisive criticism of the French affair, Paine found "absurd in its principles and outrageous in its manner." However, it was effective; and Paine set about making a reply, to defend, he said, "a system then established and operating in America and which I wished to see peaceably adopted in Europe." His *Rights of Man* (Part I, 1791) thus had three aims: to defend the American system against Burke's implied criticisms; to defend the French Revolution against Burke's direct attack; and to expound his own political theory. He argued for the necessity of a government with a written constitution, a guaranteed bill of rights, a representative and responsible legislative body, and an equalitarian society. Part II (1792) contained a number of suggestions for specific social legislation, and an implied but clear invitation for a revolt against the British monarchy and the establishment of a British republic. *The Rights of Man* sold so well that it was suppressed, and its author tried for treason and outlawed in 1792.

Paine barely escaped to France, where, as an honorary French citizen, he attended meetings of the Assembly. He opposed the Jacobins and the execution of the king, however, and was stripped

of his French citizenship and imprisoned for nearly a year, until
the American minister obtained his release. While in prison, he
completed the manuscript of the first part of *The Age of Reason*.
TEXT: William M. Van der Weyde, ed., *The Life and Works of
Thomas Paine* (New Rochelle, N.Y., 1925), VI, 249–280.

The Nature of Government

[From *The Rights of Man,* Part II, 1792]

CHAPTER II

ON THE ORIGIN OF THE PRESENT OLD GOVERNMENTS

It is impossible that such governments as have hitherto existed in
the world, could have commenced by any other means than a total
violation of every principle, sacred and moral. The obscurity in which
the origin of all the present old governments is buried, implies the
iniquity and disgrace with which they began. The origin of the
present governments of America and France will ever be remembered,
because it is honorable to record it; but with respect to the rest, even
flattery has consigned them to the tomb of time, without an inscription.

It could have been no difficult thing in the early and solitary ages
of the world, while the chief employment of men was that of attending
flocks and herds, for a banditti of ruffians to overrun a country, and
lay it under contributions. Their power being thus established, the chief
of the band contrived to lose the name of robber in that of monarch;
and hence the origin of monarchy and kings.

The origin of the government of England, so far as relates to what
is called its line of monarchy, being one of the latest, is perhaps the
best recorded. The hatred which the Norman invasion and tyranny
begat, must have been deeply rooted in the nation, to have outlived
the contrivance to obliterate it. Though not a courtier will talk of the
curfew-bell, not a village in England has forgotten it.

Those bands of robbers having parcelled out the world and divided
it into dominions, began, as is naturally the case, to quarrel with each
other. What at first was obtained by violence, was considered by
others as lawful to be taken, and a second plunderer succeeded the
first. They alternately invaded the dominions which each had assigned
to himself, and the brutality with which they treated each other
explains the original character of monarchy. It was ruffian torturing
ruffian.

The conquerer considered the conquered, not as his prisoner, but
as his property. He led him in triumph, rattling in chains, and

doomed him, at pleasure, to slavery or death. As time obliterated the history of their beginning, their successors assumed new appearances, to cut off the entail of their disgrace, but their principles and objects remained the same. What at first was plunder, assumed the softer name of revenue; and the power originally usurped, they affected to inherit.

From such beginning of governments, what could be expected, but a continual system of war and extortion? It has established itself into a trade. The vice is not peculiar to one more than to another, but is the common principle of all. There does not exist within such government sufficient stamina whereon to ingraft reformation; and the shortest, easiest, and most effectual remedy, is to begin anew.

What scenes of horror, what perfection of iniquity, present themselves in contemplating the character, and reviewing the history of such governments! If we would delineate human nature with a baseness of heart, and hypocrisy of countenance, that reflection would shudder at and humanity disown, it is kings, courts, and cabinets, that must sit for the portrait. Man, naturally as he is, with all his faults about him, is not up to the character.

Can we possibly suppose that if governments had originated in a right principle, and had not an interest in pursuing a wrong one, that the world could have been in the wretched and quarrelsome condition we have seen it? What inducement has the farmer, while following the plough, to lay aside his peaceful pursuit, and go to war with the farmer of another country? Or what inducement has the manufacturer? What is dominion to them, or to any class of men in a nation? Does it add an acre to any man's estate, or raise its value? Are not conquest and defeat each of the same price, and taxes the never failing consequence? Though this reasoning may be good to a nation, it is not so to a government. War is the faro-table of governments, and nations the dupes of the games.

If there is any thing to wonder at in this miserable scene of governments, more than might be expected, it is the progress which the peaceful arts of agriculture, manufacture and commerce have made, beneath such a long accumulating load of discouragement and oppression. It serves to show, that instinct in animals does not act with stronger impulse, than the principles of society and civilization operate in man. Under all discouragements, he pursues his object, and yields to nothing but impossibilities.

CHAPTER III

ON THE OLD AND NEW SYSTEMS OF GOVERNMENT

Nothing can appear more contradictory than the principles on which the old governments began, and the condition to which society, civilization and commerce, are capable of carrying mankind. Government on the old system is an assumption of power, for the aggrandizement of itself; on the new, a delegation of power, for the common benefit of society. The former supports itself by keeping up a system of war; the latter promotes a system of peace, as the true means of enriching a nation. The one encourages national prejudices; the other promotes universal society, as the means of universal commerce. The one measures its prosperity, by the quantity of revenue it extorts; the other proves its excellence, by the small quantity of taxes it requires.

Mr. Burke has talked of old and new Whigs. If he can amuse himself with childish names and distinctions, I shall not interrupt his pleasure. It is not to him, but to Abbé Siéyès, that I address this chapter. I am already engaged to the latter gentleman, to discuss the subject of monarchical government; and as it naturally occurs in comparing the old and new sytems, I make this the opportunity of presenting to him my observations. I shall occasionally take Mr. Burke in my way.

Though it might be proved that the system of government now called the NEW, is the most ancient in principle of all that have existed, being founded on the original inherent Rights of Man: yet, as tyranny and the sword have suspended the exercise of those rights for many centuries past, it serves better the purpose of distinction to call it a *new*, than to claim the right of calling it the old.

The first general distinction between those two systems is, that the one now called the old is *hereditary*, either in whole or in part; and the new is entirely *representative*. It rejects all hereditary government:

First, as being an imposition on mankind.

Secondly, as being inadequate to the purposes for which government is necessary.

With respect to the first of these heads. It cannot be proved by what right hereditary government could begin: neither does there exist within the compass of mortal power a right to establish it. Man has no authority over posterity in matters of personal right; and therefore, no man, or body of men, had, or can have, a right to set up hereditary government. Were even ourselves to come again into existence, instead of being succeeded by posterity, we have not now the right of taking from ourselves the rights which would then be ours. On what ground, then, do we pretend to take them from others?

All hereditary government is in its nature tyranny. An heritable crown, or an heritable throne, or by what other fanciful name such things may be called, have no other significant explanation than that mankind are heritable property. To inherit a government, is to inherit the people, as if they were flocks and herds.

With respect to the second head, that of being inadequate to the purposes for which government is necessary, we have only to consider what government essentially is, and compare it with the circumstances to which hereditary succession is subject. Government ought to be a thing always in maturity. It ought to be so constructed as to be superior to all the accidents to which individual man is subject; and therefore, hereditary succession, by being *subject to them all,* is the most irregular and imperfect of all the systems of government.

We have heard the Rights of Man called a *levelling* system; but the only system to which the word *levelling* is truly applicable, is the hereditary monarchical system. It is a system of *mental levelling.* It indiscriminately admits every species of character to the same authority. Vice and virtue, ignorance and wisdom, in short, every quality, good or bad, is put on the same level. Kings succeed each other, not as rationals, but as animals. It signifies not what their mental or moral characters are.

Can we then be surprised at the abject state of the human mind in monarchical countries, when the government itself is formed on such an abject levelling system? It has no fixed character. To-day it is one thing; to-morrow it is something else. It changes with the temper of every succeeding individual, and is subject to all the varieties of each. It is government through the medium of passions and accidents.

It appears under all the various characters of childhood, decrepitude, dotage, a thing at nurse, in leading-strings, or on crutches. It reverses the wholesome order of nature. It occasionally puts children over men, and the conceits of nonage over wisdom and experience. In short, we cannot conceive a more ridiculous figure of government than hereditary succession, in all its cases, presents.

Could it be made a decree in nature, or an edict registered in heaven, and man could know it, that virtue and wisdom should invariably appertain to hereditary succession, the objections to it would be removed; but when we see that nature acts as if she disowned and sported with the hereditary system; that the mental characters of successors, in all countries, are below the average of human understanding; that one is a tyrant, another an idiot, a third insane, and some all three together, it is impossible to attach confidence to it, when reason in man has power to act.

It is not to the Abbé Siéyès that I need apply this reasoning; he has already saved me that trouble, by giving his own opinion upon the case. "If it be asked," says he, "what is my opinion with respect to hereditary right, I answer, without hesitation, that, in good theory, an hereditary transmission of any power or office, can never accord with the laws of a true representation. Hereditaryship is, in this sense, as much an attaint upon principle, as an outrage upon society. But let us," continues he, "refer to the history of all elective monarchies and principalities: is there one in which the elective mode is not worse than the hereditary succession?"

As to debating on which is the worse of the two, is admitting both to be bad; and herein we are agreed. The preference which the Abbé has given is a condemnation of the thing he prefers. Such a mode of reasoning on such a subject is inadmissible, because it finally amounts to an accusation upon Providence, as if she had left to man no other choice with respect to government than between two evils, the best of which he admits to be "*an attaint upon principle, and an outrage upon society.*"

Passing over, for the present, all the evils and mischiefs which monarchy has occasioned in the world, nothing can more effectually prove its uselessness in a state of *civil government,* than making it hereditary. Would we make any office hereditary that required wisdom and abilities to fill it? And where wisdom and abilities are not necessary, such an office, whatever it may be, is superfluous or insignificant.

Hereditary succession is a burlesque upon monarchy. It puts it in the most ridiculous light, by presenting it as an office, which any child or idiot may fill. It requires some talents to be a common mechanic; but to be a king, requires only the animal figure of a man — a sort of breathing automaton. This sort of superstition may last a few years more, but it cannot long resist the awakened reason and interest of man.

As to Mr. Burke, he is a stickler for monarchy, not altogether as a pensioner, if he is one, which I believe, but as a political man. He has taken up a contemptible opinion of mankind, who in their turn, are taking up the same of him. He considers them as a herd of beings that must be governed by fraud, effigy, and show; and an idol would be as good a figure of monarchy with him, as a man. I will, however, do him the justice to say, that, with respect to America, he has been very complimentary. He always contended, at least in my hearing, that the people of America are more enlightened than those of England, or of any other country in Europe; and that therefore the imposition of show was not necessary in their government.

Though the comparison between hereditary and elective monarchy, which the Abbé has made, is unnecessary to the case, because the representative system rejects both; yet, were I to make the comparison, I should decide contrary to what he has done.

The civil wars which have originated from contested hereditary claims are numerous, and have been more dreadful, and of longer continuance, than those which have been occasioned by election. All the civil wars in France arose from the hereditary system; they were either produced by hereditary claims, or by the imperfection of the hereditary form, which admits of regencies, or monarchies at nurse.

With respect to England, its history is full of the same misfortunes. The contests for succession between the houses of York and Lancaster, lasted a whole century; and others of a similar nature, have renewed themselves since that period. Those of 1715 and 1745, were of the same kind. The Succession-war for the crown of Spain, embroiled almost half of Europe. The disturbances in Holland are generated from the hereditaryship of the stadtholder. A government calling itself free, with an hereditary office, is like a thorn in the flesh, that produces a fermentation which endeavors to discharge it.

But I might go further, and place also foreign wars, of whatever kind, to the same cause. It is by adding the evil of hereditary succession to that of monarchy, that a permanent family interest is created, whose constant objects are dominion and revenue. Poland, though an elective monarchy, has had fewer wars than those which are hereditary; and it is the only government that has made a voluntary essay, though but a small one, to reform the condition of the country.

Having thus glanced at a few of the defects of the old, or hereditary system of government, let us compare it with the new, or representative system.

The representative system takes society and civilization for its basis; nature, reason, and experience for its guide.

Experience, in all ages, and in all countries, has demonstrated, that it is impossible to control Nature in her distribution of mental powers. She gives them as she pleases. Whatever is the rule by which she, apparently to us, scatters them among mankind, that rule remains a secret to man. It would be as ridiculous to attempt to fix the hereditaryship of human beauty, as of wisdom.

Whatever wisdom constituently is, it is like a seedless plant; it may be reared when it appears, but it cannot be voluntarily produced. There is always a sufficiency somewhere in the general mass of society for all purposes; but with respect to the parts of society, it is continually changing its place. It rises in one to-day, in another to-morrow, and has most probably visited in rotation every family of the earth, and again withdrawn.

As this is the order of nature, the order of government must necessarily follow it, or government will, as we see it does, degenerate into ignorance. The hereditary system, therefore, is as repugnant to human wisdom, as to human rights, and is as absurd, as it is unjust.

As the republic of letters brings forward the best literary productions, by giving to genius a fair and universal chance; so the representative system of government is calculated to produce the wisest laws, by collecting wisdom where it can be found. I smile to myself when I contemplate the ridiculous insignificance into which literature and all the sciences would sink, were they made hereditary; and I carry the same idea into governments. An hereditary governor is as inconsistent as an hereditary author. I know not whether Homer or Euclid had sons; but I will venture an opinion, that if they had, and had left their works unfinished, those sons could not have completed them.

Do we need a stronger evidence of the absurdity of hereditary government, than is seen in the descendants of those men, in any line of life, who once were famous? Is there scarcely an instance in which there is not a total reverse of character? It appears as if the tide of mental faculties flowed as far as it could in certain channels, and then forsook its course, and arose in others. How irrational then is the hereditary system which establishes channels of power, in company with which wisdom refuses to flow! By continuing this absurdity, man is perpetually in contradiction with himself; he accepts, for a king, or a chief magistrate, or a legislator, a person whom he would not elect for a constable.

It appears to general observation, that revolutions create genius and talents; but those events do no more than bring them forward. There is existing in man, a mass of sense lying in a dormant state, and which, unless something excites it to action, will descend with him, in that condition, to the grave. As it is to the advantage of society that the whole of its faculties should be employed, the construction of government ought to be such as to bring forward, by a quiet and regular operation, all that extent of capacity which never fails to appear in revolutions.

This cannot take place in the insipid state of hereditary government, not only because it prevents, but because it operates to benumb. When the mind of a nation is bowed down by any political superstition in its government, such as hereditary succession is, it loses a considerable portion of its powers on all other subjects and objects.

Hereditary succession requires the same obedience to ignorance, as to wisdom; and when once the mind can bring itself to pay this indiscriminate reverence, it descends below the stature of mental manhood. It is fit to be great only in little things. It acts a treachery upon itself, and suffocates the sensations that urge to detection.

Though the ancient governments present to us a miserable picture of the condition of man, there is one which above all others exempts itself from the general description. I mean the democracy of the

Athenians. We see more to admire, and less to condemn, in that great, extraordinary people, than in any thing which history affords.

Mr. Burke is so little acquainted with constituent principles of government, that he confounds democracy and representation together. Representation was a thing unknown in the ancient democracies. In those the mass of the people met and enacted laws (grammatically speaking) in the first person.

Simple democracy was no other than the common hall of the ancients. It signifies the *form*, as well as the public principle of the government. As these democracies increased in population, and the territory extended, the simple democratical form became unwieldy and impracticable; and as the system of representation was not known, the consequence was, they either degenerated convulsively into monarchies, or became absorbed into such as then existed.

Had the system of representation been then understood, as it now is, there is no reason to believe that those forms of government, now called monarchical and aristocratical, would ever have taken place. It was the want of some method to consolidate the parts of society, after it became too populous, and too extensive for the simple democratical form, and also the lax and solitary condition of shepherds and herdsmen in other parts of the world, that afforded opportunities to begin.

As it is necessary to clear away the rubbish of errors, into which the subject of government has been thrown, I shall proceed to remark on some others.

It has always been the political craft of courtiers and court-governments, to abuse something which they called republicanism; but what republicanism was, or is, they never attempt to explain. Let us examine a little into this case.

The only forms of government are, the democratical, the aristocratical, the monarchical, and what is now called the representative.

What is called a *republic*, is not any *particular form* of government. It is wholly characteristical of the purport, matter, or object for which government ought to be instituted, and on which it is to be employed, *res-publica*, the public affairs, or the public good; or, literally translated, the *public thing*.

It is a word of a good original, referring to what ought to be the character and business of government; and in this sense it is naturally opposed to the word *monarchy*, which has a base original signification. It means arbitrary power in an individual person; in the exercise of which, *himself*, and not the *res-publica*, is the object.

Every government that does not act on the principle of a *republic*, or in other words, that does not make the *res-publica* its whole and sole object, is not a good government. Republican government is no other than government established and conducted for the interest of the public, as well individually as collectively. It is not necessarily connected with any particular form, but it most naturally associates with the representative form, as being best calculated to secure the end for which a nation is at the expense of supporting it.

Various forms of government have affected to style themselves a republic. Poland calls itself a republic, which is an hereditary aristocracy, with what is called an elective monarchy. Holland calls itself a republic which is chiefly aristocratical, with an hereditary stadt-holdership.

But the government of America, which is wholly on the system of representation, is the only real republic in character and practise, that now exists. Its government has no other object than the public business of the nation, and therefore it is properly a republic; and the Americans have taken care that *this*, and no other, shall always be the object of the government, by their rejecting everything hereditary, and establishing government on the system of representation only.

Those who have said that a republic is not a *form* of government calculated for countries of great extent, mistook, in the first place, the *business* of a government for a *form* of government; for the *res-publica* equally appertains to every extent of territory and population. And, in the second place, if they meant any thing with respect to *form*, it was the simple democratical form, such as was the mode of government in the ancient democracies, in which there was no representation. The case therefore, is not, that a republic cannot be extensive, but that it cannot be extensive on the simple democratical form; and the question naturally presents itself, *What is the best form of government for conducting the* RESPUBLICA, *or the* PUBLIC BUSINESS *of a nation, after it becomes too extensive and populous for the simple democratical form?*

It cannot be monarchy, because monarchy is subject to an objection of the same amount to which the simple democratical form was subject.

It is possible that an individual may lay down a system of principles, on which government shall be constitutionally established to any extent of territory. This is no more than an operation of the mind, acting by its own powers. But the practise upon those principles, as applying to the various and numerous circumstances of a nation, its agriculture, manufacture, trade, commerce, etc., requires a knowledge of a different kind, and which can be had only from the various parts of society.

It is an assemblage of practical knowledge, which no one individual can possess; and therefore the monarchical form is as much limited, in useful practise, from the incompetency of knowledge, as was the democratical form, from the multiplying of population. The one degenerates, by extension, into confusion; the other, into ignorance and incapacity, of which all the great monarchies are an evidence. The monarchical form, therefore, could not be a substitute for the democratical, because it has equal inconveniences.

Much less could it when made hereditary. This is the most effectual of all forms to preclude knowledge. Neither could the high democratical mind have voluntarily yielded itself to be governed by children and idiots, and all the motley insignificance of character, which attends such a mere animal system, the disgrace and the reproach of reason and of man.

As to the aristocratical form, it has the same vices and defects with the monarchical, except that the chance of abilities is better from the proportion of numbers, but there is still no security for the right use and application of them.

Referring, then, to the original simple democracy, it affords the true data from which government on a large scale can begin. It is incapable of extension, not from its principle, but from the inconvenience of its form; and monarchy and aristocracy, from their incapacity. Retaining, then, democracy as the ground, and rejecting the corrupt systems of monarchy and aristocracy, the representative system naturally presents itself; remedying at once the defects of the simple democracy as to form, and the incapacity of the other two with respect to knowledge.

Simple democracy was society governing itself without the aid of secondary means. By ingrafting representation upon democracy, we arrive at a system of government capable of embracing and confederating all the various interests and every extent of territory and population; and that also with advantages as much superior to hereditary government, as the republic of letters is to hereditary literature.

It is on this system that the American government is founded. It is representation ingrafted upon democracy. It has fixed the form by a scale parallel in all cases to the extent of the principle. What Athens was in miniature, America will be in magnitude. The one was the wonder of the ancient world; the other is becoming the admiration and model of the present. It is the easiest of all the forms of government to be understood, and the most eligible in practise; and excludes at once the ignorance and insecurity of the hereditary mode, and the inconvenience of the simple democracy.

It is impossible to conceive a system of government capable of acting over such an extent of territory, and such a circle of interests, as is immediately produced by the operation of representation. France, great and popular as it is, is but a spot in the capaciousness of the system. It adapts itself to all possible cases. It is preferable to simple democracy even in small territories. Athens, by representation, would have outrivalled her own democracy.

That which is called government, or rather that which we ought to conceive government to be, is no more than some common center, in which all the parts of society unite. This cannot be accomplished by any method so conducive to the various interests of the community, as by the representative system.

It concentrates the knowledge necessary to the interests of the parts, and of the whole. It places government in a state of constant maturity. It is, as has been already observed, never young, never old. It is subject neither to nonage, nor dotage. It is never in the cradle, nor on crutches. It admits not of a separation between knowledge and power, and is superior, as government always ought to be, to all the accidents of individual man, and is therefore superior to what is called monarchy.

A nation is not a body, the figure of which is to be represented by the human body; but is like a body contained within a circle, having a common center, in which every radius meets; and that center is formed by representation. To connect representation with what is called monarchy is eccentric government. Representation is of itself the delegated monarchy of a nation, and cannot debase itself by dividing it with another.

Mr. Burke has two or three times, in his parliamentary speeches, and in his publications, made use of a jingle of words that convey no ideas. Speaking of government, he says, "it is better to have monarchy for its basis, and republicanism for its corrective, than republicanism for its basis, and monarchy for its corrective." If he means that it is better to correct folly with wisdom, than wisdom with folly, I will not otherwise contend with him, than that it would be much better to reject the folly entirely.

But what is this thing that Mr. Burke calls monarchy? Will he explain it? All men can understand what representation is; and that it must necessarily include a variety of knowledge and talents. But what security is there for the same qualities on the part of monarchy? Or, when this monarchy is a child, where then is the wisdom? What does it know about government? Who then is the monarch, or where is the monarchy? If it is to be performed by regency, it proves to be a farce.

A regency is a mock species of republic, and the whole of monarchy deserves no better description. It is a thing as various as imagination can paint. It has none of the stable character that government ought to possess. Every succession is a revolution, and every regency a counter-revolution. The whole of it is a scene of perpetual court cabal and intrigue, of which Mr. Burke is himself an instance.

To render monarchy consistent with government, the next in succession should not be born a child, but a man at once, and that man a Solomon. It is ridiculous that nations are to wait, and government be interrupted, till boys grow to be men.

Whether I have too little sense to see, or too much to be imposed upon; whether I have too much or too little pride, or of anything else, I leave out of the question; but certain it is, that what is called monarchy, always appears to me a silly, contemptible thing. I compare it to something kept behind a curtain, about which there is a great deal of bustle and fuss, and a wonderful air of seeming solemnity; but when, by any accident, the curtain happens to open, and the company see what it is, they burst into laughter.

In the representative system of government, nothing of this can happen. Like the nation itself, it possesses a perpetual stamina, as well of body as of mind, and presents itself on the open theater of the world in a fair and manly manner. Whatever are its excellencies or its defects, they are visible to all. It exists not by fraud and mystery; it deals not in cant and sophistry; but inspires a language, that, passing from heart to heart, is felt and understood.

We must shut our eyes against reason, we must basely degrade our understanding, not to see the folly of what is called monarchy. Nature is orderly in all her works; but this is a mode of government that counteracts nature. It turns the progress of the human faculties upside down. It subjects age to be governed by children, and wisdom by folly. On the contrary, the representative system is always parallel with the order and immutable laws of nature, and meets the reason of man in every part. For example:

In the American Federal Government, more power is delegated to the President of the United States, than to any other individual member of Congress.[1] He cannot, therefore, be elected to this office under the age of thirty-five years. By this time the judgment of man becomes matured, and he has lived long enough to be acquainted with men and things, and the country with him.

But on the monarchial plan, (exclusive of the numerous chances there are against every man born into the world, of drawing a prize in the lottery of human faculties), the next in succession, whatever he may be, is put at the head of a nation, and of a government, at the age of eighteen years.

Does this appear like an act of wisdom? Is it consistent with the proper dignity and the manly character of a nation? Where is the propriety of calling such a lad the father of the people? In all other

[1] In the early days of our Republic, it was customary in Europe, especially in England, to designate the President as the "President of Congress."

cases, a person is a minor until the age of twenty-one years. Before
this period, he is not trusted with the management of an acre of land,
or with the heritable property of a flock of sheep, or an herd of swine;
but, wonderful to tell! he may, at the age of eighteen years, be trusted
with a nation.

That monarchy is all a bubble, a mere court artifice to procure
money, is evident (at least to me), in every character in which it can
be viewed. It would be impossible, on the rational system of representative government, to make out a bill of expenses to such an
enormous amount as this deception admits. Government is not of
itself a very chargeable institution. The whole expense of the Federal
Government of America, founded, as I have already said, on the
system of representation, and extending over a country nearly ten
times as large as England, is but six hundred thousand dollars, or one
hundred and thirty thousand pounds sterling.

I presume, that no man in his sober senses will compare the character of any of the kings of Europe with that of General Washington.
Yet, in France, and also in England, the expense of the civil list only,
for the support of one man, is eight times greater than the whole
expense of the Federal Government in America. To assign a reason
for this, appears almost impossible. The generality of people in
America, especially the poor, are more able to pay taxes, than the
generality of people either in France or England. But the case is,
that the representative system diffuses such a body of knowledge
throughout a nation, on the subject of government, as to explode
ignorance and preclude imposition. The craft of courts cannot be
acted on that ground. There is no place for mystery; nowhere for it
to begin. Those who are not in the representation, know as much
of the nature of business as those who are. An affectation of mysterious
importance would there be scouted. Nations can have no secrets; and
the secrets of courts, like those of individuals, are always their defects.

In the representative system, the reason for everything must publicly appear. Every man is a proprietor in government and considers
it a necessary part of his business to understand. It concerns his
interest, because it affects his property. He examines the cost, and
compares it with the advantages; and above all, he does not adopt the
slavish custom of following what in other governments are called
LEADERS.

It can only be by blinding the understanding of man, and making
him believe that government is some wonderful mysterious thing, that
excessive revenues are obtained. Monarchy is well calculated to ensure
this end. It is the popery of government; a thing kept up to amuse the
ignorant, and quiet them into paying taxes.

The government of a free country, properly speaking, is not in the persons, but in the laws. The enacting of those requires no great expense; and when they are administered, the whole of civil government is performed — the rest is all court contrivance.

⚶ Joel Barlow (1754–1812)

JOEL BARLOW, the son of a Connecticut farmer, graduated from Yale in 1778, taught school, studied law, and harbored an ambition to write the great American epic. He tried twice — in *The Vision of Columbus* (1787), later revised as *The Columbiad* (1807) — without much success. In 1788 he went to London and to France, beginning a seventeen-year stay abroad, during which time he was caught up in the great tide of revolutionary thought and activity then flooding England and Europe. For his *Letter to the National Convention of France* (1792) he was made an honorary citizen of France. His inflammatory poem *The Conspiracy of Kings* (1792) placed him under the suspicion of the British authorities. His *Advice to the Privileged Orders,* published in England in 1792, less than a year after his friend Paine published the first part of *The Rights of Man,* was so effective that it was suppressed and Barlow was forced to flee to France for haven. He ran for office in France in 1793, but lost.

Barlow made a substantial fortune trading in France, and in 1795 was appointed United States Consul at Algiers, where he did excellent diplomatic work in representing American interests during the troubles with the Barbary pirates. Returning to the United States in 1805, he lived quietly until President Madison appointed him minister to France in 1811. Barlow hoped to secure a treaty between France and the United States, and after some difficult negotiations it was arranged that Napoleon would meet him somewhere in Poland during the Russian campaign. But the Emperor was soon caught up in the disastrous retreat from Moscow, and Barlow, who had traveled to Cracow to meet him, died from a sudden illness.

Barlow's *Advice* is a powerful attack on the remnants of feudalism and aristocracy in British and European governments, and an eloquent exposition of the principle that the state is the guardian of the people's rights, rather than simply the protector of property. Like Paine's *Rights of Man,* it is essentially a reply to Edmund Burke's *Reflections on the French Revolution.*

TEXTS: Joel Barlow, *Advice to the Privileged Orders in the Several States of Europe* . . . (London, 1794). Letter to Cheetham, from E. C. Stedman and E. M. Hutchinson, *A Library of American Literature* (New York, 1889–90), IV, 56–57.

American Liberty and Equality

[From *Advice to the Privileged Orders*, 1792]

Whether men are born to govern, or to obey, or to enjoy equal liberty, depends not on the original capacity of the mind, but on the instinct of analogy, or the habit of thinking. When children of the same family are taught to believe in the unconquerable distinctions of birth among themselves, they are completely fitted for a feudal government; because their minds are familiarized with all the gradations and degradations that such a government requires. The birthright of domineering is not more readily claimed on the one hand, than it is acknowledged on the other; and the Jamaica planter is not more habitually convinced that an European is superior to an African, than he is that a Lord is better than himself.

This subject deserves to be placed in a light in which no writer, as far as I know, has yet considered it. When a person was repeating to Fontenelle the common adage, Habit is the second nature, the philosopher replied, And do me the favor to tell me which is the first. When we assert that nature has established inequalities among men, and has thus given to some the right of governing others, or when we maintain the contrary of this position, we should be careful to define what sort of nature we mean, whether the first or second nature; or whether we mean that there is but one. A mere savage, Colocolo for instance, would decide the question of equality by a trial of bodily strength, designating the man that could lift the heaviest beam to be the legislator; and unless all men could lift the same beam, they could not be equal in their rights. Aristotle would give the preference to him that excelled in mental capacity. Ulysses would make the decision upon a compound ratio of both. But there appears to me another step in this ladder, and that the habit of thinking is the only safe and universal criterion to which, in practice, the question can be referred. Indeed, when interest is laid aside, it is the only one to which, in civilized ages, it ever is referred. We never submit to a King because he is stronger than we in bodily force, nor because he is superior in understanding or in information; but because we believe him born to govern, or at least, because a majority of the society believes it.

This habit of thinking has so much of nature in it, it is so undistinguishable from the indelible marks of the man, that it is a perfectly safe foundation for any system that we may choose to build upon it; indeed it is the only foundation, for it is the only point of contact by which men communicate as moral associates. As a practical position therefore, and as relating to almost all places and almost all times, in which the experiment has yet been made, Aristotle was as right in teaching, That some are born to command, and others to be commanded, as the National Assembly was in declaring, That men are born and always continue free and equal in respect to their rights. The latter is as apparently false in the diet of Ratisbon, as the former is in the hall of the Jacobins.

Abstractly considered, there can be no doubt of the unchangeable truth of the assembly's declaration; and they have taken the right method to make it a practical truth, by publishing it to the world for discussion. A general belief that it is a truth, makes it at once practical, confirms it in one nation, and extends it to others.

A due attention to the astonishing effects that are wrought in the world by the habit of thinking, will serve many valuable purposes. I cannot therefore dismiss the subject as soon as I intended; but will mention one or two influences of these effects, and leave the reflection of the reader to make application to a thousand others.

First, it is evident that all arbitrary systems in the world are founded and supported on this second nature of man, in counteraction of the first. Systems which distort and crush and subjugate every thing that we can suppose original and characteristic in man, as an undistorted being. It sustains the most absurd and abominable theories of religion, and honors them with as many martyrs as it does those that are the most peaceful and beneficent.

But secondly, we find for our consolation, that it will likewise support systems of equal liberty and national happiness. In the United States of America, the science of liberty is universally understood, felt, and practiced, as much by the simple as the wise, the weak as the strong. Their deep-rooted and inveterate habit of thinking is, that all men are equal in their rights, that it is impossible to make them otherwise; and this being their undisturbed belief, they have no conception how any man in his senses can entertain any other. This point once settled, every thing is settled. Many operations, which in Europe have been considered as incredible tales or dangerous experiments, are but the infallible consequences of this great principle. The first of these operations is the business of election, which with that people is carried on with as much gravity as their daily labor. There is no jealousy on the occasion, nothing lucrative in office; any man in society may attain to any place in the government, and may exercise its functions. They believe that there is nothing more difficult in the management of the affairs of a nation than the affairs of a family, that it only requires more hands. They believe that it is the juggle of keeping up impositions to blind the eyes of the vulgar, that constitutes the intricacy of state. Banish the mysticism of inequality, and you banish almost all the evils attendant on human nature.

The people, being habituated to the election of all kinds of officers, the magnitude of the office makes no difficulty in the case. The president of the United States, who has more power while in office than some of the kings of Europe, is chosen with as little commotion as a churchwarden. There is a public service to be performed, and the people say who shall do it. The servant feels honored with the confidence reposed in him, and generally expresses his gratitude by a faithful performance.

Another of these operations is making every citizen a soldier, and every soldier a citizen; not only permitting every man to arm, but obliging him to arm. This fact, told in Europe previous to the French revolution, would have gained little credit; or at least it would have been regarded as a mark of an uncivilized people, extremely dangerous to a well ordered society. Men who build systems on an inversion of nature are obliged to invert every thing that is to make part of that system. It is because the people are civilized that they are safely armed. It is an effect of their conscious dignity, as citizens enjoying equal rights, that they wish not to invade the rights of others. The danger (where there is any) from armed citizens is only to the government, not to the society; and as long as they have nothing to revenge in the government (which they cannot have while it is in their own hands), there are many advantages in their being accustomed to the use of arms, and no possible disadvantage.

Power, habitually in the hands of a whole community, loses all the ordinary associated ideas of power. The exercise of power is a relative term; it supposes an opposition, — something to operate upon. We perceive no exertion of power in the motion of the planetary system, but a very strong one in the movement of a whirlwind; it is because we see obstructions to the latter, but none to the former. Where the government is not in the hands of the people, there you find opposition, you perceive two contending interests, and get an idea of the exercise of power; and whether this power be in the hands of the government or of the people, or whether it change from side to side, it is always to be dreaded. But the word *people,* in America, has a different meaning from what it has in Europe. It there means the whole community and comprehends every human creature; here it means something else, more difficult to define.

Another consequence of the habitual idea of equality is the facility of changing the structure of their government, whenever and as often as the society shall think there is any thing in it to amend. As Mr. Burke has written no "reflections on the revolution" in America, the people there have never yet been told that they have no right "to frame a government for themselves"; they have therefore done much in this business without ever affixing to it the idea of "sacrilege" or "usurpation," or any other term of rant to be found in that gentleman's vocabulary.

Within a few years the fifteen states have not only framed each its own state-constitution and two successive federal constitutions, but since the settlement of the present general government in the year 1789, three of the states, Pennsylvania, South Carolina, and Georgia, have totally new-modeled their own. And all this is done without the least confusion, the operation being scarcely known beyond the limits of the state where it is performed. Thus they are in the habit of "choosing their own governors," of "cashiering them for misconduct," of "framing a government for themselves," and all those abominable things, the mere naming of which, in Mr. Burke's opinion, has polluted the pulpit in the Old Jewry.

But it is said, These things will do very well for America where the people are less numerous, less indigent, and better instructed; but they will not apply to Europe. This objection deserves a reply, not because it is solid, but because it is fashionable. It may be answered, that some parts of Spain, much of Poland, and almost the whole of Russia, are less peopled than the settled country in the United States; that poverty and ignorance are effects of slavery rather than its causes; but the best answer to be given is the example of France. To the event of that revolution I will trust the argument. Let the people have time to become thoroughly and soberly grounded in the doctrine of equality, and there is no danger of oppression either from government or from anarchy. Very little instruction is necessary to teach a man his rights; and there is no person of common intellect, in the most ignorant corner of Europe, but receives lessons enough, if they were of the proper kind. For writing and reading are not indispensable to the object; it is thinking right which makes them act right. Every child is taught to repeat about fifty Latin prayers, which set up the Pope, the Bishop, and the King, as the trinity of his adoration; he is taught that the powers that be are ordained of God, and therefore the soldier quartered in the parish has a right to cut his throat. Half this instruction, upon opposite principles, would go a great way; in that case, nature would be assisted, while here [in Europe] she is counteracted. Engrave it on the heart of a man, that all men are equal in rights, and that the government is their own, and then persuade him to sell his crucifix and buy a musket, — and you have made him a good citizen.

Another consequence of a settled belief in the equality of rights is that under this belief there is no danger from anarchy. This word has likewise acquired a different meaning in America from what we read of it in books. In Europe it means confusion, attended with mobs and carnage, where the innocent perish with the guilty. But [it] is very different where a country is used to a representative government, though it should have an interval of no government at all. Where the people at large feel and know that they can do everything by themselves personally, they really do nothing by themselves personally. In the heat of the American revolution, when the people in some states were for a long time without the least shadow of law or government, they always acted by committees and representation. This they must call anarchy, for they know no other.

These are materials for the formation of governments, which need not be dreaded, though disjointed and laid asunder to make some repairs. They are deep-rooted habits of thinking, which almost change the moral nature of man; they are principles as much unknown to the ancient republics as to the modern monarchies of Europe.

We must not therefore rely upon systems drawn from the experimental reasonings of Aristotle, when we find them contradicted by what we feel to be the eternal truth of nature, and see them brought to the test of our own experience. Aristotle was certainly a great politician; and Claudius Ptolemy was a great geographer; but the latter has said not a word of America, the largest quarter of the globe; nor the former, of representative republics, the resource of afflicted humanity.

The Character and Genius of Thomas Paine

[Letter to James Cheetham of New York, 1809]

SIR: I have received your letter calling for information relative to the life of Thomas Paine. It appears to me that this is not the moment to publish the life of that man in this country. His own writings are his best life, and these are not read at present. The greater part of readers in the United States will not be persuaded as long as their present feelings last to consider him in any other light than as a drunkard and a deist. The writer of his life who should dwell on these topics to the exclusion of the great and estimable traits of his real character might indeed please the rabble of the age, who do not know him; the book might sell, but it would only tend to render the truth more obscure for the future biographer than it was before. But if the present writer should give us Thomas Paine complete in all his character, as one of the most benevolent and disinterested of mankind, endowed with the clearest perception, an uncommon share of original genius, and the greatest breadth of thought; if this piece of biography should analyze his literary labors, and rank him, as he ought to be ranked, among the brightest and most undeviating luminaries of the age in which he has lived, yet with a mind assailable by flattery and receiving through that weak side a tincture of vanity which he was too proud to conceal; with a mind, though strong enough to bear him up and to rise elastic under the heaviest hand of oppression, yet unable to endure the contempt of his former friends and fellow-laborers, the rulers of the country that had received his first and greatest services — a mind incapable of looking down with serene compassion as it ought on the rude scoffs of their imitators, a new generation that knew him not — a mind that shrinks from their society and unhappily seeks refuge in low company or looks for consolation in the sordid solitary bottle till it sink so far at last below its native elevation as to lose all respect for itself and to forfeit that of its best friends, disposing those friends almost to join with his enemies, and to wish, though from different motives, that he would venture to hide himself in the grave; if you are disposed and prepared to write his life thus entire, to fill up the picture, to which these hasty strokes of outline give but a rude sketch, with great vacuities, your book may be a useful one for another age, but it will not be relished nor scarcely tolerated in this.

The biographer of Thomas Paine should not forget his mathematical acquirements and his mechanical genius, his invention of the iron bridge, which led him to Europe in the year 1787, and which has procured him a great reputation in that branch of science in France and England — in both which countries his bridge has been adopted in many instances, and is now much in use. You ask whether he took the oath of allegiance to France. Doubtless the qualifications to be a member of the Convention required an oath of fidelity to that country, but involved in it no abjuration of fidelity to this. He was made a French citizen by the same decree with Washington, Hamilton, Priestley, and Sir James Mackintosh. What Mr. M. has told you relative to the circumstances of his arrestation by order of Robespierre is erroneous, at least in one point. Paine did not lodge at the house where he was arrested, but had been dining there with some Americans, of whom Mr. M. may have been one. I never heard before that Paine was intoxicated that night. Indeed, the officers brought him directly to my house, which was two miles from his lodging, and doubtless far from the place where he had been dining. He was not intoxicated when they came to me. Their object was to get me to go and assist them to examine Paine's papers. It employed us the whole of that night and the rest of the next day at Paine's lodgings, and he was not committed to prison till the next evening. You ask what company he kept. He always frequented the best, both in England and France, till he became the object of calumny in certain American papers (echoes of the English court papers) for his adherence to what he thought the cause of liberty in France; till he conceived himself neglected and despised by his former friends in the United States. From that moment he gave himself very much to drink, and consequently to companions less worthy of his better days. It is said he was always a peevish ingrate. This is possible. So was Laurence Sterne, so was Torquato Tasso, so was J. J. Rousseau. But Thomas Paine as a visiting acquaintance and as a literary friend, the only points of view in which I knew him, was one of the most instructive men I have ever known. He had a surprising memory and a brilliant fancy; his mind was a storehouse of vast and useful observation. He was full of lively anecdotes and ingenious original pertinent remarks upon almost every subject. He was always charitable to the poor beyond his means, a sure protector and friend to all Americans in distress that he found in foreign countries. And he had frequent occasion to exert his influence in protecting them during the Revolution in France. His writings will answer for his patriotism and his entire devotion to what he conceived to be the best interest and happiness of mankind.

This, sir, is all I have to remark on the subject you mention now. I have only one request to make, and that would doubtless seem impertinent were you not the editor of a newspaper. It is that you will not publish this letter nor permit a copy of it to be taken.

JOEL BARLOW.

⤳ Ezra Stiles (1727–1795)

AFTER his graduation from Yale in 1746, Ezra Stiles was appointed tutor, and he remained concerned with the college in one way or another for the rest of his many-sided life. He studied theology, was ordained, and kept up an active parish life. An excellent mathematician and astronomer, he was a lifelong friend and correspondent of Franklin and a contributing member of the American Philosophical Society. He also studied law and was admitted to the bar; later, in middle age, desiring to improve his Biblical scholarship, he learned Arabic, Hebrew, and Syriac in addition to his already excellent Greek and Latin. Appointed president of Yale in 1778, he was a staunch advocate of the revolutionary cause and an articulate supporter of the war.

In this excerpt from one of his numerous historical-theological works, President Stiles hails and justifies the prevailing revolutionary spirit and predicts a world-wide revolt against tyranny and injustice, sparked by the American and French examples. His view of the popular majority, factions, and public trust apparently lay closer to Jefferson's than to Madison's or Adams'.

TEXT: Ezra Stiles, A History of Three of the Judges of King Charles I (Hartford, 1794).

The Values of Revolutionary Societies

[From A *History of Three of the Judges of King Charles I*, 1794]

Monarchies contemplate Jacobin societies with horror and dread, and this with great reason. They need not be so viewed by republics. The Jacobin societies have proved the salvation of France. They have been the bulwark of liberty. Their excesses are to be coerced by government; but their suppression and extinction is unnecessary and impossible. "The popular societies are the columns of the revolution — They shall not be shaken," said president Cambeceres. Violent and unjust in many things though they may be, and sometimes are, congresses, assemblies, and parliaments [are] not therefore to be dissolved, for they may be generally right. Would it be wise to wish the extinction of the winds, which are salutary and beneficial for navigation and for clarifying the atmosphere, because sometimes attended with hurricanes? They may be set up against a good government indeed, but their efforts against it must ultimately be inefficacious and harmless. Because they sometimes succeed in overthrowing a tyranny, will it follow that there is even a possibility of these societies succeeding against a good policy? The experiment is yet to be made. Hitherto there has existed no good polity to try them upon. In the nature of things they will become self-correctors of their own irregularities and excesses; and the harmonization of the public sentiment must result from their diffusive deliberations.

Now the strength of a general and uniform support to the administration of a good policy must arise [from revolutionary societies]. Their discussions, circulation of intelligence, and communication of light, must eventually form, digest and unify the national judgment. None but tyrants need fear them. The national convention has not feared them, but rejoined their support. Congress in 1775 did not fear the body of the people in America, though sometimes wild and anarchical. A policy which shall have sustained their ventilation and discussion, will be firm. The end being answered, and the care of the public consigned into the hands of constitutional government, these societies will spontaneously disappear; nor rise again unless called forth on great occasions worthy [of] their attention.

I have said that men would judge of historical events according as they are principles in politics. Monarchies of all modes are contemplated with a suspicious eye, by communities at large; which in their turn contemplate republics, of any and almost every form, with attention and pleasure. There was once a time, and it is not yet past, when the sovereigns of Europe could not contemplate but with horror and disgust, the Prince of Orange and Holland, dissolving their feudal submission to their lord paramount; the revolt of the house of Braganza from Spain; the more recent erection of the federated kingdom of Prussia; or the self-created republics of Switzerland, and the United States. But all these examples come into operative and efficacious view in the present age; and are contemplated with sympathetic consolation by states struggling with the tyranny of kings.

Self-erected sovereignties, whether monarchical or republican, bid fair for considerable duration; while popular societies are either defeated, or go to rest in course, when their end is accomplished. Their coerced extinction would prove fatal to liberty and the rights of man, as the forcible suppression or extinction of letters or the liberty of the press. Both ever have done, and ever will do, much mischief; both do infinitely more good; both are the combined conservators of the public liberty, in philosophy, religion, politics. They are excellently adapted to frame the public mind to wisdom, and to an acquiescence founded in diffusive conviction and reformation of that wherein consists the public interest, the general welfare of society. There is no alternative between their right to assemble, and the abolition of liberty.

If the popular societies sometimes err, it is not always, it is not usually from malicious and inimical views, but from defective and partial information among the best disposed for the public good —, or, as I have said, from tories which covertly, insidiously, and unawares infer themselves as marplots. If well informed, it is impossible the community at large can be inimical to the public good. Enough of this general disposition for the public good can be found in every community to counteract and nullify the injuries of faction. And the common people will generally judge right, when duly informed. The general liberty is safe and secure in their hands. It is not from deficiency of abilities to judge, but from want of information, if they at any time as a body go wrong. Upon information from an abundance of enlightened characters always intermixt among them, they will ultimately always judge right, and be in the end the faithful guardians and support and security of government. Nothing will kill a faction, like the body of a people if consulted. A faction may beat a faction, at a pretty fair and even conflict; but in a fair and full contest, it can never beat the people. The great art of factions is to keep the decision from the body of the people. But let a matter be fairly brought before the people, and they will not only determine it, but will judge and determine it right. It is the insidious art of parties and politicians to keep things concealed from the people, or if they are alarmed and assemble, to excite parties, sow dissensions, and prevent as much as possible the question from coming up fair before them, instead of harmoniously endeavoring in a fair, open and candid manner to lay things clearly before them, and thus honestly endeavoring to form and obtain the public mind. And thus they ever attempt, and are too successful at deceiving, instead of a frank and open appeal to the people.

But shall this cunning prevail forever? Politicians, with too much reason, say it will. I, who am no politician but a prophet, say it will not. Almost all the civil polities on earth stand before a well formed system of revolutionary societies. Those of France and the United States will sustain them without injury or aversion. The reformation of all others, must commence in associations which by governments will be considered and treated as factionary and treasonable, but will enlarge and spread into a system of revolutionary societies. In all states these will be frowned upon, and suppressed as treasonable. Their suppression and persecution will pour oil on the flame. They will burst out again and again till they carry all before them, till revolution shall be accurately defined not to the sense of aristocrats or the present usurped reigning powers, but to the general sense of the community. And such a law of treason will be infallibly supported by the community. Thus done, every association will know what it may, and may not do, with impunity. Till this is done, the spirit of enlightened liberty is become so great, and so ready to burst forth under oppressive and intolerable irritations, that it will risk all consequences, until all present polities shall be fairly brought to the tribunal of public sense. Then no one can doubt the result.

Factionary societies begun even with the primary and direct design of overturning government, if the government or polity be supported by the general sense, will fail; otherwise they will bring on and adduce at length extensive discussions which enlighten the public, defeat insidious and partial cunning, and bring forward an open and firm support of good and acceptable government. Should they at any time surrender, or duped and outwitted by counter factions, be prevailed upon to betray the public liberty, the community will deserve slavery a little longer, until again aroused to energy, unity, and wisdom. Thus England has now for a century been suffering a national punishment or chastisement, brought upon them by their own folly, for being duped by the insidious cavalier faction, which overturned the happy constitution of Oliver's republican polity. When at length brought to their senses and a conviction of their national folly, they will break out and burst forth with united and irresistible vigor, and recover and rectify themselves. The French have for ages been duped by court factions, but have at length recovered their natural rights and liberties, by a voluntary, united, bold, and daring exertion, by an effort which makes all Europe tremble. So it will be in England. . . .

The polities of all the European nations are become so radically corrupt and oppressive, that the welfare of mankind requires that they should all be renovated. This would be best for human society. Why should despotism and oppression be entailed to subsequent generations? Why is it not just that the ages of tyranny should be succeeded by ages of liberty? Under the obstinate and persevering opposition of the reigning powers this emancipation cannot be made but by the people. This must commence, as I have said, in popular societies, connected, spreading, and growing up into a general popular exertion. If oppression occasions their rise, they must take their fate. The enterprise is arduous, but combined national enthusiasm in the cause of liberty is of great and awful force. All Europe is ripening with celerity for a great revolution; the era is commencing of a *general revolution*. The amelioration of human society must and will take place. It will be a conflict between Kings and their subjects. This war of Kings, like that of Gog and Magog, will be terrible. It will, for there is no other way, it will commence and originate in voluntary associations among subjects in all kingdoms. Eluded supplications and petitions for liberty, will be followed by armaments for the vindication of the rights of human nature. The public ardor will be kindled, and a natural spirit and exertion aroused, which undiscouraged, unsubdued by many defeats, will ultimately carry all away before it.

George Washington (1732–1799)

WASHINGTON used his last official utterance as the occasion to speak to the American people on the problem of maintaining national unity in time of stress and strain. He was especially concerned with the issue of American neutrality in the French Revolution and with the dangers of becoming involved in the embroilments and bickerings of an unsettled Europe. His speech is easily misinterpreted, if taken out of context, to mean a policy of blind isolationism; instead, Washington was explaining to the people that, by avoiding foreign entanglements, the nation could best maintain its independence, consolidate its position among nations, and gain the time it needed for adjustment and growth. He also warned of the dangers of factional bitterness and self-interest, of the need for a strong union and central government to guard against internal unrest, of the necessity for unity and stability. Though Hamilton and Madison wrote portions of the Address, the views are Washington's.

TEXT: John C. Fitzpatrick, ed., *The Writings of George Washington* (Washington, 1931–44), XXXV, 214–238.

Farewell Address
to the People of the United States
[September 17, 1796]

Friends, and Fellow-Citizens: The period for a new election of a Citizen, to Administer the Executive government of the United States, being not far distant, and the time actually arrived, when your thoughts must be employed in designating the person, who is to be cloathed with that important trust, it appears to me proper, especially as it may conduce to a more distinct expression of the public voice, that I should now apprise you of the resolution I have formed, to decline being considered among the number of those, out of whom a choice is to be made.

I beg you, at the same time, to do me the justice to be assured, that this resolution has not been taken, without a strict regard to all the considerations appertaining to the relation, which binds a dutiful citizen to his country, and that, in with drawing the tender of service which silence in my situation might imply, I am influenced by no diminution of zeal for your future interest, no deficiency of grateful respect for your past kindness; but am supported by a full conviction that the step is compatible with both.

The acceptance of, and continuance hitherto in, the office to which your Suffrages have twice called me, have been a uniform sacrifice of inclination to the opinion of duty, and to a deference for what appeared to be your desire. I constantly hoped, that it would have been much earlier in my power, consistently with motives, which I was not at liberty to disregard, to return to that retirement, from which I had been reluctantly drawn. The strength of my inclination to do this, previous to the last Election, had even led to the preparation of an address to declare it to you; but mature reflection on the then perplexed and critical posture of our Affairs with foreign Nations, and the unanimous advice of persons entitled to my confidence, impelled me to abandon the idea.

I rejoice, that the state of your concerns, external as well as internal, no longer renders the pursuit of inclination incompatible with the sentiment of duty, or propriety; and am persuaded whatever partiality may be retained for my services, that in the present circumstances of our country, you will not disapprove my determination to retire.

The impressions, with which I first undertook the arduous trust, were explained on the proper occasion. In the discharge of this trust, I will only say, that I have, with good intentions, contributed towards the Organization and Administration of the government, the best exertions of which a very fallible judgment was capable. Not unconscious, in the outset, of the inferiority of my qualifications, experience in my own eyes, perhaps still more in the eyes of others, has strengthened the motives to diffidence of myself; and every day the increasing weight of years admonishes me more and more, that the shade of retirement is as necessary to me as it will be welcome. Satisfied that if any circumstances have given peculiar value to my services, they were temporary, I have the consolation to believe, that while choice and prudence invite me to quit the political scene, patriotism does not forbid it.

In looking forward to the moment, which is intended to terminate the career of my public life, my feelings do not permit me to suspend the deep acknowledgment of that debt of gratitude which I owe to my beloved country, for the many honors it has conferred upon me; still more for the stedfast confidence with which it has supported me; and for the opportunities I have thence enjoyed of manifesting my inviolable attachment, by services faithful and persevering, though in usefulness unequal to my zeal. If benefits have resulted to our country from these services, let it always be remembered to your praise, and as an instructive example in our annals, that, under circumstances in which the Passions agitated in every direction were liable to mislead, amidst appearances sometimes dubious, vicissitudes of fortune often discouraging, in situations in which not unfrequently want of Success has countenanced the spirit of criticism, the constancy of your support was the essential prop of the efforts, and a guarantee of the plans by which they were effected. Profoundly penetrated with this idea, I shall carry it with me to my grave, as a strong incitement to unceasing vows that Heaven may continue to you the choicest tokens of its beneficence; that your Union and brotherly affection may be perpetual; that the free constitution, which is the work of your hands, may be sacredly maintained; that its Administration in every department may be stamped with wisdom and Virtue; that, in fine, the happiness of the people of these States, under the auspices of liberty, may be made complete, by so careful a preservation and so prudent a use of this blessing as will acquire to them the glory of recommending it to the applause, the affection, and adoption of every nation which is yet a stranger to it.

Here, perhaps, I ought to stop. But a solicitude for your welfare, which cannot end but with my life, and the apprehension of danger, natural to that solicitude, urge me on an occasion like the present, to offer to your solemn contemplation, and to recommend to your frequent review, some sentiments; which are the result of much reflection, of no inconsiderable observation, and which appear to me all important to the permanency of your felicity as a People. These will be offered to you with the more freedom, as you can only see in them the disinterested warnings of a parting friend, who can possibly have no personal motive to bias his counsel. Nor can I forget, as an encouragement to it, your indulgent reception of my sentiments on a former and not dissimilar occasion.[1]

Interwoven as is the love of liberty with every ligament of your hearts, no recommendation of mine is necessary to fortify or confirm the attachment.

The Unity of Government which constitutes you one people is also now dear to you. It is justly so; for it is a main Pillar in the Edifice of your real independence, the support of your tranquillity at home; your peace abroad; of your safety; of your prosperity; of that very Liberty which you so highly prize. But as it is easy to foresee, that from different causes and from different quarters, much pains will be taken, many artifices employed, to weaken in your minds the conviction of this truth; as this is the point in your political fortress against which the batteries of internal and external enemies will be most constantly and actively (though often covertly and insidiously) directed, it is of infinite moment, that you should properly estimate the immense value of your national Union to your collective and individual happiness; that you should cherish a cordial, habitual and immoveable attachment to it; accustoming yourselves to think and speak of it as of the Palladium of your political safety and prosperity; watching for its preservation with jealous anxiety; discountenancing whatever may suggest even a suspicion that it can in any event be abandoned, and indignantly frowning upon the first dawning of every attempt to alienate any portion of our Country from the rest, or to enfeeble the sacred ties which now link together the various parts.

For this you have every inducement of sympathy and interest. Citizens by birth or choice, of a common country, that country has a right to concentrate your affections. The name of AMERICAN, which belongs to you, in your national capacity, must always exalt the just pride of Patriotism, more than any appellation derived from local discriminations. With slight shades of difference, you have the same Religion, Manners, Habits and political Principles. You have in a common cause fought and triumphed together. The independence and liberty you possess are the work of joint councils, and joint efforts; of common dangers, sufferings and successes.

But these considerations, however powerfully they address themselves to your sensibility, are greatly outweighed by those which apply more immediately to your Interest. Here every portion of our country finds the most commanding motives for carefully guarding and preserving the Union of the whole.

[1] On relinquishing his command of the Army.

The *North*, in an unrestrained intercourse with the *South*, protected by the equal Laws of a common government, finds in the productions of the latter, great additional resources of Maritime and commercial enterprise and precious materials of manufacturing industry. The *South* in the same Intercourse, benefitting by the Agency of the *North*, sees its agriculture grow and its commerce expand. Turning partly into its own channels the seamen of the *North*, it finds its particular navigation envigorated; and while it contributes, in different ways, to nourish and increase the general mass of the National navigation, it looks forward to the protection of a Maritime strength, to which itself is unequally adapted. The *East*, in a like intercourse with the *West*, already finds, and in the progressive improvement of interior communications, by land and water, will more and more find a valuable vent for the commodities which it brings from abroad, or manufactures at home. The *West* derives from the *East* supplies requisite to its growth and comfort, and what is perhaps of still greater consequence, it must of necessity owe the *secure* enjoyment of indispensable *outlets* for its own productions to the weight, influence, and the future Maritime strength of the Atlantic side of the Union, directed by an indissoluble community of Interest as *one Nation*. Any other tenure by which the *West* can hold this essential advantage, whether derived from its own separate strength, or from an apostate and unnatural connection with any foreign Power, must be intrinsically precarious.

While then every part of our country thus feels an immediate and particular Interest in Union, all the parts combined cannot fail to find in the united mass of means and efforts greater strength, greater resource, proportionably greater security from external danger, a less frequent interruption of their Peace by foreign Nations; and, what is of inestimable value! they must derive from Union an exemption from those broils and Wars between themselves, which so frequently afflict neighbouring countries, not tied together by the same government; which their own rivalships alone would be sufficient to produce, but which opposite foreign alliances, attachments and intrigues would stimulate and imbitter. Hence likewise they will avoid the necessity of those overgrown Military establishments, which under any form of Government are inauspicious to liberty, and which are to be regarded as particularly hostile to Republican Liberty. In this sense it is, that your Union ought to be considered as a main prop of your liberty, and that the love of the one ought to endear to you the preservation of the other.

These considerations speak a persuasive language to every reflecting and virtuous mind, and exhibit the continuance of the UNION as a primary object of Patriotic desire. Is there a doubt, whether a common government can embrace so large a sphere? Let experience solve it. To listen to mere speculation in such a case were criminal. We are authorized to hope that a proper organization of the whole, with the auxiliary agency of governments for the respective Subdivisions, will afford a happy issue to the experiment. 'Tis well worth a fair and full experiment. With such powerful and obvious motives to Union, affecting all parts of our country, while experience shall not have demonstrated its impracticability, there will always be reason, to distrust the patriotism of those, who in any quarter may endeavor to weaken its bands.

In contemplating the causes which may disturb our Union, it occurs as matter of serious concern, that any ground should have been furnished for characterizing parties by *Geographical* discriminations: *Northern* and *Southern; Atlantic* and *Western;* whence designing men may endeavor to excite a belief that there is a real difference of local interests and views. One of the expedients of Party to acquire influence, within particular districts, is to misrepresent the opinions and aims of other Districts. You cannot shield yourselves too much against the jealousies and heart burnings which spring from these misrepresentations. They tend to render Alien to each other those who ought to be bound together by fraternal affection. The Inhabitants of our Western country have lately had a useful lesson on this head. They have seen, in the Negociation by the Executive, and in the unanimous ratification by the Senate, of the Treaty with Spain, and in the universal satisfaction at that event, throughout the United States, a decisive proof how unfounded were the suspicions propagated among them of a policy in the General Government and in the Atlantic States unfriendly to their Interests in regard to the MISSISSIPPI. They have been witnesses to the formation of two Treaties, that with G: Britain and that with Spain, which secure to them every thing they could desire, in respect to our Foreign relations, towards confirming their prosperity. Will it not be their wisdom to rely for the preservation of these advantages on the UNION by which they were procured? Will they not henceforth be deaf to those advisers, if such there are, who would sever them from their Brethren and connect them with Aliens?

To the efficacy and permanency of Your Union, a Government for the whole is indispensable. No Alliances however strict between the parts can be an adequate substitute. They must inevitably experience the infractions and interruptions which all Alliances in all times have experienced. Sensible of this momentous truth, you have improved upon your first essay, by the adoption of a Constitution of Government, better calculated than your former for an intimate Union, and for the efficacious management of your common concerns. This government, the offspring of our own choice uninfluenced and unawed, adopted upon full investigation and mature deliberation, completely free in its principles, in the distribution of its powers, uniting security with energy, and containing within itself a provision for its own amendment, has a just claim to your confidence and your support. Respect for its authority, compliance with its Laws, acquiescence in its measures, are duties enjoined by the fundamental maxims of true Liberty. The basis of our political systems is the right of the people to make and to alter their Constitutions of Government. But the Constitution which at any time exists, 'till changed by an explicit and authentic act of the whole People, is sacredly obligatory upon all. The very idea of the power and the right of the People to establish Government presupposes the duty of every Individual to obey the established Government.

All obstructions to the execution of the Laws, all combinations and Associations, under whatever plausible character, with the real design to direct, control, counteract, or awe the regular deliberation and action of the Constituted authorities are destructive of this fundamental principle and of fatal tendency. They serve to organize faction, to give it an artificial and extraordinary force; to put in the place of the delegated will of the Nation, the will of a party; often a small but artful and enterprising minority of the Community; and, according to the alternate triumphs of different parties, to make the public administration the Mirror of the ill concerted and incongruous projects of faction, rather than the organ of consistent and wholesome plans digested by common councils and modified by mutual interests. However combinations or Associations of the above description may now and then answer popular ends, they are likely, in the course of time and things, to become potent engines, by which cunning, ambitious and unprincipled men will be enabled to subvert the Power of the People, and to usurp for themselves the reins of Government; destroying afterwards the very engines which have lifted them to unjust dominion.

Towards the preservation of your Government and the permanency of your present happy state, it is requisite, not only that you steadily discountenance irregular oppositions to its acknowledged authority, but also that you resist with care the spirit of innovation upon its principles however specious the pretexts. One method of assault may be to effect, in the forms of the Constitution, alterations which will impair the energy of the system, and thus to undermine what cannot be directly overthrown. In all the changes to which you may be invited, remember that time and habit are at least as necessary to fix the true character of Governments, as of other human institutions; that experience is the surest standard, by which to test the real tendency of the existing Constitution of a country; that facility in changes upon the credit of mere hypotheses and opinion exposes to perpetual change, from the endless variety of hypotheses and opinion: and remember, especially, that for the efficient management of your common interests, in a country so extensive as ours, a Government of as much vigour as is consistent with the perfect security of Liberty is indispensable. Liberty itself will find in such a Government, with powers properly distributed and adjusted, its surest Guardian. It is indeed little else than a name, where the Government is too feeble to withstand the enterprises of faction, to confine each member of the Society within the limits prescribed by the laws and to maintain all in the secure and tranquil enjoyment of the rights of person and property.

I have already intimated to you the danger of Parties in the State, with particular reference to the founding of them on Geographical discriminations. Let me now take a more comprehensive view, and warn you in the most solemn manner against the baneful effects of the Spirit of Party, generally.

This spirit, unfortunately, is inseparable from our nature, having its root in the strongest passions of the human Mind. It exists under different shapes in all Governments, more or less stifled, controlled, or repressed; but, in those of the popular form it is seen in its greatest rankness and is truly their worst enemy.

The alternate domination of one faction over another, sharpened by the spirit of revenge natural to party dissension, which in different ages and countries has perpetrated the most horrid enormities, is itself a frightful despotism. But this leads at length to a more formal and permanent despotism. The disorders and miseries, which result, gradually incline the minds of men to seek security and repose in the absolute power of an Individual: and sooner or later the chief of some prevailing faction more able or more fortunate than his competitors, turns this disposition to the purposes of his own elevation, on the ruins of Public Liberty.

Without looking forward to an extremity of this kind (which nevertheless ought not to be entirely out of sight) the common and continual mischiefs of the spirit of Party are sufficient to make it the interest and the duty of a wise People to discourage and restrain it.

It serves always to distract the Public Councils and enfeeble the Public administration. It agitates the Community with ill founded jealousies and false alarms, kindles the animosity of one part against another, foments occasionally riot and insurrection. It opens the door to foreign influence and corruption, which find a facilitated access to the government itself through the channels of party passions. Thus the policy and the will of one country, are subjected to the policy and will of another.

There is an opinion that parties in free countries are useful checks upon the Administration of the Government and serve to keep alive the spirit of Liberty. This within certain limits is probably true, and in Governments of a Monarchical cast Patriotism may look with indulgence, if not with favour, upon the spirit of party. But in those of the popular character, in Governments purely elective, it is a spirit not to be encouraged. From their natural tendency, it is certain there will always be enough of that spirit for every salutary purpose. And there being constant danger of excess, the effort ought to be, by force of public opinion, to mitigate and assuage it. A fire not to be quenched, it demands a uniform vigilance to prevent its bursting into a flame, lest instead of warming it should consume.

It is important, likewise, that the habits of thinking in a free Country should inspire caution in those entrusted with its administration, to confine themselves within their respective Constitutional spheres; avoiding in the exercise of the Powers of one department to encroach upon another. The spirit of encroachment tends to consolidate the powers of all the departments in one, and thus to create whatever the form of government, a real despotism. A just estimate of that love of power, and proneness to abuse it, which predominates in the human heart is sufficient to satisfy us of the truth of this position. The necessity of reciprocal checks in the exercise of political power, by dividing and distributing it into different depositories, and constituting each the Guardian of the Public Weal against invasions by the others, has been evinced by experiments ancient and modern; some of them in our country and under our own eyes. To preserve them must be as necessary as to institute them. If in the opinion of the People, the distribution or modification of the Constitutional powers be in any particular wrong, let it be corrected by an amendment in the way which the Constitution designates. But let there be no change by usurpation; for though this, in one instance, may be the instrument of good, it is the customary weapon by which free governments are destroyed. The precedent must always greatly overbalance in permanent evil any partial or transient benefit which the use can at any time yield.

Of all the dispositions and habits which lead to political prosperity. Religion and morality are indispensable supports. In vain would that man claim the tribute of Patriotism, who should labour to subvert these great Pillars of human happiness, these firmest props of the duties of Men and citizens. The mere Politician, equally with the pious man ought to respect and to cherish them. A volume could not trace all their connections with private and public felicity. Let it simply be asked where is the security for property, for reputation, for life, if the sense of religious obligation *desert* the oaths, which are the instruments of investigation in Courts of Justice? And let us with caution indulge the supposition, that morality can be maintained without religion. Whatever may be conceded to the influence of refined education on minds of peculiar structure, reason and experience both forbid us to expect that National morality can prevail in exclusion of religious principle.

'Tis substantially true, that virtue or morality is a necessary spring of popular government. The rule indeed extends with more or less force to every species of free Government. Who that is a sincere friend to it, can look with indifference upon attempts to shake the foundation of the fabric?

Promote then as an object of primary importance, Institutions for the general diffusion of knowledge. In proportion as the structure of a government gives force to public opinion, it is essential that public opinion should be enlightened.

As a very important source of strength and security, cherish public credit. One method of preserving it is to use it as sparingly as possible: avoiding occasions of expence by cultivating peace, but remembering also that timely disbursements to prepare for danger frequently prevent much greater disbursements to repel it; avoiding likewise the accumulation of debt, not only by shunning occasions of expence, but by vigorous exertions in time of Peace to discharge the Debts which unavoidable wars may have occasioned, not ungenerously throwing upon posterity the burthen which we ourselves ought to bear. The execution of these maxims belongs to your Representatives, but it is necessary that public opinion should cooperate. To facilitate to them the performance of their duty, it is essential that you should practically bear in mind, that towards the payment of debts there must be Revenue; that to have Revenue there must be taxes; that no taxes can be devised which are not more or less inconvenient and unpleasant; that the intrinsic embarrassment inseparable from the selection of the proper objects (which is always a choice of difficulties) ought to be a decisive motive for a candid construction of the Conduct of the Government in making it, and for a spirit of acquiescence in the measures for obtaining Revenue which the public exigencies may at any time dictate.

Observe good faith and justice towards all Nations. Cultivate peace and harmony with all. Religion and morality enjoin this conduct; and can it be that good policy does not equally enjoin it? It will be worthy of a free, enlightened, and, at no distant period, a great Nation, to give to mankind the magnanimous and too novel example of a People always guided by an exalted justice and benevolence. Who can doubt that in the course of time and things the fruits of such a plan would richly repay any temporary advantages which might be lost by a steady adherence to it? Can it be, that Providence has not connected the permanent felicity of a Nation with its virtue? The experiment, at least, is recommended by every sentiment which ennobles human Nature. Alas! is it rendered impossible by its vices?

In the execution of such a plan nothing is more essential than that permanent, inveterate antipathies against particular Nations and passionate attachments for others should be excluded; and that in place of them just and amicable feelings towards all should be cultivated. The Nation, which indulges towards another an habitual hatred, or an habitual fondness, is in some degree a slave. It is a slave to its animosity or to its affection, either of which is sufficient to lead it astray from its duty and its interest. Antipathy in one Nation against another, disposes each more readily to offer insult and injury, to lay hold of slight causes of umbrage, and to be haughty and intractable, when accidental or trifling occasions of dispute occur. Hence frequent collisions, obstinate envenomed and bloody contests. The Nation, prompted by ill will and resentment sometimes impels to War the Government, contrary to the best calculations of policy. The Government sometimes participates in the national propensity, and adopts through passion what reason would reject; at other times, it makes the animosity of the Nation subservient to projects of hostility instigated by pride, ambition and other sinister and pernicious motives. The peace often, sometimes perhaps the Liberty, of Nations has been the victim.

So likewise, a passionate attachment of one Nation for another produces a variety of evils. Sympathy for the favourite nation, facilitating the illusion of an imaginary common interest, in cases where no real common interest exists, and infusing into one the enmities of the other, betrays the former into a participation in the quarrels and Wars of the latter, without adequate inducement or justification. It leads also to concessions to the favourite Nation of privileges denied to others, which is apt doubly to injure the Nation making the concessions; by unnecessarily parting with what ought to have been retained; and by exciting jealousy, ill will, and a disposition to retaliate, in the parties from whom equal privileges are withheld. And it gives to ambitious, corrupted, or deluded citizens (who devote themselves to the favourite Nation) facility to betray, or sacrifice the interests of their own country, without odium, sometimes even with popularity; gilding with the appearances of a virtuous sense of obligation a commendable deference for public opinion, or a laudable zeal for public good, the base or foolish compliances of ambition, corruption, or infatuation.

As avenues to foreign influence in innumerable ways, such attachments are particularly alarming to the truly enlightened and independent Patriot. How many opportunities do they afford to tamper with domestic factions, to practice the arts of seduction, to mislead public opinion, to influence or awe the public Councils! Such an attachment of a small or weak, towards a great and powerful Nation, dooms the former to be the satellite of the latter.

Against the insidious wiles of foreign influence, (I conjure you to believe me fellow citizens) the jealousy of a free people ought to be *constantly* awake; since history and experience prove that foreign influence is one of the most baneful foes of Republican Government. But that jealousy to be useful must be impartial; else it becomes the instrument of the very influence to be avoided, instead of a defence against it. Excessive partiality for one foreign nation and excessive dislike of another, cause those whom they actuate to see danger only on one side, and serve to veil and even second the arts of influence on the other. Real Patriots, who may resist the intrigues of the favourite, are liable to become suspected and odious; while its tools and dupes usurp the applause and confidence of the people, to surrender their interests.

The Great rule of conduct for us, in regard to foreign Nations is in extending our commercial relations to have with them as little *political* connection as possible. So far as we have already formed engagements let them be fulfilled, with perfect good faith. Here let us stop.

Europe has a set of primary interests, which to us have none, or a very remote relation. Hence she must be engaged in frequent controversies, the causes of which are essentially foreign to our concerns. Hence therefore it must be unwise in us to implicate ourselves, by artificial ties, in the ordinary vicissitudes of her politics, or the ordinary combinations and collisions of her friendships, or enmities.

Our detached and distant situation invites and enables us to pursue a different course. If we remain one People, under an efficient government, the period is not far off, when we may defy material injury from external annoyance; when we may take such an attitude as will cause the neutrality we may at any time resolve upon to be scrupulously respected; when belligerent nations, under the impossibility of making acquisitions upon us, will not lightly hazard the giving us provocation; when we may choose peace or war, as our interest guided by our justice shall Counsel.

Why forego the advantages of so peculiar a situation? Why quit our own to stand upon foreign ground? Why, by interweaving our destiny with that of any part of Europe, entangle our peace and prosperity in the toils of European Ambition, Rivalship, Interest, Humour or Caprice?

'Tis our true policy to steer clear of permanent Alliances, with any portion of the foreign world. So far, I mean, as we are now at liberty to do it, for let me not be understood as capable of patronising infidelity to existing engagements (I hold the maxim no less applicable to public than to private affairs, that honesty is always the best policy). I repeat it therefore, let those engagements be observed in their genuine sense. But in my opinion, it is unnecessary and would be unwise to extend them.

Taking care always to keep ourselves, by suitable establishments, on a respectably defensive posture, we may safely trust to temporary alliances for extraordinary emergencies.

Harmony, liberal intercourse with all Nations, are recommended by policy, humanity and interest. But even our Commercial policy should hold an equal and impartial hand: neither seeking nor granting exclusive favours or preferences; consulting the natural course of things; diffusing and diversifying by gentle means the streams of Commerce, but forcing nothing; establishing with Powers so disposed, in order to give to trade a stable course, to define the rights of our Merchants, and to enable the Government to support them, conventional rules of intercourse, the best that present circumstances and mutual opinion will permit, but temporary, and liable to be from time to time abandoned or varied, as experience and circumstances shall dictate; constantly keeping in view, that 'tis folly in one Nation to look for disinterested favours from another; that it must pay with a portion of its Independence for whatever it may accept under that character; that by such acceptance, it may place itself in the condition of having given equivalents for nominal favours and yet of being reproached with ingratitude for not giving more. There can be no greater error than to expect, or calculate upon real favours from Nation to Nation. 'Tis an illusion which experience must cure, which a just pride ought to discard.

In offering to you, my Countrymen, these counsels of an old and affectionate friend, I dare not hope they will make the strong and lasting impression, I could wish; that they will control the usual current of the passions, or prevent our Nation from running the course which has hitherto marked the Destiny of Nations. But if I may even flatter myself, that they may be productive of some partial benefit, some occasional good; that they may now and then recur to moderate the fury of party spirit, to warn against the mischiefs of foreign Intrigue, to guard against the Impostures of pretended patriotism; this hope will be a full recompence for the solicitude for your welfare, by which they have been dictated.

How far in the discharge of my Official duties, I have been guided by the principles which have been delineated, the public Records and other evidences of my conduct must Witness to You and to the world. To myself, the assurance of my own conscience is, that I have at least believed myself to be guided by them.

In relation to the still subsisting War in Europe, my Proclamation of the 22d. of April 1793 is the index to my Plan. Sanctioned by your approving voice and by that of Your Representatives in both Houses of Congress, the spirit of that measure has continually governed me; uninfluenced by any attempts to deter or divert me from it.

After deliberate examination with the aid of the best lights I could obtain I was well satisfied that our Country, under all the circumstances of the case, had a right to take, and was bound in duty and interest, to take a Neutral position. Having taken it, I determined, as far as should depend upon me, to maintain it, with moderation, perseverence and firmness.

The considerations, which respect the right to hold this conduct, it is not necessary on this occasion to detail. I will only observe, that according to my understanding of the matter, that right, so far from being denied by any of the Belligerent Powers has been virtually admitted by all.

The duty of holding a Neutral conduct may be inferred, without any thing more, from the obligation which justice and humanity impose on every Nation, in cases in which it is free to act, to maintain inviolate the relations of Peace and amity towards other Nations.

The inducements of interest for observing that conduct will best be referred to your own reflections and experience. With me, a predominant motive has been to endeavour to gain time to our country to settle and mature its yet recent institutions, and to progress without interruption, to that degree of strength and consistency, which is necessary to give it, humanly speaking, the command of its own fortunes.

Though in reviewing the incidents of my Administration, I am unconscious of intentional error, I am nevertheless too sensible of my defects not to think it probable that I may have committed many errors. Whatever they may be I fervently beseech the Almighty to avert or mitigate the evils to which they may tend. I shall also carry with me the hope that my Country will never cease to view them with indulgence; and that after forty-five years of my life dedicated to its Service, with an upright zeal, the faults of incompetent abilities will be consigned to oblivion, as myself must soon be to the Mansions of rest.

Relying on its kindness in this as in other things, and actuated by that fervent love towards it, which is so natural to a Man, who views in it the native soil of himself and his progenitors for several Generations; I anticipate with pleasing expectation that retreat, in which I promise myself to realize, without alloy, the sweet enjoyment of partaking, in the midst of my fellow Citizens, the benign influence of good Laws under a free Government, the ever favourite object of my heart, and the happy reward, as I trust, of our mutual cares, labours and dangers.

Nature and Deity

❦

❧ Benjamin Franklin (1706–1790)

FRANKLIN'S greatest pleasures, he said, came from his scientific pursuits, those "philosophical studies and amusements" to which he hoped to devote his life after his retirement from business. No man had greater curiosity about the world around him, and "to extend the power of man over nature" was Franklin's earliest and latest interest.

Though science was often crowded out of his life by a career in diplomacy and public service that gave him only a few years of leisure for study in middle life, Franklin was nevertheless one of the dozen or so great scientific scholars of the eighteenth century, responsible for some of the most important basic research ever performed, respected as a scientist at home and abroad. He began his first work in 1729, and in 1742 initiated the series of experiments in electricity upon which his fame later rested. He was a member of the Royal Society of London, holder of the Copley Medal for original research and of seven honorary degrees, master of five languages, member of the French, Dutch, Swedish, Italian, and Spanish academies, and author of more than a hundred papers on electricity, medicine, chemistry, botany, meteorology, engineering, hydraulics, ethnology, and agronomy. He published his first researches at twenty-three (on heat conductivity) and his last, on oceanography, at seventy-nine.

Franklin was no amateur, but a highly-trained, brilliant research scientist, a firm believer in the inductive method and controlled laboratory experimentation. His contributions to the infant science of electricity were epochal: he rejected the contemporary "two fluid" theory of electricity, recognizing the existence and function of *positive* and *negative* charges (terms which he coined); he performed basic research on the battery principle; he proved the identity of electricity in natural and manufactured form by his lightning experiment. But most of all, Franklin helped to identify, explain, and tame the strange, great force so recently discovered and so soon to change the world.

TEXTS: John Bigelow, ed., *The Works of Benjamin Franklin* (New York, 1904), I, 289–294. Albert H. Smyth, ed., *The Writings of Benjamin Franklin* (New York, 1905–7), III, 151–153; IX, 73–75. E. A. and G. L. Duyckinck, *The Cyclopaedia of American Literature* (Philadelphia, 1881), I, 185–187.

The New World of Electricity

[From *Autobiography* (1771 ff.)]

Before I proceed in relating the part I had in public affairs under this new governor's administration, it may not be amiss here to give some account of the rise and progress of my philosophical reputation.

In 1746, being at Boston I met there with a Dr. Spence who was lately arrived from Scotland, and show'd me some electric experiments. They were imperfectly perform'd as he was not very expert but, being on a subject quite new to me, they equally surpris'd and pleased me. Soon after my return to Philadelphia, our library company receiv'd from Mr. P. Collinson, Fellow of the Royal Society of London, a present of a glass tube with some account of the use of it in making such experiments. I eagerly seized the opportunity of repeating what I had seen at Boston; and, by much practice, acquir'd great readiness in performing those, also, which we had an account of from England, adding a number of new ones. I say much practice, for my house was continually full, for some time, with people who came to see these new wonders.

To divide a little this incumbrance among my friends, I caused a number of similar tubes to be blown at our glass-house, with which they furnished themselves, so that we had at length several performers. Among these, the principal was Mr. Kinnersley, an ingenious neighbor, who, being out of business, I encouraged to undertake showing the experiments for money, and drew up for him two lectures, in which the experiments were rang'd in such order, and accompanied with such explanations in such method, as that the foregoing should assist in comprehending the following. He procur'd an elegant apparatus for the purpose, in which all the little machines that I had roughly made for myself were nicely form'd by instrument-makers. His lectures were well attended and gave great satisfaction, and after some time he went thro' the colonies exhibiting them in every capital town and pick'd up some money. In the West India Islands, indeed, it was with difficulty the experiments could be made, from the general moisture of the air.

Oblig'd as we were to Mr. Collinson for his present of the tube, etc., I thought it right he should be inform'd of our success in using it, and wrote him several letters containing accounts of our experiments. He got them read in the Royal Society where they were not at first thought worth so much notice as to be printed in their Transactions. One paper, which I wrote for Mr. Kinnersley, on the sameness of lightning with electricity, I sent to Dr. Mitchel, an acquaintance of mine and one of the members also of that society, who wrote me word that it had been read, but was laughed at by the connoisseurs. The papers, however, being shown to Dr. Fothergill, he thought they were of too much value to be stifled, and advis'd the printing of them. Mr. Collinson then gave them to Cave for publication in his *Gentleman's Magazine;* but he chose to print them separately in a pamphlet and Dr. Fothergill wrote the preface. Cave, it seems, judged rightly for his profit, for by the additions that arrived afterward, they swell'd to a quarto volume which has had five editions, and cost him nothing for copy-money.

It was, however, some time before those papers were much taken notice of in England. A copy of them happening to fall into the hands of the Count de Buffon, a philosopher deservedly of great reputation in France, and, indeed, all over Europe, he prevailed with M. Dalibard to translate them into French, and they were printed at Paris. The publication offended the Abbé Nollet, preceptor in Natural Philosophy to the royal family, and an able experimenter, who had form'd and publish'd a theory of electricity, which then had the general vogue. He could not at first believe that such a work came from America, and said it must have been fabricated by his enemies at Paris, to decry his system. Afterwards, having been assur'd that there really existed such a person as Franklin at Philadelphia, which he had doubted, he wrote and published a volume of "Letters," chiefly address'd to me, defending his theory, and denying the verity of my experiments and of the positions deduc'd from them.

I once purpos'd answering the abbé, and actually began the answer, but, on consideration that my writings contain'd a description of experiments which any one might repeat and verify, and if not to be verifi'd, could not be defended; or of observations offer'd as conjectures and not delivered dogmatically, therefore not laying me under any obligation to defend them; and reflecting that a dispute between two persons, writing in different languages, might be lengthened greatly by mistranslations and thence misconceptions of one another's meaning, much of one of the abbé's letters being founded on an error in the translation, I concluded to let my papers shift for themselves, believing it was better to spend what time I could spare from public business in making new experiments, than in disputing about those already made. I therefore never answered M. Nollet, and the event gave me no cause to repent my silence; for my friend M. le Roy, of the Royal Academy of Sciences, took up my cause and refuted him; my book was translated into the Italian, German, and Latin languages, and the doctrine it contain'd was by degrees universally adopted by the philosophers of Europe in preference to that of the abbé; so that he lived to see himself the last of his sect, except Monsieur B——, of Paris, his *élève* and immediate disciple.

What gave my book the more sudden and general celebrity, was the success of one of its proposed experiments, made by Messrs. Dalibard and De Lor at Marly, for drawing lightning from the clouds. This engaged the public attention every where. M. de Lor, who had an apparatus for experimental philosophy, and lectur'd in that branch of science, undertook to repeat what he called the *Philadelphia Experiments;* and, after they were performed before the king and court, all the curious of Paris flocked to see them. I will not swell this narrative with an account of that capital experiment, nor of the infinite pleasure I receiv'd in the success of a similar one I made soon after with a kite at Philadelphia, as both are to be found in the histories of electricity.

Dr. Wright, an English physician, when at Paris, wrote to a friend, who was of the Royal Society, an account of the high esteem my experiments were in among the learned abroad, and of their wonder that my writings had been so little noticed in England. The Society, on this, resum'd the consideration of the letters that had been read to them, and the celebrated Dr. Watson drew up a summary account of them and of all I had afterwards sent to England on the subject, which he accompanied with some praise of the writer. This summary was then printed in their Transactions; and some members of the Society in London, particularly the very ingenious Mr. Canton, having verified the experiment of procuring lightning from the clouds by a pointed rod, and acquainting them with the success, they soon made me more than amends for the slight with which they had before treated me. Without my having made any application for that honor, they chose me a member, and voted that I should be excus'd the customary payments, which would have amounted to twenty-five guineas; and ever since have given me their Transactions gratis. They also presented me with the gold medal of Sir Godfrey Copley for the year 1753, the delivery of which was accompanied by a very handsome speech of the president, Lord Macclesfield, wherein I was highly honoured.

An Experiment with Lightning

[From a letter to Peter Collinson, September 1753]

At last, on the 12th of *April,* 1753, there being a smart gust of some continuance, I charg'd one phial pretty well with lightning, and the other equally, as near as I could judge, with electricity from my glass globe; and, having placed them properly, I beheld, with great surprise and pleasure, the cork ball play briskly between them, and was convinced, that one bottle was electrised *negatively.*

I repeated this experiment several times during the gust, and in eight succeeding gusts, always with the same success; and being of opinion (for reasons I formerly gave in my letter to Mr. *Kinnersley,* since printed in *London*), that the glass globe electrises *positively,* I concluded that the clouds are *always* electrised *negatively,* or have always in them less than their natural quantity of the electric fluid.

Yet notwithstanding so many experiments, it seems I concluded too soon; for at last, *June* the 6th, in a gust which continued from five o'clock, P. M., to seven, I met with one cloud that was electrised *positively,* tho' several that pass'd over my rod before, during the same gust, were in the *negative* state. This was thus discovered. . . .

But this was a single experiment, which, however, destroys my first too general conclusion, and reduces me to this: *That the clouds of a thunder-gust are most commonly in a negative state of electricity, but sometimes in a positive state.*

The latter I believe is rare; for, tho' I soon after the last experiment, set out on a journey to *Boston,* and was from home most part of the summer, which prevented my making farther trials and observations; yet Mr. *Kinnersley,* returning from the islands just as I left home, pursued the experiments during my absence, and informs me, that he always found the clouds in the *negative* state.

So that, for the most part, in thunder-strokes, *'tis the earth that strikes into the clouds, and not the clouds that strike into the earth.*

War and Science

[From a letter to Sir Joseph Banks, July 27, 1783]

DEAR SIR:

I received your very kind letter by Dr. Blagden, and esteem myself much honoured by your friendly Remembrance. I have been too much and too closely engaged in public Affairs, since his being here, to enjoy all the Benefit of his Conversation you were so good to intend me. I hope soon to have more Leisure, and to spend a part of it in those Studies, that are much more agreeable to me than political Operations.

I join with you most cordially in rejoicing at the return of Peace. I hope it will be lasting, and that Mankind will at length, as they call themselves reasonable Creatures, have Reason and Sense enough to settle their Differences without cutting Throats; for, in my opinion, *there never was a good War, or a bad Peace.* What vast additions to the Conveniences and Comforts of Living might Mankind have acquired, if the Money spent in Wars had been employed in Works of public utility! What an extension of Agriculture, even to the Tops of our Mountains; what Rivers rendered navigable, or joined by Canals: what Bridges, Aqueducts, new Roads, and other public Works, Edifices, and Improvements, rendering England a compleat Paradise, might have been obtained by spending those Millions in doing good, which in the last War have been spent in doing Mischief; in bringing Misery into thousands of Families, and destroying the Lives of so many thousands of working people, who might have performed the useful labour!

I am pleased with the late astronomical Discoveries made by our Society. Furnished as all Europe now is with Academies of Science, with nice instruments and the Spirit of Experiment, the progress of human knowledge will be rapid, and discoveries made, of which we have at present no Conception. I begin to be almost sorry I was born so soon, since I cannot have the happiness of knowing what will be known 100 years hence.

I wish continued success to the Labours of the Royal Society, and that you may long adorn their Chair; being with the highest esteem, dear Sir, &c.

B. FRANKLIN

P. S. Dr. Blagden will acquaint you with the experiment of a vast Globe sent up into the Air, much talked of here, and which, if prosecuted, may furnish means of new knowledge.

St. Jean de Crèvecoeur

Traveling with Dr. Franklin

[From St. Jean de Crèvecoeur, *Voyage dans la Haute Pennsylvanie*, 1801]

In the year 1787 I accompanied the venerable Franklin, at that time Governor of Pennsylvania, on a journey to Lancaster, where he had been invited to lay the corner-stone of a college, which he had founded there for the Germans. In the evening of the day of the ceremony, we were talking of the different nations which inhabit the continent, of their aversion to agriculture, &c., when one of the principal inhabitants of the city said to him:

"Governor, where do you think these nations came from? Do you consider them aborigines? Have you heard of the ancient fortifications and tombs which have been recently discovered in the west?"

"Those who inhabit the two Floridas," he replied, "and lower Louisiana, say, that they came from the mountains of Mexico. I should be inclined to believe it. If we may judge of the Esquimaux of the coasts of Labrador (the most savage men known) by the fairness of their complexion, the color of their eyes, and their enormous beards, they are originally from the north of Europe, whence they came at a very remote period. As to the other nations of this continent, it seems difficult to imagine from what stock they can be descended. To assign them an Asiatic and Tartar origin, to assert that they crossed Behring Straits, and spread themselves over this continent, shocks all notions of probability. How, indeed, can we conceive that men almost naked; armed with bows and arrows, could have undertaken a journey of a thousand leagues through thick forests or impenetrable marshes, accompanied by their wives and children, with no means of subsistence, save what they derived from hunting? What could have been the motives of such an emigration? If it were the severe cold of their own country, why should they have advanced to Hudson's Bay and Lower Canada? Why have they not stopped on their way at the beautiful plains on the banks of the Missouri, the Minnesota, the Mississippi, or the Illinois? But it will be said, they *did* settle there, and those with whom we are acquainted are but the surplus population of these ancient emigrations. If it were so, we should discover some analogy between their languages: and it is ascertained beyond a doubt, that the languages of the Nadouassees and Padoukas no more resemble the Chippewa, the Mohawk, or the Abenaki, than they do the jargon of Kamschatka.

"On the other hand," he continued, "how can we suppose them to be aborigines of a region like this, which produces scarcely any fruits or plants on which the primitive man could have subsisted until he had learned to make a bow and arrow, harpoon a fish, and kindle a fire? How could these first families have resisted the inclemency of the seasons, the stings of insects, the attacks of carnivorous animals? The warm climates, therefore, and those that abound in natural fruits, must have been the cradle of the human race; it was from the bosom of these favored regions that the *exuberant* portion of the early communities gradually spread over the rest of the world. Whence came the nations which inhabit this continent, those we meet with in New Zealand, New Holland, and the islands of the Pacific? Why have the people of the old world been civilized for thousands of ages, while those of the new still remain plunged in ignorance and barbarism? Has this hemisphere more recently emerged from the bosom of the waters? These questions, and a thousand others we might ask, will ever be to us, frail beings, like a vast desert where the wandering eye sees not the smallest bush on which it may repose.

"This planet is very old," he continued. "Like the works of Homer and Hesiod, who can say through how many editions it has passed in the immensity of ages? The rent continents, the straits, the gulfs, the islands, the shallows of the ocean, are but vast fragments on which, as on the planks of some wrecked vessel, the men of former generations who escaped these commotions, have produced new populations. Time, so precious to us, the creatures of a moment, is nothing to nature. Who can tell us when the earth will again experience these fatal catastrophes, to which, it appears to me, to be as much exposed in its annual revolutions, as are the vessels which cross the seas to be dashed in pieces on a sunken rock? The near approach or contact of one of those globes whose elliptical and mysterious courses are perhaps the agents of our destinies, some variation in its annual or diurnal rotation, in the inclination of its axis or the equilibrium of the seas, might change its climate, and render it long uninhabitable.

"As to your third question," continued the governor," I will give you some reflections which occurred to me on reading the papers lately presented to our philosophical society by Generals Varnum and Parsons, and Captains John Hart and Serjeant, in relation to the entrenched camps and other indications of an ancient population, of whom tradition has transmitted no account to our indigenous population. In travelling through the parts of this state beyond the Alleghanies, we often find on the high ground near the rivers remains of parapets and ditches covered with lofty trees. Almost the whole of the peninsula of Muskinghum is occupied by a vast fortified camp. It is composed of three square inclosures; the central one, which is the largest, has a communication with the former bed of the river, whose waters appear to have retreated nearly three hundred feet. These inclosures are formed by ditches and parapets of earth, in which no cut stones or brick have been found. The centre is occupied by conical elevations of different diameters and heights. Each of these inclosures appears to have had a cemetery. As a proof of the high antiquity of these works, we are assured, as an undisputed fact, that the bones are converted into calcareous matter, and that the vegetable soil with which these fortifications are covered, and which has been formed merely by the falling off of the leaves and of the fragments of trees, is almost as thick as in the places around about them. Two other camps have been likewise discovered in the neighborhood of Lexington. The area of the first is six acres, that of the second, three. The fragments of earthenware which have been found in digging are of a composition unknown to our Indians.

"On Paint Creek, a branch of the Scioto, there has been found a series of these fortified inclosures, extending as far as the Ohio, and even south of that river. Similar works have been discovered in the two Miamis, at a distance of more than twenty miles, and likewise on Big Grave Creek. These last are only a series of elevated redoubts on the banks of these rivers at unequal distances apart. Those which have been found on Big Black Creek, and at Byo Pierre, in the neighborhood of the Mississippi, appear to have been embankments intended to protect the inhabitants from the inundations of the river.

"At a distance of five hundred leagues from the sea, on the eastern shore of Lake Peppin (which is only an extension of the Mississippi),

Carver found considerable remains of entrenchments made, like the former, of earth, and covered with high woods. The barrows lately discovered in Kentucky and elsewhere, are cones of different diameters and heights; they are covered with a thick layer of earth, and resemble, although smaller, those which are still seen in Asia and some parts of Europe. The first row of bodies lies upon flat stones, with which the whole of the bottom is paved: these are covered over with new layers, serving as beds for other bodies placed like the former, and so on to the top. As in the fortifications on the Muskinghum, we meet with no signs of mortar, and no traces of the hammer. The new state of Tennessee is full of these tombs, and several caves have also been discovered there in which bones have been found.

"In the neighborhood of several Cherokee villages, in Keowe, Steccoe, Sinica, &c., there have been found terraces, pyramids, or artificial hills, of great height, whose origin was unknown to the inhabitants whom the Cherokees drove out at the time of their invasion, nearly two centuries ago. The same artificial heights, the same proofs of the residence and power of ancient nations, are also found in the two Floridas, on the banks of the Oakmulgee, at Taensa, on the Alabama, &c.

"At what period, by what people, were these works constructed? What degree of civilization had this people reached? Were they acquainted with the use of iron? What has become of them? Can we conceive that nations sufficiently powerful to have raised such considerable fortifications, and who buried their dead with such religious care, can have been destroyed and replaced by the ignorant and barbarous hordes we see about us at the present day? Could the calamities occasioned by a long state of war have effaced the last traces of their civilization and brought them back to the primitive condition of hunters? Are our Indians the descendants of that ancient people?

"Such are the doubts and conjectures which arise in our minds on contemplating the traces of the passage and existence of the nations which inhabited the regions of the west; traces which are not sufficient to guide us in the vagueness of the past. Although neither arms nor instruments of iron have yet been discovered, how can we conceive that they could dig such deep ditches, or raise such large masses of earth, without the aid of that metal? This ancient people must have had chiefs, and been subject to laws; for without the bonds of subordination, how could they have collected and kept together so great a number of workmen? They must have been acquainted with agriculture, since the products of the chase would never have sufficed to support them. The extent of these camps also proves that the number of the troops destined to defend these works, and that of the families to which, in moments of danger, they afforded an asylum was immense. The cemeteries prove that they sojourned there a long time. This

people must therefore have been much further advanced in civilization
than our Indians.

"When the population of the United States shall have spread over
every part of that vast and beautiful region, our posterity, aided by
new discoveries, may then perhaps form more satisfactory conjectures.
What a field for reflection! A new continent, which, at some unknown
period, appears to have been inhabited by agricultural and warlike
nations! Were it not for my advanced age, I would myself cross the
mountains to examine those old military works. Perhaps a careful and
minute inspection would give rise to conjectures which now elude all
the combinations of the mind."

◁ᴙ Thomas Jefferson (1743–1826)

"NATURE intended me for the tranquil pursuits of science,"
Jefferson once wrote, "by rendering them my supreme delight."
A skilled amateur rather than a professional like Franklin, Jefferson was nevertheless an accomplished botanist and mathematician,
knowledgeable in zoology, meteorology, astronomy, ethnology, and
"natural philosophy," as the life and earth sciences were custom-
arily called. He read widely in scientific journals, corresponded
with scientists everywhere, and collected specimens of every con-
ceivable kind with great enthusiasm. The theory of Buffon, the
French scientist, that animals in America were inferior to those in
Europe, especially intrigued him, and he did a great deal to dis-
prove it by his observation and collection of native fauna.

Jefferson's speculations on the mammoth are an excellent
example of how the accepted framework of eighteenth-century
concepts of nature and creation tended to predetermine scientific
conclusions. Like every other educated man of his time, Jefferson
believed that the Deity had originally established a clear and
definite hierarchy of order for all creation — that there existed a
"Great Chain of Being" in which everything was assigned a place,
and within the limits of which it stayed. The discovery of fossil
bones in America, and a lack of observable living mammoth
specimens, therefore led Jefferson to speculate about the place
of the mammoth in this chain, and its relation to other species in
the same set of links.

TEXT: A. A. Lipscomb and A. E. Bergh, eds., *The Writings of
Thomas Jefferson* (Washington, 1903–5), II, 54–61.

The Mammoth

[From *Notes on Virginia*, 1788]

Our quadrupeds have been mostly described by Linnæus and Mons.
de Buffon. Of these the mammoth, or big buffalo, as called by the
Indians, must certainly have been the largest. Their tradition is, that
he was carnivorous, and still exists in the northern parts of America.
A delegation of warriors from the Delaware tribe having visited the
Governor of Virginia, during the revolution, on matters of business,
after these had been discussed and settled in council, the Governor
asked them some questions relative to their country, and among others,
what they knew or had heard of the animal whose bones were found
at the Saltlicks on the Ohio. Their chief speaker immediately put
himself into an attitude of oratory, and with a pomp suited to what he
conceived the elevation of his subject, informed him that it was a
tradition handed down from their fathers, "That in ancient times a
herd of these tremendous animals came to the Big-bone licks, and
began an universal destruction of the bear, deer, elks, buffaloes, and
other animals which had been created for the use of the Indians; that
the Great Man above, looking down and seeing this, was so enraged
that he siezed his lightning, descended on the earth, seated himself on
a neighboring mountain, on a rock of which his seat and the print of
his feet are still to be seen, and hurled his bolts among them till the
whole were slaughtered, except the big bull, who presenting his forehead to the shafts, shook them off as they fell; but missing one at length,
it wounded him in the side; whereon, springing round, he bounded
over the Ohio, over the Wabash, the Illinois, and finally over the great
lakes, where he is living at this day." It is well known, that on the
Ohio, and in many parts of America further north, tusks, grinders, and
skeletons of unparalleled magnitude, are found in great numbers, some
lying on the surface of the earth, and some a little below it. A Mr.
Stanley, taken prisoner near the mouth of the Tennessee, relates, that
after being transferred through several tribes, from one to another, he
was at length carried over the mountains west of the Missouri to a river
which runs westwardly; that these bones abounded there, and that the
natives described to him the animal to which they belonged as still
existing in the northern parts of their country; from which description
he judged it to be an elephant. Bones of the same kind have been
lately found, some feet below the surface of the earth, in salines
opened on the North Holston, a branch of the Tennessee, about the
latitude of $36\frac{1}{2}°$ north. From the accounts published in Europe, I
suppose it to be decided that these are of the same kind with those

found in Siberia. Instances are mentioned of like animal remains found in the more southern climates of both hemispheres; but they are either so loosely mentioned as to leave a doubt of the fact, so inaccurately described as not to authorize the classing them with the great northern bones, or so rare as to found a suspicion that they have been carried thither as curiosities from the northern regions. So that, on the whole, there seem to be no certain vestiges of the existence of this animal farther south than the salines just mentioned. It is remarkable that the tusks and skeletons have been ascribed by the naturalists of Europe to the elephant, while the grinders have been given to the hippopotamus, or river horse. Yet it is acknowledged, that the tusks and skeletons are much larger than those of the elephant, and the grinders many times greater than those of the hippopotamus, and essentially different in form. Wherever these grinders are found, there also we find the tusks and skeleton; but no skeleton of the hippopotamus nor grinders of the elephant. It will not be said that the hippopotamus and elephant came always to the same spot, the former to deposit his grinders, and the latter his tusks and skeleton. For what became of the parts not deposited there? We must agree then, that these remains belong to each other, that they are of one and the same animal, that this was not a hippopotamus, because the hippopotamus had no tusks, nor such a frame, and because the grinders differ in their size as well as in the number and form of their points. That this was not an elephant, I think ascertained by proofs equally decisive. I will not avail myself of the authority of the celebrated anatomist, who, from an examination of the form and structure of the tusks, has declared they were essentially different from those of the elephant; because another anatomist, equally celebrated, has declared, on a like examination, that they are precisely the same. Between two such authorities I will suppose this circumstance equivocal. But, 1. The skeleton of the mammoth (for so the incognitum has been called) bespeaks an animal of five or six times the cubic volume of the elephant, as Mons. de Buffon has admitted. 2. The grinders are five times as large, are square, and the grinding surface studded with four or five rows of blunt points; whereas those of the elephant are broad and thin, and their grinding surface flat. 3. I have never heard an instance, and suppose there has been none, of the grinder of an elephant being found in America. 4. From the known temperature and constitution of the elephant, he could never have existed in those regions where the remains of the mammoth have been found. The elephant is a native only of the torrid zone and its vicinities; if, with the assistance of warm apartments and warm clothing, he has been preserved in the temperate climates of Europe, it has only been for a small portion of what would have been his natural period, and no instance of his multiplication in them has ever been known. But no bones of the mammoth, as I have before observed, have been ever found further south than the salines of Holston, and they have been found as far north as the Arctic circle. Those, therefore, who are of opinion that the elephant and mammoth are the same, must believe, 1. That the elephant known to us can exist and multiply in the frozen zone; or, 2. That an eternal fire may once have warmed those regions, and since abandoned them, of which, however, the globe exhibits no unequivocal indications; or, 3. That the obliquity of the ecliptic, when these elephants lived, was so great as to include within the tropics all those regions in which the bones are found; the tropics being, as is before observed, the natural limits of habitation for the elephant. But if it be admitted that this obliquity has really decreased, and we adopt the highest rate of decrease yet pretended, that is, of one minute in a century, to transfer the northern tropic to the Arctic circle, would carry the existence of these supposed elephants two hundred and fifty thousand years back; a period far beyond our conception of the duration of animal bones less exposed to the open air than these are in many instances. Besides, though these regions would then be supposed within the tropics, yet their winters would have been too severe for the sensibility of the elephant. They would have had, too, but one day and one night in the year, a circumstance to which we have no reason to suppose the nature of the elephant fitted. However, it has been demonstrated, that, if a variation of obliquity in the ecliptic takes place at all, it is vibratory, and never exceeds the limits of nine degrees, which is not sufficient to bring these bones within the tropics. One of these hypotheses, or some other equally voluntary and inadmissible to cautious philosophy, must be adopted to support the opinion that these are the bones of the elephant. For my own part, I find it easier to believe that an animal may have existed, resembling the elephant in his tusks, and general anatomy, while his nature was in other respects extremely different. From the 30th degree of south latitude to the 30th degree of north, are nearly the limits which nature has fixed for the existence and multiplication of the elephant known to us. Proceeding thence northwardly to 36½ degrees, we enter those assigned to the mammoth. The farther we advance north, the more their vestiges multiply as far as the earth has been explored in that direction; and it is as probable as otherwise, that this progression continues to the pole itself, if land extends so far. The center of the frozen zone, then, may be the acmé of their vigor, as that of the torrid is of the elephant. Thus nature seems to have drawn a belt of separation between these two tremendous animals, whose breadth, indeed, is not precisely known, though at present we may suppose it about 6½ degrees of latitude; to have assigned to the elephant the

region south of these confines, and those north to the mammoth, founding the constitution of the one in her extreme of heat, and that of the
other in the extreme of cold. When the Creator has therefore separated
their nature as far as the extent of the scale of animal life allowed to
this planet would permit, it seems perverse to declare it the same,
from a partial resemblance of their tusks and bones. But to whatever
animal we ascribe these remains, it is certain such a one has existed
in America, and that it has been the largest of all terrestrial beings.
It should have sufficed to have rescued the earth it inhabited, and the
atmosphere it breathed, from the imputation of impotence in the conception and nourishment of animal life on a large scale; to have stifled,
in its birth, the opinion of a writer, the most learned, too, of all others
in the science of animal history, that in the new world, "La nature
vivante est beaucoup moins agissante, beaucoup moins forte:"[1] that
nature is less active, less energetic on one side of the globe than she
is on the other. As if both sides were not warmed by the same genial
sun; as if a soil of the same chemical composition was less capable of
elaboration into animal nutriment; as if the fruits and grains from
that soil and sun yielded a less rich chyle, gave less extension to the
solids and fluids of the body, or produced sooner in the cartilages,
membranes, and fibres, that rigidity which restrains all further extension, and terminates animal growth. The truth is, that a pigmy and a
Patagonian, a mouse and a mammoth, derive their dimensions from
the same nutritive juices. The difference of increment depends on circumstances unsearchable to beings with our capacities. Every race of
animals seems to have received from their Maker certain laws of extension at the time of their formation. Their elaborate organs were
formed to produce this, while proper obstacles were opposed to its
further progress. Below these limits they cannot fall, nor rise above
them. What intermediate station they shall take may depend on soil,
on climate, on food, on a careful choice of breeders. But all the manna
of heaven would never raise the mouse to the bulk of the mammoth.

 Benjamin Rush (1745–1813)

DR. BENJAMIN RUSH was the most famous American physician of
his generation. Born in Philadelphia, Rush graduated from Princeton and studied medicine under Dr. Redman of his home city.
He then enrolled at the University of Edinburgh, one of Europe's
three great medical schools, and received his M.D. from that in-

[1] Buffon, xviii. 112 edit. Paris, 1764. [Jefferson's note]

stitution in 1768. The following year he was appointed Professor of Chemistry at the College of Philadelphia, and in 1791, when the College became a University, Professor of the Institute and Practice of Medicine. Rush was an early devotee of the cause of independence, served in the Continental Congress, signed the Declaration of Independence, became Surgeon-General of the Continental Army, and for fourteen years after the war was Treasurer of the National Mint. He was also interested in chemistry, engineering, theology, penology, and what would today be called psychiatry. His 1786 essay, *The Influence of Physical Causes on the Moral Faculty,* is a landmark in the history of psychiatric research.

Rush was a dedicated scientist, searching constantly for basic laws of medicine and openly critical of much of the medical knowledge of his time. Medicine was then a tangle of confusion, ignorance, and superstition. There existed no accepted theory of disease, little experimentation or research, few records, no reliable techniques of diagnosis, nor even a system of medical classification. The two most popular theories of medicine were the Cullenian and the Brunonian, named after Dr. William Cullen and Dr. John Brown, Scottish physicians. Cullen believed that disease originated in debilitation of a "life force" emanating from the brain; Brown considered illness an imbalance of "excitability" in the body. There were other widely differing theories, as well. The following essay served as an introduction to a series of lectures delivered by Rush on the state of medical knowledge near the close of the eighteenth century.

TEXT: Dagobert D. Runes, *The Selected Writings of Benjamin Rush* (New York, 1947), pp. 245–253.

Observations and Reasoning in Medicine

[A lecture of 1791]

Physicians have been divided into empirics and dogmatists. The former pretend to be guided by experience, and the latter by reasoning alone in their prescriptions. I object to both when separately employed. They lead alike to error and danger in the practice of physic. I shall briefly point out the evils which result from an exclusive reliance upon each of them.

1. Empiricism presupposes a correct and perfect knowledge of all the diseases of the human body, however varied they may be in their symptoms, seats, and force, by age, habit, sex, climate, season, and aliment. Now, it is well known, that the longest life is insufficient for the purpose of acquiring that knowledge. This will appear more evident, when we consider that it must be seated, exclusively, in the

memory; a faculty which is the most subject to decay, and the least faithful to us of any of the faculties of the mind. Few physicians, I believe, ever recollect, perfectly, the phenomena of any disease more than two years, and, perhaps, for a much shorter time, when they are engaged in extensive business.

2. Neither can the defect of experience, nor the decay, or weakness of the memory in one physician, be supplied by the experience and observations of others. Few men see the same objects through the same medium. How seldom do we find the histories of the same disease, or of the effects of the same medicine to agree, even when they are related by physicians of the most respectable characters for talents and integrity! An hundred circumstances, from the difference of treatment, produce a difference in the symptoms and issue of similar diseases, and in the operation of the same medicines. The efforts of nature, are, moreover, often mistaken for the effects of a favourite prescription; and, in some instances, the crisis of a disease has been ascribed to medicines which have been thrown out of a window, or emptied behind a fire.

3. If it were possible to obviate all the inconveniences and dangers from solitary experience which have been mentioned, an evil would arise from the nature of the human mind, which would defeat all the advantages that might be expected from it. This evil is a disposition to reason upon all medical subjects, without being qualified by education for that purpose. As well might we attempt to control the motions of the heart by the action of the will, as to suspend, for a moment, that operation of the mind, which consists in drawing inferences from facts. To observe, is to think, and to think, is to reason in medicine. Hence we find theories in the writings of the most celebrated practical physicians, even of those who preface their works by declaiming against idle and visionary speculations in our science; but, I will add, further, that I believe no empiric ever gave a medicine without cherishing a theoretical indication of cure in his mind. Some acrid humour is to be obtunded, some viscid fluid is to be thinned, some spasm is to be resolved, or debility in some part of the body is to be obviated, in all his prescriptions. To an exclusive reliance upon theory in medicine, there are an equal number of objections. I shall only mention a few of them.

1. Our imperfect knowledge of the structure of the human body, and of the laws of the animal economy.

2. The limited extent of the human understanding, which acquires truth too slowly to act with effect, in the numerous and rapid exigencies of diseases.

3. The influence of the imagination and passions, upon the understanding in its researches after truth. An opinion becomes dear to us

by being generated in our imaginations; and contradiction, by inflaming the passions, increases our attachment to error. It is for these reasons, we observe great, and even good men, so zealously devoted to their opinions, and the practice founded upon them, even after they have been exposed and refuted by subsequent discoveries in medicine.

From this view of the comparative insufficiency of experience and theory, in our science, it will be impossible to decide in favour of either of them in their separate states. The empirics and dogmatists have mutually charged each other with the want of successful practice. I believe them both, and will add, further, if an inventory of the mischief that has been done by empirics, within the present century, whether they acted under the cover of a diploma, or imposed upon the public by false and pompous advertisements, could be made out, and compared with the mischief which has been done by a practice in medicine, founded upon a belief in the archeus of Van Helmont, the anima medica of Stahl, the spasm of Hoffman, the morbid acrimonies of Boerhaave, the putrefaction of Cullen, and the debility of Brown, as the proximate causes of diseases, I am satisfied neither sect would have any cause of exultation, or triumph. Both would have more reason to lament the immense additions they have made to pestilence and the sword in their ravages upon the human race.

It is peculiar to man, to divide what was intended by the Author of nature to be indivisible. Religion and morals, government and liberty, nay, even reason and the senses, so happily paired by the Creator of the world, in the order in which they have been mentioned, have each been disunited by the caprice and folly of man. The evils which have arisen from this breach in the symmetry of the divine government cannot now be enumerated. It belongs to our present subject, only to take notice that the same hostile disposition in the human mind, to order and utility, appears in the attempts that have been made to separate experience and reasoning in medicine. They are necessarily united, and it is only by preserving and cultivating their union, that our science can be made to convey extensive and lasting blessings to mankind.

The necessity of combining theory and practice in medicine, may be illustrated, by the advantages which other sciences have derived from the union of principles and facts. The numerous benefits and pleasures we enjoy from the glasses which have been made use of to extend our vision to distant and minute objects, are the results of a knowledge of the principles of optics. The many useful inventions which are employed to shorten and facilitate labor, are the products of a knowledge of the principles of mechanics and hydraulics. The exploits of mariners in subduing the ocean, and all the benefits that have occurred to the world from the connection of the extremities of our globe by means of commerce, are the fruits of a knowledge in the principles of navigation. Equally great have been the advantages of theory in the science of medicine. It belongs to theory to accumulate facts; and hence we find the greatest stock of them is always possessed by speculative physicians. While simple observation may be compared to a power which creates an alphabet, theory resembles a power which arranges all its component parts in such a manner, as to produce words and ideas. But theory does more. It supplies in a great degree the place of experience, and thereby places youth and old age nearly upon a footing in the profession of medicine; for, with just principles, it is no more necessary for a young physician to see all the diseases of the human body before he prescribes for them, than it is for a mariner, who knows the principles of navigation, to visit all the ports in the world, in order to conduct his vessel in safety to them.

To illustrate still further the benefits of theory, I shall take notice of its influence upon the use of several celebrated and popular remedies.

Accident probably first suggested the use of cool air in the cure of fevers. For many years it was prescribed indiscriminately in every form and grade of those diseases, during which time it did as much harm as good. It was not until chemistry taught us that its good effects depended wholly upon its abstracting the heat of the body, that its application was limited to those fevers only, which are accompanied with preternatural heat, and excessive action in the blood-vessels. Since the use of cool air has been regulated by this principle, its effects have been uniformly salutary in inflammatory fevers.

While the Peruvian bark was believed to act as a specific in the cure of intermittents, it was often an ineffectual, and sometimes a destructive medicine; but since its tonic and astringent virtues have been ascertained, its injurious effects have been restrained, and its salutary operation extended to all those fevers, whether intermitting, remitting, or continual, in which a feeble morbid action takes place in the sanguiferous system.

Opium was formerly used only as an antidote to wakefulness and pain, during which time it often increased the danger and mortality of diseases; but since its stimulating virtues have been discovered, its exhibition has been regulated by the degree of excitement in the system, and hence it is now administered with uniform safety, or success.

Mercury was prescribed empirically for many years in the cure of several diseases, in which it often did great mischief; but since it has been discovered to act as a general stimulant and evacuant, such a ratio has been established between it, and the state of diseases, as to render it a safe and nearly an universal medicine.

In answer to what has been delivered in favor of the union of experience and reasoning in medicine, it has been said, that the most celebrated physicians, in all ages, have been empirics; among whom they class Hippocrates and Sydenham. This charge against the illustrious fathers of ancient and modern medicine is not just, for they both reasoned upon the causes, symptoms, and cure of diseases; and their works contain more theory, than is to be met with in many of the most popular systems of medicine. Their theories, it is true, are in many instances erroneous; but they were restrained from perverting their judgments, and impairing the success of their practice, by their great experience, and singular talents for extensive and accurate observation. This defence of Hippocrates and Sydenham does not apply to common empirics. They cure only by chance; for, by false reasoning, they detract from the advantages of their solitary experience. It is true, they often acquire reputation and wealth, but this must be ascribed to the credulity of their patients, and to the zeal with which they justify their preference of such physicians, by multiplying and exaggerating their cures, or by palliating, or denying their mistakes. It is for this reason that it has been well said, "Quacks are the greatest liars in the world, except their patients."

We are further told, in favour of empiricism, that physicians of the first character have acknowledged the fallacy of principles in medicine. I cannot assent to the truth of this assertion. It is contradicted by the history of our science in all ages and countries. The complaints of its fallacy, and even of its uncertainty, originate, I believe, in most cases, in ignorance, indolence, or imposture; and therefore were never uttered by men of eminence and integrity in our profession.

In the progress of medicine towards its present state of improvement, different theories or systems have been proposed by different authors. You will find a minute and entertaining account of such of them as have been handed down to us from antiquity in Dr. Black's History of Medicine. They are all necessarily imperfect, inasmuch as none of them embraces the numerous discoveries in anatomy, physiology, chemistry, materia medica, and natural philosophy, which have been made within the two last centuries in Europe. The systems which divide the physicians of the present day, are those of Dr. Stahl, Dr. Boerhaave, Dr. Cullen, and Dr. Brown.

1. Dr. Stahl lived and wrote in a country remarkable for the simplicity of the manners of its inhabitants. Their diseases partook of their temperate mode of living, and were often cured by the operations of nature, without the aid of medicine; hence arose Dr. Stahl's opinion of the vires naturæ medicatrices, or of the existence of an anima medica, whose business it was to watch over the health of the body. We shall show, therefore, the error of these supposed healing

powers in nature, and the extreme danger of trusting to them in the dangerous and complicated diseases, which are produced by the artificial customs of civilized life.

2. Dr. Boerhaave lived and wrote in a country in which a moist atmosphere, and an excessive quantity of unwholesome aliment, had produced an immense number of diseases of the skin. These were supposed to arise from an impure state of the blood, and hence lentor, tenuity, and acrimony in that fluid were supposed to be the proximate causes of all the diseases of the human body.

3. Dr. Cullen lived and wrote in a country in which indolence and luxury had let loose a train of diseases which appeared to be seated chiefly in the nervous system, and hence we find the laws of that system have been investigated and ascertained by him with a success which has no parallel in the annals of medicine. In his concentrated views of the nervous system he has overlooked, or but slightly glanced at the pathology of the bloodvessels, and by adopting the nosology of Sauvage, Linnæus, and Vogel, he has unfortunately led physicians to prescribe for the names of diseases, instead of their proximate cause.

4. In the system of Dr. Brown, we find clear and consistent views of the causes of animal life, also just opinions of the action of heat and cold, of stimulating, and what are called sedative medicines, and of the influence of the passions in the production and cure of diseases. But while he has thus shed light upon some parts of medicine, he has thrown a shade upon others. I shall hereafter take notice of all the errors of his system. At present I shall only say, I shall not admit with him, debility to be a disease. It is only its predisposing cause. Disease consists in morbid excitement, and is always of a partial nature: of course I shall reject his doctrine of equality of excitement in the morbid states of the body, and maintain, that the cure of diseases consists simply in restoring the equal and natural diffusion of excitement throughout every part of the system. If Dr. Cullen did harm by directing the attention of physicians, by means of his nosology, only to the names of diseases, how much more mischief has been done by Dr. Brown, by reducing them nearly to one class, and accommodating his prescriptions to the reverse state of the body, of that which constitutes their proximate cause.

A perfect system of medicine may be compared to a house, the different stories of which have been erected by different architects. The illustrious physicians who have been named, have a large claim upon our gratitude, for having, by their great, and successive labours, advanced the building to its present height. It belongs to the present and future generations to place a roof upon it, and thereby to complete the fabric of medicine.

In the following course of lectures I shall adopt such principles of Dr. Boerhaave, Dr. Cullen, and Dr. Brown, as I believe to be true, and shall add to them such others, as have been suggested to me, by my own observations and reflections.

If, in delivering new opinions, I should be so unfortunate as to teach any thing, which subsequent reflection or observation should discover to be erroneous, I shall publicly retract it. I am aware how much I shall suffer by this want of stability in error, but I have learned from one of my masters to "esteem truth the only knowledge, and that laboring to defend an error, is only striving to be more ignorant."

Upon those parts of our course on which I am unable to deliver principles, I shall lay before you a simple detail of facts. Our labor in this business will not be lost, for, however long those facts may appear to lie in a confused and solitary state, they will sooner or later unite in that order and relation to each other which was established at the creation of the world. From this union of prerelated truths, will arise, at some future period, a complete system of principles in medicine.

We live, gentlemen, in a revolutionary age. Our science has caught the spirit of the times, and more improvements have been made in all its branches, within the last twenty years, than had been made in a century before. From these events, so auspicious to medicine, may we not cherish a hope, that our globe is about to undergo those happy changes, which shall render it a more safe and agreeable abode to man, and thereby prepare it to receive the blessing of universal health and longevity; for premature deaths seem to have arisen from the operation of that infinite goodness which delivers from evils to come.

William Bartram (1739–1823)

WILLIAM BARTRAM was the son of John Bartram, himself a famous naturalist. Born in Pennsylvania of a Quaker family, raised in a household of science, William was a shy, retiring man, happiest when roaming in the forests, swamps, or fields, observing the natural life around him. From 1773 to 1777 a wealthy London physician, Dr. John Fothergill, financed Bartram for a series of field trips through the South, which was still one of the great scientifically unexplored areas of the colonies. The result was one of the great American nature books of all time, *Travels Through North and South Carolina, East and West Florida, the Cherokee Country, the Extensive Territories of the Muscoqules, or Creek Confederacy* . . . , published in Philadelphia in 1791.

Bartram's *Travels* went through three more editions, and was translated into German, French, and Dutch. A number of contemporary writers, such as Coleridge, Wordsworth, and Chateaubriand, used it as a source of information about American nature, and its literary influence was considerable in America and Europe. Bartram was almost as much romantic philosopher as scientific observer; a superb reporter of natural facts, he also saw nature as a harmonious, uncorrupted, divinely ordered creation of God.

TEXT: William Bartram, *Travels Through North and South Carolina* . . . (Philadelphia, 1791).

The Alligator

[From *Travels*, 1791]

The verges and islets of the lagoon were elegantly embellished with flowering plants and shrubs; the laughing coots with wings half spread were tripping over the little coves and hiding themselves in the tufts of grass; young broods of the painted summer teal, skimming the still surface of the waters, and following the watchful parent unconscious of danger, were frequently surprised by the voracious trout; and he, in turn, as often by the subtle, greedy alligator. Behold him rushing forth from the flags and reeds. His enormous body swells. His plaited tail, brandished high, floats upon the lake. The waters like a cataract descend from his opening jaws. Clouds of smoke issue from his dilated nostrils. The earth trembles with his thunder. When immediately, from the opposite coast of the lagoon, emerges from the deep his rival champion. They suddenly dart upon each other. The boiling surface of the lake marks their rapid course, and a terrific conflict commences. They now sink to the bottom folded together in horrid wreaths. The water becomes thick and discolored. Again they rise, their jaws clap together, re-echoing through the deep surrounding forests. Again they sink, when the contest ends at the muddy bottom of the lake, and the vanquished makes a hazardous escape, hiding himself in the muddy, turbulent waters and sedge on a distant shore. The proud victor exulting returns to the place of action. The shores and forests resound his dreadful roar, together with the triumphing shouts of the plaited tribes around, witnesses of the horrid combat.

My apprehensions were highly alarmed after being a spectator of so dreadful a battle. It was obvious that every delay would but tend to increase my dangers and difficulties, as the sun was near setting, and the alligators gathered around my harbor from all quarters. From these considerations I concluded to be expeditious in my trip to the lagoon, in order to take some fish. Not thinking it prudent to take my fusee with me, lest I might lose it overboard in case of a battle, which I had every reason to dread before my return, I therefore furnished myself with a club for my defence, went on board, and penetrating the first line of those which surrounded my harbor, they gave way; but being pursued by several very large ones, I kept strictly on the watch, and paddled with all my might towards the entrance of the lagoon, hoping to be sheltered there from the multitude of my assailants; but ere I had half-way reached the place, I was attacked on all sides, several endeavoring to overset the canoe. My situation now became precarious to the last degree: two very large ones attacked me closely, at the same instant, rushing up with their heads and part of their bodies above the water, roaring terribly and belching floods of water over me. They struck their jaws together so close to my ears, as almost to stun me, and I expected every moment to be dragged out of the boat and instantly devoured. But I applied my weapons so effectually about me, though at random, that I was so successful as to beat them off a little; when, finding that they designed to renew the battle, I made for the shore, as the only means left me for my preservation; for, by keeping close to it, I should have my enemies on one side of me only, whereas I was before surrounded by them; and there was a probability, if pushed to the last extremity, of saving myself, by jumping out of the canoe on shore, as it is easy to outwalk them on land, although comparatively as swift as lightning in the water. I found this last expedient alone could fully answer my expectations, for as soon as I gained the shore, they drew off and kept aloof. This was a happy relief, as my confidence was, in some degree, recovered by it. On recollecting myself, I discovered that I had almost reached the entrance of the lagoon, and determined to venture in, if possible, to take a few fish, and then return to my harbor, while daylight continued: for I could now, with caution and resolution, make my way with safety along shore; and indeed there was no other way to regain my camp, without leaving my boat and making my retreat through the marshes and reeds, which, if I could even effect, would have been in a manner throwing myself away, for then there would have been no hopes of ever recovering my bark, and returning in safety to any settlements of men. I accordingly proceeded, and made good my entrance into the lagoon, though not without opposition from the alligators, who formed a line across the entrance, but did not pursue me into it, nor was I molested by any there, though there were some very large ones in a cove at the upper end. I soon caught more trout than I had present occasion for, and the air was too hot and sultry to admit of their being kept for many hours, even though salted or barbecued.

I now prepared for my return to camp, which I succeeded in with but little trouble, by keeping close to the shore; yet I was opposed upon re-entering the river out of the lagoon, and pursued near to my landing (though not closely attacked), particularly by an old daring one, about twelve feet in length, who kept close after me; and when I stepped on shore and turned about, in order to draw up my canoe, he rushed up near my feet, and lay there for some time, looking me in the face, his head and shoulders out of water. I resolved he should pay for his temerity, and having a heavy load in my fusee, I ran to my camp, and returning with my piece, found him with his foot on the gunwale of the boat, in search of fish. On my coming up he withdrew sullenly and slowly into the water, but soon returned and placed himself in his former position, looking at me, and seeming neither fearful nor any way disturbed. I soon despatched him by lodging the contents of my gun in his head, and then proceeded to cleanse and prepare my fish for supper; and accordingly took them out of the boat, laid them down on the sand close to the water, and began to scale them; when, raising my head, I saw before me, through the clear water, the head and shoulders of a very large alligator, moving slowly towards me. I instantly stepped back, when, with a sweep of his tail, he brushed off several of my fish. It was certainly most providential that I looked up at that instant, as the monster would probably, in less than a minute, have seized and dragged me into the river. This incredible boldness of the animal disturbed me greatly, supposing there could now be no reasonable safety for me during the night, but by keeping continually on the watch; I therefore, as soon as I had prepared the fish, proceeded to secure myself and effects in the best manner I could. In the first place, I hauled my bark upon the shore, almost clear out of the water, to prevent their oversetting or sinking her; after this, every movable was taken out and carried to my camp, which was but a few yards off; then ranging some dry wood in such order as was the most convenient, I cleared the ground round about it, that there might be no impediment in my way, in case of an attack in the night either from the water or the land; for I discovered by this time that this small isthmus, from its remote situation and fruitfulness, was resorted to by bears and wolves. Having prepared myself in the best manner I could, I charged my gun and proceeded to reconnoitre my camp and the adjacent grounds; when I discovered that the peninsula and grove, at the distance of about two hundred yards from my encampment on the land side, were invested by a cypress swamp covered with water, which below was joined to the shore of the little lake, and above to the marshes surrounding the lagoon; so that I was confined to an islet exceedingly circumscribed, and I found there was no other retreat for me, in case of an attack, but by either ascending one of the large oaks, or pushing off with my boat.

It was by this time dusk, and the alligators had nearly ceased their roar, when I was again alarmed by a tumultuous noise that seemed to be in my harbor, and therefore engaged my immediate attention. Returning to my camp, I found it undisturbed, and then continued on to the extreme point of the promontory, where I saw a scene, new and surprising, which at first threw my senses into such a tumult, that it was some time before I could comprehend what was the matter; however, I soon accounted for the prodigious assemblage of crocodiles at this place, which exceeded everything of the kind I had ever heard of.

How shall I express myself so as to convey an adequate idea of it to the reader, and at the same time avoid raising suspicions of my veracity? Should I say, that the river (in this place) from shore to shore, and perhaps near half a mile above and below me, appeared to be one solid bank of fish, of various kinds, pushing through this narrow pass of St. Juan's into the little lake, on their return down the river, and that the alligators were in such incredible numbers, and so close together from shore to shore, that it would have been easy to have walked across on their heads, had the animals been harmless? What expressions can sufficiently declare the shocking scene that for some minutes continued, whilst this mighty army of fish were forcing the pass? During this attempt, thousands, I may say hundreds of thousands, of them were caught and swallowed by the devouring alligators. I have seen an alligator take up out of the water several great fish at a time, and just squeeze them betwixt his jaws while the tails of the great trout flapped about his eyes and lips, ere he had swallowed them. The horrid noise of their closing jaws, their plunging amidst the broken banks of fish, and rising with their prey some feet upright above the water, the floods of water and blood rushing out of their mouths, and the clouds of vapor issuing from their wide nostrils, were truly frightful. This scene continued at intervals during the night, as the fish came to the pass. After this sight, shocking and tremendous as it was, I found myself somewhat easier and more reconciled to my situation; being convinced that their extraordinary assemblage here was owing to this annual feast of fish; and that they were so well employed in their own element, that I had little occasion to fear their paying me a visit.

It being now almost night, I returned to my camp, where I had left my fish broiling, and my kettle of rice stewing; and having with me oil, pepper and salt, and excellent oranges hanging in abundance over my head (a valuable substitute for vinegar), I sat down and regaled myself cheerfully. Having finished my repast, I rekindled my fire for light, and whilst I was revising the notes of my past day's journey, I was suddenly roused with a noise behind me towards the main-land. I sprang up on my feet, and listening, I distinctly heard some creature wading in the water of the isthmus. I seized my gun and went cautiously from my camp, directing my steps towards the noise: when I had advanced about thirty yards, I halted behind a coppice of orange trees, and soon perceived two very large bears,

which had made their way through the water, and had landed in the
grove, about one hundred yards distance from me, and were advancing
towards me. I waited until they were within thirty yards of me: they
there began to snuff and look towards my camp: I snapped my piece,
but it flashed, on which they both turned about and galloped off, plunging through the water and swamp, never halting, as I suppose, until
they reached fast land, as I could hear them leaping and plunging a
long time. They did not presume to return again, nor was I molested
by any other creature, except being occasionally awakened by the
whooping of owls, screaming of bitterns, or the wood-rats running
amongst the leaves. . . .

The alligator when full grown is a very large and terrible creature,
and of prodigious strength, activity, and swiftness in the water. I have
seen them twenty feet in length, and some are supposed to be twenty-
two or twenty-three feet. Their body is as large as that of a horse;
their shape exactly resembles that of a lizard, except their tail, which
is flat or cuneiform, being compressed on each side, and gradually
diminishing from the abdomen to the extremity, which, with the whole
body is covered with horny plates or squamæ, impenetrable when on
the body of the live animal, even to a rifle-ball, except about their head
and just behind their forelegs, or arms, where it is said they are only
vulnerable. The head of a full grown one is about three feet, and the
mouth opens nearly the same length; their eyes are small in proportion
and seem sunk deep in the head, by means of the prominency of the
brows; the nostrils are large, inflated and prominent on the top, so that
the head in the water resembles, at a distance, a great chunk of wood
floating about. Only the upper jaw moves, which they raise almost
perpendicular, so as to form a right angle with the lower one. In the
forepart of the upper jaw, on each side, just under the nostrils, are two
very large, thick, strong teeth or tusks, not very sharp, but rather the
shape of a cone: these are as white as the finest polished ivory, and are
not covered by any skin or lips, and always in sight, which gives the
creature a frightful appearance: in the lower jaw are holes opposite
to these teeth, to receive them: when they clap their jaws together
it causes a surprising noise, like that which is made by forcing a heavy
plank with violence upon the ground, and may be heard at a great
distance.

But what is yet more surprising to a stranger, is the incredible loud
and terrifying roar which they are capable of making, especially in
the spring season, their breeding-time. It most resembles very heavy
distant thunder, not only shaking the air and waters, but causing the
earth to tremble; and when hundreds and thousands are roaring at the
same time, you can scarcely be persuaded but that the whole globe is
violently and dangerously agitated.

. An old champion, who is perhaps absolute sovereign of a little lake or lagoon (when fifty less than himself are obliged to content themselves with swelling and roaring in little coves round about), darts forth from the reedy coverts all at once, on the surface of the waters, in a right line; at first seemingly as rapid as lightning, but gradually more slowly until he arrives at the centre of the lake, when he stops. He now swells himself by drawing in wind and water through his mouth, which causes a loud, sonorous rattling in the throat for near a minute, but it is immediately forced out again through his mouth and nostrils, with a loud noise, brandishing his tail in the air, and the vapor ascending from his nostrils like smoke. At other times, when swollen to an extent ready to burst, his head and tail lifted up, he spins or twirls round on the surface of the water. He acts his part like an Indian chief when rehearsing his feats of war and then retiring, the exhibition is continued by others who dare to step forth, and strive to excel each other, to gain the attention of the favorite female.

⊄⊰ Samuel Latham Mitchill (1764–1831)

SAMUEL LATHAM MITCHILL, born into a well-to-do Long Island Quaker family, was privately educated and apprenticed as a medical student to Dr. Samuel Bard, one of New York City's best physicians. He studied at Edinburgh, graduated with his M.D. and high honors in 1786, and returned to New York to become one of its leading citizens. Mitchill was a charming man with friends in every walk of life, among them Robert Fulton, Charles Brockden Brown, DeWitt Clinton, James Kent, Chancellor Livingston, and Washington Irving. He was perhaps the city's most famous after-dinner speaker, a member of forty-nine clubs and societies, and at various times a member of the United States Senate and the New York legislature.

At the same time, Mitchill was a first-rate scientist. He was made Professor of Botany and Materia Medica in Columbia College of Physicians and Surgeons, and did much to introduce the new chemistry of Lavoisier into the United States. He wrote the first descriptive geology of North America, and the first authoritative study of American fishes. He did good research in agriculture, Indian languages, psychology, archaeology, and zoology; he founded *The Medical Repository*, the first medical journal in the United States, and edited it for twenty-four years. His letter to a medical student in answer to a question about hallucinations and insanity is a good example of his quick, penetrating mind.

TEXT: Courtney R. Hall, *A Scientist in the Early Republic* (New York, 1934), pp. 136–139.

The Illusions of the Human Senses

[Letter to Alexander Anderson, March 6, 1796]

Dear sir

I regret that I cannot find for you a copy of pamphlet published in Albany in 1789 on the *Illusions of Human Senses*. I must therefore endeavor to give you an abstract from my notes and from memory, together with such ideas on the subject as have occurred to me upon deeper reflection, since that time.

The principle which I endeavored to establish was this: "that conditions of the body occur, in which the organs of sense do from internal causes and without the aid of external agents, take upon themselves a configuration or impression, similar to that which is usually induced by the action of material objects and occurrences from without."

1. This sometimes happens when the person whose sensations are thus perverted is himself quite conscious of the deception, and can thus counteract in a good degree the influence of those false suggestions upon the mind, by the effects of will and the exercise of judgment. Now and then the singular state of one or more of the senses comes on in a person who is in other respects well in health; and in such cases the change wrought is feeble and fugitive. The spectra left upon the retina after looking at the sun or any other bright or highly coloured body are of this sort; and the case of our late Professor Nicoll, as he related it to me, was a very remarkable one, wherein the ears as well as the eyes were strangely affected while he was perfectly aware of the imposition. High-wrought imagination and poetic fancy seem to belong to this head.

2. Another memorable instance of such illusions is, when besides this affection of the sensorial organs there is a belief wrought, at least for the time being, of the reality of what appears. The whole of the phenomena of dreaming, incubus, and of delirium, are of this kind. In dreaming, the shapes and colours of things seen, the distinctness of notes and voices, and even in some instances the pleasurable and painful perceptions referable to the sense of feeling, oftentimes surpass anything that can be impressed upon the eye, ear, or touch, even by real objects, in a state of wakefulness. A belief of their actual existence is from the senses so operated upon, impressed upon the mind; but this belief instantly vanishes on waking; and the whole series of events that just before seemed with so much distinctness to be present is confessed to be an illusion.

In nightmare and delusion too, the person who raves, tho' firm in the persuasion for the present, that things are truly as he fancies them, acknowledges his error and stands self convicted as the fit is over. The false suggestions in these ailments are, as in dreaming, found in morbid conditions of the organs of sense induced without the customary operation of external bodies.

3. A third case is where the images presented to the sensorium by morbid sensation are not only not present, but where they are wholly different from anything which exists, and have consequently no prototype in nature. Wicked persons and such as are highly superstitious and enthusiastic, whose minds are under deep concern, or are violently agitated, and whose organs of sense are irritable, are often the subjects of this illusion. Hence devils in all imaginable forms, angels in every possible variety of shape, spectres, ghosts and apparitions, are frequently seen by persons suffering this form of disease, and visions, revelations and extraordinary communications made to them. They see invisible things, they hear sounds not audible. The irritable condition of the eyes suggests to them inward light beaming with celestial influence upon them, and giving a foretaste of Heaven; or impresses them with the notions of fires and flames threatening them with infernal torture and anticipating the pains of Hell. There is nothing hideous, deformed or monstrous which may not thus be presented to the mind originating in distempered sense and giving rise to fallacious experience.

4. There is yet another example of morbid sensation wherein the impressions made upon the senses from 'inward causes' are stronger than those occasioned by external occurrences and this condition of the organs is so permanent and obstinate that it continues during the time of wakefulness and is not to be dispelled by any effort of the will. When this happens in a single point or in a few respects it constitutes partial insanity. When false impressions ensue on many objects they constitute general or total mania. The fury of such madness will depend upon the vividity or force of the distempered sensation. Its duration will be proportional to the permanent or indelible nature of the impression. And here there is generally the strongest conviction of the truth of the false perception. From this erroneous principle proceed an endless variety of odd deductions and applications, flowing however in many instances, logically enough from the premises.

I consider the state of body to which mania belongs as a morbid sensation, wherein without corresponding exciting powers from without, a condition of some or other of the organs of sense is induced from inward causes similar to what usually happens from the operation of external agents and which probably would be brought on by these . . . [Mitchill suggests at this point that the causes of insanity may lie in the brain, in the arterial system, or in the organs of sense themselves].

As to the seat of madness, I have strong doubts of its being in the brain. The disorder of the thinking powers is secondary, and I believe always subsequent to vitiated sensations. The organs of sense, then, or sentient extremities of the nerves, which have been considered by Darwin, with great appearance of truth, to be the seats of thought, are, I apprehend, particularly and primarily diseased in madness. Dissections of the brain in manias have thrown little or no light upon this malady; and the brain has been found excessively deranged in its structure by diseases, as distention, supporation, [word illegible], and in other ailments, without producing any corresponding disorder of mind, and I consider it vain and fruitless to search the brain for cause of mania. As it is grounded in false sensation, the organs of sense must be examined with a view to detect the mischief there. The principal internal stimulus acting upon the sentient extremities of the nerves is the blood; and if an irregular distribution of blood, its circulation with too great or too little force, in quantity too large or too small, are capable of inducing disorders or morbid changes in the organs of sense, then a large share of maniacal affection is inherent in the sanguiferous system.

I am, dear sir, with much esteem and regard yours

Saml. L. Mitchill.

Alexander Wilson (1776–1813)

ALEXANDER WILSON was born into a poor Scottish family, and early in life was apprenticed to a weaver. Almost entirely self-educated, he left Scotland for America in 1794, settled in Philadelphia, and taught country school in Pennsylvania and New Jersey for some years. His next-door neighbor, William Bartram, noted his interest in nature, encouraged him, and lent him volumes from his library.

Discovering that ornithology was an undeveloped branch of natural science, Wilson began observing birds and collecting specimens. Traveling thousands of miles by every known means of transportation, he pursued his searches into the South and West. His monumental *American Ornithology* appeared in nine volumes between 1808 and 1814. Wilson was, without a doubt, the first to open the field of ornithology in the United States, and his work was immediately recognized in Europe as a scientific contribution of the first order. Though John James Audubon later extended and systematized Wilson's work, he did not supersede it.

TEXT: Alexander Wilson, *American Ornithology; or, The Natural History of the Birds of the United States* (Philadelphia, 1808–14), I, 12–17.

The Blue Jay

[From *American Ornithology*, 1808–1814]

The Blue Jay is an almost universal inhabitant of the woods, frequenting the thickest settlements, as well as the deepest recesses of the forest, where his squalling voice often alarms the deer, to the disappointment and mortification of the hunter; one of whom informed me, that he made it a point, in summer, to kill every Jay he could meet with. In the charming season of spring, when every thicket pours forth harmony, the part performed by the Jay always catches the ear. He appears to be among his fellow musicians what the trumpeter is in a band, some of his notes having no distant resemblance to the tones of that instrument. These he has the faculty of changing through a great variety of modulations, according to the particular humour he happens to be in. When disposed for ridicule, there is scarce a bird whose peculiarities of song he cannot tune his notes to. When engaged in the blandishments of love they resemble the soft chatterings of a duck, and while he nestles among the thick branches of the cedar, are scarce heard at a few paces distance; but no sooner does he discover your approach, than he sets up a sudden and vehement outcry, flying off, and screaming with all his might, as if he called the whole feathered tribes of the neighbourhood to witness some outrageous usage he had received. When he hops undisturbed among the high branches of the oak and hickory, they become soft and musical; and his calls of the female a stranger would readily mistake for the repeated creakings of an ungreased wheelbarrow. All these he accompanies with various nods, jerks, and other gesticulations, for which the whole tribe of Jays are so remarkable, that, with some other peculiarities, they might have very well justified the great Swedish naturalist in forming them into a separate genus by themselves.

The Blue Jay builds a large nest, frequently in the cedar, sometimes on an apple-tree, lines it with dry fibrous roots, and lays five eggs of a dull olive, spotted with brown. The male is particularly careful of not being heard near the place, making his visits as silently and secretly as possible. His favorite food is chestnuts, acorns, and Indian corn. He occasionally feeds on bugs and caterpillars, and sometimes pays a plundering visit to the orchard, cherry-rows, and potato patch; and has been known in times of scarcity, to venture into the barn, through openings between the weatherboards. In these cases he is extremely active and silent, and if surprised in the fact makes his escape with precipitation, but without noise, as if conscious of his criminality.

Of all birds he is the most bitter enemy of the Owl. No sooner has he discovered the retreat of one of these, than he summons the whole feathered fraternity to his assistance, who surround the glimmering *solitaire,* and attack him from all sides, raising such a shout as may be heard, in a still day, more than half a mile off. When in my hunting excursions I have passed near this scene of tumult, I have imagined to myself that I have heard the insulting party venting their respective charges with all the virulency of a Billingsgate mob; the owl, meanwhile, returning every compliment with a broad goggling stare. The war becomes louder and louder, and the owl at length forced to betake himself to flight, is followed by the whole train of his persecutors, until driven beyond the boundaries of their jurisdiction.

But the Blue Jay himself is not guiltless of similar depredations with the owl, and becomes, in his turn, the very tyrant he detested, when he sneaks through the woods, as he frequently does, and among the thickets and hedge-rows, plundering every nest he can find of its eggs, tearing up the callow young by piecemeal and spreading alarm and sorrow around him. The cries of the distressed parents soon bring together a number of interested spectators (for birds in such circumstances seem truly to sympathize with each other), and he is sometimes attacked with such spirit as to be under the necessity of making a speedy retreat.

He will sometimes assault small birds, with the intention of killing and devouring them; an instance of which I myself once witnessed over a piece of woods near the borders of Schuylkill; where I saw him engaged for more than five minutes pursuing what I took to be a species of Motacilla, wheeling, darting and doubling in the air, and at last, to my great satisfaction, got disappointed, by the escape of his intended prey. In times of great extremity, when his hoard or magazine is frozen up, buried in snow, or perhaps exhausted, he becomes very voracious, and will make a meal of whatever carrion or other animal substance comes in the way; and has been found regaling himself on the bowels of a Robin in less than five minutes after it was shot.

There are, however, individual exceptions to this general character for plunder and outrage, a proneness for which is probably often occasioned by the wants and irritations of necessity. A Blue Jay, which I have kept for some time, and with whom I am on terms of familiarity, is in reality a very notable example of mildness of disposition and sociability of manners. An accident in the woods first put me in possession of this bird, while in full plumage, and in high health and spirits; I carried him home with me, and put him into a cage already occupied by a Gold-winged Woodpecker, where he was saluted with such rudeness, and received such a drubbing from the lord of the manor, for entering his premises, that, to save his life, I was obliged to take him out again. I then put him into another cage, where the only tenant was a female Orchard Oriole. She also put on airs of alarm, as if she considered herself endangered and insulted by the intrusion; the Jay meanwhile sat mute and motionless on the bottom of the cage, either dubious of his own situation, or willing to allow time for the fears of his neighbour to subside. Accordingly in a few minutes, after displaying various threatening gestures (like some of those Indians we read of in their first interviews with the whites), she began to make her approaches, but with great circumspection, and readiness for retreat. Seeing, however, the Jay begin to pick up some crumbs of broken chestnuts in a humble and peaceable way, she also descended, and began to do the same; but at the slightest motion of her new guest, wheeled round and put herself on the defensive. All this ceremonious jealousy vanished before evening; and they now roost together, feed, and play together, in perfect harmony and good-humor. When the Jay goes to drink, his messmate very impudently jumps into the saucer to wash herself, throwing the water in showers over her companion, who bears it all patiently; venturing now and then to take a sip between every splash, without betraying the smallest token of irritation. On the contrary, he seems to take pleasure in his little fellow-prisoner, allowing her to pick (which she does very gently) about his whiskers, and to clean his claws from the minute fragments of chestnuts which happen to adhere to them. This attachment on the one part, and mild condescension on the other, may, perhaps, be partly the effect of mutual misfortunes, which are found not only to knit mankind, but many species of inferior animals, more closely together; and shews that the disposition of the Blue Jay may be humanized, and rendered susceptible of affectionate impressions, even for those birds which in a state of nature he would have no hesitation in making a meal of.

He is not only bold and vociferous, but possesses a considerable talent for mimicry, and seems to enjoy great satisfaction in mocking and teasing other birds, particularly the little hawk (*F. Sparverius*), imitating his cry wherever he sees him, and squealing out as if caught; this soon brings a number of his own tribe around him, who all join in the frolic, darting about the hawk and feigning the cries of a bird sorely wounded and already under the clutches of its devourer; while others lie concealed in bushes, ready to second their associates in the attack. But this ludicrous farce often terminates tragically. The hawk singling out one of the most insolent and provoking, sweeps upon him in an unguarded moment, and offers him up a sacrifice to his hunger and resentment. In an instant the tune is changed; all their buffoonery vanishes, and loud and incessant screams proclaim their disaster.

Wherever the Jay has had the advantage of education from man, he has not only shewn himself an apt scholar, but his suavity of manners seems equalled only by his art and contrivances, though it must be confessed that his itch for thieving keeps pace with all his other acquirements. Dr. Mease, on the authority of Colonel Postell, of South

Carolina, informs me that a Blue Jay which was brought up in the family of the latter gentleman, had all the tricks and loquacity of a parrot; pilfered every thing he could conveniently carry off, and hid them in holes and crevices; answered to his name with great sociability, when called on; could articulate a number of words pretty distinctly; and when he heard any uncommon noise or loud talking, seemed impatient to contribute his share to the general festivity (as he probably thought it) by a display of all the oratorical powers he was possessed of.

Mr. Bartram relates an instance of the Jay's sagacity worthy of remark. "Having caught a Jay in the winter season," says he, "I turned him loose in the greenhouse, and fed him with corn (zea, maize), the heart of which they are very fond of. This grain being ripe and hard, the bird at first found a difficulty in breaking it, as it would start from his bill when he struck it. After looking about, and as if considering for a moment, he picked up his grain, carried and placed it close up in a corner of the shelf, between the wall and a plant box, where being confined on three sides he soon effected his purpose, and continued afterwards to make use of this same practical expedient. The Jay," continues this judicious observer, "is one of the most useful agents in the economy of nature, for disseminating forest trees, and other ruciferous and hard-seeded vegetables on which they feed. Their chief employment during the autumnal season is foraging to supply their winter stores. In performing this necessary duty they drop abundance of seed in their flight over fields, hedges, and by fences, where they alight to deposit them in the post holes, &c. It is remarkable what numbers of young trees rise up in fields and pastures after a wet winter and spring. These birds alone are capable in a few years' time, to replant all the cleared lands."

◁ℜ Benjamin Franklin (1706–1790)

FRANKLIN, like Thomas Jefferson, preferred to keep his religious principles to himself, but he held them firmly and practiced them with deep sincerity. "Metaphysical readings," he once said, caused him "great uncertainty," so he had little interest in theological speculation or religious disputation. Since the Calvinism in which he was reared neither suited his temperament nor satisfied his scientific mind, he evolved his own set of religious principles, which met his twin tests of Christianity and rationality, and lived by them.

Franklin was, in effect, a deist who found his reasonable, beneficent, all-wise God visible in nature and in His works. The most acceptable way to worship this Deity, he believed, was to serve his fellow men; life was good to him, and Franklin felt that he could best "show his gratitude for these mercies from God by a readiness to help His other children and my brethren." He thought that Christianity ought to be translated into life. "The hearing and reading of sermons," he wrote, "may be useful; but, if men rest in hearing and praying, as many do, it is as if a tree should value itself on being watered and putting forth leaves, tho' it never produce any fruit." He contributed to a Protestant church and a Jewish synagogue, and helped his friend John Carroll to become the first Catholic archbishop in the United States. Franklin attacked no sect, praised none, and worshiped his God in his own way.

TEXTS: John Bigelow, ed., *The Works of Benjamin Franklin* (New York, 1904), I, 148–151, 185–201. Albert H. Smyth, ed., *The Writings of Benjamin Franklin* (New York, 1905–7), V. 437–438; X, 83–85.

The Faith of a Reasonable Man

[From *Autobiography* (1771 ff.)]

Before I enter upon my public appearance in business, it may be well to let you know the then state of my mind with regard to my principles and morals, that you may see how far those influenc'd the future events of my life. My parents had early given me religious impressions, and brought me through my childhood piously in the Dissenting way. But I was scarce fifteen when, after doubting by turns of several points, as I found them disputed in the different books I read, I began to doubt of Revelation itself. Some books against Deism fell into my hands; they were said to be the substance of sermons preached at Boyle's Lectures. It happened that they wrought an effect on me quite contrary to what was intended by them; for the arguments of the Deists, which were quoted to be refuted, appeared to me much stronger than the refutations; in short, I soon became a thorough Deist. My arguments perverted some others, particularly Collins and Ralph; but each of them having afterwards wrong'd me greatly without the least compunction, and recollecting Keith's conduct towards me (who was another freethinker), and my own towards Vernon and Miss Read, which at times gave me great trouble, I began to suspect that this doctrine, tho' it might be true, was not very useful. My London pamphlet, which had for its motto these lines of Dryden:

> Whatever is, is right. Though purblind man
> Sees but a part o' the chain, the nearest link:
> His eyes not carrying to the equal beam,
> That poises all above;

and from the attributes of God, his infinite wisdom, goodness, and power, concluded that nothing could possibly be wrong in the world, and that vice and virtue were empty distinctions, no such things existing, appear'd now not so clever a performance as I once thought it; and I doubted whether some error had not insinuated itself unperceiv'd into my argument, so as to infect all that follow'd, as is common in metaphysical reasonings.

I grew convinc'd that *truth, sincerity,* and *integrity* in dealings between man and man were of the utmost importance to the felicity of life; and I form'd written resolutions, which still remain in my journal book, to practice them ever while I lived. Revelation had indeed no weight with me, as such; but I entertain'd an opinion that, though certain actions might not be bad *because* they were forbidden by it, or good *because* it commanded them, yet probably those actions might be forbidden *because* they were bad for us, or commanded *because* they were beneficial to us, in their own natures, all the circumstances of things considered. And this persuasion, with the kind hand of Providence, or some guardian angel, or accidental favorable circumstances and situations, or all together, preserved me, thro' this dangerous time of youth, and the hazardous situations I was sometimes in among strangers remote from the eye and advice of my father, without any willful gross immorality or injustice that might have been expected from my want of religion. I say willful, because the instances I have mentioned had something of *necessity* in them, from my youth, inexperience, and the knavery of others. I had therefore a tolerable character to begin with; I valued it properly, and determined to preserve it. . . .

I had been religiously educated as a Presbyterian, and tho' some of the dogmas of that persuasion, such as *the eternal decrees of God, election, reprobation, etc.,* appeared to me unintelligible, others doubtful, and I early absented myself from the public assemblies of the sect, Sunday being my studying day, I never was without some religious principles. I never doubted, for instance, the existence of the Deity; that he made the world, and govern'd it by his Providence; that the most acceptable service of God was the doing good to man; that our souls are immortal; and that all crime will be punished, and virtue rewarded, either here or hereafter. These I esteem'd the essentials of every religion; and, being to be found in all the religions we had in our country, I respected them all, tho' with different degrees of respect, as I found them more or less mix'd with other articles, which, without any tendency to inspire, promote, or confirm morality, serv'd principally to divide us, and make us unfriendly to one another. This respect to all, with an opinion that the worst had some good effects, induc'd me to avoid all discourse that might tend to lessen the good opinion another might have of his own religion; and as our province increas'd in people, and new places of worship were continually wanted, and generally erected by voluntary contribution, my mite for such purpose, whatever might be the sect, was never refused.

Tho' I seldom attended any public worship, I had still an opinion of its propriety, and of its utility when rightly conducted, and I regularly paid my annual subscription for the support of the only Presbyterian minister or meeting we had in Philadelphia. He us'd to visit me sometimes as a friend, and admonish me to attend his administrations, and I was now and then prevail'd on to do so, once for five Sundays successively. Had he been in my opinion a good preacher, perhaps I might have continued, notwithstanding the occasion I had for the Sunday's leisure in my course of study; but his discourses were chiefly either polemic arguments, or explications of the peculiar doctrines of our sect, and were all to me very dry, uninteresting, and unedifying, since not a single moral principle was inculcated or enforc'd, their aim seeming to be rather to make us Presbyterians than good citizens.

At length he took for his text that verse of the fourth chapter of Philippians: *"Finally, brethren, whatsoever things are true, honest, just, pure, lovely, or of good report, if there be any virtue, or any praise, think on these things."* And I imagin'd, in a sermon on such a text, we could not miss of having some morality. But he confin'd himself to five points only, as meant by the apostle, viz.: 1. Keeping holy the Sabbath day. 2. Being diligent in reading the holy Scriptures. 3. Attending duly the publick worship. 4. Partaking of the Sacrament. 5. Paying a due respect to God's ministers. These might be all good things; but, as they were not the kind of good things that I expected from that text, I despaired of ever meeting with them from any other, was disgusted, and attended his preaching no more. I had some years before compos'd a little Liturgy, or form of prayer, for my own private use (viz., in 1728), entitled *Articles of Belief and Acts of Religion.* I return'd to the use of this, and went no more to the public assemblies. My conduct might be blameable, but I leave it, without attempting further to excuse it; my present purpose being to relate facts, and not to make apologies for them.

It was about this time I conceiv'd the bold and arduous project of arriving at moral perfection. I wish'd to live without committing any fault at any time; I would conquer all that either natural inclination, custom, or company might lead me into. As I knew, or thought I knew, what was right and wrong, I did not see why I might not always do the one and avoid the other. But I soon found I had undertaken a task of more difficulty than I had imagined. While my care was employ'd in guarding against one fault, I was often surprised by another; habit took the advantage of inattention; inclination was sometimes too strong for reason. I concluded, at length, that the mere speculative conviction that it was our interest to be completely virtuous, was not sufficient to prevent our slipping; and that the contrary habits must be broken, and good ones acquired and established, before we can have any dependence on a steady, uniform rectitude of conduct. For this purpose I therefore contrived the following method.

In the various enumerations of the moral virtues I had met with in my reading, I found the catalogue more or less numerous, as different writers included more or fewer ideas under the same name. Temperance, for example, was by some confined to eating and drinking, while by others it was extended to mean the moderating every other pleasure, appetite, inclination, or passion, bodily or mental, even to our avarice and ambition. I propos'd to myself, for the sake of clearness, to use rather more names, with fewer ideas annex'd to each, than a few names with more ideas; and I included under thirteen names of virtues all that at that time occurr'd to me as necessary or desirable, and annexed to each a short precept, which fully express'd the extent I gave to its meaning.

These names of virtues, with their precepts, were:

1. Temperance
Eat not to dullness; drink not to elevation.

2. Silence
Speak not but what may benefit others or yourself; avoid trifling conversation.

3. Order
Let all your things have their places; let each part of your business have its time.

4. Resolution
Resolve to perform what you ought; perform without fail what you resolve.

5. Frugality
Make no expense but to do good to others or yourself; i. e., waste nothing.

6. Industry
Lose no time; be always employ'd in something useful; cut off all unnecessary actions.

7. Sincerity
Use no hurtful deceit, think innocently and justly; and, if you speak, speak accordingly.

8. Justice
Wrong none by doing injuries, or omitting the benefits that are your duty.

9. Moderation

Avoid extreams; forbear resenting injuries so much as you think they deserve.

10. Cleanliness

Tolerate no uncleanliness in body, cloaths, or habitation.

11. Tranquillity

Be not disturbed at trifles, or at accidents common or unavoidable.

12. Chastity

Rarely use venery but for health or offspring, never to dullness, weakness, or the injury of your own or another's peace or reputation.

13. Humility

Imitate Jesus and Socrates.

My intention being to acquire the *habitude* of all these virtues, I judg'd it would be well not to distract my attention by attempting the whole at once, but to fix it on one of them at a time; and, when I should be master of that, then proceed to another, and so on till I had gone thro' the thirteen; and, as the previous acquisition of some might facilitate the acquisition of certain others, I arrang'd them with that view, as they stand above. *Temperance* first, as it tends to procure that coolness and clearness of head, which is so necessary where constant vigilance was to be kept up, and guard maintained against the unremitting attraction of ancient habits, and the force of perpetual temptations. This being acquir'd and establish'd, Silence would be more easy; and my desire being to gain knowledge at the same time that I improv'd in virtue, and considering that in conversation it was obtain'd rather by the use of the ears than of the tongue, and therefore wishing to break a habit I was getting into of prattling, punning, and joking, which only made me acceptable to trifling company, I gave *Silence* the second place. This and the next, *Order,* I expected would allow me more time for attending to my project and my studies. *Resolution,* once become habitual, would keep me firm in my endeavors to obtain all the subsequent virtues; *Frugality* and *Industry* freeing me from my remaining debt, and producing affluence and independence, would make more easy the practice of *Sincerity* and *Justice,* etc., etc. Conceiving, then, that, agreeably to the advice of Pythagoras in his *Golden Verses,* daily examination would be necessary, I contrived the following method for conducting that examination.

I made a little book, in which I allotted a page for each of the virtues. I rul'd each page with red ink, so as to have seven columns, one for each day of the week, marking each column with a letter for the day. I cross'd these columns with thirteen red lines, marking the beginning of each line with the first letter of one of the virtues, on which line, and in its proper column, I might mark, by a little black spot, every fault I found upon examination to have been committed respecting that virtue upon that day.

Form of the Pages

	S.	M.	T.	W.	T.	F.	S.
TEMPERANCE.							
EAT NOT TO DULLNESS; DRINK NOT TO ELEVATION.							
T.							
S.	✷	✷		✷		✷	
O.	✷ ✷	✷	✷		✷	✷	✷
R.			✷			✷	
F.		✷			✷		
I.			✷				
S.							
J.							
M.							
C.							
T.							
C.							
H.							

I determined to give a week's strict attention to each of the virtues successively. Thus, in the first week, my great guard was to avoid even the least offence against *Temperance,* leaving the other virtues to their ordinary chance, only marking every evening the faults of the day. Thus, if in the first week I could keep my first line, marked T, clear of spots, I suppos'd the habit of that virtue so much strengthen'd, and its opposite weaken'd, that I might venture extending my attention to include the next, and for the following week keep both lines clear of spots. Proceeding thus to the last, I could go thro' a course compleat in thirteen weeks, and four courses in a year. And like him who, having a garden to weed, does not attempt to eradicate all the bad herbs at once, which would exceed his reach and his strength, but works on one of the beds at a time, and, having accomplish'd the first, proceeds to a second, so I should have, I hoped, the encouraging pleasure of seeing on my pages the progress I made in virtue, by clearing successively my lines of their spots, till in the end, by a number of courses, I should be happy in viewing a clean book, after a thirteen weeks' daily examination.

This my little book had for its motto these lines from Addison's *Cato:*

> Here will I hold. If there 's a power above us
> (And that there is, all nature cries aloud
> Thro' all her works), He must delight in virtue;
> And that which He delights in must be happy.

Another from Cicero,

> O vitæ Philosophia dux! O virtutum indagatrix expultrixque vitiorum! Unus dies, bene et ex præceptis tuis actus, peccanti immortalitati est anteponendus.

Another from the Proverbs of Solomon, speaking of wisdom or virtue:

> Length of days is in her right hand, and in her left hand riches and honour. Her ways are ways of pleasantness, and all her paths are peace. — iii. 16, 17.

And conceiving God to be the fountain of wisdom, I thought it right and necessary to solicit his assistance for obtaining it; to this end I formed the following little prayer, which was prefix'd to my tables of examination, for daily use.

> *O powerful Goodness! bountiful Father! merciful Guide! Increase in me that wisdom which discovers my truest interest. Strengthen my resolutions to perform what that wisdom dictates. Accept my kind offices to thy other children as the only return in my power for thy continual favours to me.*

I used also sometimes a little prayer which I took from Thomson's *Poems*, viz.:

> Father of light and life, thou Good Supreme!
> O teach me what is good; teach me Thyself!
> Save me from folly, vanity, and vice,
> From every low pursuit; and fill my soul
> With knowledge, conscious peace, and virtue pure;
> Sacred, substantial, never-fading bliss!

The precept of *Order* requiring that *every part of my business should have its allotted time,* one page in my little book contain'd the following scheme of employment for the twenty-four hours of a natural day.

THE MORNING. *Question.* What good shall I do this day?	{	5 6 7	Rise, wash, and address *Pow- erful Goodness!* Contrive day's business, and take the resolution of the day; prosecute the pre- sent study, and breakfast.
		8 9 10 11	Work.
NOON.	{	12 1	Read, or overlook my ac- counts, and dine.
		2 3 4 5	Work.
EVENING. *Question.* What good have I done to-day?	{	6 7 8 9	Put things in their places. Supper. Music or diversion, or conversation. Examination of the day.
NIGHT.	{	10 11 12 1 2 3 4	Sleep.

I enter'd upon the execution of this plan for self-examination, and continu'd it with occasional intermissions for some time. I was surpris'd to find myself so much fuller of faults than I had imagined; but I had the satisfaction of seeing them diminish. To avoid the trouble of renewing now and then my little book, which, by scraping out the marks on the paper of old faults to make room for new ones in a new course, became full of holes, I transferr'd my tables and precepts to the ivory leaves of a memorandum book, on which the lines were drawn with red ink, that made a durable stain, and on those lines I mark'd my faults with a black-lead pencil, which marks I could easily wipe out with a wet sponge. After a while I went thro' one course only in a year, and afterward only one in several years, till at length I omitted them entirely, being employ'd in voyages and business abroad, with a multiplicity of affairs that interfered; but I always carried my little book with me.

My scheme of ORDER gave me the most trouble; and I found that, tho' it might be practicable where a man's business was such as to leave him the disposition of his time, that of a journeyman printer, for instance, it was not possible to be exactly observed by a master who must mix with the world and often receive people of business at their own hours. *Order,* too, with regard to places for things, papers, etc., I found extreamly difficult to acquire. I had not been early accustomed to it, and, having an exceeding good memory, I was not so sensible of the inconvenience attending want of method. This article, therefore costs me so much painful attention and my faults in it vexed me so much, and I made so little progress in amendment, and had such frequent relapses that I was almost ready to give up the attempt, and content myself with a faulty character in that respect, like the man who, in buying an ax of a smith, my neighbour, desired to have the whole of its surface as bright as the edge. The smith consented to grind it bright for him if he would turn the wheel; he turn'd while the smith press'd the broad face of the ax hard and heavily on the stone which made the turning of it very fatiguing. The man came every now and then from the wheel to see how the work went on and at length would take his ax as it was, without farther grinding. "No," said the smith, "turn on, turn on; we shall have it bright by and by; as yet, it is only speckled." "Yes," says the man, *"but I think I like a speckled ax best."* And I believe this may have been the case with many who, having, for want of some such means as I employ'd, found the difficulty of obtaining good and breaking bad habits in other points of vice and virtue, have given up the struggle, and concluded that *"a speckled ax was best";* for something, that pretended to be reason, was every now and then suggesting to me that such extream nicety as I exacted of myself might be a kind of foppery in morals, which, if it were known, would make me ridiculous; that a perfect character might be attended with the inconvenience of being envied and hated; and that a benevolent man should allow a few faults in himself, to keep his friends in countenance.

In truth, I found myself incorrigible with respect to Order; and now I am grown old and my memory bad, I feel very sensibly the want of it. But, on the whole, tho' I never arrived at the perfection I had been so ambitious of obtaining, but fell far short of it, yet I was, by the endeavour, a better and a happier man than I otherwise should have been if I had not attempted it; as those who aim at perfect writing by imitating the engraved copies, tho' they never reach the wish'd-for excellence of those copies, their hand is mended by the endeavour, and is tolerable while it continues fair and legible.

It may be well my posterity should be informed that to this little artifice, with the blessing of God, their ancestor ow'd the constant felicity of his life, down to his 79th year, in which this is written.

What reverses may attend the remainder is in the hand of Providence; but, if they arrive, the reflection on past happiness enjoy'd ought to help his bearing them with more resignation. To Temperance he ascribes his long-continued health, and what is still left to him of a good constitution; to Industry and Frugality, the early easiness of his circumstances and acquisition of his fortune, with all that knowledge that enabled him to be a useful citizen, and obtained for him some degree of reputation among the learned; to Sincerity and Justice, the confidence of his country, and the honorable employs it conferred upon him; and to the joint influence of the whole mass of virtues, even in the imperfect state he was able to acquire them, all that evenness of temper, and that cheerfulness in conversation, which makes his company still sought for and agreeable even to his younger acquaintances. I hope, therefore, that some of my descendants may follow the example and reap the benefit.

It will be remark'd that, tho' my scheme was not wholly without religion, there was in it no mark of any of the distinguishing tenets of any particular sect. I had purposely avoided them; for, being fully persuaded of the utility and excellence of my method, and that it might be serviceable to people in all religions, and intending some time or other to publish it, I would not have any thing in it that should prejudice any one, of any sect, against it. I purposed writing a little comment on each virtue, in which I would have shown the advantages of possessing it, and the mischiefs attending its opposite vice; and I should have called my book THE ART OF VIRTUE,[1] because it would have shown the means and manner of obtaining virtue, which would have distinguished it from the mere exhortation to be good, that does not instruct and indicate the means, but is like the apostle's man of verbal charity, who only, without showing to the naked and hungry how or where they might get clothes or victuals, exhorted them to be fed and clothed. — James ii. 15, 16.

But it so happened that my intention of writing and publishing this comment was never fulfilled. I did, indeed, from time to time, put down short hints of the sentiments, reasonings, etc., to be made use of in it, some of which I have still by me; but the necessary close attention to private business in the earlier part of my life, and public business since, have occasioned my postponing it; for, it being connected in my mind with *a great and extensive project* that required the whole man to execute, and which an unforeseen succession of employs prevented my attending to, it has hitherto remain'd unfinish'd.

In this piece it was my design to explain and enforce this doctrine, that vicious actions are not hurtful because they are forbidden, but forbidden because they are hurtful, the nature of man alone considered;

[1] Nothing so likely to make a man's fortune as virtue. [*Marg. Note* — Franklin]

that it was, therefore, every one's interest to be virtuous who wish'd to be happy even in this world; and I should, from this circumstance (there being always in the world a number of rich merchants, nobility, states, and princes, who have need of honest instruments for the management of their affairs, and such being rare), have endeavored to convince young persons that no qualities were so likely to make a poor man's fortune as those of probity and integrity.

Two Letters on Religion
[To Joseph Priestley, September 19, 1772; and to
Ezra Stiles, March 9, 1790]

DEAR SIR,

In the Affair of so much Importance to you, wherein you ask my Advice, I cannot, for want of sufficient Premises, counsel you *what* to determine: but, if you please, I will tell you *how*. When those difficult Cases occur, they are difficult, chiefly because, while we have them under Consideration, all the Reasons *pro* and *con* are not present to the Mind at the same time; but sometimes one Set present themselves, and at other times another, the first being out of Sight. Hence the various Purposes or Inclinations that alternately prevail, and the Uncertainty that perplexes us.

To get over this, my Way is, to divide half a Sheet of Paper by a Line into two Columns; writing over the one *pro* and over the other *con;* then during three or four Days' consideration, I put down under the different Heads short Hints of the different Motives, that at different times occur to me *for* or *against* the Measure. When I have thus got them all together in one View, I endeavor to estimate their respective Weights; and, where I find two (one on each side), that seem equal, I strike them both out. If I find a Reason *pro* equal to some *two* Reasons *con*, I strike out the *three*. If I judge some *two* Reasons *con,* equal to some *three* Reasons *pro,* I strike out the *five;* and thus proceeding I find at length where the Balance lies; and if, after a Day or two of farther Consideration, nothing new that is of Importance occurs on either side, I come to a Determination accordingly. And, though the Weight of Reasons cannot be taken with the Precision of Algebraic quantities, yet, when each is thus considered separately and comparatively, and the whole lies before me, I think I can judge better, and am less liable to make a rash Step; and in fact I have found great advantage for this kind of Equation, in what may be called *moral* or *prudential algebra*. . . .

B. FRANKLIN.

[To Joseph Priestley]

REVEREND AND DEAR SIR,

I received your kind Letter of Jan'y 28, and am glad you have at length received the portrait of Gov'r Yale from his Family, and deposited it in the College Library. He was a great and good Man, and had the Merit of doing infinite Service to your Country by his Munificence to that Institution. The Honour you propose doing me by placing mine in the same Room with his, is much too great for my Deserts; but you always had a Partiality for me, and to that it must be ascribed. I am however too much obliged to Yale College, the first learned Society that took Notice of me and adorned me with its Honours, to refuse a Request that comes from it thro' so esteemed a Friend. But I do not think any one of the Portraits you mention, as in my Possession, worthy of the Place and Company you propose to place it in. You have an excellent Artist lately arrived. If he will undertake to make one for you, I shall cheerfully pay the Expence; but he must not delay setting about it, or I may slip thro' his fingers, for I am now in my eighty-fifth year, and very infirm.

I send with this a very learned Work, as it seems to me, on the antient Samaritan Coins, lately printed in Spain, and at least curious for the Beauty of the Impression. Please to accept it for your College Library. I have subscribed for the Encyclopædia now printing here, with the Intention of presenting it to the College. I shall probably depart before the Work is finished, but shall leave Directions for its Continuance to the End. With this you will receive some of the first numbers.

You desire to know something of my Religion. It is the first time I have been questioned upon it. But I cannot take your Curiosity amiss, and shall endeavour in a few Words to gratify it. Here is my Creed. I believe in one God, Creator of the Universe. That he governs it by his Providence. That he ought to be worshipped. That the most acceptable Service we render to him is doing good to his other Children. That the soul of Man is immortal, and will be treated with Justice in another Life respecting its Conduct in this. These I take to be the fundamental Principles of all sound Religion, and I regard them as you do in whatever Sect I meet with them.

As to Jesus of Nazareth, my Opinion of whom you particularly desire, I think the System of Morals and his Religion, as he left them to us, the best the World ever saw or is likely to see; but I apprehend it has received various corrupting Changes, and I have, with most of the present Dissenters in England, some Doubts as to his Divinity; tho' it is a question I do not dogmatize upon, having never studied it, and think it needless to busy myself with it now, when I expect soon an Opportunity of knowing the Truth with less Trouble. I see no harm, however, in its being believed, if that Belief has the good Consequence, as probably it has, of making his Doctrine more respected and better observed; especially as I do not perceive, that the Supreme takes it amiss, by distinguishing the Unbelievers in his Government of the World with any peculiar Marks of his Displeasure.

I shall only add, respecting myself, that, having experienced the Goodness of that Being in conducting me prosperously thro' a long life, I have no doubt of its Continuance in the next, though without the smallest Conceit of meriting such Goodness. My Sentiments on this Head you will see in the Copy of an old Letter enclosed, which I wrote in answer to one from a zealous Religionist, whom I had relieved in a paralytic case by electricity, and who, being afraid I should grow proud upon it, sent me his serious though rather impertinent Caution. I send you also the Copy of another Letter, which will shew something of my Disposition relating to Religion. With great and sincere Esteem and Affection, I am, Your obliged old Friend and most obedient humble Servant

B. FRANKLIN.

P.S. Had not your College some Present of Books from the King of France? Please to let me know, if you had an Expectation given you of more, and the Nature of that Expectation? I have a Reason for the Enquiry.

I confide, that you will not expose me to Criticism and censure by publishing any part of this Communication to you. I have ever let others enjoy their religious Sentiments, without reflecting on them for those that appeared to me unsupportable and even absurd. All Sects here, and we have a great Variety, have experienced my good will in assisting them with Subscriptions for building their new Places of Worship; and, as I have never opposed any of their Doctrines, I hope to go out of the World in Peace with them all.

[To Ezra Stiles]

Thomas Jefferson (1743–1826)

RELIGION, Jefferson once wrote, "is a matter which lies solely between a man and his God." Though frequently attacked for what seemed to some to be unorthodox doctrines, Jefferson preferred to be reticent about what he believed, so much so that his grandson said that his own family was never quite sure of his actual religious views. Jefferson was an Episcopalian, born, married, and buried under the rites of his church, and a faithful, lifelong parishioner of it. However, he once remarked, "I am a sect by myself, as far as I know," and privately he held beliefs fairly close to eighteenth-century deism.

Jefferson believed deeply in the excellence of New Testament Christianity, feeling that the moral and ethical doctrines of Jesus were the "most pure and perfect" of all religious teachings and the best possible guides to mankind. He made his own "bible," in fact, for his personal use, consisting of the words of Jesus extracted from the Gospels and arranged for study and contemplation. Most of all, Jefferson believed it to be "a truth, and a natural right, that the exercise of religion should be free," and he considered his part in the establishment of Virginia's Statute of Religious Freedom as one of the great achievements of his life.

TEXTS: A. A. Lipscomb and A. E. Bergh, eds., *The Writings of Thomas Jefferson* (Washington, 1903–5), II, 300–303; VI, 256–262. Paul L. Ford, ed., *The Writings of Thomas Jefferson* (New York, 1892–99), VIII, 223–226.

Liberty of Mind and Faith

[An Act for establishing Religious Freedom, passed in the
Assembly of Virginia in the beginning of the year 1786]

Well aware that Almighty God hath created the mind free; that all attempts to influence it by temporal punishments or burdens, or by civil incapacitations, tend only to beget habits of hypocrisy and meanness, and are a departure from the plan of the Holy Author of our religion, who being Lord both of body and mind, yet chose not to propagate it by coercions on either, as was in his Almighty power to do; that the impious presumption of legislators and rulers, civil as well as ecclesiastical, who, being themselves but fallible and uninspired men have assumed dominion over the faith of others, setting up their own opinions and modes of thinking as the only true and infallible, and as such endeavoring to impose them on others, hath established and maintained false religions over the greatest part of the world, and through all time; that to compel a man to furnish contributions of money for the propagation of opinions which he disbelieves, is sinful and tyrannical; that even the forcing him to support this or that teacher of his own religious persuasion, is depriving him of the comfortable liberty of giving his contributions to the particular pastor whose morals he would make his pattern, and whose powers he feels most persuasive to righteousness, and is withdrawing from the ministry those temporal rewards, which proceeding from an approbation of their personal conduct, are an additional incitement to earnest and unremitting labors for the instruction of mankind; that our civil rights have no dependence on our religious opinions, more than our opinions in physics or geometry; that, therefore, the proscribing any citizen as unworthy the public confidence by laying upon him an incapacity of being called to the offices of trust and emolument, unless he profess or renounce this or that religious opinion, is depriving him injuriously of those privileges and advantages to which in common with his fellow citizens he has a natural right; that it tends also to corrupt the principles of that very religion it is meant to encourage, by bribing, with a monopoly of worldly honors and emoluments, those who will externally profess and conform to it; that though indeed these are criminal who do not withstand such temptation, yet neither are those innocent who lay the bait in their way; that to suffer the civil magistrate to intrude his powers into the field of opinion and to restrain the profession or propagation of principles, on the supposition of their ill tendency, is a dangerous fallacy, which at once destroys all religious liberty, because he being of course judge of that tendency, will make his opinions the rule of judgment, and approve or condemn the sentiments of others only as they shall square with or differ from his own; that it is time enough for the rightful purposes of civil government, for its offices to interfere when principles break out into overt acts against peace and good order; and finally, that truth is great and will prevail if left to herself, that she is the proper and sufficient antagonist to error, and has nothing to fear from the conflict, unless by human interposition disarmed of her natural weapons, free argument and debate, errors ceasing to be dangerous when it is permitted freely to contradict them.

Be it therefore enacted by the General Assembly, That no man shall be compelled to frequent or support any religious worship, place or ministry whatsoever, nor shall be enforced, restrained, molested, or burthened in his body or goods, nor shall otherwise suffer on account of his religious opinions or belief; but that all men shall be free to profess, and by argument to maintain, their opinions in matters of religion, and that the same shall in nowise diminish, enlarge, or affect their civil capacities.

And though we well know this Assembly, elected by the people for the ordinary purposes of legislation only, have no power to restrain the acts of succeeding assemblies, constituted with the powers equal to our own, and that therefore to declare this act irrevocable, would be of no effect in law, yet we are free to declare, and do declare, that the rights hereby asserted are of the natural rights of mankind, and that if any act shall be hereafter passed to repeal the present or to narrow its operation, such act will be an infringement of natural right.

The Basis of Moral Education

[Letter to Peter Carr, August 10, 1787]

DEAR PETER, — I have received your two letters of December the 30th and April the 18th, and am very happy to find by them, as well as by letters from Mr. Wythe, that you have been so fortunate as to attract his notice and good will; I am sure you will find this to have been one of the most fortunate events of your life, as I have ever been sensible it was of mine. I enclose you a sketch of the sciences to which I would wish you to apply, in such order as Mr. Wythe shall advise; I mention, also, the books in them worth your reading, which submit to his correction. Many of these are among your father's books, which you should have brought to you. As I do not recollect those of them not in his library, you must write to me for them, making out a catalogue of such as you think you shall have occasion for, in eighteen months from the date of your letter, and consulting Mr. Wythe on the subject. To this sketch, I will add a few particular observations:

1. Italian. I fear the learning this language will confound your French and Spanish. Being all of them degenerated dialects of the Latin, they are apt to mix in conversation. I have never seen a person speaking the three languages, who did not mix them. It is a delightful language, but late events having rendered the Spanish more useful, lay it aside to prosecute that.

2. Spanish. Bestow great attention on this, and endeavor to acquire an accurate knowledge of it. Our future connections with Spain and Spanish America, will render that language a valuable acquisition. The ancient history of that part of America, too, is written in that language. I send you a dictionary.

3. Moral Philosophy. I think it lost time to attend lectures on this branch. He who made us would have been a pitiful bungler, if he had made the rules of our moral conduct a matter of science. For one man of science, there are thousands who are not. What would have become of them? Man was destined for society. His morality, therefore, was to be formed to this object. He was endowed with a sense of right and wrong, merely relative to this. This sense is as much a part of his nature, as the sense of hearing, seeing, feeling; it is the true foundation of morality, and not the το καλον, truth, &c., as fanciful writers have imagined. The moral sense, or conscience, is as much a part of man as his leg or arm. It is given to all human beings in a stronger or weaker degree, as force of members is given them in a greater or less degree. It may be strengthened by exercise, as may any particular limb of the body. This sense is submitted, indeed, in some

degree, to the guidance of reason; but it is a small stock which is required for this: even a less one than what we call common sense. State a moral case to a ploughman and a professor. The former will decide it as well, and often better than the latter, because he has not been led astray by artificial rules. In this branch, therefore, read good books, because they will encourage, as well as direct your feelings. The writings of Sterne, particularly, form the best course of morality that ever was written. Besides these, read the books mentioned in the enclosed paper; and, above all things, lose no occasion of exercising your dispositions to be grateful, to be generous, to be charitable, to be humane, to be true, just, firm, orderly, courageous, &c. Consider every act of this kind, as an exercise which will strengthen your moral faculties and increase your worth.

4. Religion. Your reason is now mature enough to examine this object. In the first place, divest yourself of all bias in favor of novelty and singularity of opinion. Indulge them in any other subject rather than that of religion. It is too important, and the consequences of error may be too serious. On the other hand, shake off all the fears and servile prejudices, under which weak minds are servilely crouched. Fix reason firmly in her seat, and call to her tribunal every fact, every opinion. Question with boldness even the existence of a God; because, if there be one, he must more approve of the homage of reason, than that of blindfolded fear. You will naturally examine first, the religion of your own country. Read the Bible, then, as you would read Livy or Tacitus. The facts which are within the ordinary course of nature, you will believe on the authority of the writer, as you do those of the same kind in Livy and Tacitus. The testimony of the writer weighs in their favor, in one scale, and their not being against the laws of nature, does not weigh against them. But those facts in the Bible which contradict the laws of nature, must be examined with more care, and under a variety of faces. Here you must recur to the pretensions of the writer to inspiration from God. Examine upon what evidence his pretensions are founded, and whether that evidence is so strong, as that its falsehood would be more improbable than a change in the laws of nature, in the case he relates. For example, in the book of Joshua, we are told, the sun stood still several hours. Were we to read that fact in Livy or Tacitus, we should class it with their showers of blood, speaking of statues, beasts, etc. But it is said, that the writer of that book was inspired. Examine, therefore, candidly, what evidence there is of his having been inspired. The pretension is entitled to your inquiry, because millions believe it. On the other hand, you are astronomer enough to know how contrary it is to the law of nature that a body revolving on its axis, as the earth does, should have stopped, should not, by that sudden stoppage, have prostrated animals,

trees, buildings, and should after a certain time have resumed its revolution, and that without a second general prostration. Is this arrest of the earth's motion, or the evidence which affirms it, most within the law of probabilities? You will next read the New Testament. It is the history of a personage called Jesus. Keep in your eye the opposite pretensions: 1, of those who say he was begotten by God, born of a virgin, suspended and reversed the laws of nature at will, and ascended bodily into heaven; and 2, of those who say he was a man of illegitimate birth, of a benevolent heart, enthusiastic mind, who set out without pretensions to divinity, ended in believing them, and was punished capitally for sedition, by being gibbeted, according to the Roman law, which punished the first commission of that offence by whipping, and the second by exile, or death *in furea*. See this law in the Digest, Lib. 48. tit. 19. § 28.3. and Lipsius Lib. 2. de cruce. cap. 2. These questions are examined in the books I have mentioned, under the head of Religion, and several others. They will assist you in your inquiries; but keep your reason firmly on the watch in reading them all. Do not be frightened from this inquiry by any fear of its consequences. If it ends in a belief that there is no God, you will find incitements to virtue in the comfort and pleasantness you feel in its exercise, and the love of others which it will procure you. If you find reason to believe there is a God, a consciousness that you are acting under his eye, and that he approves you, will be a vast additional incitement; if that there be a future state, the hope of a happy existence in that increases the appetite to deserve it; if that Jesus was also a God, you will be comforted by a belief of his aid and love. In fine, I repeat, you must lay aside all prejudice on both sides, and neither believe nor reject anything, because any other persons, or description of persons, have rejected or believed it. Your own reason is the only oracle given you by heaven, and you are answerable, not for the rightness, but uprightness of the decision. I forgot to observe, when speaking of the New Testament, that you should read all the histories of Christ, as well as those whom a council of ecclesiastics have decided for us, to be Pseudo-evangelists, as those they named Evangelists. Because these Pseudo-evangelists pretended to inspiration, as much as the others, and you are to judge their pretensions by your own reason, and not by the reason of those ecclesiastics. Most of these are lost. There are some, however, still extant, collected by Fabricius, which I will endeavor to get and send you.

5. Travelling. This makes men wiser, but less happy. When men of sober age travel, they gather knowledge, which they may apply usefully for their country; but they are subject ever after to recollections mixed with regret; their affections are weakened by being extended over more objects; and they learn new habits which cannot be

gratified when they return home. Young men, who travel, are exposed to all these inconveniences in a higher degree, to others still more serious, and do not acquire that wisdom for which a previous foundation is requisite, by repeated and just observations at home. The glare of pomp and pleasure is analogous to the motion of the blood; it absorbs all their affection and attention, they are torn from it as from the only good in this world, and return to their home as to a place of exile and condemnation. Their eyes are forever turned back to the object they have lost, and its recollection poisons the residue of their lives. Their first and most delicate passions are hackneyed on unworthy objects here, and they carry home the dregs, insufficient to make themselves or anybody else happy. Add to this, that a habit of idleness, an inability to apply themselves to business is acquired, and renders them useless to themselves and their country. These observations are founded in experience. There is no place where your pursuit of knowledge will be so little obstructed by foreign objects, as in your own country, nor any, wherein the virtues of the heart will be less exposed to be weakened. Be good, be learned, and be industrious, and you will not want the aid of travelling, to render you precious to your country, dear to your friends, happy within yourself. I repeat my advice, to take a great deal of exercise, and on foot. Health is the first requisite after morality. Write to me often, and be assured of the interest I take in your success, as well as the warmth of those sentiments of attachment with which I am, dear Peter, your affectionate friend.

The Teachings of Jesus

[Letter to Dr. Benjamin Rush, April 21, 1803]

DEAR SIR, — In some of the delightful conversations with you, in the evenings of 1798-99, and which served as an anodyne to the afflictions of the crisis through which our country was then laboring, the Christian religion was sometimes our topic; and I then promised you, that one day or other, I would give you my views of it. They are the result of a life of inquiry and reflection, and very different from that anti-Christian system imputed to me by those who know nothing of my opinions. To the corruptions of Christianity I am, indeed, opposed; but not to the genuine precepts of Jesus himself. I am a Christian, in the only sense in which he wished any one to be; sincerely attached to his doctrines, in preference to all others; ascribing to himself every *human* excellence; and believing he never claimed any other. At the short interval since these conversations, when I could justifiably abstract my mind from public affairs, the subject has been under my contemplation. But the more I considered it, the more it expanded beyond the measure of either my time or information. In the moment of my late departure from Monticello, I received from Dr. Priestley, his little treatise of "Socrates and Jesus Compared." This being a section of the general view I had taken of the field, it became a subject of reflection while on the road, and unoccupied otherwise. The result was, to arrange in my mind a syllabus, or outline of such an estimate of the comparative merits of Christianity, as I wished to see executed by some one of more leisure and information for the task, than myself. This I now send you, as the only discharge of my promise I can probably ever execute. And in confiding it to you, I know it will not be exposed to the malignant perversions of those who make every word from me a text for new misrepresentations and calumnies. I am moreover averse to the communication of my religious tenets to the public; because it would countenance the presumption of those who have endeavored to draw them before that tribunal, and to seduce public opinion to erect itself into that inquisition over the rights of conscience, which the laws have so justly proscribed. It behooves every man who values liberty of conscience for himself, to resist invasions of it in the case of others; or their case may, by change of circumstances, become his own. It behooves him, too, in his own case, to give no example of concession, betraying the common right of independent opinion, by answering questions of faith, which the laws have left between God and himself. Accept my affectionate salutations.

Syllabus of an Estimate of the Merit of the Doctrines of Jesus,
compared with those of others.

In a comparative view of the Ethics of the enlightened nations of antiquity, of the Jews and of Jesus, no notice should be taken of the corruptions of reason among the ancients, to wit, the idolatry and superstition of the vulgar, nor of the corruptions of Christianity by the learned among its professors.

Let a just view be taken of the moral principles inculcated by the most esteemed of the sects of ancient philosophy, or of their individuals; particularly Pythagoras, Socrates, Epicurus, Cicero, Epictetus, Seneca, Antoninus.

I. Philosophers. 1. Their precepts related chiefly to ourselves, and the government of those passions which, unrestrained, would disturb our tranquillity of mind. In this branch of philosophy they were really great.

2. In developing our duties to others, they were short and defective. They embraced, indeed, the circles of kindred and friends, and in-

culcated patriotism, or the love of our country in the aggregate, as a primary obligation: towards our neighbors and countrymen they taught justice, but scarcely viewed them as within the circle of benevolence. Still less have they inculcated peace, charity and love to our fellow men, or embraced with benevolence the whole family of mankind.

II. Jews. 1. Their system was Deism; that is, the belief in one only God. But their ideas of him and of his attributes were degrading and injurious.

2. Their Ethics were not only imperfect, but often irreconcilable with the sound dictates of reason and morality, as they respect intercourse with those around us; and repulsive and anti-social, as respecting other nations. They needed reformation, therefore, in an eminent degree.

III. Jesus. In this state of things among the Jews, Jesus appeared. His parentage was obscure; his condition poor; his education null; his natural endowments great; his life correct and innocent; he was meek, benevolent, patient, firm, disinterested, and of the sublimest eloquence.

The disadvantages under which his doctrines appear are remarkable.

1. Like Socrates and Epictetus, he wrote nothing himself.

2. But he had not, like them, a Xenophon or an Arrian to write for him. I name not Plato, who only used the name of Socrates to cover the whimsies of his own brain. On the contrary, all the learned of his country, entrenched in its power and riches, were opposed to him, lest his labors should undermine their advantages; and the committing to writing his life and doctrines fell on unlettered and ignorant men; who wrote, too, from memory, and not till long after the transactions had passed.

3. According to the ordinary fate of those who attempt to enlighten and reform mankind, he fell an early victim to the jealousy and combination of the altar and the throne, at about thirty-three years of age, his reason having not yet attained the *maximum* of its energy, nor the course of his preaching, which was but of three years at most, presented occasions for developing a complete system of morals.

4. Hence the doctrines which he really delivered were defective as a whole, and fragments only of what he did deliver have come to us mutilated, misstated, and often unintelligible.

5. They have been still more disfigured by the corruptions of schismatizing followers, who have found an interest in sophisticating and perverting the simple doctrines he taught, by engrafting on them the mysticisms of a Grecian sophist, frittering them into subtleties, and obscuring them with jargon, until they have caused good men to reject the whole in disgust, and to view Jesus himself as an imposter.

Notwithstanding these disadvantages, a system of morals is presented to us, which, if filled up in the style and spirit of the rich fragments he left us, would be the most perfect and sublime that has ever been taught by man.

The question of his being a member of the Godhead, or in direct communication with it, claimed for him by some of his followers, and denied by others, is foreign to the present view, which is merely an estimate of the intrinsic merits of his doctrines.

1. He corrected the Deism of the Jews, confirming them in their belief of one only God, and giving them juster notions of his attributes and government.

2. His moral doctrines, relating to kindred and friends, were more pure and perfect than those of the most correct of the philosophers, and greatly more so than those of the Jews; and they went far beyond both in inculcating universal philanthropy, not only to kindred and friends, to neighbors and countrymen, but to all mankind, gathering all into one family, under the bonds of love, charity, peace, common wants and common aids. A development of this head will evince the peculiar superiority of the system of Jesus over all others.

3. The precepts of philosophy, and of the Hebrew code, laid hold of actions only. He pushed his scrutinies into the heart of man; erected his tribunal in the region of his thoughts, and purified the waters at the fountain head.

4. He taught, emphatically, the doctrines of a future state, which was either doubted, or disbelieved by the Jews; and wielded it with efficacy, as an important incentive, supplementary to the other motives to moral conduct.

⌲ Ethan Allen (1738–1789)

ETHAN ALLEN, Revolutionary patriot and soldier, was born in Connecticut, but after service in the French and Indian wars he settled in Vermont. New York claimed ownership of certain Vermont lands, and in the ensuing argument Allen organized a group of Vermonters into the "Green Mountain Boys," who so harassed the New York militia that the Governor of New York offered a hundred pounds for Allen's arrest. However, the onset of the Revolution brought Allen and his Vermonters into the Continental Army before the reward could be collected. Ordered to take the British-held fort at Ticonderoga, Allen did so, demanding its surrender "in the name of the Great Jehovah and the Continental Congress." He was captured later in an expedition against Montreal, but was finally exchanged before the end of the war.

Though not formally educated, Ethan Allen read rather widely in theology and became deeply interested in science. His deistic tract, *Reason the Only Oracle of Man; or a Compenduous System of Natural Religion* (1784), a direct attack on orthodox Calvinistic theology, elicited a number of replies to its "infidelity," and was attacked by Timothy Dwight as "the first formal publication in the United States openly directed against the Christian religion." There is reason to believe, however, that much of the book was written by Dr. Thomas Young, a physician and neighbor of Allen's who died in 1777.

TEXT: Ethan Allen, *Reason the Only Oracle of Man* . . . (Bennington, Vt., 1784).

A Universe of Perfect Order

[From *Reason the Only Oracle of Man*, 1784]

When we consider our solar system, attracted by its fiery center, and moving in its several orbits with regular, majestic, and periodical revolution, we are charmed at the prospect and contemplation of those worlds of motion, and adore the wisdom and the power by which they are attracted, and their velocity regulated and perpetuated. And when we reflect that the blessings of life are derived from and dependent on the properties, qualities, constructions, proportions, and movements of that stupendous machine, we gratefully acknowledge the divine beneficence. When we extend our thoughts (through our external sensations) to the vast regions of the starry heavens, we are lost in the immensity of God's works; some stars appear fair and luminous, and other scarcely discernible to the eye, which by the help of glasses make a brilliant appearance, bringing the knowledge of others far remote within the verge of our feeble discoveries, which merely by the eye could not have been discerned or distinguished. These discoveries of the works of God naturally prompt the inquisitive mind to conclude that the author of this astonishing part of creation, which is displayed to our view, has still extended his creation; so that if it were possible that any of us could be transported to the farthest extended star which is perceptible to us here, we should from thence survey worlds as distant from that, as that is from this, and so on *ad infinitum.*

Furthermore, it is altogether reasonable to conclude that the heavenly bodies, *alias* worlds, which move or are situate within the circle of our knowledge, as well as all others throughout immensity, are each and every one of them possessed or inhabited by some intelligent agents or other, however different their sensations or manner of receiving or communicating their ideas may be from ours, or however different from each other. For why would it not have been as wise or as consistent with the perfections which we adore in God, to have neglected giving being to intelligences in this world as in those other worlds, interspersed with either of various qualities in his immense creation? And inasmuch as this world is thus replenished, we may with the highest rational certainty infer that as God has given us to rejoice and adore him for our being, he has acted consistent with his goodness, in the display of his providence throughout the universality of worlds.

To suppose that God Almighty has confined his goodness to this world, to the exclusion of all others, is much similar to the idle fancies of some individuals in this world, that they and those of their communion or faith are the favorites of heaven exclusively; but these are narrow and bigoted conceptions, which are degrading to a rational nature and utterly unworthy of God, of whom we should form the most exalted ideas. Furthermore, there could be no display of goodness or of any of the moral perfections of God, merely in repleting immensity with a stupid creation of elements or sluggish, senseless, and incogitative matter, which by nature may be supposed to be incapable of sensation, reflection, and enjoyment: undoubtedly elements and material compositions were designed by God to subserve rational beings, by constituting or supporting them in their respective modes of existence, in this or those other numerous worlds.

There may be in God's boundless empire of nature and providence as many different sorts of modified sensation as there are different worlds and temperatures in immensity, or at least sensation may more or less vary; but whether their sensations agree in any or many respects or not, or whether they agree with ours, or if in part, how far, are matters unknown to us; but that there are intelligent orders of beings interspersed through the creation of God, is a matter of the highest degree of rational certainty of any thing that falls short of mathematical demonstration or of proofs which come within the reach of our outward sensations, called sensible demonstration. For if this is the only world that is replenished with life and reason, it includes the whole circumference of God's providence; and there would be no display of wisdom or goodness merely in governing rude elements and senseless matter, nor could there be any valuable end proposed by such a supposed government, or any happiness, instruction, or subserviency to being in general, for any reason assigned by such a creation (for it cannot be a providence) should have had the divine approbation; and consequently we may be morally certain that rational beings are interspersed co-extensive with the creation of God.

Although the various orders of intelligences throughout infinitude differ ever so much in their manner of sensation, and consequently in their manner of communication or of receiving ideas, yet reason and consciousness must be the same in all, but not the same with respect to the various objects of the several worlds, though in nature the same.

For instance, a person born blind cannot possibly have an idea of colors, though his sensibility of sound and feeling may be as acute as ours; and since there are such a variety of modes of sensation in this world, how vastly numerous may we apprehend them to be in immensity! We shall soon, by pondering on these things, feel the insufficiency of our imagination to conceive of the immense possibility of the variety of their modes of sensation and the manner of intercourse of cogitative beings.

It may be objected that a man cannot subsist in the sun; but does it follow from thence that God cannot or has not constituted a nature peculiar to that fiery region, and caused it to be as natural and necessary for it to suck in and breathe out flames of fire, as it is for us to do the like in air? Numerous are the kinds of fishy animals which can no other way subsist but in the water, in which other animals would perish (amphibious ones excepted); while other animals, in a variety of forms, either swifter or slower, move on the surface of the earth or wing the air: of these there are sundry kinds which during the seasons of winter live without food; and many of the insects which are really possessed of animal life remain frozen, and as soon as they are let loose by the kind influence of the sun, they again assume their wonted animal life; and if animal life may differ so much in the same world, what inconceivable variety may be possible in worlds innumerable, as applicable to mental, cogitative, and organized beings! Certain it is, that any supposed obstructions concerning the quality or temperature of any or every of those worlds could not have been any bar in the way of God Almighty, with regard to his replenishing his universal creation with moral agents. The unlimited perfection of God could perfectly well adapt every part of his creation to the design of whatever rank or species of constituted beings his Godlike wisdom and goodness saw fit to impart existence to; so that as there is no deficiency of absolute perfection in God, it is rationally demonstrative that the immense creation is replenished with rational agents, and that it has been eternally so, and that the display of divine goodness must have been as perfect and complete in the antecedent, as it is possible to be in the subsequent eternity.

From this theological way of arguing on the creation and providence of God, it appears that the whole, which we denominate by the term *nature*, which is the same as creation perfectly regulated, was eternally connected together by the creator to answer the same all-glorious purpose, *to wit:* the display of the divine nature, the consequences of which are existence and happiness to being in general, so that creation, with all its productions, operates according to the laws of nature and is sustained by the self-existent eternal cause in perfect order and decorum, agreeable to the eternal wisdom, unalterable rectitude, impartial justice, and immense goodness of the divine nature, which is a summary of God's providence. It is from the established order of nature that summer and winter, rainy and fair seasons, monsoons, refreshing breezes, seed time and harvest, day and night, interchangeably succeed each other and diffuse their extensive blessings to man. Every enjoyment and support of life is from God, delivered to his creatures in and by the tendency, aptitude, disposition, and operation of those laws. — Nature is the medium or intermediate instrument through which God dispenses his benignity to mankind. The air we breathe in, the light of the sun, and the waters of the murmuring rills evince his providence; and well it is that they are given in so great profusion that they cannot by the monopoly of the rich be engrossed from the poor.

When we copiously pursue the study of nature, we are certain to be lost in the immensity of the works and wisdom of God; we may nevertheless, in a variety of things, discern their fitness, happifying tendency, and sustaining quality to us-ward, from all which, as rational and contemplative beings, we are prompted to infer that God is universally uniform and consistent in his infinitude of creation and providence; although we cannot comprehend all that consistency, by reason of infirmity, yet we are morally sure that of all possible plans, infinite wisdom must have eternally adopted the best, and infinite goodness have approved it, and infinite power have perfected it. And as the good of being in general must have been the ultimate end of God in his creation and government of his creatures, his omniscience could not fail to have it always present in his view. Universal nature must therefore be ultimately attracted to this single point, and infinite perfection must have eternally displayed itself in creation and providence. From hence we infer that God is as eternal and infinite in his goodness as his self-existent and perfect nature is omnipotently great.

OF THE IMPORTANCE OF THE EXERCISE OF REASON AND PRACTICE OF MORALITY, IN ORDER TO THE HAPPINESS OF MANKIND

The period of life is very uncertain, and at the longest is but short; a few years bring us from infancy to manhood, a few more to a dissolution; pain, sickness, and death are the necessary consequences of animal life. Through life we struggle with physical evils, which eventually are certain to destroy our earthly composition; and well would it be for us did evils end here; but alas! moral evil has been more or less predominant in our agency; and though natural evil is unavoidable, yet moral evil may be prevented or remedied by the exercise of virtue. Morality is therefore of more importance to us than any or all other attainments, as it is a habit of mind, from a retrospective conscious-

ness of our agency in this life, we should carry with us into our succeeding state of existence, as an acquired appendage of our rational
nature and as the necessary means of our mental happiness. Virtue
and vice are the only things in this world which, with our souls, are
capable of surviving death; the former is the rational and only procuring cause of all intellectual happiness, and the latter of conscious guilt
and misery; and therefore our indispensable duty and ultimate interest
is to love, cultivate, and improve the one, as the means of our greatest
good, and to hate and abstain from the other, as productive of our
greatest evil. And in order thereto, we should so far divest ourselves
of the incumbrances of this world (which are too apt to engross our
attention) as to enquire a consistent system of the knowledge of
religious duty, and make it our constant endeavor in life to act conformably to it. The knowledge of the being, perfections, creation, and
providence of God, and of the immortality of our souls, is the foundation of religion, which has been particularly illustrated in the four
first chapters of this discourse. And as the pagan, Jewish, Christian,
and Mahometan countries of the world have been overwhelmed with
a multiplicity of revelations diverse from each other, and which, by
their respective promulgators, are said to have been immediately
inspired into their souls by the spirit of God, or immediately communicated to them by the intervening agency of angels (as in the
instance of the invisible Gabriel to Mahomet), and as those revelations
have been received and credited by far the greater part of the inhabitants of the several countries of the world (on whom they have
been obtruded) as supernaturally revealed by God or angels; and
which, in doctrine and discipline, are in most respects repugnant to
each other, it fully evinces their imposture and authorizes us, without
a lengthly course of arguing, to determine with certainty that not more
than one, if any one, of them had their original from God, as they
clash with each other, which is ground of high probability against the
authenticity of each of them.

A revelation that may be supposed to be really of the institution of
God must also be supposed to be perfectly consistent or uniform, and
to be able to stand the test of truth; therefore such pretended revelations as are tendered to us as the contrivance of heaven, which do not
bear that test, we may be morally certain, [were] either originally a
deception or [have] since, by adulteration, become spurious. Furthermore, should we admit that among the numerous revelations on which
the respective priests have given the stamp of divinity, some one of
them was in reality of divine authority, yet we could no otherwise, as
rational beings, distinguish it from others, but by reason.

Reason therefore must be the standard by which we determine the
respective claims of revelation; for otherwise we may as well subscribe

to the divinity of the one as of the other, or to the whole of them, or to none at all. So likewise, on this thesis, if reason rejects the whole of those revelations, we ought to return to the religion of nature and reason.

Undoubtedly it is our duty, and for our best good, that we occupy and improve the faculties with which our Creator has endowed us; but so far as prejudice or prepossession of opinion prevails over our minds, in the same proportion reason is excluded from our theory or practice. Therefore, if we would acquire useful knowledge, we must first divest ourselves of those impediments and sincerely endeavor to search out the truth and draw our conclusions from reason and just argument, which will never conform to our inclination, interest, or fancy; but we must conform to that if we would judge rightly. As certain as we determine contrary to reason, we make a wrong conclusion; therefore, our wisdom is to conform to the nature and reason of things, as well in religious matters as in other sciences. Preposterously absurd would it be to negative the exercise of reason in religious concerns and yet be actuated by it in all other and less occurrences of life. All our knowledge of things is derived from God, in and by the order of nature, out of which we cannot perceive, reflect, or understand anything whatsoever; our external senses are natural and so are our souls; by the instrumentality of the former we perceive the objects of sense, and with the latter we reflect on them. And those objects are also natural; so that ourselves, and all things about us, and our knowledge collected therefrom is natural, and not supernatural, as argued in the Sixth Chapter.

We may, and often do, connect or arrange our ideas together in a wrong or improper manner for the want of skill or judgment, or through mistake or the want of application, or through the influence of prejudice; but in all such cases the error does not originate from the ideas themselves but from the composer; for a system, or an arrangement of ideas justly composed, always contain[s] the truth, but an unjust composition never fails to contain error and falsehood. Therefore an unjust connection of ideas is not derived from nature but from the imperfect composition of man. Misconnection of ideas is the same as misjudging, and has no positive existence, being merely a creature of the imagination; but nature and truth are real and uniform, and the rational mind, by reasoning, discerns the uniformity and is thereby enabled to make a just composition of ideas which will stand the test of truth. But the fantastical illuminations of the credulous and superstitious part of mankind proceed from weakness, and as far as they take place in the world, subvert the religion of Reason and Truth.

⟁ Thomas Paine (1737–1809)

THOMAS PAINE was born in England of a Quaker family, but he early adopted a free-thinking, independent attitude toward orthodox religious belief. After emigrating to America, and serving with distinction in the cause of independence, Paine returned to England and France, where he became deeply involved in the political and intellectual arguments of the French Revolution. In 1794 he began, in *The Age of Reason* (1794, 1796), an attack on orthodox, conservative religion, which in his opinion supported tyranny, superstition, and human misery everywhere.

Paine advocated instead a "religion of reason," which held out to man the promise of intellectual, personal, and political freedom. Drawing his ideas from contemporary science and philosophy, he summarized and clarified the doctrines of deism in a manner everybody could understand. His tactlessness and his polemics, however, alienated many readers and obscured the fact that his primary aim was to save "true Christianity" from "false systems of government, and false theology," lest men "lose sight of morality, of humanity, and of the theology that is true."

The Age of Reason stirred up tremendous controversy. There were more than thirty-five replies to it within a decade. Paine was attacked in press and pulpit as Satan's emissary, an atheist, a drunkard, and a traitor. Yet in retrospect it is clear that he was a genuinely religious man in his own fashion, and that his book is the best and most carefully reasoned exposition of eighteenth-century deism produced during the times.

TEXT: William M. Van der Weyde, ed., *The Life and Works of Thomas Paine* (New Rochelle, N.Y., 1925), VIII, 3–13, 41–45, 52–57, 68–73.

From
The Age of Reason
[Part I, 1794]

THE AUTHOR'S PROFESSION OF FAITH

It has been my intention, for several years past, to publish my thoughts upon religion. I am well aware of the difficulties that attend the subject, and from that consideration, had reserved it to a more advanced period of life. I intended it to be the last offering I should make to my fellow-citizens of all nations, and that at a time when the purity of the motive that induced me to it could not admit of a question, even by those who might disapprove the work. The circumstance that has now taken place in France of the total abolition of the whole national order of priesthood, and of everything appertaining to compulsive systems of religion, and compulsive articles of faith, has not only precipitated my intention, but rendered a work of this kind exceedingly necessary, lest in the general wreck of superstition, of false systems of government and false theology, we lose sight of morality, of humanity and of the theology that is true.

As several of my colleagues, and others of my fellow-citizens of France, have given me the example of making their voluntary and individual profession of faith, I also will make mine; and I do this with all that sincerity and frankness with which the mind of man communicates with itself.

I believe in one God, and no more; and I hope for happiness beyond this life.

I believe in the equality of man; and I believe that religious duties consist in doing justice, loving mercy, and endeavoring to make our fellow-creatures happy.

But, lest it should be supposed that I believe many other things in addition to these, I shall, in the progress of this work, declare the things I do not believe, and my reasons for not believing them.

I do not believe in the creed professed by the Jewish Church, by the Roman Church, by the Greek Church, by the Turkish Church, by the Protestant Church, nor by any church that I know of. My own mind is my own church.

All national institutions of churches, whether Jewish, Christian or Turkish, appear to me no other than human inventions, set up to terrify and enslave mankind, and monopolize power and profit.

I do not mean by this declaration to condemn those who believe otherwise; they have the same right to their belief as I have to mine. But it is necessary to the happiness of man that he be mentally faithful to himself. Infidelity does not consist in believing, or in disbelieving; it consists in professing to believe what he does not believe.

It is impossible to calculate the moral mischief, if I may so express it, that mental lying has produced in society. When a man has so far corrupted and prostituted the chastity of his mind as to subscribe his professional belief to things he does not believe he has prepared himself for the commission of every other crime.

He takes up the trade of a priest for the sake of gain, and in order to qualify himself for that trade he begins with a perjury. Can we conceive any thing more destructive to morality than this?

Soon after I had published the pamphlet "Common Sense," in America, I saw the exceeding probability that a revolution in the system of government would be followed by a revolution in the system of religion. The adulterous connection of church and state, wherever it has taken place, whether Jewish, Christian or Turkish, has so effectually prohibited by pains and penalties every discussion upon established creeds, and upon first principles of religion, that until the system of government should be changed, those subjects could not be brought fairly and openly before the world; but that whenever this should be done, a revolution in the system of religion would follow. Human inventions and priestcraft would be detected; and man would return to the pure, unmixed and unadulterated belief of one God, and no more.

Concerning Missions and Revelations

Every national church or religion has established itself by pretending some special mission from God, communicated to certain individuals. The Jews have their Moses; the Christians their Jesus Christ, their apostles and saints; and the Turks their Mahomet, as if the way to God was not open to every man alike.

Each of those churches show certain books, which they call *revelation*, or the Word of God. The Jews say that their Word of God was given by God to Moses, face to face; the Christians say that their Word of God came by divine inspiration; and the Turks say that their Word of God (the Koran) was brought by an angel from heaven. Each of those churches accuses the other of unbelief; and for my own part, I disbelieve them all.

As it is necessary to affix right ideas to words, I will, before I proceed further into the subject, offer some observations on the word *revelation*. Revelation, when applied to religion, means something communicated *immediately* from God to man.

No one will deny or dispute the power of the Almighty to make such a communication, if He pleases. But admitting, for the sake of a case, that something has been revealed to a certain person, and not revealed to any other person, it is revelation to that person only. When he tells it to a second person, a second to a third, a third to a fourth, and so on, it ceases to be a revelation to all those persons. It is revelation to the first person only, and *hearsay* to every other, and consequently they are not obliged to believe it.

It is a contradiction in terms and ideas, to call anything a revelation that comes to us at second-hand, either verbally or in writing. Revelation is necessarily limited to the first communication — after this it is only an account of something which that person says was a revelation made to him; and though he may find himself obliged to believe it, it cannot be incumbent on me to believe it in the same manner; for it was not a revelation made to *me*, and I have only his word for it that it was made to him. When Moses told the children of Israel that he received the two tables of the commandments from the hands of God, they were not obliged to believe him, because they had no other authority for it than his telling them so; and I have no other authority for it than some historian telling me so. The commandments carry no internal evidence of divinity with them; they contain some good moral precepts, such as any man qualified to be a lawgiver, or a legislator, could produce himself, without having recourse to supernatural intervention.[1]

When I am told that the Koran was written in heaven and brought to Mahomet by an angel, the account comes too near the same kind of hearsay evidence and second-hand authority as the former. I did not see the angel myself and, therefore, I have a right not to believe it.

When also I am told that a woman called the Virgin Mary, said, or gave out, that she was with child without any cohabitation with a man, and that her betrothed husband, Joseph, said that an angel told him so, I have a right to believe them or not; such a circumstance required a much stronger evidence than their bare word for it; but we have not even this — for neither Joseph nor Mary wrote any such matter themselves; it is only reported by others that *they said so* — it is hearsay upon hearsay, and I do not choose to rest my belief upon such evidence.

It is, however, not difficult to account for the credit that was given to the story of Jesus Christ being the Son of God. He was born at a time when the heathen mythology had still some fashion and repute in the world, and that mythology had prepared the people for the belief of such a story. Almost all the extraordinary men that lived under the heathen mythology were reputed to be the sons of some of their gods. It was not a new thing, at that time, to believe a man to have been celestially begotten; the intercourse of gods with women was then a matter of familiar opinion.

Their Jupiter, according to their accounts, had cohabited with hundreds: the story, therefore, had nothing in it either new, wonderful or obscene; it was comfortable to the opinions that then prevailed among the people called Gentiles, or Mythologists, and it was those people only that believed it.

The Jews, who had kept strictly to the belief of one God, and no more, and who had always rejected the heathen mythology, never credited the story.

It is curious to observe how the theory of what is called the Christian Church sprung out of the tail of the heathen mythology. A direct

1 It is, however, necessary to except the declaration which says that God *visits the sins of the fathers upon the children;* it is contrary to every principle of moral justice. [Paine's note]

incorporation took place in the first instance, by making the reputed founder to be celestially begotten. The trinity of gods that then followed was no other than a reduction of the former plurality, which was about twenty or thirty thousand; the statue of Mary succeeded the statue of Diana of Ephesus; the deification of heroes changed into the canonization of saints; the Mythologists had gods for everything; the Christian Mythologists had saints for everything; the Church became as crowded with the one as the Pantheon had been with the other, and Rome was the place of both. The Christian theory is little else than the idolatry of the ancient Mythologists, accommodated to the purposes of power and revenue; and it yet remains to reason and philosophy to abolish the amphibious fraud.

An Appreciation of the Character of Jesus Christ, and His History

Nothing that is here said can apply, even with the most distant disrespect, to the real character of Jesus Christ. He was a virtuous and an amiable man. The morality that he preached and practised was of the most benevolent kind; and though similar systems of morality had been preached by Confucius, and by some of the Greek philosophers, many years before; by the Quakers since; and by many good men in all ages, it has not been exceeded by any.

Jesus Christ wrote no account of himself, of his birth, parentage, or anything else; not a line of what is called the New Testament is of his own writing. The history of him is altogether the work of other people; and as to the account given of his resurrection and ascension, it was the necessary counterpart to the story of his birth. His historians, having brought him into the world in a supernatural manner, were obliged to take him out again in the same manner, or the first part of the story must have fallen to the ground.

The wretched contrivance with which this latter part is told exceeds every thing that went before it. The first part, that of the miraculous conception, was not a thing that admitted of publicity; and therefore the tellers of this part of the story had this advantage, that though they might not be credited, they could not be detected. They could not be expected to prove it, because it was not one of those things that admitted of proof, and it was impossible that the person of whom it was told could prove it himself.

But the resurrection of a dead person from the grave, and his ascension through the air, is a thing very different as to the evidence it admits of, to the invisible conception of a child in the womb. The resurrection and ascension, supposing them to have taken place, admitted of public and ocular demonstration, like that of the ascension of a balloon, or the sun at noon-day, to all Jerusalem at least.

A thing which everybody is required to believe requires that the proof and evidence of it should be equal to all, and universal; and as the public visibility of this last related act was the only evidence that could give sanction to the former part, the whole of it falls to the ground, because that evidence never was given. Instead of this, a small number of persons, not more than eight or nine, are introduced as proxies for the whole world to say they saw it, and all the rest of the world are called upon to believe it. But it appears that Thomas did not believe the resurrection, and, as they say, would not believe without having ocular and manual demonstration himself. *So neither will I*, and the reason is equally as good for me, and for every other person, as for Thomas. . . .

DEFINING THE TRUE REVELATION

But some, perhaps, will say: Are we to have no Word of God — no revelation? I answer, Yes; there is a Word of God; there is a revelation.

THE WORD OF GOD IS THE CREATION WE BEHOLD and it is in *this word*, which no human invention can counterfeit or alter, that God speaketh universally to man.

Human language is local and changeable, and is therefore incapable of being used as the means of unchangeable and universal information. The idea that God sent Jesus Christ to publish, as they say, the glad tidings to all nations, from one end of the earth unto the other, is consistent only with the ignorance of those who knew nothing of the extent of the world, and who believed, as those world-saviors believed, and continued to believe for several centuries (and that in contradiction to the discoveries of philosophers and the experience of navigators), that the earth was flat like a trencher, and that man might walk to the end of it.

But how was Jesus Christ to make anything known to all nations? He could speak but one language, which was Hebrew, and there are in the world several hundred languages. Scarcely any two nations speak the same language, or understand each other; and as to translations, every man who knows anything of languages knows that it is impossible to translate from one language into another, not only without losing a great part of the original, but frequently mistaking the sense; and besides all this, the art of printing was wholly unknown at the time Christ lived.

It is always necessary that the means that are to accomplish any end be equal to the accomplishment of that end, or the end cannot be accomplished. It is in this that the difference between finite and infinite power and wisdom discovers itself. Man frequently fails in accomplishing his ends, from a natural inability of the power to the purpose, and frequently from the want of wisdom to apply power properly. But it is impossible for infinite power and wisdom to fail as man faileth. The means it uses are always equal to the end; but human language, more especially as there is not an universal language, is incapable of being used as an universal means of unchangeable and uniform information, and therefore it is not the means that God uses in manifesting himself universally to man.

It is only in the CREATION that all our ideas and conceptions of a *Word of God* can unite. The Creation speaks a universal language, independently of human speech or human language, multiplied and various as they be. It is an ever-existing original which every man can read. It cannot be forged; it cannot be counterfeited; it cannot be lost; it cannot be altered; it cannot be suppressed. It does not depend upon the will of man whether it shall be published or not; it publishes itself from one end of the earth to the other. It preaches to all nations and to all worlds; and this *Word of God* reveals to man all that is necessary for man to know of God.

Do we want to contemplate His power? We see it in the immensity of the creation. Do we want to contemplate His wisdom? We see it in the unchangeable order by which the incomprehensible whole is governed. Do we want to contemplate His munificence? We see it in the abundance with which He fills the earth. Do we want to contemplate His mercy? We see it in His not withholding that abundance even from the unthankful. In fine, do we want to know what God is? Search not the book called the Scripture, which any human hand might make, but the Scripture called the creation.

CONCERNING GOD, AND THE LIGHTS CAST ON HIS EXISTENCE AND ATTRIBUTES BY THE BIBLE

The only idea man can affix to the name of God is that of a *first cause*, the cause of all things. And incomprehensible and difficult as it is for a man to conceive what a first cause is, he arrives at the belief of it from the tenfold greater difficulty of disbelieving it.

It is difficult beyond description to conceive that space can have no end; but it is more difficult to conceive an end. It is difficult beyond the power of man to conceive an eternal duration of what we call time; but it is more impossible to conceive a time when there shall be no time.

In like manner of reasoning, everything we behold carries in itself the internal evidence that it did not make itself. Every man is an evidence to himself that he did not make himself; neither could his father make himself, nor his grandfather, nor any of his race; neither could any tree, plant or animal make itself; and it is the conviction arising from this evidence that carries us on, as it were, by necessity to the belief of a first cause eternally existing, of a nature totally different to any material existence we know of, and by the power of which all things exist; and this first cause man calls God.

It is only by the exercise of reason that man can discover God. Take away that reason, and he would be incapable of understanding anything; and, in this case, it would be just as consistent to read even the book called the Bible to a horse as to a man. How, then, is it that people pretend to reject reason? . . .

TRUE THEOLOGY AND THAT OF SUPERSTITION

. . . .

The scientific principles that man employs to obtain the foreknowledge of an eclipse, or of anything else relating to the motion of the heavenly bodies, are contained chiefly in that part of science which is called trigonometry, or the properties of a triangle, which, when applied to the study of the heavenly bodies, is called astronomy; when applied to direct the course of a ship on the ocean it is called navigation; when applied to the construction of figures drawn by rule and compass it is called geometry; when applied to the construction of plans or edifices it is called architecture; when applied to the measurement of any portion of the surface of the earth it is called land surveying. In fine, it is the soul of science; it is an eternal truth; it contains the *mathematical demonstration* of which man speaks, and the extent of its uses is unknown.

It may be said that man can make or draw a triangle, and therefore a triangle is a human invention.

But the triangle, when drawn, is no other than the image of the principle; it is a delineation to the eye, and from thence to the mind, of a principle that would otherwise be imperceptible. The triangle does not make the principle, any more than a candle taken into a room that was dark makes the chairs and tables that before were invisible. All the properties of a triangle exist independently of the figure, and existed before any triangle was drawn or thought of by man. Man had no more to do in the formation of these properties or principles than he had to do in making the laws by which the heavenly bodies move; and therefore the one must have the same divine origin as the other.

In the same manner, as it may be said, that man can make a triangle, so also, may it be said, he can make the mechanical instrument called a lever; but the principle by which the lever acts is a thing distinct from the instrument, and would exist if the instrument did not; it attaches itself to the instrument after it is made; the instrument, therefore, cannot act otherwise than it does act; neither can all the efforts of human invention make it act otherwise — that which, in all such cases, man calls the *effect* is no other than the principle itself rendered perceptible to the senses.

Since, then, man cannot make principles, from whence did he gain a knowledge of them, so as to be able to apply them, not only to things on earth, but to ascertain the motion of bodies so immensely distant from him as all the heavenly bodies are? From whence, I ask, *could* he gain that knowledge, but from the study of the true theology?

It is the structure of the universe that has taught this knowledge to man. That structure is an ever-existing exhibition of every principle upon which every part of mathematical science is founded. The offspring of this science is mechanics; for mechanics is no other than the principles of science applied practically.

The man who proportions the several parts of a mill uses the same scientific principles as if he had the power of constructing a universe; but as he cannot give to matter that invisible agency by which all the component parts of the immense machine of the universe have influence upon each other and act in motional unison together, without any apparent contact, and to which man has given the name of attraction, gravitation and repulsion, he supplies the place of that agency by the humble imitation of teeth and cogs.

All the parts of a man's microcosm must visibly touch; but could he gain a knowledge of that agency so as to be able to apply it in practise we might then say that another *canonical book* of the Word of God had been discovered.

If man could alter the properties of the lever, so also could he alter the properties of the triangle, for a lever (taking that sort of lever which is called a steelyard, for the sake of explanation) forms, when in motion, a triangle. The line it descends from (one point of that line being in the fulcrum), the line it descends to, and the chord of the arc which the end of the lever describes in the air, are the three sides of a triangle.

The other arm of the lever describes also a triangle; and the corresponding sides of those two triangles, calculated scientifically or measured geometrically, and also the sines, tangents and secants generated from the angles, and geometrically measured, have the same proportions to each other as the different weights have that will balance each other on the lever, leaving the weight of the lever out of the case.

It may also be said that man can make a wheel and axis; that he can put wheels of different magnitudes together, and produce a mill. Still the case comes back to the same point, which is that he did not make the principle that gives the wheels those powers. That principle is as unalterable as in the former cases, or rather it is the same principle under a different appearance to the eye.

The power that two wheels of different magnitudes have upon each other is in the same proportion as if the semi-diameter of the two wheels were joined together and made into that kind of lever I have described, suspended at the part where the semi-diameters join; for the two wheels, scientifically considered, are no other than the two circles generated by the motion of the compound lever.

It is from the study of the true theology that all our knowledge of science is derived, and it is from that knowledge that all the arts have originated.

The Almighty Lecturer, by displaying the principles of science in the structure of the universe, has invited man to study and to imitation. It is as if He had said to the inhabitants of this globe that we call ours, "I have made an earth for man to dwell upon, and I have rendered the starry heavens visible, to teach him science and the arts. He can now provide for his own comfort, AND LEARN FROM MY MUNIFICENCE TO ALL, TO BE KIND TO EACH OTHER."

Of what use is it, unless it be to teach man something, that his eye is endowed with the power of beholding to an incomprehensible distance an immensity of worlds revolving in the ocean of space? Of what use is it that this immensity of worlds is visible to man? What has man to do with the Pleiades, with Orion, with Sirius, with the star he calls the North Star, with the moving orbs he has named Saturn, Jupiter, Mars, Venus, and Mercury, if no uses are to follow from their being visible? A less power of vision would have been sufficient for man, if the immensity he now possesses were given only to waste itself, as it were, on an immense desert of space glittering with shows.

It is only by contemplating what he calls the starry heavens, as the book and school of science, that he discovers any use in their being visible to him, or any advantage resulting from his immensity of vision. But when he contemplates the subject in this light, he sees an additional motive for saying, that *nothing was made in vain;* for in vain would be this power of vision if it taught man nothing.

COMPARING CHRISTIANISM WITH PANTHEISM

.   .   .   .

My father being of the Quaker profession, it was my good fortune to have an exceedingly good moral education, and a tolerable stock of useful learning. Though I went to the grammar school, I did not learn Latin, not only because I had no inclination to learn languages, but because of the objection the Quakers have against the books in which the language is taught. But this did not prevent me from being acquainted with the subjects of all the Latin books used in the school.

The natural bent of my mind was to science. I had some turn, and I believe some talent, for poetry; but this I rather repressed than encouraged, as leading too much into the field of imagination. As soon as I was able I purchased a pair of globes, and attended the philosophical lectures of Martin and Ferguson, and became afterward acquainted with Dr. Bevis, of the society called the Royal Society, then living in the Temple, and an excellent astronomer.

I had no disposition for what is called politics. It presented to my mind no other idea than as contained in the word Jockeyship. When, therefore, I turned my thoughts toward matter of government I had to form a system for myself that accorded with the moral and philosophic principles in which I have been educated. I saw, or at least I thought I saw, a vast scene opening itself to the world in the affairs of America, and it appeared to me that unless the Americans changed the plan they were pursuing with respect to the government of England, and declared themselves independent, they would not only involve themselves in a multiplicity of new difficulties, but shut out the prospect that was then offering itself to mankind through their means. It was from these motives that I published the work known by the name of "Common Sense," which was the first work I ever did publish; and so far as I can judge of myself, I believe I should never have been known in the world as an author on any subject whatever had it not been for the affairs of America. I wrote "Common Sense" the latter end of the year 1775, and published it the first of January, 1776. Independence was declared the fourth of July following.

Any person who has made observations on the state and progress of the human mind by observing his own cannot but have observed that there are two distinct classes of what are called thoughts — those that we produce in ourselves by reflection and the act of thinking, and those that bolt into the mind of their own accord. I have always made it a rule to treat these voluntary visitors with civility, taking care to examine, as well as I was able, if they were worth entertaining, and it is from them I have acquired almost all the knowledge that I have. As to the learning that any person gains from school education, it serves only, like a small capital, to put him in a way of beginning learning for himself afterward.

Every person of learning is finally his own teacher, the reason of which is that principles, being a distinct quality to circumstances, cannot be impressed upon the memory; their place of mental residence is the understanding and they are never so lasting as when they begin by conception. Thus much for the introductory part.

From the time I was capable of conceiving an idea and acting upon it by reflection, I either doubted the truth of the Christian system or thought it to be a strange affair; I scarcely knew which it was, but I well remember, when about seven or eight years of age, hearing a sermon read by a relation of mine, who was a great devotee of the Church, upon the subject of what is called *redemption by the death of the Son of God.*

After the sermon was ended, I went into the garden, and as I was going down the garden steps (for I perfectly recollect the spot) I revolted at the recollection of what I had heard, and thought to myself that it was making God Almighty act like a passionate man who killed His son when He could not revenge Himself in any other way, and, as I was sure a man would be hanged who did such a thing, I could not see for what purpose they preached such sermons.

This was not one of that kind of thoughts that had anything in it of childish levity; it was to me a serious reflection, arising from the idea I had that God was too good to do such an action, and also too almighty to be under any necessity of doing it. I believe in the same manner at this moment; and I moreover believe that any system of religion that has anything in it that shocks the mind of a child cannot be a true system.

It seems as if parents of the Christian profession were ashamed to tell their children anything about the principles of their religion. They sometimes instruct them in morals and talk to them of the goodness of what they call Providence, for the Christian mythology has five deities — there is God the Father, God the Son, God the Holy Ghost, the God Providence and the Goddess Nature. But the Christian story of God the Father putting His son to death, or employing people to do it (for that is the plain language of the story) cannot be told by a parent to a child; and to tell him that it was done to make mankind happier and better is making the story still worse — as if mankind could be improved by the example of murder; and to tell him that all this is a mystery is only making an excuse for the incredibility of it.

How different is this to the pure and simple profession of Deism! The true Deist has but one Deity, and his religion consists in contemplating the power, wisdom and benignity of the Deity in His works, and in endeavoring to imitate Him in everything moral, scientifical and mechanical.

The religion that approaches the nearest of all others to true Deism, in the moral and benign part thereof, is that professed by the Quakers; but they have contracted themselves too much by leaving the works of God out of their system. Though I reverence their philanthropy, I cannot help smiling at the conceit that if the taste of a Quaker could have been consulted at the Creation what a silent and drab-colored Creation it would have been! Not a flower would have blossomed its gayeties, nor a bird been permitted to sing. . . .

ॐ Elihu Palmer (1764–1806)

ELIHU PALMER was born and brought up in Connecticut, and educated at Dartmouth. He studied for the Presbyterian ministry, obtained a pulpit on Long Island in 1788, and within six months was forced out by his congregation for his liberal theological views. He moved to Philadelphia, where he joined the Universalist church, but his parishioners nearly mobbed him for his "radicalism."

Palmer was in fact, by 1790, neither Presbyterian nor Universalist, but a pronounced and militant deist. Discouraged, he turned to the study of law and was admitted to the bar in 1793, but just as he was about to begin practice an attack of yellow fever left him permanently blind. After a long period of travel as a deist lecturer, Palmer settled in New York City and organized a deist society. Later he founded similar groups in Philadelphia and Baltimore and published a deist newspaper called *The Temple of Reason.* He also planned a Temple of Nature in New York, as a kind of deist church, but died before it could be completed.

A skillful organizer and a powerful speaker, Palmer did much to propagate the principles of deism during its brief period of popularity (1790–1810) among intellectuals. His *Principles of Nature; or a Development of the Moral Causes of Happiness and Misery among the Human Species* (1802) is the most complete statement of his beliefs.

TEXT: Elihu Palmer, *Principles of Nature* . . . (London, 1823).

The Origin of Moral Evil, and the Means of Its Extinction

[From *Principles of Nature,* 1802]

The facts in the physical world are, many of them, difficult of solution: those of the moral world have perplexed still more the operations of the human understanding. The subtilty, the abstruseness, the incognizable character of moral existence, place it beyond the power of clear intellectual perception, and the mind loses itself in those metaphysical combinations, whose successive variations are incalculable. But the difficulties which nature has thrown in the way of this inquiry are much less numerous than those presented by superstition. A design has been formed, and carried into effect, whose object it was to cover the moral world with a mantle of mystery, and exclude it wholly from the view of vulgar eyes, and common comprehension. It is only necessary to conceal the real nature and character of a thing, and then deformities and distortions may be made to pass for positive properties, or essential qualities inherent in any specific mode of existence. If the subtilty of thought, and the difficulty of moral discrimination, have in many cases presented to human investigation a barrier to farther progress; the intentional malignant descriptions of superstition have, in almost every age and country, terrified the mind of man, and prevented the development of substantial moral principle. Nature furnishes some difficulties, but supernatural theology exhibits many more.

In no one instance is this remark more substantially verified, than in the inquiries which man has made concerning the source or origin of moral evil. Reason and theology, philosophy and superstition, are at war upon this subject. The believers in the Christian religion, following the examples of their theological and fanatic predecessors, have searched the universe in quest of a satisfactory solution to that long altercated question — Whence came moral evil? One religious sectary, willing to screen the divinity from any just accusation relative to so nefarious a concern, have descended into hell, and discovered there all the characters and distorted machinery necessary to the production of such an effect: but here metaphysical and fanatic invention indulged itself in all the extravagance of delusion. It was necessary first to create this *infernal* country, and then to create inhabitants suited to the nature of the climate, and the unfortunate condition in which they were to reside. The idea of a Devil was accordingly formed, and the reality of his existence rendered an indubitable truth by the reiterated assertions of superstition. Ignorance and fanaticism greedily swallowed the foolish *infernal* dose which had been administered.

There is a remarkable disposition in the human mind to remove the point of intellectual difficulty as far from the reality of the case as possible, and then it triumphantly imagines that a solution has been given. This is a fact particularly in theological inquiry, in which a few retrogressive efforts of the mind have been considered as an ample illustration of all the difficulties relative to the subject of Theism, and the existence of the physical universe. Similar to this idea is the doctrine concerning moral evil, and the disposition which theologians have exhibited to remove the burden from their own shoulders, and place it upon the devil's back. The whole *infernal* machinery with which we are presented by superstition, serves only to detach the mind from the true and real source of moral evil. While reflection is directed to another world, it is incompetent to a clear view of the facts existing in this, and the habit of such reveries produces a fanatic delirium subversive of all correctness of judgment. The existence of hell, and the beings that dwell therein, being only supported by what is called divine revelation, it follows, of course, that if this revelation is not true, a belief in any thing that is a mere result of that system cannot be substantially founded. Since then it is presumed, that in these chapters a competent refutation is given to the doctrine contained in the sacred books of the Jews and Christians, the idea of descending into hell, or having recourse to a devil, in search of moral evil, is futile and inconsistent.

Another part of the Christian world, willing to avoid difficulties which their antagonists had thrown in their way, abandoned the *infernal* abodes, and ascended into the celestial world, in quest of the origin of evil. They exhibited ingenious metaphysical reasoning upon the subject, declaring that God was the Creator of all things; that sin was something and not nothing, and therefore he must be the Creator of sin or moral evil. This puzzled the advocates of the *hell scheme* and a clerical warfare was engendered concerning two theological opinions, neither of which had any kind of existence in the nature of things. After heaven and hell had been searched through and through to find something which did not belong to either of them, the terror-struck inquirer, as if fatigued with his atmospheric journey, seated himself once more upon the earth, and saw, or might have seen, in the very bosom of society, and the perverted character of man, a clear and satisfactory solution of that difficult question, which, for so long a time, had occupied his attention in distant regions. It is in this manner, that the plainest subject is rendered mysterious, when a superstitious religion is industriously employed in subverting the independent power of thought. It is neither in the upper nor lower regions; it is not in heaven nor in hell, that the origin of moral evil will be discovered; it is to be found only among those intelligent beings who exist upon the earth. *Man has created it, and man must destroy it.*

But it is necessary to exhibit the proofs of this last assertion, and convince Christian theology of the innumerable errors, which for ages past have been imposed upon a credulous and deluded world. What is it, then, that constitutes a moral evil? It is the violation of a law of justice or utility, by any one of the human species, competent to distinguish between right and wrong. We have no other cognizable idea upon this subject. Facts and practice are presented continually to the view of the human mind; the decision of a correct mind is always according to the nature and character of the case. The character of a human being is made either good or bad by the actions he commits. If these actions are conformable to the principles of justice and universal benevolence, they are with great propriety denominated good; if they are unjust, cruel, and destructive to sensitive and intellectual life, they are denominated bad. There are certain fundamental laws, suitable for the government of rational beings, and it is a departure from these laws that vitiates the human character. It is proved in another part of this work, that virtue and vice are personal qualities and that they result from personal adherence to, or personal infraction of moral law.

It is only necessary in this place to call the attention once more to the nature of human actions, and to the characteristic difference between them, in order to establish the position principally assumed in this inquiry; for it ought to be recollected, that even if it *could* be proved, which by the way it cannot, that even a deity or a devil had violated moral law, this would not affect the decision upon the subject in regard to man; because that evil could not be transferred from a different kind of beings in the other world, to those who exist upon earth. As the moral properties of all intelligent agents are personal; are essentially their own and not another's; as there can be no justifiable transfer between man and man, so it follows that there can be none between man and devil. Every intellectual being must depend upon himself: must rest upon his own energies and be responsible for himself. Man must, therefore, relinquish that position, which has been assumed by Christian theology, relative to the transferable nature of moral qualities. Christianity presents us with two grand leading characters, to whom we are always referred in our inquiries upon the subject of moral evil. Adam and Jesus are these persons, and in them is said to have been concentred the sin and righteousness of the human race. The new Testament declares that, *as in Adam all die, even so in Christ shall all be made alive.* This is a sweeping clause, in regard to the moral existence of man, and flies in the face of universal experience. Facts are at war with this scriptural declaration, and it is impossible to reduce the sentiment to practice, without producing in common life the grossest violation of justice. Admitting for a moment the existence of such a man as Adam, which by the way is extremely problematical, it will not follow, that there was in him either a moral or physical death of the human race. Physically it is impossible, and morally it is unjust. If Christian theology has made a recurrence to Adam, to aid the solution of difficulties, relative to the origin of moral evil; if it has by this idea perverted the eternal principles of discriminative justice, it has also been equally unfortunate in calling in the righteous Jesus to its assistance, in expectation of ultimately destroying the immorality of the world. The scriptures invite us to behold the Lamb of God, that taketh away the sins of the world. The Lamb is Jesus, the only begotten of the Father; he is reputed to be divine and uncontaminated with any kind of moral turpitude. He is made the victim of Jehovah's wrath, and falls a sacrifice to the vindictive fury of his benevolent father, and all this for the purpose of removing crimes for which apostate man should have been scourged and afflicted. Means more unsuitable or incompetent to the production of such an effect, could never have been invented by the delirious brain of fanaticism itself; but the absurd and incompetent methods which Christian theology has invented for the destruction of moral evil, are not so much the objects of the present investigation, as the means which reason has in view to effectuate the moral renovation of the species. . . .

The most important step which can be taken for the extermination of vice and misery, is to destroy the artificial causes by which such evils are perpetuated. If other causes should be found to exist in the constitution of nature, they will be progressively removed by the light and power of science, and a more comprehensive view of the true interest of the human species. But efforts tending to make the individuals of a nation virtuous and happy, will never succeed extensively till the civil and religious tyranny under which they groan shall be completely annihilated. This will lead to the application of force in the political revolutions of the world; an expedient, however, the rectitude of which some benevolent philosophers have called in question. . . .

It is sufficient at this time to remark, that despotism gives no encouragement to any kind of improvement, and the hope of human amelioration from this quarter will ever prove to be fallacious. Reason, righteous and immortal reason, with the argument of the printing types in one hand, and the keen argument of the sword in the other, must attack the thrones and the hierarchies of the world, and level them with the dust of the earth; then the emancipated slave must be raised by the power of science into the character of an enlightened citizen; thus possessing a knowledge of his rights, a knowledge of his duties will consequently follow, and he will discover the intimate and essential union between the highest interests of existence, and the practice of an exalted virtue. If civil and ecclesiastical despotism were destroyed, knowledge would become universal, and its progress inconceivably accelerated. It would be impossible, in such a case, that moral virtue should fail of a correspondent acceleration, and the ultimate extirpation of vice would become an inevitable consequence. Ages must elapse before the accomplishment of an object so important to the elevated concerns of intelligent life; but the causes are already in operation, and nothing can arrest or destroy the benignant effects which they are calculated to produce. The power of reason, the knowledge of printing, the overthrow of political and ecclesiastical despotism, the universal diffusion of the light of science, and the universal enjoyment of republican liberty; these will become the harbingers and procuring causes of real virtue in every individual, and universal happiness will become the lot of man.

☙ Timothy Dwight (1752–1817)

TIMOTHY DWIGHT, Jonathan Edwards' grandson, was generally accepted after 1790 as the leader of conservative theology in New England, at a time when orthodox Calvinism seemed threatened by a rising tide of "infidelity" — the term usually applied to deism, Unitarianism, or religious liberalism of any kind. The appeal of the new "natural" or "rational" religion was especially strong to young intellectuals; and college professors leveled their guns against it in class, sermon, and discussion. The Harvard authorities distributed copies of Bishop Watson's defense of the Bible as an antidote; Dwight, who became president of Yale in 1795, preached more than two hundred sermons against "infidelity" and wrote a savagely satiric poem, *The Triumph of Infidelity* (1788). The theologically orthodox, frightened by the religious radicalism of the French Revolution and the influence of "certain skeptical philosophers of France" (as the Reverend Samuel Miller called them), placed much of the blame for deism's popularity on Jefferson, Paine, Barlow, and other known French sympathizers. Dwight's analysis of the history of infidelity and the current situation, in a sermon preached at Yale in 1801, is typical of the orthodox point of view.

TEXT: Timothy Dwight, *A Discourse on Some Events of the Last Century* (New Haven, 1801).

The Present Dangers of Infidelity

[From *A Discourse on Some Events,* 1801]

The religion of this country has exhibited a very commendable spirit of catholicism and moderation during the past century, a spirit extended perhaps as far as can be reasonably expected from men, and producing a general and happy harmony of sentiment and conduct. In no country, it is presumed, can be found a more general decency and liberality of conduct in the various classes of religious towards each other. Indeed, the existing error appears to be a tendency, in many persons, towards what is emphatically called *modern liberality;* which is no other than mere indifference to truth and error, virtue and vice: a more dangerous and fatal character than the most contemptible enthusiasm, or the most odious bigotry. Toleration, strictly understood, has no existence here; for all religious denominations are placed on the same equal and independent ground. This, if it can be preserved, as there is hitherto much reason to believe, is certainly an improvement in human affairs, and ought to be regarded both as an honor, and a blessing, to our country.

In the course of this period GOD has, in various instances, been pleased to revive his glorious work of sanctification, and to extend it through many parts of the land. I know that a number of men, and some of much respectability, have entertained unfavorable ideas of what are called revivals of religion; but I cannot help thinking their opinions of this subject rather formed in the closet than derived from facts, or warranted by the scriptures. Seasons of enthusiasm about various subjects have indeed often existed, and probably in every civilized country. In these seasons the human mind has not unfrequently exhibited many kinds and degrees of weakness, error, and deformity. Hence, perhaps, sober men have, in some instances, been led to believe that wherever enthusiasm exists these evils exist also. As therefore revivals of religion have frequently been more or less accompanied by enthusiasm, they have, I think without sufficient grounds, determined that all which existed was enthusiasm, and that nothing would flow from it but these evils.

That the mind under the first clear, strong, and solemn views of its own sins should be deeply affected, and greatly agitated, is to be expected from the nature of man. He is always thus affected by the first strong view taken of any object deeply interesting, and always thus agitated when such an object is seen in an uncertain, suspended state. No object can be so interesting, or more entirely suspended, than the state of the soul in the case specified.

When these emotions, thus excited by objects of such immense importance, and in so absolute a state of suspense, as the guilt, the condemnation, and the salvation of an immortal mind, are attended with some degree of enthusiasm and extravagance; when they are followed by seasons of deep despondence, and successive transport; nothing takes place, but that, which sound philosophy must presuppose; as similar emotions are, in all similar cases, followed, especially in ardent minds, by the same consequences. All this, however, will go no length towards proving that nothing exists beyond enthusiasm; and that, amid several irregular and excessive exertions of the mind, there is not to be found a real change of the disposition, a real assumption of piety. To me it is evident that revivals of religion are often what they are called, if not always; and that the proof abundantly exists (where alone it ought to be looked for) in the real and permanent melioration of the moral character of multitudes, who then become serious and professedly religious.

Of the last of these revivals of religion, that which still extensively exists, it ought to be observed that it has absolutely, or at least very nearly, been free from every extravagance. I speak not here to infidels, nor to libertines. All religion is extravagance, enthusiasm, and super-stition, with them. But no man of common candor can hesitate to admit that vice is not the only sober and rational state of a moral being; and that impiety is an unhappy proof of real wisdom. In this great and auspicious event of which I have spoken, thousands have been already happily concerned, and thousands more will, it is hoped, hereafter claim a share.

But, with the rest of mankind, we have abused our blessings. Loose opinions and loose practices have found their place here also. The first considerable change in the religious character of the people of this country was accomplished by the war which began in 1755. War is at least as fatal to morals as to life, or happiness. The officers and soldiers of the British armies, then employed in this country, although probably as little corrupted as those of most armies, were yet loose patterns of opinions and conduct, and were unhappily copied by con-siderable numbers of our own countrymen, united with them in military life. These, on their return, spread the infection through those around them. Looser habits of thinking began then to be adopted, and were followed, as they always are, by looser conduct. The American war increased these evils. Peace had not, at the commencement of this war, restored the purity of life which existed before the preceding war. To the depravation still remaining was added a long train of immoral doctrines and practices, which spread into every corner of the country. The profanation of the Sabbath, before unusual, profaneness of language, drunkenness, gambling, and lewdness, were exceedingly increased; and, what is less commonly remarked, but is perhaps not less mischievous than any of them, a light, vain method of thinking, concerning sacred things, a cold, contemptuous indifference toward every moral and religious subject. In the meantime, that enormous evil, a depreciating currency, gave birth to a new spirit of fraud, and opened numerous temptations, and a boundless field for its operations; while a new and intimate correspondence with corrupted foreigners introduced a multiplicity of loose doctrines, which were greedily embraced by licentious men, as the means of palliating and justifying their sins.

At this period Infidelity began to obtain, in this country, an exten-sive currency and reception. As this subject constitutes far the most interesting and prominent characteristic of the past century, it will not be amiss to exhibit it with some degree of minuteness, and to trace through several particulars the steps of its progress.

Infidelity has been frequently supposed to be founded on an appre-hended deficiency of the evidence which supports a divine Revelation. No opinion can be more erroneous than this. That solitary instances may have existed, in which men did not believe the scriptures to be the word of God, because they doubted of the evidence in *their* possession, I am ready to admit; but that this has been the common fact is, at least in my view, a clear impossibility.

Our Saviour informs us, that "This is the condemnation, that light is come into the world, and men loved darkness rather than light, because their deeds were evil:" and subjoins, that "he who doth evil hateth the light, neither cometh to the light, lest his deeds should be reproved." Here one of the two great causes of Infidelity is distinctly and exactly alleged, viz., *the opposition of a heart which loves sin, and dreads the punishment of it, to that truth which, with infinite authority, and under an immense penalty, demands of all men a holy life.* The other great cause of Infidelity is frequently mentioned by the inspired writers, particularly St. Paul, St. Peter, and St. Jude. In the following passages of St. Peter it is exhibited with peculiar force. "For when they speak great swelling words of vanity, they allure through the lusts of the flesh, through much wantonness, them that were clean escaped from them, that live in error. While they promise them liberty, they themselves are the servants (bond-slaves) of corruption." "There shall come in the last days scoffers, walking after their own lusts, and saying, Where is the promise of his coming? for, since the fathers fell asleep, all things continue as they were from the beginning of the creation."

The Infidels, here referred to, are plainly *philosophists; the authors of vain and deceitful philosophy; of science falsely so called; always full of vanity in their discourses: scoffers, walking after their own lusts, and alluring others, through the same lusts, to follow them; promising them liberty, as their reward, and yet being themselves, and making their disciples, the lowest and most wretched of all slaves, the slaves of corruption. Philosophistical pride* and *the love of sinning in security and peace* are, therefore, the two great causes of Infidelity, according to the scriptures.

A more exact account of this subject, as existing in fact, could not even now be given. Infidelity has been assumed because it was *loved,* and not because it was *supported by evidence;* and has been maintained and defended, *to quiet the mind in sin,* and *to indulge the pride of talents and speculation.*

The form which it has received has varied in the hands of almost every distinguished Infidel. It was first *Theism, or natural Religion,* then *mere Unbelief,* then *Animalism,* then *Scepticism,* then *partial,* and then *total Atheism.* Yet it has, in three things at least, preserved a general consistency: *opposition to Christianity, devotion to sin and lust,* and a *pompous profession of love to Liberty.* To a candid and logical opposition to Christianity, consisting of facts and arguments fairly stated and justly exhibited, no reasonable objection can be made.

It is to be wished that this had been the conduct of the opposition actually made; but nothing has been more unlike that conduct. The war has been the desultory attack of a barbarian, not of a civilized soldier; an onset of passion, pride, and wit; a feint of conjectures and falsified facts; an incursion of sneers, jests, gross banter, and delicate ridicule; a parade of hints and insinuations; and a vigorous assault on fancy, passion, and appetite. These were never the weapons of sober conviction; this was never the conduct of honest men.

In the earlier periods of this controversy there were, however, more frequent efforts at argumentation, on the part of Infidels. For the last twenty or thirty years they seem to have despaired of success in this field, and have betaken themselves to that of action and influence. In this field they have wrought with a success totally unprecedented. Nor is this at all to be wondered at, if we consider the opportunity of succeeding presented to them, during the latter half of the last century, by the state of society in Europe. The excessive wealth of that division of the eastern Continent has generated an enormous luxury, the multiplied enjoyments of which have become not only the ruling objects of desire, and the governing motives of action, but, in the view of a great part of the inhabitants, the necessary means of even a comfortable existence. On these life is employed, ambition fastened, ardor exhausted, and energy spent. Voluptuousness and splendor, formed on the Asiatic scale, engross men in public and private stations, in the university, the camp, the shop, and the desk, as well as the court and the cabinet. To glitter with diamonds, to roll in pomp, to feast on dainties, to wanton in amusements, to build palaces, and to fashion wildernesses of pleasure, are the supreme objects of millions apparently destined to the grave, still, and humble walks of life, as well as of those who were high born and highly endowed. Science toils, ingenuity is stretched on the rack, and art is wearied through all her refinements, to satisfy the universal demand for pleasure; the mines of Golconda are ransacked, the caverns of Mexico emptied, and the mountains of Potosi transported across the ocean.

Of this universal devotion to pleasure and shew, modern Infidels have availed themselves to the utmost. To a mind, to a nation, dissolved in sloth, enervated by pleasure, and fascinated with splendor, the Gospel is preached, and heaven presented, in vain. The eye is closed, the ear stopped, and the heart rendered gross and incapable of healing. The soul is of course unconscious of danger, impatient of restraint, and insensible to the demands of moral obligation. It is, therefore, prepared to become an Infidel, without research, and without conviction. Hence, more sagacious than their predecessors, the later Infidels have neither labored, nor wished, to convince the understanding, but have bent all their efforts to engross the heart.

In the meantime other events, highly favorable to their designs, have taken place both in America and Europe. The American Revolution, an august, solemn, and most interesting spectacle, drew towards it at this time the eyes of mankind. The novelty of the scene, the enchanting sound of Liberty, to which the pulse of man instinctively beats, the sympathy ever excited for the feebler and suffering party, embarked deeply in the American cause a great part of the civilized world. Benevolent men, of all countries, hoped, when the contest was ended prosperously for us, and ardent men boldly pronounced, that a new era had arrived in human things, that "the iron rod of the oppressor was broken," and that "the oppressed would soon be universally set free."

Among the agents in the American Revolution were many natives of France; men, in numerous instances, of ardent minds and daring speculations; who either imbibed here new sentiments of liberty, or ripened those which they had already adopted at home. These men, returning to their own country, diffused extensively the enthusiasm which they had cherished here, and thus hastened the crisis to which France was otherwise approaching. . . .

The door thus opened, Infidels entered in mass, and labored with a zeal, activity, and perseverance unrivaled since the days of the apostles. In every possible instance they possessed themselves of every office of honor and power, of instruction and influence; secured the literary society and the secret club, engrossed the press and the stage, debauched the prince and the peasant, the noble and the ecclesiastic, deceived the aged, and ensnared the young. The authority of the monarch, the address of the courtier, the gravity of the apostate divine, and the abstract jugglery of the sophist, the mysterious trade of the bookseller, and the humble lessons of the schoolmaster, were all employed to support, to spread, and to rivet Infidelity.

Their writers have been no less assiduous and persevering. A part of their labors has been presented to the world under the form of new systems of philosophy; which, if believed, are utterly subversive of Christianity, but in which no direct attack is made on Christianity. These, though ushered into public view with great pomp and solemnity, have been mere theories of the closet; often ingenious, but always unsupported by fact or evidence. The terms employed in them are so wholly abstract, and the phraseology so mysterious and perplexed, that the reader, engaged by the ingenuity of the writer, is lost in a mist of doubtful expressions and unsettled sentiments. His faith is constantly solicited to gravely described dreams; and his eye is required to fix on the form of a cloud, varying its shape through every moment of his inspection. From the highway of common sense he is invited into bypaths where indeed nothing worthy of his curiosity is

ever seen, but where, he is continually informed, something of vast
importance is in the end to be seen. Whatever he reads is uttered
with the gravity and confidence of superior wisdom, and an imposing
air of mystery, and with continual hints of something, immensely important, in due time to be revealed. Thus he wanders on, a dupe to
artfully excited expectation, and loses himself in "a wilderness, where
there is no way." He is not informed, but allured; not convinced, but
perplexed; yet he is often, perhaps usually, by his own curiosity,
pride, and self-consistency, and by the doubt and ridicule artfully
thrown in against Revelation, so thoroughly estranged from truth and
virtue as never to return. To ruin in this way are surely led most
readers of a particular class, and that a numerous one; readers pleased
with reasoning extended to a certain degree, and conducted with a due
mixture of brilliancy; readers fond of novelty, and esteeming singularity of thought a proof of superior understanding.

This, however, has been but one, and that a very partial object of
their reliance. Their writings have assumed every form, and treated
every subject of thought. From the lofty philosophical discourse it
has descended through all the intervening gradations to the newspaper
paragraph; from the sermon to the catechism; from regular history to
the anecdote; from the epic poem to the song; and from the formal
satire to the jest of the buffoon. Efforts in vast numbers have also
been made to diffuse Infidelity in a remark unexpectedly found in a
discourse, when a totally different subject was under consideration;
in a note subjoined to a paper on criticism or politics; in a hint in a
book of travels; or a stroke in a letter of civility. In these and the like
cases the reader was intended to be taken by surprise, and to yield his
judgment before he was aware that he was called to judge. The number and variety of the efforts have also been increased beyond example;
have poured from innumerable presses, and from all civilized countries; have been sold at the lowest prices, and given gratuitously; and
have been circulated with vast industry, and by innumerable hands,
throughout Christendom. The intention of this amazing multitude of
exertions has plainly been to astonish and discourage their adversaries,
to amaze and overwhelm their readers, and to persuade, insensibly,
the mass of mankind, that the world was converted to Infidelity.

But the pen has been a far less important and successful instrument
than action and influence. This has been exerted with immense vigor,
employed in every place, and addressed to every mind. In consequence of the prospects of triumph opened to them, during the latter
part of the Century under consideration, they loudly proclaimed themselves the champions of liberty, and the friends of persecuted man.
No knight-errant ever offered himself to an affrighted damsel with
more generosity, as her protector, than they to the human race. The

common people, never honored by Voltaire with any higher title than the rabble, or the mob, yet as they possessed the physical strength of man suddenly beheld these philanthropic gentlemen starting up in the form of their guardians and foster fathers, and volunteering in the humane employment of vindicating their wrongs and asserting their rights. The tale, which in the mind of every sober man awakened no emotions but indignation and contempt, roused, nevertheless, in the feelings of the ignorant, the ardent, and the enthusiastic, a frenzied expectation of good, unknown indeed, but certain and immense. An universal thrill was felt, a millennium seen already dawning in the horizon. All the weak, the tender, the doubting, the boding, the eager, the daring passions of the human mind were now attacked, successively, by the persuasion of eloquence, the stings of ridicule, the parade of argument, the alarm of danger, the hope of safety, and the promise of reward.

In this great moral convulsion Royalty and Christianity sunk in the kingdom of France. Emboldened beyond every fear by this astonishing event, Infidelity, which anciently had hidden behind a mask, walked forth in open day, and displayed her genuine features to the sun. Without a blush she now denied the existence of moral obligation, annihilated the distinction between virtue and vice, challenged and authorized the indulgence of every lust, trod down the barriers of truth, perjured herself daily in the sight of the universe, lifted up her front in the face of heaven, denied the being, and dared the thunder of the Almighty. Virtue and truth, her native enemies, and the objects of all her real hatred, she hunted from every cell and solitude; and, whenever they escaped her fangs, she followed them with the execrations of malice, the finger of derision, and the hisses of infamy.

Elevated now, for the first time to the chair of dominion, she ushered forth her edicts with the gravity of deliberation and the authority of law, and executed them by the oppressive hand of the jailor, the axe of the executioner, and the sword of the warrior. All rights fell before her, all interests were blasted by her breath, and happiness and hope were together swept away by her besom of destruction.

In the midst of all this effrontery, Infidels forgot not their arts and impositions. As occasion dictated, or ingenuity whispered, they availed themselves of every disguise, and of every persuasive. As if they had designed to give the last wound to virtue, they assumed all her titles and challenged all her attributes to their own conduct. Daily forsworn, and laughing at the very distinction between right and wrong, they proclaimed themselves the assertors of justice, and the champions of truth. While they converted a realm into a Bastille, they trumpeted their inviolable attachment to liberty; while they "cursed their GOD, and looked upward," they announced themselves worshippers of the *Supreme Being*. With a little finger, thicker than the loins of both the monarchy and the hierarchy, encircled with three millions of corpses, and in the center of a kingdom changed into a stall of slaughter, they hung themselves over with labels of philanthropy. Nay, they have far outgone all this. Two of their philosophers, independently of each other, have declared that, to establish their favorite system, the sacrifice of all the existing race of man would be a cheap price: an illustrious instance of Infidel benevolence, and of the excellence of their daring maxim, that "the end sanctifies the means."

These, however, are but a small portion of their arts. They have, as the state of things required, disguised their designs; disavowed them; doubted their existence; wondered at those who believed them real; ridiculed the belief; and professed themselves amazed at such credulity. This conduct has been even reduced to a system, and taught and enjoined on their followers, as a code of policy, and as being often the most effectual means of spreading their opinions. . . .

In all these and the like forms, Infidelity has been seasoned and served up; in all these and the like methods, it is insinuated, urged, and forced on mankind. To these things ought to be added, that the magic of the pencil, the skill of the architect, the chisel of the sculptor, the gaiety of public festivals, the pomp of processions, the splendor and fascination of the theatre, and the all-commanding power of fashion, have been engaged, and engrossed, to adorn, to solemnize, and to impress on every mind the sentiments of Infidelity. Even the fair sex, whose intercourse and elegance of mind have so exceedingly refined and improved men, are embarked in the great business of corruption, and lend their wit, their accomplishments, and their persons to promote the ruin of human society.

Such is the astonishing state of moral things, in several parts of Europe, which, within a short time, has opened upon the view of our countrymen. The strong sympathy which, unhappily, and on no rational grounds, prevailed here towards those who were leaders in the French Revolution, and towards the Revolution itself, prepared us to become the miserable dupes of their principles and declarations. They were viewed merely as *human beings, embarked deeply in the glorious cause of liberty;* and not at all as *Infidels,* as the *abettors of falsehood,* and the *enemies of Righteousness, of Truth, and of* GOD. Hence all their concerns were felt, and all their conduct covered with the veil of charity. They were viewed as *having adventured,* and *suffered, together with ourselves,* and as *now enlisted for the support of a kindred cause.* The consequences of these prejudices were such as would naturally be expected. A general and unexampled confidence was soon felt, and manifested, by every licentious man. Every Infidel, particularly, claimed a new importance, and treated religion with enhanced contempt. The graver ones, indeed, through an affected tenderness for the votaries of Christianity, adopted a more decent manner of despising it; but all were secure of a triumph, and satisfied that talents, character, and the great world were on their side. The young, the ardent, the ambitious, and the voluptuous were irresistibly solicited to join a cause which harmonized with all their corruptions, pointed out the certain road to reputation, and administered the necessary opiates to conscience; and could not refuse to unite themselves with men who *spoke great swelling words of vanity, who allured them through much wantonness, and promised them* the unbounded *liberty* of indulging every propensity to pleasure. The timid at the same time were terrified, the orderly let loose, the sober amazed, and the religious shocked beyond example; while the floating part of our countrymen, accustomed to swim with every tide, moved onward in obedience to the impulse. Thus principles were yielded, useful habits were relaxed, and a new degree of irreligion extensively prevailed.

Happily for us, the source whence these peculiar evils flowed furnished us in some degree with a remedy. It was soon discovered that *the liberty of Infidels was not the liberty of New England;* that France, instead of being free, merely changed through a series of tyrannies, at the side of which all former despotisms whitened into moderation and humanity; and that of the immeasurable evils under which she and her neighbors agonized, Infidelity was the genuine source, the Vesuvius from whose mouth issued those rivers of destruction which deluged and ruined all things in their way. It was seen that man, unrestrained by law and religion, is a mere beast of prey; that licentiousness, although adorned with the graceful name of liberty, is yet the spring of continual alarm, bondage, and misery; and that the restraints imposed by equitable laws, and by the religion of the scriptures, were far less burthensome and distressing than the boasted freedom of Infidels.

Even sober Infidels began to be alarmed for their own peace, safety, and enjoyments; and to wish that other men might continue still to be Christians; while Christians saw with horror their God denied, their Saviour blasphemed, and war formally declared against Heaven.

To all this was added a complete development of the base and villainous designs of the French government against our country, their piratical plunder of our property, and their inhuman treatment of our seamen. Persons who thought nothing, who felt nothing, concerning religion, felt these things exquisitely; and rationally concluded that men who could do these things, could and would do everything else that was evil and unjust; and that their moral principles, which produced and sanctioned these crimes, could not fail to merit contempt and detestation. Such persons, therefore, began now to lean towards the side of Christianity, and to seek in it a safety and peace which they beheld Infidelity destroy.

Thus *having* in the midst of these enormous dangers *obtained help of God, we continue until the present time;* and this part of our country, at least, has escaped not only tributary bondage, but the infinitely more dreadful bondage of Infidelity, corruption, and moral ruin.

It ought, here and forever, to be remembered with peculiar gratitude that GOD has, during the past Century, often and wonderfully interposed in our behalf, and snatched us from the jaws of approaching destruction. The instances of this interposition are too numerous to be now recounted, and are happily too extraordinary to be either unknown or forgotten. We have been frequently on the brink of destruction; but although *cast down, we have not been destroyed.* Perhaps we have so often been, and are still, suffered to stand on this precipice, that we may see, and feel, and acknowledge the hand of our Preserver.

In such a period as the present, when the state of society is so disturbed, when the minds of men are so generally set afloat, and when so many ancient landmarks, so many standards of opinion and practice, are thrown down; when ambition, avarice, and sensuality, deliberate and decree, and violence and cruelty are charged with the execution, throughout a great part of the civilized world; a contemplative and serious mind cannot but ask, *What shall the end of these things be?*

‹R Peter Cartwright (1785–1872)

PETER CARTWRIGHT, born in Virginia into a poor family, moved with his parents to Logan County, Kentucky, where he grew up as a wild frontier youth, almost illiterate. At sixteen he was converted at a Methodist revival, joined the church, and began to preach. He was given an "exhorter's license" after a little schooling, and in 1803 became a traveling "circuit rider," or itinerant preacher, with Kentucky and parts of Indiana, Ohio, and Tennessee as his circuit.

In 1824, because of his growing dislike of slavery, Cartwright asked to be transferred to Illinois, where he became a prominent figure in both church and politics. He was twice elected to the Illinois legislature, and suffered his only political defeat from Abraham Lincoln, who ran against him for Congress in 1846. In almost fifty years as a preacher, Cartwright baptized eight thousand children and four thousand adults, founded two colleges, and reared eight children of his own in the faith. He wrote of his experiences in his *Autobiography* (1857) and *Fifty Years as a Presiding Elder* (1871).

TEXT: W. P. Strickland, ed., *Autobiography of Peter Cartwright, the Backwoods Preacher* (New York, 1857).

A Muscular Christian

[From *Autobiography*, 1857]

My appointment, during 1805–6, was on the Scioto Circuit, Ohio State and District. John Sale was presiding elder, and James Quinn was senior preacher, or preacher in charge. The reader will see how greatly I was favored the first two years of my regular itinerant life, to be placed under two such men as Benjamin Lakin and James Quinn, and more, two such presiding elders as William M'Kendree and John Sale. These four men were able ministers of Jesus Christ, lived long, did much good, witnessed a good confession, died happy, and are all now safely housed in heaven. Peace to their memory forever!

Scioto Circuit extended from the Ohio River to Chillicothe, situated on that river; and crossed it near the mouth, at what is now called Portsmouth. It was a four-weeks' circuit, and there were four hundred and seventy-four members on it. Dr. Tiffin, who was governor of the state, was a local preacher; and both he and his wife were worthy members of our Church. He lived at Chillicothe, then the seat of government for the state.

There were two incidents happened while I was on the east end of this circuit, which I will relate.

We had an appointment near Eagle Creek. Here the Shakers broke in Mr. Dunlevy, whom we have mentioned elsewhere as having been a regular Presbyterian minister, who had left that Church and joined the New Lights. His New Light increased so fast, that he lost what little sense he had, and was now a ranting Shaker. He came up here, and roared and fulminated a while, led many astray, flourished for some time, and then his influence died away, and he left for parts unknown.

On the southeastern part of the circuit, we took in a new preaching-place, at a Mr. Moor's. We gave them Sunday preaching. Mr. Moor had built a large hewn log-house, two stories high. There was no partition in the second story; but it was seated, and he gave it to us to preach in. Not far from this place lived a regularly educated Presbyterian preacher, who had a fine family, and was in many respects a fine man, but, unhappily, he had contracted a love for strong drink. He had preached in this neighborhood, and was much beloved, for he was withal a very good preacher.

In making my way on one occasion to Mr. Moor's, to my Sunday appointment, I got lost and was belated, and when I arrived, there was a large assembly collected, and this minister was preaching to them, and he preached well, and I was quite pleased with the sermon so far as I heard it. When he was done, he undertook to make a public apology for a drunken spree he had got into a few days before. "Well," thought I, "*this* is right; all right, I suppose!" But to excuse himself for his unaccountable love of whisky, he stated that he had been informed by his mother that before he was born she longed for whisky; and he supposed that this was the cause of his appetite for strong drink, for he had loved it from his earliest recollection. This was the substance of his apology.

I felt somewhat indignant at this; and when I rose to close after him, I stated to the congregation that I thought the preacher's apology for drunkenness was infinitely worse than the act of drunkenness itself; that I looked upon it as a lie, and a downright slander on his mother; and that I believed his love of whisky was the result of the intemperate use of it, in which he had indulged until he formed the habit; and that I, for one, was not willing to accept or believe the truth of his apology; that I feared the preacher would live and die a drunkard, and be damned at last; and that I hoped the people there would not receive him as a preacher until he gave ample evidence that he was entirely cured of drunkenness.

After I made these statements, I felt that God was willing to bless the people there and then; and, raising my voice, gave them as warm an exhortation as I could command. Suddenly an awful power fell on the congregation, and they instantly fell right and left, and cried aloud for mercy. I suppose there were not less than thirty persons smitten down; the young, the old, and middle-aged indiscriminately, were operated on in this way. My voice at that day was strong and clear; and I could sing, exhort, pray, and preach almost all the time, day and night. I went through the assembly, singing, exhorting, praying, and directing poor sinners to Christ. While I was thus engaged, the Presbyterian minister left.

There were a few scattered members of the Church around this place, who got happy and shouted aloud for joy, and joined in and exhorted sinners, and they helped me very much. Indeed, our meeting lasted all night, and the greater part of next day. Between twenty and thirty professed religion, and joined the Church; and fully as many more went home under strong conviction and in deep distress. Many of them afterward obtained religion, and joined the Church.

There was a very remarkable case that I will mention here. There was one lady about forty-five years old, who was a member of the Presbyterian Church, and a very rigid predestinarian. Her husband was a Methodist, and several of their children had obtained religion among the young converts. This lady got powerfully convicted, and concluded that she never had any religion. She had fallen to the floor under the mighty power of God. She prayed and agonized hard for days. At length the devil tempted her to believe that she was a reprobate, and that there was no mercy for her. She went into black despair under this temptation of the devil, and such was the desperate state of her mind that at length she conceived that she was Jesus Christ, and took it upon her, in this assumed character, to bless and curse any and all that came to see her.

The family were, of course, greatly afflicted, and the whole neighborhood were in great trouble at this afflictive dispensation. Her friends and all of us used every argument in our power, but all in vain. She at length utterly refused to eat, or drink, or sleep. In this condition she lingered for thirteen days and nights, and then died without ever returning to her right mind. A few persecutors and opposers of the Methodists tried to make a great fuss about this affair, but they were afraid to go far with it, for fear the Lord would send the same affliction on them.

The Hockhocking River lay immediately north of us, the Scioto River between us. John Meek and James Axley were appointed to that circuit. The circuit reached from the Scioto to Zanesville, on the Muskingum River. It was a hard and laborious circuit. Brother Meek's health failed, and Brother Sale, our presiding elder, moved me from Scioto, and placed me on this circuit with Brother Axley. I was sorry to leave the brethren in Scioto Circuit, and especially Brother Quinn, whom I dearly loved; but Brother Sale was still my presiding elder, and Brother Quinn's family lived in Hockhocking Circuit, and a precious family it was.

I got to see Brother Quinn every round. Brother Axley and myself were like Jonathan and David. There were no parsonages in those days, and Brother Quinn lived in a little cabin on his father-in-law's land. He had several children, and his cabin was small. When the preachers would come to see him, they would eat and converse with Brother Quinn and family, but would sleep at old Father Teel's, Brother Quinn's father-in-law. The first time I came round, I spent the afternoon with Brother Quinn. He made some apologies, and told me I could sleep better at Father Teel's. "But," said he, "I will tell you how you must do. You will sleep, at Father Teel's, in one part of his double cabin; he and his family will sleep in the other. His custom is to rise early. As soon as ever he dresses himself he commences giving out a hymn, sings, and then goes to prayer; he does not even wait for his family to get up. He serves the preachers the same way. He never was known to wait a minute for any preacher except Bishop Asbury. You must rise early, dress quickly, and go right into the other room if you want to be at morning prayer. I thought I would tell you beforehand, that you might not be taken by surprise."

I thanked him. "But," said I, "why don't the preachers cure the old man of this disorderly way?"

"O, he is old and set in his way," said Brother Quinn.

"You may rest assured I will cure him," said I.

"O, no," said he, "you cannot."

So I retired to old Father Teel's to sleep. We had family prayer, and I retired to rest. I had no fear about the matter, for I was a constant early riser, and always thought it very wrong for preachers to sleep late and keep the families waiting on them. Just as day broke I awoke, rose up, and began to dress, but had not nigh accomplished it when I distinctly heard Teel give out his hymn and commence singing, and about the time I had got dressed I heard him commence praying. He gave thanks to God that they had been spared through the night, and were all permitted to see the light of a new day, and at the same time I suppose every one of his family was fast asleep. I deliberately opened the door and walked out to the well, washed myself, and then walked back to my cabin. Just as I got to the door, the old brother opened his door, and seeing me, said:

"Good morning, sir. Why, I did not know you were up."

"Yes," said I; "I have been up some time."

"Well, brother," said he, "why did you not come in to prayers?"

"Because," said I, "it is wrong to pray of a morning in the family before we wash."

The old brother passed on, and no more was said at that time. That evening, just before we were about to retire to rest, the old brother set out the book and said to me:

"Brother, hold prayers with us."

"No, sir," said I.

Said he: "Come, brother, take the book and pray with us."

"No, sir," said I; "you love to pray so well you may do it yourself."

He insisted, but I persistently refused, saying,

"You are so fond of praying yourself, that you even thanked God this morning that he had spared you all to see the light of a new day, when your family had not yet opened their eyes, but were all fast asleep. And you have such an absurd way of holding prayers in your family, that I do not wish to have anything to do with it."

He then took up the book, read and said prayers, but you may rely on it the next morning things were much changed. He waited for me, and had all his family up in order. He acknowledged his error, and told me it was one of the best reproofs he ever got. I then prayed with the family, and after that all went on well.

Our last quarterly-meeting was a camp-meeting. We had a great many tents, and a large turn-out for a new country, and, perhaps, there never was a greater collection of rabble and rowdies. They came drunk, and armed with dirks, clubs, knives, and horse-whips, and swore they would break up the meeting. After interrupting us very much on Saturday night, they collected early on Sunday morning, determined on a general riot. At eight o'clock I was appointed to preach. About the time I was half through my discourse, two very fine-dressed young men marched into the congregation with loaded whips, and hats on, and rose up and stood in the midst of the ladies, and began to laugh and talk. They were near the stand, and I requested them to desist and get off the seats; but they cursed me, and told me to mind my own business, and said they would not get down. I stopped trying to preach, and called for a magistrate. There were two at hand, but I saw they were both afraid. I ordered them to take these men into custody, but they said they could not do it. I told them, as I left the stand, to command me to take them, and I would do it at the risk of my life. I advanced toward them. They ordered me to stand off, but I advanced. One of them made a pass at my head with his whip, but I closed in with him, and jerked him off the seat. A regular scuffle ensued. The congregation by this time were all in commotion. I heard the magistrates giving general orders, commanding all friends of order to aid in suppressing the riot. In the scuffle I threw my prisoner down, and held him fast; he tried his best to get loose; I told him to be quiet, or I would pound his chest well. The mob rose, and rushed to the rescue of the two prisoners, for they had taken the other young man also. An old and drunken magistrate came up to me, and ordered me to let my prisoner go. I told him I should not. He swore if I did not, he would knock me down. I told him to crack away. Then one of my friends, at my request, took hold of my prisoner, and the drunken justice made a pass at me; but I parried the stroke, and seized him by the collar and the hair of the head, and fetching him a sudden jerk forward, brought him to the ground, and jumped on him. I told him to be quiet, or I would pound him well. The mob then rushed to the scene; they knocked down seven magistrates, and several preachers and others. I gave up my drunken prisoner to another, and threw myself in front of the friends of order. Just at this moment the ring-leader of the mob and I met; he made three passes at me, intending to knock me down. The last time he struck at me, by the force of his own effort he threw the side of his face toward me. It seemed at that moment I had not power to resist temptation, and I struck a sudden

blow in the burr of the ear and dropped him to the earth. Just at that
moment the friends of order rushed by hundreds on the mob, knocking
them down in every direction. In a few minutes, the place became too
strait for the mob, and they wheeled and fled in every direction; but
we secured about thirty prisoners, marched them off to a vacant tent,
and put them under guard till Monday morning, when they were tried,
and every man was fined to the utmost limits of the law. The aggregate
amount of fines and costs was near three hundred dollars. They fined
my old drunken magistrate twenty dollars, and returned him to court,
and he was cashiered of his office. On Sunday, when we had vanquished the mob, the whole encampment was filled with mourning;
and although there was no attempt to resume preaching till evening,
yet, such was our confused state, that there was not then a single
preacher on the ground willing to preach, from the presiding elder,
John Sale, down. Seeing we had fallen on evil times, my spirit was
stirred within me. I said to the elder, "I feel a clear conscience, for
under the necessity of the circumstances we have done right, and now
I ask to let me preach."

"Do," said the elder, "for there is no other man on the ground
can do it."

The encampment was lighted up, the trumpet blown, I rose in the
stand, and required every soul to leave the tents and come into the
congregation. There was a general rush to the stand. I requested the
brethren, if ever they prayed in all their lives, to pray now. My voice
was strong and clear, and my preaching was more of an exhortation
and encouragement than anything else. My text was, "The gates of
hell shall not prevail." In about thirty minutes the power of God fell
on the congregation in such a manner as is seldom seen; the people
fell in every direction, right and left, front and rear. It was supposed
that not less than three hundred fell like dead men in mighty battle;
and there was no need of calling mourners, for they were strewed all
over the camp-ground; loud wailing went up to heaven from sinners
for mercy, and a general shout from Christians, so that the noise was
heard afar off. Our meeting lasted all night, and Monday and Monday
night; and when we closed on Tuesday, there were two hundred who
had professed religion, and about that number joined the Church.

The Beginnings of a
National Literature

The Nationalistic Impulse

↜ Noah Webster (1758–1843)

NOAH WEBSTER touched the life of his times on many sides. He was born in Connecticut, educated at Yale, and admitted to the bar as a lawyer. He began teaching school at Goshen, New York, and in 1782 wrote his famous *Spelling Book* for use in the schools, a book which sold more than seventy million copies over the next century. Its influence on the spelling and pronunciation of the English language in America has been virtually immeasurable. Strongly nationalistic in his views, Webster continued to labor for the creation of an American variety of English; in 1784 he published an English grammar on American principles and in 1785 a reader for American schools.

Webster next conducted a magazine and a newspaper, but abandoned journalism in 1803 to begin work on his *Compendious Dictionary of the English Language,* which appeared in 1806. He thereupon immediately began on a larger edition, which, after twenty-two years of labor, appeared as *An American Dictionary of the English Language* (1828). Then, at the age of seventy, he began a revised edition of the Bible, which came out in 1833.

TEXT: Noah Webster, *Dissertations on the English Language* (Boston, 1789).

A National Language

[From *Dissertations on the English Language*, 1789]

A regular study of language has, in all civilized countries, formed a part of a liberal education. The Greeks, Romans, Italians and French successively improved their native tongues, taught them in Academies at home, and rendered them entertaining and useful to the foreign student.

281

The English tongue, tho later in its progress towards perfection, has attained to a considerable degree of purity, strength and elegance, and been employed, by an active and scientific nation, to record almost all the events and discoveries of ancient and modern times.

This language is the inheritance which the Americans have received from their British parents. To cultivate and adorn it, is a task reserved for men who shall understand the connection between language and logic, and form an adequate idea of the influence which a uniformity of speech may have on national attachments.

It will be readily admitted that the pleasures of reading and conversing, the advantage of accuracy in business, the necessity of clearness and precision in communicating ideas, require us to be able to speak and write our own tongue with ease and correctness. But there are more important reasons, why the language of this country should be reduced to such fixed principles, as may give its pronunciation and construction all the certainty and uniformity which any living tongue is capable of receiving.

The United States were settled by emigrants from different parts of Europe. But their descendants mostly speak the same tongue; and the intercourse among the learned of the different States, which the revolution has begun, and an American Court will perpetuate, must gradually destroy the differences of dialect which our ancestors brought from their native countries. This approximation of dialects will be certain; but without the operation of other causes than an intercourse at Court, it will be slow and partial. The body of the people, governed by habit, will still retain their respective peculiarities of speaking; and for want of schools and proper books, fall into many inaccuracies, which, incorporating with the language of the state where they live, may imperceptibly corrupt the national language. Nothing but the establishment of schools and some uniformity in the use of books, can annihilate differences in speaking and preserve the purity of the American tongue. A sameness of pronunciation is of considerable consequence in a political view; for provincial accents are disagreeable to strangers and sometimes have an unhappy effect upon social affections. All men have local attachments, which lead them to believe their own practice to be the least exceptionable. Pride and prejudice incline men to treat the practice of their neighbors with some degree of contempt. Thus small differences in pronunciation at first excite ridicule — a habit of laughing at the singularities of strangers is followed by disrespect — and without respect friendship is a name, and social intercourse a mere ceremony.

These remarks hold equally true, with respect to individuals, to small societies and to large communities. Small causes, such as a nick-name, or a vulgar tone in speaking, have actually created a dissocial spirit between the inhabitants of the different states, which is often discoverable in private business and public deliberations. Our political harmony is therefore concerned in a uniformity of language.

As an independent nation, our honor requires us to have a system of our own, in language as well as government. Great Britain, whose children we are, and whose language we speak, should no longer be our standard; for the taste of her writers is already corrupted, and her language on the decline. But if it were not so, she is at too great a distance to be our model, and to instruct us in the principles of our own tongue.

It must be considered further, that the English is the common root or stock from which our national language will be derived. All others will gradually waste away — and within a century and a half, North America will be peopled with a hundred millions of men, *all speaking the same language.* Place this idea in comparison with the present and possible future bounds of the language in Europe — consider the Eastern Continent as inhabited by nations, whose knowledge and intercourse are embarrassed by differences of language; then anticipate the period when the people of one quarter of the world, will be able to associate and converse together like children of the same family. Compare this prospect, which is not visionary, with the state of the English language in Europe, almost confined to an Island and to a few millions of people; then let reason and reputation decide, how far America should be dependent on a transatlantic nation, for her standard and improvements in language.

Let me add, that whatever predilection the Americans may have for their native European tongues, and particularly the British descendants for the English, yet several circumstances render a future separation of the American tongue from the English, necessary and unavoidable. The vicinity of the European nations, with the uninterrupted communication in peace, and the changes of dominion in war, are gradually assimilating their respective languages. The English with others is suffering continual alterations. America, placed at a distance from those nations, will feel, in a much less degree, the influence of the assimilating causes; at the same time, numerous local causes, such as a new country, new associations of people, new combinations of ideas in arts and science, and some intercourse with tribes wholly unknown in Europe, will introduce new words into the American tongue. These causes will produce, in a course of time, a language in North America, as different from the future language of England, as the modern Dutch, Danish and Swedish are from the German, or from one another: Like remote branches of a tree springing from the same stock; or rays of light, shot from the same center, and diverging from each other, in proportion to their distance from the point of separation.

Whether the inhabitants of America can be brought to a perfect uniformity in the pronunciation of words, it is not easy to predict; but it is certain that no attempt of the kind has been made, and an experiment begun and pursued on the right principles, is the only way to decide the question. Schools in Great Britain have gone far towards demolishing local dialects — commerce has also had its influence — and in America these causes, operating more generally, must have a proportional effect.

In many parts of America, people at present attempt to copy the English phrases and pronunciation — an attempt that is favored by their habits, their prepossessions and the intercourse between the two countries. This attempt has, within the period of a few years, produced a multitude of changes in these particulars, especially among the leading classes of people. These changes make a difference between the language of the higher and common ranks; and indeed between the *same* ranks in *different* states; as the rage for copying the English, does not prevail equally in every part of North America.

But besides the reasons already assigned to prove this imitation absurd, there is a difficulty attending it, which will defeat the end proposed by its advocates; which is, that the English themselves have no standard of pronunciation, nor can they ever have one on the plan they propose. The Authors, who have attempted to give us a standard, make the practice of the court and stage in London the sole criterion of propriety in speaking. An attempt to establish a standard on this foundation is both *unjust* and *idle*. It is unjust, because it is abridging the nation of its rights: The *general practice* of a nation is the rule of propriety, and this practice should at least be consulted in so important a matter, as that of making laws for speaking. While all men are upon a footing and no singularities are accounted vulgar or ridiculous, every man enjoys perfect liberty. But when a particular set of men, in exalted stations, undertake to say, "we are the standards of propriety and elegance, and if all men do not conform to our practice, they shall be accounted vulgar and ignorant," they take a very great liberty with the rules of the language and the rights of civility.

But an attempt to fix a standard on the practice of any particular class of people is highly absurd: As a friend of mine once observed, it is like fixing a light house on a floating island. It is an attempt to *fix* that which is in itself *variable;* at least it must be variable so long as it is supposed that a local practice has no standard but a *local practice;* that is, no standard but *itself*. While this doctrine is believed, it will be impossible for a nation to follow as fast as the standard changes —

for if the gentlemen at court constitute a standard, they are above it themselves, and their practice must shift with their passions and their whims.

But this is not all. If the practice of a few men in the capital is to be the standard, a knowledge of this must be communicated to the whole nation. Who shall do this? An able compiler perhaps attempts to give this practice in a dictionary; but it is probable that the pronunciation, even at court, or on the stage, is not uniform. The compiler therefore must follow his particular friends and patrons; in which case he is sure to be opposed and the authority of his standard called in question; or he must give two pronunciations as the standard, which leaves the student in the same uncertainty as it found him. Both these events have actually taken place in England, with respect to the most approved standards; and of course no one is universally followed.

Besides, if language must vary, like fashions, at the caprice of a court, we must have our standard dictionaries republished, with the fashionable pronunciation, at least one in five years; otherwise a gentleman in the country will become intolerably vulgar, by not being in a situation to adopt the fashion of the day. The *new* editions of them will supersede the *old,* and we shall have our pronunciation to re-learn, with the polite alterations, which are generally corruptions.

Such are the consequences of attempting to make a *local* practice the *standard* of language in a *nation.* The attempt must keep the language in perpetual fluctuation, and the learner in uncertainty.

If a standard therefore cannot be fixed on local and variable custom, on what shall it be fixed? If the most eminent speakers are not to direct our practice, where shall we look for a guide? The answer is extremely easy; the *rules of the language itself,* and the *general practice of the nation,* constitute propriety in speaking. If we examine the structure of any language, we shall find a certain principle of analogy running through the whole. We shall find in English that similar combinations of letters having usually the same pronunciation and that words, having the same terminating syllable, generally have the accent at the same distance from the termination. These principles of analogy were not the result of design — they must have been the effect of accident, or that tendency which all men feel towards uniformity. But the principles, when established, are productive of great convenience, and become an authority superior to the arbitrary decisions of any man or class of men. There is one exception only to this remark: When a deviation from analogy has become the universal practice of a nation, it then takes place of all rules and becomes the standard of propriety.

The two points therefore, which I conceive to be the basis of a standard in speaking, are these; *universal undisputed practice,* and the *principle of analogy. Universal practice* is generally, perhaps always, a rule of propriety; and in disputed points where people differ in opinion and practice, *analogy* should always decide the controversy.

These are authorities to which all men will submit — they are superior to the opinions and caprices of the great, and to the negligence and ignorance of the multitude. The authority of individuals is always liable to be called in question — but the unanimous consent of a nation, and a fixed principle interwoven with the very construction of a language, coeval and coextensive with it, are like the common laws of a land, or the immutable rules of morality, the propriety of which every man, however refractory, is forced to acknowledge, and to which most men will readily submit. Fashion is usually the child of caprice and the being of a day; principles of propriety are founded in the very nature of things, and remain unmoved and unchanged, amidst all the fluctuations of human affairs and the revolutions of time.

It must be confessed that languages are changing, from age to age, in proportion to improvements in science. Words, as Horace observes, are like leaves of trees; the old ones are dropping off and new ones growing. These changes are the necessary consequence of changes in customs, the introduction of new arts, and new ideas in the sciences. Still the body of a language and its general rules remain for ages the same, and the new words usually conform to these rules; otherwise they stand as exceptions, which are not to overthrow the principle of analogy already established. . . .

Altho stile, or the choice of words and manner of arranging them, may be necessarily liable to change, yet it does not follow that pronunciation and orthography cannot be rendered in a great measure permanent. An orthography, in which there would be a perfect correspondence between the spelling and pronunciation, would go very far towards effecting this desirable object. The Greek language suffered little or no change in these particulars, for about a thousand years; and the Roman was in a great degree fixed for several centuries.

Rapid changes of language proceed from violent causes; but these causes cannot be supposed to exist in North America. It is contrary to all rational calculation, that the United States will ever be conquered by any one nation, speaking a different language from that of the country. Removed from the danger of corruption by conquest, our language can change only with the slow operation of the causes beforementioned and the progress of arts and sciences, unless the folly of imitating our parent country should continue to govern us, and lead us into endless innovation. This folly however will lose its influence gradually, as our particular habits of respect for that country shall wear away, and our *amor patriae* acquire strength and inspire us with a suitable respect for our own national character.

We have therefore the fairest opportunity of establishing a national language, and of giving it uniformity and perspicuity, in North America, that ever presented itself to mankind. Now is the time to begin the plan. The minds of the Americans are roused by the events of a revolution; the necessity of organizing the political body and of forming constitutions of government that shall secure freedom and property, has called all the faculties of the mind into exertion; and the danger of losing the benefits of independence, has disposed every man to embrace any scheme that shall tend, in its future operation, to reconcile the people of America to each other, and weaken the prejudices which oppose a cordial union. . . .

. . . A *national language* is a bond of *national union*. Every engine should be employed to render the people of this country *national;* to call their attachments home to their own country; and to inspire them with the pride of national character. However they may boast of Independence, and the freedom of their government, yet their *opinions* are not sufficiently independent; an astonishing respect for the arts and literature of their parent country, and a blind imitation of its manners, are still prevalent among the Americans. Thus an habitual respect for another country, deserved indeed and once laudable, turns their attention from their own interests, and prevents their respecting themselves. . . .

. . . America is in a situation the most favorable for great reformations; and the present time is, in a singular degree, auspicious. The minds of men in this country have been awakened. New scenes have been, for many years, presenting new occasions for exertion; unexpected distresses have called forth the powers of invention; and the application of new expedients has demanded every possible exercise of wisdom and talents. Attention is roused; the mind expanded; and the intellectual faculties invigorated. Here men are prepared to receive improvements, which would be rejected by nations, whose habits have not been shaken by similar events.

Now is the time, and *this* the country, in which we may expect success, in attempting changes favorable to language, science and government. Delay, in the plan here proposed, may be fatal; under a tranquil general government, the minds of men may again sink into indolence; a national acquiescence in error will follow; and posterity be doomed to struggle with difficulties, which time and accident will perpetually multiply.

Let us then seize the present moment and establish a *national language,* as well as a national government. Let us remember that there is a certain respect due to the opinions of other nations. As an inde-

pendent people, our reputation abroad demands that, in all things, we
should be federal; be *national;* for if we do not respect *ourselves,* we
may be assured that *other nations* will not respect us. In short, let
it be impressed upon the mind of every American, that to neglect the
means of commanding respect abroad, is treason against the character
and dignity of a brave independent people.

✒ Philip Freneau (1752–1832)

FRENEAU, a Princeton graduate of 1771, served in the Continental
Army, was imprisoned in a British prison ship, and after the war
sailed as a captain in the coastal trade. He determined quite early
to be a poet, but made his living, precarious as it often was, as a
sailor and a journalist. Though better known (and deservedly so)
as a poet, he contributed essays to various journals in the early
stages of his career, publishing many of them in the papers he
edited — *The Freeman's Journal, The Daily Advertiser, The
National Gazette, The Jersey Chronicle,* and his own miscellany,
The Timepiece and Literary Companion. Some of these pieces
were reprinted in *The Miscellaneous Works of Mr. Philip Freneau*
(1788) and others in a volume which appeared in 1799, but for
the most part Freneau's essays have remained uncollected until
our own day. They reflect the prevailing fashions in this particular
prose form — romantic nostalgia, eccentricity, nationalism, dependence on British models (in Freneau's case *The Spectator* and
Goldsmith) and a diffuse, sentimental style. They are, however,
among the better examples of their kind, and indicate Freneau's
gift for expression which made him much more successful as a
poet.

TEXT: Philip Marsh, ed., *The Prose of Philip Freneau* (New
Brunswick, N.J., 1955).

The Future of America

[From *The Philosopher of the Forest,* No. X, 1782]

When nature first brought forth her infant, the American world,
to enjoy the blessings and vivifying influences of the new created sun,
as if conscious of the injuries this part of her creation was to suffer
in future ages, she seemed particularly industrious, she took especial
care to plant it in such a situation that many hundreds of centuries, an
immense number of years must elapse, before it could possibly be
discovered by the greedy natives of the eastern continent. — "Till

more than five thousand years have passed away (said she) it shall be inaccessible to all, except a few tribes of wandering Tartars, who from time to time may find their way thither by accident; literally *the children of nature,* wild as the wind and waves, and free as the animals that wander in the woody or watry waste. The magnet alone, continued she, shall enable the polished people of the eastern regions to discover and ravage the delectable lands I have formed in the opposite hemisphere; but that fossil, the invaluable loadstone, I will bury deep in the earth, unobserved its wonderful properties, till destiny and over-ruling fate, whose decrees no one can obviate, to my extremest grief, shall disclose it to the eye of avarice, ambition, and scrutinizing curiosity, and prompt a bold and daring *Columbus* to go in quest of those shores which it will not be in my power any longer to conceal." —

So spoke NATURE, the mother of all men, and all things. In the mean time ages rolled away: the old world was peopled, unpeopled, and peopled again. Nations grew and flourished: they quarrelled, they fought, and made peace: the *four great monarchies* succeeded each other, and fell again into decay, with their emperors, kings and heroes, by far less durable than the lifeless marble columns which to this day mark the spot where their proudest capitals stood, or where their most famous battles were fought. These nations had their ages of politeness and barbarism, ignorance and science, misery and felicity: the follies of one age were acted over again by another, and each retired in its turn to the receptacles of silence, solitude and darkness, to make room for succeeding generations.

But still America lay unknown and undiscovered, with all her islands, lakes, mountains, woods, plains, capacious harbours and extended shores. Here the fish sported in the waters, undisturbed by hooks or nets, and the beasts of the forest enjoyed a secure repose. The poets of the eastern world were in the mean time amusing their iron hearted cotemporaries [sic] with the fictions of a golden age; their fabulous Arcadias and Saturnian kingdoms; the ideas and notions of which must have owed their existence to the magic power of fancy alone, as they were wholly ignorant that the happy scenes, the innocent people and pastoral ages, of which they sung, were at that moment realizing in another quarter of the globe, as yet unexplored and unknown. — But, in process of time, as nature had foreseen, this immense continent was at length raised from its long night of obscurity to the view of astonished nations: the inhabitants, like the country, seemed to be a new race of mortals, of different natures, ideas and inclinations from those already known. They, also, gazed at the Europeans as a species of men differing in all respects from themselves, and, as far as regarded power and abilities, beings of a superior nature.

As the Europeans had the *means,* they of course conceived they had also the *right* to extirpate the innocent natives, or drive them from the sea coasts to the interior parts of the country. The most specious pretext for this procedure seems to have been, that the Aborigines, or old inhabitants of America, did not sufficiently exert themselves to cultivate and improve the lands nature had so liberally bestowed upon them: they were content with the productions of the simple genius of the earth, and *therefore* were scarcely to be considered, according to these casuists, as legal proprietors of the immense territories that were now discovered.

Full of this idea, the Europeans flocked over, and carefully examined the soil and productions of this new-found region: the best lands in North America were observed to lie in a temperate climate, and the new-comers soon found it their interest to cultivate and improve a soil that promised so much to the hand of industry. This roused the jealousy of the natives, who, unwilling to part with their pleasant abodes in the neighbourhood of the sea, made many attempts, (and sometimes not unsuccessfully) to annihilate these intruding strangers; but, as the several divisions of the old world were at that time over-stocked with inhabitants, who constantly waged bloody wars with each other, notwithstanding the devastation and destruction of the human species occasioned thereby, it became absolutely necessary that many should emigrate. Providence gave permission to the arm of tyranny to expel thousands from their native lands; and many, in hopes of better-ing their fortunes, submitted to become voluntary exiles. Among the rest, Britain seemed very busy in virtually banishing and expelling her subjects to this remote region, who chose the northern coast, as know-ing of no other asylum, excepting the grave, from the scourge of oppression. These, with a mixture of adventurers from various nations, at length humbled the savage tribes, and by the mere force of indus-try rendered a large proportion of this new country rich and flourishing. Britain soon cast a greedy eye upon the hard-earned possessions of this exiled race; she claimed them as subjects, and took them under her protection; but at the same time said in her heart, *They shall hereafter be my slaves.*

The children of the first emigrants immediately forgot the wrongs and injuries their forefathers had experienced, and strictly united themselves to her, not as yet aware of her insidious designs: but nature disregarded the connexion; and whispering in the ear of reason, was heard to say, "The union cannot be lasting."

Her words have proved true: the people of the present age have seen the unnatural bonds in a moment dissolved, the union broken, and the connexion at an end! Tell me, ye advocates for the dependence of these states upon the remote island of Britain; ye who assert that their happiness, their interest, and their glory is bound up in such a dependence, would you not esteem him a madman who should attempt amidst the rage of contending winds and waves to bind together two bulky ships with a single thread of silk for their mutual safety? Just as reasonable is it to suppose that America and the comparatively paltry and oppositely interested island of Britain can be happily united under one and the same sovereign.

What a spectacle of derision do the infatuated Britons now exhibit to the world, in seriously attempting to subjugate a country to which nature never gave them a shadow of right, and whose immense extent is, of itself, a standing and insurmountable obstacle to their success! An island, situated on the extremities of the ocean, on the verge of polar darkness, incumbered with rugged mountains, traversed by uncouth savages of horrid mien; barren heaths, and useless, broken lands; a spot, whose strength is merely artificial, sending out on impracticable conquests her fleets and armies, the flower of her youth and her ablest commanders, who, the moment they come within the vortex, the sphere of attraction of this huge unwieldy body, the American world, are instantly swallowed up, like straws in a whirlpool, and irrecoverably lost!

What a nation of numerous and ingenious mechanics and manufacturers were the English only ten years ago! With the fleeces of their sheep they warmed the inhabitants of either frigid zone: the fine linnens [sic] of their island were in high estimation in every clime; but in order to prosecute their mad scheme of reducing to unconditional submission or desolating a country naturally invincible, they have taken the weaver from the loom and the cobler from his stall; the back of the pedlar is released from its burden, and he who of yore was honestly and profitably occupied in fitting garments to the shoulders of his brethren, fancying himself on a sudden an *Alexander* or an *Hernando Cortez,* in search of glory, in quest of never-fading laurels, and for the support of his idol, Royalty, traverses the wide extended ocean, and leads to imaginary conquests and devastations in the trans-Atlantic world!

It is not easy to conceive what will be the greatness and importance of North America in a century or two to come, if the present fabric of Nature is upheld, and the people retain those bold and manly sentiments of freedom, which actuate them at this day. Agriculture, the basis of a nation's greatness, will here, most probably, be advanced to its summit of perfection; and its attendant, commerce, will so agreeably and usefully employ mankind, that wars will be forgotten; nations, by a free intercourse with this vast and fertile continent, and this continent with the whole world, will again become brothers after so many centuries of hatred and jealousy, and no longer treat each other as savages and monsters. The iron generation will verge to decay, and those days of felicity advance which have been so often wished for by all good men, and which are so beautifully described by the prophetic sages of ancient times.

My friend the clergyman informs me, that after passing a ridge of lofty mountains extending on the western frontiers of these republics, a new and most enchanting region opens, of inexpressible beauty and fertility. The lands are *there* of a quality far superior to those situated in the neighbourhood of the sea coast: the trees of the forest are stately and tall, the meadows and pastures spacious, supporting vast herds of the native animals of the country; which own no master, nor expect their sustenance from the hands of men. The climate, he says, is moderate and agreeable; there the rivers no longer bend their courses eastward to the Atlantic, but inclining to the west and south, and moving with a gentle current through the channels that Nature has opened, fall at length into that grand repository of a thousand streams, *Mississippi*, who collecting his waters, derived from a source remote and unknown, rolls onward through the frozen regions of the north, and stretching his prodigiously extended arms to the east and west, embraces those savage groves and dreary solitudes, as yet uninvestigated by the traveller, unsung by the poet, and unmeasured by the chain of the geometrician; till uniting with the *Ohio* and turning due south, receiving afterwards the *Missori* [sic] and a hundred others, this prince of rivers, in comparison of whom the *Nile* is but a small rivulet, and the *Danube* a ditch, hurries with his immense flood of waters into the Mexican sea, laving the shores of many fertile countries in his passage, inhabited by savage nations to this day almost unknown and without a name.

It is a standing rule in philosophy, that Nature does nothing in vain. A potent nation, now at war with these republics, has proclaimed her resolution *to lay waste what she cannot reclaim by conquest, and schemes are projected to oblige such to re-emigrate to Europe as shall escape the fury of the destroyers.* But if this new world was not to become at some time or another the receptacle of numerous civilized nations, from one extremity to the other, for what visible purpose could Nature have formed these vast lakes in the bosom of her infant empire, which surprise and astonish the traveller, who, leaving the salt ocean behind him to the east, finds, unexpectedly, new oceans of a prodigious extent in those tracts where Fancy would have surmised nothing but endless hills, inhospitable wilds and dreary forests existed? These lakes having, severally, a communication with each other, and lastly with the Atlantic ocean, towards the north-east; approaching also very near, by the west, to several of the navigable branches of the Mississippi, form an easy communication through a long tract of country, the intercourse between the various parts of which would, in future times, at least for the purposes of commerce, be extremely difficult and laborious, were it not for this continuation of waters, that for ages have been waiting to receive the barque of traffic, urged forward by the sail or the stroke of the springy oar; as the soil bordering thereon has no less impatiently expected the operations of the industrious plough.

During a very considerable part of the year, the south west wind blows unremittedly on the face of this serpentine river, the Ohio; and even at other times, the current of air is more prevalent in that direction than in any other, which being directly opposed to the course of the stream, moving at the rate of one mile hourly, is it not evident that Providence, Nature, or Fate, has so ordered this matter, that the commercial vessels hereafter sailing northward thereon may have favourable gales to make an answerable progress against a current that is still contrary and the same, and that those bound to the south may have the assistance of the ebbing stream to combat the adverse winds with more advantage. — It would carry me far beyond the bounds of a a short essay, to point out every particular, indicating the future importance of this newly discovered country; and it is really astonishing, as I intimated before, that a nation endued with the divine gift of reason, if they would exercise that gift, should at this day entertain a serious thought of reducing, by force of arms, this immense continent to their absolute sway; a continent beholding two hemispheres, abounding with a hardy and active race of inhabitants, producing every thing within itself proper for its own maintenance and defence; a continent extending thro' such a number of degrees of latitude and longitude, from the limits of the torrid zone, the circle of the northern tropic, to those frozen streams and icy mountains, where, chilled with the extreme rigours of perpetual winter, Nature seems to have lost her vegetative powers; and where a few of the human race, the natives of the polar regions, that are found to exist in those unjoyous climes, bear so little resemblance in the features of the mind to what the civilized world calls a *man,* that they scarcely deserve the name.

⟨⟩ Fisher Ames (1758–1808)

FISHER AMES, chief spokesman of conservative New England Federalism, had very little faith in democracy as a means of producing either political stability or artistic excellence. Unlike many of his contemporaries, who hailed the "coming glory" of American literature and confidently awaited the appearance of native Popes and Miltons, Ames saw no hope of cultural excellence in a Jeffersonian society which, he believed, leveled all men to the same mediocrity.

TEXT: Seth Ames, ed., *The Works of Fisher Ames* (Boston, 1854), II, 428–442.

The Future of American Literature

[From *Works*, 1809]

Few speculative subjects have exercised the passions more or the judgment less, than the inquiry, what rank our country is to maintain in the world for genius and literary attainments. Whether in point of intellect we are equal to Europeans, or only a race of degenerate creoles; whether our artists and authors have already performed much and promise every thing; whether the muses, like the nightingales, are too delicate to cross the salt water, or sicken and mope without song if they do, are themes upon which we Americans are privileged to be eloquent and loud. It might indeed occur to our discretion, that as the only admissible proof of literary excellence is the measure of its effects, our national claims ought to be abandoned as worthless the moment they are found to need asserting.

Nevertheless, by a proper spirit and constancy in praising ourselves, it seems to be supposed, the doubtful title of our vanity may be quieted in the same manner as it was once believed the currency of the continental paper could, by a universal agreement, be established at par with specie. Yet such was the unpatriotic perverseness of our citizens, they preferred the gold and silver, for no better reason than because the paper bills were not so good. And now it may happen, that from spite or envy, from want of attention or the want of our sort of information, foreigners will dispute the claims of our preëminence in genius and literature, notwithstanding the great convenience and satisfaction we should find in their acquiescence.

In this unmanageable temper or indocile ignorance of Europe, we may be under the harsh necessity of submitting our pretensions to a scrutiny; and as the world will judge of the matter with none of our partiality, it may be discreet to anticipate that judgment, and to explore the grounds upon which it is probable the aforesaid world will frame it. And after all, we should suffer more pain than loss, if we should in the event be stripped of all that does not belong to us; and especially if, by a better knowledge of ourselves, we should gain that modesty which is the first evidence, and perhaps the last, of a real improvement. For no man is less likely to increase his knowledge than the coxcomb, who fancies he has already learned out. An excessive national vanity, as it is the sign of mediocrity, if not of barbarism, is one of the greatest impediments to knowledge.

It will be useless and impertinent to say, a greater proportion of our citizens have had instruction in schools than can be found in any European state. It may be true that neither France nor England can boast of so large a portion of their population who can read and write, and who are versed in the profitable mystery of the rule of three. This is not the footing upon which the inquiry is to proceed. The question is not, what proportion are stone blind, or how many can see, when the sun shines, but what geniuses have arisen among us, like the sun and stars to shed life and splendor on our hemisphere.

This state of the case is no sooner made, than all the firefly tribe of our authors perceive their little lamps go out of themselves, like the flame of a candle when lowered into the mephitic vapor of a well. Excepting the writers of two able works on our politics, we have no authors. To enter the lists in single combat against Hector, the Greeks did not offer the lots to the nameless rabble of their soldiery; all eyes were turned upon Agamemnon and Ajax, upon Diomed and Ulysses. Shall we match Joel Barlow against Homer or Hesiod? Can Thomas Paine contend against Plato? Or could Findley's history of his own insurrection vie with Sallust's narrative of Catiline's? There is no scarcity of spelling-book makers, and authors of twelve-cent pamphlets; and we have a distinguished few, a sort of literary nobility, whose works have grown to the dignity and size of an octavo volume. We have many writers who have read, and who have the sense to understand, what others have written. But a right perception of the genius of others is not genius; it is a sort of business talent, and will not be wanting where there is much occasion for its exercise. Nobody will pretend that the Americans are a stupid race; nobody will deny that we justly boast of many able men, and exceedingly useful publications. But has our country produced one great original work of genius? If we tread the sides of Parnassus, we do not climb its heights; we even creep in our path, by the light that European genius has thrown upon it. Is there one luminary in our firmament that shines with unborrowed rays? Do we reflect how many constellations blend their beams in the history of Greece, which will appear bright to the end of time, like the path of the zodiac, bespangled with stars?

If, then, we judge of the genius of our nation by the success with which American authors have displayed it, our country has certainly hitherto no pretensions to literary fame. The world will naturally enough pronounce its opinion, that what we have not performed we are incapable of performing.

It is not intended to proceed in stripping our country's honors off, till every lover of it shall turn with disgust from the contemplation of its nakedness. Our honors have not faded — they have not been won. Genius no doubt exists in our country, but it exists, like the unbodied soul on the stream of Lethe, unconscious of its powers, till the causes to excite and the occasions to display it shall happen to concur.

What were those causes that have forever consecrated the name of Greece? We are sometimes answered, she owes her fame to the republican liberty of her states. But Homer, and Hesiod, to say nothing of Linus, Orpheus, Musæus, and many others, wrote while kings governed those states. Anacreon and Simonides flourished in the court of Pisistratus, who had overthrown the democracy of Athens. Nor, we may add in corroboration, did Roman genius flourish till the republic fell. France and England are monarchies, and they have excelled all modern nations by their works of genius. Hence we have a right to conclude the form of government has not a decisive, and certainly not an exclusive influence, on the literary eminence of a people.

If climate produces genius, how happens it that the great men who reflected such honor on their country appeared only in the period of a few hundred years before the death of Alexander? The melons and figs of Greece are still as fine as ever; but where are the Pindars?

In affairs that concern morals, we consider the approbation of a man's own conscience as more precious than all human rewards. But in the province of the imagination, the applause of others is of all excitements the strongest. This excitement is the cause; excellence, the effect. When every thing concurs, and in Greece every thing did concur, to augment its power, a nation wakes at once from the sleep of ages. It would seem as if some Minerva, some present divinity, inhabited her own temple in Athens, and by flashing light and working miracles had conferred on a single people, and almost on a single age of that people, powers that are denied to other men and other times. The admiration of posterity is excited and overstrained by an effulgence of glory, as much beyond our comprehension as our emulation. The Greeks seem to us a race of giants, Titans, the rivals, yet the favorites of their gods. We think their apprehension was quicker, their native taste more refined, their prose poetry, their poetry music, their music enchantment. We imagine they had more expression in their faces, more grace in their movements, more sweetness in the tones of conversation than the moderns. Their fabulous deities are supposed to have left their heaven to breathe the fragrance of their groves, and to enjoy the beauty of their landscapes. The monuments of heroes must have excited to heroism; and the fountains, which the muses had chosen for their purity, imparted inspiration.

It is indeed almost impossible to contemplate the bright ages of Greece, without indulging the propensity to enthusiasm.

We are ready to suspect the delusion of our feelings, and to ascribe its fame to accident, or to causes which have spent their force. Genius, we imagine, is forever condemned to inaction by having exhausted its power, as well as the subjects upon which it has displayed itself. Another Homer or Virgil could only copy the Iliad and Æneid; and can the second poets, from cinders and ashes, light such a fire as still glows in the writings of the first. Genius, it will be said, like a conflagration on the mountains, consumes its fuel in its flame. Not so. It is a spark of elemental fire that is unquenchable, the contemporary of this creation, and destined with the human soul to survive it. As well might the stars of heaven be said to expend their substance by their lustre. It is to the intellectual world what the electric fluid is to nature, diffused everywhere, yet almost everywhere hidden, capable by its own mysterious laws of action and by the very breath of applause, that like the unseen wind excites it, of producing effects that appear to transcend all power, except that of some supernatural agent riding in the whirlwind. In an hour of calm we suddenly hear its voice, and are moved with the general agitation. It smites, astonishes, and confounds, and seems to kindle half the firmament.

It may be true, that some departments in literature are so filled by the ancients, that there is no room for modern excellence to occupy. Homer wrote soon after the heroic ages, and the fertility of the soil seemed in some measure to arise from its freshness: it had never borne a crop. Another Iliad would not be undertaken by a true genius, nor equally interest this age, if he executed it. But it will not be correct to say, the field is reduced to barrenness from having been overcropped. Men have still imagination and passions, and they can be excited. The same causes that made Greece famous, would, if they existed here, quicken the clods of our valleys, and make our Bœotia sprout and blossom like their Attica.

In analyzing genius and considering how it acts, it will be proper to inquire how it is acted upon. It feels the power it exerts, and its emotions are contagious, because they are fervid and sincere. A single man may sit alone and meditate, till he fancies he is under no influence but that of reason. Even in this opinion, however, he will allow too little for prejudice and imagination; and still more must be allowed when he goes abroad and acts in the world. But masses and societies of men are governed by their passions.

The passion that acts the strongest, when it acts at all, is fear; for in its excess, it silences all reasoning and all other passions. But that which acts with the greatest force, because it acts with the greatest constancy, is the desire of consideration. There are very few men who are greatly deceived with respect to their own measure of sense and abilities, or who are much dissatisfied on that account; but we scarcely see any who are quite at ease about the estimate that other people make of them. Hence it is, that the great business of mankind is to fortify or create claims to general regard. Wealth procures respect, and more wealth would procure more respect. The man who, like Midas, turns all he touches into gold, who is oppressed and almost buried in its superfluity, who lives to get, instead of getting to live, and at length belongs to his own estate and is its greatest encumbrance, still toils and contrives to accumulate wealth, not because he is deceived in regard to his wants, but because he knows and feels, that one of his wants, which is insatiable, is that respect which follows its possession. After engrossing all that the seas and mountains conceal, he would be still unsatisfied, and with some good reason, for of the treasures of esteem who can ever have enough? Who would mar or renounce one half his reputation in the world?

At different times, the opinions of men in the same country will vary with regard to the objects of prime consideration, and in different countries there will ever be a great difference; but that which is the first object of regard will be the chief object of pursuit. Men will be most excited to excel in that department which offers to excellence the highest reward in the respect and admiration of mankind. It was this strongest of all excitements that stimulated the literary ages of Greece.

In the heroic times, it is evident, violence and injustice prevailed. The state of society was far from tranquil or safe. Indeed, the traditional fame of the heroes and demigods is founded on the gratitude that was due for their protection against tyrants and robbers. Thucydides tells us, that companies of travellers were often asked whether they were thieves. Greece was divided into a great number of states, all turbulent, all martial, always filled with emulation, and often with tumult and blood. The laws of war were far more rigorous than they are at present. Each state, and each citizen in the state, contended for all that is dear to man. If victors, they despoiled their enemies of every thing; the property was booty, and the people were made slaves. Such was the condition of the Helots and Messenians under the yoke of Sparta. There was every thing, then, both of terror and ignominy, to rouse the contending states to make every effort to avoid subjugation.

The fate of Platæa, a city that was besieged and taken by the Spartans, and whose citizens were massacred in cold blood, affords a terrible illustration of this remark. The celebrated siege of Troy is an instance more generally known, and no less to the purpose. With what ardent love and enthusiasm the Trojans viewed their Hector, and the Greeks their Ajax and Achilles, is scarcely to be conceived. It cannot be doubted, that to excel in arms was the first of all claims to the popular admiration.

Nor can it escape observation, that in times of extreme danger the internal union of a state would be most perfect. In these days we can have no idea of the ardor of ancient patriotism. A society of no great extent was knit together like one family by the ties of love, emulation, and enthusiasm. Fear, the strongest of all passions, operated in the strongest of all ways. Hence we find, that the first traditions of all nations concern the champions who defended them in war.

This universal state of turbulence and danger, while it would check the progress of the accurate sciences, would greatly extend the dominion of the imagination. It would be deemed of more importance, to rouse or command the feelings of men, than to augment or correct their knowledge.

In this period it might be supposed, that eloquence displayed its power; but this was not the case. Views of refined policy, and calculations of remote consequences were not adapted to the taste or capacity of rude warriors, who did not reason at all, or only reasoned from their passions. The business was not to convince, but to animate; and this was accomplished by poetry. It was enough to inspire the poet's enthusiasm, to know beforehand that his nation would partake it.

Accordingly, the bard was considered as the interpreter and favorite of the gods. His strains were received with equal rapture and reverence as the effusions of an immediate inspiration. They were made the vehicles of their traditions, to diffuse and perpetuate the knowledge of memorable events and illustrious men.

We grossly mistake the matter, if we suppose that poetry was received of old with as much apathy as it is at the present day. Books are now easy of access; and literary curiosity suffers oftener from repletion than from hunger. National events slip from the memory to our records; they miss the heart, though they are sure to reach posterity.

It was not thus the Grecian chiefs listened to Phemius or Demodocus, the bards mentioned by Homer. It was not thus that Homer's immortal verse was received by his countrymen. The thrones of Priam and Agamemnon were both long ago subverted; their kingdoms and those of their conquerors have long since disappeared, and left no wreck nor memorial behind; but the glory of Homer has outlived his country and its language, and will remain unshaken like Teneriffe or Atlas, the ancestor of history, and the companion of time to the end of his course. O! had he in his lifetime enjoyed, though in imagination, but a glimpse of his own glory, would it not have swelled his bosom with fresh enthusiasm, and quickened all his powers? What will not ambition do for a crown? and what crown can vie with Homer's?

Though the art of alphabetic writing was known in the east in the time of the Trojan war, it is nowhere mentioned by Homer, who is so exact and full in describing all the arts he knew. If his poems were in writing, the copies were few; and the knowledge of them was diffused, not by reading, but by the rhapsodists, who made it a profession to recite his verses.

Poetry, of consequence, enjoyed in that age, in respect to the vivacity of its impressions, and the significance of the applauses it received, as great advantages as have ever since belonged to the theatre. Instead of a cold perusal in a closet, or a still colder confinement unread, in a bookseller's shop, the poet saw with delight his work become the instructor of the wise, the companion of the brave and the great. Alexander locked up the Iliad in the precious cabinet of Darius, as a treasure of more value than the spoils of the king of Persia.

But though Homer contributed so much and so early to fix the language, to refine the taste, and inflame the imagination of the Greeks, his work, by its very excellence, seems to have quenched the emulation of succeeding poets to attempt the epic. It was not till long after his age, and by very slow degrees, that Æschylus, Sophocles, and Euripides carried the tragic art to its perfection.

For many hundred years, there seems to have been no other literary taste, and indeed no other literature, than poetry. When there was so much to excite and reward genius, as no rival to Homer appeared, it is a clear proof, that nature did not produce one. We look back on the history of Greece, and the names of illustrious geniuses thicken on the page, like the stars that seem to sparkle in clusters in the sky. But if with Homer's own spirit we could walk the milky-way, we should find that regions of unmeasured space divide the bright luminaries that seem to be so near. It is no reproach to the genius of America, if it does not produce ordinarily such men as were deemed the prodigies of the ancient world. Nature has provided for the propagation of men — giants are rare; and it is forbidden by her laws that there should be races of them.

If the genius of men could have stretched to the giant's size, there was every thing in Greece to nourish its growth and invigorate its force. After the time of Homer, the Olympic and other games were established. All Greece, assembled by its deputies, beheld the contests of wit and valor, and saw statues and crowns adjudged to the victors, who contended for the glory of their native cities as well as for their own. To us it may seem, that a handful of laurel leaves was a despicable prize. But what were the agonies, what the raptures of the contending parties, we may read, but we cannot conceive. That reward, which writers are now little excited to merit, because it is doubtful and distant, "the estate which wits inherit after death," was in Greece a present possession. That public so terrible by its censure, so much more terrible by its neglect, was then assembled in person, and the happy genius who was crowned victor was ready to expire with the transports of his joy.

There is reason to believe, that poetry was more cultivated in those early ages than it ever has been since. The great celebrity of the only two epic poems of antiquity, was owing to the peculiar circumstances of the ages in which Homer and Virgil lived; and without the concurrence of those circumstances their reputation would have been confined to the closets of scholars, without reaching the hearts and kindling the fervid enthusiasm of the multitude. Homer wrote of war to heroes and their followers, to men who felt the military passion stronger than the love of life; Virgil, with art at least equal to his genius, addressed his poem to Romans, who loved their country with sentiment, with passion, with fanaticism. It is scarcely possible, that a modern epic poet should find a subject that would take such hold of the heart, for no such subject worthy of poetry exists. Commerce has supplanted war, as the passion of the multitude; and the arts have divided and contracted the objects of pursuit. Societies are no longer under the power of single passions, that once flashed enthusiasm through them all at once like electricity. Now the propensities of mankind balance and neutralize each other, and, of course, narrow the range in which poetry used to move. Its coruscations are confined, like the northern light, to the polar circle of trade and politics, or like a transitory meteor blaze in a pamphlet or magazine.

The time seems to be near, and perhaps is already arrived, when poetry, at least poetry of transcendent merit, will be considered among the lost arts. It is a long time since England has produced a first rate poet. If America has not to boast at all what our parent country boasts no longer, it will not be thought a proof of the deficiency of our genius.

It is a proof that the ancient literature was wholly occupied by poetry, that we are without the works, and indeed without the names, of any other very ancient authors except poets. Herodotus is called the father of history; and he lived and wrote between four and five hundred years after Homer. Thucydides, it is said, on hearing the applauses bestowed at the public games on the recital of the work of Herodotus, though he was then a boy, shed tears of emulation. He afterwards excelled his rival in that species of writing.

Excellent, however, as these Grecian histories will ever be esteemed, it is somewhat remarkable, that political science never received much acquisition in the Grecian democracies. If Sparta should be vouched as an exception to this remark, it may be replied, Sparta was not a democracy. Lest that however should pass for an evasion of the point, it may be further answered, the constitution of Lycurgus seems to have been adapted to Sparta rather as a camp than a society of citizens. His whole system is rather a body of discipline than of laws whose whole object it was, not to refine manners or extend knowledge but to provide for the security of the camp. The citizens, with whom any portion of political power was intrusted, were a military caste or class; and the rigor of Lycurgus's rules and articles was calculated and intended to make them superior to all other soldiers. The same strictness, that for so long a time preserved the Spartan government, secures the subordination and tranquillity of modern armies. Sparta was, of course, no proper field for the cultivation of the science of politics. Nor can we believe, that the turbulent democracies of the neighboring states favored the growth of that kind of knowledge, since we are certain it never did thrive in Greece. How could it be, that the assemblies of the people, convened to hear flattery or to lavish the public treasures for plays and shows to amuse the populace, should be any more qualified, than inclined, to listen to political disquisitions, and especially to the wisdom and necessity of devising and putting in operation systematical checks on their own power, which was threatened with ruin by its licentiousness and excess, and which soon actually overthrew it? It may appear bold, but truth and history seem to warrant the assertion, that political science will never become accurate in popular states; for in *them* the most salutary truths must be too offensive for currency or influence.

It may be properly added, and in perfect consistency with the theory before assumed that fear is the strongest of all passions, that in democracies writers will be more afraid *of* the people, than afraid *for* them. The principles indispensable to liberty are not therefore to be discovered, or if discovered, not to be propagated and established in such a state of things. But where the chief magistrate holds the sword, and is the object of reverence, if not of popular fear, the direction of prejudice and feeling will be changed. Supposing the citizens to have privileges, and to be possessed of influence, or in other words, of some power in the state, they will naturally wish so to use the power they have, as to be secure against the abuse of that which their chief possesses; and this universal propensity of the public wishes will excite and reward the genius, that discovers the way in which this may be done. If we know any thing of the true theory of liberty, we owe it to the wisdom, or perhaps more correctly, to the experience of those nations whose public sentiment was employed to check rather than to guide the government.

It is then little to be expected that American writers will add much to the common stock of political information.

It might have been sooner remarked, that the dramatic art has not afforded any opportunities for native writers. It is but lately that we have had theatres in our cities; and till our cities become large, like London and Paris, the progress of taste will be slow, and the rewards of excellence unworthy of the competitions of genius.

Nor will it be charged, as a mark of our stupidity, that we have produced nothing in history. Our own is not yet worthy of a Livy; and to write that of any foreign nation where could an American author collect his materials and authorities? Few persons reflect, that all our universities would not suffice to supply them for such a work as Gibbon's.

The reasons why we yet boast nothing in the abstruse sciences, are of a different and more various nature. Much, perhaps all, that has been discovered in these, is known to some of our literati. It does not appear that Europe is now making any advances. But to make a wider diffusion of these sciences, and to enlarge their circle, would require the learned leisure, which a numerous class enjoy in Europe, but which cannot be enjoyed in America. If wealth is accumulated by commerce, it is again dissipated among heirs. Its transitory nature no doubt favors the progress of luxury, more than the advancement of letters. It has among us no uses to found families, to sustain rank, to purchase power, or to pension genius. The objects on which it must be employed are all temporary, and have more concern with mere appetite or ostentation than with taste or talents. Our citizens have not been accustomed to look on rank or titles, on birth or office, as capable of the least rivalship with wealth, mere wealth, in pretensions to respect. Of course the single passion that engrosses us, the only avenue to consideration and importance in our society, is the accumulation of property; our inclinations cling to gold, and are bedded in it, as deeply as that precious ore in the mine. Covered as our genius is in this mineral crust, is it strange that it does not sparkle? Pressed down to earth, and with the weight of mountains on our heads, is it surprising, that no sons of ether yet have spread their broad wings to the sky, like Jove's own eagle, to gaze undazzled at the sun, or to perch on the top of Olympus, and partake the banquet of the gods?

At present the nature of our government inclines all men to seek popularity, as the object next in point of value to wealth; but the acquisition of learning and the display of genius are not the ways to obtain it. Intellectual superiority is so far from conciliating confidence, that it is the very spirit of a democracy, as in France, to proscribe the aristocracy of talents. To be the favorite of an ignorant multitude, a man must descend to their level; he must desire what they desire, and detest all that they do not approve; he must yield to their prejudices, and substitute them for principles. Instead of enlightening their errors, he must adopt them; he must furnish the sophistry that will propagate and defend them.

Surely we are not to look for genius among demagogues; the man who can descend so low, has seldom very far to descend. As experience evinces that popularity, in other words, consideration and power, is to be procured by the meanest of mankind, the meanest in spirit and understanding, and in the worst of ways, it is obvious, that at present the excitement to genius is next to nothing. If we had a Pindar, he would be ashamed to celebrate our chief, and would be disgraced, if he did. But if he did not, his genius would not obtain his election for a selectman in a democratic town. It is party that bestows emolument, power, and consideration; and it is not excellence in the sciences that obtains the suffrages of party.

But the condition of the United States is changing. Luxury is sure to introduce want; and the great inequalities between the very rich and the very poor will be more conspicuous, and comprehend a more formidable host of the latter. The rabble of great cities is the standing army of ambition. Money will become its instrument, and vice its agent. Every step, (and we have taken many,) towards a more complete, unmixed democracy is an advance towards destruction; it is treading where the ground is treacherous and excavated for an explosion. Liberty has never yet lasted long in a democracy; nor has it ever ended in any thing better than despotism. With the change of our government, our manners and sentiments will change. As soon as our emperor has destroyed his rivals, and established order in his army, he will desire to see splendor in his court, and to occupy his subjects with the cultivation of the sciences.

If this catastrophe of our public liberty should be miraculously delayed or prevented, still we shall change. With the augmentation of wealth, there will be an increase of the numbers who may choose a literary leisure. Literary curiosity will become one of the new appetites of the nation; and as luxury advances, no appetite will be denied. After some ages we shall have many poor and a few rich, many grossly ignorant, a considerable number learned, and a few eminently learned. Nature, never prodigal of her gifts, will produce some men of genius, who will be admired and imitated.

◈ James Kirke Paulding (1778–1860)

BORN into the Hudson River Dutch aristocracy in Dutchess County, New York, Paulding was one of the well-to-do, sophisticated, wealthy "young men about town" who formed Irving's sprightly Knickerbocker group in New York City shortly after the turn of the century. Paulding joined Washington and William Irving in writing the *Salmagundi* series, and continued to produce an amazing number of poems, sketches, plays, essays, and novels throughout a long life. His *Diverting History of John Bull and Brother Jonathan* (1812) was a popular anti-British satire. His long epic poem, *The Backwoodsman* (1818), though an artistic failure, was nevertheless an important early effort to use the American frontier as literary material. Among his other works were *Koningsmarke* (1823), *Westward Ho!* (1832), and *The Old Continentals* (1846), three good novels; *The Bucktails* (1847), a successful play; *A Sketch of Old England* (1822), a well-written travel book; *Letters from the South, by a Northern Man* (1817), a series of essays on Southern society; and *A Life of Washington* (1835).

TEXT: James K. Paulding, *Works* (New York, 1835–36), IV, 265–272.

A National Literature

[From *Salmagundi, Second Series,* Saturday, August 19, 1820]

It has been often observed by such as have attempted to account for the scarcity of romantic fiction among our native writers, that the history of the country affords few materials for such works, and offers little in its traditionary lore to warm the heart or elevate the imagination. The remark has been so often repeated that it is now pretty generally received with perfect docility, as an incontrovertible truth, though it seems to me without the shadow of a foundation. It is in fact an observation that never did nor ever will apply to any nation, ancient or modern.

Wherever there are men, there will be materials for romantic adventure. In the misfortunes that befall them; in the sufferings and vicissitudes which are everywhere the lot of human beings; in the struggles to counteract fortune, and in the conflicts of the passions, in every situation of life, he who studies nature and draws his pictures from her rich and inexhaustible sources of variety, will always find enough of those characters and incidents which give a relish to works of fancy. The aid of superstition, the agency of ghosts, fairies, goblins, and all that antiquated machinery which till lately was confined to the nursery, is not necessary to excite our wonder or interest our feelings; although it is not the least of incongruities, that in an age which boasts of having by its scientific discoveries dissipated almost all the materials of superstition, some of the most popular fictions should be founded upon a superstition which is now become entirely ridiculous, even among the ignorant.

The best and most perfect works of imagination appear to me to be those which are founded upon a combination of such characters as every generation of men exhibits, and such events as have often taken place in the world, and will again. Such works are only fictions, because the tissue of events which they record never perhaps happened in precisely the same train, and to the same number of persons, as are exhibited and associated in the relation. Real life is fraught with adventures, to which the wildest fictions scarcely afford a parallel; and it has this special advantage over its rival, that these events, however extraordinary, can always be traced to motives, actions, and passions, arising out of circumstances no way unnatural, and partaking of no impossible or supernatural agency.

Hence it is, that the judgment and the fancy are both equally gratified in the perusal of this class of fictions, if they are skilfully conducted; while in those which have nothing to recommend them but appeals to the agency of beings in whose existence nobody believes, and whose actions of course can have no alliance either with nature or probability, it is the imagination alone that is satisfied, and that only by the total subjection of every other faculty of the mind.

It must be acknowledged, however, that these probable and consistent fictions are by far the most difficult to manage. It is easy enough to bring about the most improbable, not to say impossible catastrophe, by the aid of beings whose power is without limit, and whose motives are inscrutable, though in my opinion it is always proof of want of power in the writer when he is thus compelled to call upon Hercules to do what he cannot perform himself. It is either an indication that his judgment is inadequate to the arrangement of his materials and the adjustment of his plans, or that he is deficient in the invention of rational means to extricate himself from his difficulties.

On the contrary, nothing is more easy than the management of this machinery of ghosts, goblins, and fairies, who are subject neither to Longinus, Quintilian, or Dryden (whom I look upon as the best critic of modern times); who are always within call, and can be made active or passive, without the trouble of putting them or the author to the inconvenience of being governed by any rational motive whatever. Events that would be extraordinary, if they were not impossible, are thus brought about in a trice, without any preparatory and laborious arrangements of causes and effects, and the fiction becomes thus complete in its kind, by being equally elevated beyond our comprehension and belief.

The rare and happy combination of invention, judgment, and experience, requisite to produce such a work as *Tom Jones,* is seldom twice found in the same country; while thousands of mere romance-writers flourish and are forgotten in every age.

In the raw material for the latter species of fiction, it must be acknowledged this country is quite deficient. Fairies, giants, and goblins are not indigenous here, and with the exception of a few witches that were soon exterminated, our worthy ancestors brought over with them not a single specimen of Gothic or Grecian mythology.

The only second-sight they possessed was founded on the solid basis of a keen recollection of the past, a rational anticipation of the future. They acknowledged no agency above that of the physical and intellectual man, except that of the Being that created him; and they relied for protection and support on their own resolute perseverance, aided by the blessings of God. But if I mistake not, there is that in the peculiarities of their character; in the motives which produced the resolution to emigrate to the wilderness; in the courage and perseverance with which they consummated this gallant enterprise; and in the wild and terrible peculiarities of their intercourse, their adventures, and their contests with the savages, amply sufficient for all the purposes of those higher works of imagination, which may be called Rational Fictions.

That these materials have as yet been little more than partially interwoven into the few fictions which this country has given birth to, is not owing to their being inapplicable to that purpose, but to another cause entirely. We have been misled by bad models, or the suffrages of docile critics, who have bowed to the influence of rank and fashion, and given testimony in favour of works which their better judgment must have condemned. We have cherished a habit of looking to other nations for examples of every kind, and debased the genius of this new world by making it the ape and the tributary of that of the old. We have imitated where we might often have excelled; we have overlooked our own rich resources, and sponged upon the exhausted treasury of our empoverished neighbours; we were born rich, and yet have all our lives subsisted by borrowing. Hence it has continually occurred, that those who might have gone before had they chosen a new path, have been content to come last, merely by following the old track. Many a genius that could and would have attained an equal height, in some new and unexplored region of fancy, has dwindled into insignificance and contempt by stooping to track some inferior spirit, to whom fashion had assigned a temporary elevation. They ought to be told, that though fashion may give a momentary popularity to works that neither appeal to national attachments, domestic habits, or those feelings which are the same yesterday, today, forever, and everywhere, still it is not by imitation they can hope to equal any thing great. It appears to me that the young candidate for the prize of genius, in the regions of invention and fancy, has but one path open to fame. He cannot hope to wing his way above those immortal works that have stood the test of ages, and are now with one consent recognised as specimens beyond which the intellect of man is not permitted to soar. But a noble prize is yet within his grasp, and worthy of the most aspiring ambition.

By freeing himself from a habit of servile imitation; by daring to think and feel, and express his feelings; by dwelling on scenes and events connected with our pride and our affections; by indulging in those little peculiarities of thought, feeling, and expression which belong to every nation; by borrowing from nature, and not from those who disfigure or burlesque her — he may and will in time destroy the ascendency of foreign taste and opinions, and elevate his own in the place of them. These causes lead to the final establishment of a national literature, and give that air and character of originality which it is sure to acquire, unless it is debased and expatriated by a habit of servile imitation.

The favourite, yet almost hopeless object of my old age, is to see this attempt consummated. For this purpose, it is my delight to furnish occasionally such hints as may turn the attention of those who have leisure, health, youth, genius, and opportunities, to domestic subjects on which to exercise their powers. Let them not be disheartened, even should they sink into a temporary oblivion in the outset. This country is not destined to be always behind in the race of literary glory. The time will assuredly come, when that same freedom of thought and action which has given such a spur to our genius in other respects, will achieve similar wonders in literature. It is then that our early specimens will be sought after with avidity, and that those who led the way in the rugged discouraging path will be honoured, as we begin to honour the adventurous spirits who first sought, explored, and cleared this western wilderness.

These remarks will, we think, most especially apply to the fictions of the late Mr. Charles Brockden Brown, which are among the most vigorous and original efforts of our native literature. Indeed, it appears to us that few if any writers of the present day exceed, or even approach him in richness of imagination, depth of feeling, command of language, and the faculty of exciting a powerful and permanent interest in the reader. They constitute a class of fictions standing alone by themselves; they are the product of our soil, the efforts of one of our most blameless and esteemed fellow-citizens, and they do honour to any country. Yet they want the stamp of fashion and notoriety; they have never been consecrated by the approbation of foreign criticism; and, in all probability, a large portion of our readers are ignorant that they were ever written.

Yet we hazard little in predicting that the period is not far distant when they will be rescued from oblivion by the hand of some kindred spirit, and the people of the United States become sufficiently independent to dare to admire and to express their admiration of a writer who will leave many followers, but few equals; and whose future fame will furnish a bright contrast to the darkness in which he is now enveloped.

The Beginnings of the American Novel

Hugh Henry Brackenridge (1748–1816)

SCOTTISH-BORN Hugh Henry Brackenridge, brought to Pennsylvania by his parents in 1753, acquired what education he could on the frontier. When he was fifteen he moved to Gunpowder Falls, Maryland, to teach school for five years before entering the College of New Jersey, now Princeton University, in 1768. There his love of classical literature was encouraged by classmates like James Madison and Philip Freneau, with whom he formed a political and literary club called the Whig Literary Society, combining the two interests that dominated his later career. With Freneau he wrote an early piece of prose fiction called *Father Bombo's Pilgrimage to Mecca* (1770), and for their commencement the two collaborated on a prophetic poem, *The Rising Glory of America* (1771). Three years later, when Brackenridge returned to take his M.A., he delivered his *Poem on Divine Revelation,* but by then he knew that he was no poet. He taught school for a time; became an army chaplain (1776–78); edited the short-lived *United States Magazine* in Philadelphia in 1779; and at last began the study of law, moving in 1781 to Pittsburgh, where he lived for twenty years, actively engaged in political and economic affairs. Elected to the State Assembly (1786), he was soon ousted for failing to support his constituency, and did not again run for office until 1798, when he was defeated in a bitter campaign. But for his service in organizing and leading the Republicans in western Pennsylvania, he was made a justice of the Pennsylvania Supreme Court (1799). He spent much of the remainder of his life as a defender of the judiciary and the common law, both of which were long under vigorous attack.

Brackenridge's personal experience in the economic, legal, and political turmoil following the Revolution was not, for the most part, pleasant. But not satisfied to vent his personal pique and disillusionment directly upon his antagonists, he fortunately put on the satiric mask he had discovered in the work of Lucian,

Rabelais, Cervantes, Samuel Butler, Swift, Sterne, Smollett, and Fielding. The result was the most popular piece of prose fiction to come out of the region west of the Alleghenies before the nineteenth century. *Modern Chivalry* began as a Hudibrastic satire on Brackenridge's political opponents in the Pennsylvania legislature (1787), expanded into a narrative poem called *The Modern Chevalier* (1788–89), and by 1790 had turned into prose, which Brackenridge thought "was a more humble and might be a safer walk." The first two volumes, published in 1792, introduce the Quixotic characters of Captain John Farrago and his troublesome Irish servant Teague O'Regan, who encounter a series of adventures closely paralleling Brackenridge's main political interests — public elections, tax collecting, the Whiskey Rebellion, frontier pretensions to learning, the French Revolution, the scurrility of the American press, and the Federal Constitution. Six volumes of adventures, interspersed with brief essays, had appeared by 1805. The entire romance was issued in an enlarged, complete edition in 1815, the year before Brackenridge died.

    Text: Hugh Henry Brackenridge, *Modern Chivalry*, ed. Claude M. Newlin (New York, 1937), pp. 13–17, 20–22, 125–128.

From
Modern Chivalry

HOW DEMOCRACY WORKS

[Vol. I, Bk. I, Chap. III]

    The Captain rising early next morning, and setting out on his way, had now arrived at a place where a number of people were convened, for the purpose of electing persons to represent them in the legislature of the state. There was a weaver who was a candidate for this appointment, and seemed to have a good deal of interest among the people. But another, who was a man of education, was his competitor. Relying on some talent of speaking which he thought he possessed, he addressed the multitude.

    Said he, Fellow citizens, I pretend not to any great abilities; but am conscious to myself that I have the best good will to serve you. But it is very astonishing to me, that this weaver should conceive himself qualified for the trust. For though my acquirements are not great, yet his are still less. The mechanical business which he pursues, must necessarily take up so much of his time, that he cannot apply himself to political studies. I should therefore think it would be more answerable to your dignity, and conducive to your interest, to be represented by a man at least of some letters, than by an illiterate handicraftsman like this. It will be more honourable for himself, to remain at his loom and knot threads, than to come forward in a legislative capacity: because, in the one case, he is in the sphere where God and nature has placed him; in the other, he is like a fish out of water, and must struggle for breath in a new element.

Is it possible he can understand the affairs of government, whose mind has been concentered to the small object of weaving webs; to the price by the yard, the grist of the thread, and such like matters as concern a manufacturer of cloths? The feet of him who weaves, are more occupied than the head, or at least as much; and therefore the whole man must be, at least, but in half accustomed to exercise his mental powers. For these reasons, all other things set aside, the chance is in my favour, with respect to information. However, you will decide, and give your suffrages to him or to me, as you shall judge expedient.

The Captain hearing these observations, and looking at the weaver, could not help advancing, and undertaking to subjoin something in support of what had been just said. Said he, I have no prejudice against a weaver more than another man. Nor do I know any harm in the trade; save that from the sedentary life in a damp place, there is usually a paleness of the countenance: but this is a physical, not a moral evil. Such usually occupy subterranean apartments; not for the purpose, like Demosthenes, of shaving their heads, and writing over eight times the history of Thucydides, and perfecting a stile of oratory; but rather to keep the thread moist; or because this is considered but as an inglorious sort of trade, and is frequently thrust away into cellars, and damp outhouses, which are not occupied for a better use.

But to rise from the cellar to the senate house, would be an unnatural hoist. To come from counting threads, and adjusting them to the splits of a reed, to regulate the finances of a government, would be pre-posterous; there being no congruity in the case. There is no analogy between knotting threads and framing laws. It would be a reversion of the order of things. Not that a manufacturer of linen or woolen, or other stuff, is an inferior character, but a different one, from that which ought to be employed in affairs of state. It is unnecessary to enlarge on this subject; for you must all be convinced of the truth and propriety of what I say. But if you will give me leave to take the manufacturer aside a little, I think I can explain to him my ideas on the subject; and very probably prevail with him to withdraw his pretensions. The people seeming to acquiesce, and beckoning to the weaver, they drew aside, and the Captain addressed him in the following words:

Mr. Traddle, said he, for that was the name of the manufacturer, I have not the smallest idea of wounding your sensibility; but it would seem to me, it would be more your interest to pursue your occupation, than to launch out into that of which you have no knowledge. When you go to the senate house, the application to you will not be to warp a web; but to make laws for the commonwealth. Now, suppose that the making these laws, requires a knowledge of commerce, or of the interests of agriculture, or those principles upon which the different manufactures depend, what service could you render. It is possible you might think justly enough; but could you speak? You are not in the habit of public speaking. You are not furnished with those common place ideas, with which even very ignorant men can pass for knowing something. There is nothing makes a man so ridiculous as to attempt what is above his sphere. You are no tumbler, for instance; yet should you give out that you could vault upon a man's back; or turn head over heels, like the wheel of a cart; the stiffness of your joints would encumber you; and you would fall upon your backside to the ground. Such a squash as that would do you damage. The getting up to ride on the state is an unsafe thing to those who are not accustomed to such horsemanship. It is a disagreeable thing for a man to be laughed at, and there is no way of keeping ones self from it but by avoiding all affectation.

While they were thus discoursing, a bustle had taken place among the crowd. Teague hearing so much about elections, and serving the government, took it into his head, that he could be a legislator himself. The thing was not displeasing to the people, who seemed to favour his pretensions; owing, in some degree, to there being several of his countrymen among the croud; but more especially to the fluctuation of the popular mind, and a disposition to what is new and ignoble. For though the weaver was not the most elevated object of choice, yet he was still preferable to this tatter-demalion, who was but a menial servant, and had so much of what is called the brogue on his tongue, as to fall far short of an elegant speaker.

The Captain coming up, and finding what was on the carpet, was greatly chagrined at not having been able to give the multitude a better idea of the importance of a legislative trust; alarmed also, from an apprehension of the loss of his servant. Under these impressions he resumed his address to the multitude. Said he, This is making the matter still worse, gentlemen: this servant of mine is but a bog-trotter; who can scarcely speak the dialect in which your laws ought to be written; but certainly has never read a single treatise on any political subject; for the truth is, he cannot read at all. The young people of the lower class, in Ireland, have seldom the advantage of a good education; especially the descendants of the ancient Irish, who have most of them a great assurance of countenance, but little information, or literature. This young man, whose family name is Oregan, has been my servant for several years. And, except a too great fondness for women, which now and then brings him into scrapes, he has demeaned himself in a manner tolerable enough. But he is totally ignorant of the great principles of legislation; and more especially, the particular interests of the government. A free government is a noble possession to a people: and this freedom consists in an equal right to make laws, and to have the benefit of the laws when made. Though doubtless, in such a government, the lowest citizen may become chief magistrate; yet it is sufficient to possess the right; not absolutely necessary to exercise it. Or even if you should think proper, now and then, to shew your privilege, and exert, in a signal manner, the democratic prerogative, yet is it not descending too low to filch away from me a hireling, which I cannot well spare, to serve your purposes? You are surely carrying the matter too far, in thinking to make a senator of this hostler; to take him away from an employment to which he has been bred, and put him to another, to which he has served no apprenticeship: to set those hands which have been lately employed in currying my horse, to the draughting-bills, and preparing business for the house.

The people were tenacious of their choice, and insisted on giving Teague their suffrages; and by the frown upon their brows, seemed to indicate resentment at what had been said; as indirectly charging them with want of judgment; or calling in question their privilege to do what they thought proper. It is a very strange thing, said one of them, who was a speaker for the rest, that after having conquered Burgoyne and Cornwallis, and got a government of our own, we cannot put in it whom we please. This young man may be your servant, or another man's servant; but if we chuse to make him a delegate, what is that to you. He may not be yet skilled in the matter, but there is a good day a-coming. We will impower him; and it is better to trust a plain man like him, than one of your high flyers, that will make laws to suit their own purposes.

Said the Captain, I had much rather you would send the weaver, though I thought that improper, than to invade my household, and thus detract from me the very person that I have about me to brush my boots, and clean my spurs. The prolocutor of the people gave him to understand that his surmises were useless, for the people had determined on the choice, and Teague they would have for a representative.

Finding it answered no end to expostulate with the multitude, he requested to speak a word with Teague by himself. Stepping aside, he said to him, composing his voice, and addressing him in a soft manner; Teague, you are quite wrong in this matter they have put into your head. Do you know what it is to be a member of a deliberative body? What qualifications are necessary? Do you understand any thing of geography? If a question should be, to make a law to dig a canal in some part of the state, can you describe the bearing of the mountains, and the course of the rivers? Or if commerce is to be pushed to some new quarter, by the force of regulations, are you competent to decide in such a case? There will be questions of law, and astronomy on the carpet. How you must gape and stare like a fool, when you come to be asked your opinion on these subjects? Are you acquainted with the abstract principles of finance; with the funding public securities; the ways and means of raising the revenue; providing for the discharge of the public debts, and all other things which respect the economy of the government? Even if you had knowledge, have you a facility of speaking? I would suppose you would have too much pride to go to the house just to say, Ay, or No. This is not the fault of your nature, but of your education; having been accustomed to dig turf in your early years, rather than instructing yourself in the classics, or common school books.

When a man becomes a member of a public body, he is like a rac-coon, or other beast that climbs up the fork of a tree; the boys pushing at him with pitch-forks, or throwing stones, or shooting at him with an arrow, the dogs barking in the mean time. One will find fault with your not speaking; another with your speaking, if you speak at all. They will have you in the news papers, and ridicule you as a perfect beast. There is what they call the caricatura; that is, representing you with a dog's head, or a cat's claw. As you have a red head, they will very probably make a fox of you, or a sorrel horse, or a brindled cow, or the like. It is the devil in hell to be exposed to the squibs and crackers of the gazette wits and publications. You know no more about these matters than a goose; and yet you would undertake rashly, without advice, to enter on the office; nay, contrary to advice. For I would not for a thousand guineas, though I have not the half of it to spare, that the breed of the Oregans should come to this; bringing on them a worse stain than stealing sheep; to which they are addicted. You have nothing but your character, Teague, in a new country to depend upon. Let it never be said, that you quitted an honest livelihood, the taking care of my horse, to follow the new fangled whims of the times, and to be a statesman.

Teague was moved chiefly with the last part of the address, and consented to give up the object.

The Captain, glad of this, took him back to the people, and announced his disposition to decline the honour which they had intended him.

Teague acknowledged that he had changed his mind, and was willing to remain in a private station.

The people did not seem well pleased with the Captain; but as nothing more could be said about the matter, they turned their atten-tion to the weaver, and gave him their suffrages.

CONTAINING REFLECTIONS

[Vol. I, Bk. I, Chap. V]

A democracy is beyond all question the freest government: because under this, every man is equally protected by the laws, and has equally a voice in making them. But I do not say an equal voice; because some men have stronger lungs than others, and can express more forcibly their opinions of public affairs. Others, though they may not speak very loud, yet have a faculty of saying more in a short time; and even in the case of others, who speak little or none at all, yet what they do say containing good sense, comes with greater weight; so that all things considered, every citizen has not, in this sense of the word, an equal voice. But the right being equal, what great harm if it is unequally exercised? is it necessary that every man should become a statesman? No more than that every man should become a poet or a painter. The sciences are open to all; but let him only who has taste and genius pursue them. If any man covets the office of a bishop, says St. Paul, he covets a good work. But again, he adds this caution, Ordain not a novice, lest being lifted up with pride, he falls into the condemnation of the devil. It is indeed making a devil of a man to lift him up to a state to which he is not suited. A ditcher is a respectable character, with his over-alls on, and a spade in his hand; but put the same man to those offices which require the head, whereas he has been accustomed to impress with his foot, and there appears a contrast between the man and the occupation.

There are individuals in society, who prefer honour to wealth; or cultivate political studies as a branch of literary pursuits; and offer themselves to serve public bodies, in order to have an opportunity of discovering their knowledge, and exercising their judgment. It must be chagrining to these, and hurtful to the public, to see those who have no talent this way; and ought to have no taste, preposterously obtrude themselves upon the government. It is the same as if a brick-layer should usurp the office of a taylor, and come with his square and perpendicular, to make the measure of a pair of breeches.

It is proper that those who cultivate oratory, should go to the house of orators. But for an Ay and No man to be ambitious of that place, is to sacrifice his credit to his vanity.

I would not mean to insinuate that legislators are to be selected from the more wealthy of the citizens, yet a man's circumstances ought to be such as afford him leisure for study and reflection. There is often wealth without taste or talent. I have no idea, that because a man lives in a great house, and has a cluster of bricks or stones about his backside, that he is therefore fit for a legislator. There is so much pride and arrogance with those who consider themselves the first in a government, that it deserves to be checked by the populace, and the evil most usually commences on this side. Men associate with their own persons, the adventitious circumstances of birth and fortune: So that a fellow blowing with fat and repletion, conceives himself superior to the poor lean man, that lodges in an inferior mansion. But as in all cases, so in this, there is a medium. Genius and virtue are independent of rank and fortune; and it is neither the opulent, nor the indigent, but the man of ability and integrity that ought to be called forth to serve his country: and while, on the one hand, the aristocratic part of the government arrogates a right to represent; on the other hand, the democratic contends the point; and from this conjunction and opposition of forces, there is produced a compound resolution, which carries the object in an intermediate direction. When we see therefore, a Teague Oregan lifted up, the philosopher will reflect, that it is to balance some purse-proud fellow, equally as ignorant, that comes down from the sphere of the aristocratic interest.

But every man ought to consider for himself, whether it is his use to be this draw-back, on either side. For as when good liquor is to be distilled, you throw in some material useless in itself to correct the effervescence of the spirit; so it may be his part to act as a sedative. For though we commend the effect, yet still the material retains but its original value.

But as the nature of things is such, let no man, who means well to the commonwealth, and offers to serve it, be hurt in his mind when some one of meaner talents is preferred. The people are a sovereign, and greatly despotic; but, in the main, just.

I have a great mind, in order to elevate the composition, to make quotations from the Greek and Roman history. And I am conscious to myself, that I have read over the writers on the government of Italy and Greece, in ancient, as well as modern times. But I have drawn a great deal more from reflection on the nature of things, than from all the writings I have ever read. Nay, the history of the election, which I have just given, will afford a better lesson to the American mind, than all that is to be found in other examples. We have seen here, a weaver a favoured candidate, and in the next instance, a bog-trotter superseding him. Now it may be said, that this is fiction; but fiction, or no fiction, the nature of the thing will make it a reality. But I return to the adventures of the Captain, whom I have upon my hands; and who, as far as I can yet discover, is a good honest man; and means what is benevolent and useful; though his ideas may not comport with the ordinary manner of thinking, in every particular.

A VISIT TO THE UNIVERSITY

[Vol. II, Bk. V, Chap. VI]

It was about three or four o'clock in the afternoon, that some one, who read the advertisement respecting Teague, came to the Captain, and informed him, that a person, answering the description, had been lately employed to teach Greek in the University. Struck with the idea, that the bog-trotter might have passed himself for a Greek scholar, whereas he understood only Irish, he set out to the University, to make enquiry. Knocking at the door of the principal, he was admitted; and being seated, addressed him as follows: Said he, sir, a pedeseque of mine, (for talking to the rector of a college, he did not chuse to use the vulgar terms, waiter, or bog-trotter,) a pedeseque of mine, whom I have found useful, save that he is somewhat trouble-some in pretending to places of appointment for which he is not qualified; a thing, by the bye, too common in this country; where men, without the aid of academic knowledge, thrust themselves into places requiring great learning and ability: (This he said to flatter the man of letters; as if a man could know but little, that had not been forged or furbished at his school): I say, this pedeseque of mine, has absconded for some days; and I have been able to collect no account of him until last evening, that a person, having read an advertisement of mine in the gazette, came to me, and informed, that one answering the descrip-tion I had given, both as to appearance and accomplishments, had been lately employed, as professor of the Greek language, in this University. Now, though I well know this Pady, as I may call him, to understand no Greek; yet, as he speaks Irish, and has much assurance, and little honesty in matters where his ambition is concerned, I did not know, but he might have imposed himself upon you, for a Greek scholar, and obtained a professorship.

The principal made answer, that it was true that a person from Ireland had been lately employed in that capacity; and that should he be discovered to be an imposter, it would be using the university very ill. The Captain thought so too; and taking it for granted that it was Teague, expressed his surprise that they had not examined him, before he was admitted; or at least had such proof by letters as would have had ascertained his being qualified. The principal observed, that as to examination they had no one at hand to examine, as there were none of the trustees or professors of other branches in the university under-stood Greek; as for himself he did not, having not studied it in early life, and for a series of years, having given himself to politics and mathematics; so that unless they could send out for a Roman Catholic priest, or a Scotch clergyman, there was none to examine. The improbability of any person passing himself, above all things, for a master of the Greek language on the score of understanding Irish, was such, that it never came into their heads to suspect it, so as to demand letters.

Had you known said the Captain, this bog-trotter of mine, (here he forgot the word pedeseque) as well as I do, you would not be surprised at his attempting any thing; and that he should be now in your academy giving Greek lectures, understanding nothing but the vernacular tongue of his own country. Here he gave an account of his setting up for Congress, &c. as explained in the preceding part of this narrative.

However, wishing to see the raggamuffin, that he might unkennel him, he was accompanied by the principal to the chamber of the pseudo professor, considering as he went along, in what manner he should accost him; whether he should break out upon him with a direct invective, or with ironical words; such as, Mr. Professor, you must be a very learned man, not only to understand Irish, but Greek: but perhaps the Greek and Irish language are much the same. It must be so; for I know that a few days ago, you did not understand a word of this, and to acquire a dead language in such a short time would be impossible, unless the living tongue was a good deal a-kin to it. But I had never understood that Irish had any more affinity to the language of Athens and Sparta, than the Erse, or the German, or the Welsh; however, we must live and learn, as the saying is; you have shewn us what we never knew before.

Conning a speech of this sort in his own mind, with a view to divert the principal, and amuse himself with Teague, he entered the chamber of the professor; who sat in an elbow chair with Thucydides before him.

What was the surprise of the Captain to find that it was not Teague.

In fact it was a person not wholly unlike him, especially in a tinge of the brogue which he betrayed in his discourse; for though the professor was really a man of education, having been early sent to St. Omer's, where he had studied, being intended for a priest, and understood not only the Greek, and Latin, but spoke French; yet in the pronunciation of the English tongue, he had that prolongation of the sound of a word, and articulation of the vowel O, which constitutes what is vulgarly called the brogue, as being the pronunciation of the native Irish; who being a depressed people, are most of them poor, and wear a kind of mean shoe, which they call a brogue.

After an apology to the professor for mistaking him for a certain Teague O'Regan, whom he had in his employment, at the request of the professor, the principal and the Captain took seats.

The professor said, His name was not O'Regan, being O'Dougherty; but he knew the O'Regans very well in Ireland. There was a Pady O'Regan in the same class with him at St. Omers, when he read Craike.

That he was a good scholar, and understood Craike very well; and he would be glad if he was over in this country to teach Craike here; it appeared to be a very scarce language; but he had become a praste, and was now a missionary to Paraguay, in Sout America.

The Captain punning on his pronunciation of the work Greek; and willing to amuse himself a little with the professor, could not help observing, that he was under a mistake, as to the scarceness of the Craike language in these States. That there were whole tribes who spoke the Craike language; there was that of the heron, and the raven, and several other fowls. A German professor, who was present, apprehending the Captain to be under a mistake, and willing to correct him, observed — It is, said he, the Creek language, that the professor means. As to that, said the Captain, it is also spoken plentifully in America. There is a whole nation of Indians, on the borders of South Carolina and Georgia, that speak the Creek language; men, women, and children.

The professor, knowing more of the classics than of the geography of these United States, and of the heathen gods more than of the aborigines of this country, expressed astonishment. If what you tell me be a trut, said he, it is a crate discovery; perhaps dese may have de fragments o' de books o' de philosophers and poets that are lost, and de professors cannot come acrass in deir own countries; but I have tought dat de Craike language was spake only in de Morea, and a little in Russia, and Constantinople.

The Captain assured him, the principal favouring the mistake, by a grave face, and bowing as the Captain spoke, that it was absolutely the vernacular language of these people.

Why den, said the other, do dey not get professors from amongst dese, to tache Craike in deir colleges?

Because, said the Captain, we have been heretofore on hostile terms with these Indians, and it is but of late that we have made a peace. But now, it is to be presumed, we shall have it in our power to procure from them able teachers.

The professor was alarmed at this; as supposing it would supercede the necessity of his services; or, at least, much reduce the price of his tuition. He could have wished he had not come to this quarter of the world; and was almost ready, in his own mind, to bind up what he had, and go back to Clogher.

So ended their visit to the University, and the Captain withdrew.

ᶜᷨ Susannah Haswell Rowson (1762–1824)

UNPROTECTED by copyright and widely reprinted, British novels
dominated the leisure of American women, who devoured the
sensational, sentimental tales of seduction, incest, shame, and
suicide made popular by Samuel Richardson's *Pamela* and *Clarissa*.
Attacked as morally dangerous by the press and the clergy, and
defended in prefatory notes as object lessons against vice, such
novels quickly gained a wide public in the new nation, a public
of which writers like Susannah Rowson were quick to take advantage.

Susannah Haswell, the daughter of a British naval officer, was
born in England and came to America with her family shortly
before the Revolution. During the war the Haswells were forced
to move several times as the fortunes of the conflict turned against
the British, and at its conclusion they returned to England, where
Susannah in 1786 married William Rowson, a hardware merchant
who was also a trumpeter in the Horse Guards. After his business
failed, Rowson and his wife went on the stage with moderate success, coming to Philadelphia in 1793 for an engagement at the
Chestnut Street Theater in Philadelphia. They remained in Philadelphia until 1797, when Mrs. Rowson opened a girls' school in
Boston. Thereafter she pursued a successful career as school-
mistress, editor and contributor to magazines, poet, playwright,
and Bostonian.

Mrs. Rowson wrote several novels before coming to America,
among them *Victoria* (1786), *Mary, or the Test of Honour* (1787),
and *The Inquisitors* (1788). *Charlotte Temple: A Tale of Truth*,
based upon an actual experience in her family, appeared in London in 1791 and in an American edition in 1794. It began
slowly, with three editions before the turn of the century, and
then its popularity grew — fifty thousand copies sold before 1810,
and ultimately some two hundred editions in the next century.
Mrs. Rowson continued to write novels, such as *Trials of the
Human Heart, Reuben and Rachel,* and *Lucy Temple, or The
Three Orphans,* the story of Charlotte's daughter. None, however, approached the popularity of *Charlotte,* which, with William
Hill Brown's epistolary *Power of Sympathy* (1789) and Hannah
Foster's *The Coquette* (1797), remains a classic example of the
sentimental novel — exaggerated in emotion, moralistic in tone,
inflated in style, and "refined" in sentiment.

Mrs. Rowson's tale is told simply and directly. Charlotte, the
daughter of respectable upper-middle-class parents and a student
at Madame Du Pont's School for Girls in England, meets Montraville, a young officer, shortly before his departure for the

American wars. With the help of a devilish brother officer, Belcour, and a depraved Frenchwoman, Mademoiselle La Rue, the well-meaning but weak Montraville persuades Charlotte to elope with him to New York on promise of marriage. He becomes enamored of Julia Franklin, a young American girl; and through the machinations of Belcour, who wants Charlotte for himself, abandons Charlotte and her illegitimate child. Belcour immediately loses interest, and the dying Charlotte sinks deeper into virtuous poverty until she finds refuge at the hut of a poor servant family. Here her true friend, Mrs. Beauchamp, her grieving father, and Montraville find her, too late.

TEXT: Susannah Rowson, *Charlotte Temple, A Tale of Truth* (New York, 1897).

From
Charlotte Temple

THE AUTHOR'S PREFACE

For the perusal of the young and thoughtless of the fair sex this Tale of Truth is designed; and I could wish my fair readers to consider it as not merely the effusion of Fancy, but as a reality. The circumstances on which I have founded this novel were related to me some little time since by an old lady who had personally known Charlotte, tho she concealed the real names of the characters and likewise the place where the unfortunate scenes were acted: yet, as it was impossible to offer a relation to the public in such an imperfect state, I have thrown over the whole a slight veil of fiction, and substituted names and places according to my own fancy. The principal characters in this little tale are now consigned to the silent tomb: it can therefore hurt the feelings of no one, and may, I flatter myself, be of service to some who are so unfortunate as to have neither friends to advise or understanding to direct them through the various and unexpected evils that attend a young and unprotected woman in her first entrance into life.

While the tear of compassion still trembled in my eye for the fate of the unhappy Charlotte, I may have children of my own, said I, to whom this recital may be of use, and if to your own children, said Benevolence, why not to the many daughters of Misfortune who, deprived of natural friends or spoilt by a mistaken education, are thrown on an unfeeling world without the least power to defend themselves from the snares, not only of the other sex, but from the more dangerous arts of the profligate of their own?

Sensible as I am that a novel writer, at a time when such a variety of works are ushered into the world under that name, stands but a poor chance for fame in the annals of literature, but conscious that I wrote with a mind anxious for the happiness of that sex whose morals and conduct have so powerful an influence on mankind in general; and convinced that I have not wrote a line that conveys a wrong idea to the head, or a corrupt wish to the heart, I shall rest satisfied in the purity of my own intentions, and if I merit not applause, I feel that I dread not censure.

If the following tale should save one hapless fair one from the errors which ruined poor Charlotte, or rescue from impending misery the heart of one anxious parent, I shall feel a much higher gratification in reflecting on this trifling performance than could possibly result from the applause which might attend the most elegant, finished piece of literature whose tendency might deprave the heart or mislead the understanding.

THE VOICE OF THE TEMPTRESS

[Chapter VI]

Madame Du Pont was a woman in every way calculated to take care of young ladies, had that care entirely devolved on herself; but it was impossible to attend to the education of a numerous school without proper assistants; and those assistants were not always the kind of people whose conversations and morals were exactly such as parents of delicacy and refinement would wish a daughter to copy.

Among the teachers at Madame Du Pont's school was Mademoiselle La Rue, who added to a pleasing person and insinuating address a liberal education and the manners of a gentlewoman. She was recommended to the school by a lady whose humanity overstepped the bounds of discretion; for, though she knew Miss La Rue had eloped from a convent with a young officer, and on coming to England had lived in open defiance of all moral and religious duties, yet, finding her reduced to the most abject want, and believing the penitence which she professed to be sincere, she took her into her own family, and thence recommended her to Madame Du Pont, as thinking the situation more suitable for a woman of her abilities.

But Mademoiselle possessed too much the spirit of intrigue to remain long without adventures. At church, where she constantly appeared, her person attracted the attention of a young man who was upon a visit at a gentleman's seat in the neighborhood; she had met him several times clandestinely, and being invited to come out that evening and eat some fruit and pastry in a summer-house belonging to the gentleman he was visiting, and requested to bring some of the ladies with her, Charlotte, being her favorite, was fixed on to accompany her.

The mind of youth easily catches at promised pleasure. Pure and innocent by nature, it thinks not of the dangers lurking beneath those pleasures until too late to avoid them.

When Mademoiselle asked Charlotte to go with her, she mentioned the gentleman as a relation, and spoke in such high terms of the elegance of his gardens, the sprightliness of his conversation, and the liberality with which he entertained his guests, that Charlotte thought only of the pleasure she should enjoy in the visit, not of the imprudence of going without her governess' knowledge, or of the danger to which she exposed herself in visiting the house of a young man of fashion.

Madame Du Pont had gone out for the evening, and the rest of the ladies had retired to rest, when Charlotte and the teacher stole out of the back gate, and in crossing the field, were accosted by Montraville, as mentioned in the first chapter.

Charlotte was disappointed at the pleasure she had promised herself from this visit. The levity of the gentlemen and the freedom of their conversation disgusted her. She was astonished at the liberties Mademoiselle permitted them to take, grew thoughtful and uneasy, and heartily wished herself at home again, in her own chamber.

Perhaps one cause of that wish might be an earnest desire to see the contents of the letter which had been put into her hand by Montraville.

Any reader, who has the least knowledge of the world, will easily imagine the letter was made up of encomiums on her beauty, and vows of everlasting love and constancy, nor will he be surprised that a heart open to every gentle, generous sentiment, should feel itself warmed by gratitude for a man who professed to feel so much for her, nor is it improbable that her mind might revert to the agreeable person and martial appearance of Montraville.

In affairs of love, a young heart is never in more danger than when attacked by a handsome young soldier. A man of indifferent appearance will, when arrayed in a military habit, show to advantage, but when beauty of person, elegance of manner, and an easy method of paying compliments are united to the scarlet coat, smart cockade, and military sash — ah! well-a-day for the poor girl who gazes upon him; she is in imminent danger, but if she listens to him with pleasure, 'tis all over with her, and from that moment she has neither eyes nor ears for any other object.

Now, my dear, sober matron — if a sober matron should deign to turn over these pages before she trusts them to the eyes of a darling daughter — let me entreat you not to put on a grave face and throw down the book in a passion, and declare 'tis enough to turn the heads of half the girls in England. I do solemnly protest, my dear madam, I mean no more by what I have here advanced than to ridicule those girls who foolishly imagine a red coat and a silver epaulet constitute a fine gentleman; and should that fine gentleman make half a dozen fine speeches to them they will imagine themselves so much in love as to fancy it a meritorious act to jump out of a two-pair stairs window, abandon their friends, and trust entirely to the honor of a man who, perhaps, hardly knows the meaning of the word, and if he does, will be too much the modern man of refinement to practise it in their favor.

Gracious Heaven! when I think of the miseries that must rend the heart of a doting parent, when he sees the darling of his age at first seduced from his protection, and afterwards abandoned by the very wretch whose promises of love decoyed her from the paternal roof — when he sees her poor and wretched, her bosom torn between remorse for her crime and love for her foul betrayer — when fancy paints to me the good old man stooping to raise the weeping penitent, while every tear from her eye is numbered by drops from his bleeding heart, my bosom glows with honest indignation, and I wish for power to extirpate these monsters of seduction from the earth.

Oh, my dear girls — for to such only am I writing — listen not to the voice of love, unless sanctioned by paternal approbation; be assured, it is now past the days of romance; no woman can be run away with contrary to her own inclination; then kneel down each morning and request kind Heaven to keep you free from temptation; or should it please to suffer you to be tried, pray for fortitude to resist the impulse of natural inclination, when it runs counter to the precepts of religion and virtue.

NATURAL SENSE OF PROPRIETY INHERENT IN THE FEMALE BOSOM

[Chapter VII]

"I cannot think we have done exactly right in going out this evening, Mademoiselle," said Charlotte, seating herself, when she entered her apartment; "nay, I am sure it was not right; for I expected to be very happy, but was sadly disappointed."

"It was your own fault, then," replied Mademoiselle; "for I am sure my cousin omitted nothing that could serve to render the evening agreeable."

"True," said Charlotte, "but I thought the gentlemen were very free in their manner; I wonder you would suffer them to behave as they did."

"Prithee, don't be such a foolish little prude," said the artful woman, affecting anger. "I invited you to go, in hopes it would divert you, and be an agreeable change of scene; however, if your delicacy was hurt by the behavior of the gentlemen, you need not go again; so there let it rest."

"I do not intend to go again," said Charlotte, gravely, taking off her bonnet, and beginning to prepare for bed. "I am sure, if Madame Du Pont knew we had been out to-night, she would be very angry; and it is ten to one but she hears of it by some means or other."

"Nay, miss," said La Rue, "perhaps your mighty sense of propriety may lead you to tell her yourself, and in order to avoid the censure you would incur should she hear of it by accident, throw the blame on me; but I confess I deserve it; it will be a very kind return for that partiality which led me to prefer you before any of the rest of the ladies, but perhaps it will give you pleasure," continued she, letting fall some hypocritical tears, "to see me deprived of bread, and for an action which by the most rigid could be esteemed but an inadvertency, lose my place and character, and be driven again into the world, where I have already suffered all the evils attendant on poverty."

This was touching Charlotte in the most vulnerable part; she arose from her seat, and taking Mademoiselle's hand — "You know, my dear La Rue," said she, "I love you too well to do anything that would injure you in my governess' opinion; I am only sorry we went out this evening."

"I don't believe it, Charlotte," said she, assuming a little vivacity, "for, if you had not gone out, you would not have seen the gentleman who met us crossing the field, and I rather think you were pleased with his conversation."

"I had seen him once before," replied Charlotte, "and thought him an agreeable man, and you know one is always pleased to see a person with whom one has passed several cheerful hours. But," said she, pausing and drawing the letter from her pocket, while a general suffusion of vermilion tinged her neck and face, "he gave me this letter; what shall I do with it?"

"Read it, to be sure," returned Mademoiselle.

"I am afraid I ought not," said Charlotte. "My mother has often told me I should never read a letter given me by a young man without first giving it to her."

"Lord bless you, my dear girl!" cried the teacher, smiling, "have you a mind to be in leading strings all your lifetime? Prithee, open the letter, read it, and judge for yourself. If you show it to your mother, the consequence will be, you will be taken from school, and a strict guard kept over you, so you will stand no chance of ever seeing the smart young officer again."

"I should not like to leave school yet," replied Charlotte, "till I have attained a greater proficiency in my Italian and music. But you can, if you please, Mademoiselle, take the letter back to Montraville, and tell him I wish him well, but cannot, with any propriety, enter into a clandestine correspondence with him."

She laid the letter on the table, and began to undress herself.

"Well," said La Rue, "I vow you are an unaccountable girl. Have you no curiosity to see the inside now? For my part, I could no more let a letter addressed to me lie unopened so long than I could work miracles; he writes a good hand," continued she, turning the letter to look at the superscription.

"'Tis well enough," said Charlotte, drawing it towards her.

"He is a genteel young fellow," said La Rue, carelessly, folding up her apron at the same time; "but I think he is marked with the smallpox."

"Oh, you are greatly mistaken," said Charlotte, eagerly; "he has a remarkably clear skin and a fine complexion.

"His eyes, if I should judge by what I saw," said La Rue, "are gray, and want expression."

"By no means," replied Charlotte; "they are the most expressive eyes I ever saw."

"Well, child, whether they are gray or black is of no consequence; you have determined not to read his letter, so it is likely you will never either see or hear from him again."

Charlotte took up the letter, and Mademoiselle continued:

"He is most probably going to America; and if ever you should hear any account of him it may possibly be that he is killed; and though he loved you ever so fervently, though his last breath should be spent in a prayer for your happiness, it can be nothing to you; you can feel nothing for the fate of the man whose letter you will not open, and whose sufferings you will not alleviate, by permitting him to think you would remember him when absent and pray for his safety."

Charlotte still held the letter in her hand; her heart swelled at the conclusion of Mademoiselle's speech, and a tear dropped on the wafer that closed it.

"The wafer is not dry yet," said she, "and sure there can be no great harm —" She hesitated. La Rue was silent. "I may read it, Mademoiselle, and return it afterwards."

"Certainly," replied Mademoiselle.

"At any rate, I am determined not to answer it," continued Charlotte, as she opened the letter.

Here let me stop to make one remark, and trust me, my very heart aches while I write it; but certain I am that when once a woman has stifled the sense of shame in her own bosom — when once she has lost sight of the basis on which reputation, honor, everything that should be dear to the female heart, rests — she grows hardened in guilt, and will spare no pains to bring down innocence and beauty to the shocking level with herself; and this proceeds from that diabolical spirit of envy which repines at seeing another in full possession of that respect and esteem which she can no longer hope to enjoy.

Mademoiselle eyed the unsuspecting Charlotte, as she perused the letter, with malignant pleasure. She saw that the contents had awakened new emotions in her youthful bosom.

She encouraged her hopes, calmed her fears, and before they parted for the night, it was determined that she should meet Montraville on the ensuing evening.

DEATH AND PUNISHMENT

[Chapter XXXIII]

When Mrs. Beauchamp entered the apartment of the poor sufferer, she started back in horror. On a wretched bed, without hangings and poorly supplied with covering, lay the emaciated figure of what still retained the semblance of a lovely woman, though sickness had so altered her features that Mrs. Beauchamp had not the least recollection of her person.

In a corner of a room stood a woman washing, and shivering over a small fire, two healthy, but half-naked children. The infant was asleep beside its mother, and on a chair by the bedside stood a porringer and wooden spoon containing a little gruel, and a tea-cup with about two spoonsful of wine in it.

Mrs. Beauchamp had never before beheld such a scene of poverty; she shuddered involuntarily, and exclaiming, "Heaven preserve us!" leaned on the back of the chair, ready to sink to the earth.

The doctor repented having so precipitately brought her into this affecting scene; but there was no time for apologies.

Charlotte caught the sound of her voice, and starting almost out of bed, exclaimed:

"Angel of peace and mercy, art thou come to deliver me? Oh, I know you are, for whenever you were near me I felt eased of half my sorrows; but you don't know me, nor can I, with all the recollection that I am mistress of, remember your name just now; but I know that benevolent countenance and the softness of that voice, which has so often comforted the wretched Charlotte."

Mrs. Beauchamp had, during the time Charlotte was speaking, seated herself on the bed; and taking one of her hands, she looked at her attentively, and at the name of Charlotte she perfectly conceived the whole affair. A faint sickness came over her.

"Gracious Heaven!" said she, "is this possible?" and bursting into tears, she reclined the burning head of Charlotte on her own bosom, and folding her arms about her, wept over her in silence.

"Oh," said Charlotte, "you are very good to weep thus for me; it is a long time since I shed a tear for myself; my head and heart are both on fire; but these tears of yours seem to cool and refresh me.

"Oh, now I remember you said you would send a letter to my poor father; do you think he ever received it? or perhaps you may have brought me an answer; why don't you speak, madam?

"Does he say I may go home? Well, he is very good; I shall soon be ready."

She then made an effort to get out of bed; but being prevented, her frenzy again returned, and she raved with the greatest wildness and incoherence.

Mrs. Beauchamp, finding it was impossible for her to be removed, contented herself with ordering the apartment to be made more comfortable, and procuring a proper nurse for both mother and child; and having learned the particulars of Charlotte's fruitless application to Mrs. Crayton[1] from honest John, she amply rewarded him for his benevolence, and returned home with a heart oppressed with many painful sensations, but yet rendered easy by the reflection that she had performed her duty towards a distressed fellow-creature.

Early next morning she again visited Charlotte, and found her tolerably composed; she called her by name, thanked her for her goodness, and when her child was brought to her, pressed it in her arms, wept over it, and called it the offspring of disobedience.

Mrs. Beauchamp was delighted to see her so much amended, and began to hope she might recover, and in spite of her former errors, become a useful and respectable member of society; but the arrival of the doctor put an end to these delusive hopes; he said nature was making her last effort, and a few hours would most probably consign the unhappy girl to her kindred dust.

Being asked how she found herself, she replied:

"Why, better, much better, doctor. I hope now I have but little more to suffer. I had last night a few hours' sleep, and when I awoke recovered the whole power of recollection. I am quite sensible of my weakness; I feel I have but little longer to combat with the shafts of affliction. I have an humble confidence in the mercy of Him who died to save the world, and trust that my sufferings in this state of mortality, joined to my unfeigned repentance, through His mercy, have blotted my offences from the sight of my offended Maker. I have but one care — my poor infant! Father of mercy!" continued she, raising her eyes, "of thy infinite goodness, grant that the sins of the parent be not visited on the unoffending child. May those who taught me to despise Thy laws be forgiven; lay not my offences to their charge I beseech

---

[1] The married name of Mademoiselle La Rue.

Thee; and oh! shower the choicest of Thy blessings on those whose pity
has soothed the afflicted heart, and made easy even the bed of pain
and sickness."

She was exhausted by this fervent address to the throne of mercy,
and though her lips still moved, her voice became inarticulate; she lay
for some time, as it were, in a doze, and then recovering, faintly
pressed Mrs. Beauchamp's hand, and then requested that a clergyman
might be sent for.

On his arrival, she joined fervently in the pious office, frequently
mentioning her ingratitude to her parents as what lay most heavy at
her heart.

When she had performed the last solemn duty, and was preparing
to lie down, a little bustle outside the door occasioned Mrs. Beauchamp
to open it and inquire the cause.

A man, in appearance about forty, presented himself, and asked for
Mrs. Beauchamp.

"That is my name, sir," said she.

"Oh, then, my dear madam," cried he, "tell me where I may find my
poor, ruined, but repentant child."

Mrs. Beauchamp was surprised and much affected; she knew not
what to say; she foresaw the agony this interview would occasion Mr.
Temple, who had just arrived in search of Charlotte, and yet was
sensible that the pardon and blessing of the father would soften even
the agonies of death to the daughter.

She hesitated.

"Tell me, madam," said he, wildly, "tell me, I beseech thee, does
she live? Shall I see my darling once again? Perhaps she is in this
house. Lead — lead me to her, that I may bless her, and then lie down
and die."

The ardent manner in which he uttered these words occasioned him
to raise his voice.

It caught the ear of Charlotte; she knew the beloved sound, and
uttering a loud shriek, she sprang forward as Mr. Temple entered the
room.

"My adored father!"

"My long lost child!"

Nature could support no more, and they both sank lifeless into the
arms of the attendants.

Charlotte was again put into bed, and a few moments restored Mr.
Temple; but to describe the agonies of his sufferings is past the power
of any one. Though we can readily conceive, we cannot delineate the
dreadful scene.

Every eye gave testimony of what each other felt — but all were
silent.

When Charlotte recovered, she found herself supported in her father's arms.

She cast upon him a most impressive look, but was unable to speak.

A reviving cordial was administered.

She then asked in a low voice for her child.

It was brought to her; she put it in her father's arms.

"Protect her," said she, "and bless your dying —"

Unable to finish the sentence, she sunk back on her pillow; her countenance was serenely composed; she regarded her father as he pressed the infant to his breast, with a steadfast look; a sudden beam of joy passed across her languid features: she raised her eyes to heaven — and then closed them forever.

RETRIBUTION

[Chapter XXXIV]

In the meantime, Montraville had received orders to return to New York, arrived, and having some feeling of compassionate tenderness for the woman whom he regarded as brought to shame by himself he went in search of Belcour, to inquire whether she was safe, and whether the child lived.

He found him immersed in dissipation, and could gain no other intelligence than that Charlotte had left him, and that he knew not what had become of her.

"I cannot believe it possible," said Montraville, "that a mind once so pure as Charlotte Temple's should so suddenly become the mansion of vice. Beware, Belcour," continued he, "beware if you have dared to behave either unjustly or dishonorably to that poor girl, your life shall pay the forfeit; I will avenge her cause."

He immediately went into the country, to the house where he had left Charlotte. It was desolate.

After much inquiry he at length found the servant girl who had lived with her.

From her he learned the misery Charlotte had endured from the complicated evils of illness, poverty, and a broken heart, and that she had set out for New York on a cold winter's evening; but she could inform him no further.

Tortured almost to madness by this shocking account, he returned to the city, but before he reached it, the evening was drawing to a close.

In entering the town, he was obliged to pass several little huts, the residences of poor women, who supported themselves by washing the clothes of the officers and soldiers.

It was nearly dark; he heard from a neighboring steeple a solemn toll that seemed to say, some poor mortal was going to their last mansion; the sound struck on the heart of Montraville, and he involuntarily stopped, when from one of the houses he saw the appearance of a funeral.

Almost unknowing what he did, he followed at a small distance; and as they let the coffin into the grave, he inquired of a soldier, who stood by, and had just wiped off a tear that did honor to his heart, who it was that was just buried.

"An' please your honor," said the man, " 'tis a poor girl that was brought from her friends by a cruel man, who left her when she was big with a child, and married another."

Montraville stood motionless, and the man proceeded.

"I met her myself, not a fortnight since, one night, all cold and wet in the street; she went to Madam Crayton's, but she would not take her in and so the poor thing went raving mad."

Montraville could bear no more; he struck his hands against his forehead with violence, and exclaiming, "poor murdered Charlotte!" ran with precipitation towards the place where they were heaping the earth on her remains.

"Hold — hold! one moment," said he, "close not the grave of the injured Charlotte Temple, till I have taken vengeance on her murderer."

"Rash young man," said Mr. Temple, "who art thou that thus disturbest the last mournful rites of the dead, and rudely breakest in upon the grief of an afflicted father?"

"If thou art the father of Charlotte Temple," said he, gazing at him with mingled horror and amazement — "if thou art her father — I am Montraville."

Then, falling on his knees, he continued: "Here is my bosom. I bare it to receive the stroke I merit. Strike — strike now, and save me from the misery of reflection."

"Alas!" said Mr. Temple, "if thou wert the seducer of my child, thy own reflections be thy punishment. I wrest not the power from the hand of Omnipotence. Look on that little heap of earth; there hast thou buried the only joy of a fond father. Look at it often; and may thy heart feel such sorrow as shall merit the mercy of Heaven."

He turned from him, and Montraville, starting up from the ground where he had thrown himself, and that instant remembering the perfidy of Belcour, flew like lightning to his lodgings. Belcour was intoxicated; Montraville impetuous; they fought, and the sword of the latter entered the heart of his adversary.

He fell, and expired almost instantly. Montraville had received a slight wound, and, overcome with the agitation of his mind, and loss of blood, was carried in a state of insensibility to his distracted wife.

A dangerous illness and obstinate delirium ensued, during which he raved incessantly for Charlotte, but a strong constitution, and the tender assiduities of Julia, in time overcame the disorder.

He recovered, but to the end of his life was subject to severe fits of melancholy, and while he remained in New York, frequently retired to the churchyard, where he wept over the grave, and regretted the untimely fate of the lovely Charlotte Temple.[1]

CONCLUSION

[Chapter XXXV]

Shortly after the interment of his daughter, Mr. Temple, with his dear little charge and her nurse, set forward for England.

It would be impossible to do justice to the meeting-scene between him and his Lucy, and her aged father. Every heart of sensibility can easily conceive their feelings.

After the first tumult of grief was subsided, Mrs. Temple gave up the chief of her time to her grandchild, and as she grew up and improved, began almost to fancy she again possessed her Charlotte.

It was about ten years after these painful events, that Mr. and Mrs. Temple, having buried their father, were obliged to come to London on particular business, and brought the little Lucy with them.

They had been walking one evening, when, on their return they found a poor wretch sitting on the steps of the door.

She attempted to rise as they approached, but from extreme weakness was unable, and after several fruitless efforts fell back in a fit.

Mr. Temple was not one of those men who stand to consider whether by assisting an object of distress they shall not inconvenience themselves, but, instigated by a noble, feeling heart, immediately ordered her to be carried into the house and proper restoratives applied.

She soon recovered, and fixing her eye on Mrs. Temple, cried:

"You know not, madam, what you do; you know not whom you are relieving, or you would curse me in the bitterness of your heart. Come not near me, madam, I shall contaminate you. I am the viper that stung your peace. I am the woman who turned the poor Charlotte out to perish in the street. Heaven have mercy! I see her now," continued she, looking at Lucy; "such — such was the fair bud of innocence that my vile arts blasted ere it was half blown."

It was in vain that Mr. and Mrs. Temple entreated her to be composed and take some refreshment.

She only drank half a glass of wine, and then told them she had been separated from her husband seven years, the chief of which she

[1] The grave of Charlotte Stanley, in Trinity Churchyard in New York, was long presumed to be that of the original of Charlotte Temple.

passed in riot, dissipation and vice, till, overtaken by poverty and sickness, she had been reduced to part with every valuable, and thought only of ending her life in prison, when a benevolent friend paid her debts and released her; but that, her illness increasing, she had no possible means of supporting herself, and her friends were weary of relieving her. "I have fasted," said she, "two days, and last night laid my aching head on the cold pavement; indeed, indeed, it was but just that I should experience those miseries myself, which I unfeelingly inflicted on others."

Greatly as Mr. Temple had reason to detest Mrs. Crayton, he could not behold her in this distress without some emotions of pity.

He gave her shelter that night beneath his hospitable roof, and the next day got her admission into a hospital, where, having lingered a few weeks, she died, a striking example that vice, however prosperous in the beginning, in the end leads on to misery and shame.

◅ Charles Brockden Brown (1771–1810)

PHILADELPHIA was the center of American intellectual activity in the early years of the Republic. With wartime tensions relaxed, its society was looking for diversion and seeking to assert a cultural as well as a political independence. As a Philadelphian, Charles Brockden Brown was singularly well situated to become the father of the American novel, the first professional man of letters in America. Educated at the Quaker Latin School of Robert Proud, Brown turned to the study of law, but by the age of nineteen found himself much more attracted to literature, and by 1795 had completely given up the law. Fascinated by poetry — he had, before he was sixteen, planned several long epics — he met the brilliant Dr. Elihu Hubbard Smith, who introduced him to Timothy Dwight among other Connecticut Wits and, in New York, to William Dunlap and the literary society known as the Friendly Club. But surrendering poetry for the essay and prose fiction (he considered himself a "story-telling moralist"), he published *Alcuin,* a defense of women's rights, in 1798; and he spent the next four years producing the six novels on which his fame rests — *Wieland* (1798), *Edgar Huntly* (1799), *Ormond* (1799), *Arthur Mervyn* (1799–1800), *Clara Howard* (1801), and *Jane Talbot* (1801). He returned to Philadelphia, kept store, edited periodicals, renounced the novel as a form, contributed regularly to his own *American Register, or General Repository of History, Politics, and Science,* and died of tuberculosis at thirty-nine.

Brown managed to weave sensation, Gothic mystery, sentiment, extravagant adventure, high terror, and native scenes into stories that remain compelling in spite of his often turgid style and clumsy structure. The novels evince Brown's interest in gimmicks like ventriloquism and death by spontaneous combustion in *Wieland*, or Edgar Huntly's discovery (following the episode given here) that he suffers from sleepwalking; his delight in Poesque ratiocination and horror; and a proclivity for sensational episodes like the plague scenes in *Ormond* and *Arthur Mervyn*. But always behind his extravagant inventions is the sturdy social philosophy Brown derived from the eighteenth-century rationalism of Mary Wollstonecraft and William Godwin.

TEXTS: Charles Brockden Brown, *Edgar Huntly, or Memoirs of a Sleep-Walker* (Philadelphia, 1887); *The Monthly Magazine*, III, 7–10 (July 1800).

The Novelist and the Patron

[Letter to Thomas Jefferson, December 15, 1798; letter from Jefferson to Brown, January 15, 1799][1]

Sir:

After some hesitation a stranger to the person, though not to the character of Thomas Jefferson, ventures to entreat his acceptance of the volume by which this is accompanied. He is unacquainted with the degree in which your time and attention is engrossed by your public office; he knows not in what way your studious hours are distributed and whether mere works of imagination and invention are not excluded from your notice. He is even doubtful whether this letter will be opened or read, or, if read, whether its contents will not be instantly dismissed from your memory; so much a stranger is he, though a citizen of the United States, to the private occupations and modes of judging of the most illustrious of his fellow citizens.

To request your perusal of a work [*Wieland*] which at the same time is confessed to be unworthy of perusal will be an uncommon proof of absurdity. In thus transmitting my book to you I tacitly acknowledge my belief that it is capable of affording you pleasure and of entitling the writer to some portion of your good opinion. If I had not this belief, I should unavoidably be silent.

I am conscious, however, that this form of composition may be regarded by you with indifference or contempt, that social and intellectual theories, that the history of facts in the processes of nature and the operations of government may appear to you the only laudable pursuits; that fictitious narratives in their own nature or in the manner

[1] From David Lee Clark, *Charles Brockden Brown, Pioneer Voice of America* (Durham, N.C., 1952), pp. 163–164.

in which they have been hitherto conducted may be thought not to deserve notice, and that, consequently, whatever may be the merit of my book as a fiction, yet it is to be condemned because it is a fiction.

I need not say that my own opinions are different. I am therefore obliged to hope that an artful display of incidents, the powerful delineation of characters and the train of eloquent and judicious reasoning which may be combined in a fictitious work, will be regarded by Thomas Jefferson with as much respect as they are regarded by me.

No man holds a performance which he has deliberately offered to the world in contempt; but, if he be a man of candor and discernment, his favorable judgment of his own work will always be attended by diffidence and fluctuation. I confess I foster the hope that Mr. Jefferson will be induced to open the book that is here offered him; that when he has begun it he will find himself prompted to continue, and that he will not think the time employed upon it tediously or uselessly consumed.

With more than this I dare not flatter myself. That he will be pleased to any uncommon degree, and that, by his recommendation, he will contribute to diffuse the knowledge of its author, and facilitate a favorable reception to future performances, is a benefit far beyond the expectations, though certainly the object of the fondest wishes of

CHARLES B. BROWN

[Exactly a month later, Jefferson answered.]

Sir:

I received on my arrival here some days ago the copy of the book you were so kind as to send me together with your letter, for which be pleased to accept my thanks. As soon as I am in a situation to admit it (which is hardly the case here), I shall read it, and I doubt not with great pleasure. Some of the most agreeable moments of my life have been spent in reading works of imagination, which have this advantage over history, that the incidents of the former may be dressed in the most interesting form, while those of the latter must be confined to fact. They cannot therefore possess virtue in the best and vice in the worst forms possible, as the former may. I have the honor to be with great consideration, Sir.

Your most obed. servt.
TH. JEFFERSON

On a Scheme for Describing American Manners;
Addressed to a Foreigner

[From *The Monthly Magazine,* July 1800]

What strange project is this which you describe? A picture of American manners! A view of our social, domestic, economical state! Such as foreign and future observers, as well as contemporary ones, shall point to and say, "This is the scene displayed by four millions of actors on the vast stage bounded by the Ocean, Florida, Mississippi, and St. Lawrence, for the three lustrums ensuing the revolution which made the Anglo-Belgico-Teutonico-North Americans a nation." Are you aware of the many difficulties attending such a scheme?

Only reflect upon the motleyness, the endless variety of habits, ranks, and conditions in our country. The theatre itself is too wide for you to traverse: a thousand miles one way, and fifteen hundred the other: various in climate from the ceaseless ardors of the tropic to the horrors of the arctic winter: divided into near a score of separate states, in each of which there are very great peculiarities of constitution and laws; each of which has climate, soil, productions, distributions of property and rank somewhat different from those of its neighbors.

To know the manners of a people, their domestic maxims and habits, their social principles and prejudices, it is not sufficient to travel through their country. You must be the inmate of their houses and bosoms; you must have time to cultivate their confidence, to mark the steps of their education, the gradual unfolding of their character, as new connections, situations, and temptations successively arise. . . .

To estimate the manners, the social and political state of my country, it is not enough that I am born and reared in it. That can only make me acquainted with what immediately surrounds my birthplace or my dwelling, and this is no adequate specimen of the whole. If I am resident in the vicinity of Cape Cod, I am as little qualified to describe the state of universal manners, their state at Pittsburgh or Savannah, for example, as that of Toulon or Archangel. To fit me for this task, I must be multiplied an hundredfold, and be born and educated at once, if that were possible, at Charleston, Baltimore, and Salem. I must be, at the same time, a Catholic of Maryland, a Quaker of Pennsylvania, an English Episcopalian of New York, and a Congregationalist of Connecticut.

More than one traveler from Europe has undertaken to describe the state of society in the United States. Whatever he sees in an hasty journey through a small part of it, is instantly seized upon, and held up as a specimen of the whole. From incidents happening at an inn, or in a stagecoach, between one maritime city and another, or an object casually noticed by the way, an inference is confidently drawn in relation to the whole territory. "Such," says he, "is the practice in *America;* such is the ignorance or knowledge, the independence or prejudice, of *Americans.*" And his conclusions are just as sagacious as those of him who should infer the state of cultivation and manners in Turkey or Poland, or even in Ireland or Scotland, from what he meets with in a journey from Falmouth to London.

Look at the guise and manners of a tiller of the field in New Hampshire. What circumstance in his condition can give us the slightest knowledge of the tiller of the field in Georgia? The serfs in Bohemia are far more like the freeholders of Middlesex, in complexion, habits, liberty, knowledge, temperature, and products, than the New Hampshire ploughman is like the corn-planter of Roanoke or the rice-sower of Santee.

The [American] observer has, however, one advantage over the foreigner. His parentage and kindred are, at least, within the country; and, while he enjoys similar or better opportunities of surveying the whole, he is of necessity intimately and domestically acquainted with a part. He has had American parents and kinsfolk, tutors, playfellows, and friends. He has a family, a neighborhood, a study and profession, fellow citizens, and fellow sectaries. He is, to a small extent, therefore, practically versed in the effects of our social maxims and political condition. He himself is a product of the soil, is a sample of the beings which a North American climate, government, and education will produce. Those who are inquisitive as to their effects will closely and eagerly examine him, and he may contribute much to improve the science of human nature, and somewhat to a picture of his age and country, by minutely and faithfully portraying himself.

The Strange Adventures of a Sleepwalker

[From *Edgar Huntly,* 1799]

CHAPTER XV

Here, my friend, thou must permit me to pause. The following incidents are of a kind to which the most ardent invention has never conceived a parallel. Fortune, in her most wayward mood, could scarcely be suspected of an influence like this. The scene was pregnant with astonishment and horror. I cannot, even now, recall it without reviving the dismay and confusion which I then experienced. . . .

I have said that I slept. My memory assures me of this; it informs me of the previous circumstances of my laying aside my clothes, of placing the light upon a chair within reach of my pillow, of throwing myself upon the bed, and of gazing on the rays of the moon reflected on the wall and almost obscured by those of the candle. I remember my occasional relapses into fits of incoherent fancies, the harbingers of sleep. I remember, as it were, the instant when my thoughts ceased to flow and my senses were arrested by the leaden wand of forgetfulness.

My return to sensation and to consciousness took place in no such tranquil scene. I emerged from oblivion by degrees so slow and so faint, that their succession cannot be marked. When enabled at length to attend to the information which my senses afforded, I was conscious for a time of nothing but existence. It was unaccompanied with lassitude or pain, but I felt disinclined to stretch my limbs or raise my eyelids. My thoughts were wildering and mazy, and, though consciousness was present, it was disconnected with the locomotive or voluntary power.

From this state a transition was speedily effected. I perceived that my posture was supine, and that I lay upon my back. I attempted to open my eyes. The weight that oppressed them was too great for a slight exertion to remove. The exertion which I made cost me a pang more acute than any which I ever experienced. My eyes, however, were opened; but the darkness that environed me was as intense as before.

I attempted to rise, but my limbs were cold, and my joints had almost lost their flexibility. My efforts were repeated, and at length I attained a sitting posture. I was now sensible of pain in my shoulders and back. I was universally in that state to which the frame is reduced by blows of a club, mercilessly and endlessly repeated; my temples throbbed, and my face was covered with clammy and cold drops: but that which threw me into deepest consternation was my inability to see. I turned my head to different quarters; I stretched my eyelids, and exerted every visual energy, but in vain. I was wrapped in the murkiest and most impenetrable gloom.

The first effort of reflection was to suggest the belief that I was blind: that disease is known to assail us in a moment and without previous warning. This, surely, was the misfortune that had now befallen me. Some ray, however fleeting and uncertain, could not fail to be discerned, if the power of vision were not utterly extinguished. In what circumstances could I possibly be placed, from which every particle of light should, by other means, be excluded?

This led my thoughts into a new train. I endeavoured to recall the past; but the past was too much in contradiction to the present, and my intellect was too much shattered by external violence, to allow me accurately to review it.

Since my sight availed nothing to the knowledge of my condition, I betook myself to other instruments. The element which I breathed was stagnant and cold. The spot where I lay was rugged and hard. I was neither naked nor clothed: a shirt and trousers composed my dress, and the shoes and stockings, which always accompanied these, were now wanting. What could I infer from this scanty garb, this chilling atmosphere, this stony bed?

I had awakened as from sleep. What was my condition when I fell asleep? Surely it was different from the present. Then I inhabited a lightsome chamber and was stretched upon a down bed; now I was supine upon a rugged surface and immersed in palpable obscurity. Then I was in perfect health; now my frame was covered with bruises and every joint was racked with pain. What dungeon or den had received me, and by whose command was I transported hither?

After various efforts I stood upon my feet. At first I tottered and staggered. I stretched out my hands on all sides, but met only with vacuity. I advanced forward. At the third step my foot moved something which lay upon the ground: I stooped and took it up, and found, on examination, that it was an Indian tomahawk. This incident afforded me no hint from which I might conjecture my state.

Proceeding irresolutely and slowly forward, my hands at length touched a wall. This, like the flooring, was of stone, and was rugged and impenetrable. I followed this wall. An advancing angle occurred at a short distance, which was followed by similar angles. I continued to explore this clue, till the suspicion occurred that I was merely going round the walls of a vast and irregular apartment.

The utter darkness disabled me from comparing directions and distances. This discovery, therefore, was not made on a sudden, and was still entangled with some doubt. My blood recovered some warmth, and my muscles some elasticity; but in proportion as my sensibility returned, my pains augmented. Overpowered by my fears and my agonies, I desisted from my fruitless search, and sat down, supporting my back against the wall.

My excruciating sensations for a time occupied my attention. These, in combination with other causes, gradually produced a species of delirium. I existed, as it were, in a wakeful dream. With nothing to correct my erroneous perceptions, the images of the past occurred in capricious combinations and vivid hues. Methought I was the victim of some tyrant who had thrust me into a dungeon of his fortress, and left me no power to determine whether he intended I should perish with famine, or linger out a long life in hopeless imprisonment. Whether the day was shut out by insuperable walls, or the darkness that surrounded me was owing to the night and to the smallness of those crannies through which daylight was to be admitted, I conjectured in vain.

Sometimes I imagined myself buried alive. Methought I had fallen into seeming death, and my friends had consigned me to the tomb, from which a resurrection was impossible. That, in such a case, my limbs would have been confined to a coffin, and my coffin to a grave, and that I should instantly have been suffocated, did not occur to destroy my supposition. Neither did this supposition overwhelm me with terror or prompt my efforts at deliverance. My state was full of tumult and confusion, and my attention was incessantly divided between my painful sensations and my feverish dreams.

There is no standard by which time can be measured but the succession of our thoughts and the changes that take place in the external world. From the latter I was totally excluded. The former made the lapse of some hours appear like the tediousness of weeks and months. At length, a new sensation recalled my rambling meditations, and gave substance to my fears. I now felt the cravings of hunger, and perceived that, unless my deliverance were speedily effected, I must suffer a tedious and lingering death.

I once more tasked my understanding and my senses to discover the nature of my present situation and the means of escape. I listened to catch some sound. I heard an unequal and varying echo, sometimes near and sometimes distant, sometimes dying away and sometimes swelling into loudness. It was unlike any thing I had before heard, but it was evident that it arose from wind sweeping through spacious halls and winding passages. These tokens were incompatible with the result of the examination I had made. If my hands were true, I was immured between walls through which there was no avenue.

I now exerted my voice, and cried as loud as my wasted strength would admit. Its echoes were sent back to me in broken and confused sounds and from above. This effort was casual, but some part of that uncertainty in which I was involved was instantly dispelled by it. In passing through the cavern on the former day, I have mentioned the verge of the pit at which I arrived. To acquaint me as far as was possible with the dimensions of the place, I had hallooed with all my force, knowing that sound is reflected according to the distance and relative positions of the substances from which it is repelled.

The effect produced by my voice on this occasion resembled, with remarkable exactness, the effect which was then produced. Was I, then, shut up in the same cavern? Had I reached the brink of the same precipice and been thrown headlong into that vacuity? Whence else could arise the bruises which I had received, but from my fall? Yet all remembrance of my journey hither was lost. I had determined to explore this cave on the ensuing day, but my memory informed me not that this intention had been carried into effect. Still, it was only possible to conclude that I had come hither on my intended expedition, and had been thrown by another, or had, by some ill chance, fallen, into the pit.

This opinion was conformable to what I had already observed. The pavement and walls were rugged like those of the footing and sides of the cave through which I had formerly passed.

But if this were true, what was the abhorred catastrophe to which I was now reserved? The sides of this pit were inaccessible; human footsteps would never wander into these recesses. My friends were unapprized of my forlorn state. Here I should continue till wasted by famine. In this grave should I linger out a few days in unspeakable agonies, and then perish forever.

The inroads of hunger were already experienced; and this knowledge of the desperateness of my calamity urged me to frenzy. I had none but capricious and unseen fate to condemn. The author of my distress, and the means he had taken to decoy me hither, were incomprehensible. Surely my senses were fettered or depraved by some spell. I was still asleep, and this was merely a tormenting vision; or madness had seized me, and the darkness that environed and the hunger that afflicted me existed only in my own distempered imagination.

The consolation of these doubts could not last long. Every hour added to the proof that my perceptions were real. My hunger speedily became ferocious. I tore the linen of my shirt between my teeth and swallowed the fragments. I felt a strong propensity to bite the flesh from my arm. My heart overflowed with cruelty, and I pondered on the delight I should experience in rending some living animal to pieces, and drinking its blood and grinding its quivering fibres between my teeth.

This agony had already passed beyond the limits of endurance. I saw that time, instead of bringing respite or relief, would only aggravate my wants, and that my only remaining hope was to die before I should be assaulted by the last extremes of famine. I now recollected that a tomahawk was at hand, and rejoiced in the possession of an instrument by which I could so effectually terminate my sufferings.

I took it in my hand, moved its edge over my fingers, and reflected on the force that was required to make it reach my heart. I investigated the spot where it should enter, and strove to fortify myself with resolution to repeat the stroke a second or third time, if the first should prove insufficient. I was sensible that I might fail to inflict a mortal wound, but delighted to consider that the blood which would be made to flow would finally release me, and that meanwhile my pains would be alleviated by swallowing this blood.

You will not wonder that I felt some reluctance to employ so fatal though indispensable a remedy. I once more ruminated on the possibility of rescuing myself by other means. I now reflected that the upper termination of the wall could not be at an immeasurable distance from the pavement. I had fallen from a height; but if that height had been considerable, instead of being merely bruised, should I not have been dashed into pieces?

Gleams of hope burst anew upon my soul. Was it not possible, I asked, to reach the top of this pit? The sides were rugged and uneven. Would not their projectures and abruptnesses serve me as steps by which I might ascend in safety? This expedient was to be tried without delay. Shortly my strength would fail, and my doom would be irrevocably sealed.

I will not enumerate my laborious efforts, my alternations of despondency and confidence, the eager and unwearied scrutiny with which I examined the surface, the attempts which I made, and the failures which, for a time, succeeded each other. A hundred times, when I had ascended some feet from the bottom, I was compelled to relinquish my undertaking by the *untenable* smoothness of the spaces which remained to be gone over. A hundred times I threw myself, exhausted by fatigue and my pains, on the ground. The consciousness was gradually restored that, till I had attempted every part of the wall, it was absurd to despair, and I again drew my tottering limbs and aching joints to that part of the wall which had not been surveyed.

At length, as I stretched my hand upward, I found somewhat that seemed like a recession in the wall. It was possible that this was the top of the cavity, and this might be the avenue to liberty. My heart leaped with joy, and I proceeded to climb the wall. No undertaking could be conceived more arduous than this. The space between this verge and the floor was nearly smooth. The verge was higher from the bottom than my head. The only means of ascending that were offered me were by my hands, with which I could draw myself upward so as, at length, to maintain my hold with my feet.

My efforts were indefatigable, and at length I placed myself on the verge. When this was accomplished, my strength was nearly gone. Had I not found space enough beyond this brink to stretch myself at length, I should unavoidably have fallen backward into the pit, and all my pains had served no other end than to deepen my despair and hasten my destruction.

What impediments and perils remained to be encountered I could not judge. I was now inclined to forebode the worst. The interval of repose which was necessary to be taken, in order to recruit my strength, would accelerate the ravages of famine, and leave me without the power to proceed.

In this state, I once more consoled myself that an instrument of death was at hand. I had drawn up with me the tomahawk, being sensible that, should this impediment be overcome, others might remain that would prove insuperable. Before I employed it, however, I cast my eyes wildly and languidly around. The darkness was no less intense than in the pit below, and yet two objects were distinctly seen.

They resembled a fixed and obscure flame. They were motionless. Though lustrous themselves, they created no illumination around them. This circumstance, added to others, which reminded me of similar objects noted on former occasions, immediately explained the nature of what I beheld. These were the eyes of a panther.

Thus had I struggled to obtain a post where a savage was lurking and waited only till my efforts should place me within reach of his fangs. The first impulse was to arm myself against this enemy. The desperateness of my condition was, for a moment, forgotten. The weapon which was so lately lifted against my own bosom was now raised to defend my life against the assault of another.

There was no time for deliberation and delay. In a moment he might spring from his station and tear me to pieces. My utmost speed might not enable me to reach him where he sat, but merely to encounter his assault. I did not reflect how far my strength was adequate to save me. All the force that remained was mustered up and exerted in a throw.

No one knows the powers that are latent in his constitution. Called forth by imminent dangers, our efforts frequently exceed our most sanguine belief. Though tottering on the verge of dissolution, and apparently unable to crawl from this spot, a force was exerted in this throw, probably greater than I had ever before exerted. It was resistless and unerring. I aimed at the middle space between those glowing orbs. It penetrated the skull, and the animal fell, struggling and shrieking, on the ground.

My ears quickly informed me when his pangs were at an end. His cries and his convulsions lasted for a moment and then ceased. The effect of his voice, in these subterranean abodes, was unspeakably rueful.

The abruptness of this incident, and the preternatural exertion of my strength, left me in a state of languor and sinking, from which slowly and with difficulty I recovered. The first suggestion that occurred was to feed upon the carcass of this animal. My hunger had arrived at that pitch where all fastidiousness and scruples are at an end. I crept to the spot. I will not shock you by relating the extremes to which dire necessity had driven me. I review this scene with loathing and horror. Now that it is past I look back upon it as on some hideous dream. The whole appears to be some freak of insanity. No alternative was offered, and hunger was capable of being appeased even by a banquet so detestable.

If this appetite has sometimes subdued the sentiments of nature, and compelled the mother to feed upon the flesh of her offspring, it will not excite amazement that I did not turn from the yet warm blood and reeking fibres of a brute.

One evil was now removed, only to give place to another. The first sensations of fulness had scarcely been felt when my stomach was seized by pangs, whose acuteness exceeded all that I ever before experienced. I bitterly lamented my inordinate avidity. The excruciations of famine were better than the agonies which this abhorred meal had produced.

Death was now impending with no less proximity and certainty, though in a different form. Death was a sweet relief for my present miseries, and I vehemently longed for its arrival. I stretched myself on the ground. I threw myself into every posture that promised some alleviation of this evil. I rolled along the pavement of the cavern, wholly inattentive to the dangers that environed me. That I did not fall into the pit whence I had just emerged must be ascribed to some miraculous chance.

How long my miseries endured, it is not possible to tell. I cannot even form a plausible conjecture. Judging by the lingering train of my sensations, I should conjecture that some days elapsed in this deplorable condition; but nature could not have so long sustained a conflict like this.

Gradually my pains subsided, and I fell into a deep sleep. I was visited by dreams of a thousand hues. They led me to flowing streams and plenteous banquets, which, though placed within my view, some power forbade me to approach. From this sleep I recovered to the fruition of solitude and darkness, but my frame was in a state less feeble than before. That which I had eaten had produced temporary distress, but on the whole had been of use. If this food had not been provided for me I should scarcely have avoided death. I had reason, therefore, to congratulate myself on the danger that had lately occurred.

I had acted without foresight, and yet no wisdom could have prescribed more salutary measures. The panther was slain, not from a view to the relief of my hunger, but from the self-preserving and involuntary impulse. Had I foreknown the pangs to which my ravenous and bloody meal would give birth, I should have carefully abstained;

and yet these pangs were a useful effort of nature to subdue and convert to nourishment the matter I had swallowed.

I was now assailed by the torments of thirst. My invention and my courage were anew bent to obviate this pressing evil. I reflected that there was some recess from this cavern, even from the spot where I now stood. Before, I was doubtful whether in this direction from this pit any avenue could be found; but, since the panther had come hither, there was reason to suppose the existence of some such avenue.

I now likewise attended to a sound, which, from its invariable tenor, denoted somewhat different from the whistling of a gale. It seemed like the murmur of a running stream. I now prepared to go forward and endeavour to move along in that direction in which this sound apparently came.

On either side, and above my head, there was nothing but vacuity. My steps were to be guided by the pavement, which, though unequal and rugged, appeared, on the whole, to ascend. My safety required that I should employ both hands and feet in exploring my way.

I went on thus for a considerable period. The murmur, instead of becoming more distinct, gradually died away. My progress was arrested by fatigue, and I began once more to despond. My exertions produced a perspiration, which, while it augmented my thirst, happily supplied me with imperfect means of appeasing it.

This expedient would, perhaps, have been accidentally suggested; but my ingenuity was assisted by remembering the history of certain English prisoners in Bengal, whom their merciless enemy imprisoned in a small room, and some of whom preserved themselves alive merely by swallowing the moisture that flowed from their bodies. This experiment I now performed with no less success.

This was slender and transitory consolation. I knew that, wandering at random, I might never reach the outlet of this cavern, or might be disabled, by hunger and fatigue, from going farther than the outlet. The cravings which had lately been satiated would speedily return, and my negligence had cut me off from the resource which had recently been furnished. I thought not till now that a second meal might be indispensable.

To return upon my footsteps to the spot where the dead animal lay was a heartless project. I might thus be placing myself at a hopeless distance from liberty. Besides, my track could not be retraced. I had frequently deviated from a straight direction for the sake of avoiding impediments. All of which I was sensible was, that I was travelling up an irregular acclivity. I hoped some time to reach the summit, but had no reason for adhering to one line of ascent in preference to another.

To remain where I was was manifestly absurd. Whether I mounted or descended, a change of place was most likely to benefit me. I resolved to vary my direction, and instead of ascending, keep along the side of what I accounted a hill. I had gone some hundred feet when the murmur, before described, once more saluted my ear.

This sound, being imagined to proceed from a running stream, could not but light up joy in the heart of one nearly perishing with thirst. I proceeded with new courage. The sound approached no nearer, nor became more distinct; but, as long as it died not away, I was satisfied to listen and to hope.

I was eagerly observant if any the least glimmering of light should visit this recess. At length, on the right hand, a gleam, infinitely faint, caught my attention. It was wavering and unequal. I directed my steps towards it. It became more vivid and permanent. It was of that kind, however, which proceeded from a fire, kindled with dry sticks, and not from the sun. I now heard the crackling of flames.

This sound made me pause, or, at least, to proceed with circumspection. At length the scene opened, and I found myself at the entrance of a cave. I quickly reached a station, when I saw a fire burning. At first no other object was noted, but it was easy to infer that the fire was kindled by men, and that they who kindled it could be at no great distance.

CHAPTER XVI

Thus was I delivered from my prison, and restored to the enjoyment of the air and the light. Perhaps the chance was almost miraculous that led me to this opening. In any other direction, I might have involved myself in an inextricable maze and rendered my destruction sure; but what now remained to place me in absolute security? Beyond the fire I could see nothing; but, since the smoke rolled rapidly away, it was plain that on the opposite side the cavern was open to the air.

I went forward, but my eyes were fixed upon the fire: presently, in consequence of changing my station, I perceived several feet, and the skirts of blankets. I was somewhat startled at these appearances. The legs were naked, and scored into uncouth figures. The *moccasins* which lay beside them, and which were adorned in a grotesque manner, in addition to other incidents, immediately suggested the suspicion that they were Indians. No spectacle was more adapted than this to excite wonder and alarm. Had some mysterious power snatched me from the earth, and cast me, in a moment, into the heart of the wilderness? Was I still in the vicinity of my parental habitation, or was I thousands of miles distant?

Were these the permanent inhabitants of this region, or were they wanderers and robbers? While in the heart of the mountain, I had entertained a vague belief that I was still within the precincts of Norwalk. This opinion was shaken for a moment by the objects which I now beheld, but it insensibly returned: yet how was this opinion to be reconciled to appearances so strange and uncouth, and what measure did a due regard to my safety enjoin me to take?

I now gained a view of four brawny and terrific figures, stretched upon the ground. They lay parallel to each other, on their left sides; in consequence of which their faces were turned from me. Between each was an interval where lay a musket. Their right hands seemed placed upon the stocks of their guns, as if to seize them on the first moment of alarm.

The aperture through which these objects were seen was at the back of the cave, and some feet from the ground. It was merely large enough to suffer a human body to pass. It was involved in profound darkness, and there was no danger of being suspected or discovered as long as I maintained silence and kept out of view.

It was easily imagined that these guests would make but a short sojourn in this spot. There was reason to suppose that it was now night, and that, after a short repose, they would start up and resume their journey. It was my first design to remain shrouded in this covert till their departure, and I prepared to endure imprisonment and thirst somewhat longer.

Meanwhile my thoughts were busy in accounting for this spectacle. I need not tell thee that Norwalk is the termination of a sterile and narrow tract which begins in the Indian country. It forms a sort of rugged and rocky vein, and continues upwards of fifty miles. It is crossed in a few places by narrow and intricate paths, by which a communication is maintained between the farms and settlements on the opposite sides of the ridge.

During former Indian wars, this rude surface was sometimes traversed by the red men, and they made, by means of it, frequent and destructive inroads into the heart of the English settlements. During the last war, notwithstanding the progress of population, and the multiplied perils of such an expedition, a band of them had once penetrated into Norwalk, and lingered long enough to pillage and murder some of the neighbouring inhabitants.

I have reason to remember that event. My father's house was placed on the verge of this solitude. Eight of these assassins assailed it at the dead of night. My parents and an infant child were murdered in their beds; the house was pillaged, and then burnt to the ground. Happily, myself and my two sisters were abroad upon a visit. The preceding day had been fixed for our return to our father's house; but a storm occurred, which made it dangerous to cross the river, and, by obliging us to defer our journey, rescued us from captivity or death.

Most men are haunted by some species of terror or antipathy, which they are, for the most part, able to trace to some incident which befell them in their early years. You will not be surprised that the fate of my parents, and the sight of the body of one of this savage band, who, in the pursuit that was made after them, was overtaken and killed, should produce lasting and terrific images in my fancy. I never looked upon or called up the image of a savage without shuddering.

I knew that, at this time, some hostilities had been committed on the frontier; that a long course of injuries and encroachments had lately exasperated the Indian tribes; that an implacable and exterminating war was generally expected. We imagined ourselves at an inaccessible distance from the danger; but I could not but remember that this persuasion was formerly as strong as at present, and that an expedition which had once succeeded might possibly be attempted again. Here was every token of enmity and bloodshed. Each prostrate figure was furnished with a rifled musket, and a leathern bag tied round his waist, which was, probably, stored with powder and ball.

From these reflections, the sense of my own danger was revived and enforced; but I likewise ruminated on the evils which might impend over others. I should, no doubt, be safe by remaining in this nook; but might not some means be pursued to warn others of their danger? Should they leave this spot without notice of the approach being given to the fearless and pacific tenants of the neighbouring district, they might commit, in a few hours, the most horrid and irreparable devastation.

The alarm could only be diffused in one way. Could I not escape, unperceived, and without alarming the sleepers, from this cavern? The slumber of an Indian is broken by the slightest noise; but, if all noise be precluded, it is commonly profound. It was possible, I conceived, to leave my present post, to descend into the cave, and issue forth without the smallest signal. Their supine posture assured me that they were asleep. Sleep usually comes at their bidding, and if, perchance, they should be wakeful at an unseasonable moment, they always sit upon their haunches, and leaning their elbows on their knees, consume the tedious hours in smoking. My peril would be great. Accidents which I could not foresee, and over which I had no command, might occur to awaken some one at the moment I was passing the fire. Should I pass in safety, I might issue forth into a wilderness, of which I had no knowledge, where I might wander till I perished with famine, or where my footsteps might be noted and pursued and overtaken by these implacable foes. These perils were enormous and imminent; but I likewise considered that I might be at no great distance from the habitations of men, and that my escape might rescue them from the most dreadful calamities. I determined to make this dangerous experiment without delay.

I came nearer to the aperture, and had, consequently, a larger view of this recess. To my unspeakable dismay, I now caught a glimpse of one seated at the fire. His back was turned towards me, so that I could distinctly survey his gigantic form and fantastic ornaments.

My project was frustrated. This one was probably commissioned to watch and to awaken his companions when a due portion of sleep had been taken. That he would not be unfaithful or remiss in the performance of the part assigned to him was easily predicted. To pass him without exciting his notice (and the entrance could not otherwise be reached) was impossible. Once more I shrunk back, and revolved with hopelessness and anguish the necessity to which I was reduced.

This interval of dreary foreboding did not last long. Some motion in him that was seated by the fire attracted my notice. I looked, and beheld him rise from his place and go forth from the cavern. This unexpected incident led my thoughts into a new channel. Could not some advantage be taken of his absence? Could not this opportunity be seized for making my escape? He had left his gun and hatchet on the ground. It was likely, therefore, that he had not gone far, and would speedily return. Might not these weapons be seized, and some provision be thus made against the danger of meeting him without, or of being pursued?

Before a resolution could be formed, a new sound saluted my ear. It was a deep groan, succeeded by sobs that seemed struggling for utterance but were vehemently counteracted by the sufferer. This low and bitter lamentation apparently proceeded from some one within the cave. It could not be from one of this swarthy band. It must, then, proceed from a captive, whom they had reserved for torment or servitude, and who had seized the opportunity afforded by the absence of him that watched to give vent to his despair.

I again thrust my head forward, and beheld, lying on the ground, apart from the rest, and bound hand and foot, a young girl. Her dress was the coarse russet garb of the country, and bespoke her to be some farmer's daughter. Her features denoted the last degree of fear and anguish, and she moved her limbs in such a manner as showed that the ligatures by which she was confined produced, by their tightness, the utmost degree of pain.

My wishes were now bent not only to preserve myself and to frustrate the future attempts of these savages, but likewise to relieve this miserable victim. This could only be done by escaping from the cavern and returning with seasonable aid. The sobs of the girl were likely to rouse the sleepers. My appearance before her would prompt her to testify her surprise by some exclamation or shriek. What could hence be predicted but that the band would start on their feet and level their unerring pieces at my head?

I know not why I was insensible to these dangers. My thirst was rendered by these delays intolerable. It took from me, in some degree, the power of deliberation. The murmurs which had drawn me hither continued still to be heard. Some torrent or cascade could not be far distant from the entrance of the cavern, and it seemed as if one draught of clear water was a luxury cheaply purchased by death itself. This, in addition to considerations more disinterested, and which I have already mentioned, impelled me forward.

The girl's cheek rested on the hard rock, and her eyes were dim with tears. As they were turned towards me, however, I hoped that my movements would be noticed by her gradually and without abruptness. This expectation was fulfilled. I had not advanced many steps before she discovered me. This moment was critical beyond all others in the course of my existence. My life was suspended, as it were, by a spider's thread. All rested on the effect which this discovery should make upon this feeble victim.

I was watchful of the first movement of her eye which should indicate a consciousness of my presence. I laboured, by gestures and looks, to deter her from betraying her emotion. My attention was, at the same time, fixed upon the sleepers, and an anxious glance was cast towards the quarter whence the watchful savage might appear.

I stooped and seized the musket and hatchet. The space beyond the fire was, as I expected, open to the air. I issued forth with trembling steps. The sensations inspired by the dangers which environed me, added to my recent horrors, and the influence of the moon, which had now gained the zenith, and whose lustre dazzled my long-benighted senses, cannot be adequately described.

For a minute, I was unable to distinguish objects. This confusion was speedily corrected, and I found myself on the verge of a steep. Craggy eminences arose on all sides. On the left hand was a space that offered some footing, and hither I turned. A torrent was below me, and this path appeared to lead to it. It quickly appeared in sight, and all foreign cares were, for a time, suspended.

This water fell from the upper regions of the hill, upon a flat projecture which was continued on either side, and on part of which I was now standing. The path was bounded on the left by an inaccessible wall, and on the right terminated, at the distance of two or three feet from the wall, in a precipice. The water was eight or ten paces distant, and no impediment seemed likely to rise between us. I rushed forward with speed.

My progress was quickly checked. Close to the falling water, seated on the edge, his back supported by the rock, and his legs hanging over the precipice, I now beheld the savage who left the cave before me. The noise of the cascade and the improbability of interruption, at least from this quarter, had made him inattentive to my motions.

I paused. Along this verge lay the only road by which I could reach the water, and by which I could escape. The passage was completely occupied by this antagonist. To advance towards him, or to remain where I was, would produce the same effect. I should, in either case, be detected. He was unarmed; but his outcries would instantly summon his companions to his aid. I could not hope to overpower him, and pass him in defiance of his opposition. But, if this were effected, pursuit would be instantly commenced. I was unacquainted with the way. The way was unquestionably difficult. My strength was nearly annihilated; I should be overtaken in a moment, or their deficiency in speed would be supplied by the accuracy of their aim. Their bullets, at least, would reach me.

There was one method of removing this impediment. The piece which I held in my hand was cocked. There could be no doubt that it was loaded. A precaution of this kind would never be omitted by a warrior of this hue. At a greater distance than this, I should not fear to reach the mark. Should I not discharge it, and, at the same moment, rush forward to secure the road which my adversary's death would open to me?

Perhaps you will conceive a purpose like this to have argued a sanguinary and murderous disposition. Let it be remembered, however, that I entertained no doubts about the hostile designs of these men. This was sufficiently indicated by their arms, their guise, and the captive who attended them. Let the fate of my parents be, likewise, remembered. I was not certain but that these very men were the assassins of my family, and were those who had reduced me and my sisters to the condition of orphans and dependents. No words can describe the torments of my thirst. Relief to these torments, and safety to my life, were within view. How could I hesitate?

Yet I did hesitate. My aversion to bloodshed was not to be subdued but by the direst necessity. I knew, indeed, that the discharge of a musket would only alarm the enemies who remained behind; but I had another and a better weapon in my grasp. I could rive the head of my adversary, and cast him headlong, without any noise which should be heard, into the cavern.

Still I was willing to withdraw, to re-enter the cave, and take shelter in the darksome recesses from which I had emerged. Here I might remain, unsuspected, till these detested guests should depart. The hazards attending my re-entrance were to be boldly encountered, and the torments of unsatisfied thirst were to be patiently endured, rather than imbrue my hands in the blood of my fellow-men. But this expedient would be ineffectual if my retreat should be observed by this savage. Of that I was bound to be incontestably assured. I retreated, therefore, but kept my eye fixed at the same time upon the enemy.

Some ill fate decreed that I should not retreat unobserved. Scarcely had I withdrawn three paces when he started from his seat, and, turning towards me, walked with a quick pace. The shadow of the rock, and the improbability of meeting an enemy here, concealed me for a moment from his observation. I stood still. The slightest motion would have attracted his notice. At present, the narrow space engaged all his vigilance. Cautious footsteps, and attention to the path, were indispensable to his safety. The respite was momentary, and I employed it in my own defence.

How otherwise could I act? The danger that impended aimed at nothing less than my life. To take the life of another was the only method of averting it. The means were in my hand, and they were used. In an extremity like this, my muscles would have acted almost in defiance of my will.

The stroke was quick as lightning, and the wound mortal and deep. He had not time to descry the author of his fate, but, sinking on the path, expired without a groan. The hatchet buried itself in his breast, and rolled with him to the bottom of the precipice.

Never before had I taken the life of a human creature. On this head I had, indeed, entertained somewhat of religious scruples. These scruples did not forbid me to defend myself, but they made me cautious and reluctant to decide. Though they could not withhold my hand when urged by a necessity like this, they were sufficient to make me look back upon the deed with remorse and dismay.

I did not escape all compunction in the present instance, but the tumult of my feelings was quickly allayed. To quench my thirst was a consideration by which all others were supplanted. I approached the torrent, and not only drank copiously, but laved my head, neck, and arms, in this delicious element.

Early American Poetry

ᛉ John Trumbull (1750–1831)

THE poets and essayists known as the Hartford or Connecticut Wits were essentially a nucleus of four or five figures, who met at Yale College shortly before the Revolution, rejoined one another after the Revolution, and in the confusion caused by (or allowed by) the Articles of Confederation, commented on the social, political, and economic chaos in a series of poetic satires under the title *American Antiquities* (1786–87) — a pretended discovery of an ancient prophetic document called *The Anarchiad: A Poem on the Restoration of Chaos and Substantial Night.* Though its twenty-four books supported the Federalist position and were sent to persons of the highest rank in government, the work never amounted to much as a hoax, as a political instrument, or as poetry.

John Trumbull, the oldest of the group, came from a preacher's house (his mother was Jonathan Edwards' cousin), entered Yale at thirteen (having passed the entrance examinations at seven), took his B.A. in 1767, and continued at Yale for three more years. There he met Timothy Dwight in 1765 and David Humphreys in 1767; Joel Barlow joined the group somewhat later, as did other "wits," Lemuel Hopkins, Richard Alsop, Theodore Dwight, Elihu H. Smith, and Mason F. Cogswell. Trumbull gained the admiration of his younger colleagues by his graceful Addisonian essays and his satire on Yale in the Tom Brainless section of *The Progress of Dulness* (1772), written when he was a tutor. To placate the offended college officials, Trumbull added two more sections, which toned down the satire of the first part by generalizing the subjects into the typical eighteenth-century coquette and fop, Harriet Simper and Dick Hairbrain. He also excused himself by pointing out that the ideal end of satire is to "expose vice by general animadversions, and not to brand characters by personal satire."

353

Trumbull was admitted to the bar in 1773, and entered the Boston law office of John Adams; the following year he moved his practice to New Haven. In 1776 he issued the first two cantos of *M'Fingal*, which quickly became the most popular anti-Tory poem of the Revolution, going through thirty editions in sixty years. A distinguished judge of the Supreme Court of Errors and a state legislator until 1819, Trumbull revised his works in 1820, moved to Detroit five years later, and died there in 1831.

TEXT: John Trumbull, *Poetical Works* (Hartford, 1820), II, 11–33.

The Saga of Tom Brainless

[Part I of *The Progress of Dulness,* 1772]

"Our Tom has grown a sturdy boy;
His progress fills my heart with joy;
A steady soul, that yields to rule,
And quite ingenious too, at school.
Our master says, (I'm sure he's right,)
There's not a lad in town so bright.
He'll cypher bravely, write and read,
And say his catechism and creed,
And scorns to hesitate or falter
In Primer, Spelling-book or Psalter.
Hard work indeed, he does not love it;
His genius is too much above it.
Give him a good substantial teacher,
I'll lay he'd make a special preacher.
I've loved good learning all my life;
We'll send the lad to college, wife."
    Thus sway'd by fond and sightless passion,
His parents hold a consultation;
If on their couch, or round their fire,
I need not tell, nor you enquire.
    The point's agreed; the boy well pleased,
From country cares and labor eased;
No more to rise by break of day
To drive home cows, or deal out hay;
To work no more in snow or hail,
And blow his fingers o'er the flail,
Or mid the toils of harvest sweat
Beneath the summer's sultry heat,
Serene, he bids the farm, good-bye,
And quits the plough without a sigh.
Propitious to their constant friend,

The pow'rs of idleness attend.
   So to the priest in form he goes,
Prepared to study and to doze.
The parson, in his youth before,
Had run the same dull progress o'er;
His sole concern to see with care
His church and farm in good repair.
His skill in tongues, that once he knew,
Had bid him long, a last adieu;
Away his Latin rules had fled,
And Greek had vanish'd from his head.
   Then view our youth with grammar teazing,
Untaught in meaning, sense or reason;
Of knowledge e'er he gain his fill, he
Must diet long on husks of Lily,[1]
Drudge on for weary months in vain,
By mem'ry's strength, and dint of brain;
From thence to murd'ring Virgil's verse,
And construing Tully into farce,
Or lab'ring with his grave preceptor,
In Greek to blunder o'er a chapter.
The Latin Testament affords
The needed help of ready words;
At hand the Dictionary laid,
Gives up its page in frequent aid;
Hard by, the Lexicon and Grammar,
Those helps of mem'ry when they stammer;
The lesson's short; the priest contented;
His task to hear is sooner ended.
He lets him mind his own concerns,
Then tells his parents how he learns.
   Two years thus spent in gathering knowledge,
The lad sets forth t' unlade at college,
While down his sire and priest attend him,
To introduce and recommend him;
Or if detain'd, a letter's sent
Of much apocryphal content,
To set him forth, how dull soever,
As very learn'd and very clever;
A genius of the first emission,
With burning love for erudition;
So studious he'll outwatch the moon
And think the planets set too soon.
He had but little time to fit in;
Examination too must frighten.
Depend upon't he must do well,
He knows much more than he can tell;

---

[1] Lily's was the only Latin Grammar then in use. [Trumbull's note]

Admit him, and in little space
He'll beat his rivals in the race;
His father's incomes are but small,
He comes now, if he come at all.
    So said, so done, at college now
He enters well, no matter how;
New scenes awhile his fancy please,
But all must yield to love of ease.
In the same round condemn'd each day,
To study, read, recite and pray;
To make his hours of business double —
He can't endure th' increasing trouble;
And finds at length, as times grow pressing,
All plagues are easier than his lesson.
With sleepy eyes and count'nance heavy,
With much excuse of *non paravi*,[2]
Much absence, *tardes* and *egresses*,
The college-evil on him seizes.
Then ev'ry book, which ought to please,
Stirs up the seeds of dire disease;
Greek spoils his eyes, the print's so fine,
Grown dim with study, or with wine;
Of Tully's latin much afraid,
Each page, he calls the doctor's aid;
While geometry, with lines so crooked,
Sprains all his wits to overlook it.
His sickness puts on every name,
Its cause and uses still the same;
'Tis tooth-ache, cholic, gout or stone,
With phases various as the moon;
But though through all the body spread,
Still makes its cap'tal seat, the head.
In all diseases, 'tis expected,
The weakest parts be most infected.
    Kind head-ache hail! thou blest disease,
The friend of idleness and ease;
Who mid the still and dreary bound
Where college walls her sons surround,
In spite of fears, in justice' spite,
Assumest o'er laws dispensing right,
Sett'st from his task the blunderer free,
Excused by dulness and by thee.
Thy vot'ries bid a bold defiance
To all the calls and threats of science,
Slight learning human and divine,

---

[2] *Non paravi,* I have not prepared for recitation — an excuse commonly given; *tardes* and *egresses,* were terms used at college, for coming in late and going out before the conclusion of service. [Trumbull's note]

And hear no prayers, and fear no fine.
　And yet how oft the studious gain,
The dulness of a letter'd brain;
Despising such low things the while,
As English grammar, phrase and style;
Despising ev'ry nicer art,
That aids the tongue, or mends the heart;
Read ancient authors o'er in vain,
Nor taste one beauty they contain;
Humbly on trust accept the sense,
But deal for words at vast expense;
Search well how every term must vary
From Lexicon to Dictionary;
And plodding on in one dull tone,
Gain ancient tongues and lose their own,
Bid every graceful charm defiance,
And woo the skeleton of science.
　Come ye, who finer arts despise,
And scoff at verse as heathen lies;
In all the pride of dulness rage
At Pope, or Milton's deathless page;
Or stung by truth's deep-searching line,
Rave ev'n at rhymes as low as mine;
Say ye, who boast the name of wise,
Wherein substantial learning lies.
Is it, superb in classic lore,
To speak what Homer spoke before,
To write the language Tully wrote,
The style, the cadence and the note?
Is there a charm in sounds of Greek,
No language else can learn to speak;
That cures distemper'd brains at once,
Like Pliny's rhymes for broken bones?
Is there a spirit found in Latin,
That must evap'rate in translating?
And say are sense and genius bound
To any vehicles of sound?
Can knowledge never reach the brains,
Unless convey'd in ancient strains?
While Homer sets before your eyes
Achilles' rage, Ulysses' lies,
Th' amours of Jove in masquerade,
And Mars entrapp'd by Phœbus' aid;
While Virgil sings, in verses grave,
His lovers meeting in a cave,
His ships turn'd nymphs, in pagan fables,
And how the Trojans eat their tables;
While half this learning but displays

The follies of the former days;
And for our linguists, fairly try them,
A tutor'd parrot might defy them.
    Go to the vulgar — 'tis decreed,
There you must preach and write or plead;
Broach every curious Latin phrase
From Tully down to Lily's days:
All this your hearers have no share in,
Bate but their laughing and their staring.
Interpreters must pass between,
To let them know a word you mean.
    Yet could you reach that lofty tongue
Which Plato wrote and Homer sung;
Or ape the Latin verse and scanning,
Like Vida, Cowley or Buchanan;
Or bear ten phrase-books in your head;
Yet know, these languages are dead,
And nothing, e'er, by death, was seen
Improved in beauty, strength or mien,
Whether the sexton use his spade,
Or sorcerer wake the parted shade.
Think how would Tully stare or smile
At these wan spectres of his style,
Or Horace in his jovial way
Ask what these babblers mean to say.
    Let modern Logic next arise
With newborn light to glad your eyes,
Enthroned on high in Reason's chair,
Usurp her name, assume her air,
Give laws, to think with quaint precision,
And deal out loads of definition.
    Sense, in dull syllogisms confined,
Scorns these weak trammels of the mind,
Nor needs t' enquire by logic's leave
What to reject and what receive;
Throws all her trifling bulwarks down,
Expatiates free; while from her frown
Alike the dunce and pedant smart,
The fool of nature, or of art.
    On books of Rhetorick turn your hopes,
Unawed by figures or by tropes.
What silly rules in pomp appear!
What mighty nothings stun the ear!
Athroismos, Mesoteleuton,
Symploce and *Paregmenon!*[3]
Thus, in such sounds high rumbling, run
The names of jingle and of pun;

[3] Exaggerated figures of speech.

Thus shall your pathos melt the heart,
And shame the Greek and Roman art.
Say then, where solid learning lies
And what the toil that makes us wise!
Is it by mathematic's aid
To count the worlds in light array'd,
To know each star, that lifts its eye,
To sparkle in the midnight sky?
Say ye, who draw the curious line
Between the useful and the fine,
How little can this noble art
Its aid in human things impart,
Or give to life a cheerful ray,
And force our pains, and cares away.
Is it to know whate'er was done
Above the circle of the sun?
Is it to lift the active mind
Beyond the bounds by heaven assign'd;
And leave our little world at home,
Through realms of entity to roam;
Attempt the secrets dark to scan,
Eternal wisdom hid from man;
And make religion but the sign
In din of battle when to join?
Vain man, to madness still a prey,
Thy space a point, thy life a day,
A feeble worm, that aim'st to stride
In all the foppery of pride!
The glimmering lamp of reason's ray
Was given to guide thy darksome way.
Why wilt thou spread thy insect wings,
And strive to reach sublimer things?
Thy doubts confess, thy blindness own,
Nor vex thy thoughts with scenes unknown.
Indulgent heaven to man below,
Hath all explain'd we need to know;
Hath clearly taught enough to prove
Content below, and bliss above.
Thy boastful wish how proud and vain,
While heaven forbids the vaunting strain!
For metaphysics rightly shown
But teach how little can be known:
Though quibbles still maintain their station,
Conjecture serves for demonstration,
Armies of pens draw forth to fight,
And **** and **** write.[4]
Oh! might I live to see that day,

4 Unidentified authors.

When sense shall point to youths their way;
Through every maze of science guide;
O'er education's laws preside;
The good retain, with just discerning
Explode the quackeries of learning;
Give ancient arts their real due,
Explain their faults, and beauties too;
Teach where to imitate, and mend,
And point their uses and their end.
Then bright philosophy would shine,
And ethics teach the laws divine;
Our youths might learn each nobler art,
That shews a passage to the heart;
From ancient languages well known
Transfuse new beauties to our own;
With taste and fancy well refin'd,
Where moral rapture warms the mind,
From schools dismiss'd, with lib'ral hand,
Spread useful learning o'er the land;
And bid the eastern world admire
Our rising worth, and bright'ning fire.
    But while through fancy's realms we roam,
The main concern is left at home;
Return'd, our hero still we find
The same, as blundering and as blind.
    Four years at college dozed away
In sleep, and slothfulness and play,
Too dull for vice, with clearest conscience,
Charged with no fault but that of nonsense,
And nonsense long, with serious air,
Has wander'd unmolested there,
He passes trial, fair and free,
And takes in form his first degree.
    A scholar see him now commence
Without the aid of books or sense;
For passing college cures the brain,
Like mills to grind men young again.
The scholar-dress, that once array'd him,
The charm, *Admitto te ad gradum*,[5]
With touch of parchment can refine,
And make the veriest coxcomb shine,
Confer the gift of tongues at once,
And fill with sense the vacant dunce.
So kingly crowns contain quintessence
Of worship, dignity and presence;
Give learning, genius, virtue, worth,

---

[5] *Admitto te ad gradum*, I admit you to a degree; part of the words used in conferring the honours of college. [Trumbull's note]

Wit, valor, wisdom, and so forth;
Hide the bald pate, and cover o'er
The cap of folly worn before.
 Our hero's wit and learning now may
Be proved by token of diploma,
Of that diploma, which with speed
He learns to construe and to read;
And stalks abroad with conscious stride,
In all the airs of pedant pride,
With passport sign'd for wit and knowledge,
And current under seal of college.
 Few months now past, he sees with pain
His purse as empty as his brain;
His father leaves him then to fate,
And throws him off, as useless weight;
But gives him good advice, to teach
A school at first and then to preach.
 Thou reason'st well; it must be so;
For nothing else thy son can do.
As thieves of old, t' avoid the halter,
Took refuge in the holy altar;
Oft dulness flying from disgrace
Finds safety in that sacred place;
There boldly rears his head, or rests
Secure from ridicule or jests;
Where dreaded satire may not dare
Offend his wig's[6] extremest hair;
Where scripture sanctifies his strains,
And reverence hides the want of brains.
 Next see our youth at school appear,
Procured for forty pounds a year;
His ragged regiment round assemble,
Taught, not to read, but fear and tremble.
Before him, rods prepare his way,
Those dreaded antidotes to play.
Then throned aloft in elbow chair,
With solemn face and awful air,
He tries, with ease and unconcern,
To teach what ne'er himself could learn;
Gives law and punishment alone,
Judge, jury, bailiff, all in one;
Holds all good learning must depend
Upon his rod's extremest end,
Whose great electric virtue's such,
Each genius brightens at the touch;
With threats and blows, incitements pressing,

---

[6] A wig was then an essential part of the clerical dress. None appeared in
the pulpit without it. [Trumbull's note]

Drives on his lads to learn each lesson;
Thinks flogging cures all moral ills,
And breaks their heads to break their wills.
　　The year is done; he takes his leave;
The children smile; the parents grieve;
And seek again, their school to keep,
One just as good and just as cheap.
　　Now to some priest, that's famed for teaching,
He goes to learn the art of preaching;
And settles down with earnest zeal
Sermons to study, and to steal.
Six months from all the world retires
To kindle up his cover'd fires;
Learns, with nice art, to make with ease
The scriptures speak whate'er he please;
With judgment, unperceived to quote
What Pool explain'd, or Henry wrote;
To give the gospel new editions,
Split doctrines into propositions,
Draw motives, uses, inferences,
And torture words in thousand senses;
Learn the grave style and goodly phrase,
Safe handed down from Cromwell's days,
And shun, with anxious care, the while,
The infection of a modern style;
Or on the wings of folly fly
Aloft in metaphysic sky;
The system of the world explain,
Till night and chaos come again;
Deride what old divines can say,
Point out to heaven a nearer way;
Explode all known establish'd rules,
Affirm our fathers all were fools;
The present age is growing wise,
But wisdom in her cradle lies;
Late, like Minerva, born and bred,
Not from a Jove's, but scribbler's head,
While thousand youths their homage lend her,
And nursing fathers rock and tend her.
　　Round him much manuscript is spread,
Extracts from living works, and dead,
Themes, sermons, plans of controversy,
That hack and mangle without mercy,
And whence to glad the reader's eyes,
The future dialogue[7] shall rise.
　　At length, matured the grand design,

[7] Writing in dialogue was then a fashionable mode among the controversial divines. [Trumbull's note]

He stalks abroad, a grave divine.
    Mean while, from every distant seat,
At stated time the clergy meet.
Our hero comes, his sermon reads,
Explains the doctrine of his creeds,
A licence gains to preach and pray,
And makes his bow and goes his way.
    What though his wits could ne'er dispense
One page of grammar, or of sense;
What though his learning be so slight,
He scarcely knows to spell or write;
What though his skull be cudgel-proof!
He's orthodox, and that's enough.
    Perhaps with genius we'd dispense;
But sure we look at least for sense.
    Ye fathers of our church attend
The serious counsels of a friend,
Whose utmost wish, in nobler ways,
Your sacred dignity to raise.
Though blunt the style, the truths set down
Ye can't deny — though some may frown.
    Yes, there are men, nor these a few,
The foes of virtue and of you;
Who, nurtured in the scorner's school,
Make vice their trade, and sin by rule;
Who deem it courage heav'n to brave,
And wit, to scoff at all that's grave;
Vent stolen jests, with strange grimaces,
From folly's book of common-places;
While mid the simple throng around
Each kindred blockhead greets the sound,
And, like electric fire, at once,
The laugh is caught from dunce to dunce.
    The deist's scoffs ye may despise;
Within yourselves your danger lies;
For who would wish, neglecting rule,
To aid the triumphs of a fool?
From heaven at first your order came,
From heaven received its sacred name,
Indulged to man, to point the way,
That leads from darkness up to day.
Your highborn dignity attend,
And view your origin and end.
    While human souls are all your care,
By warnings, counsels, preaching, prayer,
In bands of christian friendship join'd,
Where pure affection warms the mind,
While each performs the pious race,

Nor dulness e'er usurps a place;
No vice shall brave your awful test,
Nor folly dare to broach the jest,
Each waiting eye shall humbly bend,
And reverence on your steps attend.
　But when each point of serious weight
Is torn with wrangling and debate,
When truth, mid rage of dire divisions,
Is left, to fight for definitions,
And fools assume your sacred place,
It threats your order with disgrace;
Bids genius from your seats withdraw,
And seek the pert, loquacious law;
Or deign in physic's paths to rank,
With every quack and mountebank;
Or in the ways of trade content,
Plod ledgers o'er of cent. per cent.
　While in your seats so sacred, whence
We look for piety and sense,
Pert dulness raves in school-boy style,
Your friends must blush, your foes will smile;
While men, who teach the glorious way,
Where heaven unfolds celestial day,
Assume the task sublime, to bring
The message of th' Eternal King,
Disgrace those honours they receive,
And want that sense, they aim to give.
Now in the desk, with solemn air,
Our hero makes his audience stare;
Asserts with all dogmatic boldness,
Where impudence is yoked to dulness;
Reads o'er his notes with halting pace,
Mask'd in the stiffness of his face;
With gestures such as might become
Those statues once that spoke at Rome,
Or Livy's ox, that to the state
Declared the oracles of fate,
In awkward tones, nor said, nor sung,
Slow rumbling o'er the falt'ring tongue,
Two hours his drawling speech holds on,
And names it preaching, when he's done.
　With roving tired, he fixes down
For life, in some unsettled town.
People and priest full well agree,
For why — they know no more than he.
Vast tracts of unknown land he gains,
Better than those the moon contains;
There deals in preaching and in prayer,

And starves on sixty pounds a year,
And culls his texts, and tills his farm,
Does little good, and little harm;
On Sunday, in his best array,
Deals forth the dulness of the day,
And while above he spends his breath,
The yawning audience nod beneath.
   Thus glib-tongued Merc'ry in his hand
Stretch'd forth the sleep-compelling wand,
Each eye in endless doze to keep —
The God of speaking, and of sleep.

⚫ Timothy Dwight (1752–1817)

THE Reverend Timothy Dwight, poet, preacher, and president
of Yale, came under the influence of John Trumbull when the
two were Yale undergraduates. His earliest major literary attempt
was a grand Biblical epic, the first of its kind in America, defined by Dwight as "A Fable related by a Poet, in order to raise
the Admiration, and inspire the love of Virtue, by representing
to us the Action of a Hero favour'd by Heaven, who brings
about a great Enterprize, notwithstanding the Obstacles he meets
in his way." The finished poem was a tumultuous, largely
Miltonic treatment of the wars of Joshua, in which Joshua turns
out so much the American hero that later readers insisted on
confusing him with George Washington. "In short," writes
Professor Leon Howard of the poem, "Dwight's poem was full
of eighteenth-century Americans with Hebrew names who talked
like Milton's angels and fought like prehistoric Greeks." Titled
The Conquest of Canaan, the poem was published in 1785.

   Dwight opened an academy in Greenfield, Connecticut, where
he was also Congregational pastor, in 1783. In 1787 he began
a seven-part poem on the happiness of America, which he published as *Greenfield Hill* in 1794, celebrating the beauties of the
countryside, the admirability of Connecticut institutions, and the
romance of local history. But as happy as America might be,
especially by contrast with Goldsmith's "Deserted Village," it had
its baleful side, which Dwight portrayed in a malevolent satire,
The Triumph of Infidelity (1788). From 1795 until his death
he was president of Yale, attracting many younger men to poetry
from this prominence.

   TEXTS: Vernon L. Parrington, ed., *The Connecticut Wits* (New
York, 1926).

Columbia

Columbia, Columbia, to glory arise,
The queen of the world, and child of the skies!
Thy genius commands thee; with rapture behold,
While ages on ages thy splendors unfold.
Thy reign is the last, and the noblest of time,
Most fruitful thy soil, most inviting thy clime;
Let the crimes of the east ne'er encrimson thy name.
Be freedom, and science, and virtue, thy fame.

To conquest, and slaughter, let Europe aspire;
Whelm nations in blood, and wrap cities in fire;
Thy heroes the rights of mankind shall defend,
And triumph pursue them, and glory attend.
A world is thy realm: for a world be thy laws,
Enlarg'd as thine empire, and just as thy cause;
On Freedom's broad basis, that empire shall rise,
Extend with the main, and dissolve with the skies.

Fair Science her gates to thy sons shall unbar,
And the east see thy morn hide the beams of her star.
New bards and new sages, unrival'd shall soar
To fame, unextinguish'd, when time is no more;
To fame, the last refuge of virtue design'd,
Shall fly from all nations the best of mankind;
Here, grateful to heaven, with transport shall bring
Their incense, more fragrant than odours of spring.

Nor less shall thy fair ones to glory ascend,
And Genius and Beauty in harmony blend;
The graces of form shall awake pure desire,
And the charms of the soul ever cherish the fire;
Their sweetness unmingled, their manners refin'd
And virtue's bright image, instamp'd on the mind,
With peace, and soft rapture, shall teach life to glow,
And light up a smile in the aspect of woe.

Thy fleets to all regions thy pow'r shall display,
The nations admire, and the ocean obey;
Each shore to thy glory its tribute unfold,
And the east and the south yield their spices and gold.
As the day-spring unbounded, thy splendor shall flow,
And earth's little kingdoms before thee shall bow,
While the ensigns of union, in triumph unfurl'd,
Hush the tumult of war, and give peace to the world.

Thus, as down a lone valley, with cedars o'erspread,
From war's dread confusion I pensively stray'd —
The gloom from the face of fair heav'n retir'd;
The winds ceas'd to murmur; the thunders expir'd;
Perfumes, as of Eden, flow'd sweetly along,
And a voice, as of angels, enchantingly sung;
"Columbia, Columbia, to glory arise,
The queen of the world, and the child of the skies."

(1777)

The Village Church and School

[From *Greenfield Hill*, 1794]

Beside yon church, that beams a modest ray,
With tidy neatness reputably gay,
When, mild and fair, as Eden's seventh-day light,
In silver silence, shines the Sabbath bright,
In neat attire, the village household come,
And learn the path-way to the eternal home.
Hail solemn ordinance! worthy of the SKIES;
When thousand richest blessings daily rise;
Peace, order, cleanliness, and manners sweet,
A sober mind, to rule submission meet,
Enlarging knowledge, life from guilt refin'd,
And love to God, and friendship to mankind.
In the clear splendour of thy vernal morn,
New-quicken'd man to light, and life, is born;
The desert of the mind with virtue blooms;
Its flowers unfold, its fruits exhale perfumes;
Proud guilt dissolves, beneath the searching ray,
And low debasement, trembling, creeps away;
Vice bites the dust; foul Error seeks her den;
And God, descending, dwells anew with men.
Where yonder humbler spire salutes the eye,
Its vane slow turning in the liquid sky,
Where, in light gambols, healthy striplings sport,
Ambitious learning builds her outer court;
A grave preceptor, there, her usher stands,
And rules, without a rod, her little bands.
Some half-grown sprigs of learning grac'd his brow:
Little he knew, though much he wish'd to know,
Inchanted hung o'er Virgil's honey'd lay,
And smiled, to see desipient Horace play;
Glean'd scraps of Greek; and, curious, trac'd afar,
Through Pope's clear glass, the bright Maeonian star.
Yet oft his students at his wisdom star'd,

For many a student to his side repair'd,
Surpriz'd, they heard him Dilworth's knots untie,
And tell, what lands beyond the Atlantic lie.

Many his faults; his virtues small, and few;
Some little good he did, or strove to do;
Laborious still, he taught the early mind,
And urg'd to manners meek, and thoughts refin'd;
Truth he impress'd, and every virtue prais'd;
While infant eyes, in wondering silence, gaz'd;
The worth of time would, day by day, unfold,
And tell them, every hour was made of gold.
Brown Industry he lov'd; and oft declar'd
How hardly Sloth, in life's sad evening, far'd; . . . .

The Parade of Satan's Army,
and His Final Defeat

[From *The Triumph of Infidelity*, 1788]

And now the morn arose; when o'er the plain
Gather'd, from every side, a numerous train;
To quell those fears, that rankled still within,
And gain new strength, and confidence, to sin.
There the half putrid Epicure was seen,
His cheeks of port, and lips with turtle green,
Who hop'd a long eternity was given,
To spread good tables, in some eating heaven.
The leacher there his lurid visage shew'd,
The imp of darkness, and the foe of good;
Who fled his lovely wife's most pure embrace,
To sate on hags, and breed a mongrel race;
A high-fed horse, for others wives who neigh'd;
A cur, who prowl'd around each quiet bed;
A snake, far spreading his impoison'd breath,
And charming innocence to guilt, and death.
Here stood Hypocrisy, in sober brown,
His sabbath face all sorrow'd with a frown.
A dismal tale he told of dismal times,
And this sad world brimful of saddest crimes,
Furrow'd his cheeks with tears for other's sin,
But clos'd his eyelids on the hell within.
There smil'd the smooth Divine, unus'd to wound
The sinners heart, with hell's alarming sound.
No terrors on his gentle tongue attend:
No grating truths the nicest ear offend.

That strange new-birth, that methodistic grace,
Nor in his heart, nor sermons, found a place.
Plato's fine tales he clumsily retold,
Trite, fireside, moral seesaws, dull as old;
His Christ, and bible, plac'd at good remove,
Guilt hell-deserving, and forgiving love.
'Twas best, he said, mankind should cease to sin;
Good fame requir'd it; so did peace within
Their honours, well he knew, would ne'er be driven;
But hop'd they still would please to go to heaven.
Each week, he paid his visitation dues;
Coax'd, jested, laugh'd; rehears'd the private news;
Smok'd with each goody, thought her cheese excell'd;
Her pipe he lighted, and her baby held.
Or plac'd in some great town, with lacquer'd shoes,
Trim wig, and trimmer gown, and glistening hose,
He bow'd, talk'd politics, learn'd manners mild;
Most meekly questioned, and most smoothly smil'd;
At rich men's jests laugh'd loud, their stories prais'd;
Their wives new patterns gaz'd, and gaz'd, and gaz'd;
Most daintily on pamper'd turkies din'd;
Nor shrunk with fasting, nor with study pin'd:
Yet from their churches saw his brethren driven,
Who thunder'd truth, and spoke the voice of heaven,
Chill'd trembling guilt, in Satan's headlong path,
Charm'd the feet back, and rous'd the ear of death.
"Let fools," he cried, "starve on, while prudent I
Snug in my nest shall live, and snug shall die."
   There stood the infidel of modern breed,
Blest vegetation of infernal seed,
Alike no Deist, and no Christian, he;
But from all principle, all virtue, free.
To him all things the same, as good or evil;
Jehovah, Jove, the Lama, or the Devil
Mohammed's braying, or Isaiah's lays;
The Indian's powaws, or the Christian's praise.
With him all *natural* desires are good;
His[1] thirst for stews; the Mohawk's thirst for blood:
Made, not to know, or love, the all beauteous mind;
Or wing thro' heaven his path to bliss refin'd:
But his dear self, choice Dagon! to adore;
To dress, to game, to swear, to drink, to whore;
To race his steeds; or cheat, when others run;
Pit tortur'd cocks, and swear 'tis glorious fun:
His soul not cloath'd with attributes divine;
But a nice watch-spring to that grand machine,

1 Both justified, as all other crimes are, on the great principle that they are
natural. [Dwight's note]

That work more nice than Rittenhouse can plan,
The body; man's chief part; himself, the man;
Man, that illustrious brute of noblest shape,
A swine unbristled, and an untail'd ape:
To couple, eat, and die — his glorious doom —
The oyster's church-yard, and the capon's tomb.
  There[2] —— grinn'd, his conscience fear'd anew,
And scarcely wish'd the doctrine false or true;
Scarce smil'd, himself secure from God to know,
So poor the triumph o'er so weak a foe.
In the deep midnight of his guilty mind,
Where not one solitary virtue shin'd,
Hardly, at times, his struggling conscience wrought
A few, strange intervals of lucid thought,
Holding her clear and dreadful mirrour nigher,
Where villain glow'd, in characters of fire.
Those few the tale dispers'd: His soul no more
Shall, once a year, the Beelzebub rum o'er;
Nor more shall J —— n's ghost her infant show,
Saw his hard nerves, and point the hell below;
Fixed in cold death, no more his eyeballs stare,
Nor change to upright thorns his bristly hair.
  There Demas smil'd, who once the Christian name
Gravely assum'd, and wore with sober fame.
Meek, modest, decent, in life's lowly vale,
Pleas'd he walk'd on; nor now had grac'd this tale;
But, borne beyond the Atlantic ferry, he
Saw wondrous things, his schoolmates did not see.
Great houses, and great men, in coaches carried;
Great Ladies, great Lords' wives, tho' never married;
Fine horses, and fine pictures, and fine plays,
And all the finest things of modern days.
Camelion like, he lost his former hue,
And, mid such great men, grew a great man too;
Enter'd the round of silly, vain parade;
His hair he powder'd, and his bow he made.
Shall powder'd heads, he cried, be sent to hell?
Shall men in vain in such fine houses dwell?
  There Euclio[3] — Ah my Muse, let deepest shame
Blush on thy cheek, at that unhappy name!
Oh write it not, my hand! the name appears
Already written: Wash it out, my tears!
Still, Oh all pitying Saviour! let thy love,
Stronger than death, all heights, and heaven above,
That on the accursed tree, in woes severe,

---

[2] Dwight's targets among contemporary ministers and theological writers remain largely unidentified.

[3] Possibly the Reverend Pierrepont Edwards, Dwight's uncle.

The thief's dire guilt extinguish'd with a tear,
Yearn o'er that mind, that, with temptations dire,
Rank appetites, and passions fraught with fire,
By each new call without, each thought within,
Is forc'd to folly, and is whirl'd to sin;
In conscience' spite, tho' arm'd with hissing fears,
Strong pangs of soul, and all his country's tears,
Is charm'd to madness by the old serpent's breath,
And hurried swiftly down the steep of death.
Burst, burst, thou charm! wake, trembler wake again,
Nor let thy parent's dying prayers be vain!
   The hour arriv'd, th' infernal trumpet blew;
Black from its mouth a cloud sulphureous flew;
The caverns groan'd; the startled throng gave way,
And forth the chariot rush'd to gloomy day.
On every side, expressive emblems rose,
The man, the scene, the purpose to disclose.
Here wrinkled dotage, like a fondled boy,
Titter'd, and smirk'd its momentary joy:
His crumbs there avarice grip'd, with lengthen'd nails,
And weigh'd clipp'd half pence in unequal scales.
Trim vanity her praises laugh'd aloud,
And snuff'd for incense from the gaping crowd.
While Age an eye of anguish cast around,
His crown of glory prostrate on the ground.
There C —— sate; aloud his voice declar'd,
Hell is no more, or no more to be fear'd.
What tho' the Heavens, in words of flaming fire,
Disclose the vengeance of eternal ire,
Bid anguish o'er the unrepenting soul,
In waves succeeding waves, forever roll;
The strongest terms, each language knows, employ
To teach us endless woe, and endless joy:
'Tis all a specious irony, design'd,
A harmless trifling with the human kind;
Or, not to charge the sacred books with lies,
A wile most needful of the ingenious skies,
On this bad earth their kingdom to maintain,
And curb the rebel, man; but all in vain.
First Origen, then Tillotson, then I
Learned their profoundest cunning to descry,
And shew'd this truth, tho' nicely cover'd o'er,
That hell's broad path leads round to heaven's door.
See[4] *kai's* and *epi's* build the glorious scheme!

---

4 How much alike are great men, still say I? The Doctor has found a whole system of divinity, in three or four Greek adverbs, and prepositions; as Lord Coke had before discovered, that there is much curious and cunning kind of learning, in an etc. . . . [Dwight's note]

And *gar's* and *pro's* unfold their proof supreme!
But such nice proof, as none but those can know,
Who oft have read the sacred volume thro',
And read in Greek: but chiefly those, who all
The epistles oft have search'd of cunning Paul.
He, he alone, the mystery seem'd to know,
And none but wizard eyes can peep him thro'.
Then here, at second hand, receive from me
What in the sacred books you'll never see.
For[5] tho' the page reveal'd our cause sustains,
When search'd with cunning, and when gloss'd with pains,
Yet our first aids from human passions rise,
Blest friends to error, and blest props to lies!
And chief, that ruling principle within,
The love of sweet security in sin:
Beneath whose power all pleasing falsehoods blind,
And steal, with soft conviction, on the mind.
No good more luscious than their truth she knows.
And hence their evidence will ne'er oppose.
Aided by this, she mounts the Eternal Throne,
And makes the universe around her own.
Decides the rights of Godhead with her nod,
And wields for him dominion's mighty rod.
Whate'er he ought, or ought not, she descries,
Beholds all infinite relations rise,
Th' immense of time and space surveys serene,
And tells whate'er the bible ought to mean;
Whate'er she wishes, sees him bound to do,
Else is his hand unjust, his word untrue.
      Then would you lay your own, or others fears,
Search your own bosoms, or appeal to theirs.
Know, what those bosoms wish Heaven must reveal;
And sure no bosom ever wish'd a hell.
But, lest sustain'd by underpinning frail,
Our hopes and wits, our proofs and doctrines fail,
Admit a hell; but from its terrors take
Whate'er commands the guilty heart to quake.
Again the purgatorial whim revive,
And bid the soul by stripes and penance live.
And now, with search most deep, and wits most keen,
I've learn'd, that hell is but a school for sin;
Which yields, to heaven, the soul from guile refin'd,

---

[5] Witness Matthew vii. 13–14 — *Strait is the gate, and narrow the way, that leadeth to destruction, and no body there is, who goes in thereat:*
Because wide is the gate, and broad is the way, that leadeth unto life, and all they be, who find it. Murray's new version of the Bible, very proper to be kept by thieves, whoremongers, idolaters, and all liars; with others, who mean to go to heaven, via hell. [Dwight's note]

And, tho' it mars the devil's, mends mankind.
And thus the matter stands. When God makes man,
He makes him *here* religious, if he can;
If he cannot, he bids him farther go,
And try to be religious, down below;
But as his failure is his fault, ordains
His soul to suffer dire repentance' pains,
Repentance, fearful doom of sinners vile!
The law's whole curse, and nature's highest ill!
If there the wretch repent, the work is done;
If not, he plunges to a lower zone,
A lower still, and still a lower, tries,
'Til with such sinking tir'd, he longs to rise;
And finding there the fashion to repent,
He joins the throng, and strait to heaven is sent.
Heaven now his own he claims; nor can the sky
Preserve its honour, and its claim deny.
Thus stands the fact; and if the proof should fail,
Let Heaven, next time, some better proof reveal.
I've done my part; I've given you here the pith;
The rest, the bark and sap, I leave to ——
   Thus spoke the sage; a shout, from all the throng,
Roll'd up to heaven, and roar'd the plains along;
Conscience, a moment, ceas'd her stings to rear,
And joy excessive whelm'd each rising fear.
But soon reflection's glass again she rear'd,
Spread out fell sin; and all her horrors bar'd;
There anguish, guilt, remorse, her dreadful train,
Tremendous harbingers of endless pain,
Froze the sad breast, amaz'd the withering eye,
And forc'd the soul to doubt the luscious lie.
   Yet soon sophistic wishes, fond and vain,
The scheme review'd, and lov'd, and hop'd again;
Soon, one by one, the flames of hell withdrew;
Less painful conscience, sin less dangerous grew;
Less priz'd the day, to man for trial given,
Less fear'd Jehovah, and less valued heaven.
   No longer now by conscience' calls unmann'd,
To sin, the wretch put forth a bolder hand;
More freely cheated, lied, defam'd, and swore;
Nor wish'd the night to riot, drink, or whore;
Look'd up, and hiss'd his God; his parent stung,
And sold his friend, and country, for a song.
The new-fledg'd infidel of modern brood
Climb'd the next fence, clapp'd both his wings, and crow'd;
Confess'd the doctrines were as just, as new,
And doubted if the bible were not true.
The decent christian threw his mask aside,

And smil'd, to see the path of heaven so wide,
To church, the half of each fair sunday, went,
The rest, in visits, sleep, or dining, spent;
To vice and error nobly liberal grew;
Spoke kindly of all doctrines, but the true;
All men, but saints, he hop'd to heaven might rise,
And thought all roads, but virtue, reach'd the skies,
    There truth and virtue stood, and sigh'd to find
New gates of falshood open'd on mankind;
New paths to ruin strew'd with flowers divine,
And other aids, and motives, gain'd to sin.
    From a dim cloud, the spirit[6] eyed the scene,
Now proud with triumph, and now vex'd with spleen,
Mark'd all the throng, beheld them all his own,
And to his cause no friend of virtue won:
Surpriz'd, enrag'd, he wing'd his sooty flight,
And hid beneath the pall of endless night.

[6] Satan.

Joel Barlow (1754–1812)

JOEL BARLOW, another of the Connecticut group, graduated from Yale in 1778 in the same class as Noah Webster. He studied law and divinity, and served in the Revolution as chaplain to the Fourth Massachusetts Brigade. After the war he drifted in and out of the law, ran a bookstore, edited a newspaper, and published a Congregational psalm book. He was also writing and publishing poetry, including a revision of his Yale graduation poem, "The Prospect of Peace," and a long patriotic epic in nine books and five thousand lines called *The Vision of Columbus* (1787). In 1788 he went to Europe as agent for the Scioto Land Company of Ohio, into the middle of the ferment that was about to erupt in the French Revolution. Barlow was soon involved with the French radical leaders, and after meeting Tom Paine and others in England in 1792 became more deeply committed than ever to the revolutionary cause. His long poem *The Conspiracy of Kings* (1792) celebrated revolution, and his powerful prose analysis of European politics, *Advice to the Privileged Orders* (1792), was accounted to be so subversive by the Pitt government that it was suppressed in England.

Barlow served as United States Consul at Algiers from 1795 to 1805 and as minister to France from 1811 until his death the next year. Between 1805 and 1811 he lived quietly in the United

States, pursuing his interests in poetry and politics. In 1807 he produced *The Columbiad,* an American epic which included reworked portions of his earlier *Vision of Columbus,* but which was not much more successful as a work of poetic art.

TEXT: Joel Barlow, *The Columbiad* (Philadelphia, 1807).

A Warning to Americans

[From *The Columbiad,* 1807]

You scorn the Titan's threat; nor shall I strain
The powers of pathos in a task so vain
As Afric's wrongs to sing; for what avails
To harp for you these known familiar tales?
To tongue mute misery, and re-rack the soul
With crimes oft copied from that bloody scroll
Where Slavery pens her woes; tho tis but there
We learn the weight that mortal life can bear.
The tale might startle still the accustom'd ear,
Still shake the nerve that pumps the pearly tear,
Melt every heart, and thro the nation gain
Full many a voice to break the barbarous chain.
But why to sympathy for guidance fly,
(Her aids uncertain and of scant supply)
When your own self-excited sense affords
A guide more sure, and every sense accords?
Where strong self-interest, join'd with duty, lies,
Where doing right demands no sacrifice,
Where profit, pleasure, life-expanding fame
League their allurements to support the claim,
Tis safest there the impleaded cause to trust;
Men well instructed will be always just.
From slavery then your rising realms to save,
Regard the master, notice not the slave;
Consult alone for freemen, and bestow
Your best, your only cares, to keep them so.
Tyrants are never free; and, small and great,
All masters must be tyrants soon or late;
So nature works; and oft the lordling knave
Turns out at once a tyrant and a slave,
Struts, cringes, bullies, begs, as courtiers must,
Makes one a god, another treads in dust,
Fears all alike, and filches whom he can,
But knows no equal, finds no friend in man.
Ah! would you not be slaves, with lords and kings,
Then be not masters; there the danger springs.

The whole crude system that torments this earth,
Of rank, privation, privilege of birth,
False honor, fraud, corruption, civil jars,
The rage of conquest and the curse of wars,
Pandora's total shower, all ills combined
That erst o'erwhelm'd and still distress mankind,
Box'd up secure in your deliberate hand,
Wait your behest, to fix or fly this land.
   Equality of Right is nature's plan;
And following nature is the march of man.
Whene'er he deviates in the least degree,
When, free himself, he would be more than free,
The baseless column, rear'd to bear his bust,
Falls as he mounts, and whelms him in the dust.
   See Rome's rude sires, with autocratic gait,
Tread down their tyrant and erect their state;
Their state secured, they deem it wise and brave
That every freeman should command a slave,
And, flusht with franchise of his camp and town,
Rove thro the world and hunt the nations down;
Master and man the same vile spirit gains,
Rome chains the world, and wears herself the chains.
   Mark modern Europe with her feudal codes,
Serfs, villains, vassals, nobles, kings and gods,
All slaves of different grades, corrupt and curst
With high and low, for senseless rank athirst,
Wage endless wars; not fighting to be free,
But *cujum pecus*, whose base herd they'll be.
   Too much of Europe, here transplanted o'er,
Nursed feudal feelings on your tented shore,
Brought sable serfs from Afric, call'd it gain,
And urged your sires to forge the fatal chain.
But now, the tents o'erturn'd, the war dogs fled,
Now fearless Freedom rears at last her head
Matcht with celestial Peace, — my friends, beware
To shade the splendors of so bright a pair;
Complete their triumph, fix their firm abode,
Purge all privations from your liberal code,
Restore their souls to men, give earth repose,
And save your sons from slavery, wars and woes.
   Based on its rock of Right your empire lies,
On walls of wisdom let the fabric rise;
Preserve your principles, their force unfold,
Let nations prove them and let kings behold.
EQUALITY, your first firm-grounded stand;
Then FREE ELECTION; then your FEDERAL BAND;
This holy Triad should forever shine
The great compendium of all rights divine,

Creed of all schools, whence youths by millions draw
Their themes of right, their decalogues of law;
Till men shall wonder (in these codes inured)
How wars were made, how tyrants were endured.

The Progress of American Culture

[From *The Columbiad*, 1807]

To nurse the arts and fashion freedom's lore
Young schools of science rise along the shore;
Great without pomp their modest walls expand,
Harvard and Yale and Princeton grace the land,
Penn's student halls his youths with gladness greet,
On James's bank Virginian Muses meet,
Manhattan's mart collegiate domes command,
Bosom'd in groves, see growing Dartmouth stand;
Bright o'er its realm reflecting solar fires,
On yon tall hill Rhode Island's seat aspires.
Thousands of humbler name around them rise,
Where homebred freedmen seize the solid prize;
Fixt in small spheres, with safer beams to shine,
They reach the useful and refuse the fine,
Found, on its proper base, the social plan,
The broad plain truths, the common sense of man,
His obvious wants, his mutual aids discern,
His rights familiarize, his duties learn,
Feel moral fitness all its force dilate,
Embrace the village and comprise the state.
Each rustic here who turns the furrow'd soil,
The maid, the youth that ply mechanic toil,
In equal rights, in useful arts inured,
Know their just claims, and see their claims secured;
They watch their delegates, each law revise,
Its faults designate and its merits prize,
Obey, but scrutinize; and let the test
Of sage experience prove and fix the best.
Here, fired by virtue's animating flame,
The preacher's task persuasive sages claim,
To mould religion to the moral mind,
In bands of peace to harmonize mankind,
To life, to light, to promised joys above
The soften'd soul with ardent hope to move.
No dark intolerance blinds the zealous throng,
No arm of power attendant on their tongue;
Vext Inquisition, with her flaming brand,

Shuns their mild march, nor dares approach the land.
Tho different creeds their priestly robes denote,
Their orders various and their rites remote,
Yet one their voice, their labors all combined,
Lights of the world and friends of humankind.
So the bright galaxy o'er heaven displays
Of various stars the same unbounded blaze;
Where great and small their mingling rays unite,
And earth and skies exchange the friendly light.

And lo, my son, that other sapient band,
The torch of science flaming in their hand!
Thro nature's range their searching souls aspire,
Or wake to life the canvass and the lyre.
Fixt in sublimest thought, behold them rise
World after world unfolding to their eyes,
Lead, light, allure them thro the total plan,
And give new guidance to the paths of man.

Yon meteor-mantled hill see Franklin tread,
Heaven's awful thunders rolling o'er his head;
Convolving clouds the billowy skies deform,
And forky flames emblaze the blackening storm.
See the descending streams around him burn,
Glance on his rod and with his finger turn;
He bids conflicting fulminants expire
The guided blast, and holds the imprison'd fire.
No more, when doubling storms the vault o'erspread,
The livid glare shall strike thy race with dread,
Nor towers nor temples, shuddering with the sound,
Sink in the flames and shake the sheeted ground.
His well tried wires, that every tempest wait,
Shall teach mankind to ward the bolts of fate,
With pointed steel o'ertop the trembling spire,
And lead from untouch'd walls the harmless fire;
Fill'd with his fame while distant climes rejoice,
Wherever lightning shines or thunder rears its voice.

And see sage Rittenhouse,[1] with ardent eye,
Lift the long tube and pierce the starry sky;
Clear in his view the circling planets roll,
And suns and satellites their course control.
He marks what laws the widest wanderers bind,
Copies creation in his forming mind,
Sees in his hall the total semblance rise,
And mimics there the labors of the skies.
There student youths without their tubes behold
The spangled heavens their mystic maze unfold,
And crowded schools their cheerful chambers grace

[1] David Rittenhouse, Philadelphia astronomer.

With all the spheres that cleave the vast of space.
To guide the sailor in his wandering way,
See Godfrey's[2] glass reverse the beams of day.
His lifted quadrant to the eye displays
From adverse skies the counteracting rays;
And marks, as devious sails bewilder'd roll,
Each nice gradation from the stedfast pole.

West[3] with his own great soul the canvass warms,
Creates, inspires, impassions human forms,
Spurns critic rules, and seizing safe the heart,
Breaks down the former frightful bounds of Art;
Where ancient manners, with exclusive reign,
From half mankind withheld her fair domain.
He calls to life each patriot, chief or sage,
Garb'd in the dress and drapery of his age.
Again bold Regulus to death returns,
Again her falling Wolfe Britannia mourns;
Lahogue, Boyne, Cressy, Nevilcross demand
And gain fresh lustre from his copious hand;
His Lear stalks wild with woes, the gods defies,
Insults the tempest and outstorms the skies;
Edward in arms to frowning combat moves,
Or, won to pity by the queen he loves,
Spares the devoted *Six*, whose deathless deed
Preserves the town his vengeance doom'd to bleed.

With rival force, see Copley's[4] pencil trace
The air of action and the charms of face.
Fair in his tints unfold the scenes of state,
The senate listens and the peers debate;
Pale consternation every heart appals,
In act to speak, when death-struck Chatham falls.
He bids dread Calpe cease to shake the waves,
While Elliott's arm the host of Bourbon saves;
O'er sail-wing'd batteries sinking in the flood,
Mid flames and darkness, drench'd in hostile blood,
Britannia's sons extend their generous hand
To rescue foes from death, and bear them to the land.

Fired with the martial deeds that bathed in gore
His brave companions on his native shore,
Trumbull[5] with daring hand their fame recalls;
He shades with night Quebec's beleagured walls,
Thro flashing flames, that midnight war supplies,
The assailants yield, their great Montgomery dies.
On Bunker height, thro floods of hostile fire,

2 Thomas Godfrey, Philadelphia glazier who invented an improved quadrant.
3 Benjamin West, painter of historical scenes.
4 John Singleton Copley, portrait painter.
5 John Trumbull (1756–1843), painter of Revolutionary scenes.

His Putnam toils till all the troops retire,
His Warren, pierced with balls, at last lies low,
And leaves a victory to the wasted foe.
Britannia too his glowing tint shall claim,
To pour new splendor on her Calpean fame;
He leads her bold sortie, and from their towers
O'erturns the Gallic and Iberian powers.

See rural seats of innocence and ease,
High tufted towers and walks of waving trees,
The white waves dashing on the craggy shores,
Meandring streams and meads of mingled flowers,
Where nature's sons their wild excursions tread,
In just design from Taylor's[6] pencil spread.

Stuart and Brown[7] the moving portrait raise,
Each rival stroke the force of life conveys;
Heroes and beauties round their tablets stand,
And rise unfading from their plastic hand;
Each breathing form preserves its wonted grace,
And all the soul stands speaking in the face.

Two kindred arts the swelling statue heave,
Wake the dead wax, and teach the stone to live.
While the bold chisel claims the rugged strife,
To rouse the sceptred marble into life.
See Wright's[8] fair hands the livelier fire control,
In waxen forms she breathes impassion'd soul;
The pencil'd tint o'er moulded substance glows,
And different powers the peerless art compose.
Grief, rage and fear beneath her fingers start,
Roll the wild eye and pour the bursting heart;
The world's dead fathers wait her wakening call,
And distant ages fill the storied hall.

To equal fame ascends thy tuneful throng,
The boast of genius and the pride of song;
Caught from the cast of every age and clime,
Their lays shall triumph o'er the lapse of time.

With lynx-eyed glance thro nature far to pierce,
With all the powers and every charm of verse,
Each science opening in his ample mind,
His fancy glowing and his taste refined,
See Trumbull[9] lead the train. His skilful hand
Hurls the keen darts of satire round the land.
Pride, knavery, dullness feel his mortal stings,

6 Perhaps William Taylor (1764–1841), Yale graduate, merchant, and land-
scape painter.
7 Gilbert Stuart, famed portraitist of George Washington and other prominent
figures; Mather Brown, Stuart's disciple, a miniaturist.
8 Patience Lovell Wright, wax sculptress.
9 John Trumbull the poet; see p. 353.

And listening virtue triumphs while he sings;
Britain's foil'd sons, victorious now no more,
In guilt retiring from the wasted shore,
Strive their curst cruelties to hide in vain;
The world resounds them in his deathless strain.
   On wings of faith to elevate the soul
Beyond the bourn of earth's benighted pole,
For Dwight's[10] high harp the epic Muse sublime
Hails her new empire in the western clime.
Tuned from the tones by seers seraphic sung,
Heaven in his eye and rapture on his tongue,
His voice revives old Canaan's promised land,
The long-fought fields of Jacob's chosen band.
In Hanniel's fate, proud faction finds its doom,
Ai's midnight flames light nations to their tomb,
In visions bright supernal joys are given,
And all the dark futurities of heaven.
   While freedom's cause his patriot bosom warms,
In counsel sage, nor inexpert in arms,
See Humphreys[11] glorious from the field retire,
Sheathe the glad sword and string the soothing lyre;
That lyre which erst, in hours of dark despair,
Roused the sad realms to finish well the war.
O'er fallen friends, with all the strength of woe,
Fraternal sighs in his strong numbers flow;
His country's wrongs, her duties, dangers, praise,
Fire his full soul and animate his lays:
Wisdom and War with equal joy shall own
So fond a votary and so brave a son.

10 Timothy Dwight; see p. 365.
11 David Humphreys, another of the Connecticut Wits.

Philip Freneau (1752–1832)

A GRADUATE of the College of New Jersey (Princeton) in the same class (1771) with James Madison and Aaron Burr, the New York-born Freneau soon acquired a reputation as a bright young poet. With another classmate — Hugh Henry Brackenridge — he collaborated on the prose tale *Father Bombo's Pilgrimage* and the prophetic commencement poem *The Rising Glory of America* (1771). Though he was determined from the first to be a poet ("To write was my sad destiny, / The worst of trades, we all agree") he first served a sentence on a British prison ship, enlisted in the Revolutionary Army, sailed in the coastal trade as a sea-captain, and spent a number of years in political journalism as a Jeffersonian partisan editor and publicist.

Freneau's verse, issued in collected editions in 1786, 1788, 1809, and 1815, falls into fairly clear divisions. His wartime poetry reflects the heated passions of the time and his hatred of the British, whose treatment of him on the prison ship he never forgot or forgave. His political satires, directed against the Federalists, were expert and effective, so much so that Washington himself called him "that rascal Freneau." An avowed radical, Freneau threw himself into a number of reform causes and wrote verses about them. His lyric verse, dealing with themes of nature, transience, the past, and personal experience, shows him to have been a poet of genuine gifts and imagination. Though he obviously echoed Collins, Gray, Akenside, and other English pre-Romantics, there is in his best verse a freshness, originality, and haunting beauty unsurpassed in the poetry of the period. Late in life, Freneau began to write an unusual kind of rough, realistic, local color verse, somewhat parallel to that of Robert Burns. He also produced a small body of deist-Unitarian poetry of excellent quality. But most of all, Freneau's importance lies in the fact that he alone, of his American generation, broke out of the constrictions of neo-classical imitativeness to look at life around him directly, read it imaginatively, and record it sensitively.

TEXTS: Harry Hayden Clark, ed., *Poems of Freneau* (New York, 1929). "The Republican Genius of Europe" from F. L. Pattee, ed., *The Poems of Philip Freneau* (Princeton, 1902–7), III, 129–130.

⌘

POEMS OF FANCY

The Power of Fancy

Wakeful, vagrant, restless thing
Ever wandering on the wing,
Who thy wondrous source can find,
FANCY, regent of the mind;
A spark from Jove's resplendent throne,
But thy nature all unknown.
    THIS spark of bright, celestial flame,
From Jove's seraphic altar came,

And hence alone in man we trace,
Resemblance to the immortal race.

Ah! what is all this mighty WHOLE,
These suns and stars that round us roll!
What are they all, where'er they shine,
But *Fancies* of the Power Divine!
What is this *globe*, these *lands*, and *seas*,
And *heat*, and *cold*, and *flowers*, and *trees*,
And *life*, and *death*, and *beast*, and *man*,
And *time*, — that with the *sun* began —
But thoughts on reason's scale combin'd,
Ideas of the Almighty mind?

On the surface of the brain
Night after night she walks unseen,
Noble fabrics doth she raise
In the woods or on the seas,
On some high, steep, pointed rock,
Where the billows loudly knock
And the dreary tempests sweep
Clouds along the uncivil deep.

Lo! she walks upon the moon,
Listens to the chimy tune
Of the bright, harmonious spheres,
And the song of angels hears;
Sees this earth a distant star,
Pendant, floating in the air;
Leads me to some lonely dome,
Where Religion loves to come,
Where the bride of Jesus dwells,
And the deep ton'd organ swells
In notes with lofty anthems join'd,
Notes that half distract the mind.

Now like lightning she descends
To the prison of the fiends,
Hears the rattling of their chains,
Feels their never ceasing pains —
But, O never may she tell
Half the frightfulness of hell.

Now she views Arcadian rocks,
Where the shepherds guard their flocks,
And, while yet her wings she spreads,
Sees chrystal streams and coral beds,
Wanders to some desert deep,
Or some dark, enchanted steep,
By the full moonlight doth shew
Forests of a dusky blue,
Where, upon some mossy bed,
Innocence reclines her head.

SWIFT, she stretches o'er the seas
To the far off Hebrides,
Canvas on the lofty mast
Could not travel half so fast —
Swifter than the eagle's flight
Or instantaneous rays of light!
Lo! contemplative she stands
On Norwegia's rocky lands —
Fickle Goddess, set me down
Where the rugged winters frown
Upon Orca's howling steep,
Nodding o'er the northern deep,
Where the winds tumultuous roar,
Vext that *Ossian* sings no more.
Fancy, to that land repair,
Sweetest Ossian slumbers there;
Waft me far to southern isles
Where the soften'd winter smiles,
To Bermuda's orange shades,
Or Demarara's lovely glades;
Bear me o'er the sounding cape,
Painting death in every shape,
Where daring *Anson*[1] spread the sail
Shatter'd by the stormy gale —
Lo! she leads me wide and far,
Sense can never follow her —
Shape thy course o'er land and sea,
Help me to keep pace with thee,
Lead me to yon' chalky cliff,
Over rock and over reef,
Into Britain's fertile land,
Stretching far her proud command.
Look back and view, thro' many a year,
Caesar, Julius Caesar, there.
    Now to Tempe's verdant wood,
Over the mid ocean flood
Lo! the islands of the sea
— Sappho, Lesbos mourns for thee:
Greece, arouse thy humbled head,
Where are all thy mighty dead,
Who states to endless ruin hurl'd
And carried vengeance through the world? —
Troy, thy vanish'd pomp resume,
Or, weeping at thy Hector's tomb,
Yet those faded scenes renew,
Whose memory is to *Homer* due.

[1] George Anson, leader of a British naval expedition to the South Pacific.

Fancy, lead me wandering still
Up to Ida's cloud-topt hill;
Not a laurel there doth grow
But in vision thou shalt show, —
Every sprig on Virgil's tomb
Shall in livelier colours bloom,
And every triumph Rome has seen
Flourish on the years between.

Now she bears me far away
In the east to meet the day,
Leads me over Ganges' streams,
Mother of the morning beams —
O'er the ocean hath she ran,
Places me on *Tinian;*
Farther, farther in the east,
Till it almost meets the west,
Let us wandering both be lost
On Taitis sea-beat coast,
Bear me from that distant strand,
Over ocean, over land,
To California's golden shore —
Fancy, stop, and rove no more.

Now, tho' late, returning home,
Lead me to *Belinda's* tomb;
Let me glide as well as you
Through the shroud and coffin too,
And behold, a moment, there,
All that once was good and fair —
Who doth here so soundly sleep?
Shall we break this prison deep? —
Thunders cannot wake the maid,
Lightnings cannot pierce the shade,
And tho' wintry tempests roar,
Tempests shall disturb no more.

YET must those eyes in darkness stay,
That once were rivals to the day — ?
Like heaven's bright lamp beneath the main
They are but set to rise again.

FANCY, thou the muses' pride,
In thy painted realms reside
Endless images of things,
Fluttering each on golden wings,
Ideal objects, such a store,
The universe could hold no more:
Fancy, to thy power I owe
Half my happiness below;
By thee Elysian groves were made,
Thine were the notes that Orpheus play'd;

By thee was Pluto charm'd so well
While rapture seiz'd the sons of hell —
Come, O come — perceiv'd by none,
You and I will walk alone.

(1770, 1786)

The Vanity of Existence

To Thyrsis

In youth, gay scenes attract our eyes,
   And not suspecting their decay
Life's flowery fields before us rise,
   Regardless of its winter day.

But vain pursuits, and joys as vain,
   Convince us life is but a dream.
Death is to wake, to rise again
   To that true life you best esteem.

So nightly on some shallow tide,
   Oft have I seen a splendid show;
Reflected stars on either side,
   And glittering moons were seen below.

But when the tide had ebbed away,
   The scene fantastic with it fled,
A bank of mud around me lay,
   And sea-weed on the river's bed.

(1781)

On a Honey Bee

DRINKING FROM A GLASS OF WINE, AND DROWNED THEREIN

Thou, born to sip the lake or spring,
Or quaff the waters of the stream,
Why hither come on vagrant wing? —
Does Bacchus tempting seem —
Did he, for you, this glass prepare? —
Will I admit you to a share?

Did storms harass or foes perplex,
Did wasps or king-birds bring dismay —
Did wars distress, or labours vex,
Or did you miss your way? —

A better seat you could not take
Than on the margin of this lake.

Welcome! — I hail you to my glass:
All welcome, here, you find;
Here, let the cloud of trouble pass,
Here, be all care resigned. —
This fluid never fails to please,
And drown the griefs of men or bees.

What forced you here, we cannot know,
And you can scarcely tell —
But cheery we would have you go
And bid a fond farewell:
On lighter wings we bid you fly,
Your dart will now all foes defy.

Yet take not, oh! too deep a drink,
And in this ocean die;
Here bigger bees than you might sink,
Even bees full six feet high.
Like Pharaoh, then, you would be said
To perish in a sea of red.

Do as you please, your will is mine;
Enjoy it without fear —
And your grave will be this glass of wine,
Your epitaph — a tear —
Go, take your seat in Charon's boat,
We'll tell the hive, you died afloat.

(1809)

The Indian Burying Ground

In spite of all the learned have said,
I still my old opinion keep;
The *posture*, that *we* give the dead,
Points out the soul's eternal sleep.

Not so the ancients of these lands —
The Indian, when from life released,
Again is seated with his friends,
And shares again the joyous feast.[1]

1 The North American Indians bury their dead in a sitting posture; decorating
the corpse with wampum, the images of birds, quadrupeds, &c: And (if that
of a warrior) with bows, arrows, tomahawks and other military weapons.
[Freneau's note]

His imaged birds, and painted bowl,
And venison, for a journey dressed,
Bespeak the nature of the soul,
ACTIVITY, that knows no rest.

His bow, for action ready bent,
And arrows, with a head of stone,
Can only mean that life is spent,
And not the old ideas gone.

Thou, stranger, that shalt come this way,
No fraud upon the dead commit —
Observe the swelling turf, and say
They do not *lie*, but here they *sit*.

Here still a lofty rock remains,
On which the curious eye may trace
(Now wasted, half, by wearing rains)
The fancies of a ruder race.

Here still an aged elm aspires,
Beneath whose far-projecting shade
(And which the shepherd still admires)
The children of the forest played!

There oft a restless Indian queen
(Pale *Shebah*, with her braided hair)
And many a barbarous form is seen
To chide the man that lingers there.

By midnight moons, o'er moistening dews,
In habit for the chase arrayed,
The hunter still the deer pursues,
The hunter and the deer, a shade!

And long shall timorous fancy see
The painted chief, and pointed spear,
And Reason's self shall bow the knee
To shadows and delusions here.

(1788)

To an Author

Your leaves bound up compact and fair,
In neat array at length prepare,
To pass their hour on learning's stage,
To meet the surly critic's rage;

The statesman's slight, the smatterer's sneer —
Were these, indeed, your only fear,
You might be tranquil and resigned:
What most should touch your fluttering mind,
Is that, few critics will be found
To sift your works, and deal the wound.

Thus, when one fleeting year is past
On some bye-shelf *your* book is cast —
Another comes, with *something new*,
And drives you fairly out of view:
With some to praise, *but more to blame*,
The mind returns to — whence it came;
And some alive, who *scarce could read*
Will publish satires on the dead.

Thrice happy Dryden, who could meet
Some rival bard in every street!
When all were bent on writing well
It was some credit to excel: —

Thrice happy Dryden, who could find
A *Milbourne* for his sport designed —
And *Pope*, who saw the harmless rage
Of *Dennis* bursting o'er his page
Might justly spurn the *critic's aim*,
Who only helped to swell his fame.

On these bleak climes by Fortune thrown,
Where rigid *Reason* reigns alone,
Where lovely *Fancy* has no sway,
Nor magic forms about us play —
Nor nature takes her summer hue
Tell me, what has the muse to do? —

An age employed in edging steel
Can no poetic raptures feel;
No solitude's attracting power,
No leisure of the noon day hour,
No shaded stream, no quiet grove
Can this fantastic century move;

The muse of love in no request —
Go — try your fortune with the rest,
One of the nine you should engage,
To meet the follies of the age: —
On *one*, we fear, your choice must fall —
The least engaging of them all —
Her visage stern — an angry style —

A clouded brow — malicious smile —
A mind on *murdered victims* placed —
She, only she, can please the taste!

(1788)

The Wild Honey Suckle

Fair flower, that dost so comely grow,
Hid in this silent, dull retreat,
Untouched thy honied blossoms blow,
Unseen thy little branches greet:
    No roving foot shall crush thee here,
    No busy hand provoke a tear.

By Nature's self in white arrayed,
She bade thee shun the vulgar eye,
And planted here the guardian shade,
And sent soft waters murmuring by;
    Thus quietly thy summer goes,
    Thy days declining to repose.

Smit with those charms, that must decay,
I grieve to see your future doom;
They died — nor were those flowers more gay,
The flowers that did in Eden bloom;
    Unpitying frosts, and Autumn's power
    Shall leave no vestige of this flower.

From morning suns and evening dews
At first thy little being came:
If nothing once, you nothing lose,
For when you die you are the same;
    The space between, is but an hour,
    The frail duration of a flower.

(1786)

On the Sleep of Plants

When suns are set, and stars in view,
Not only *man* to slumber yields;
But Nature grants this blessing too,
To yonder *plants*, in yonder fields.

The Summer heats and lengthening days
(To them the same as toil and care)
Thrice welcome make the evening breeze,
That kindly does their strength repair.

At early dawn each plant survey,
And see, revived by Nature's hand,
With youthful vigour, fresh and gay,
Their blossoms blow, their leaves expand.

Yon' garden plant, with weeds o'er-run,
Not void of *thought*, perceives its hour,
And, watchful of the parting sun,
Throughout the night conceals her flower.

Like us, the slave of cold and heat,
She too enjoys her little span —
With *Reason*, only less complete
Than *that* which makes the boast of *man*.

Thus, moulded from one common clay,
A varied life adorns the plain;
By Nature subject to decay,
BY NATURE MEANT TO BLOOM AGAIN.

(1790)

The Sea Voyage

From a gay island green and fair,
With gentle blasts of southern air,
   Across the deep we held our way,
Around our barque smooth waters played,
   No envious clouds obscur'd the day,
Serene came on the evening shade.

Still farther to the north we drew,
And Porto Rico's mountains blue,
   Were just decaying on the eye,
When from the main arose the sun;
   Before his ray the shadows fly,
As we before the breezes run.

Now northward of the tropic pass'd,
The fickle skies grew black at last;
   The ruffian winds began to roar,
The sea obey'd their tyrant force,
   And we, alas! too far from shore,
Must now forsake our destin'd course.

The studding sails at last to hand,
The vent'rous captain gave command;
   But scarcely to the task went they

When a vast billow o'er us broke,
  And tore the sheets and tacks away,
Nor could the booms sustain the stroke.

Still vaster rose the angry main,
The winds through every shroud complain;
  The topsails we could spread no more,
Though doubly reef'd, the furious blast
  Away the fluttering canvas bore,
And vow'd destruction to the mast.

When now the northern storm was quell'd,
A calm ensued — but ocean swell'd
  Beyond the towering mountain's height,
Till from the south new winds arose;
  Our sails we spread at dead of night,
And fair, though fierce, the tempest blows.

When morning rose, the skies were clear,
The gentle breezes warm and fair,
  Convey'd us o'er the wat'ry road;
A ship o'ertook us on the way,
  Her thousand sails were spread abroad,
And flutter'd in the face of day.

At length, through many a climate pass'd,
Caesaria's hills we saw at last,
  And reach'd the land of lovely dames;
My charming Caelia there I found,
  'Tis she my warmest friendship claims,
The fairest maid that treads the ground.

                              (1779)

ৠৡৠ

POEMS OF PATRIOTISM AND REVOLUTION

A Political Litany

Libera Nos, Domine. — DELIVER US O LORD, *not only from British Dependence, but also,*

From a junto that labour with absolute power,
Whose schemes disappointed have made them look sour,
From the lords of the council, who fight against freedom,
Who still follow on where delusion shall lead them.

From the group at St. James's, who slight our petitions,
And fools that are waiting for further submissions —
From a nation whose manners are rough and severe,
From scoundrels and rascals, — do keep us all clear.

From pirates sent out by command of the king
To murder and plunder, but never to swing;
From *Wallace* and *Greaves*, and *Vipers* and *Roses*,[1]
Who, if heaven pleases, we'll give bloody noses.

From the valiant *Dunmore*, with his crew of banditti,
Who plunder Virginians at *Williamsburg* city,
From hot-headed *Montague*, mighty to swear,
The little fat man, with his pretty white hair.

From bishops in Britain, who butchers are grown,
From slaves, that would die for a smile from the throne,
From assemblies that vote against *Congress proceedings,*
(Who now see the fruit of their stupid misleadings.)

From *Tryon* the mighty, who flies from our city,
And swelled with importance disdains the committee:
(But since he is pleased to proclaim us his foes,
What the devil care we where the devil he goes.)

From the caitiff, lord *North,* who would bind us in chains,
From a royal king Log, with his tooth-full of brains,

---

[1] Captains and ships in the British navy, then employed on the American coast. [Freneau's note]

Who dreams, and is certain (when taking a nap)
He has conquered our lands, as they lay on his map.

From a kingdom that bullies, and hectors, and swears,
We send up to heaven our wishes and prayers
That we, disunited, may freemen be still,
And Britain go on — to be damned if she will.

(1775)

To the Memory of the Brave Americans

Under General Greene, in South Carolina, who fell in the action of September 8, 1781

At Eutaw springs the valiant died:
Their limbs with dust are cover'd o'er —
Weep on, ye springs, your tearful tide;
How many heroes are no more!

If in this wreck of ruin, they
Can yet be thought to claim a tear,
O smite thy gentle breast, and say
The friends of freedom slumber here!

Thou, who shalt trace this bloody plain,
If goodness rules thy generous breast,
Sigh for the wasted rural reign;
Sigh for the shepherds, sunk to rest!

Stranger, their humble graves adorn;
You too may fall, and ask a tear:
'Tis not the beauty of the morn
That proves the evening shall be clear —

They saw their injur'd country's woe;
The flaming town, the wasted field;
Then rush'd to meet the insulting foe;
They took the spear — but left the shield,

Led by thy conquering genius, GREENE,
The Britons they compell'd to fly:
None distant view'd the fatal plain,
None griev'd, in such a cause, to die —

But, like the Parthian, fam'd of old,
Who, flying, still their arrows threw;

These routed Britons, full as bold,
Retreated, and retreating slew.

Now rest in peace, our patriot band;
Though far from Nature's limits thrown,
We trust, they find a happier land,
A brighter sun-shine of their own.

(1781, 1795)

From

On the Fall of General Earl Cornwallis

A Chieftain join'd with Howe, Burgoyne, and Gage,
Once more, nor this the last, provokes my rage —
Who saw these Nimrods first for conquest burn!
Who has not seen them to the dust return?
This ruffian next, who scour'd our ravag'd fields,
Foe to the human race, Cornwallis yields! —
None e'er before essay'd such desperate crimes,
Alone he stood, arch-butcher of the times,
Rov'd uncontroul'd this wasted country o'er,
Strew'd plains with dead, and bath'd his jaws with gore.
    'TWAS thus the wolf, who sought by night his prey,
And plunder'd all he met with on his way,
Stole what he could, and murder'd as he pass'd,
Chanc'd on a trap, and lost his head at last.
    WHAT pen can write, what human tongue can tell
The endless murders of this man of hell!
Nature in him disgrac'd the form divine;
Nature mistook, she meant him for a — swine:
That eye his forehead to her shame adorns;
Blush! nature, blush — bestow him tail and horns! —
By him the orphans mourn — the widow'd dame
Saw ruin spreading in the wasteful flame;
Gash'd o'er with wounds beheld with streaming eye
A son, a brother, or a consort, die! —
Through ruin'd realms bones lie without a tomb,
And souls be sped to their eternal doom,
Who else had liv'd, and seen their toils again
Bless'd by the genius of the rural reign.
    BUT turn your eyes, and see the murderer fall,
Then say — "Cornwallis has atchiev'd it all." —
Yet he preserves the honour and the fame
That vanquish'd heroes only ought to claim —
Is he a hero! — Read, and you will find

Heroes are beings of a different kind: —
Compassion to the worst of men is due,
And mercy heaven's first attribute, 'tis true;
Yet most presume it was *too nobly* done
To grant mild terms to *Satan's first-born son.*
    CONVINC'D we are, no foreign spot of earth
But Britain only, gave this reptile birth.
That white-cliff'd isle, the vengeful dragon's den,
Has sent us monsters where we look'd for men.
When memory paints their horrid deeds anew,
And brings these murdering miscreants to your view,
Then ask the leaders of these bloody bands,
Can they expect compassion at our hands? —
    BUT may this year, the glorious eighty-one,
Conclude successful, as it first begun;
This brilliant year their total downfall see,
And what Cornwallis *is,* may Clinton *be.*

(1781)

Literary Importation

However we wrangled with Britain awhile
We think of her now in a different stile,
And many fine things we receive from her isle;
Among all the rest,
Some demon possessed
Our dealers in knowledge and sellers of sense
To have a good *bishop* imported from thence.

The words of *Sam Chandler*[1] were thought to be vain,
When he argued so often and proved it *so plain*
"That Satan must flourish till bishops should reign:"
Though he went to the wall
With his project and all,
Another bold Sammy,[2] in bishop's array,
Has got something more than his pains for his pay.

It seems we had spirit to humble a throne,
Have genius for science inferior to none,
But hardly encourage a plant of our own:
If a college be planned,
'Tis all at a stand
'Till in Europe we send at a shameful expense,
To send us a book-worm to teach us some sense.

1 Who laboured for the establishment of an American Episcopacy, previously
to the revolutionary war. [Freneau's note]
2 Bishop Samuel Seabury of Connecticut.

Can we never be thought to have learning or grace
Unless it be brought from that horrible place
Where tyranny reigns with her impudent face;
And popes and pretenders,
And sly faith-defenders
Have ever been hostile to reason and wit,
Enslaving a world that shall conquer them yet.

'Tis folly to fret at the picture I draw:
And I say what was said by a *Doctor Magraw*;[3]
"If they give us their Bishops, they'll give us their law."
How that will agree
With such people as we,
Let us leave to the learned to reflect on awhile,
And say what they think in a handsomer stile.

(1786)

On the Emigration to America

and
Peopling the Western Country

To western woods, and lonely plains,
Palemon from the crowd departs,
Where Nature's wildest genius reigns,
To tame the soil, and plant the arts —
What wonders there shall freedom show,
What mighty STATES successive grow!

From Europe's proud, despotic shores
Hither the stranger takes his way,
And in our new found world explores
A happier soil, a milder sway,
Where no proud despot holds him down,
No slaves insult him with a crown.

What charming scenes attract the eye,
On wild Ohio's savage stream!
There Nature reigns, whose works outvie
The boldest pattern art can frame;
There ages past have rolled away,
And forests bloomed but to decay.

From these fair plains, these rural seats,
So long concealed, so lately known,

[3] A noted practitioner in physic, formerly of N. York. [Freneau's note]

The unsocial Indian far retreats,
To make some other clime his own,
When other streams, less pleasing flow,
And darker forests round him grow.

Great Sire[1] of floods; whose varied wave
Through climes and countries takes its way,
To whom creating Nature gave
Ten thousand streams to swell thy sway!
No longer shall *they* useless prove,
Nor idly through the forests rove;

Nor longer shall your princely flood
From distant lakes be swelled in vain,
Nor longer through a darksome wood
Advance, unnoticed, to the main,
Far other ends, the heavens decree —
And commerce plans new freights for thee.

While virtue warms the generous breast,
There heaven-born freedom shall reside,
Nor shall the voice of war molest,
Nor Europe's all-aspiring pride —
There Reason shall new laws devise,
And order from confusion rise.

Forsaking kings and regal state,
With all their pomp and fancied bliss,
The traveller owns, convinced though late,
No realm so free, so blest as this —
The east is half to slaves consigned,
Where kings and priests enchain the mind.

O come the time, and haste the day,
When man shall man no longer crush,
When Reason shall enforce her sway,
Nor these fair regions raise our blush,
Where still the *African* complains,
And mourns his yet unbroken chains.

Far brighter scenes a future age,
The muse predicts, these States will hail,
Whose genius may the world engage,
Whose deeds may over death prevail,
And happier systems bring to view,
Than all the eastern sages knew.

(1784)

[1] Mississippi. [Freneau's note]

Stanzas

To the memory of General WASHINGTON, *who died December 14,* 1799

Terra tegit, populus moeret, coelum habet!

Departing with the closing age
    To virtue, worth, and freedom true,
The chief, the patriot, and the sage
    To Vernon bids his last adieu:
        To reap in some exalted sphere
        The just rewards of virtue here.

Thou, Washington, by heaven design'd
    To act a part in human things
That few have known among mankind,
    And far beyond the task of kings;
        We hail you now to heaven received,
        Your mighty task on earth achieved.

While sculpture and her sister arts,
    For thee their choicest wreaths prepare,
Fond gratitude her share imparts
    And begs thy bones for burial there;
        Where, near Virginia's northern bound
        Swells the vast pile on federal ground.

To call from their obscure abodes
    The grecian chief, the roman sage,
The kings, the heroes, and the gods
    Who flourish'd in time's earlier age,
        Would be to class them not with you, —
        Superior far, in every view.

Those ancients of ferocious mould,
    Blood their delight, and war their trade,
Their oaths profaned, their countries sold,
    And fetter'd nations prostrate laid;
        Could these, like you, assert their claim
        To honor and immortal fame?

Those monarchs, proud of pillaged spoils,
    With nations shackled in their train,
Returning from their desperate toils
    With trophies, — and their thousands slain;

In all they did no traits are known
Like those that honor'd Washington.

Who now will save our shores from harms,
   The task to him so long assign'd?
Who now will rouse our youth to arms
   Should war approach to curse mankind?
      Alas! no more the word you give,
      But in your precepts you survive.

Ah, gone! and none your place supply,
   Nor will your equal soon appear;
But that great name can only die
   When memory dwells no longer here,
      When man and all his systems must
      Dissolve, like you, and turn to dust.

                                    (1799)

The Republican Genius of Europe

Emperors and kings! in vain you strive
   Your torments to conceal —
The age is come that shakes your thrones,
Tramples in dust despotic crowns,
   And bids the spectre fail.

In western worlds the flame began:
   From thence to France it flew —
Through Europe, now, it takes its way,
Beams an insufferable day,
   And lays all tyrants low.

Genius of France! pursue the chace
   Till Reason's laws restore
Man to be Man, in every clime; —
That Being, active, great, sublime
   Debas'd in dust no more.

In dreadful pomp he takes his way
   O'er ruin'd crowns, demolish'd thrones —
      Pale tyrants shrink before his blaze —
Round him terrific lightnings play —
   With eyes of fire, he looks them through,
   Crushes the vile despotic crew,
      And Pride in ruin lays.

                                    (1795)

On Mr. Paine's Rights of Man

Thus briefly sketched the sacred RIGHTS OF MAN,
How inconsistent with the ROYAL PLAN!
Which for itself exclusive honour craves,
Where some are masters born, and millions slaves.
With what contempt must every eye look down
On that base, childish bauble called a *crown*,
The gilded bait, that lures the crowd, to come,
Bow down their necks, and meet a slavish doom;
The source of half the miseries men endure,
The quack that kills them, while it seems to cure.
   Roused by the REASON of his manly page,
Once more shall PAINE a listening world engage:
From Reason's source, a bold reform he brings,
In raising up *mankind*, he pulls down *kings*,
Who, source of discord, patrons of all wrong,
On blood and murder have been fed too long:
Hid from the world, and tutored to be base,
The curse, the scourge, the ruin of our race,
Their's was the task, a dull designing few,
To shackle beings that they scarcely knew,
Who made this globe the residence of slaves,
And built their thrones on systems formed by knaves.
— Advance, bright years, to work their final fall,
And haste the period that shall crush them all.
   Who, that has read and scann'd the historic page
But glows, at every line, with kindling rage,
To see by them the rights of men aspersed,
Freedom restrain'd, and Nature's law reversed,
Men, ranked with beasts, by monarchs *will'd* away,
And bound young fools, or madmen to obey:
Now driven to wars, and now oppressed at home,
Compelled in crowds o'er distant seas to roam,
From India's climes the plundered prize to bring
To glad the strumpet, or to glut the king.
   COLUMBIA, hail! immortal be thy reign:
Without a king, we till the smiling plain;
Without a king, we trace the unbounded sea,
And traffic round the globe, through each degree;
Each foreign clime our honour'd flag reveres,
Which asks no monarch, to support the STARS:
Without a *king*, the laws maintain their sway,
While honour bids each generous heart obey.
Be ours the task the ambitious to restrain,
And this great lesson teach — that kings are vain;

That warring realms to certain ruin haste,
That kings subsist by war, and wars are waste:
So shall our nation, form'd on Virtue's plan,
Remain the guardian of the Rights of Man,
A vast Republic, famed through every clime,
Without a king, to see the end of time.

(1792, 1795)

Stanzas

On the decease of Thomas Paine, who died at New York, on the 8th of June, 1809

Princes and kings decay and die
   And, instant, rise again:
But this is not the case, trust me,
   With men like THOMAS PAINE.

In vain the democratic host
   His *equal* would attain:
For years to come they will not boast
   A second Thomas Paine.

Though many may his name assume;
   Assumption is in vain;
For every man has not *his* plume —
   Whose name is *Thomas Paine.*

Though heaven bestow'd on all its sons
   Their *proper* share of brain,
It gives to few, ye simple ones,
   The mind of Thomas Paine.

To tyrants and the tyrant crew,
   Indeed, he was the bane;
He writ, and gave them all their due,
   And signed it, — THOMAS PAINE.

Oh! how we loved to see him write
   And curb the race of Cain!
They hope and wish that Thomas P ——
   May never rise again.

What idle hopes! — yes — such a man
   May yet appear again. —
When *they* are dead, they die for aye:
   — Not so with Thomas Paine.

(1809)

Reflections

ON THE GRADUAL PROGRESS OF NATIONS FROM DEMOCRATICAL
STATES TO DESPOTIC EMPIRES

Mantua vae miserae nimium vicina Cremonae!   Virgil.

Oh fatal day! when to the Atlantic shore
European despots sent the doctrine o'er,
That man's vast race was born to lick the dust;
Feed on the Winds, or toil through life accurst;
Poor and despised, that rulers might be great
And swell to monarchs, to devour the state.

Whence came these ills, or from what causes grew,
This vortex vast, that only spares the few,
Despotic sway, where every plague combined,
Distracts, degrades, and swallows up mankind;
Takes from the intellectual sun its light,
And shrouds the world in universal night?

Accuse not nature for the dreary scene,
That glooms her stage or hides her heaven serene,
She, equal still in all her varied ways,
An equal blessing to the world displays.
The suns that now on northern climates glow,
Will soon retire to melt Antarctic snow,
The seas she robb'd to form her clouds and rain,
Return in rivers to that source again;
But man, wrong'd man, borne down, deceived and vex'd,
Groans on through life, bewilder'd and perplex'd;
No suns on him but suns of misery shine,
Now march'd to war, now grovelling in the mine.
Chain'd, fetter'd, prostrate, sent from earth a slave,
To seek rewards in worlds beyond the grave.

If in her general system, just to all,
We nature an impartial parent call,
Why did she not on man's whole race bestow,
Those fine sensations angels only know;
Who, sway'd by reason, with superior mind
In nature's state all nature's blessings find,
Which shed through all, does all their race pervade,
In streams not niggard by a despot made?

Leave this a secret in great nature's breast,
Confess that all her works tend to the best,

Or own that man's neglected culture here
Breeds all the mischiefs that we feel or fear.
In all, except the skill to rule her race,
Man, wise and skillful, gives each part its place:
Each nice machine he plans, to reason true,
Adapting all things to the end in view,
But taught in this, the art himself to rule
His sense is folly, and himself a fool.

Where social strength resides, there rests, 'tis plain,
The power, mankind to govern and restrain:
This strength is not but in the social plan
Controling all, the common good of man,
That power concentred by the general voice,
In honest men, an honest people's choice,
With frequent change, to keep the patriot pure,
And from vain views of power the heart secure:
Here lies the secret, hid from Rome or Greece,
That holds a state in awe, yet holds in peace.

See through the world, in ages now retired,
Man foe to man, as policy required:
At some proud tyrant's nod what millions rose,
To extend their sway, and make a world their foes.
View Asia ravaged, Europe drench'd with blood,
In feuds whose cause no nation understood.
The cause we fear, of so much misery sown,
Known at the helm of state, and there alone.

Left to himself, wherever man is found,
In peace he aims to walk life's little round;
In peace to sail, in peace to till the soil,
Nor force false grandeur from a brother's toil.
All but the base, designing, scheming, few,
Who seize on nations with a robber's view,
With crowns and sceptres awe his dazzled eye,
And priests that hold the artillery of the sky;
These, these, with armies, navies, potent grown,
Impoverish man and bid the nations groan.
These with pretended balances of states
Keep worlds at variance, breed eternal hates,
Make man the poor base slave of low design,
Degrade his nature to its last decline,
Shed hell's worse blots on his exalted race,
And make them poor and mean, to make them base.

Shall views like these assail our happy land,
Where embryo monarchs thirst for wide command,

Shall a whole nation's strength and fair renown
Be sacrificed, to prop a tottering throne,
That, ages past, the world's great curse has stood,
Has throve on plunder, and been fed on blood. —
Americans! will you control such views?
Speak — for you must — you have no hour to lose.

(1815)

ᕔᔤᕗ

THE COMMON TOUCH

Tobacco

(Supposed to be written by a Young Beginner)

This *Indian weed,* that once did grow
On fair *Virginia's* fertile plain,
From whence it came — again may go,
To please some happier swain:
Of all the plants that Nature yields
This, least beloved, shall shun my fields.

In evil hour I first essayed
To chew this vile forbidden leaf,
When, half ashamed, and half afraid,
I touched, and tasted — to my grief:
Ah me! the more I was forbid,
The more I wished to take a *quid.*

But when I smoaked, in thought profound,
And raised the spiral circle high,
My heart grew sick, my head turned round —
And what can all this mean, (said I) —
Tobacco surely was designed
To poison, and destroy mankind.

Unhappy they, whom choice, or fate
Inclines to prize this bitter weed;
Perpetual source of female hate;
On which no beast — but man will feed;
That sinks my heart, and turns my head,
And sends me, reeling, home to bed!

(1790)

The Indian Convert

An Indian, who lived at *Muskingum,* remote,
Was teazed by a parson to join his dear flock,
To throw off his blanket and put on a coat,
And of grace and religion to lay in a stock.

The Indian long slighted an offer so fair,
Preferring to preaching his fishing and fowling;
A *sermon* to him was a heart full of care,
And singing but little superior to howling.

At last by persuasion and constant harassing
Our Indian was brought to consent to be *good;*
He saw that the malice of *Satan* was pressing,
And the *means* to repel him not yet understood.

Of heaven, one day, when the parson was speaking,
And painting the beautiful things of the place,
The *convert,* who something substantial was seeking,
Rose up, and confessed he had doubts in the case. —

Said he, *Master Minister,* this place that you talk of,
Of things for the stomach, pray what has it got;
Has it liquors in plenty? — if so I'll soon walk off
And put myself down in the heavenly spot.

You fool (said the preacher) no liquors are there!
The place I'm describing is most like our meeting,
Good people, all singing, with preaching and prayer;
They live upon these without eating or drinking.

But the doors are all locked against folks that are wicked:
And you, I am fearful, will never get there: —
A life of REPENTANCE must purchase the ticket,
And few of you, Indians, can buy it, I fear.

Farewell (said the Indian) I'm none of your mess;
On victuals, so airy, I faintish should feel,
I cannot consent to be lodged in a place
Where there's nothing to eat and but little to steal.

(1797)

The Drunkard's Apology

"You blame the blushes on my nose,
And yet admire the blushing rose;
On CELIA's cheek the bloom you prize,
And yet, on mine, that bloom despise.

"The world of spirits you admire,
To which all holy men aspire:
Yet, me with curses you requite,
Because in *spirits* I delight.

"Whene'er I fall, and crack my crown,
You blame me much for *falling down* —
Yet to some *god*, that you adore,
You, too, fall prostrate on the floor.

"You call me fool, for drinking hard;
And yet old HUDSON you regard,
Who fills his jug from yonder bay,
And drinks his guts-full, every day!" —
                                        (1795)

Jack Straw, or the Forest Beau

When first to feel Love's fire JACK STRAW begins
He combs his hair, and cocks his hat with pins,
Views in some stream, his face, with fond regard,
Plucks from his upper lip the bristly beard,
With soap and sand his homely visage scowers
(Rough from the joint attack of sun and showers)
The sheepskin breeches stretch'd upon his thighs, —
Next on his back the homespun coat he tries;
Round his broad breast he wraps the jerkin blue,
And sews a spacious soal on either shoe.
Thus, all prepar'd, the fond adoring swain
Cuts from his groves of pine a ponderous cane;
In thought a beau, a savage to the eye,
Forth, from his mighty bosom, heaves the sigh;
Tobacco is the present for his fair,
This he admires, and this best pleases her —
The bargain struck — few cares his bosom move
How to maintain, or how to lodge his love;
Close at his hand the piny forest grows,

Thence for his hut a slender frame he hews,
With art, (not copied from *Palladio's* rules,)
A hammer and an axe, his only tools,
By Nature taught, a hasty hut he forms
Safe in the woods, to shelter from the storms; —
There sees the summer pass and winter come,
Nor envies Britain's king his loftier home.

(1795)

❦

THREE POEMS OF FAITH

On the Religion of Nature

The power, that gives with liberal hand
   The blessings man enjoys, while here,
And scatters through a smiling land
   Abundant products of the year;
      That power of nature, ever bless'd,
      Bestow'd religion with the rest.

Born with ourselves, her early sway
   Inclines the tender mind to take
The path of right, fair virtue's way
   Its own felicity to make.
      This universally extends
      And leads to no mysterious ends.

Religion, such as nature taught,
   With all divine perfection suits;
Had all mankind this system sought
   Sophists would cease their vain disputes,
      And from this source would nations know
      All that can make their heaven below.

This deals not curses on mankind,
   Or dooms them to perpetual grief,
If from its aid no joys they find,
   It damns them not for unbelief;
      Upon a more exalted plan
      Creatress nature dealt with man —

Joy to the day, when all agree
   On such grand systems to proceed,

From fraud, design, and error free,
　And which to truth and goodness lead:
　　Then persecution will retreat
　　And man's religion be complete.

(1815)

On the Universality and Other Attributes
of the God of Nature

All that we see, about, abroad,
What is it all, but nature's God?
In meaner works discover'd here
No less than in the starry sphere.

In seas, on earth, this God is seen;
All that exist, upon him lean;
He lives in all, and never stray'd
A moment from the works he made:

His system fix'd on general laws
Bespeaks a wise creating cause;
Impartially he rules mankind
And all that on this globe we find.

Unchanged in all that seems to change,
Unbounded space is his great range;
To one vast purpose always true,
No time, with him, is old or new.

In all the attributes divine
Unlimited perfectings shine;
In these enwrapt, in these complete,
All virtues in that centre meet.

This power who doth all powers transcend,
To all intelligence a friend,
Exists, the *greatest and the best*
Throughout all worlds, to make them blest.

All that he did he first approved
He all things into *being* loved;
O'er all he made he still presides,
For them in life, or death provides.

(1815)

On the Uniformity and Perfection of Nature

On one fix'd point all nature moves,
Nor deviates from the track she loves;
Her system, drawn from reason's source,
She scorns to change her wonted course.

Could she descend from that great plan
To work unusual things for man,
To suit the insect of an hour —
This would betray a want of power,

Unsettled in its first design
And erring, when it did combine
The parts that form the vast machine,
The figures sketch'd on nature's scene.

Perfections of the great first cause
Submit to no contracted laws,
But all-sufficient, all-supreme,
Include no trivial views in them.

Who looks through nature with an eye
That would the scheme of heaven descry,
Observes her constant, still the same,
In all her laws, through all her frame.

No imperfection can be found
In all that is, above, around, —
All, nature made, in reason's sight
Is order all, and *all is right.*

(1815)

An American Play

◁ℜ William Dunlap (1766–1839)

WILLIAM DUNLAP, born in New Jersey, showed early talent as a painter. At sixteen he was already a successful portrait artist, with George and Martha Washington among his subjects. He spent three years in London as a student of Benjamin West's, and returned to continue his artistic career. However, he saw Royall Tyler's play, *The Contrast;* imitated it successfully in a comedy of manners called *The Father* (1789); and chose a career in the theater instead.

Dunlap wrote a play a year (including one opera) until he purchased a share of the Old American Theater Company in New York in 1796, thereupon becoming its manager, bookkeeper, and business agent. He also managed the Park Theater and stayed with the Old American Company until it went bankrupt in 1805. He continued to write, but he found greater success in translating and adapting German and French plays: of the sixty-odd plays credited to him, about half are original; the rest are adaptations of Kotzebue, Schiller, and various French playwrights. After his company failed, Dunlap took up miniature painting, managed another theater, attempted to edit a magazine, wrote a novel and a biography of his friend Charles Brockden Brown, and helped to found the National Academy of Design (1826) where he served as professor of historical painting. His *History of the American Theater* (1832) is one of the most important works on early American theatrical history, and his *History of the Rise and Progress of the Arts of Design in the United States* (2 vols., 1834) is still indispensable for the study of early American art.

Major John André was hanged on October 2, 1780, at the age of twenty-nine, after a military board headed by General Greene (and including Lafayette) had pronounced him a spy, which he undoubtedly was. Dunlap's play *André* was produced on March

30, 1798; Benedict Arnold was still alive in London, and Washington survived the play by more than a year and a half. The play was presented in the Park Theater in New York by the Old American Company, with Hodgkinson, who was also one of the Company's shareholders, taking the part of André. The first night was a moderate success (except that Mr. Cooper, as Bland, forgot far too many of his lines) and the receipts were $817. After a brief run the company moved on to other productions, but Dunlap returned to *André* twice more, revising and using parts of it in other plays in 1803 and 1807.

The story of André still had great appeal to the American public, eighteen years after his execution. Dunlap no doubt saw in it, as other authors did, the elements of irony, nationalism, tragedy, and moral tension which made prime dramatic material. First of all, it was a spy story of the late Revolution, and thus doubly appealing to an audience. Second, André himself was an interesting figure — young, handsome, a talented amateur artist and poet, a likable and respected young man who had a good many friends on the American side. Furthermore, he had actually suffered a broken romance with a young English girl, Honora Seward, whose parents had forbidden their marriage, a love story that Dunlap pulled into the plot to good advantage. Then, too, Arnold's escape and André's capture lent tragic irony to the affair. Arnold, for his treachery, received a brigadier's commission, a reward, and an annuity for his wife and family, and was at the moment living peacefully in London. Young André, who was only a go-between, captured almost by accident, paid with his life for Arnold's treason. Finally, of course, the action included, as a perfect center for the story, the godlike figure of George Washington, whose choice it ultimately was that the young man should die. It is little wonder that Dunlap, as he wrote in the preface to the published version, spent nine years working on the play before he succeeded in fusing its elements into a dramatic whole.

André is first and foremost a nationalistic, patriotic play, a historical *tour de force* intended to bring cheers from the audience at climactic points. As Washington speaks in Act I:

> O patriotism!
> Thou wondrous principle of godlike action,
> Where liberty is found, there reigns
> The love of country. Now the self-same spirit
> Which fill'd the breast of great Leonidas
> Swells in the hearts of thousands on these plains,
> Thousands who never heard the hero's tale.
> 'Tis this alone which saves thee, O my country!
> And, till that spirit flies these western shores,
> No power on earth shall crush thee.

Nationalistic pride is clearly a major theme of the play and the reason for its being. Yet it is noticeable that the enemy are dealt with as gentlemen, that Washington views Sir Henry Clinton as another professional soldier who knows what duty is, and that André, the spy, is treated with respect and affection. The British do set Colonel Bland free, despite their threats, and M'Donald, in the final speech, closes the play with a plea for tolerance and forgiveness toward the one-time enemy.

André is also a problem play. The central conflict of the action lies between head and heart, reason and sentiment, duty and friendship. It is also, despite its militaristic heroics, a play about "the folly, guilt, and madness" of war, as Melville muses to himself in his moody opening speech. Dunlap sets the young cavalryman Bland — impetuous, emotional, a friend of André's — against the older M'Donald, the Scotsman of "deliberate judgment" who has already lost a son in the war, but who places duty, painful as the act may be, above friendship, emotion, or abstract justice. If André's death, or the whole "accurs'd times" of war can make "this new world, / A resting spot for man, while Europe howls about him," the sacrifice is worth it.

At the moral center of the play stands Washington, who must make the choice about which Bland and M'Donald disagree. He will not deny Bland's despairing charge that the ways of war are "cruel and unjust"; like M'Donald, however, he sees André's fate in a larger context, for he believes that

. . . the destiny of millions, millions
Yet unborn, depends upon the rigor of this moment.

Washington must actually make a double choice: first, to permit the tragic but necessary death of young André; and second, by so doing to condemn to death his friend Colonel Bland, held hostage by the British. He resists the impassioned appeal of young Bland, the romantic grief of Honora, and the quiet bravery of Mrs. Bland, the good soldier's wife. It is a hard decision, but Washington makes it, as Colonel Bland himself does, by the standards of duty, that iron taskmaster of soldiers and statesmen.

Dunlap, hurried and harried through his theatrical career by impending bankruptcy, never again approached the level of skill he displayed in *André*. It remains the best example of the early American historical play, and a lonely landmark in the American drama of the 1790's.

TEXT: Arthur H. Quinn, *Representative American Plays*, 3d ed. (New York, 1925).

Alexander Hamilton

The Fate of Major André

[From a letter to Lieutenant-Colonel John Laurens,
October 1780][1]

Never, perhaps, did a man suffer death with more justice, or
deserve it less. The first step he took after his capture was to write to
General Washington, conceived in terms of dignity without insolence,
and apology without meanness. The scope of it was to vindicate
himself from the imputation of having assumed a mean character for
treacherous or interested purposes; asserting that he had been involuntarily an imposter; that contrary to his intention, which was to meet a
person for intelligence on neutral ground, he had been betrayed
within our posts, and forced into the vile condition of an enemy in disguise; soliciting only that, to whatever rigor policy might devote him,
a decency of treatment might be observed, due to a person who,
though unfortunate, had been guilty of nothing dishonorable. His
request was granted in its full extent; for, in the whole progress of
the affair, he was treated with the most scrupulous delicacy. When
brought before the Board of Officers he met with every mark of
indulgence, and was required to answer no interrogatory which could
even embarrass his feelings. On his part, while he carefully concealed
every thing that might involve others, he frankly confessed all the
facts relating to himself; and, upon his confession, without the trouble
of examining a witness, the Board made their report. The members
of it were not more impressed with the candor and firmness, mixed
with a becoming sensibility, which he displayed, than he was penetrated with their liberality and politeness. He acknowledged the
generosity of the behavior towards him in every respect, but particularly in this, in the strongest terms of manly gratitude. In a
conversation with a gentleman who visited him after his trial, he said
he flattered himself he had never been illiberal; but if there were any
remains of prejudice in his mind, his present experience must obliterate
them.

In one of the visits I made to him (and I saw him several times
during his confinement), he begged me to be the bearer of a request
to the General, for permission to send an open letter to Sir Henry
Clinton. "I foresee my fate," said he, "and though I pretend not to
play the hero, or to be indifferent about life, yet I am reconciled to

[1] From *Works*, ed. H. C. Lodge (New York, 1885–86), VIII, 23–27.

whatever may happen, conscious that misfortune, not guilt, has brought it upon me. There is only one thing that disturbs my tranquillity. Sir Henry Clinton has been too good to me; he has been lavish of his kindness. I am bound to him by too many obligations, and love him too well, to bear the thought that he should reproach himself, or that others should reproach him, on the supposition of my having conceived myself obliged, by his instructions, to run the risk I did. I would not for the world leave a sting in his mind that should imbitter his future days." He could scarce finish the sentence, bursting into tears in spite of his efforts to suppress them, and with difficulty collected himself enough afterwards to add, "I wish to be permitted to assure him I did not act under this impression, but submitted to a necessity imposed upon me, as contrary to my own inclination as to his orders." His request was readily complied with, and he wrote the letter annexed, with which I dare say you will be as much pleased as I am, both for the diction and sentiment.

When his sentence was announced to him he remarked that since it was his lot to die, there was still a choice in the mode, which would make a material difference in his feelings, and he would be happy, if possible, to be indulged with a professional death. He made a second application, by letter, in concise but persuasive terms. It was thought this indulgence, being incompatible with the customs of war, could not be granted, and it was therefore determined, in both cases, to evade an answer, to spare him the sensations which a certain knowledge of the intended mode would inflict.

In going to the place of execution, he bowed familiarly as he went along, to all those with whom he had been acquainted in his confinement. A smile of complacency expressed the serene fortitude of his mind. Arrived at the fatal spot, he asked, with some emotion, "Must I then die in this manner?" He was told that it had been unavoidable. "I am reconciled to my fate," said he, "but not to the mode." Soon, however, recollecting himself, he added: "It will be but a momentary pang," and, springing upon the cart, performed the last offices to himself, with a composure that excited the admiration and melted the hearts of the beholders. Upon being told that the final moment was at hand, and asked if he had any thing to say, he answered: "Nothing but to request you will witness to the world that I die like a brave man." Among the extraordinary circumstances that attended him, in the midst of his enemies, he died universally esteemed and universally regretted.

There was something singularly interesting in the character and fortunes of André. To an excellent understanding, well improved by education and travel, he united a peculiar elegance of mind and manners, and the advantage of a pleasing person. 'T is said he possessed a pretty taste for the fine arts, and had himself attained some proficiency in poetry, music, and painting. His knowledge appeared without ostentation, and embellished by a diffidence that rarely accompanies so many talents and accomplishments: which left you to suppose more than appeared. His sentiments were elevated, and inspired esteem: they had a softness that conciliated affection. His elocution was handsome; his address easy, polite, and insinuating. By his merit he had acquired the unlimited confidence of his general, and was making a rapid progress in military rank and reputation. But in the height of his career, flushed with new hopes from the execution of a project, the most beneficial to his party that could be devised, he was at once precipitated from the summit of prosperity, and saw all the expectations of his ambition blasted, and himself ruined.

The character I have given of him, is drawn partly from what I saw of him myself, and partly from information. I am aware that a man of real merit is never seen in so favorable a light as through the medium of adversity: the clouds that surround him are shades that set off his good qualities. Misfortune cuts down the little vanities that in prosperous times serve as so many spots in his virtues; and gives a tone of humility that makes his worth more amiable. His spectators, who enjoy a happier lot, are less prone to detract from it, through envy, and are more disposed, by compassion, to give him the credit he deserves, and perhaps even to magnify it.

I speak not of André's conduct in this affair as a philosopher, but as a man of the world. The authorized maxims and practices of war are the satires of human nature. They countenance almost every species of seduction as well as violence; and the general who can make most traitors in the army of his adversary is frequently most applauded. On this scale we acquit André; while we could not but condemn him, if we were to examine his conduct by the sober rules of philosophy and moral rectitude. It is, however, a blemish on his fame, that he once intended to prostitute a flag: about this, a man of nice honor ought to have had a scruple; but the temptation was great: let his misfortunes cast a veil over his error.

André

By William Dunlap

CHARACTERS

GENERAL, dress, American staff uniform, blue, faced with buff, large gold epaulets, cocked hat, with the black and white cockade, indicating the union with France, buff waistcoat and breeches, boots ....Mr. Hallam

M'DONALD, a man of forty years of age, uniform nearly the same as the first ....Mr. Tyler

SEWARD, a man of thirty years of age, staff uniform ......Mr. Martin

ANDRÉ, a man of twenty-nine years of age, full British uniform after the first scene ....Mr. Hodgkinson

BLAND, a youthful but military figure, in the uniform of a Captain of horse — dress, a short blue coat, faced with red, and trimmed with gold lace, two small epaulets, a white waistcoat, leather breeches, boots and spurs; over the coat, crossing the chest from the right shoulder, a broad buff belt, to which is suspended a manageable hussar sword; a horseman's helmet on the head, decorated as usual, and the union cockade affixed ....Mr. Cooper

MELVILLE, a man of middle age, and grave deportment; his dress a Captain's uniform when on duty; a blue coat with red facings, gold epaulet, white waistcoat and breeches, boots and cocked hat, with the union cockade
Mr. Williamson

BRITISH OFFICER ....Mr. Hogg

AMERICAN OFFICER ....Mr. Miller

CHILDREN ....Master Stockwell and Miss Hogg

AMERICAN SERGEANT ....Mr. Seymour

AMERICAN OFFICERS AND SOLDIERS, &c.

MRS. BLAND ....Mrs. Melmoth

HONORA ....Mrs. Johnson

Scene, the Village of Tappan, Encampment, and adjoining country.
Time, ten hours.

PROLOGUE

Spoken by Mr. Martin.

A Native Bard, a native scene displays,
And claims your candour for his daring lays:
Daring, so soon, in mimic scenes to shew,
What each remembers as a real woe.
Who has forgot when gallant André died?
A name by Fate to Sorrow's self allied.
Who has forgot, when o'er the untimely bier,
Contending armies paus'd, to drop a tear.

Our Poet builds upon a fact to-night;
Yet claims, in building, every Poet's right;
To choose, embellish, lop, or add, or blend,
Fiction with truth, as best may suit his end;
Which, he avows, is pleasure to impart,
And move the passions but to mend the heart.

O, may no party spirit blast his views,
Or turn to ill the meanings of the Muse;
She sings of wrongs long past, Men as they were,
To instruct, without reproach, the Men that are;
Then judge the Story by the genius shown,
And praise, or damn it, for its worth alone.

ACT FIRST

SCENE 1. *A Wood seen by star-light; an Encampment at a distance appearing between the trees.*

(*Enter* MELVILLE.)

MELVILLE. The solemn hour, "when night and morning meet,"
Mysterious time, to superstition dear,
And superstition's guides, now passes by;
Deathlike in solitude. The sentinels,
In drowsy tones, from post to post send on
The signal of the passing hour. "All's well,"
Sounds through the camp. Alas, all is not well;
Else, why stand I, a man, the friend of man,
At midnight's depth, deck'd in this murderous guise,
The habiliment of death, the badge of dire
Necessitous coercion. 'T is not well.
— In vain the enlighten'd friends of suffering man
Point out, of war, the folly, guilt, and madness.
Still, age succeeds to age, and war to war;
And man, the murderer, marshals out in hosts
In all the gaiety of festive pomp,
To spread around him death and desolation.
How long! how long! —
— Methinks I hear the tread of feet this way.
My meditating mood may work me woe.   (*Draws.*)
Stand, whoso'er thou art. Answer. Who's there?

(*Enter* BLAND.)

BLAND. A friend.
MELVILLE.   Advance and give the countersign.
BLAND. Hudson.
MELVILLE.   What, Bland!
BLAND.   Melville, my friend, you *here?*
MELVILLE. And *well*, my brave young friend. But why do you,
At this dead hour of night, approach the camp
On foot, and thus alone?
BLAND.   I have but now
Dismounted, and from yon sequester'd cot,
Whose lonely taper through the crannied wall
Sheds its faint beams and twinkles midst the trees,

Have I, adventurous, grop'd my darksome way.
My servant and my horses, spent with toil,
There wait till morn.
MELVILLE.   Why waited not yourself?
BLAND. Anxious to know the truth of those reports
Which, from the many mouths of busy fame,
Still, as I pass'd, struck varying on my ear,
Each making th' other void. Nor does delay
The color of my hasteful business suit.
I bring dispatches for our great Commander;
And hasted hither with design to wait
His rising, or awake him with the sun.
MELVILLE. You will not need the last, for the blest sun
Ne'er rises on his slumbers; by the dawn
We see him mounted gaily in the field,
Or find him wrapt in meditation deep,
Planning the welfare of our war-worn land.
BLAND. Prosper, kind Heaven, and recompense his cares.
MELVILLE. You're from the South, if I presume aright?
BLAND. I am; and, Melville, I am fraught with news.
The South teems with events — convulsing ones.
The Briton, there, plays at no mimic war;
With gallant face he moves, and gallantly is met.
Brave spirits, rous'd by glory, throng our camp;
The hardy hunter, skill'd to fell the deer,
Or start the sluggish bear from covert rude;
And not a clown that comes, but from his youth
Is trained to pour from far the leaden death,
To climb the steep, to struggle with the stream,
To labor firmly under scorching skies,
And bear, unshrinking, winter's roughest blast.
This, and that heaven-inspir'd enthusiasm
Which ever animates the patriot's breast,
Shall far outweigh the lack of discipline.
MELVILLE. Justice is ours; what shall prevail against her?
BLAND. But as I pass'd along, many strange tales
And monstrous rumors have my ears assail'd:
That Arnold had prov'd false; but he was ta'en
And hung, or to be hung — I know not what.
Another told that all our army, with their
Much-lov'd Chief, sold and betray'd, were captur'd.
But as I nearer drew, at yonder cot
'T was said that Arnold, traitor like, had fled;
And that a Briton, tried and prov'd a spy,

Was, on this day, as such, to suffer death.

MELVILLE. As you drew near, plain truth advanced to meet you.
'T is even as you heard, my brave young friend.
Never had people on a single throw
More interest at stake; when he who held
For us the die prov'd false and play'd us foul.
But for a circumstance of that nice kind,
Of cause so microscopic that the tongues
Of inattentive men call it the effect
Of chance, we must have lost the glorious game.

BLAND. Blest, blest be heaven! whatever was the cause!

MELVILLE. That blow ere this had fallen that would have bruis'd
The tender plant which we have striven to rear,
Crush'd to the dust, no more to bless this soil.

BLAND. What warded off the blow?

MELVILLE. The brave young man, who this day dies, was seiz'd
Within our bounds, in rustic garb disguis'd.
He offer'd bribes to tempt the band that seiz'd him;
But the rough farmer, for his country arm'd,
That soil defending which his ploughshare turn'd,
Those laws his father chose and he approv'd,
Cannot, as mercenary soldiers may,
Be brib'd to sell the public weal for gold.

BLAND. 'T is well. Just Heaven! O grant that thus may fall
All those who seek to bring this land to woe,
All those, who, or by open force, or dark
And secret machinations, seek to shake
The Tree of Liberty, or stop its growth,
In any soil where thou hast pleased to plant it.

MELVILLE. Yet not a heart but pities and would save him;
For all confirm that he is brave and virtuous;
Known, but till now, the darling child of Honor.

BLAND. (*Contemptuously.*) And how is call'd this — honorable spy?

MELVILLE. André's his name.

BLAND. (*Much agitated.*) André!

MELVILLE. Aye! Major André.

BLAND. André! — O no, my friend, you're sure deceiv'd —
I'll pawn my life, my ever sacred fame,
My General's favor, or a soldier's honor,
That gallant André never yet put on
The guise of falsehood. O, it cannot be!

MELVILLE. How might I be deceiv'd? I've heard him, seen him,
And what I tell, I tell from well-prov'd knowledge;
No second tale-bearer who heard the news.

BLAND. Pardon me, Melville. O, that well-known name,
 So link'd with circumstances infamous!
 My friend must pardon me. Thou wilt not blame
 When I shall tell what cause I have to love him;
 What cause to think him nothing more the pupil
 Of Honor stern, than sweet Humanity.
 Rememberest thou, when cover'd o'er with wounds
 And left upon the field, I fell the prey
 Of Britain? To a loathsome prison-ship
 Confin'd, soon had I sunk, victim of death,
 A death of aggravated miseries;
 But, by benevolence urg'd, this best of men,
 This gallant youth, then favor'd, high in power,
 Sought out the pit obscene of foul disease,
 Where I and many a suffering soldier lay,
 And, like an angel, seeking good for man,
 Restor'd us light and partial liberty.
 Me he mark'd out his own. He nurst and cur'd,
 He lov'd and made his friend. I liv'd by him,
 And in my heart he liv'd, till, when exchang'd,
 Duty and honor call'd me from my friend.
 Judge how my heart is tortur'd. — Gracious Heaven,
 Thus, thus to meet him on the brink of death —
 A death so infamous. Heav'n grant my prayer.   (*Kneels.*)
 That I may save him, O inspire my heart
 With thoughts, my tongue with words that move to pity. (*Rises.*)
 Quick, Melville, show me where my André lies.
MELVILLE. Good wishes go with you.
BLAND. I'll save my friend.   (*Exeunt.*)

    SCENE, *the Encampment by star-light.*

   (*Enter the* GENERAL, M'DONALD, *and* SEWARD.)

GENERAL. 'T is well. Each sentinel upon his post
 Stands firm, and meets me at the bayonet's point;
 While in his tent the weary soldier lies,
 The sweet reward of wholesome toil enjoying;
 Resting secure as erst within his cot
 He careless slept, his rural labor o'er;
 Ere Britons dar'd to violate those laws,
 Those boasted laws by which themselves are govern'd,
 And strove to make their fellow-subjects slaves.
SEWARD. They know to whom they owe their present safety.

GENERAL. I hope they know that to themselves they owe it;
   To that good discipline which they observe,
   The discipline of men to order train'd
   Who know its value, and in whom 't is virtue;
   To that prompt hardihood with which they meet
   Or toil or danger, poverty or death.
   Mankind who know not whence that spirit springs,
   Which holds at bay all Britain's boasted power,
   Gaze on their deeds astonish'd. See the youth
   Start from his plough and straightway play the hero;
   Unmurmuring bear such toils as veterans shun;
   Rest all content upon the dampsome earth;
   Follow undaunted to the deathful charge;
   Or, when occasion asks, lead to the breach,
   Fearless of all the unusual din of war,
   His former peaceful mates. O patriotism!
   Thou wondrous principle of godlike action.
   Wherever liberty is found, there reigns
   The love of country. Now the self-same spirit
   Which fill'd the breast of great Leonidas
   Swells in the hearts of thousands on these plains,
   Thousands who never heard the hero's tale.
   'T is this alone which saves thee, O my country!
   And, till that spirit flies these western shores,
   No power on earth shall crush thee.
SEWARD.   'T is wondrous!
   The men of other climes from this shall see
   How easy 't is to shake oppression off;
   How all-resistless is a union'd people;
   And hence, from our success (which, by my soul,
   I feel as much secur'd as though our foes
   Were now within their floating prisons hous'd,
   And their proud prows all pointing to the east),
   Shall other nations break their galling fetters,
   And re-assume the dignity of man.
M'DONALD. Are other nations in that happy state,
   That, having broke Coercion's iron yoke,
   They can submit to Order's gentle voice,
   And walk on earth self-ruled? I much do fear it.
   As to ourselves, in truth, I nothing see,
   In all the wondrous deeds which we perform,
   But plain effects from causes full as plain.
   Rises not man forever 'gainst oppression?
   It is the law of life; he can't avoid it.

But when the love of property unites
With sense of injuries past and dread of future,
Is it then wonderful that he should brave
A lesser evil to avoid a greater?
GENERAL. (*Sportively.*) 'T is hard, quite hard, we may not please
    ourselves,
By our great deeds ascribing to our virtue.
SEWARD. M'Donald never spares to lash our pride.
M'DONALD. In truth I know of naught to make you proud.
I think there's none within the camp that draws
With better will his sword than does M'Donald.
I have a home to guard. My son is — butcher'd —
SEWARD. Hast thou no nobler motives for thy arms
Than love of property and thirst for vengeance?
M'DONALD. Yes, my good Seward, and yet nothing wondrous.
I love this country for the sake of man.
My parents, and I thank them, cross'd the seas,
And made me native of fair Nature's world,
With room to grow and thrive in. I have thriven;
And feel my mind unshackled, free, expanding,
Grasping with ken unbounded mighty thoughts,
At which, if chance my mother had, good dame,
In Scotia, our revered parent soil,
Given me to see the day, I should have shrunk
Affrighted. Now, I see in this new world
A resting spot for man, if he can stand
Firm in his place, while Europe howls around him,
And all unsettled as the thoughts of vice,
Each nation in its turn threats him with feeble malice.
One trial, now, we prove; and I have met it.
GENERAL. And met it like a man, my brave M'Donald.
M'DONALD. I hope so; and I hope my every act
Has been the offspring of deliberate judgment;
Yet feeling seconds reason's cool resolves.
O! I could hate, if I did not more pity
These bands of mercenary Europeans,
So wanting in the common sense of nature,
As, without shame, to sell themselves for pelf
To aid the cause of darkness; murder man —
Without inquiry murder, and yet call
Their trade the trade of honor — high-soul'd honor —
Yet honor shall accord in act with falsehood.
O! that proud man should e'er descend to play
The tempter's part, and lure men to their ruin!

Deceit and honor badly pair together.

SEWARD. You have much shew of reason; yet, methinks
What you suggest of one, whom fickle Fortune,
In her changeling mood, hath hurl'd, unpitying,
From her topmost height to lowest misery,
Tastes not of charity. André, I mean.

M'DONALD. I mean him, too; sunk by misdeed, not fortune.
Fortune and chance, O, most convenient words!
Man runs the wild career of blind ambition,
Plunges in vice, takes falsehood for his buoy,
And when he feels the waves of ruin o'er him,
Curses, "in good set terms," poor Lady Fortune.

GENERAL. (*Sportively to* SEWARD.) His mood is all untoward; let us
leave him.
Tho' he may think that he is bound to rail,
We are not bound to hear him. (*To* M'DONALD.) Grant you that?

M'DONALD. O, freely, freely! You I never rail on.

GENERAL. No thanks for that; you've courtesy for office.

M'DONALD. You slander me.

GENERAL. Slander that would not wound.
Worthy M'Donald, though it suits full well
The virtuous man to frown on all misdeeds,
Yet ever keep in mind that man is frail;
His tide of passion struggling still with Reason's
Fair and favorable gale, and adverse
Driving his unstable Bark upon the
Rocks of error. Should he sink thus shipwreck'd,
Sure, it is not Virtue's voice that triumphs
In his ruin. I must seek rest. Adieu!

> (*Exeunt* GENERAL *and* SEWARD.)

M'DONALD. Both good and great thou art; first among men;
By nature, or by early habit, grac'd
With that blest quality which gives due force
To every faculty, and keeps the mind
In healthful equipoise, ready for action;
Invaluable temperance — by all
To be acquired, yet scarcely known to any.   (*Exit.*)

END OF THE FIRST ACT.

ACT SECOND

SCENE, *a Prison*. ANDRÉ *discovered, in a pensive posture, sitting at a table; a book by him and candles; his dress neglected, his hair dishevelled; he rises and comes forward.*

ANDRÉ. Kind Heaven be thank'd for that I stand alone
In this sad hour of life's brief pilgrimage!
Single in misery; no one else involving,
In grief, in shame, and ruin. 'T is my comfort.
Thou, my thrice honor'd sire, in peace went'st down
Unto the tomb, nor knew to blush, nor knew
A pang for me. And thou, revered matron,
Could'st bless thy child, and yield thy breath in peace!
No wife shall weep, no child lament my loss.
Thus may I consolation find in what
Was once my woe. I little thought to joy
In not possessing, as I erst possest,
Thy love, Honora! André's death, perhaps,
May cause a cloud pass o'er thy lovely face;
The pearly tear may steal from either eye;
For thou mayest feel a transient pang, nor wrong
A husband's rights: more than a transient pang
O mayest thou never feel! The morn draws nigh
To light me to my shame. Frail nature shrinks —
And *is* death then so fearful? I have brav'd
Him, fearless, in the field, and steel'd my breast
Against his thousand horrors; but his cool,
His sure approach, requires a fortitude
Which naught but conscious rectitude can give.
                                    (*Retires, and sits leaning.*)

(*Enter* BLAND, *unperceived by* ANDRÉ.)

BLAND. And is that André? O, how changed! Alas!
Where is that martial fire, that generous warmth,
Which glow'd his manly countenance throughout,
And gave to every look, to every act,
The tone of high chivalrous animation?
André, my friend, look up!
ANDRÉ.   Who calls *me* friend?
BLAND. Young Arthur Bland.
ANDRÉ. (*Rising.*) That name sounds like a friend's. (*With emotion.*)

I have inquired for thee — wish'd much to see thee —
I prythee take no note of these fool's tears —
My heart was full — and seeing thee —
BLAND. (*Embracing him.*)   O André!
I have but now arrived from the South —
Nor heard — till now — of this — I cannot speak.
Is this a place? — O, thus to find my friend!
ANDRÉ. Still dost thou call me friend? I, who dared act
Against my reason, my declared opinion;
Against my conscience and a soldier's fame?
Oft in the generous heat of glowing youth,
Oft have I said how fully I despis'd
All bribery base, all treacherous tricks in war:
Rather my blood should bathe these hostile shores,
And have it said, "he died a gallant soldier,"
Than with my country's gold encourage treason,
And thereby purchase gratitude and fame.
BLAND. Still mayest thou say it, for thy heart's the same.
ANDRÉ. Still is my heart the same, still may I say it;
But now my deeds will rise against my words;
And should I dare to talk of honest truth,
Frank undissembling probity and faith,
Memory would crimson o'er my burning cheek,
And actions retrospected choak the tale.
Still is my heart the same. But there has past
A day, an hour, which ne'er can be recall'd.
Unhappy man! Tho' all thy life pass pure;
Mark'd by benevolence thy every deed;
The out-spread map, which shows the way thou'st trod,
Without one devious track or doubtful line;
It all avails thee naught, if in one hour,
One hapless hour, thy feet are led astray; —
Thy happy deeds all blotted from remembrance;
Cancel'd the record of thy former good.
Is it not hard, my friend? Is 't not unjust?
BLAND. Not every record cancel'd. — O, there are hearts
Where Virtue's image, when 't is once engraved,
Can never know erasure.
ANDRÉ.   Generous Bland!   (*Takes his hand.*)
The hour draws nigh which ends my life's sad story.
I should be firm —
BLAND.   By heaven, thou shalt not die!
Thou dost not sure deserve it. Betray'd, perhaps —
Condemn'd without due circumstance made known?

Thou didst not mean to tempt our officers?
Betray our yeoman soldiers to destruction?
Silent! Nay, then 't was from a duteous wish
To serve the cause thou wast in honor bound. —
ANDRÉ. Kind is my Bland, who to his generous heart
Still finds excuses for his erring friend.
Attentive hear and judge me. —
Pleas'd with the honors daily shower'd upon me,
I glow'd with martial heat my name to raise
Above the vulgar herd, who live to die,
And die to be forgotten. Thus I stood,
When avarice or ambition Arnold tempted,
His country, fame, and honor to betray,
Linking his name to infamy eternal.
In confidence it was to me propos'd
To plan with him the means which should ensure
Thy country's downfall. Nothing then I saw
But confidential favor in the service,
My country's glory, and my mounting fame;
Forgot my former purity of thought,
And high-ton'd honor's scruples disregarded.
BLAND. It was thy duty so to serve thy country.
ANDRÉ. Nay, nay; be cautious ever to admit
That duty can beget dissimulation.
On ground, unoccupied by either part,
Neutral esteem'd, I landed, and was met.
But ere my conference was with Arnold clos'd,
The day began to dawn; I then was told
That till the night I must my safety seek
In close concealment. Within your posts convey'd,
I found myself involved in unthought dangers.
Night came. I sought the vessel which had borne
Me to the fatal spot; but she was gone.
Retreat that way cut off, again I sought
Concealment with the traitors of your army.
Arnold now granted passes, and I doff'd
My martial garb, and put on curs'd disguise.
Thus in a peasant's form I pass'd your posts;
And when, as I conceiv'd, my danger o'er,
Was stopt and seiz'd by some returning scouts.
So did ambition lead me, step by step,
To treat with traitors, and encourage treason;
And then, bewilder'd in the guilty scene,
To quit my martial designating badges,

Deny my name, and sink into the spy.

BLAND. Thou didst no more than was a soldier's duty,
To serve the part on which he drew his sword.
Thou shalt not die for this. Straight will I fly —
I surely shall prevail —

ANDRÉ. It is in vain.
All has been tried. Each friendly argument —

BLAND. All has not yet been tried. The powerful voice
Of friendship in thy cause has not been heard.
My General favors *me*, and loves my father —
My gallant father! would that he were here!
But he, perhaps, now wants an André's care,
To cheer his hours — perhaps now languishes
Amidst those horrors whence thou sav'd'st his son.
The present moment claims my thought. André,
I fly to save thee!

ANDRÉ. Bland, it is in vain.
But, hold — there is a service thou may'st do me.

BLAND. Speak it.

ANDRÉ. O, think, and as a soldier think,
How I must die — the *manner* of my death —
Like the base ruffian, or the midnight thief,
Ta'en in the act of stealing from the poor,
To be turn'd off the felon's — murderer's cart,
A mid-air spectacle to gaping clowns; —
To run a short, an envied course of glory,
And end it on a gibbet. —

BLAND. Damnation!

ANDRÉ. Such is my doom. O, have the manner changed,
And of mere death I'll think not. Dost thou think —?
Perhaps thou canst gain *that* —?

BLAND. (*Almost in a phrenzy.*) Thou shalt not die.

ANDRÉ. Let me, O, let me die a soldier's death,
While friendly clouds of smoke shroud from all eyes
My last convulsive pangs, and I'm content.

BLAND. (*With increasing emotion.*) Thou shalt not die!
Curse on the laws of war!
If worth like thine must thus be sacrificed
To policy so cruel and unjust,
I will forswear my country and her service;
I'll hie me to the Briton, and with fire,
And sword, and every instrument of death
Or devastation, join in the work of war!
What! shall worth weigh for nought? I will avenge thee!

ANDRÉ. Hold, hold, my friend; thy country's woes are full.
What! wouldst thou make me cause another traitor?
No more of this; and, if I die, believe me,
Thy country for my death incurs no blame.
Restrain thy ardor — but ceaselessly entreat
That André may at least die as he lived,
A soldier.

BLAND.   By heaven thou shalt not die!

> (BLAND *rushes off;* ANDRÉ *looks after him with
> an expression of love and gratitude, then
> retires up the stage. Scene closes.*)

SCENE, *the* GENERAL'S *Quarters.*

(*Enter* M'DONALD *and* SEWARD, *in conversation.*)

M'DONALD. (*Coming forward.*) Three thousand miles the Atlantic
wave rolls on,
Which bathed Columbia's shores, ere, on the strand
Of Europe, or of Africa, their continents,
Or sea-girt isles, it chafes.

SEWARD.   O, would to heaven
That in midway between these sever'd worlds
Rose barriers, all impassable to man,
Cutting off intercourse, till either side
Had lost all memory of the other!

M'DONALD. What spur now goads thy warm imagination?

SEWARD. Then might, perhaps, one land on earth be found,
Free from th' extremes of poverty and riches;
Where ne'er a scepter'd tyrant should be known,
Or tyrant lordling, curses of creation; —
Where the faint shrieks of woe-exhausted age,
Raving, in feeble madness, o'er the corse
Of a polluted daughter, stained by lust
Of viand-pampered luxury, might ne'er be heard;
Where the blasted form of much abused
Beauty, by villainy seduced, by knowledge
All unguarded, might ne'er be viewed, flitting
Obscene, 'tween lamp and lamp, i' th' midnight street
Of all-defiling city; where the child —

M'DONALD. Hold! Shroud thy raven imagination.
Torture not me with images so curst!

SEWARD. Soon shall our foes, inglorious, fly these shores.
Peace shall again return. Then Europe's ports
Shall pour a herd upon us, far more fell
Than those, her mercenary sons, who now

Threaten our sore chastisement.

M'DONALD. Prophet of ill,
  From Europe shall enriching commerce flow,
  And many an ill attendant; but from thence
  Shall likewise flow blest science. Europe's knowledge,
  By sharp experience bought, we should appropriate;
  Striving thus to leap from that simplicity,
  With ignorance curst, to that simplicity,
  By knowledge blest; unknown the gulf between.

SEWARD. Mere theoretic dreaming.

M'DONALD. Blest wisdom
  Seems, from out the chaos of the social world,
  Where good and ill in strange commixture float,
  To rise, by strong necessity impell'd;
  Starting, like Love divine, from womb of Night,
  Illuming all, to order all reducing;
  And showing by its bright and noontide blaze
  That happiness alone proceeds from justice.

SEWARD. Dreams, dreams! Man can know naught but ill on earth.

M'DONALD. I'll to my bed, for I have watch'd all night;
  And may my sleep give pleasing repetition
  Of these my waking dreams! Virtue's incentives. (*Exit.*)

SEWARD. Folly's chimeras rather: guides to error.

(*Enter* BLAND, *preceded by a Sergeant.*)

SERGEANT. Pacquets for the General. (*Exit.*)

BLAND. Seward, my friend!

SEWARD. Captain, I'm glad to see the hue of health
  Sit on a visage from the sallow south.

BLAND. The lustihood of youth hath yet defied
  The parching sun, and chilling dew of even.
  The General — Seward —?

SEWARD. I will lead you to him.

BLAND. Seward, I must make bold. Leave us together,
  When occasion offers. 'T will be friendly.

SEWARD. I will not cross your purpose. (*Exeunt.*)

SCENE, *a Chamber.*

(*Enter* MRS. BLAND.)

MRS. BLAND. Yes, ever be this day a festival
  In my domestic calendar. This morn
  Will see my husband free. Even now, perhaps,
  Ere yet Aurora flies the eastern hills,
  Shunning the sultry sun, my Bland embarks.

Already, on the Hudson's dancing wave,
He chides the sluggish rowers, or supplicates
For gales propitious; that his eager arms
May clasp his wife, may bless his little ones.
O, how the tide of joy makes my heart bound,
Glowing with high and ardent expectation!

(*Enter two* CHILDREN.)

FIRST CHILD. Here we are, Mamma, up, and dress'd already.

MRS. BLAND. And why were ye so early?

FIRST CHILD. Why, did not you tell us that Papa was to be home to-day?

MRS. BLAND. I said, perhaps.

SECOND CHILD. (*Disappointed.*) Perhaps!

FIRST CHILD. I don't like perhaps's.

SECOND CHILD. No, nor I neither; nor "may-be-so's."

MRS. BLAND. We make not certainties, my pretty loves;
I do not like "perhaps's" more than you do.

SECOND CHILD. O, don't say so, Mama! for I'm sure I hardly ever ask you anything but you answer me with "may be so," — "perhaps," — or "very likely." "Mamma, shall I go to the camp to-morrow, and see the General?" "May be so, my dear." Hang "may be so," say I!

MRS. BLAND. Well said, Sir Pertness!

FIRST CHILD. But I am sure, Mama, you said, that, to-day, Papa would have his liberty.

MRS. BLAND. So your dear father, by his letters, told me.

SECOND CHILD. Why, then, *I am sure* he will be here to-day. When he can come to *us,* I'm sure he will not stay among those strange Englishmen and Hessians. I often wish'd that I had wings to fly, for then I would soon be with him.

MRS. BLAND. Dear boy!

(*Enter* SERVANT, *and gives a letter to* MRS. BLAND.)

SERVANT. An express, Madam, from New York to Head-quarters, in passing, delivered this.

SECOND CHILD. Papa's coming home to-day, John.

(*Exeunt* SERVANT *and* CHILDREN.)

MRS. BLAND. What fears assail me! O, I did not want
A letter now!
(*She reads in great agitation, exclaiming, while her eyes are fixed on the paper:*)
My husband! doomed to die! Retaliation!
(*She looks forward with wildness, consternation, and horror.*)
To die, if André dies! *He* dies to-day!

My husband to be murdered! And to-day!
To-day, if André dies! Retaliation!
O curst contrivance! Madness relieve me!
Burst, burst, my brain! Yet — André is not dead;
My husband lives. (*Look at the letter.*) "One man has power."
I fly to save the father of my children!   (*Rushes out.*)

END OF THE SECOND ACT.

ACT THIRD

Scene, *the* General's *quarters.*

The General *and* Bland *come forward.*

General. (*Papers in his hand.*) Captain, you are noted here with
    honorable
Praises. Depend upon that countenance
From me, which you have prov'd yourself so richly
Meriting. Both for your father's virtues
And your own, your country owes you honor —
The sole return the poor can make for service.
Bland. If from my country aught I've merited,
    Or gain'd the approbation of her champion,
    At any other time I should not dare,
    Presumptuously, to show my sense of it;
    But now my tongue, all shameless, dares to name
    The boon, the precious recompense, I wish,
    Which, granted, pays all service, past or future,
    O'erpays the utmost I can e'er achieve.
General. Brief, my young friend, briefly, your purpose.
Bland. If I have done my duty as a soldier;
    If I have brav'd all dangers for my country;
    If my brave father has deserved aught;
    Call all to mind — and cancel all — but grant
    My one request — mine, and humanity's.
General. Be less profuse of words, and name your wish;
    If fit, its fitness is the best assurance
    That not in vain you sue; but, if unjust,
    Thy merits, nor the merits of thy race,
    Cannot its nature alter, nor my mind,
    From its determined opposition change.

BLAND. You hold the fate of my most lov'd of friends;
   As gallant soldier as e'er fac'd a foe,
   Bless'd with each polish'd gift of social life,
   And every virtue of humanity.
   To me, a savior from the pit of death,
   To me, and many more, my countrymen.
   Oh, could my words pourtray him what he is!
   Bring to your mind the blessings of his deeds,
   While thro' the fever-heated, loathsome holds
   Of floating hulks, dungeons obscene, where ne'er
   The dewy breeze of morn, or evening's coolness,
   Breath'd on our parching skins, he pass'd along,
   Diffusing blessings; still his power exerting,
   To alleviate the woes which ruthless war,
   Perhaps thro' dire necessity, heap'd on us;
   Surely the scene would move you to forget
   His late intent — (tho' only serving then
   As duty prompted) — and turn the rigor
   Of War's iron law from him, the best of men,
   Meant only for the worst.
GENERAL.   Captain, no more.
BLAND. If André lives, the prisoner finds a friend;
   Else helpless and forlorn —
   All men will bless the act, and bless thee for it.
GENERAL. Think'st thou thy country would not curse the man
   Who, by a clemency ill-tim'd, ill-judg'd,
   Encourag'd treason? That *pride* encourag'd,
   Which, by denying us the rights of nations,
   Hath caus'd those ills which thou hast now pourtray'd?
   Our prisoners, brave and generous peasantry,
   As rebels have been treated, not as men.
   'T is mine, brave yeomen, to assert your rights;
   'T is mine to teach the foe, that, though array'd
   In rude simplicity, ye yet are men,
   And rank among the foremost. Oft their scouts,
   The very refuse of the English arms,
   Unquestion'd, have your countrymen consign'd
   To death, when captur'd, mocking their agonies.
BLAND. Curse them! (*Checking himself*). Yet, let not censure fall on
     André.
   O, there are Englishmen as brave, as good,
   As ever land on earth might call its own;
   And gallant André is among the best!
GENERAL. Since they have hurl'd war on us, we must show

That by the laws of war we will abide;
And have the power to bring their acts for trial
To that tribunal, eminent 'mongst men,
Erected by the policy of nations,
To stem the flood of ills, which else fell war
Would pour, uncheck'd, upon the sickening world,
Sweeping away all trace of civil life.

BLAND. To pardon him would not encourage ill.
His case is singular; his station high;
His qualities admir'd; his virtues lov'd.

GENERAL. No more, my good young friend: it is in vain.
The men entrusted with thy country's rights
Have weigh'd, attentive, every circumstance.
An individual's virtue is by them
As highly prized as it can be by thee.
I know the virtues of this man and love them.
But the destiny of millions, millions
Yet unborn, depends upon the rigor
Of this moment. The haughty Briton laughs
To scorn our armies and our councils. Mercy,
Humanity, call loudly, that we make
Our now despised power be felt, vindictive.
Millions demand the death of this young man.
My injur'd country, he his forfeit life
Must yield, to shield thy lacerated breast
From torture. (*To* BLAND.) Thy merits are not overlook'd.
Promotion shall immediately attend thee.

BLAND. (*With contemptuous irony.*) Pardon me, sir, I never shall
    deserve it.
(*With increasing heat.*) The country that forgets to reverence
    virtue;
That makes no difference 'twixt the sordid wretch
Who, for reward, risks treason's penalty,
And him unfortunate, whose duteous service
Is, by mere accident, so chang'd in form
As to assume guilt's semblance, I serve not:
Scorn to serve. I have a soldier's honor,
But 't is in union with a freeman's judgment,
And when I act, both prompt. Thus from my helm
I tear what once I proudly thought, the badge
Of virtuous fellowship. (*Tears the cockade from his helmet.*) My
    sword I keep. (*Puts on his helmet.*)
Would, André, thou hadst never put thine off.
Then hadst thou through opposers' hearts made way

To liberty, or bravely pierc'd thine own!   (*Exit.*)
GENERAL. Rash, headstrong, maddening boy!
  Had not this action past without a witness,
  Duty would ask that thou shouldst rue thy folly —
  But, for the motive, be the deed forgotten.   (*Exit.*)

SCENE, *a Village. At a distance some tents. In front muskets, drums,
and other indications of soldiers' quarters...*

(*Enter* MRS. BLAND *and* CHILDREN, *attended by* MELVILLE.)

MELVILLE. The General's doors to you are ever open.
  But why, my worthy friend, this agitation?
  Our colonel, your husband —
MRS. BLAND. (*In tears, gives him the letter.*) Read, Melville.
FIRST CHILD. Do not cry, Mama, for I'm sure if Papa said he would
  come home to-day, he will come yet; for he always does what he
  says he will.
MRS. BLAND. He cannot come, dear love; they will not let him.
SECOND CHILD. Why, then, they told him lies. O, fye upon them!
MELVILLE. (*Returning the letter.*) Fear nothing, Madam, 't is an
    empty threat:
  A trick of policy. They dare not do it.
MRS. BLAND. Alas, alas! what dares not power to do?
  What art of reasoning, or what magic words,
  Can still the storm of fears these lines have raised?
  The wife's, the mother's fears? Ye innocents,
  Unconscious on the brink of what a perilous
  Precipice ye stand, unknowing that to-day
  Ye are cast down the gulph, poor babes, ye weep
  From sympathy. Children of sorrow, nurst,
  Nurtur'd, 'midst camps and arms; unknowing man,
  But as man's fell destroyer; must ye now,
  To crown your piteous fate, be fatherless?
  O, lead me, lead me to him! Let me kneel,
  Let these, my children, kneel, till André, pardon'd,
  Ensures to me a husband, them a father.
MELVILLE. Madam, duty forbids further attendance.
  I am on guard to-day. But see your son;
  To him I leave your guidance. Good wishes
  Prosper you.   (*Exit* MELVILLE.)
             (*Enter* BLAND.)

MRS. BLAND. My Arthur, O my Arthur!
BLAND. My mother!   (*Embracing her.*)

MRS. BLAND. My son, I have been wishing
For you —   (*Bursts into tears, unable to proceed.*)
BLAND. But whence this grief, these tears, my mother?
Why are these little cheeks bedew'd with sorrow?
                  (*He kisses the children, who exclaim, Brother, brother!*)
Have I done aught to cause a mother's sadness?
MRS. BLAND. No, my brave boy! I oft have fear'd, but never
Sorrow'd for thee.
BLAND. High praise! Then bless me, Madam;
For I have pass'd through many a bustling scene
Since I have seen a father or a mother.
MRS. BLAND. Bless thee, my boy! O, bless him, bless him, Heaven!
Render him worthy to support these babes,
So soon, perhaps, all fatherless — dependant.
BLAND. What mean'st thou, Madam? Why these tears?
MRS. BLAND.   Thy father —
BLAND. A prisoner of war — I long have known it —
But made so without blemish to his honor,
And soon exchang'd, returns unto his friends,
To guard these little ones, and point and lead
To virtue and to glory.
MRS. BLAND.   Never, never!
His life, a sacrifice to André's manes,[1]
Must soon be offer'd. Even now, endungeon'd,
Like a vile felon on the earth he lies,
His death expecting. André's execution
Gives signal for the murder of thy father —
André now dies!
BLAND. (*Despairingly.*) My father and my friend!
MRS. BLAND. There is but one on earth can save my husband —
But one can pardon André.
BLAND.   Haste, my mother!
Thou wilt prevail. Take with thee in each hand
An unoffending child of him thou weep'st.
Save — save them both! This way — haste — lean on me.
                                        (*Exeunt.*)

SCENE, *the* GENERAL'S *Quarters.*

(*Enter the* GENERAL *and* M'DONALD.)

GENERAL. *Here* have I intimation from the foe.
That still they deem the spy we have condemn'd,

[1] Shade.

Merely a captive; by the laws of arms
From death protected; and retaliation,
As they term it, threaten, if we our purpose hold.
Bland is the victim they have singled out,
Hoping his threaten'd death will André save.

M'Donald. If I were Bland I boldly might advise
My General how to act. Free, and in safety,
I will now suppose my counsel needless.

(*Enter an* American Officer.)

Officer. Another flag hath from the foe arrived,
And craves admittance.

General.   Conduct it hither.   (*Exit* Officer.)
Let us, unwearied hear, unbias'd judge,
Whate'er against our martial court's decision,
Our enemies can bring.

(*Enter* British Officer, *conducted by the* American Officer.)

General.   You are welcome, sir.
What further says Sir Henry?

British Officer.   This from him.
He calls on you to think what weighty woes
You now are busy bringing on your country.
He bids me say, that if your sentence reach
The prisoner's life (prisoner of arms he deems him,
And no spy) on him alone it falls not.
He bids me loud proclaim it, and declare,
If this brave officer, by cruel mockery
Of war's stern law, and justice' feign'd pretence,
Be murder'd; the sequel of our strife, bloody,
Unsparing and remorseless, you will make.
Think of the many captives in our power.
Already one is mark'd; for André mark'd; —
And when his death, unparallel'd in war,
The signal gives, then Colonel Bland must die.

General. 'T is well, sir; bear this message in return.
Sir Henry Clinton knows the laws of arms:
He is a soldier, and, I think, a brave one.
The prisoners he retains he must account for.
Perhaps the reckoning's near. I, likewise, am
A soldier; entrusted by my country.
What I shall judge most for that country's good,
That shall I do. When doubtful, I consult
My country's friends; never her enemies.
In André's case there are no doubts; 't is clear:
Sir Henry Clinton knows it.

British Officer. Weigh consequences.

GENERAL. In strict regard to consequence I act;
 And much should doubt to call that action right,
 Howe'er specious, whose apparent end
 Was misery to man. That brave officer
 Whose death you threaten, for himself drew not
 His sword — his country's wrongs arous'd his mind;
 Her good alone his aim; and if his fall
 Can further fire that country to resistance,
 He will, with smiles, yield up his glorious life,
 And count his death a gain; and tho' Columbians
 Will lament his fall, they will lament in blood.
     (GENERAL *walks up the stage.*)
M'DONALD. Hear this, hear this, mankind!
BRITISH OFFICER. Thus am I answered?
    (*Enter a* SERGEANT *with a letter.*)
SERGEANT. Express from Colonel Bland   (*Delivers it and exit.*)
GENERAL. With your permission.   (*Opens it.*)
BRITISH OFFICER. Your pleasure, sir. It may my mission further.
M'DONALD. O Bland, my countryman, surely I know thee!
GENERAL. 'T is short; I will put form aside, and read it.
(*Reads.*) "Excuse me, my Commander, for having a moment doubted
 your virtue; but you love me. If you waver, let this confirm you.
 My wife and children, to you and my country. Do *your* duty."
 Report this to your General.
BRITISH OFFICER. I shall, sir.
    (*Bows, and exit with* AMERICAN OFFICER.)
GENERAL. O Bland, my countryman!   (*Exit, with emotion.*)
M'DONALD. Triumph of virtue!
 Like him and thee, still be Americans.
 Then, tho' all-powerful Europe league against us,
 And pour in arms her legions on our shores;
 Who is so dull would doubt their shameful flight?
 Who doubt our safety, and our glorious triumph?

SCENE, *the Prison.*

(*Enter* BLAND.)

BLAND. Lingering, I come to crush the bud of hope
 My breath has, flattering, to existence warmed.
 Hard is the task to friendship! hard to say
 To the lov'd object, there remains no hope,
 No consolation for thee; thou *must* die
 The worst of deaths, no circumstance abated.
    (*Enter* ANDRÉ, *in his uniform and dress'd.*)
ANDRÉ. Is there that state on earth which friendship cannot cheer?

Bland. Little *I* bring to cheer thee, André.

André. I understand. 'T is well. 'T will soon be past.
Yet, 't was not much I asked. A soldier's death,
A trifling change of form.

Bland.   Of that I spoke not.
By vehemence of passion hurried on,
I pleaded for thy precious life alone;
The which denied, my indignation barr'd
All further parley. But strong solicitation
Now is urg'd to gain the wish'd-for favor.

André. What is 't o'clock?

Bland.   'T is past the stroke of nine.

André. Why, then, 't is almost o'er. But to be hung —
Is there no way to escape that infamy?
What then *is* infamy? — no matter — no matter.

Bland. Our General hath received another flag.

André. Soliciting for me?

Bland.   On thy behalf.

André. I have been ever favor'd.

Bland.   Threat'nings, now;
No more solicitations. Harsh, indeed,
The import of the message; harsh, indeed.

André. I am sorry for it. Would that I were dead,
And all was well with those I leave behind.

Bland. Such a threat! Is it not enough, just Heaven,
That I must lose this man? Yet there was left
One for my soul to rest on. But, to know
That the same blow deprives them both of life —

André. What mean'st thou, Bland? Surely my General
Threats not retaliation. In vengeance
Dooms not some better man to die for me?

Bland. The best of men.

André.   Thou hast a father, captive —
I dare not ask —

Bland.   That father dies for thee.

André. Gracious Heaven, how woes are heap'd upon me!
What! cannot one, so trifling in life's scene,
Fall, without drawing such a ponderous ruin?
Leave me, my friend, awhile — I yet have life —
A little space of life — let me exert it
To prevent injustice. — From death to save
Thy father, thee to save from utter desolation.

Bland. What mean'st thou, André?

André.   Seek thou the messenger

Who brought this threat. I will my last entreaty
Send by him. My General, sure, will grant it.
BLAND. To the last thyself!   *(Exit.)*
ANDRÉ.   If, at this moment,
When the pangs of death already touch me,
Firmly my mind against injustice strives,
And the last impulse to my vital powers
Is given by anxious wishes to redeem
My fellow-men from pain; surely my end,
Howe'er accomplish'd, is not infamous.   *(Exit.)*

END OF THE THIRD ACT.

ACT FOURTH

SCENE, *the Encampment.*

(*Enter* M'DONALD *and* BLAND.)

BLAND. It doth in truth appear, that as a — spy —
Detested word! — brave André must be view'd.
His sentence he confesses strictly just.
Yet sure, a deed of mercy from *thy* hand,
Could never lead to ill. By such an act,
The stern and blood-stain'd brow of War
Would be disarm'd of half its gorgon horrors;
More humanized customs be induced;
And all the race of civilized man —
Yet sure, a deed of mercy, from *thy* suit;
'T will well become thy character and station.
M'DONALD. Trust me, young friend, I am alone the judge
Of what becomes my character and station;
And having judg'd that this young Briton's death,
Even 'though attended by thy father's murder,
Is necessary, in these times accurs'd,
When every thought of man is ting'd with blood,
I will not stir my finger to redeem them.
Nay, much I wonder, Bland, having so oft
The reasons for this necessary rigor
Enforced upon thee, thou wilt still persist
In vain solicitations. Imitate
Thy father!

BLAND.   My father knew not André.
  I know his value; owe to him my life;
  And gratitude, that first, that best of virtues, —
  Without the which man sinks beneath the brute, —
  Binds me in ties indissoluble to him.
M'DONALD. That man-created virtue blinds thy reason.
  Man owes to man all love; when exercised,
  He does no more than duty. Gratitude,
  That selfish rule of action, which commands
  That we our preference make of men,
  Not for their worth, but that they did *us* service,
  Misleading reason, casting in the way
  Of justice stumbling-blocks, cannot be virtue.
BLAND. Detested sophistry! 'T was André sav'd me.
M'DONALD. He sav'd thy life, and thou art grateful for it.
  How self intrudes, delusive, on man's thoughts.
  He sav'd thy life, yet strove to damn thy country;
  Doom'd millions to the haughty Briton's yoke;
  The best and foremost in the cause of virtue
  To death, by sword, by prison, or the halter;
  His sacrifice now stands the only bar
  Between the wanton cruelties of war
  And our much-suffering soldiers; yet when weigh'd
  With gratitude, for that he sav'd *thy* life,
  These things prove gossamer, and balance air; —
  Perversion monstrous of man's moral sense!
BLAND. Rather perversion monstrous of all good
  Is thy accurs'd, detestable opinion.
  Cold-blooded reasoners, such as thee, would blast
  All warm affection; asunder sever
  Every social tie of humanized man.
  Curst be thy sophisms, cunningly contriv'd
  The callous coldness of thy heart to cover,
  And screen thee from the grave man's detestation!
M'DONALD. Boy, boy!
BLAND. Thou knowest that André's not a spy.
M'DONALD. I know him one. Thou hast acknowledg'd it.
BLAND. Thou liest!
M'DONALD. Shame on thy ruffian tongue! How passion
  Mars thee! I pity thee. Thou canst not harm,
  By words intemperate, a virtuous man.
  I pity thee; for passion sometimes sways
  My older frame, through former uncheck'd habit;
  But when I see the havoc which it makes

In others, I can shun the snare accurst,
And nothing feel but pity.

BLAND. (*Indignantly.*) Pity me! (*Approaches him, and speaks in an under voice.*)

Thou canst be cool, yet, trust me, *passion* sways thee.
Fear does not warm the blood, yet 't is a *passion*.
Hast thou no feeling? I have call'd thee liar!

M'DONALD. If thou could'st make me one, I then might grieve.

BLAND. Thy coolness goes to freezing; thou 'rt a coward!

M'DONALD. Thou knowest thou tell'st a falsehood.

BLAND.   Thou shalt know
None with impunity speaks thus of me.
That to rouse thy courage! (*Touches him gently with his open hand, in crossing him.* M'DONALD *looks at him unmoved.*)
Dost thou not yet feel?

M'DONALD. For *thee* I feel. And, tho' another's acts
Cast no dishonor on the worthy man,
I still feel for thy father. Yet, remember,
I may not, haply, ever be thus guarded;
I may not always the distinction make,
However just, between the blow intended
To provoke, and one that's meant to injure.

BLAND. Hast thou no sense of honor?

M'DONALD.   Truly, yes:
For I am honor's votary. Honor, with me,
Is worth; 't is truth; 't is virtue; 't is a thing
So high preëminent, that a boy's breath,
Or brute's, or madman's blow can never reach it.
My honor is so much, so truly mine,
That none hath power to wound it, save myself.

BLAND. I will proclaim thee through the camp a coward.

M'DONALD. Think better of it. Proclaim not thine own shame.

BLAND. I'll brand thee, — damnation!   (*Exit.*)

M'DONALD.   O passion, passion!
A man who values fame far more than life;
A brave young man; in many things a good;
Utters vile falsehoods; adds injury to insult;
Striving with blood to seal such foul injustice;
And all from impulse of unbridled feeling. (*Pause.*)
Here comes the mother of this headstrong boy.
Severely rack'd. What shall allay her torture?
For common consolation, *here*, is insult.

(*Enter* MRS. BLAND *and* CHILDREN.)

Mrs. Bland. O my good friend!

M'Donald. (*Taking her hand.*)
                I know thy cause of sorrow.
   Art thou now from our Commander?

Mrs. Bland. (*Drying her tears and assuming dignity.*)   I am.
   But vain is my entreaty. All unmov'd
   He hears my words, he sees my desperate sorrow.
   Fain would I blame his conduct, — but I cannot.
   Strictly examin'd, with intent to mark
   The error which so fatal proves to *me,*
   My scrutiny but ends in admiration.
   Thus when the prophet from the hills of Moab,
   Look'd down upon the chosen race of Heaven,
   With fell intent to curse, ere yet he spake,
   Truth all resistless, emanation bright
   From great Adonai, fill'd his froward mind,
   And chang'd the curses of his heart to blessings.

M'Donald. Thou payest high praise to virtue. Whither now?

Mrs. Bland. I still must hover round this spot until
   My doom is known.

M'Donald. Then to my quarters, lady;
   There shall my mate give comfort and refreshment:
   One of your sex can best your sorrows soothe.   (*Exeunt.*)

Scene, *the prison.*

(*Enter* Bland.)

Bland. Where'er I look, cold desolation meets me.
   My father — André — and self-condemnation.
   Why seek I André now? Am *I* a man
   To soothe the sorrows of a suffering friend?
   The weather-cock of passion! fool inebriate!
   Who could with ruffian hand strive to provoke
   Hoar wisdom to intemperance! who could lie!
   Aye, swagger, lie, and brag! — Liar! Damnation!
   O, let me steal away and hide my head,
   Nor view a man, condemned to harshest death,
   Whose words and actions, when by mine compar'd,
   Show white as innocence and bright as truth.
   I now would shun him, but that his shorten'd
   Thread of life gives me no line to play with.
   He comes with smiles, and all the air of triumph,
   While *I* am sinking with remorse and shame;
   Yet *he* is doom'd to death, and *I* am free.

(*Enter* André.)

ANDRÉ. Welcome, my Bland! Cheerly, a welcome hither!
　　I feel assurance that my last request
　　Will not be slighted. Safely thy father
　　Shall return to thee. (*Holding out a paper.*) See what employment
　　For a dying man. Take thou these verses;
　　And, after my decease, send them to her
　　Whose name is woven in them; whose image
　　Hath controul'd my destiny. Such tokens
　　Are rather out of date. Fashions
　　There are in love as in all else; they change
　　As variously. A gallant knight, erewhile,
　　Of Cœur de Lion's day, would, dying, send
　　His heart home to its mistress; degenerate
　　Soldier, I send but some blotted paper.
BLAND. If 't would not damp thy present cheerfulness,
　　I would require the meaning of thy words.
　　I ne'er till now did hear of André's mistress.
ANDRÉ. Mine is a story of that common kind,
　　So often told, with scanty variation,
　　That the pall'd ear loaths the repeated tale.
　　Each young romancer chuses for his theme
　　The woes of youthful hearts, by the cold hand
　　Of frosty age, arm'd with parental power,
　　Asunder torn. But I long since have ceas'd
　　To mourn; well satisfied that she I love,
　　Happy in holy union with another,
　　Shares not my wayward fortunes. Nor would I
　　Now these tokens send, remembrance to awaken,
　　But that I know her happy; and the happy
　　Can think on misery and share it not.
BLAND. (*Agitated.*)
　　Some one approaches.
ANDRÉ.　　　　　　　　Why, 't is near the time!
　　But tell me, Bland, say, — is the manner chang'd?
BLAND. I hope it, but I yet have no assurance.
ANDRÉ. Well, well!
HONORA. (*Without.*) I must see him.
ANDRÉ.　　　　　　　　　　　Whose voice was that?
　　My senses! — Do I dream? (*Leans on* BLAND.)

　　　　　　　　　(*Enter* HONORA.)

HONORA.　　　　Where is he?
ANDRÉ.　　　　　　　　　　'T is she!
　　(*Starts from* BLAND *and advances towards* HONORA; *she rushes into
　　　his arms.*)

Honora. It is enough! He lives, and *I* shall save him.
             (*She faints in the arms of* André.)
André. She sinks — assist me, Bland! O, save her, save her!
(*Places her in a chair and looks tenderly on her.*)
Yet, why should she awake from that sweet sleep?
Why should she ope her eyes — (*wildly*) — to see me hung!
What does she here? Stand off — (*tenderly*) — and let her die.
How pale she looks! How worn that tender frame! —
She has known sorrow! Who could injure her?
Bland. She revives — André — soft, bend her forward.
                  (André *kneels and supports her.*)
Honora. André! —
André.   Lov'd excellence!
Honora.   Yes, it is André!
         (*Rises and looks at him.*)
No more deceived by visionary forms,
By him supported — (*Leans on him.*)
André.   Why is this?
Thou dost look pale, Honora — sick and wan —
Languid thy fainting limbs —
Honora.   All will be well.
But was it kind to leave me as thou did'st?
So rashly to desert thy vow-link'd wife?
André. When made another's both by vows and laws —
Honora. (*Quitting his support.*) What meanest thou?
André.   Did'st thou not marry him?
Honora. Marry!
André. Did'st thou not give thy hand away
From me?
Honora. O, never, never.
André.   Not married?
Honora. To none but thee, and but in will to thee.
André. O blind, blind wretch! — Thy father told me —
Honora. Thou wast deceived. They hurried me away,
Spreading false rumors to remove thy love —
(*Tenderly.*) Thou did'st too soon believe them.
André.   Thy father —
How could I but believe Honora's father?
And he did tell me so. I reverenc'd age,
Yet knew age was not virtue. I believed
His snowy locks, and yet they did deceive me!
I have destroy'd myself and thee! — Alas,
Ill-fated maid, why did'st thou not forget me?
Hast thou rude seas and hostile shores explor'd

For this? To see my death? Witness my shame?

HONORA. I come to bless thee, André, and shall do it.
I bear such offers from thy kind Commander
As must prevail to save thee. Thus the daughter
May repair the ills her cruel sire inflicted.
My father, dying, gave me cause to think
That arts were us'd to drive thee from thy home;
But what those arts I knew not. An heiress left,
Of years mature, with power and liberty,
I straight resolv'd to seek thee o'er the seas.
A long-known friend, who came to join her lord,
Yielded protection and lov'd fellowship. —
Indeed, when I did hear of thy estate,
It almost kill'd me; — I was weak before —

ANDRÉ. 'T is I have murder'd thee!

HONORA.   All shall be well.
Thy General heard of me, and instant form'd
The plan of this my visit. I am strong,
Compar'd with what I was. Hope strengthens me;
Nay, even solicitude supports me now;
And when thou shalt be safe, *thou* wilt support me.

ANDRÉ. Support thee! — O Heaven! What! — and *must* I die?
Die! — and leave her *thus* — suffering — unprotected!

(*Enter* MELVILLE *and* GUARD.)

MELVILLE. I am sorry that my duty should require
Service, at which my heart revolts; but, sir,
Our soldiers wait in arms. All is prepar'd —

HONORA. To death! Impossible! Has my delay,
Then, murder'd him? A momentary respite —

MELVILLE. Lady, I have no power.

BLAND.   Melville, my friend,
This lady bears dispatches of high import.
Touching this business; — should they arrive too late —

HONORA. For pity's sake, and heaven's, conduct me to him;
And wait the issue of our conference.
O, 't would be murder of the blackest dye,
Sin execrable, not to break thy orders —
Inhuman, thou art not.

MELVILLE.   Lady, thou say'st true;
For rather would I lose my rank in arms,
And stand cashier'd for lack of discipline,
Than gain 'mongst military men all praise,
Wanting the touch of sweet humanity.

HONORA. Thou grantest my request?

MELVILLE.   Lady, I do.

  Retire!   (*Soldiers go out.*)

BLAND. I know not what excuse, to martial men,
  Thou canst advance for this; but to thy heart
  Thou wilt need none, good Melville.

ANDRÉ.   O Honora!

HONORA. Cheer up, I feel assur'd. Hope wings my flight,
  To bring thee tidings of much joy to come.

                (*Exit* HONORA, *with* BLAND *and* MELVILLE.)

ANDRÉ. Eternal blessings on thee, matchless woman! —
  If Death now comes, he finds the veriest coward
  That e'er he dealt withal. I cannot think
  Of dying. Void of fortitude, each thought
  Clings to the world that holds Honora!   (*Exit.*)

END OF THE FOURTH ACT.

ACT FIFTH

SCENE, *the Encampment.*

(*Enter* BLAND.)

BLAND.   Suspence — uncertainty — man's bane and solace!
  How racking now to me! My mother comes.
  Forgive me, O my father, if in this war,
  This wasting conflict of my 'wildering passions,
  Memory of thee holds here a second place!
  M'Donald comes with her. I would not meet him;
  Yet I *will* do it. Summon up some courage —
  Confess my fault, and gain, if not his love,
  At least the approbation of *my* judgment.

     (*Enter* MRS. BLAND *and* CHILDREN, *with* M'DONALD.)

BLAND. Say, Madam, is there no change of counsel,
  Or new determination?

MRS. BLAND.   *Nought new,* my son.
  The tale of misery is told unheard.
  The widow's and the orphans' sighs
  Fly up, unnoted by the eye of man,

And mingle, undistinguish'd, with the winds.
My friend (*to* M'DONALD), attend thy duties. I must away.

SECOND CHILD. You need not cry, Mama, the General will do it, I am
  sure, for I saw him cry. He turn'd away his head from *you,* but
  I saw it.

MRS. BLAND. Poor thing! Come, let us home and weep. Alas!
  I can no more, for war hath made men rocks.

> (*Exeunt* MRS. BLAND *and* CHILDREN.)

BLAND. Colonel, I used thee ill this morning.

M'DONALD.   No!
  Thyself thou used'st most vilely, I remember.

BLAND. Myself sustained the injury, most true;
  But the intent of what I said and did
  Was ill to thee alone; I'm sorry for it.
  See'st thou these blushes? They proceed from warmth
  As honest as the heart of man e'er felt;
  But not with shame unmingled, while I force
  This tongue, debased, to own it slander'd thee,
  And utter'd — I could curse it — utter'd falsehood.
  Howe'er misled by passion, still my mind
  Retains that sense of honest rectitude
  Which makes the memory of an evil deed
  A troublesome companion. I was wrong.

M'DONALD. Why, now, this glads me; for thou *now* art right.
  O, may thy tongue, henceforward, utter naught
  But Truth's sweet precepts, in fair Virtue's cause!
  Give me thy hand. (*Takes his hand.*) Ne'er may it grasp a sword
  But in defence of justice.

BLAND.   Yet, erewhile,
  A few short hours scarce past, when this vile hand
  Attempted on *thee* insult; and was raised
  Against thy honor; ready to be raised
  Against thy life. If this my deep remorse —

M'DONALD. No more, no more! 'T is past. Remember it
  But as thou would'st the action of another,
  By thy enlighten'd judgment much condemn'd;
  And serving as a beacon in the storms
  Thy passions yet may raise. Remorse is vice;
  Guard thee against its influence debasing.
  Say to thyself: "I *am* not what I *was;*
  I am not *now* the instrument of vice;
  I'm changed; I am a man; Virtue's firm friend;
  Sever'd forever from my former self;

No link, but in remembrance salutary."
<Bland.[1] How all men tower above me!
M'Donald.   Nay, not so.
Above what once thou wast, some few do rise;
None above what thou art.
Bland. It shall be so.
M'Donald.   It is so.
Bland.   Then to prove it.
For I must yet a trial undergo,
That will require a consciousness of virtue.   (*Exit.*)
M'Donald. O, what a temper doth in man reside!
How capable of yet unthought perfection!   (*Exit.*)>

Scene, *the General's quarters.*

(*Enter* General *and* Seward.)

General. Ask her, my friend, to send by thee her pacquets.
          (*Exit* Seward.)

[1] The lines marked < > were omitted after the first night and the following were inserted.

Bland. Noble M'Donald, truth and honor's champion!
Yet think not strange that my intemperance wrong'd thee:
Good as thou art! for, would'st thou, can'st thou, think it?
My tongue unbridled, hath the same offence,
With action violent, and boisterous tone,
Hurl'd on that glorious man, whose pious labors
Shield from every ill his grateful country.
That man, whom friends to adoration love,
And enemies revere. Yes, M'Donald,
Even in the presence of the first of men
Did I abjure the service of my country,
And reft my helmet of that glorious badge
Which graces even the brow of Washington.
How shall I see him more?

M'Donald. Alive himself to every generous impulse,
He hath excused the impetuous warmth of youth,
In expectation that thy fiery soul,
Chasten'd by time and reason, will receive
The stamp indelible of godlike virtue.
To me, in trust, he gave this badge disclaim'd,
With power, when thou should'st see thy wrongful error,
From him, to reinstate it in thy helm,
And thee in his high favor.
    (*Gives the cockade.*)
Bland. (*Takes the cockade and replaces it.*) Shall I speak my thoughts of thee and him?
No! let my actions henceforth show what thou
And he have made me. Ne'er shall my helmet
Lack again its proudest, noblest ornament,
Until my country knows the rest of peace,
Or Bland the peace of death.
       (*Exit.*)

O, what keen struggles must I undergo!
Unbless'd estate! to have the power to pardon;
The court's stern sentence to remit; — give life;
Feel the strong wish to use such blessed power;
Yet know that circumstances strong as fate
Forbid to obey the impulse. O, I feel
That man should never shed the blood of man!

(*Enter* SEWARD.)

SEWARD. Naught can the lovely suitor satisfy,
But conference with thee, and much I fear
Refusal would cause madness.
GENERAL. Yet to admit,
To hear, be tortur'd, and refuse at last —
SEWARD. Sure never man such spectacle of sorrow
Saw before. Motionless the rough-hewn soldiers
Silent view her, or walk aside and weep.
GENERAL. (*After a pause.*) Admit her. (SEWARD *goes out.*) O, for
the art, the precious art,
To reconcile the sufferer to his sorrows!
(HONORA *rushes in, and throws herself wildly on her knees before
him; he endeavors to raise her.*)
HONORA. Nay, nay, here is my place, or here, or lower,
Unless thou grant'st his life. All forms away!
Thus will I clasp thy knees, thus cling to thee —
I am his wife — 't is I have ruin'd him —
O, save him! Give him to me! Let us cross
The mighty seas, far, far — ne'er to offend again —
(*The* GENERAL *turns away, and hides his eyes with his hand.*)
(*Enter* SEWARD *and an* OFFICER.)
GENERAL. Seward, support her; my heart is torn in twain.
(HONORA, *as if exhausted, suffers herself to be raised, and leans
on* SEWARD.)
OFFICER. This moment, sir, a messenger arrived
With well confirm'd and mournful information,
That gallant Hastings, by the lawless scouts
Of Britain taken, after cruel mockery
With show of trial and of condemnation,
On the next tree was hung.
HONORA. (*Wildly.*) O, it is false.
GENERAL. Why, why, my country, did I hesitate? (*Exit.*)
(HONORA *sinks, faints, and is borne off by* SEWARD *and* OFFICER.)

SCENE, *the Prison.*

(ANDRÉ *meeting* BLAND.)

ANDRÉ. How speeds Honora? (*Pause.*) Art thou silent, Bland?
  Why, then, I know my task. The mind of man,
  If not by vice debas'd, debilitated,
  Or by disease of body quite unton'd,
  Hath o'er its thoughts a power — energy divine.
  Of fortitude the source and every virtue —
  A godlike power, which e'en o'er circumstance
  Its sov'reignty exerts. Now from my thoughts,
  Honora! Yet she is left alone — expos'd —
BLAND. O, André, spurn me, strike me to the earth;
  For what a wretch am I in André's mind,
  That he can think he leaves his love alone,
  And I retaining life!
ANDRÉ.   Forgive me, Bland.
  My thoughts glanc'd not on thee. Imagination
  Pictur'd only, then, her orphan state, helpless;
  Her weak and grief-exhausted frame. Alas!
  This blow will kill her.
BLAND. (*Kneeling.*) Here, do I myself
  Devote, my fortune consecrate, to thee,
  To thy remembrance, and Honora's service.
ANDRÉ. Enough! Let me not see her more — nor think of her —
  Farewell, farewell, sweet image! Now for death.
BLAND. Yet that thou should'st the felon's fate fulfil —
  Damnation! My blood boils. Indignation
  Makes the current of my life course wildly
  Through its round and maddens each emotion.
ANDRÉ. Come, come, it matters not.
BLAND.   I do remember,
  When a boy at school, in our allotted tasks,
  We, by our puny acts, strove to pourtray
  The giant thoughts of Otway. I was Pierre.
  O, thou art Pierre's reality — a soldier,
  On whose manly brow sits fortitude enamor'd;
  A Mars, abhorring vice, yet doom'd to die
  A death of infamy; thy corse expos'd
  To vulgar gaze — halter'd — distorted — oh —
  (*Pauses, and then adds in a low hollow voice:*)
  Pierre had a friend to save him from such shame —
  And so hast thou.

ANDRÉ   No more, as thou dost love me.

BLAND. I have a sword, and arm, that never fail'd me.

ANDRÉ. Bland, such an act would justly thee involve,
   And leave that helpless one thou sworest to guard
   Expos'd to every ill. O, think not of it!

BLAND. If thou wilt not my aid — take it thyself.
                              (*Draws and offers his sword.*)

ANDRÉ. No, men will say that cowardice did urge me.
   In my mind's weakness, I did wish to shun
   That mode of death which error represented
   Infamous: now let me rise superior;
   And with a fortitude too true to start
   From mere appearances, show your country
   That she, in me, destroys a man who might
   Have liv'd to virtue.

BLAND. (*Sheathing his sword.*) I will not think more of it;
   I was again the sport of erring passion.

ANDRÉ. Go thou and guide Honora from this spot.

HONORA. (*Entering.*) Who shall oppose his wife? I will have way!
   They, cruel, would have kept me from thee, André.
   Say, am I not thy wife? Wilt thou deny me?
   Indeed I am not dress'd in bridal trim.
   But I have travelled far: — rough was the road —
   Rugged and rough — that must excuse my dress.
   (*Seeing* ANDRÉ's *distress.*) Thou art not glad to see me.

ANDRÉ.   Break my heart!

HONORA. Indeed, I feel not much in spirits. I wept but now.

(*Enter* MELVILLE *and* GUARD.)

BLAND. (*To* MELVILLE.) Say nothing.

ANDRÉ.   I am ready.

HONORA. (*Seeing the* GUARD.)   Are *they* here?
   Here again — the *same* — but they shall not harm me.
   I am with *thee*, my André — I am safe —
   And *thou* art safe with me. Is it not so?   (*Clinging to him.*)

(*Enter* MRS. BLAND.)

MRS. BLAND. Where is this lovely victim?

BLAND.   Thanks, my mother.

MRS. BLAND. M'Donald sent me hither. My woes are past.
   Thy father, by the foe released, already
   Is in safety. This be forgotten now;
   And every thought be turn'd to this sad scene.
   Come, lady, home with me.

HONORA.   Go home with thee?
   Art thou my André's mother? We will home
   And rest, for thou art weary — very weary.

(Leans on MRS. BLAND.)

     (ANDRÉ retires to the GUARD, and goes off with them, looking
     on her to the last, and with an action of extreme tenderness
     takes leave of her. MELVILLE and BLAND accompany him.)
HONORA. Now we will go. Come, love! Where is he?
   All gone! — I do remember — I awake —
   They have him. Murder! Help! O, save him! save him!
     (HONORA attempts to follow, but falls. MRS. BLAND kneels to
     assist her. Scene closes.)

SCENE, the Encampment.

     (Procession to the execution of ANDRÉ. First enter Pioneers —
     Detachment of Infantry — Military Band of Music — Infantry.
     The Music having passed off, enter ANDRÉ between MELVILLE
     and AMERICAN OFFICER; they sorrowful, he cheerfully con-
     versing as he passes over the stage.)

ANDRÉ. It may in me be merely prejudice,
   The effect of young opinion deep engraved
   Upon the tender mind by care parental;
   But I must think your country has mistook
   Her interests. Believe me, but for this I should
   Not willingly have drawn a sword against her.

(They bow their heads in silence.)

   Opinion must, nay, ought to sway our actions;
   Therefore —
     (Having crossed the stage, he goes out as still conversing with
     them. Another detachment of Infantry, with muffled and
     craped drums, closes the procession; as soon as they are off —

SCENE.

   draws and discovers the distant view of the encampment.)
     (Procession enters in same order as before, proceeds up the stage,
     and goes off the opposite side.)

     (Enter M'DONALD, leading BLAND, who looks wildly back.)

BLAND. I dare not thee resist. Yet why, O why
   Thus hurry me away? —
M'DONALD.   Would'st thou behold —
BLAND. O, name it not!

M'DONALD.　　　　　Or would'st thou, by thy looks
　And gestures wild, o'erthrow that manly calmness
　Which, or assumed or felt, so well becomes thy friend?
BLAND. What means that cannon's sound?
M'DONALD. (*After a pause.*)　　　　Signal of death
　Appointed. André, thy friend, is now no more.
BLAND. Farewell, farewell, brave spirit! O! let my countrymen,
　Henceforward when the cruelties of war
　Arise in their remembrance; when their ready
　Speech would pour forth torrents in their foe's dispraise,
　Think on this act accurst, and lock complaint in silence.
　　　　　　　　　　(BLAND *throws himself on the earth.*)
M'DONALD. Such are the dictates of the heart, not head.
　O, may the children of Columbia still
　Be taught by every teacher of mankind,
　Each circumstance of calculative gain,
　Or wounded pride, which prompted our oppressors;
　May every child be taught to lisp the tale;
　And may, in times to come, no foreign force,
　No European influence, tempt to mis-state,
　Or awe the tongue of eloquence to silence.
　Still may our children's children deep abhor
　The motives, doubly deep detest the actors;
　Ever remembering that the race who plann'd,
　Who acquiesced, or did the deeds abhor'd,
　Has pass'd from off the earth; and, in its stead,
　Stand men who challenge love or detestation
　But from their proper, individual deeds;
　Never let memory of the sire's offence
　Descend upon the son.

　　　　　　　CURTAIN DROPS.

INDEX OF AUTHORS